ROSE ELLIOT'S
Complete Vegetarian Cookbook

ROSE ELLIOT'S
Complete Vegetarian Cookbook

HarperCollins*Publishers*

First published in this hardback edition in 1985 by
William Collins Sons & Co. Ltd
London · Glasgow · Sydney · Auckland · Toronto · Johannesburg
Reprinted 1986, 1987, 1989, 1990

Reprinted by HarperCollins*Publishers* 1992 (twice)

Most of the recipes in this book first appeared in Fontana paperbacks
Copyright © Rose Elliot 1967, 1972, 1975, 1977, 1979,
1981, 1982, 1983, 1984, 1985

Illustrations by Vana Haggerty and Ken Lewis

British Library Cataloguing in Publication Data

Elliot, Rose
Rose Elliot's complete vegetarian cookbook:
over 1,000 selected recipes.
1. Vegetarian cookery
I. Title
641.5′636   TX837
ISBN 0-00-412009-4

Set in Ehrhardt
by Centracet
Printed and bound in Great Britain
by HarperCollins *Manufacturing*, Glasgow

CONTENTS

INTRODUCTION

When I was sixteen and a half I took off my school uniform for the last time and became the cook at a retreat centre run by my parents. It wasn't that I had any great aspirations to be a cook, but that I'd met and fallen head-over-heels in love with Robert, a man twelve years older than me, and couldn't get away from school fast enough. By a stroke of luck (for me), just at that very time the vegetarian cook at the retreat centre left. In those days (1960s) vegetarian cooks were few and far between, and my parents were desperate for a replacement. So they reluctantly gave in to my pleas for the job, on condition that I continued to study for my A levels at home. And that is what I did, and how I took the first step to becoming a cookery writer.

To everyone's surprise, including my own, I really enjoyed the cooking. Many of the guests at the retreat centre were experiencing vegetarian food for the first time and I enjoyed the challenge of presenting it to them in a way which would appeal. I started by using family recipes and an old recipe book, called *Household Non-Flesh Cookery*, but once I got into my stride I discovered that the ideas started to flow, and I began creating many new recipes. I found great satisfaction in the blending and balancing of colours and textures. Visitors to the retreat centre kept clamouring for recipes, but I was too busy with the cooking and my A levels to do anything other than scribble them down on odd scraps of paper.

I married Robert in the summer of my eighteenth birthday, and in due course had two daughters in quick succession. It was at this time, while I was tied to the home and cradle, that I decided to do what everyone kept asking me to do (for once!) and put my recipes together. So I wrote a book, and the religious charity which ran the retreat centre published it. The book was called *Simply Delicious* – the title was my father's brilliant idea – and the initial print run was either 4000 or 5000 (I can't remember which). Very timidly, I sent out four copies for review: one to my favourite programme, 'Woman's Hour'; one to Katie Stewart, then cookery editor of *The Times*; one to *Ideal Home* magazine; and one to the local newspaper. All gave the book wonderful reviews and orders flowed in from booksellers all over the country, especially as a result of the 'Woman's Hour' review. A reprint was immediately ordered; I was interviewed for the first time on television; and I accepted an invitation to give a cookery demonstration to an audience of 200 people. The die was cast!

Requests for more cookery demonstrations followed. One of the most rewarding – and taxing – was a series I did at the store which was then called Marshall and Snelgrove in London. This consisted of seven half-hour demonstrations, each on a different topic, over three consecutive days. When you're demonstrating, the hard part isn't the actual demonstration, it's all the preparation of ingredients and the collecting together of equipment which has to be done beforehand, and the washing up afterwards! However, my sister, Jenny, and another dear friend, Alison, helped me, the audience was wonderful, and I look back on my 'Marshall and Snelgrove demonstrations' as a happy experience and an important stepping-stone in my career. Not that I or anyone else really thought of my cookery writing as a career then; it was still a hobby which I fitted in around my toddlers. Out of my demonstrating, entertaining and general family cookery, however, was growing another book, *Not Just a Load of Old Lentils*, which my parents' religious organization also published, in the autumn of 1972.

People often ask me how I arrived at the title of this book. It happened like this. I very much wanted some illustrations in the book, so I asked an artistic friend, Willow, if she could take on this task for me. She kindly agreed, and being the thorough worker she is, went to a kitchen shop in Petersfield to do some research on equipment. The manager of the shop was most helpful, but roared with laughter when she said that it was for a *vegetarian* cookery book (such was the image, still, in those days). This so provoked Willow that she came out with the immortal phrase, 'Well, it's not just a load of old lentils you know.' When she recounted this tale to me later I suddenly thought what a great title it would make, and after some persuasion my publishers agreed. It was quite fortuitous because Fontana, who subsequently asked if they could publish the book in paperback, later told me that it was the title which clinched the idea with them.

It was after *Not Just a Load of Old Lentils* was published in paperback that I started experimenting seriously with the range of dried beans and lentils which were appearing in my local health shop. I realized that at that time there was no recipe book for these on the market. Fontana were enthusiastic when I suggested the idea to them, and so my third full-length book, and my all-time best-seller, *The Bean Book*, was written. By this time I was unexpectedly pregnant with what turned out to be my third daughter, Claire, and I completed the manuscript within a few days of her birth. I think it must have been at this point, too, that I became the workaholic that I am today, because in the six and a half years since Claire's birth, in addition to looking after her myself and caring for the rest of my family, I have written four more full-length books (*Vegetarian Dishes of the World*, subsequently published in paperback as *A Foreign Flavour*, *Your Very Good Health*, *Gourmet Vegetarian Cooking* and *Rose Elliot's Vegetarian Mother and Baby Book*), my series of eight 64-page *Little Books* and a wholefood guide for beginners called *Beanfeast*. As well as these I have also been doing quite a lot of magazine articles, broadcasting, television and cookery demonstrations, and, wearing my other career-hat, taking on the astrological pages in *Woman's Realm* and *Here's Health* magazine, and writing around a million words for a computer-astrology project which my husband and I have launched together.

But, to get back to cookery. One of the very nicest things about being a cookery writer is that, because people have used your recipes in their kitchen, they begin to think of you as a friend. They write you wonderful letters, send you tips, recipes, and sometimes strange ingredients, and come up and hug you at book-signings and after demonstrations. I've even had letters from complete strangers inviting me to meals. I can't begin to say how happy this makes me. One of the loveliest things which happened to me recently was when a reader came up to me after I'd done a cookery demonstration in London and told me she had made the long journey from the north of England specially because she wanted to thank me personally for my books! Apparently two years previously she had been told by her doctor that she had a chronic digestive condition and would be on drugs for the rest of her life. At about that time she had started using one of my cookery books and to her surprise found that her symptoms began to get better. So she began reducing the drugs until she had stopped taking them completely. Her progress continued, and she told me she felt completely rejuvenated. 'Your books have changed my life,' she told me.

Of course I can't really take credit for this: that should go to the wholefood/
vegetarian diet (and I've got many letters from other readers which tell the same story:
people who've lost weight, cured arthritis, heart problems, high blood pressure, eczema,
digestive problems and so on). So it's a way of eating that is undoubtedly healthy, and
the medical discoveries of the past few years, together with the backing given by an
increasing number of official reports which have also confirmed these views, have given
me special pleasure. Today, instead of being regarded as eccentric and odd, as my
style of cooking was when I first started, it's recognized as being both healthy and
delicious. You can buy wholewheat bread, decent muesli mix, brown rice and a range
of beans and lentils in any supermarket, and increasingly restaurants are ensuring that
they have at least one vegetarian dish always on the menu. In this context, I must say
that another thing which gives me a warm glow of pleasure and pride is when a
restaurant I know uses my recipes gets into one of the good food guides. But the
popularity of vegetarianism really came home to me last time I was doing the usual
round of press and radio interviews following the publication of my latest book, and I
realized instead of having to defend and justify my views to them, most of the
journalists interviewing me were themselves vegetarian and users of my books!

People often tell me of their culinary successes and their favourite recipes from my
books – and how they wish they were published in a more long-lasting form than a
paperback book 'which falls apart with use'. So I was delighted when my hardback
publisher, Collins, suggested the idea of this complete book, and I do hope that you
will like it too. The book contains the best and most popular recipes from all my books,
plus a few new ones which are being published for the first time. When I started
writing the book, I was amazed to find that there were nearly 2000 recipes to choose
from, so the task of selection was not as easy as I'd envisaged. I know from reader-
reaction that some recipes are perennially popular, so they've gone in, and that was
easy. My criteria in choosing the rest were, firstly, that they should be delicious to eat,
and secondly, that they should be healthy, quick and easy to make, and reasonably
economical. I don't say that every recipe meets every criterion (except the deliciousness
one, I hope) – there are one or two recipes which have crept in for fun and pleasure
rather than for health, and a few which are a bit fiddly to make and/or extravagant, but
wonderful for a special occasion – but I hope you'll agree that most of them do.

Writing this book has been a most enjoyable task, has brought back many happy
memories and been quite revealing in some ways. For instance, I was surprised to see
how addicted I was to the inclusions of bay leaves and lemon rind in the *Not Just a
Load of Old Lentils* recipes. All these early recipes – even those in *The Bean Book* –
relied much more heavily on the use of fat than subsequent ones, and my use of
polyunsaturated margarine and butter has varied from book to book, according to my
own thoughts on the relative health merits of the two. These thoughts have changed as
new evidence has come to light, and may well do so again in the future, but at the
moment my opinion on the matter is as follows.

First of all, too much of any fat – saturated or unsaturated – is unhealthy, and it makes
good sense to cut out fat in your diet wherever you can; by using a skimmed or semi-
skimmed milk in place of ordinary milk; using skimmed-milk yoghurt and low-fat cheeses;
cutting down on the amount of fat you put on bread; using smaller amounts of a stronger-
tasting cheese; and watching out for (and limiting consumption of) 'hidden' fats in cakes,
crisps, chocolate and pastries. Having done that, my own preference is for unsalted butter,

used sparingly on the table and in some cooking, such as pastry and the occasional cake, and a good-quality cold-pressed olive oil for all frying and salad dressings. The only cooking task that this does not allow for is deep-frying; for this it is necessary to use a good-quality corn or sunflower oil (not cold-pressed), though ideally deep-frying should be kept to the minimum in a healthy diet.

Let me explain the reason for my choice of fats. When vegetable oils are heated, as happens during the refining process and in the making of margarine, the chemical structure of the molecules is altered, and the valuable 'cis' fatty acids, which the body needs, are altered so that they become 'trans' fatty acids, which are harmful to health. There appears to be a link between high intake of 'trans' fatty acids and some cancers, just as there appears to be a link between high intake of saturated fat and heart disease. It is because butter and olive oil are more stable from this point of view when heated, that I prefer to use them for cooking, since the fatty acids in margarines have already been altered by the manufacturing process, and those in other cold-pressed oils are altered once you heat them.

Having said that, I must stress that the most important thing is to reduce your overall fat intake. This does not mean giving up delicious things like quiches, chocolate, chips and strawberries and cream; it just means you have to plan for them. If you know you're going to have a dish that's high in fat, in the evening perhaps, have a cereal and fruit breakfast with skimmed milk, and a salad lunch without fats. Then you can really enjoy your quiche (or whatever) for your evening meal, with steamed vegetables dressed with lemon juice and lots of chopped herbs, and a fatless fresh-fruit pudding, such as peaches in a strawberry purée, to follow. That way you can have your fat sometimes and, hopefully, stay slim and healthy!

With this in mind, I must say it's been a pleasure to have been able to update many early recipes by including ingredients such as smooth white skimmed milk cheese or quark, which simply weren't available in those days – there I was sieving cottage cheese . . . ! Come to think of it, even cottage cheese was quite difficult to get when I was writing *Simply Delicious*! For much the same reason, too, I used many more canned vegetables in those early books – the fresh red peppers, aubergines and courgettes which we can now take for granted in most parts of Britain weren't readily available then. I was also able to trace my decreasing use of sugar, and to update the earlier recipes in this respect, too. Another development since I wrote the early books has been the use of the deep-freeze, and I've given general freezing notes where applicable at the beginning of each chapter and added the F freezer symbol to recipes which are suitable for freezing.

So that's it, except that I'd also like to take this opportunity to say 'thank you' to Collins (and especially to Robin Wood) for giving me the opportunity to write this book; and, most of all, to you, for buying my books and for your encouragement and support over the years. I hope you will like this collection and find all your favourite recipes here – and perhaps some which are less familiar, too. They come to you with my love, the hope that you'll enjoy making and eating them, and my very best wishes for your health and happiness in the future.

Rose Elliot
May 1985

1

SOUPS
HOT AND CHILLED

I know cookery writers like me are always saying this, but soups are so easy to make that I think it's surprising that more people don't make more of them more of the time! A lentil soup, like the one on page 21, for instance, the potato soup, on page 26, or the celery and tomato soup, on page 16, can be prepared in moments, and make a wonderful basis for a meal. Serve them with some wholemeal rolls which you warm in the oven while the soup is simmering, a piece of cheese, perhaps, and some fresh fruit, and you've got an easy, delicious and healthy meal. A warming soup also makes the perfect accompaniment to a vitamin-rich salad meal in winter and a welcoming first course for a special meal. Chilled soups are special favourites of mine for entertaining, especially the rich ruby-red beetroot soup on page 13, the chilled cucumber soups, and the curried lentil and apple soup.

At the beginning of this chapter you'll find a good recipe for vegetarian stock. But don't be put off making soup because you haven't time for this.

You can get very good results using just water (and I often do this), or one of the excellent vegetarian stock concentrates you can buy. I specially like a Swiss one which comes in a small tin and seems expensive when you buy it but goes a long way; and a bouillon powder made by a firm called Marigold.

Many homemade soups freeze excellently, and you'll find the freezer symbol [F] against those suitable for this. It's best to make the soup with less liquid than the recipe says, so that it's more compact for freezing, then add the rest later when you use the soup. Ideally, if you're methodical, you should label the soup and make a note of the quantity of liquid to be added later.

Having said all that, soup from the deep freeze is no emergency meal, because it takes for ever to thaw – it's quicker to whizz up some soup from scratch! It is handy to have some soup in the freezer, however, for entertaining and when you've got friends staying, as long as you remember to get it out of the freezer the night before you want to use it.

When you serve the soup, you can easily turn it into something special by adding a simple, contrasting garnish. A swirl of cream or yoghurt and some chopped fresh green basil make a simple, home-made tomato soup look and taste extra good; some chopped mint adds the finishing touch to a smooth green pea soup, while a delicately-flavoured white soup, like creamy cauliflower or artichoke, is delicious with chopped chives, crunchy golden croutons or flaked nuts on top. To make croutons, just fry 6mm (¼in) cubes of soft wholemeal bread in a little butter until they're crisp and golden, then drain well on kitchen paper. Or, for a fatless version, cut crisp wholemeal toast into little cubes. Both kinds will keep in the freezer, ready for instant use.

VEGETARIAN STOCK

Although you can now buy excellent vegetarian stock powder and concentrate, home-made stock is easy to make. It only takes about 10 minutes to prepare (followed by 1 hour slow simmering) and it keeps perfectly for a week in a jug in the bottom of the refrigerator. You can add some garlic, peppercorns and other herbs, such as a bay leaf and some thyme, but this is a good basic recipe that works well for most purposes.

MAKES ABOUT 1.2 LITRES (2 PINTS) F
1 onion, peeled and roughly sliced
1 stick of celery, washed and roughly chopped
1 large carrot, scrubbed and roughly chopped
1 medium-sized potato, scrubbed and roughly chopped
2 or 3 sprigs of parsley
2.5 litres (4 pints) water

Put the vegetables and parsley into a large saucepan and add the water. Bring to the boil, then turn the heat down, cover and leave to simmer for 1 hour. Strain through a sieve.

CHILLED APPLE SOUP

SERVES 4 F
700g (1½ lb) cooking apples
850ml (1½ pints) water
pared rind ½ lemon
piece of cinnamon stick
sugar or clear honey to taste
2 teaspoons cornflour
fresh or soured cream
finely chopped apple mint

Peel, core and finely slice apples. Simmer gently in the water with the thinly pared lemon rind and cinnamon until tender. Remove cinnamon, and liquidize all but one good ladleful of apple slices, which remain to give texture to the soup. Sweeten to taste with sugar or honey, then pour in cornflour blended with a little cold water, and stir until thickened. Simmer for a further 5 minutes. Chill. Ladle into chilled bowls; add a whirl of cream – soured or fresh, according to taste, into each bowl, and finish with a sprinkling of chopped apple mint for a refreshing, cooling first course.

Variation

CHILLED PLUM SOUP

Make in exactly the same way, using 700g (1½ lb) ripe stoned red plums instead of apples.

ARTICHOKE SOUP

Jerusalem artichokes make a beautiful creamy white soup with a delicate flavour which I think is delicious. They are quite easy to peel if you use a potato peeler and are fairly ruthless about cutting off the little lumps. Put them into a bowl of cold water as they're done, to preserve their colour.

SERVES 6 F
25g (1oz) butter
1 onion, peeled and chopped
900g (2 lb) Jerusalem artichokes, peeled and cut into even-sized chunks
1.2 litres (2 pints) light vegetable stock *or* water
275ml (10 fl oz) milk
150ml (5 fl oz) single cream – optional
sea salt
freshly ground black pepper
freshly grated nutmeg
fresh chives *or* parsley, chopped

Melt the butter in a large saucepan and add the onion; fry for 5–7 minutes until fairly soft but not browned, then put in the artichoke and cook for a further 2–3 minutes, stirring often. Pour in the stock or water and bring up to the boil, then turn the heat down, put a lid on the saucepan and leave to simmer for about 20 minutes until the artichoke is soft. Liquidize or sieve the mixture, then add enough of the milk to bring the soup to the right consistency, together with the cream if you're using it, and some salt, pepper and freshly grated nutmeg to taste. Reheat, and serve with some chopped chives or parsley sprinkled on top.

ASPARAGUS SOUP

This is one of those soups with a bonus, because you can use the lower part of the asparagus stalks to make it, saving the tops for something else, perhaps a special flan. Or the tips can be wrapped in wholemeal bread (page 54) and served alongside the soup – a delicious combination. This soup is equally good served hot or chilled.

SERVES 4 F
450g (1 lb) fresh or frozen asparagus
25g (1oz) butter
1 large onion, chopped
about 1 litre (1¾ pints) water
4 tablespoons single cream
2 tablespoons lemon juice
sea salt
freshly ground black pepper

If you're using fresh asparagus, wash it well to remove any grit. Then cut off the tips of the asparagus. Trim off the coarsest part of the rest of the stems, then cut the stems into 2cm (1in) pieces. With frozen asparagus, just remove the upper half of the stalks. Cook the asparagus tips in a little boiling water until tender, then drain, reserving water. The tips are not needed for this recipe, just their cooking water. The tips can be used in the ways suggested above.

Melt the butter in a large saucepan and fry the onion gently for 5 minutes, but don't let it get brown. Then put in the asparagus stems and cook very gently, with a lid on the pan, for a further 5–10 minutes. Make the asparagus liquid up to 1.2 litres (2 pints) with cold water, and add to the onion and asparagus. Bring to the boil, then leave to simmer gently for about 30 minutes, until the asparagus is tender. Liquidize the soup and, if necessary, pass it through a sieve. Add the single cream, lemon juice, and salt and pepper to taste. Serve hot or chilled.

CHILLED AVOCADO SOUP

This soup is very easy to make (with a liquidizer or food processor) and comes out a creamy very pale green colour. It's best not to make it more than about 45 minutes in advance in case it discolours.

SERVES 6
2 large ripe avocado pears – make sure they feel slightly soft all over when you hold them in the palm of your hand
1 tablespoon lemon juice
850ml (1½ pints) ice-cold skimmed milk
sea salt
freshly ground black pepper
2 tablespoons chopped chives

Cut the avocados in half, then twist the two halves apart and remove the stones. Carefully peel off the skin. Cut the avocados into chunks and put these into the liquidizer goblet with the lemon juice and milk. Blend at medium speed until the mixture is smooth. Season with salt and pepper. Put the soup into the fridge to chill until it's needed; if there's room it's a good idea to put the soup bowls in too.

When you're ready to serve ladle the soup into the bowls and sprinkle generously with chopped chives.

BEAN AND CARROT SOUP

The recipe for this soup is based on a wartime one. The result is a pretty, pale golden soup with a creamy consistency, and the combination of beans and milk is excellent from the protein point of view.

SERVES 4–5 F
125g (4oz) haricot beans, soaked, drained and rinsed
850ml (1½ pints) unsalted stock or water
1 large onion, peeled and sliced
1 stick of celery, sliced
2 large carrots, scraped and diced
a bouquet garni – a sprig or two of parsley, a sprig of thyme and a bay leaf, tied together
25g (1oz) butter
25g (1oz) flour
275ml (10 fl oz) milk
sea salt
freshly ground black pepper
grated nutmeg
a little chopped parsley

Put the beans into a large saucepan with the stock or water and simmer them gently for 45 minutes, then add the onion, celery, carrots and the bouquet garni and cook them all for another 30 minutes or so until the beans and vegetables are tender. Remove the bouquet garni and sieve or liquidize the soup.

Melt the butter in a large, clean saucepan and stir in the flour; when it 'froths', remove the saucepan from the heat and stir in the puréed soup. Put the saucepan back on the heat and stir the soup until it has thickened; leave it to simmer gently for 10–15 minutes to cook the flour, then mix in the milk and season the soup with sea salt, freshly ground black pepper and some grated nutmeg. Reheat the soup, but don't let it boil. Serve it sprinkled with chopped parsley.

BEETROOT SOUP

This is a beautiful ruby red soup that looks mouthwatering with its swirl of creamy white topping. In hot weather this soup is also very good served chilled – in fact, I think that's how I like it best.

SERVES 4 [F]
1 onion
1 large potato – about 225g (8oz)
1 tablespoon olive oil
450g (1 lb) cooked beetroot – get the kind that is still in its skin, not beetroot which has been peeled and preserved in vinegar
1.2 litres (2 pints) water
sea salt
freshly ground black pepper
1 tablespoon lemon juice
½ teaspoon grated lemon rind
3 tablespoons thick natural yoghurt or soured cream

Peel and chop the onion; peel and dice the potatoes. Heat the oil in a fairly large saucepan and fry the onion, without browning, for about 5 minutes, then add the potatoes, turn them in the oil and cook gently for about 5 minutes more. Meanwhile slip the skin off the beetroot and dice the flesh. Add the beetroot to the saucepan and stir in the water or stock. Bring up to the boil then leave the soup to simmer, with a lid on the saucepan, for about 20 minutes until the potatoes are soft. Liquidize the soup, then return it to the saucepan and flavour with salt, pepper and the lemon juice and rind. Reheat gently. Spoon some yoghurt or soured cream on top of each bowl of soup just before serving.

RUSSIAN BEETROOT SOUP

The Russian way to serve this soup is with the little curd cheese tarts on page 248. I think this makes a very pleasant combination for a light supper.

SERVES 4–6 [F]
2 large onions
2 large carrots
2 stalks celery
125g (4oz) cabbage
2 tablespoons olive oil
1 litre (1¾ pints) water or vegetable stock
225g (8oz) can tomatoes
450g (1 lb) cooked beetroot (not beetroot in vinegar)
sea salt
sugar
150ml (5 fl oz) carton soured cream or thick natural yoghurt (optional)
fresh dill or chives (optional)

Peel and chop the onions; scrape and dice the carrots and slice the celery and cabbage. Heat the oil in a good-sized saucepan and add the prepared vegetables; stir them so that they all get coated with the oil, then leave them to fry over a gentle heat for about 10 minutes, stirring from time to time. Stir in the water or vegetable stock and tomatoes, bring up to the boil, then cover the saucepan and leave the soup to simmer for about 20 minutes until all the vegetables are tender. (I sometimes use a pressure-cooker for this in which case it takes about 5 minutes.)

While this is happening rub the peel off the beetroot and cut them into dice. Add the beetroot to the soup and season well with salt and a little sugar. Bring the soup up to the boil again and let it simmer gently for 3–4 minutes. You can serve the borsch like this, but I prefer to liquidize about half of it, which makes the soup slightly thicker while still retaining a nice texture. If using the soured cream or yoghurt whisk it lightly with a fork to make it creamy, then swirl a little into each bowl. Sprinkle with chopped dill if you've got some; or you can use chopped chives.

CREAM OF BUTTER BEAN SOUP

As this soup has a smooth, creamy texture, I like to serve it with some crunchy croûtons of fried bread or crisp wholemeal toast scattered over the top.

SERVES 4–6 F
125g (4oz) butter beans
1 large onion
1 medium-sized potato
2 carrots
2 sticks celery
25g (1oz) butter
850ml (1½ pints) water *or* unsalted stock
275ml (10 fl oz) milk
a bouquet garni – a couple of sprigs of parsley, a sprig of thyme and a bay leaf, tied together
4–6 tablespoons cream
sea salt
freshly ground black pepper
grated nutmeg
a few croûtons of fried bread or cubes of crisp wholemeal toast

Soak the butter beans, then drain and rinse them. Peel and chop the onion and potato; scrape and chop the carrots; slice the celery. Melt the butter in a large saucepan and add the vegetables; sauté them for 7–8 minutes, but don't let them brown, then add the butter beans, water or stock, the milk and the bouquet garni. Simmer gently, with a lid half on the saucepan, for about 1¼ hours, or until the butter beans are tender. Remove the herbs, then liquidize the soup, stir in the cream and add sea salt, freshly ground black pepper and nutmeg to taste. Reheat the soup, but don't let it boil. Serve each bowl sprinkled with croûtons.

BUTTER BEAN AND TOMATO SOUP

Served with garlic bread and a salad or some fruit, this hearty soup makes a complete meal.

SERVES 3–4 F
225g (8oz) butter beans
850ml (1½ pints) water *or* unsalted stock
1 bay leaf
2 large onions
25g (1oz) butter
450g (1 lb) tomatoes, peeled and chopped (or use canned ones)
sea salt
freshly ground black pepper
a little sugar
chopped parsley

Soak the butter beans in cold water for several hours, then drain and rinse them as usual. Put them into a large saucepan with the water or stock and the bay leaf and simmer them until tender – about 1¼ hours. Meanwhile, peel and slice the onions and fry them lightly in the butter until they're soft, about 10 minutes, then add them to the cooked butter beans, together with the tomatoes and some sea salt and freshly ground black pepper. Bring them up to the boil and simmer gently for about 10 minutes. Check seasoning, adding more sea salt and freshly ground pepper and a little sugar if you think it needs them. Serve sprinkled with the parsley. You can liquidize this soup, if you prefer – remove the bay leaf first!

CARROT, APPLE AND CHERVIL SOUP

Feathery leaves of chervil have a beautifully delicate flavour which I think makes this soup special. But if you can't get chervil you could use other fresh herbs instead: tarragon, lovage or fennel would be good or even ordinary mint. This soup is also good chilled, but in this case it is best to use oil instead of butter (2 tablespoons).

SERVES 4–6 F
25g (1oz) butter
1 onion, peeled and chopped
225g (8oz) carrots, scraped and sliced
125g (4oz) cooking apple, peeled, cored and sliced
1 stick celery, washed and sliced
1.2 litres (2 pints) light vegetable stock *or* water
sea salt
freshly ground black pepper
sugar
2 tablespoons chopped fresh chervil

Melt the butter in a large saucepan and add the onion; fry for 5–7 minutes until fairly soft but not browned, then put in the carrot, apple and celery and cook for a further 2–3 minutes, stirring often. Pour in the stock or water and bring to the boil, then turn the heat down, put a lid on the saucepan and leave to simmer for about 20 minutes, until the carrots are soft. Liquidize or sieve the mixture, and add a little extra stock if necessary to make a fairly thin, creamy consistency. Season with salt, pepper and perhaps just a touch of sugar. Reheat, and serve each bowl with a good sprinkling of chopped chervil on top – the bright green looks very pretty against the orange soup.

CARROT AND LEMON SOUP

The sweet carrots and sharp lemon are a pleasant combination.

SERVES 4 F
1 onion, chopped
2 sticks celery, diced
6 medium-sized carrots
15g (½oz) butter
1 bay leaf
1 teaspoon grated lemon rind
2 tablespoons lemon juice
850ml (1½ pints) water *or* stock
sea salt
freshly ground black pepper
chopped parsley to serve

Fry the onion, celery and carrot gently in the butter for 5–10 minutes until beginning to soften but not brown. Add the bay leaf, half the lemon rind and water and simmer for about 20–25 minutes until vegetables are cooked. Liquidize, add lemon juice to taste and the rest of the lemon rind and some salt and pepper. Serve sprinkled with chopped parsley.

CAULIFLOWER SOUP WITH ALMONDS

Cauliflower makes a surprisingly satisfactory soup, creamy and delicately flavoured. It goes very well with the herb bread on page 339, but if you haven't time to do this, hot garlic bread (page 54) is also good.

SERVES 6 F
25g (1oz) butter
1 onion, peeled and chopped
1 medium-sized potato, about 150g (5oz)
½ fairly small cauliflower – about 225g (8oz), washed and broken in florets
1.2 litres (2 pints) light vegetable stock *or* water
150 ml (5 fl oz) single cream – optional
sea salt
freshly ground black pepper
grated nutmeg
2 tablespoons flaked roasted almonds

Melt the butter in a large saucepan and add the onion; fry for 5–7 minutes until fairly soft but not browned, then put in the potato and cauliflower and cook for a further 2–3 minutes, stirring often: the vegetables for this soup mustn't brown or the delicate flavour will be spoilt. Pour in the stock or water and bring up to the boil, then turn the heat down, put a lid on the saucepan and leave to simmer for about 20 minutes, until the vegetables are soft. Liquidize or sieve the mixture, then add the cream, if you're using it, and season well with salt and plenty of freshly grated pepper and nutmeg. Reheat, and serve with some crisp flaked almonds on top of each portion.

CELERY SOUP WITH LOVAGE

The flavour of lovage is often described as being like that of celery: but it is much more pungent and aromatic. However it does go very well with celery and together I think they make a lovely soup. Made with the first of the English celery and the last of the lovage from the garden, it's a perfect soup for a crisp autumn day. If you can't get hold of any lovage, use some of the celery leaves, finely chopped, instead.

SERVES 6 F
25g (1oz) butter
1 onion, peeled and chopped
outside sticks from 1 head of celery – about 450g (1 lb), washed and sliced
225g (8oz) potatoes, peeled and cut into even-sized chunks
1.2 litres (2 pints) light vegetable stock *or* water
2 tablespoons chopped fresh lovage
150ml (5 fl oz) single cream – optional
sea salt
freshly ground black pepper

Melt the butter in a large saucepan and add the onion; fry for 5–7 minutes until fairly soft but not browned, then put in the celery and potato and cook for a further 2–3 minutes, stirring often. Pour in the stock or water and bring up to the boil, then turn the heat down, put a lid on the saucepan and leave to simmer for about 20 minutes until the vegetables are soft. Liquidize or sieve the mixture, then add the lovage, the cream if you're using it, and a good seasoning of salt and pepper. Reheat before serving. Or serve each bowl of soup with a swirl of cream and some chopped lovage on top.

CELERY AND TOMATO SOUP

SERVES 4
3 onions, chopped
outside stalks from 1 head celery, chopped
1 tablespoon olive oil
400g (14oz) can tomatoes
1 bay leaf
575ml (1 pint) water *or* vegetable stock
sea salt
freshly ground black pepper
sugar
2 tablespoons lemon juice
1 tablespoon chopped celery leaves

Fry the onions and celery together in the oil without browning for 5–10 minutes. Add tomatoes, roughly chopped, bay leaf and water, and simmer for 30 minutes, until celery is tender.

Add salt, pepper, sugar and lemon juice to taste. Add chopped celery leaves, and serve each bowl garnished with chopped celery leaves.

CHEESE AND ONION SOUP

Although the ingredients used in this Italian soup are very similar to those of French onion soup, the result is quite different because it is white with a smooth texture, and the cheese is stirred in just before serving to thicken and flavour it. It's a filling, protein-rich soup, lovely before a salad meal, or buttery pasta and green salad.

SERVES 4
700g (1½ lb) onions
850ml (1½ pints) water
25g (1oz) butter
sea salt
freshly ground black pepper
125–175g (4–6oz) grated cheese
25g (1oz) Parmesan cheese
cubes of wholemeal toast

Peel and chop onions, then put them into a large saucepan with the water and simmer them gently until tender – 15–20 minutes. Liquidize the soup, then return it to the rinsed out saucepan and add the butter and a little seasoning. When you're ready to serve the soup reheat it until bubbling hot. Take it off the heat and stir in the cheeses. Check the seasoning and serve the soup immediately, with some cubes of wholemeal toast on top.

If you reheat the soup once the cheese has been added don't let it boil or it might get stringy. Also be careful not to over-season the soup before you add the cheese because the cheese will make it taste saltier.

CHILLED CHERRY SOUP

No one finds it odd to start a meal with melon and really a fruit soup is only taking this a stage further! Anyway, this black cherry soup looks so delicious with its topping of soured cream or yoghurt that I don't think you'll have much trouble persuading people to try it. I usually use frozen black cherries but of course fresh ones would be better if you can get them.

SERVES 6
450g (1 lb) frozen black cherries
850ml (1½ pints) water
caster sugar or honey to taste
2 tablespoons arrowroot
150ml (5 fl oz) dry red wine
a little lemon juice – optional
a little soured cream

Stone the cherries by halving them and digging out the stones with a sharp knife; or use a cherry stoner if you've got one.

Put the cherries into a saucepan with the water, bring to the boil and simmer gently until tender. Sweeten to taste. Mix the arrowroot with a little cold water to make a smooth paste, then stir a ladleful of the hot cherry liquid into the arrowroot mixture. When blended add it to the saucepan and simmer for 2–3 minutes. Take the saucepan off the heat and pour the soup into a bowl. When it's cool stir in the wine, then chill it before serving. Taste and add a little more sugar if necessary or possibly a drop or two of lemon juice to sharpen the flavour slightly; it should be sweet but refreshing. Swirl soured cream on top before serving.

CHESTNUT SOUP

The starchy texture and slightly sweet flavour of chestnuts go well with hot vegetables and make this a very warming winter soup. You can use fresh chestnuts if you've got time to prepare them but I must admit I usually use the dried ones which you can get easily now in health shops and some supermarkets.

SERVES 4–6 F
700g (1½ lb) fresh chestnuts *or* 225g (8oz) dried chestnuts
1 large onion
2 large carrots
1 turnip
2 celery stalks
25g (1oz) butter
1 litre (1¾ pints) stock *or* water
1 tablespoon chopped parsley
sea salt
freshly ground black pepper

If you're using fresh chestnuts make a little cut in them with a sharp knife, then simmer them in boiling water until the cut opens – about 10 minutes. Remove the skins with a sharp, pointed knife – keep the chestnuts in the water until you're ready to peel them because the skins will firm up as they cool. If you're using dried chestnuts soak them in cold water for an hour or so then simmer them gently in plenty of water until they're really tender. I find this takes a good hour or more. Drain the cooked dried chestnuts, saving the liquid.

Peel and chop the onion, carrots and turnip; wash and dice the celery. Melt the butter in a large saucepan and fry the onion for 5 minutes, then add the rest of the vegetables and cook for a further 5 minutes before pouring in the stock. (If you're using dried chestnuts, make the reserved cooking liquid up to 1 litre (1¾ pints) with water or stock and use this.) Simmer the soup for about 40 minutes until the chestnuts and vegetables are tender. Stir in the parsley and season the soup with salt and pepper.

SPANISH CHICK PEA SOUP WITH GARLIC AND MINT

In this Spanish soup, 'sopa de panela', the flavour of chick peas combines beautifully with the mint and garlic. You need a liquidizer or food processor for this recipe.

SERVES 4 F
225g (8oz) chick peas *or* 2 × 400g (14oz) cans
2 garlic cloves, crushed
a handful of mint, stalks removed
a small handful of parsley, stalks removed
6 tablespoons olive oil
sea salt
freshly ground black pepper
2 slices of bread, crusts removed

If you're using dried chick peas, soak and cook them as usual. Drain the chick peas (home-cooked or canned) and measure the liquid. Put the chick peas, 850ml (1½ pints) of their liquid (made up with extra water if necessary), the garlic, mint, parsley and half the oil into the liquidizer or food processor (it may be necessary to do this in two batches) and blend at high speed until smooth. Season with sea salt and freshly ground black pepper and reheat gently. While this is happening, cut the bread into little cubes and fry it in the remaining oil until golden brown. Serve the soup sprinkled with the fried bread croûtons.

CHILLED CUCUMBER SOUP (1)

This refreshing chilled soup makes a beautiful light, low-fat starter. You can make a richer-tasting soup for a special occasion by using half yoghurt and half soured cream.

SERVES 4
1 cucumber
425g (15 fl oz) natural yoghurt
8 sprigs mint
4 sprigs parsley
1 teaspoon sea salt
4 sprigs mint

Peel the cucumber, then cut it into rough chunks. Put the chunks into the liquidizer goblet with the yoghurt. Wash the mint and parsley and remove the stalks; add the leaves to the cucumber and yoghurt together with the salt. Blend at medium speed until you've got a smooth purée. Transfer the purée to a bowl and place it in the fridge until it's really cold. Check the seasoning and add more salt if necessary – chilling tends to dull the flavour – then serve the soup in individual bowls with a sprig of mint floating on top of each.

CHILLED CUCUMBER SOUP (2)

SERVES 4–6 [F]
1 large cucumber
1 small onion or shallot
850ml (1½ pints) vegetable stock or water
½ teaspoon dill – optional
1 level dessertspoon arrowroot
4 tablespoons cream *or* evaporated milk
sea salt
freshly ground black pepper
1 sprig mint

Peel cucumber thinly and cut into small pieces; peel and chop onion and place both in a pan with the stock and dill. Bring to the boil and cover, simmering for 10–15 minutes. Pass through a sieve or liquidizer, and return to the pan. Blend the arrowroot with a little milk or cream and stir into the mixture in the pan. Bring to the boil, stirring all the time, and cook for a few seconds until thickened slightly. Add seasoning to taste. Chill thoroughly, and serve in chilled bowls, garnished with a slice of cucumber and chopped parsley or fresh sprigs of mint.

BULGARIAN CHILLED CUCUMBER SOUP

Yoghurt, cucumber, walnuts and dill sound like rather a strange mixture but actually the combination of smooth creamy yoghurt and chewy walnut with refreshing cucumber and dill works well.

SERVES 4
1 large cucumber
1 garlic clove, peeled and crushed in a little salt
425ml (15 fl oz) natural yoghurt
25g (1oz) walnut pieces
sea salt
freshly ground black pepper
1 tablespoon chopped fresh dill weed *or* parsley (*or* 1 teaspoon dried dill weed and 2 teaspoons chopped fresh parsley)

Peel the cucumber (if you leave the skin on it can make the soup taste rather bitter), then cut it into rough chunks. Put the chunks into the liquidizer with the garlic, yoghurt, walnuts, about half a teaspoon of sea salt and a grinding of pepper and blend until you've got a smoothish purée. Taste the mixture and add some more salt and pepper if you think it needs it, then pour the soup into a bowl and chill it thoroughly.

To serve the soup ladle it into individual bowls and sprinkle each with the chopped green herbs.

DAL SOUP

One of my favourite soups, this is ideal for serving before a rice and curry meal because the pulse protein complements the rice, giving first-class nourishment. You can use either split peas or split red lentils. This recipe makes quite a thin soup; for a thicker one, use 225g (8oz) split peas or lentils.

SERVES 4 [F]
175g (6oz) yellow split peas *or* split red lentils
1 large onion
2 tablespoons oil
1 garlic clove, crushed
1 teaspoon turmeric
1 teaspoon ground ginger
1 bay leaf
1 litre (1¾ pints) water
1 lemon
sea salt
freshly ground black pepper

Cover the split peas or split red lentils with water and leave them to soak for a few hours; drain and rinse them. Peel and chop the onion and fry it in the oil in a large saucepan for 5 minutes, then add the garlic, turmeric, ginger and bay leaf and fry for a further 5 minutes. Stir in the split peas or lentils and the water. Bring the mixture up to the boil, then let it simmer gently, with a lid on the saucepan, for about 30 minutes, or until the lentils or split peas are soft. Remove the bay leaf and liquidize the soup. Wash the lemon, then cut four or five circles from it, one to garnish each bowl of soup. Squeeze the rest of the lemon and add enough of the juice to the soup to sharpen it; season carefully with sea salt and freshly ground black pepper. Reheat the soup and serve each bowl with a circle of lemon floating in it.

EGG AND ONION SOUP

This is a soothing soup, and a pleasant blend of flavours. Serve with some crisp wholemeal toast for a complete light supper dish.

SERVES 4
6 medium-sized onions, chopped
25g (1oz) butter
2 tablespoons flour
1 litre (1¾ pints) milk and water, mixed
1 bay leaf
a little powdered mace
sea salt
freshly ground black pepper
4 hard boiled eggs, chopped
chopped parsley

Fry the onions gently in the butter without browning for 10 minutes; add flour, stir until blended, then gradually add the liquid. Simmer gently with a bay leaf for 15 minutes, then season with mace, salt and pepper. Add the hard boiled eggs, and heat through gently. Sprinkle with chopped parsley before serving.

FASOLADA

This is a Greek-style bean soup – and it's very filling! Serve with chunks of wholemeal bread or garlic bread.

SERVES 4 F
6 tablespoons olive oil
1 large onion, peeled and chopped
2 sticks celery, sliced
2 carrots, scraped and chopped
1 garlic clove, crushed
225g (8oz) haricot beans, soaked, thoroughly rinsed and then drained
1 litre (1¾ pints) unsalted stock or water
1 tablespoon tomato purée
2 tablespoons chopped parsley
sea salt
freshly ground black pepper
a little lemon juice

Heat the oil in a large saucepan and fry the onion, celery, carrot and garlic for 5 minutes, stirring them from time to time to prevent sticking. Then stir in the drained beans, stock or water, tomato purée and parsley and bring the mixture up to the boil. Cover the saucepan with a lid, reduce heat and simmer soup gently for about 1 hour, until the beans are tender. Season with sea salt and freshly ground black pepper to taste and a little lemon juice if you think it needs it.

This soup can be served as it is, or liquidized; personally I think it's nicest when it's been liquidized.

FLAGEOLET SOUP

Creamy and delicate, this soup is equally nice served hot or cold. If serving it cold, use oil, not butter, chill the soup well, and garnish it with extra cream and some chopped chives. The green leek helps to accentuate the natural green colour of the beans. You need a liquidizer or food processor for this one.

SERVES 4 F
125g (4oz) flageolet beans
1 small onion, chopped
1 leek, sliced
25g (1oz) butter
850ml (1½ pints) unsalted stock or water
2–4 tablespoons double cream
1 tablespoon chopped parsley
sea salt
freshly ground black pepper
a little chopped fresh parsley

Soak, rinse and drain the beans as usual. Fry the onion and leek gently together in the butter in a good-sized saucepan for about 10 minutes. Add the beans to the onion and leek, together with the stock or water, and simmer gently for about 1 hour, until the beans are tender. Put the soup into the liquidizer or food processor with the cream and parsley and blend to a smooth, creamy consistency. Season with sea salt and freshly ground black pepper. Reheat but do not boil soup; serve garnished with extra chopped parsley.

GAZPACHO

A quick and easy version of this chilled Spanish 'salad soup'. If you keep a can of tomatoes in the fridge in the summer you can make this soup in a matter of moments. It's nice served with some crunchy cubes of fried bread or crisp wholemeal toast.

SERVES 6
1 large onion, peeled and cut into rough chunks
2 large garlic cloves, peeled and crushed in a little salt
792g (1 lb 12oz) can tomatoes
4 tablespoons olive oil
2 teaspoons wine vinegar
sea salt
freshly ground black pepper
about 10cm (4in) cucumber
1 small green or red pepper
1 tablespoon chopped fresh chives
1 tablespoon chopped fresh mint
a few cubes of bread fried in oil

Put the onion and garlic into the liquidizer or food processor together with the tomatoes, olive oil, vinegar, some salt and a grinding of pepper and blend to a purée. (If you haven't got a liquidizer, grate the onion finely and pass the tomatoes through a vegetable mill, then mix them together and add the garlic, oil, vinegar and seasoning.) Chill the mixture.

Just before you want to serve the soup dice the cucumber and de-seed and finely chop the pepper. Stir the cucumber and pepper pieces into the soup, together with the freshly chopped herbs, then ladle the soup into individual bowls and hand round the croûtons of fried bread or toast separately.

GOLDEN SOUP

SERVES 4 [F]
1 onion, chopped
1 carrot, coarsely grated
15g (½oz) butter
1 bay leaf
400g (14oz) can tomatoes
575ml (1 pint) water *or* stock
½ teaspoon grated lemon rind
1–2 tablespoons lemon juice
sea salt
freshly ground black pepper

Fry the onion and carrot in the butter with the bay leaf for 10 minutes until slightly softened, but not browned. Add the tomatoes, roughly chopped, the water or stock, and lemon rind. Simmer gently for 30 minutes. Remove bay leaf. Liquidize two-thirds of the soup, add to rest of soup. Flavour with lemon juice, salt and pepper.

Because of its refreshing lemon flavour, this soup is also good served chilled. In summer, after liquidizing this soup, I sometimes throw in a few fresh french beans broken into 2cm (1in) lengths, and cook gently until tender. As well as adding their own flavour they give a pleasant texture and colour contrast.

LEEK SOUP

You can liquidize this soup, leave it as it is, or liquidize half or two-thirds and leave the rest to give some texture.

SERVES 4 [F]
450g (1 lb) potatoes
2 medium-sized leeks
1 tablespoon olive oil
850ml (1½ pints) water *or* light stock
sea salt
freshly ground black pepper
2 tablespoons single cream – optional
1 tablespoon chopped parsley

Peel and dice the potatoes; trim, thoroughly wash and slice the leeks. Heat the oil in a fairly large saucepan and add the potatoes and leeks. Turn them in the oil for a couple of minutes, being careful not to let them get brown. Stir in the water or stock. Bring up to the boil then leave the soup to simmer, with a lid on the saucepan, for about 20 minutes, until the vegetables are cooked. Liquidize some or all of the soup as desired, then season and reheat, with the cream if you're using it. Sprinkle the parsley over the top of each portion just before serving.

LEEK AND CARROT SOUP

SERVES 4 [F]
2 large carrots, sliced
4 leeks, sliced
15g (½oz) butter
850ml (1½ pints) stock *or* water
grated nutmeg
sea salt
freshly ground black pepper
1 tablespoon chopped parsley

Fry the carrots and leeks together in the butter for 10 minutes without browning. Add the stock or water and cook gently for 30–40 minutes until the vegetables are tender. Liquidize all but a good ladleful of soup, which can be left as it is, to give texture and colour. Season with nutmeg, salt and pepper; add chopped parsley.

THICK LEEK AND POTATO SOUP

This is a main course soup that's useful for a quick-to-make meal. Serve it with grated cheese or some sunflower seeds sprinkled on top or eat it as it is, sprinkled with lots of chopped parsley, with a protein course such as biscuits and cheese, yoghurt, or a handful of nuts and raisins to follow.

SERVES 4 [F]
15g (½oz) butter
1 tablespoon olive oil
1 large onion, chopped
900g (2 lb) potatoes, peeled and cut into chunky pieces
700g (1½ lb) leeks, washed, trimmed and sliced
575ml (1 pint) water
1 vegetable stock cube
sea salt
freshly ground black pepper
chopped parsley – optional

Heat the butter and oil in a large saucepan. When the butter has melted, put in the onion and fry gently for 5 minutes. Then add the potatoes and leeks and fry gently for a further 5 minutes, stirring often. Pour in the water, crumble in the stock cube, stir and bring to the boil. Then cover and leave to cook gently for about 15 minutes, until the vegetables are just tender. Mash some of the potatoes with a fork, to thicken soup, check seasoning, then serve, sprinkled with chopped parsley if you like.

Variation

THICK MUSHROOM AND POTATO SOUP

For this version, leave out the leeks and use instead 225g (8oz) sliced mushrooms.

LEEK AND POTATO SOUP – BONUS VERSION

This interesting recipe was given to me by a friend, and she, in turn, had been given it by a French cook in Paris. It's a soup recipe with a bonus, because from the following ingredients not only can a delicious soup be made but also a leek vinaigrette salad. Obviously one would not serve both dishes at the same meal.

SERVES 6 [F]
1.2 litres (2 pints) water *or* stock
6 good-sized leeks
2 large floury potatoes
sea salt
freshly ground black pepper
25–50g (1–2oz) butter

For leek vinaigrette
3 tablespoons olive oil
1 tablespoon wine vinegar

Put the water into a large saucepan and bring to the boil. Meanwhile remove roots from leeks, slit down one side and clean carefully under running water. Cut off green parts and chop those that are worth keeping. Peel and dice potatoes. Throw whole leeks, chopped green part and potatoes into the boiling water and simmer for 15 minutes or so until leeks are very tender. Using perforated spoon, remove the six whole leeks and drain back into soup. These are the salad. Place them on a flat dish into which has been mixed 3 tablespoons olive oil; 1 tablespoon white wine vinegar, and salt and milled black pepper

to taste. Baste leeks with this vinaigrette and leave until quite cold.

To finish soup pass through a medium coarse mouli or liquidizer, season and serve with a piece of butter in each bowl.

LENTIL SOUP

I think this smooth, golden soup is the most comforting of all. It is also extremely easy to make, nourishing and high in fibre. It was the first solid food I gave my youngest daughter when she was six months old and she still adores it – in fact it's a great favourite with everyone. The soup takes about 15 minutes to make from start to finish with a pressure-cooker, about 30 minutes without, and, with wholemeal bread or rolls, makes a filling meal.

SERVES 4 [F]
1 large onion, peeled and chopped
1 tablespoon olive oil
225g (8oz) split red lentils
1 litre (1¾ pints) stock *or* water
1–2 tablespoons lemon juice
sea salt
freshly ground black pepper

Heat the oil in a fairly large saucepan and fry the onion for about 5 minutes, until it's lightly browned. Add the lentils and water and bring up to the boil, then leave the soup to simmer gently for about 20 minutes, or pressure-cook for 5 minutes, until the lentils are soft and beige-gold. Liquidize the soup, add lemon juice and season with salt and plenty of black pepper. Reheat before serving.

Variations

LENTIL SOUP WITH GARLIC AND CUMIN

Make as above, then, just before serving, fry 3 or 4 tablespoons finely chopped onion in a little butter with 2 crushed garlic cloves and 1–2 teaspoons cumin. Stir this mixture into the soup before serving.

LENTIL SOUP WITH CURRIED CROÛTONS

Make soup as above. Just before serving, cut 3 slices of wholemeal bread into 6mm (¼in) dice. Heat a little olive oil in a frying pan and put in the diced bread. Sprinkle with a teaspoon of curry powder. Turn the pieces of bread frequently so that they get crisp all over and the curry powder is well distributed. Serve each bowl of soup with a few of the croûtons on top.

CURRIED LENTIL AND APPLE SOUP

This is a delectable soup which can be served hot or chilled. I think it's especially good chilled with a little cream on top.

SERVES 4 F
25g (1oz) butter
1 onion, chopped
1 carrot, scraped and chopped
125g (4oz) cooking apple, peeled and chopped
2 teaspoons curry powder
175g (6oz) red lentils
1 bay leaf
850ml (1½ pints) water *or* stock
1 tablespoon lemon juice
sea salt
freshly ground black pepper

Heat the butter in a large saucepan and fry the onion, carrot, apple and curry powder for 10 minutes, without browning. Then stir in the lentils, bay leaf and stock or water. Bring up to the boil, then simmer gently for 20–30 minutes, until lentils and vegetables are cooked. Remove bay leaf. Liquidize soup, then return to saucepan, add lemon juice and season. Reheat, or chill before serving.

CONTINENTAL LENTIL AND MUSHROOM SOUP

The lentils and mushrooms in this soup blend beautifully in flavour and texture – if they don't know, people may think they're just eating mushroom soup, but of course the lentils make it full of nourishment.

SERVES 4–5 F
125g (4oz) continental lentils
1 large onion
1 large garlic clove
25g (1oz) butter
125g (4oz) mushrooms
850ml (1½ pints) water *or* unsalted stock
sea salt
freshly ground black pepper
2 tablespoons chopped parsley

Wash, soak, drain and rinse the continental lentils as usual. Peel and chop the onion and crush the garlic, then fry them together in the butter in a large saucepan for 5 minutes. Wash and chop the mushrooms and add them to the onions and garlic in the saucepan; fry for a further 4–5 minutes, then add the rinsed and drained lentils and the water or stock. Simmer gently, with a lid on the saucepan, for about an hour, until the lentils are tender. Then liquidize the soup and season it with sea salt and freshly ground black pepper. Return the soup to the rinsed-out saucepan to reheat it, and serve it sprinkled with the parsley.

LENTIL AND TOMATO SOUP

Although it's generally best to avoid cooking pulses with tomatoes because the acid can prevent them from softening properly, in this recipe the presence of a good quantity of stock, and the fact that split red lentils are quick-cooking, means that one can get away with it and the result is a lovely tasty soup.

SERVES 4 F
1 large onion, chopped
1 stick of celery, chopped
2 tablespoons olive oil
125g (4oz) split red lentils, washed
400g (14oz) can tomatoes
850ml (1½ pints) unsalted stock *or* water
sea salt
freshly ground black pepper
1–2 tablespoons lemon juice
a little chopped parsley

Heat the oil in a large saucepan and fry the onion and celery for 7–10 minutes without browning them, then stir in the lentils and mix for a minute or two so that the lentils get coated with the oil. Add the tomatoes and stock or water to the saucepan and bring up to the boil. Half-cover with a lid and simmer gently for 25–30 minutes, by which time the lentils should be cooked. Liquidize the soup then return it to the rinsed-out saucepan and season it with sea salt, freshly ground black pepper and lemon juice to taste. Reheat the soup, then serve it garnished with chopped parsley.

CONTINENTAL LENTIL AND VEGETABLE SOUP

You can liquidize this soup if you want to, but personally I prefer not to; it looks attractive with the whole brown lentils and the colourful pieces of vegetable.

SERVES 4–5 [F]
125g (4oz) continental lentils
25g (1oz) butter
1 onion, peeled and chopped
1 large garlic clove, crushed
2 large carrots, scraped and cut into small dice
2 sticks celery, thinly sliced
2 tomatoes, skinned and chopped
50g (2oz) mushrooms, wiped and chopped
75–125g (3–4oz) cabbage, washed and chopped
1 litre (1¾ pints) unsalted stock
a bouquet garni – a couple of sprigs of parsley, a sprig of thyme and a bay leaf, tied together
2 tablespoons chopped parsley
sea salt
freshly ground black pepper

Soak the lentils in water for several hours, then drain and rinse them. Melt the butter in a large saucepan and fry the onion for 5 minutes, but don't brown it, then add the garlic and all the other vegetables and cook them very gently for a further 5 minutes, stirring often to prevent sticking. Mix in the drained lentils and stir for a minute or two so that the lentils get coated with the butter, then put in the stock and the bouquet garni. Bring the mixture up to the boil, then cover it and leave it to simmer for about 1¼ hours, or until the lentils are tender. Remove the bunch of herbs; stir in the chopped parsley and some sea salt and freshly ground black pepper to taste. This soup is nice served with grated cheese and some warm, crusty rolls.

LETTUCE SOUP

I like this soup because it's such a good way of using up those outer lettuce leaves you feel so guilty about throwing away. It's also got a nice fresh summery flavour. For a special occasion it's lovely with the single cream added but for everyday you can leave it out and use extra milk instead.

SERVES 4 [F]
1 onion
450g (1 lb) potatoes
Outside leaves of 2 or 3 lettuces
25g (1oz) butter
575ml (1 pint) water
425ml (15 fl oz) milk
150ml (5 fl oz) single cream
sea salt
freshly ground black pepper
nutmeg

Peel and chop the onion and potatoes. Wash the lettuce leaves and cut them up. Melt the butter in a large saucepan and fry the onion and potato gently for 5 minutes, but don't brown them. Then add the lettuce leaves and stir them for a minute or two so that they get all buttery. Add the water and milk and let the soup simmer gently for 15–20 minutes, until the vegetables are cooked.

Liquidize the soup and stir in the cream if you're using it. Season it with salt, pepper and a grating of nutmeg. Reheat it but don't let it boil after you've added the cream.

MUSHROOM SOUP

You can vary the character of this soup according to the type of mushrooms you use. Open mushrooms, or wild field mushrooms make a dark, richly-flavoured soup, while little white button mushrooms give a delicate, pale, creamy result. In either case, if you want to make the soup a bit special, add a tablespoon of sherry at the end.

SERVES 4 F
225g (8oz) mushrooms
small piece of onion, peeled
1 bay leaf
1 garlic clove, peeled and sliced
a few parsley stalks
575ml (1 pint) stock
50g (2oz) butter
40g (1½oz) flour
about 575ml (1 pint) milk
sea salt
freshly ground black pepper
nutmeg
cayenne pepper
1 tablespoon sherry – optional

Wash the mushrooms and remove the stalks. If you're using field mushrooms take off the skins too – but this isn't necessary with cultivated mushrooms. Put the stalks (and skins if you've removed them) into a medium-sized saucepan together with the piece of onion, bay leaf, garlic, parsley stalks and stock and bring up to the boil, then leave to simmer for 10 minutes to extract the flavours. Strain the liquid into a measuring jug and make the quantity up to 850ml (1½ pints) with the milk. (You won't need the mushrooms stalks, etc.)

Melt three-quarters of the butter in the saucepan and stir in the flour. After a moment or two, when it looks bubbly, pour in a quarter of the milk mixture and stir over a fairly high heat until it has thickened. Repeat the process with the rest of the milk in three more batches. Now chop or slice the mushrooms, fry them lightly in the remaining butter and add them to the thickened milk, together with salt, pepper, a grating of nutmeg, a pinch of cayenne pepper and the sherry if you're using it. Let the soup simmer for 3–4 minutes to give the flavours a chance to blend before serving.

MINESTRONE SOUP, VEGETARIAN-STYLE

A filling, main-course soup.

SERVES 4 F
3 medium onions, chopped
25g (1oz) butter
1 large potato, peeled and diced
1 large carrot, diced
2 sticks celery, sliced
a few leaves cabbage, chopped
2 garlic cloves, crushed
400g (14oz) can tomatoes
850ml (1½ pints) stock *or* water
bouquet garni – 1 bay leaf, few parsley stalks, sprig thyme
225g (8oz) haricot beans, cooked, *or* 2 × 400g (14oz) cans cannellini beans
50g (2oz) macaroni
sea salt
freshly ground black pepper
chopped fresh basil, if available
grated cheese

Fry the onion gently in the butter for 5 minutes, then add other vegetables and the garlic and cook for a further 5 minutes. Add tomatoes, roughly chopped, stock or water and bouquet garni. Simmer for 20–30 minutes, until vegetables are just tender. Ten minutes before serving add the drained cooked beans and macaroni in 5cm (2in) lengths, and cook until the macaroni is just tender. Season with salt and pepper, sprinkle with chopped fresh basil leaves when available, and serve very hot with grated cheese.

GOLDEN ONION SOUP WITH CHEESE

I don't quite know why, but this soup always makes me feel festive; maybe it's because I associate it with happy times in France or perhaps it's something to do with the sherry. Anyway, it makes a lovely winter lunch or late-night supper and although it's filling, it's not too high in calories.

SERVES 4 F
450g (1 lb) onions
1 tablespoon oil
1 tablespoon flour
850ml (1½ pints) water
1 vegetable stock cube
3 tablespoons cheap sherry
1 large garlic clove, peeled and crushed
4 teaspoons Dijon mustard
sea salt
freshly ground black pepper
4 slices wholemeal bread
75–125g (3–4oz) cheese, grated

Peel the onions and slice them into fairly thin rings. Heat the oil in a large saucepan and fry the onions slowly for 15–20 minutes, until they're golden, stirring them from time to time. Add the flour and cook for a few seconds before putting in the water, stock cube, sherry, garlic, mustard and a seasoning of salt and pepper. Bring mixture up to the boil, then let it simmer gently for 30 minutes. Just before the soup is ready, warm four heatproof soup bowls and lightly toast a slice of bread for each; put the toast, roughly broken up, into the bowls. Prepare a moderately hot grill. When the soup is ready, check the seasoning, then ladle it into the bowls, scatter the grated cheese on top and place the bowls under the grill to melt the cheese; serve immediately.

GREEN PEA SOUP WITH MINT AND CREAM

Frozen peas make a vivid green soup with a very smooth texture. It looks lovely swirled with cream and flecked with dark green chopped mint, and is good either hot or chilled.

SERVES 6 F
25g (1oz) butter or
2 tablespoons oil if you're planning to serve it chilled
1 onion, peeled and chopped
900g (2 lb) frozen peas
1.2 litres (2 pints) light vegetable stock or water
a few sprigs of thyme, if available
sea salt
freshly ground black pepper
150 ml (5 fl oz) single cream – optional
2 tablespoons chopped fresh mint

Melt the butter or oil in a large saucepan and add the onion; fry for 5–7 minutes until fairly soft but not browned, then put in the peas and cook for a further 2–3 minutes, stirring often. Pour in the stock or water, add the thyme, and bring mixture up to the boil, then turn the heat down, put a lid on the saucepan and leave to simmer for about 20 minutes until the vegetables are soft. Liquidize, then sieve, pushing through as much of the pea purée as you can. Tip the soup back in the saucepan and season carefully with salt and pepper. Reheat, then serve in bowls, swirling a spoonful of cream over the top of each, if using, and sprinkling with the chopped fresh mint.

PISTOU SOUP

This delicious soup from southern France makes a filling main course with warm crusty bread.

SERVES 6 F
2 onions, chopped
7 tablespoons olive oil
225g (8oz) haricot beans, cooked, or use 2 × 400g (14oz) cans cannellini beans
2 carrots, chopped
2 potatoes, peeled and diced
225g (8oz) courgettes, sliced
125g (4oz) green beans, sliced
450g (1 lb) tomatoes, peeled and chopped
1.7 litres (3 pints) unsalted stock or water
50g (2oz) vermicelli
sea salt
freshly ground black pepper
5 garlic cloves, crushed
leaves from a bunch of basil

Fry onions in 3 tablespoons of oil for 5 minutes. Add haricot beans and vegetables and cook for 5 minutes. Pour in stock, simmer for 20–30 minutes. Then add vermicelli and cook for 10 minutes. Season. Liquidize remaining oil, garlic and basil; stir into soup just before serving or put into a bowl for people to add themselves.

PARSNIP SOUP

Parsnips make a beautiful soup with a slightly sweet flavour which I think is very pleasant.

SERVES 4 F
225g (8oz) parsnips
1 carrot
1 potato
1 onion
1 bay leaf
15g (½oz) butter
425ml (15 fl oz) water
425ml (15 fl oz) milk
ground mace
sea salt
freshly ground black pepper
chopped fresh herbs or croûtons

Peel and chop parsnip, carrot, potato and onion. Fry with the bay leaf in the butter for 10 minutes without browning. Add the milk and water and cook for 30 minutes, remove bay leaf. Liquidize, and season with a little ground mace, salt and pepper. Serve garnished with chopped fresh herbs or croûtons.

POTATO SOUP WITH FRESH HERBS

Although this is a simple soup, it always tastes good, with its smooth creamy texture and topping of fresh green herbs. You can make the soup even creamier by adding the *fromage blanc*, rather as you would add cream, and you can also swirl some over the top of the soup, as in the beetroot soup recipe, for an attractive garnish.

SERVES 4 F
15g (½oz) butter
1 onion, peeled and chopped
450g (1 lb) potatoes, peeled and diced
850ml (1½ pints) water
sea salt
freshly ground black pepper
2 tablespoons single cream *or fromage blanc*
2 tablespoons chopped fresh herbs – whatever you can get – tarragon, chervil or lovage are particularly good, or parsley and/or chives

Heat the butter in a fairly large saucepan and fry the onions for 3–4 minutes, stirring often – don't let it get brown. Then add the potato and stir over the heat for a further 2–3 minutes. Pour in the water, bring up to the boil and leave to simmer for about 15 minutes, until the potatoes are tender. Liquidize or sieve, then season with salt and pepper. Reheat, stir in the cream or *fromage blanc* if you're using it and serve sprinkled with the herbs.

PUMPKIN SOUP

Pumpkin makes a very delicious soup, golden in colour with a delicate yet distinctive flavour. It's lovely sprinkled with chopped parsley and served with garlic bread at Hallowe'en.

SERVES 6 F
1 kilo (2¼ lb) pumpkin (this weight includes the skin and pips)
2 large onions
2 large garlic cloves
15g (½oz) butter
1 litre (1¾ pints) stock
sea salt
freshly ground black pepper
150ml (5 fl oz) single cream *or* top of the milk
fresh parsley

Cut the skin off the pumpkin and scoop out the seeds; cut the flesh into even-sized pieces. Peel and chop the onion; peel and crush the garlic.

Melt the butter in a heavy saucepan and cook the chopped onions for about 5 minutes, then put in the garlic and pumpkin and cook for a further 5 minutes. Add the stock and some salt and pepper; bring to the boil and simmer until the pumpkin is tender – this takes about 15–20 minutes. Sieve or liquidize the soup then stir in the single cream or top of the milk. Reheat the soup gently. Serve in individual bowls with some chopped parsley on top.

CHILLED RASPBERRY AND REDCURRANT SOUP

This soup makes an unusual, refreshing starter. Rich ruby red, swirled with soured cream or yoghurt and sprinkled with fresh chopped mint, it looks really beautiful. It can be made very successfully from frozen raspberries and the redcurrant juice can be bought in cartons from large supermarkets and delicatessens.

SERVES 4–6
350g (12oz) fresh *or* frozen raspberries
850ml (1½ pints) redcurrant juice
2 tablespoons arrowroot
lemon juice
25–50g (1–2oz) sugar
soured cream or thick natural yoghurt – optional
2 tablespoons chopped fresh mint

Liquidize about two thirds of the raspberries with some of the juice, then pass the purée through a sieve to remove the pips. Put into a saucepan with most of the remaining juice and bring to the boil. Meanwhile, put the arrowroot into a small bowl and mix to a smooth cream with the rest of the juice. Pour the hot raspberry mixture over the arrowroot cream, stir, then return the mixture to the saucepan and stir over the heat until it has thickened. Remove from the heat and add the rest of the raspberries and a little lemon juice and sugar to taste. Cool, then chill the soup. When you're ready to serve the soup, ladle it into individual bowls, stir the soured cream or yoghurt to make it smooth, then pour a teaspoonful over each portion and sprinkle with the mint.

RED SOUP

I love the rich, ruby colour of this wartime soup. It's cheap and a bit different and certainly worth trying, especially if you can serve each bowlful in a most un-wartime way, with a swirl of single cream.

SERVES 6 F
2 tablespoons olive oil
1 onion, chopped
1 cooked beetroot, skinned
1 tomato, chopped
1 stick celery, chopped
125g (4oz) split red lentils
1 litre (1¾ pints) water *or* unsalted vegetable stock
sea salt
freshly ground black pepper
1 tablespoon lemon juice

Heat the oil in a large saucepan and fry all the prepared vegetables gently for about 5 minutes, stirring from time to time. Wash the lentils and add them to the vegetables, along with the water or stock. Bring up to the boil, then simmer the soup gently for about 30 minutes, or until everything is cooked. Liquidize the soup, then season it carefully with sea salt, freshly ground black pepper and lemon juice. Return the soup to the rinsed-out saucepan and reheat it before serving.

SPINACH SOUP

SERVES 4 F
1 potato, peeled and chopped
1 onion, chopped
15g (½oz) butter
450g (1 lb) spinach
850ml (1½ pints) water *or* stock
grated nutmeg
sea salt
freshly ground black pepper
1 teaspoon lemon juice
4 tablespoons single cream

Fry the onion and potato lightly in the butter without browning for 5 minutes. Add the well-washed and chopped spinach, and water. Simmer for 15–20 minutes until potatoes are tender. Liquidize, season with nutmeg, salt and pepper, and lemon juice. Pour into heated bowls and pour a little cream into each bowl immediately before serving in a swirl of white against the dark green soup.

SPINACH AND LENTIL SOUP

Richly flavoured and satisfying, this warming soup is quite different from the previous one.

SERVES 4 F
125g (4oz) continental lentils
1 large onion, chopped
15g (½oz) butter
1 large garlic clove, crushed
1 litre (1¾ pints) unsalted stock *or* water
225g (8oz) spinach
sea salt
freshly ground black pepper
2–3 teaspoons lemon juice
croûtons *or* a little single cream

Wash the lentils and pick them over carefully, then put them into a bowl, cover them with cold water and leave to soak for several hours. Then drain and rinse them. Peel and chop the onion and fry it in the butter in a large saucepan for 10 minutes, until it's soft but not browned. Add the rinsed and drained lentils and the garlic and stir them for a minute or two so that they all get coated with the butter, then pour in the stock or water. Bring the mixture up to the boil, then let it simmer gently for about 45 minutes, until the lentils are soft. (You can of course use a pressure cooker for this, and in fact I usually do. In this case, fry the onion in the pressure cooker pan and proceed as above, cooking the soup under pressure for about 15 minutes.)

While the lentils are cooking, wash the spinach in several changes of cold water, then chop it roughly. Add the spinach to the cooked lentil mixture, cover and simmer gently for about 10 minutes, until the spinach is soft. Liquidize the soup, then return it to the rinsed-out saucepan and season it with sea salt, freshly ground black pepper and plenty of lemon juice. This soup is very nice as it is, but it's even better if you serve it topped with some crispy fried bread croûtons or a swirl of single cream.

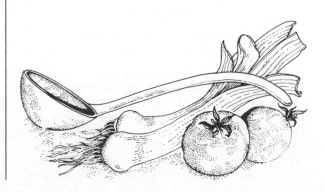

GREEN SPLIT PEA SOUP

A thick, warming winter soup.

SERVES 4 [F]
175g (6oz) green split peas – you can get these at
health shops and you needn't soak them before
cooking
1.2 litres (2 pints) water
1 onion, chopped
2 medium-sized potatoes, peeled and sliced
2 celery stalks, chopped
2 small leeks, sliced
½ teaspoon dried savory *or* marjoram
sea salt
freshly ground black pepper

Wash the split peas and put them into a large
saucepan with the water. Add the vegetables, bring
up to the boil and simmer gently until the peas are
tender – about 40 minutes. Stir in the savory or
marjoram and season the soup carefully with salt
and pepper. You can serve the soup as it is but I
think it's best to liquidize it or to liquidize half of it
to make a good base and leave the remainder to give
some texture.

CHILLED SPLIT GREEN PEA SOUP WITH MINT

If you normally think of pulse soup as filling, cold-
weather food, do try this elegant soup which comes
from the USA and is served chilled.

SERVES 4 [F]
2 tablespoons olive oil
1 large onion, peeled and chopped
1 stick of celery, chopped
8 sprigs of fresh mint
125g (4oz) split green peas, washed
1 litre (1¾ pints) unsalted stock
pinch of ground cloves
1 bay leaf
sea salt
freshly ground black pepper
a little single cream

Heat the oil in a large saucepan, add the onion and
celery and fry them gently, without browning, for
about 10 minutes. Meanwhile remove the leaves
from the stems of the mint; chop the leaves and put
them on one side. Tie the stalks together and put
them into the saucepan with the onion and celery,
together with the split peas, the stock, ground cloves
and bay leaf. Half-cover the saucepan with a lid and

let it simmer gently for about 40 minutes, until the
split peas are tender. Remove the bay leaf and mint
stalks and liquidize the soup; season it carefully to
taste. Put the soup into a bowl and leave it to cool,
then chill it. Taste the soup before serving (chilling
tends to dull the flavour of food). Spoon the soup
into individual bowls and top each portion with a
swirl of cream and the reserved chopped mint leaves.

YELLOW SPLIT PEA SOUP

This is quite a simple soup but it has a good flavour.
The split pea purée is thickened slightly with some
butter and flour which gives the soup a smooth
texture and a buttery flavour.

SERVES 4–6 [F]
225g (8oz) yellow split peas
1.7 litres (3 pints) water
25g (1oz) butter
1 large *or* 2 medium onions, peeled and finely
chopped
1 garlic clove, peeled and crushed
25g (1oz) wholemeal flour
sea salt
freshly ground black pepper

Put the split peas into a saucepan with the water; let
them simmer gently for 40–50 minutes until they're
tender then liquidize them. Melt the butter in the
rinsed out saucepan and fry the onion until it's
golden, then stir in the garlic and flour. Cook for a
minute or two, then gradually pour in the split pea
purée, stirring until you have a smooth mixture. Let
the soup simmer for 5–10 minutes to cook the flour,
then season with salt and pepper to taste. This
makes quite a thick soup; if you want it thinner you
can always add more liquid.

You will need to use a large saucepan for boiling
the split peas because of the way they bubble up as
they cook. Adding a couple of tablespoons of oil to
the cooking water helps, or if your saucepan isn't
quite big enough you can cook the peas using only
1.2 litres (2 pints) of water and add the rest when
you liquidize the soup.

SWEETCORN SOUP

A pretty, pale golden soup. You can make this using 850ml (1½pints) milk and water mixed and leave out the cream if you prefer.

SERVES 4 [F]
1 onion, chopped
15g (½oz) butter
225g (8oz) sweetcorn kernels
700ml (1¼ pints) water
150ml (5 fl oz) single cream
paprika
lemon juice
sea salt
freshly ground black pepper
thin slices of green pepper to garnish

Fry the onion without browning in the butter for 10 minutes. Add the sweetcorn and water and simmer for 30 minutes. Liquidize all but a good ladleful which is left to give texture, then stir in the cream, paprika and a little lemon juice, salt and pepper to taste. The bowls look pretty with thin slices of green pepper floating on top.

TOMATO AND FRESH BASIL SOUP WITH CREAM

When it's made from fresh tomatoes with basil from the garden, this has to be one of the best soups of all. If you haven't any basil, use chopped tarragon or chives instead. This is another soup which I like chilled in the summer. You can use a 400g (14oz) can of tomatoes instead of fresh ones, but the flavour isn't quite so good.

SERVES 4–6 [F]
25g (1oz) butter *or* 2 tablespoons oil if you're going to serve it chilled
1 onion, peeled and chopped
350g (12oz) potatoes, peeled and cut into even-sized chunks
450g (1 lb) tomatoes, peeled and chopped
1.2 litres (2 pints) light vegetable stock *or* water
sea salt
freshly ground black pepper
sugar
150ml (5 fl oz) single cream
2 tablespoons chopped fresh basil

Melt the butter or oil in a large saucepan and add the onion; fry for 5–7 minutes until fairly soft but not browned, then put in the potatoes and cook for a further 2–3 minutes, stirring often. Put in the tomatoes, mix them around, then pour in the stock or water and bring up to the boil. Turn the heat down, put a lid on the saucepan and leave to simmer for about 20 minutes, until the potatoes are soft. Liquidize the soup then pour it through a sieve into a clean saucepan to remove the seeds of the tomatoes. Season with salt, pepper and about ½ teaspoon sugar. Reheat and serve each bowl topped with a swirl of cream and a sprinkling of basil.

CLEAR VEGETABLE SOUP

The better the stock, the better this soup will be. If you haven't any home-made stock the vegetable bouillon powder or the vegetable stock concentrate described on page 10 also give very good results.

SERVES 4
2 sticks celery, chopped
2 onions, chopped
2 carrots, shaped and diced
other vegetables as available, a few French beans, a little cabbage
2 teaspoons olive oil
1 teaspoon yeast extract
1 teaspoon tomato purée
1 bay leaf
850ml (1½ pints) vegetable stock
salt
freshly ground black pepper
2 tablespoons chopped fresh chives

Fry the celery, onion and carrot together in the oil without browning for 5 minutes. Then add the beans, broken into short lengths, and the cabbage, shredded. Cook over a gentle heat for a further 5 minutes. Add yeast extract, tomato purée, bay leaf and stock and simmer for 20–30 minutes. Season with salt and freshly ground black pepper. Sprinkle with the chopped chives.

Variation

CLEAR MUSHROOM SOUP

For this pleasant variation, leave out the carrots, beans and cabbage, and add 225g (8oz) chopped mushrooms to the onions and celery after thay have been frying for 5 minutes. Add stock and simmer for 10–15 minutes, then stir in 2 heaped tablespoons of chopped parsley before serving.

WINTER VEGETABLE SOUP

This is a good winter soup, filling and nourishing yet light in texture and delicate in flavour. If you serve big bowls of it with home-made bread, cheese and fruit, it makes a complete meal, but it's also good as a first course on a cold day.

SERVES 4 F
1.2 litres (2 pints) water
2 fairly large carrots
2 onions
2 medium-sized potatoes
1 swede – about 225g (8oz)
1 turnip – about 225g (8oz)
4 sticks celery
15g (½oz) butter
sea salt
freshly ground black pepper

Put the water into a large saucepan and bring to the boil while you prepare the vegetables, cutting them into fairly small chunks; add them to the water, together with some salt, and simmer gently, with a lid on the saucepan, until they're all tender – about 30 minutes.

Scoop out two big ladlefuls of the soup and liquidize or mouli it with the butter, then pour it back into the saucepan and stir it into the rest of the soup. This thickens the soup while the pieces of whole vegetable give it body and interest. Check the seasoning, adding a little more salt if necessary and grinding in some black pepper, then reheat the soup before serving.

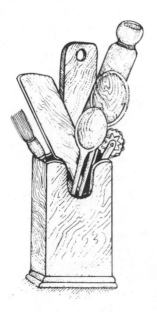

VICHYSSOISE

I've often thought it surprising that you can make such good chilled soup from what are really winter vegetables – leeks and potatoes! It's rather a pity really that these vegetables start coming into season just when the days are getting crisp and you're thinking more of soups to warm you up than cool you down. But vichyssoise is so creamy and delicious that it always seems to be popular. If the weather gets really cold you can always serve it hot, when I think it's every bit as good.

SERVES 6 F
1 onion, peeled and chopped
15g (½oz) butter
225g (8oz) potatoes, peeled and diced
700g (1½ lb) leeks, sliced
575ml (1 pint) water
sea salt
575ml (1 pint) milk
freshly ground black pepper
150ml (5 fl oz) single cream
2 tablespoons chopped chives

Fry the onion in the butter for about 5 minutes in a large saucepan but don't let it get at all brown. Then add the potato and leek to the onion and mix so that everything gets coated in the butter. Let it all cook gently for a further 4–5 minutes but be very careful you don't let it brown. Stir in the water and a little sea salt and bring up to the boil; then put a lid on the saucepan and leave the soup to simmer for 20–30 minutes until the vegetables are tender. Liquidize the soup, adding some of the milk if you like, to make the process easier, then tip the soup into a bowl or jug which will fit your fridge and add the remaining milk. Taste and season the soup then chill it.

You can stir the cream into the soup before you serve it, or swirl some over the top of each bowlful then sprinkle with the chopped chives. It looks very pretty – palest green with the darker chives on top. It's a good idea to check the seasoning after you've chilled the soup and add some more salt and pepper if necessary, as chilling seems to dull the flavour a little.

Variation

VICHYSSOISE – HEALTHY VERSION

Make as above, but use thick natural yoghurt or *fromage blanc* instead of the single cream.

WATERCRESS SOUP

This is an easy soup to make and is fresh-tasting and delicious. You do need a liquidizer or food processor.

SERVES 4 [F]
1 bunch watercress
1 onion, peeled and chopped
450g (1 lb) potatoes, peeled and diced
15g (1oz) butter
850ml (1½ pints) water *or* stock
sea salt
freshly ground black pepper
a little single cream – optional

Wash the watercress carefully, separating the stalks from the leaves; chop the stalks roughly. Heat the butter in a large saucepan and add the onion; cook gently for 5 minutes but don't let it get brown, then put in the potato and watercress stalks (keep the leaves on one side for later). Stir the vegetables over a gentle heat for a minute or two so that they all get coated with the fat, then pour in the water, bring the mixture up to the boil and let it simmer gently for about 15 minutes or until the potato is soft. Put the soup into the liquidizer or food processor together with the watercress leaves and a little salt and pepper and blend until smooth. Check seasoning; reheat gently. It's nice with a little single cream stirred into it for a special occasion.

CHILLED YOGHURT AND SPRING ONION SOUP

Cool, creamy-tasting natural yoghurt and spring onions make a beautiful chilled soup that's not nearly as strange as it sounds and couldn't be easier to make.

SERVES 4
425ml (15 fl oz) thick natural yoghurt
275ml (10 fl oz) skimmed milk
9–12 spring onions, washed, trimmed and chopped
sea salt
freshly ground black pepper

Put the yoghurt into a large bowl and stir in the milk. Add the spring onions and season to taste. Chill until ready to serve. If you keep the yoghurt and milk in the fridge they will of course be already chilled when you mix them and the soup can be served straight away – an almost instant soup.

2

FIRST COURSES, DIPS, SANDWICHES, SNACKS AND DRINKS

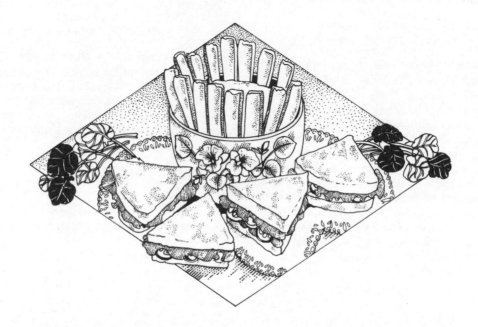

As the mother of two student daughters, I know all about kids rushing home, often accompanied by two or three friends, with cries of 'Mum, we're starving, could you get us something to eat NOW, we've got to be at the pub/drama rehearsal/Steve's house in half an hour'. This is the time when you've hit the jackpot if you've got some of the quick pizzas (page 344) in the freezer or (as far as one of my daughters, Katy, is concerned) can rustle up some pancakes (page 275) which is her favourite 'filler' under these circumstances. Cheese dip, in this section (page 44) is also a top favourite, with lots of hot wholemeal toast, or, better still, melba toast, if there's some made. My own favourites under such circumstances (not that I rush around in quite that frenzied way – well, maybe sometimes) are hummus (page 47) whizzed up from a can of chick peas and served with black olives from the fridge and pitta bread from the freezer; or a warm wholemeal pitta bread filled with salad and beansprouts if there are any around. And of course you can always fall back on

'something on toast', a plate of sandwiches (ideas on pages 52–3), a bowl of yoghurt with energy-extras like nuts, raisins, sunflower seeds, wheatgerm and sliced banana, or, for days when you (or they) are really eating 'on the wing', one of the nourishing drinks (which are also useful for a quick breakfast) or a handful of nuts and raisins to grab on the way out of the door. Yes, from the health point of view I know you should sit down calmly and eat slowly, but try telling that to an energetic teenager with a hectic social life!

The time, hopefully, for enjoying relaxed, unhurried eating is when you're entertaining friends to a meal, and that's the other situation that I've considered this section, or, rather, the first part of the meal. Many of the dips which make such good snacks, also make marvellous first courses, suitably presented. Also in this section you'll find ideas for mousses, moulds and pâtes; some interesting ways of serving those old favourites, avocado, melon and grapefruit; and some piquant and colourful salads and vegetable mixtures. Most of them are easy to make and can be prepared well beforehand so that there's one thing less for you to have to think about nearer the time. You'll find other ideas and recipes for first courses in the Soups, Salads, Flans and Savoury Pies and Pasta sections of this book, too, so there's plenty of scope!

This chapter is divided into four sections:
- bread-based recipes, sandwiches and 'things on toast';
- drinks;
- dips, spreads and pâtes;
- first course dishes

Sandwiches freeze well except when the filling contains hardboiled eggs or salad. Most of the dips would freeze very well except for the fact that they contain garlic. The flavour of this, for some strange reason, intensifies in the freezer, so, if you want to freeze a dip, either be prepared, or add the garlic later, just before using. I've put the [F] freezer symbol by those which will freeze but with the above proviso if the recipe contains garlic.

FIRST COURSES

ARTICHOKES WITH SOURED CREAM FILLING

For this, the artichokes are cooked, cooled and served with a piquant, soured cream and chive filling. They are messy to eat, so finger bowls are a good idea.

SERVES 6
6 globe artichokes
150ml (5 fl oz) soured cream
2 tablespoons mayonnaise
2 tablespoons fresh chives, chopped
sea salt
freshly ground black pepper

First prepare the artichokes. Wash them very well under cold running water, then cut the stems level with the base. Next take a pair of sharp scissors and snip the points off the leaves to square them off and make them less prickly to cope with. You will probably need two large saucepans for cooking the artichokes (or you could do them in two batches, as they're served cold). Put the artichokes into the saucepan and add enough cold water to cover them, then bring to the boil and let them simmer, with a lid half on the pan, for about 40 minutes. They are done when you can pull a leaf off easily. Drain the artichokes and leave them upside down in a colander to cool and let any remaining water drain away.

Meanwhile make the filling, by simply mixing the soured cream and mayonnaise to a smooth consistency, then adding the chives and a little seasoning as necessary.

When the artichokes are cold you will probably need to remove the inner prickly 'choke'. This isn't always necessary if the artichokes are young and tender, but you need to open the artichoke and have a look. To do this, take the artichoke and pull back the leaves, like the petals of a flower, so that you can see the centre. Take the soft central leaves in your hand and pull them away – they should come out quite easily – then use a teaspoon to scrape out any spiky centre or choke. Rinse the artichoke to remove any remaining bits of choke, then dry the inside with kitchen paper. Put the artichokes on individual plates, trimming the bases slightly if necessary to make them stand firm, then spoon the filling into the centre, where the choke was, dividing it between them.

ANTISPASTO SALAD

A colourful first course, in the Italian style.

SERVES 6
225g (8oz) button mushrooms
2 tablespoons olive oil
1 small pepper
2 teaspoons wine vinegar
sea salt
freshly ground black pepper
1 bunch radishes
½ bunch spring onions
2 heads chicory
½ cucumber
6 tomatoes
4 hardboiled eggs
12 black olives
french dressing to serve

Wash and slice mushrooms; fry lightly in 1 tablespoon olive oil for 5 minutes – leave to cool. Slice red pepper very thinly, discarding seeds. Place on a flat dish and sprinkle with remaining oil and wine or cider vinegar, season with salt and pepper. If possible, leave for 1–2 hours to soften. Meanwhile, wash and trim radishes and spring onions; slice chicory downwards into quarters, and cucumber, tomatoes and eggs into circles. Arrange all attractively on individual dishes, garnish with olives and serve with french dressing.

AUBERGINE FRITTERS WITH TOMATO SAUCE

This is one of the simplest ways of preparing aubergines, but one of my favourites, and I think it is tasty enough to serve as an extra course on its own: almost the equivalent of a fish course. The only disadvantage is that the aubergine does need to be fried just before serving, but this is quite a quick job and most of the preparation can be done well in advance.

SERVES 6
450g (1 lb) aubergines
sea salt
wholemeal flour
freshly ground black pepper
olive oil for shallow frying
grated Parmesan cheese
lemon wedges
watercress
425ml (15 fl oz) home-made tomato sauce *or* soured cream and herb sauce *or* mayonnaise sauce

Wash the aubergines and remove the stems, then cut the aubergines into 6mm (¼ in) slices. Put these into a colander, sprinkle them with salt and then place a plate and a weight on top and leave for at least 30 minutes. After that, rinse the pieces of aubergine under the cold tap and squeeze them gently to remove excess water. Dip the slices of aubergine in seasoned wholemeal flour.

To finish the aubergine fritters, heat a little olive oil in a frying pan and fry the slices, a few at a time, on both sides, until the outside is crisp and the inside feels tender when pierced with the point of a sharp knife. As the fritters are ready put them in a baking tin which has been lined with crumpled kitchen paper and keep them warm under the grill or in a cool oven until they are all ready. Serve the fritters sprinkled with a little grated Parmesan and garnished with wedges of lemon and sprigs of watercress. Hand round the sauce separately.

AVOCADO WITH CURD CHEESE AND CASHEW NUT BALLS IN TOMATO DRESSING

This is an unusual starter, little balls of curd cheese and roasted cashew nuts served in a piquant tomato sauce with slices of avocado. The cheese balls and the dressing can be made in advance and stored in the fridge so that you only have to prepare the avocado and assemble the dish just before the meal. You can use bought roasted salted cashew nuts, but I prefer to buy plain ones and roast them by putting them on a dry baking sheet and baking them in a fairly hot oven for about 10 minutes, until they're golden brown.

SERVES 6
225g (8oz) curd cheese
75g (3oz) cashew nuts, roasted and cooled
1 small garlic clove, crushed in a little salt
sea salt
freshly ground black pepper
½ teaspoon tomato purée
½–1 teaspoon caster sugar
¼ teaspoon paprika pepper
2 tablespoons red wine vinegar
6 tablespoons olive oil
2 large ripe avocados
juice of ½ lemon
2 tablespoons fresh chives, chopped
crisp lettuce leaves
melba toast

Put the curd cheese into a bowl and mash with a fork. Grate the cashew nuts – a liquidizer is good for this – and add to the curd cheese, together with the crushed garlic and salt and pepper to taste. Mix well, then form into 24 small balls, about the size of hazel nuts. Leave on one side until ready to assemble the dish. (They can be made in advance and kept in a polythene container in the fridge.)

Make the dressing by mixing the tomato purée, ½ teaspoon of sugar, paprika and vinegar, then gradually add the oil. Add some salt, pepper, and a little more sugar if necessary.

Just before you want to serve the meal, peel the avocados and remove the stones. Cut the flesh into pieces and put them into a bowl with the lemon juice, chives and a little salt and pepper. Add the curd cheese balls. Mix everything very gently so that the ingredients are well distributed.

Arrange one or two crisp lettuce leaves on each serving dish and spoon the avocado mixture carefully on top. Give the tomato dressing another stir, then spoon a little over each plateful and serve immediately, accompanied by melba toast.

AVOCADO AND GRAPEFRUIT SALAD

SERVES 6
2 grapefruit
2 oranges
2 avocado pears
½ lettuce
1 tablespoon chopped mint if available

Using serrated knife cut peel and pith from grapefruit and oranges and slice out segments. Thinly peel, stone and slice avocados, and add to the grapefruit and oranges. Pile on to lettuce leaves and serve chilled and sprinkled with chopped mint if available, or halve grapefruit to remove flesh and serve mixture in the skins.

You may like to add a little sugar, but the salad should be refreshing, not too sweet.

AVOCADO AND MUSHROOM SALAD WITH BROWN BREAD AND BUTTER

This is a pleasant mixture of flavours, textures and colours.

SERVES 4
1 large ripe avocado pear
2 tablespoons lemon juice
450g (1 lb) very fresh white button mushrooms
1 tablespoon best quality olive oil
1 tablespoon wine vinegar
sea salt
freshly ground black pepper
a few chopped chives
lightly buttered brown bread

Cut the avocado in half and remove the stone and peel. Slice the flesh and sprinkle with the lemon juice. Wash and thinly slice the mushrooms. Put the mushrooms into a bowl with the avocado and add the oil, vinegar and some salt and pepper. Mix everything together lightly. Serve on individual dishes with some chives snipped over the top.

STUFFED AVOCADO STARTER

SERVES 4
2 large avocados
juice ½ lemon
4 tomatoes
225g (8oz) button mushrooms
1 tablespoon olive oil
25g (1oz) chopped walnuts
lemon slices, watercress and lettuce to serve

Cut the avocados in half and remove stones and skin. Brush cut surfaces with lemon juice. Skin and slice tomatoes; wipe and finely chop the mushrooms and fry lightly in the oil; when tender mix with the tomatoes and walnuts. Pile into avocado halves, garnish with lemon slices and serve on a bed of lettuce and watercress.

SURPRISE AVOCADOS

'Surprise', because the avocados are completely covered in a sharp, creamy, lemon mayonnaise dressing, and it isn't until you slice one that you find the buttery-soft avocado and the piquant herb filling in the centre. You can make the filling and the dressing in advance, but don't prepare the avocados more than 1 hour in advance or they may discolour.

SERVES 6
3 ripe avocado pears – they should feel just soft all over when you cradle them in the palm of your hand.
juice of 1 lemon
125g (4oz) curd cheese
1 tablespoon fresh parsley, finely chopped
1 tablespoon fresh chives, finely chopped
sea salt
freshly ground black pepper
3 tablespoons mayonnaise
3 tablespoons natural yoghurt
lettuce leaves
paprika pepper
lemon slices

Cut the avocados in half and remove stones and skin. Brush the avocados all over with the lemon juice. To make the filling, mix the curd cheese and the herbs, season with a little salt and pepper. For the dressing, mix the mayonnaise and yoghurt.

To assemble the dish, put two or three small crisp lettuce leaves on each plate. Press a little of the curd cheese mixture into the cavity of each avocado half, dividing it between them. Put the avocados cut-side down on the lettuce leaves and pour the dressing over to cover them. Sprinkle with paprika pepper and garnish each plate with a wedge of lemon.

CHEESE MOUSSE

I have a special affection for this recipe. I always associate it with the wedding of a friend at a country hotel, on an idyllic summer's day. As most of the guests were vegetarian, she arranged a wonderful lunch using recipes from one of my books, and this was the first course, perfectly made and presented by the hotel chef.

SERVES 4–6
4 tablespoons liquid – milk or dry white wine
50g (2oz) grated gruyère cheese
50g (2oz) grated Parmesan cheese
3 eggs, separated
275ml (10 fl oz) single cream
1 garlic clove
3 teaspoons agar agar*
tiny pinch mustard
lettuce, black olives, tomato slices, paprika

* vegetarian gelatine from health shops

Heat 4 tablespoons liquid in pan, remove from heat, add cheese and stir until melted. Beat in egg yolks. Bring cream to the boil with garlic clove; when boiling sprinkle on agar agar. Cook for 1 minute, remove garlic, and pour milk over cheese mixture, add mustard and lastly fold in egg whites. Turn into wetted individual ramekins or moulds.

Turn mould out onto a base of lettuce, and decorate with black olives and tomato slices. Or top ramekins with a dusting of paprika and a black olive.

CREAMY CARROT SALAD WITH WHOLEMEAL ROLLS

A simple, healthy, low-calorie first course.

SERVES 4
350g (12oz) finely grated carrot
2 tablespoons natural yoghurt
125g (4oz) curd cheese
2 teaspoons olive oil
½ teaspoon wine vinegar
25g (1oz) raisins
25g (1oz) roasted hazel nuts
sea salt
freshly ground black pepper
warm wholemeal rolls

Put the grated carrot into a bowl and mix in all the other ingredients. Serve piled up in a pottery dish and let everyone help themselves, eating the salad with the rolls.

EGG AND CUCUMBER STARTER

Another pretty, refreshing starter.

SERVES 4–6
3 eggs, hardboiled
½ cucumber
150ml (5 fl oz) natural yoghurt
2 tablespoons chopped chives
sea salt
freshly ground black pepper
pinch dill – optional
4 lettuce leaves

Chop the eggs finely. Peel and chop cucumber into 6mm (¼in) dice. Combine eggs, cucumber, yoghurt and chives and season with salt and pepper and a pinch of dill if liked. Chill until required, then serve each portion on a lettuce leaf.

EGG MOULDS

A light, attractive first course.

SERVES 4–6
4 hardboiled eggs
½ teaspoon yeast extract
1½ teaspoons agar agar*
275ml (10 fl oz) water
150ml (5 fl oz) milk or single cream
¼ teaspoon mace
sea salt
freshly ground black pepper
½ tablespoon chopped parsley
watercress, lettuce and tomato

* vegetarian gelatine from health shops

Shell eggs and chop finely. Dissolve yeast extract in the water and when it is boiling sprinkle agar agar over and whisk until dissolved; boil gently for 1–2 minutes. Remove from heat, add eggs, milk or single cream, mace and salt and pepper. Pour into wetted individual moulds (e.g. paper cups, half filled) to set. Turn out, sprinkle with chopped parsley, and surround with a little watercress or lettuce and sliced tomato.

STUFFED EGGS

A simple but tasty first course.

SERVES 6
6 hardboiled eggs
1 large can Tartex vegetable pâté
or
125g (4oz) curd cheese
2 drops tabasco
1 teaspoon lemon juice
1 teaspoon tomato purée
1 tablespoon mayonnaise
sea salt
freshly ground black pepper
chopped parsley or chives
a little lemon to garnish

Halve eggs lengthwise and remove yolks. Mash well with Tartex or curd cheese, tabasco, lemon juice, tomato purée and mayonnaise. Pipe or spoon into the egg whites. Garnish with chopped parsley or chives, and a small piece of sliced lemon. Serve on individual plates, prettily garnished with some colourful salad items – a little lettuce, a sprig of watercress, a thin circle of red pepper, a small quantity of cooked sweetcorn kernels, for example.

FLAGEOLET BEANS IN AVOCADOS

These avocados, with their pale green filling of flageolet beans, make a good first course or light lunch with thin brown bread and butter.

SERVES 4
2 large avocados
75g (3oz) flageolet beans, cooked and drained
2 tablespoons chopped chives
4 teaspoons wine vinegar
4 tablespoons olive oil
sea salt
freshly ground black pepper
8 crisp lettuce leaves
4 sprigs watercress

Halve the avocados and remove stones, then carefully scoop out the flesh with a spoon, putting skins aside. Cut the flesh into even-sized pieces and put into a bowl with the flageolet beans and chives. Mix together the vinegar and oil, adding some salt and pepper to make a dressing. Pour this over avocado and beans and mix gently. Check seasoning. Put two lettuce leaves on each individual plate and place avocado skins on top. Divide bean mixture between skins, piling up well, and garnish with a sprig of watercress.

HAZLENUT MOULD

This mould is a light, jellied nutmeat and it makes an attractive first course served on individual plates on a pool of soured cream dressing, decorated with colourful salad items.

SERVES 6
1 medium onion
25g (1 oz) butter
1 dessertspoon agar agar*
425ml (15 fl oz) vegetable stock *or* water
125g (4oz) hazel nuts
1 dessertspoon yeast extract (*or* 1 teaspoon if using vegetable stock)
¼ teaspoon garlic salt
freshly ground black pepper

* vegetarian gelatine from health food shops

Finely grate onion and fry in butter until golden brown. Dissolve agar agar in a dessertspoon of cold water and gradually add to the vegetable stock (or seasoned water). Pour into onion and bring to boil for 5 minutes. Remove from the heat and add the hazel nuts which have been first placed in a moderately hot oven for about 10 minutes to loosen skins, then rubbed in a clean cloth to remove most of skins and milled finely. Add seasoning to mixture and cook for another 5 minutes. Pour into previously rinsed mould or moulds. If liked, moulds may be lined with slices of tomato and cucumber, in which case first brush mould with the mixture, then arrange the vegetables, then pour a little mixture over sides of mould and allow to set before adding the rest of the mixture.

MINTED GRAPEFRUIT WITH ORANGE

A pleasant, refreshing combination of flavours and colours.

SERVES 4
2 oranges
2 grapefruit
4 sprigs fresh mint
1 drop of oil of peppermint – optional
caster sugar to taste

Peel the oranges and chop flesh into small pieces. Cut grapefruits in half and scoop out flesh. Chop finely, removing pips and pith. Mix oranges and grapefruit, add caster sugar to taste, and a drop of oil of peppermint. Pile this mixture into grapefruit shells, and sprinkle with chopped fresh mint. Leave in a cool place until required.

Variation

PINK GRAPEFRUIT WITH GRAPES

Use pink grapefruits; leave out the oranges, mint and peppermint. Cut the grapefruits in half, scoop out all the flesh and remove pieces of skin and any pips as above. Add 175g (6oz) halved and stoned red or black grapes to the grapefruit flesh and mix together. Pile grapefruit and grape mixture back into the grapefruit skins and place in individual bowls.

GRAPEFRUIT ROSE BASKETS

You may feel this is too romantic an idea but I think you will agree it provides a conversation piece. I have to admit that I love it because it looks so pretty and different and is just the starter for a celebration meal in summer. It consists of whole pink grapefruits each cut into the shape of a basket (which is quite easy to do); then filled with the flesh which has been scooped out, chopped and mixed with rosewater and a few fresh pink rose petals, which are perfectly edible and taste delicious! For a final touch each basket can be garnished with a small pink rose bud. You could make this in the spring using a few fragrant violets, which are also edible, and leaving out the rosewater.

SERVES 6
6 pink grapefruits
3–4 tablespoons rosewater
a few pink rose petals
sugar
rose leaves and, if possible 6 small pink rosebuds to garnish

Using a sharp knife, make two cuts in the grapefruit about 3mm (⅛in) each side of the stalk, going half way down the fruit. Insert the point of the knife at the base of one of these cuts and slice round, across the grapefruit until you get to the other cut. Remove the knife, then re-insert it the other side and repeat the process. These two sections of grapefruit should then fall away, leaving a basket shape. Now cut the fruit from the section under the 'handle'.

Remove the grapefruit flesh from the 'bowl' of the basket in the usual way with a grapefruit knife. Prepare all the grapefruits in this way, then cut the white skin and pith from the scooped-out chunks of fruit. Put this fruit into a bowl and add rosewater to taste, a few rose petals, snipped with kitchen scissors or shredded, and just a very little sugar if you think it's needed.

Stand each grapefruit basket on a plate, cutting a slice from the base of the grapefruit if necessary to make it stand up, then spoon the rose petal mixture into the baskets. Tuck a few fresh rose leaves round the base of the baskets and lay a small pink rose bud on top of each basket, or alongside it on the plate.

MELON WITH GINGER

SERVES 6
1 honeydew melon
2 pieces preserved stem ginger
4 tablespoons liquid from ginger
lemon to garnish

Cut the melon in half; remove the seeds, chop the flesh or make into balls, using a vegetable scoop. Chop the ginger finely and mix with the melon, adding the liquid from the ginger. Sweeten to taste if necessary – not too much – and serve in individual glasses, garnished with lemon, if liked.

HALF MELONS WITH STRAWBERRIES

Although it's so simple, I think this makes a perfect first course (or pudding) in summer. My favourite melons are charentais with their fragrant orange flesh that melts in your mouth, but any small, ripe, round melons would do.

SERVES 6
3 small, ripe melons – preferably charentais *or* small cantaloupe, ogen *or* gallia
225g (8oz) strawberries, washed and hulled

Cut the melons in half and scoop out the seeds. Put the melon halves on individual plates. Cut any large strawberries in halves or quarters so that they are all roughly the same size. Put the strawberries in the centre of the melons, dividing them between them. Serve with sugar.

Variation

MELON WITH PORT

Port connoisseurs may look askance at this suggestion, but I personally love this combination of flavours. Prepare baby melons as above. Put the melon halves on individual plates. Just before serving pour a spoonful of port into the centre of each melon half.

MELON WEDGE STARTER

This recipe consists of wedges of sweet ripe melon with a creamy low-fat dressing of fromage blanc and grapes or strawberries spooned over it. I invented it before fromage blanc and quark were available in this country, and I used sieved cottage cheese beaten with a little cream instead. Now it's much easier to do, and delicious.

SERVES 6
1 melon, honeydew type
225g (8oz) *fromage blanc or* similar smooth low-fat white cheese
125g (4oz) black grapes, halved and stoned *or* strawberries, sliced
lettuce

Halve and then slice melon, remove seeds. Put on individual plates on lettuce leaves. Mix *fromage blanc* with grapes or strawberries. Spoon mixture over melon slices.

MINIATURE CURRIED LENTIL RISSOLES WITH YOGHURT AND SOURED CREAM SAUCE

These little lentil rissoles can be served hot or cold; they make a good starter and are also good for a drinks party or buffet.

MAKES ABOUT 50, SERVES 6 AS A STARTER [F]
175g (6oz) split orange lentils
350ml (12 fl oz) water
2 tablespoons olive oil
1 onion, peeled and sliced
1 large garlic clove, peeled and crushed
2 teaspoons ground coriander
sea salt
freshly ground black pepper
flour to coat
a little butter and oil for shallow-frying
2 tablespoons natural yoghurt
2 tablespoons mayonnaise
2 tablespoons soured cream
lemon slices, sprigs of watercress

Put the lentils and water into a saucepan and bring to the boil, then turn down the heat and leave to cook very gently for 20–30 minutes, until soft and pale golden-beige. The lentils should be fairly dry so that they can be formed into rissoles; if they seem a bit on the wet side, leave the saucepan over the heat for a few minutes longer, stirring often.

Meanwhile heat the oil in a medium-sized saucepan and fry the onion for 10 minutes until softened and lightly browned. Add the garlic and coriander and cook for a further minute or two, then add the lentils, and a good seasoning of salt and pepper. Leave until cold, then form into small balls about the size of large hazel nuts and roll each in flour. Heat a knob of butter and a tablespoon of oil in a frying pan and shallow-fry the rissoles until they are crisp and brown. They are rather fragile and so need to be cooked carefully: I find it best to do only a few at a time. Drain the rissoles on crumpled kitchen paper.

To make the sauce, simply mix the yoghurt, mayonnaise and cream together and season with salt and pepper.

Serve the rissoles hot or cold on small plates, garnished with lemon slices and watercress; or, for a buffet, put each little rissole on a cocktail stick and serve on a plate or stuck into a grapefruit or cabbage 'hedgehog'. Offer the sauce in a small bowl so that people can help themselves to a spoonful and dip the rissoles into it as they eat them. The lentil rissoles will freeze, but not the sauce.

MARINATED MUSHROOMS

Serve these spicy, piquant mushrooms well chilled, accompanied by lightly buttered wholemeal bread or crusty rolls.

SERVES 4
450g (1 lb) small white button mushrooms
2 tablespoons olive oil
2 teaspoons ground coriander
1 bay leaf
2 garlic cloves, peeled and crushed
sea salt
2 tablespoons lemon juice
freshly ground black pepper
crisp lettuce leaves, chopped
fresh parsley

Wash the mushrooms, halving or quartering any larger ones, then fry them in the olive oil with the coriander, bay leaf and garlic for about 2 minutes, stirring all the time. Turn the mushrooms straight into a large bowl to prevent further cooking, then add the lemon juice and a grinding of black pepper. Cool then chill the mixture. Check the seasoning before serving the mushrooms piled up on lettuce leaves on individual plates.

MUSHROOM SALAD

This makes a pleasant starter particularly if accompanied by soft warm wholemeal rolls. Use very fresh white button mushrooms.

SERVES 4 AS A STARTER
450g (1 lb) fresh white button mushrooms
2 tablespoons lemon juice
sea salt
freshly ground black pepper
4 tablespoons soured cream *or* natural yoghurt
lettuce leaves
fresh chives

Wash the mushrooms, then pat them dry and slice thinly. Put the slices into a bowl and sprinkle them with lemon juice and some salt and pepper. Add the soured cream or natural yoghurt and stir gently. Chill, then check the seasoning. To serve the salad, spoon it on to lettuce leaves on individual plates and sprinkle some chopped chives over the top.

The mushrooms will give off some liquid after you've sprinkled them with the lemon juice and salt and this will blend with the cream to make a thin dressing. If you would prefer a thicker dressing, sprinkle the lemon juice and salt on the mushrooms an hour or so before the meal, then drain off the juice which will have accumulated and fold the mushrooms through the cream just before serving them, checking the seasoning. (The mushroom liquid makes good stock.)

PEARS WITH CREAMY TOPPING

Comice pears are perfect for this recipe if you can get them. They must be really ripe so that they slice easily with the spoon and melt in your mouth as you eat them.

SERVES 4
2 tablespoons natural yoghurt
175g (6 oz) curd cheese *or* quark
1 tablespoon best quality olive oil
2 teaspoons wine vinegar
½ teaspoon Dijon mustard
sea salt
freshly ground black pepper
2 ripe comice pears
8 lettuce leaves
a little paprika pepper

First make the topping: mix together the yoghurt, cheese, oil, wine vinegar and mustard; season with salt and pepper. Arrange a few lettuce leaves on four small serving dishes. Just before the meal, peel, halve and core the pears and arrange one half, core side down, on each dish. Spoon the topping over the pears, covering them completely, and sprinkle each with a little paprika.

PINEAPPLE WEDGES

A ripe, juicy pineapple makes a beautiful starter, especially before a rich meal. Look for a pineapple that's the right size to slice down in wedges, like a melon, and, if necessary, keep it in the airing cupboard for a day or two to ripen up. It's best if you prepare the pineapple just before you want to serve it.

SERVES 6–8
1 medium-large pineapple

Slice off the leafy top, then cut the pineapple downwards in half, then cut each half down into three or four pieces. Put the wedges on individual plates, then slip a sharp knife along between the flesh and the skin to loosen the flesh. Slice off any hard core, then cut the flesh down into segments that are the right size for eating easily.

SALSIFY WITH BUTTER, PARSLEY AND LEMON

Salsify – and its close relative, scorzonera – look like long, rather dirty roots when you see them in the shops, but when they're peeled and cooked they have a most delicate flavour, which I think makes them ideal as a hot first course.

SERVES 4–6
1 kilo (2¼ lb) salsify *or* scorzonera – this might seem a lot but you lose a great deal in peeling
lemon juice
sea salt
25g (1oz) butter
2 tablespoons chopped fresh parsley
freshly ground black pepper

Peel the roots, keeping them under cold water to preserve the colour. Cut them into 2.5cm (1in) pieces and put them straight into a bowl of cold water with a tablespoonful of lemon juice, again to help keep them white. When they're all prepared, bring 2.5cm (1in) of salted water to the boil in a large saucepan and cook them for about 10 minutes, or until just tender.

Drain and add the butter, a tablespoonful of lemon juice, the parsley and salt and pepper to taste. Heat gently to melt the butter then serve at once. Some thinly sliced wholemeal bread and butter is nice with it.

SALSIFY FRITTERS

These delicate fritters make a perfect first course.

SERVES 4–6
700g (1½ lb) salsify
3 tablespoons wine vinegar
1–2 tablespoons chopped fresh herbs
sea salt
freshly ground pepper
125g (4oz) plain flour
1 tablespoon olive oil
2 eggs, separated
150ml (5 fl oz) water
oil for deep-frying
lemon slices

Prepare and cook the salsify as described in the previous recipe. Drain well, then sprinkle with the vinegar, herbs and some salt and pepper.

Mix together the flour, oil, seasoning, egg yolks and water; whisk the egg whites, then fold into the batter mixture.

Heat the oil to 190°C (275°F) (or when the batter sizzles if dropped into the oil). Coat salsify in batter, fry until browned. Drain and serve with lemon.

SALSIFY MAYONNAISE

SERVES 6
700g (1½ lb) salsify
2 tablespoons lemon juice
3 tablespoons mayonnaise
3 tablespoons yoghurt
1 tablespoon parsley
watercress to garnish
sliced tomatoes

Peel and cook salsify until tender. While still hot, add the lemon juice, mayonnaise and yoghurt. Cool. Pile in the centre of serving dish and sprinkle with parsley. Surround with watercress and tomato slices.

CREAMY TOMATOES WITH HORSERADISH

In this recipe sliced tomatoes are topped with a piquant creamy horseradish dressing.

SERVES 6
6 large firm tomatoes
sea salt
freshly ground black pepper
125g (4oz) curd cheese
2 tablespoons natural yoghurt
2 teaspoons olive oil
½ teaspoon wine vinegar
2 teaspoons horseradish sauce or 1 teaspoon grated
horseradish
chopped fresh green herbs as available

Peel the tomatoes then slice them, cutting out any hard bits. Put the slices into six little dishes and season lightly with salt and pepper. To make the topping, put the curd cheese, yoghurt, oil, vinegar and horseradish sauce into a bowl and mix together until creamy. Season, then pour this mixture over the tomatoes and sprinkle with bright green herbs – chopped fresh basil, if you have it, otherwise chives, parsley or mint.

STUFFED TOMATOES

This is a good way to serve firm, fragrant summer tomatoes. I think they're best with the skins removed, although I do sometimes leave them on if the tomatoes are very fresh and perfect.

SERVES 4
4 medium-sized tomatoes
sea salt
125g (4oz) quark
4 black olives
a few leaves of lettuce and sprigs of watercress

Skin the tomatoes, or just wash them and remove the stalks, whichever you prefer. Halve the tomatoes widthwise and scoop out the centres (these will not be needed for this recipe). Sprinkle the inside of each tomato with a little salt. Mix the quark with a fork, just to break it up a little, then spoon or pipe it into the tomato halves. Halve the olives, removing the stones. Top each tomato half with a piece of olive. Arrange the tomato halves on lettuce leaves on individual plates and garnish with a sprig or two of watercress.

DIPS AND SPREADS

AÏOLI WITH CRUDITÉS

Crisp raw vegetables dipped in smooth garlic-flavoured mayonnaise make a delicious starter or can become a complete salad meal with a lentil or vegetable soup and some wholemeal bread or rolls.

If you want to serve aïoli but hesitate on account of all the calories it contains you might like to do what I usually do and use half mayonnaise and half natural yoghurt; or add some garlic to the dressing given for the Russian cucumber salad with soured cream and hardboiled eggs and use that instead of the mayonnaise. It tastes surprisingly like mayonnaise but contains no oil.

The *crudités* can be a gloriously colourful selection of whatever fresh vegetables are available: crunchy red radishes served whole with some of the green part still attached; bright orange carrot cut into matchsticks; red or green pepper de-seeded and cut into strips; tiny crimson cubes of raw beetroot; sprigs of pearly cauliflower; small very fresh mushrooms; baby green Brussels sprouts served whole or bigger ones (as long as they're firm) cut into halves or quarters; spring onions, shiny white and just trimmed; pieces of crunchy fennel bulb; juicy cucumber in chunks; crisp leaves of chicory or sticks of celery; quarters of firm red tomatoes.

SERVES 4–6

For the crudités
A selection of vegetables as above; about 4 or 5 different types.

For the aïoli
1 egg
2–4 garlic cloves, peeled and crushed
¼ teaspoon sea salt
¼ teaspoon dry mustard
¼ teaspoon pepper
2 teaspoons wine vinegar
2 teaspoons lemon juice
200ml (7 fl oz) olive oil

Break the egg into the liquidizer goblet and add the garlic, salt, mustard, pepper, vinegar and lemon juice. Blend at medium speed for about 1 minute. Then turn the speed to high and gradually add the oil, drop by drop, through the top of the goblet lid. When about half the oil has been added and you hear the sound of the mixture change you can add the oil more quickly in a thin stream. If the mixture is very thick you can thin it by stirring in a little hot water; or if you're doing the yoghurt version add this now, stirring it gently into the mayonnaise. Spoon the aïoli into a bowl and stand it on a large plate or small tray with the *crudités* arranged around it. People can then help themselves to a spoonful of the aïoli and some of the vegetables and eat them together.

AUBERGINE AND SESAME PÂTÉ

In this Middle Eastern pâté the intense, subtle flavour of the aubergine goes well with the rich, earthy taste of the sesame cream and the texture is substantial without being at all heavy. I think it's nice with fingers of crisp toast or some warm pitta bread. It makes a good light lunch dish after lentil soup.

SERVES 4–6 F
2 medium aubergines – about 450g (1 lb)
2 heaped tablespoons sesame cream (*tahini*)
1 tablespoon lemon juice
1 large garlic clove, peeled and crushed
sea salt
freshly ground black pepper
crisp lettuce leaves
olive oil
sesame seeds, if available
fresh parsley and chives
fingers of hot wholemeal toast *or* some warm pitta bread

Prick the aubergines, then place them on a baking sheet and bake in a fairly hot oven – say 200°C (400°F), gas mark 6. But don't heat it specially; the aubergines will bake with something else and adapt to any temperature from about 160°C (325°F), gas mark 3 to 230°C (450°F), gas mark 8. They'll take about 20–30 minutes, depending on the temperature, and are done when they can be pierced easily with the point of a sharp knife. Let them cool, then remove the stalks. Chop the aubergine flesh as finely as you can then mix it with all the other ingredients, or put the aubergine into the liquidizer goblet with the sesame cream, lemon juice and garlic and blend until fairly smooth. You will probably have to do this in several short bursts, stopping the machine and stirring the mixture in between, as it is fairly thick. Season the mixture with salt and pepper, then chill it.

To serve, spoon the pâté into little dishes and smooth the tops, or arrange a bed of lettuce leaves on small plates and spoon it on top. Pour a little olive oil over the pâté, sprinkle with some whole sesame seeds, if you have them, and snip some parsley and chives over the top of everything. Hand round hot fingers of wholemeal toast or warm pitta bread.

CREAMY BUTTER BEAN DIP WITH SESAME TOAST

This is a creamy dip with a tangy flavour. If you use canned beans it's very quick to make and useful for emergencies.

SERVES 6 F
125g (4oz) dried butter beans, soaked and cooked until tender (page 178) or 400g (14oz) can butter beans
1 small garlic clove, peeled and crushed – optional
2 tablespoons olive oil
2–3 teaspoons lemon juice or wine vinegar
sea salt
freshly ground black pepper
tabasco
lettuce leaves
lemon wedges
watercress
6 slices wholemeal bread
butter
sesame seeds

Drain the butter beans, reserving the liquid. Put the butter beans into a blender, adding enough of the reserved liquid to make a thick creamy purée; or mash them with a fork and beat in the liquid. Stir in the garlic, if you're using it, olive oil and enough lemon juice or wine vinegar to sharpen the mixture. Season well with salt and pepper and add a few drops of tabasco. Chill the mixture, then just before you want to serve the pâté, spoon it into individual ramekin dishes which have been lined with lettuce leaves, and garnish with a wedge of lemon and a sprig of watercress. Serve with the hot sesame toasts.

To make the sesame toasts, set the oven to 200°C (400°F), gas mark 6. Cut the crusts off the bread and roll each slice with a rolling pin to flatten it a bit. Spread the bread with butter and sprinkle a good layer of sesame seeds on top, pressing them in with a knife. Cut the bread into fingers and place on a baking sheet. Bake for 10–15 minutes, until crisp and golden brown. Serve at once, with the creamy butter bean dip.

Variations

BUTTER BEAN AND BLACK OLIVE DIP

Make exactly as above, but add 12 black olives, stoned and finely chopped, to the mixture, or whizz them with the beans in the food processor or liquidizer.

BEAN AND BLACK OLIVE DIP WITH HARD BOILED EGGS

For this variation, cut 4 hardboiled eggs into wedges and arrange on 6 small plates lined with some shredded lettuce. Spoon the bean and black olive dip on top and sprinkle with a little paprika pepper. Decorate each plate with a sprig or two of watercress and a wedge of lemon.

AVOCADO DIP

I don't know whether it has something to do with the fact that everyone is eating with their fingers, but I find a meal always seems to get off to a particularly friendly, lively start when I serve a dip, and this is a specially good one.

SERVES 6
225g (8oz) *fromage blanc or* curd cheese
1 garlic clove, crushed
sea salt
freshly ground black pepper
tabasco
2 large, ripe avocados
1 tablespoon lemon vinegar
a little wine vinegar

Mix together the *fromage blanc* or curd cheese, garlic and some salt, pepper and tabasco. Just before serving, peel and mash the avocados with the lemon juice; add to the creamy cheese, mixing well. Check seasoning, adding a dash of wine vinegar.

Either spoon the dip on to a plate, decorate the top with the prongs of a fork and sprinkle with paprika pepper to give a nice touch of scarlet against the pale green, or arrange lettuce leaves on small individual plates and spoon the dip on top of that. Serve with crisp wholemeal melba toast, *crudités* as on page 42, or Mexican corn chips. It's best made just before you need it; don't keep it waiting more than 1 hour or the avocado will begin to discolour.

ROASTED CASHEWNUT PÂTÉ

You can use bought roasted cashewnuts for this tasty pâté but it's better to use ordinary ones which you can roast by putting on a dry baking sheet in a moderate oven for 15–20 minutes until golden.

SERVES 6 [F]
1 garlic clove
225g (8oz) quark
4 tablespoons milk
125g (4oz) roasted cashewnuts
dash of tabasco
1 teaspoon fresh garden herbs as available
freshly ground black pepper

Crush garlic and beat with quark and milk until smooth. Grate half of the nuts and chop the rest. Stir into the cheese mixture with tabasco, fresh herbs, and a grating of pepper. Press into a pottery crock and chill.

CHEDDAR CHEESE AND RED WINE DIP

The wine give this dip an intriguing flavour and a pretty pink colour. It's delicious for a special occasion served with hot fingers of wholemeal toast or slices of crisp melba toast.

SERVES 6 [F]
225g (8oz) Cheddar cheese, finely grated
25g (1oz) soft butter
125ml (4 fl oz) dry red wine – or you could use cider
½ teaspoon tabasco
sea salt
freshly ground black pepper

Put the grated cheese into a bowl with the butter and the wine and beat them together to make a light, fluffy mixture. Add the tabasco, some freshly ground black pepper and a little salt if necessary – it may not need any as the cheese is quite salty. Spoon the mixture into a small bowl or pâté dish and leave in a cool place until required. Serve with fingers of hot toast or melba toast.

CHEESE DIP

A less heady version and a great favourite with all my daughters.

MAKES ABOUT 200G (7OZ) [F]
40g (1½oz) butter
150g (5oz) grated cheese
6 tablespoons milk
pinch cayenne pepper or a few drops tabasco sauce
sea salt
freshly ground black pepper

Put all the ingredients into a food processor and blend to a creamy consistency. Or put butter into a bowl and beat until soft, then gradually beat in cheese and milk. Season with a pinch of cayenne or a few drops of tabasco and some salt and pepper. Spoon into a small dish or other container. Serve with wholemeal melba toast (page 55) or *crudités* (page 42). It's also useful as a sandwich spread.

CHEESE AND PIMENTO DIP

A friend invented this dip and gave the recipe to me. I don't often use canned red peppers these days, and, food snob that I've become, I look slightly askance at all that tomato ketchup/chutney. But this is a pleasant, piquant recipe, which is why I've included it in this book. I think it's best on wholemeal toast, or with fingers of hot crisp wholemeal toast.

SERVES 2–4 [F]
1 medium onion
15g (½oz) butter
saltspoon celery salt or celery seed
pinch pepper
pinch paprika pepper
125g (4oz) grated cheese (preferably Cheshire)
½ small bottle tomato chutney or ketchup
225g (8oz) can tomatoes
200g (7oz) can pimentos (red peppers)

Chop the onion *very* finely. Slightly warm butter and beat seasonings in, then mix in onion and grated cheese, chutney and tomatoes (mashed with a fork). Either cut the pimentos small or crush them with a fork and add to the above. Use either as a spread for sandwiches or toast or as a savoury on a green salad. If a small quantity is required, make half and use the rest of the pimentos in a rice, onion, sweetcorn and greenpea savoury.

CREAM CHEESE AND SOURED CREAM DIP

An American friend gave me this recipe which she serves on Thanksgiving Day as a first course. Like the aïoli, it's superb with a colourful selection of crisp fresh vegetables for dipping into the creamy mixture. The recipe as I've given it makes a luxurious-tasting dip; for an even richer version you could use cream cheese (which was used in the original recipe); alternatively, for a less calorific dip, you could use natural yoghurt in place of the soured cream.

SERVES 6
For the dip:
225g (8oz) low-fat quark
2 × 150g (5 fl oz) cartons soured cream
1 garlic clove, peeled and crushed
2 tablespoons finely chopped chives
sea salt
freshly ground black pepper

For the crudités:
A selection of about 5 different vegetables of contrasting colours, like those described for the aïoli on page 42.

Put the quark into a bowl and break it up with a fork, then stir in the soured cream, garlic and chives and mix to a smooth consistency. Season with salt and pepper. Spoon the dip into a serving dish and chill it until required. Arrange the colourful vegetables around the dip and let everyone help themselves to a spoonful of the creamy mixture and some crisp *crudités*.

EGG AND AVOCADO PÂTÉ

An interesting pâté with lots of variations.

SERVES 4–6
4 eggs, hardboiled
2 tablespoons mayonnaise
2 tablespoons thick yoghurt
2 tablespoons lemon juice
1 garlic clove
sea salt
freshly ground black pepper
1 avocado pear
1 tablespoon chopped parsley
few drops tabasco
lemon slices, fresh parsley and lettuce leaves to serve

Liquidize the hardboiled eggs with mayonnaise, yoghurt and 1 tablespoon of lemon juice. Wipe cut clove of garlic round mixing bowl and mix egg in this. Cut avocado in half, peel as thinly as possible and remove stone. Cut into small slices and sprinkle with the remaining lemon juice, then add to the egg mixture; season to taste and add parsley and a drop or two of tabasco. Spoon into a pottery crock and chill, or heap on to lettuce leaves and garnish with lemon twists. Serve with melba toast.

Variations

EGG AND MUSHROOM PÂTÉ

Omit avocado; use 175g (6oz) sliced and sautéed mushrooms.

EGG AND PEPPER PÂTÉ

Use 1 finely chopped large green pepper instead of the avocado.

EGG AND ASPARAGUS PÂTÉ

Use 125g (4oz) cooked asparagus spears, drained and chopped instead of avocado.

FERMENTED NUT 'CHEESE'

This can best be described as a nutty version of cottage cheese, but it's a delicious product in its own right. It's also very good for you, because, like real live yoghurt, it contains lactic acid which encourages your gut to produce helpful bacteria which then get rid of the bad ones. (Meat, by the way, does exactly the opposite; it encourages the baddies.)

MAKES 300G (10OZ)
50g (2oz) blanched almonds
75g (3oz) walnuts
50g (2oz) sunflower seeds
125g (4 fl oz) water
seasonings as required: fresh chopped herbs, a little tahini

Grind the nuts and sunflower seeds finely, add the water and mix well. Stir in the herbs and tahini, if used. Place in a bowl covered with a tea towel and leave to ferment for about 12 hours in a warm place.

FIELD BEAN PÂTÉ

This was an exciting discovery I made while testing recipes for my Little Book of Beans and Lentils. I felt I ought to feature field beans, which are the kind which more industrious people than me grow in their gardens in this country, but I couldn't get up any enthusiasm for them, with their tough brown skins and atmosphere of home-spun worthiness. Then in desperation I put some in my food processor, and, voilà, my whole feeling about them changed when this wonderful coarse-textured pâté with a delicious earthy flavour was the result! It's very economical and good as a light supper dish or first course, with fingers of hot wholemeal toast and a tomato salad, but you do need a food processor or strong blender to chop the beans. You can also use dried broad beans which you sometimes see in Middle Eastern shops (and in any Greek supermarket) for this recipe.

SERVES 4 F
225g (8oz) field beans, soaked and cooked
2 garlic cloves, chopped
bunch of parsley
4 teaspoons wine vinegar
2 tablespoons olive oil
sea salt
freshly ground black pepper

Drain the beans, reserving liquid. Put beans, garlic, parsley, vinegar and oil into a food processor or blender and blend thoroughly to break down skins and make a coarse-textured purée. Add a little of the cooking liquid if necessary to make a consistency like thick whipped cream. Add salt and pepper to taste, then spoon mixture into a shallow pottery bowl or pâté dish.

GOAT CHEESE AND HERB SPREAD

If you can't get goat cheese I find that crumbly white Wensleydale makes a good alternative, although it's not as salty. This pâté looks attractive heaped up into a cone shape in the centre of a serving dish and surrounded with tangy black olives, whole radishes, crunchy spring onions and quartered tomatoes.

SERVES 4 AS A STARTER F
125g (4 oz) feta cheese (or use crumbly white Wensleydale)
125g (4oz) unsalted butter, softened
1 tablespoon chopped chives
1 tablespoon chopped green fennel, if available
1 tablespoon chopped parsley
pinch each of paprika and caraway seeds

Crumble the cheese finely. Put the butter into a bowl and cream it with a wooden spoon, then gradually beat in the crumbled cheese and the herbs and spices. Chill the spread, then serve it as suggested above or use it as a sandwich filling or a topping for savoury biscuits.

HARICOT BEAN AND GARLIC SPREAD

This makes a pleasant sandwich filling and is also good on little cocktail biscuits, decorated with small pieces of olive, etc. The basic mixture can be varied in a number of ways.

SERVES 4 F
125g (4 oz) haricot beans, cooked until tender, then cooled
25g (1oz) soft butter
1 garlic clove, crushed
a few drops of lemon juice
sea salt
freshly ground black pepper

Mash the beans to a smooth paste with a fork, then gradually blend in the butter, garlic and lemon juice. Season well with sea salt and freshly ground black pepper.

Variations

HARICOT BEAN AND PARSLEY SPREAD

Omit garlic from the recipe and add instead 2 tablespoons of chopped fresh parsley.

HARICOT BEAN AND FRESH HERB SPREAD

Instead of the garlic add 2 tablespoons of chopped fresh herbs: parsley, chives, tarragon, mint, fennel or lovage, whatever is available.

HARICOT BEAN AND OLIVE SPREAD

Make as above, leaving out the garlic and using instead 4–6 black olives, stoned and mashed to a smooth paste.

HAZEL NUT AND CREAM CHEESE PÂTÉ LOAF

This is an unusual dish, a loaf of creamy low-fat white cheese and hazel nuts flavoured with the tang of lemon and coated with crisp breadcrumbs. People usually start by wondering what it is and end by asking for the recipe! I invented it one day when I was feeling rather lazy and didn't want to cook, so it's easy to make and keeps well in either the fridge or the freezer. Serve it with lots of fresh salad, or in slices as an interesting first course.

SERVES 4–6 F
250g (8¾oz) low-fat quark
125g (4oz) hazel nuts roasted on a dry baking sheet in a moderate oven until golden then grated – the liquidizer is good for this
juice and grated rind of ½ small lemon
2 tablespoons chopped parsley
sea salt
freshly ground black pepper
paprika pepper
50g (2oz) crisp wholemeal breadcrumbs
crisp lettuce, tomatoes, cucumber, grated carrot, sprigs of watercress as desired.

Put the quark, hazel nuts, lemon juice and rind and parsley into a bowl and mix until well combined. Add salt and pepper to taste and one or two pinches of paprika pepper. Have ready a square of grease-proof paper or foil sprinkled with dried crumbs. Turn the cream cheese mixture on to this; form it into a loaf shape, making sure that it is completely coated with the crumbs. You can use the paper to help you form the roll shape. Then wrap the roll in the paper and put into the fridge to chill for several hours. It firms up as it chills. To serve, place the roll on a bed of crisp, dry lettuce and surround with sliced tomato, cucumber, grated carrot, watercress and anything else you fancy or serve in slices on individual plates, on a pool of chilled tomato sauce (page 65) for an elegant first course.

HAZEL NUT SPREAD

MAKES ABOUT 225G (8OZ) F
125g (4oz) hazel nuts
125g (4oz) sunflower seeds
15g (½oz) butter
4 tablespoons hot water
1 garlic clove, crushed
1 tablespoon Shoyu soy sauce, from health shops
sea salt
freshly ground black pepper

Toast nuts and sunflower seeds under a hot grill or in a moderate oven until golden brown. If nuts still have brown skins on, remove these after toasting by rubbing nuts gently in a soft, clean cloth. Grind nuts and sunflower seeds finely in a coffee grinder or blender. Mix nuts and sunflower seeds with the butter, water, garlic and soy sauce. Beat until smooth and creamy. Season with salt and pepper. Spoon into a small dish.

HUMMUS

Hummus is delicious served with warm wholemeal pitta bread, which you break off and use to scoop up the hummus. It's an excellent first course, particularly before a vegetable casserole, but is a nourishing and irresistible snack any time! Tahini, or sesame cream, can be bought from health shops but omit it if necessary: the hummus will still be very good.

SERVES 4 F
225g (8 oz) chick peas, soaked and cooked or 2 × 400g (14oz) cans
2 garlic cloves, crushed
2 tablespoons olive oil
4 teaspoons tahini
2 tablespoons lemon juice
sea salt
freshly ground black pepper
extra olive oil, paprika, lemon wedges and black olives

Drain chick peas, reserving liquid. Liquidize chick peas with garlic, oil, tahini, lemon juice and 240ml (8–9 fl oz) of the liquid, to make a purée about the consistency of lightly whipped cream. Season. Divide between four flat plates, spreading out the hummus to a depth of 1cm (½in). Indent top lightly with prongs of fork. Pour a little olive oil over the top, sprinkle with paprika and garnish with lemon wedges and black olives.

CURRIED LENTIL SPREAD

This is a good mixture for sandwiches or little savoury biscuits.

SERVES 4
125g (4oz) split red lentils
200ml (7 fl oz) water
1 small onion, peeled and finely chopped
25g (1oz) butter
2 teaspoons curry powder
sea salt
freshly ground black pepper

Wash the lentils and cook them in the water until they're tender and have absorbed all the water (20–30 minutes), then mash them roughly with a fork. Fry the onion in the butter until it's tender, then add the curry powder and fry for another 1–2 minutes. Blend this mixture into the cooked lentils to make a fairly smooth paste, then season to taste and leave the spread to get cold before using it.

LENTIL AND MUSHROOM PÂTÉ

This curiously pleasant mixture can be served as part of a salad, piled on crisp lettuce leaves, sprinkled with a little olive oil and some onion rings and surrounded by wedges of hardboiled eggs; or, in smaller portions on individual dishes, it makes a delicious starter. Alternatively it can be served in a pâté dish, with melba toast and butter, or thin brown bread and butter. It also makes a good sandwich filling, with or without the addition of thin slices of crisp raw onion or cucumber, tomato or other salad ingredients.

SERVES 2 AS A SALAD MEAL, 4–6 AS A STARTER,
PÂTÉ OR SANDWICH FILLING F
125g (4oz) continental lentils
50g (2oz) button mushrooms
1 garlic clove
40g (1½oz) butter
1 tablespoon chopped parsley
sea salt
freshly ground black pepper
2–4 teaspoons lemon juice

Soak, drain, rinse and cook the lentils in the usual way until very tender and beginning to disintegrate. Drain off any extra liquid (it won't be needed for this recipe, but keep it for a gravy or soup or something as it's full of flavour and nourishment). Wipe the mushrooms and chop them up fairly finely; crush the garlic. Melt the butter in a small saucepan

and fry the mushrooms and garlic for 2–3 minutes, then remove them from the heat and mix in the lentils and parsley. Season with sea salt, freshly ground black pepper and lemon juice. Chill before using.

LENTIL AND TOMATO SPREAD

SERVES 4 F
125g (4oz) split red lentils
200ml (7 fl oz) water
25g (1oz) softened butter
1 tablespoon tomato purée
a few drops lemon juice
sea salt
freshly ground black pepper

Cook the lentils in the water for 20–30 minutes, until they're tender and there's no water left, then let them cool. Mash the butter, tomato purée, a few drops of lemon juice and some sea salt and freshly ground black pepper into the cooked lentils to make a smoothish paste. This is nice in sandwiches with some raw onion, chutney or sliced tomato.

Variations

LENTIL AND CHIVE SPREAD

Make this as above but leave out the tomato purée and add 1–2 tablespoons of chopped chives instead.

LENTIL AND PARSLEY SPREAD

Make as above, leaving out the tomato purée and adding 2 tablespoons of chopped parsley. Some chopped spring onions are nice in this, too.

LIPTAUER CHEESE

This mixture of cottage cheese, soft butter and flavourings is popular in Austria, Hungary, Yugoslavia and Holland. It makes a good starter with hot fingers of toast. You don't need extra butter with it and it's quick to spread, so it's also good in sandwiches or on little cracker biscuits.

SERVES 4–6 [F]
25g (1oz) butter, softened
225g (8oz) low-fat quark
1 teaspoon paprika pepper
1 teaspoon chopped capers
1 tablespoon chopped chives
½ teaspoon French mustard
sea salt
freshly ground black pepper

Beat the butter until it's soft and light, then gradually mix in the quark and continue to beat until it's well blended. Add the paprika, capers, chives and mustard, then season to taste with salt and a grinding of black pepper. Put the mixture into a small bowl or pottery crock and serve it chilled; people can take a portion from the bowl and eat it with hot toast.

MOCK CAVIAR

This always-popular Russian dip is made from aubergines. It has an interesting, slightly smoky taste and a creamy consistency which goes beautifully with rye bread or wholemeal toast. It makes an unusual starter. Be sure to char the aubergine skin thoroughly.

SERVES 4–6 [F]
1 large aubergine – about 450g (1 lb)
1 large garlic clove, peeled and crushed
3 tablespoons olive oil
1 tablespoon lemon juice
sea salt
freshly ground black pepper

Before you make this dip you need to char the aubergine – this gives the dip its slightly smoky flavour. The easiest way to do it is to put the aubergine on the prongs of a fork and turn it over a gas flame until the skin is black and the inside is soft. Or you can place it under a hot grill, turning it round from time to time so that it gets evenly burnt. Then carefully scrape off the skin (you don't need this!) and mash, chop or liquidize the aubergine. Put this purée into a bowl and stir in the garlic, oil, lemon juice and a seasoning of salt and pepper. Mix everything well together, then spoon the mixture into a small dish – or individual dishes – and chill until required.

PEANUT BUTTER

MAKES 225G (8OZ) [F]
225g (8oz) shelled raw peanuts
cold-pressed vegetable oil, preferably ground nut

Spread the nuts out on a baking sheet and let them roast gently at the bottom of the oven while it's on for something else. They're done when the nuts under the skins are golden brown. Rub skins off, using a soft cloth. Grind nuts as finely as possible in a blender, electric coffee grinder or food processor. Then put into a bowl and beat in enough oil to make a spreading consistency. (I find this method better than adding oil to the nuts in the blender, which usually results in a sticky mess when I do it.) Homemade peanut butter, as well as being cheaper, avoids the additives which are slipped into most commercial peanut butters (including sugar). Keep the peanut butter in the fridge. The oil will separate, but this just proves you've got a really natural product without stabilizers and emulsifiers. . . . Simply give the peanut butter a stir before you use it.

When using any nuts it's important to make sure they're fresh; with peanuts it's specially important to check there are no signs of mould, which is poisonous. This shouldn't be a problem if you buy small quantities of fresh peanuts from a reputable shop, store them in a tin or jar in a dry place, and use them up fairly quickly.

CURRIED SOYA BEAN AND APPLE SPREAD

A nutritious spread with a pleasant sweet and sour flavour.

MAKES ABOUT 500G (1 LB 2OZ)
1 small onion, finely chopped
15g (½oz) butter
125g (4oz) peeled and cored cooking apple, finely chopped
1 tablespoon curry powder
300g (10oz) cooked soya beans
sea salt
freshly ground black pepper

Fry the onion in the butter for 5 minutes, then add the apple and curry powder, and fry, covered, for a further 5 minutes, until onion and apple are soft. Remove from heat and add soya beans. Mash well, adding a little water if necessary to make a soft consistency (use the water in which the beans were cooked, if you have it). Spoon mixture into a small container.

HARD SOYA CHEESE

This recipe developed by the Vegan Society, and published here by their kind permission, makes a useful substitute for hard cheese if you don't eat dairy produce.

MAKES 225G (8OZ) [F]
125g (4oz) Tomor Margarine *or* Nutter white
vegetable fat
1 teaspoon yeast extract
125g (4oz) soya flour

Put the butter and yeast extract into a saucepan and heat gently until melted. Remove from the heat and stir in the soya flour; mix well. Pour into a mould or boil to set. The result will be a hard cheese that you can slice or grate, and even toast under the grill. Soya cheese and wholemeal bread are complementary proteins, like ordinary cheese with bread.

STILTON PÂTÉ WITH PEARS

The Stilton cheese gives this creamy pâté its tangy flavour. I like to serve it on individual plates with slices of ripe pear and a few fresh walnuts.

SERVES 6 [F] – for the pâté
150g (5oz) Stilton cheese
225g (8oz) curd cheese
4 tablespoons milk
3 really ripe pears, preferably comice
juice of 1 lemon
6 crisp lettuce leaves
25g (1oz) fresh, shelled walnuts, chopped

Grate the cheese finely, then put it into a bowl with the curd cheese and milk and mix well to a creamy consistency. Form the mixture into a fat sausage shape and wrap it in a piece of foil, twisting the two ends like a cracker. Chill the roll for at least 2 hours.

Just before you are ready to serve the pâté, peel and core the pears, then cut them into thin slices. Sprinkle the slices with the lemon juice, making sure they are all coated, to prevent them from discolouring.

To serve the dish, put a lettuce leaf on each plate and arrange the pear slices on top. Unwrap the pâté, cut the roll into six slices and put one on each plate on top of the pears. Sprinkle the walnuts on top and serve as soon as possible.

STRIPY PÂTÉ

This dish consists of different coloured layers pressed into a loaf tin and chilled overnight. When the pâté is turned out and sliced it looks most attractive and impressive, yet it's very simple to make. Serve with hot fingers of toast, or some crisp melba toast.

SERVES 6–8
For the first layer (yellow)
175g (6oz) grated orange-coloured cheese, such as
double Gloucester – *or* vegetarian Cheddar
50g (2oz) butter
4 tablespoons milk
tabasco
sea salt
freshly ground black pepper

For the second layer (green)
125g (4oz) curd cheese
1 medium-sized ripe avocado pear
1 tablespoon lemon juice
tabasco
sea salt
freshly ground black pepper

For the third layer (white)
225g (8oz) curd cheese
1 large garlic clove, peeled and crushed – optional

To finish
6 stuffed olives, halved
4 tablespoons finely chopped parsley *or* chives
paprika pepper
watercress
sea salt
freshly ground black pepper

First fold some kitchen paper into about eight layers to fit neatly into the base of a 450g (1 lb) loaf tin – this will absorb any liquid which seeps out of the pâté and ensure that it will be firm and easy to cut later. Then put a long strip of silicon paper on top of this, to cover the base and extend up the narrow sides of the tin.

Next make the mixture for the first layer: put the grated cheese into a bowl and beat in the other ingredients to make a smooth cream. Season with salt, pepper and tabasco.

For the avocado layer: put the cheese into a bowl and mash lightly with a fork. Cut the avocado in half and remove the stone and skin, then slice the flesh roughly and add to the curd cheese. Mash the avocado into the cheese, with the lemon juice, until you have a smooth green purée. Season with salt and pepper and add a few drops of tabasco to taste.

To make the third layer, beat together the curd cheese and garlic, if you're using it, and add salt and pepper to taste.

Put the sliced olives, cut side down, in the base of the tin, right down the centre, then carefully spoon the yellow cheese mixture in on top, pressing it down lightly and levelling it with the back of a spoon. Cover completely with the chopped chives in a thick layer. Then spoon the avocado mixture on top and sprinkle with a thin but even layer of paprika pepper. Cover this with the white curd cheese, smooth with the back of a spoon, then press another wad of paper on top. Put a weight on top and leave in the fridge overnight. (It's a good idea to replace the top layer of kitchen paper with a new one after an hour or so as it will have absorbed a good deal of moisture.)

To serve the pâté, remove the kitchen paper, slip a knife down the edges of the tin to loosen, then invert the tin over a serving dish, turn the pâté out and strip off the remaining layers of paper: the stuffed olives should now be on top, looking attractive against the yellow cheese mixture. Decorate with sprigs of watercress round the edge. You need a sharp knife to cut the pâté into thick slices; this is a slightly tricky operation, so you might prefer to cut it first and serve it in slices on individual plates – lay the slices flat, to show off the pretty stripes and decorate each with a sprig or two of watercress. It's also nice with the yoghurt and herb or yoghurt and spring onion sauce on page 68, or served on top of a pool of fresh tomato sauce (page 65) and chilled before using. This gives a pretty colour-contrast.

CURRIED VEGETABLE AND NUT PÂTÉ WITH YOGHURT SAUCE

Another easy one to make, this pâté consists of crunchy vegetables and nuts, flavoured with curry and garlic.

SERVES 6
25g (1oz) butter
1 medium-sized onion, peeled and finely chopped
1 carrot, about 50g (2oz), scraped and finely chopped
1 stick of celery, washed and chopped
½ green pepper, about 50g (2oz), de-seeded and chopped
½ red pepper, about 50g (2oz), de-seeded and chopped
1 garlic clove, peeled and crushed
1 tablespoon mild curry powder
125g (4oz) hazel nuts, roasted and chopped
225g (8oz) curd cheese
sea salt
freshly ground black pepper
5cm (2in) cucumber
200ml (7 fl oz) natural yoghurt
3 tablespoons fresh mint, finely chopped
lettuce leaves
sliced tomato

Line a 450g (1 lb) loaf tin with a strip of silicon paper to cover the base and come up the two narrow sides. Melt the butter in a large saucepan and fry the vegetables for 2–3 minutes: they should soften a little, but still be very crunchy. Add the curry powder and cook for a further minute. Remove from the heat and stir in the rest of the ingredients. Spoon mixture into the prepared loaf tin – it won't fill it – and smooth the top. Cover with foil and chill for several hours. Meanwhile make the dressing. Peel and finely chop the cucumber and mix with the yoghurt and mint. Season with salt and pepper.

When you're ready to serve the dish, put two or three small crisp lettuce leaves on individual plates. Slip a knife round the edges of the pâté to loosen it, then turn it out of the tin and cut into slices. Place one slice on each plate. Give the dressing a quick stir, then spoon a little on to each plate. Or serve in slices on top of a pool of the sauce, nouvelle cuisine fashion. Garnish the plates with sliced tomato. Serve the rest of the dressing in a small jug.

SANDWICHES – SAVOURY AND SWEET

One of the questions people most frequently ask is 'what can I use for vegetarian sandwiches?', so here are some suggestions. By varying both the filling and the type of bread used – wholemeal bread, pitta bread, wholemeal rolls, wholemeal French stick, for instance, many different combinations are possible. For the fillings, 'think salad' is a good maxim for health, with other more concentrated ingredients added for flavour. Here are some ideas:

SAVOURY SANDWICH IDEAS

Yeast extract, tahini, peanut butter or low-fat white cheese with lettuce, bean sprouts, tomato, cress, cucumber or grated carrot;

Cheese spread, page 46, or grated cheese bound with yoghurt, soft white cheese or mayonnaise, with any of the above salad items;

Finely chopped hardboiled egg, bound with yoghurt, mayonnaise, soft white cheese or milk, with any of the salad suggestions;

Tofu mashed, seasoned and mixed with the salad items above;

Any of the lentil, bean or nut dips, with salad;

Salad mixtures such as Greek salad, vitality salad, soya bean salad or red bean salad, in a pocket of pitta bread;

Slices of cold nut or lentil loaf with salad and/or pickle;

Lentil rissoles or burgers in a soft wholemeal bap

SWEET SANDWICH IDEAS

Clear honey mixed with finely grated nuts

Curd cheese with chopped crystallized ginger

Curd cheese with chopped 'canned in its own juice' pineapple

125g (4oz) dates softened by heating in 5 tablespoons water then beaten smooth

Dates softened as above with chopped nuts added, or some curd cheese beaten in peanut butter and sliced banana (don't freeze)

Cottage or yoghurt cheese with chopped banana, apple, dates or raisins;

Dates softened in a little boiling water then mixed with chopped or grated nuts;

The date filling on page 314 or the sugarless apricot conserve, page 314;

Sliced banana, perhaps with a sprinkling of grated nuts or desiccated coconut, or with some tahini;

Tahini mixed with honey.

OPEN SANDWICHES

A tray of colourful open sandwiches looks really mouthwatering and is a surprisingly practical way of feeding a large group of people. If you want to make the meal more substantial serve mugs or bowls of soup as well with a choice of different puddings laid out on a separate table for people to help themselves. Medium-sized plates and forks will be needed for eating the sandwiches and plenty of paper napkins are advisable.

It's fun to make the open sandwiches and not difficult to make them look pretty. I think the easiest way to do them is to prepare a really good assortment of different ingredients and spread them all out in front of you so that you can create different combinations as you go along.

For the base:
Wholemeal bread, rye bread or pumpernickel
Butter
Crisp lettuce leaves

For the toppings:
Finely grated cheese mixed to a paste with mayonnaise, cream or milk
Sliced hardboiled egg
Chopped hardboiled egg mixed with mayonnaise or low-fat quark
Cold scrambled egg
Peanut butter
Cottage cheese
Quark or cream cheese
Any of the dips on pages 42–51 (*hummus*, mock caviar, Liptauer cheese and avocado dip are particularly good)
Cold bean or lentil salads are also excellent

For the garnishes:
Slices of lemon, tomato, avocado (tossed in lemon juice) onion, red and green pepper, cooked beetroot, cucumber, radishes, spring onions
Sprigs of parsley, mint or watercress
Chopped chives
Pineapple cubes or rings
Chopped apple, sliced banana tossed in lemon juice
Raisins, dates, chopped dried apricots
Black or green grapes

Black or green olives
Chopped walnuts and flaked almonds
Chopped stem ginger
Mango chutney
Olive oil
Mayonnaise
Paprika pepper

Butter the bread fairly generously and place it on the tray from which it will be served. Cover each piece of bread with a lettuce leaf, pressing it down so that the butter sticks it on to the bread. Now arrange your toppings and garnishes on the lettuce leaf, covering each as generously as possible whilst making them practical to eat. Here are some ideas for different combinations:

1. Avocado (dipped in lemon juice), watercress, a spoonful of mayonnaise, quark or cottage cheese, chopped walnuts.
2. Peanut butter, coarsely grated carrot, green pepper rings, sliced onion.
3. Quark or cottage cheese, pineapple rings, black grapes, toasted flaked almonds.
4. Sliced cooked beetroot, onion rings, chopped walnuts, cream cheese or quark
5. Cold lentil salad, mango chutney, chopped apple, parsley.
6. *Hummus*, onion rings, paprika, sliced tomato, parsley.
7. Mock caviar or aubergine and sesame pâté, sliced tomato, onion rings, olive oil.
8. Liptauer cheese, tomato, black olives, parsley sprigs.
9. Goat cheese and herb spread, sliced cucumber and radishes.
10. Avocado dip, coarsely grated carrot, sliced tomato, chopped walnuts.
11. Cubes of cold spicy fritters, mango chutney, tomato, onion rings, garlic mayonnaise.
12. Quark or cream cheese, apple, chopped stem ginger, walnuts.

MINIATURE OPEN SANDWICHES

Miniature open sandwiches make an excellent first course or nibble for a drinks or buffet party. Make sure that the topping is pressed firmly on to the bread or else they can be rather messy to eat. If you're serving these as a first course, allow three to four for each person.

MAKES 24–36 SMALL OPEN SANDWICHES
6 slices of dark rye bread *or* other flat firm bread
butter
6–8 lettuce leaves

EGG AND OLIVE TOPPING
2 hardboiled eggs
2 tablespoons mayonnaise
8 black olives, stoned
watercress

TOMATO AND BUTTER BEAN TOPPING
225g (8oz) can butter beans
1 tablespoon olive oil
2 teaspoons lemon juice
sea salt
freshly ground black pepper
1 small tomato, cut into thin wedges
fresh chives, chopped

AVOCADO TOPPING
1 small avocado pear
lemon juice
sea salt
freshly ground black pepper
2 tablespoons mayonnaise
1 small carrot, scraped and coarsely grated
watercress
paprika pepper

Butter the slices of bread and cut each into four or six pieces. Press a piece of lettuce on top of each to cover and make a base for the toppings.

First make the egg and olive sandwiches; slice the hardboiled eggs and arrange them on top of a third of the number of bread slices. Spoon a little mayonnaise over and decorate each open sandwich with an olive and a little watercress.

For the tomato and butter bean sandwiches, drain the butter beans, reserving the liquid. Then make the beans into a dip by mashing them with the oil, lemon juice and about a tablespoonful of the reserved liquid to make a soft consistency. Season with salt and pepper. Spoon this mixture on top of another third of the bread slices and decorate each with a tomato slice and some chopped chives.

Finally, for the avocado sandwiches, cut the avocado in half and remove the stone and skin. Put the avocado into a medium-sized bowl with the lemon juice and mash until smooth. Season with salt and pepper. Spoon this mixture on to the remaining pieces of lettuce-lined bread and top each with a little mayonnaise, a few shreds of grated carrot, a sprig of watercress and a dusting of paprika pepper.

These look prettiest served on a large plate or wooden platter.

PINWHEELS

These pinwheels are good for serving at drinks parties and similar functions; they look attractive, like slices from miniature savoury swiss rolls. I like to make two batches, with contrasting fillings.

MAKES ABOUT 50 F
about 10 slices from a large sliced wholemeal loaf

For a green filling
125g (4oz) soft butter
curd cheese
4 tablespoons fresh parsley, finely chopped
1 tablespoon hot water

For an orange filling
125g (4oz) orange cheese, such as double Gloucester,
finely grated
25g (1oz) butter *or* polyunsaturated margarine
2–3 tablespoons milk
tabasco
salt
freshly ground black pepper

First make the fillings for the pinwheels. Beat together the butter or curd cheese, parsley and hot water to make a light, creamy mixture. Put the orange cheese into another bowl and beat in the butter or margarine and enough milk to make a soft consistency; add a drop or two of tabasco and a little salt and pepper.

Cut the crusts off the bread and flatten each slice with a rolling pin. Spread half the slices generously with the green butter mixture and the rest of the slices with the orange mixture. Roll the slices up like swiss rolls and if possible chill them for an hour or so. Then cut each roll into about five fairly thin slices.

ASPARAGUS ROLLS

These are one of my favourite sandwich-type party foods: moist spears of asparagus rolled in thin wholemeal bread.

MAKES ABOUT 40 F
350g (12oz) canned asparagus tips, drained *or* 225g
(8oz) fresh asparagus, cooked and drained
1 sliced wholemeal loaf
butter

Cut the crusts from the bread and roll each slice with a rolling pin to make it thinner and more flexible. Butter the bread. Put one spear of asparagus on each slice of bread and roll the bread round the asparagus. Cut each roll into two or three pieces so that they are a manageable size for eating. Keep in a cool place, covered with foil, until needed.

SNACKS

GARLIC BREAD

Hot bread with melted butter and garlic is a wonderful accompaniment to soups and creamy dips, particularly those containing lentils and beans. French bread is of course the type that is normally used for garlic bread, and there's no doubt that this is delicious, with a crisp crust and tender crumb, and you can use either the traditional white type or one of the wholemeal sticks which you can get quite easily now. For quick wholemeal garlic bread for just one or two people you can also spread slices of wholemeal bread with garlic butter, lay them out individually on a baking sheet or grill pan without any foil covering and heat them in the oven or under the grill until the butter has melted and the bread is just crispy round the edges.

SERVES 4–6
1 French loaf *or* 1 small wholemeal loaf
3–4 garlic cloves
salt
125g (4oz) butter, softened

Set the oven to 200°C (400°F), gas mark 6. Slice the French loaf almost through into chunky pieces – they should just hold together at the base. Cut the stick or loaf right through into slices – don't make them too thick. Make the garlic butter by peeling the garlic and crushing it in a little salt, then mixing it into the butter. Spread this butter on both sides of the slices of bread. Pile the bread back into the loaf shape. Wrap the loaf in foil and place it on a baking sheet in the oven. Bake it for about 20 minutes, until it's heated right through and crisp on the outside. Serve at once.

HOT GARLIC CHICKPEAS IN PITTA BREAD

SERVES 4–6
2 × 400g (14oz) cans chickpeas
self-raising wholemeal flour to coat
sea salt
freshly ground black pepper
6 tablespoons olive oil
2–4 garlic cloves, crushed
4–6 pieces warm wholemeal pitta bread to serve

Spread chickpeas out on a large plate and sprinkle with the flour and a little salt and pepper. Turn them gently so that each one is coated with flour. Heat the oil in a large frying pan; add chickpeas and garlic. Fry chickpeas gently until crisp and golden, turning them often. You may need to do them in more than one batch. Slit open the tops of the pitta bread, fill with the hot chickpeas and serve immediately. Some sliced firm tomatoes and mild onion rings are nice in the pitta bread with the chickpeas, and a dollop of natural yoghurt on top makes a pleasant finishing touch. Serve with a crisp green salad for more of a meal.

MELBA TOAST

You can make excellent melba toast from sliced wholemeal bread and it makes a lovely crunchy accompaniment to creamy dips and pâtés. It's delicious, and people always eat more than you think they will, so make plenty!

1 or 2 slices ready-sliced wholemeal bread for each person

Set the oven to 200°C (400°F), gas mark 6. Make the bread into toast in the usual way, then lay the pieces of toast flat on a board and, using a sharp knife and a sawing motion, cut the bread in half horizontally. Place the toast halves, uncooked side upper-most, on a baking sheet and bake for about 7–10 minutes, until they are crisp and brown all over, and curling up at the edges. Cool.

QUICK BREAD PIZZA (1)

Wholemeal pitta bread makes an excellent base for a quick pizza. Serve with watercress or lettuce salad.

SERVES 4
4 wholemeal pitta breads
225g (8oz) cottage cheese
8 tomatoes, skinned and sliced
125–175g (4–6oz) grated cheese
sea salt
freshly ground black pepper
oregano

Set oven to 200°C (400°F), gas mark 6, or prepare a hot grill. Put the pitta bread on a baking sheet. Spread each with cottage cheese, arrange the tomato slices on top and scatter grated cheese over them. Sprinkle with salt, pepper and oregano. Bake in the oven for about 20 minutes, or place under grill for about 10 minutes, until filling has heated through and cheese has melted and browned.

QUICK BREAD PIZZA (2)

An oval wholemeal loaf, split in half, makes a good crisp, crunchy base for a quick pizza. I like to top the bread with lots of fried onion, tomato, cheese and black olives. If you have a freezer and keep a couple of these loaves in it, already split as described in the recipe, you can make this pizza in next to no time.

SERVES 4
1 oval wholemeal loaf, about 450g (1 lb)
2 large onions, peeled and sliced
1 tablespoon olive oil
2 very large tomatoes, weighing about 450g (1 lb) together, *or* 425g (15oz) can
sea salt
freshly ground black pepper
dried basil or oregano
125g (4oz) grated Cheshire cheese
8 black olives

Set the oven to 200°C (400°F), gas mark 6. Slice the loaf in half lengthwise and scoop out the soft crumb – this won't be needed, but can be made into breadcrumbs and used in other recipes. Fry the onions in the oil for 10 minutes, until soft and lightly browned. Put the two halves of the loaf on a baking sheet and cover with the onions. Slice the tomatoes, if you're using fresh ones, or drain canned tomatoes. Arrange the tomatoes on top of the onions and season well with salt and pepper. Sprinkle with the cheese and herbs and bake for 20 minutes, until the crust is very crisp and the cheese melted and beginning to brown. Decorate with the olives and serve immediately, with a crisp green salad.

SAVOURIES ON TOAST

'Something on toast' makes a welcome quick snack. Before my two eldest daughters left for university, I seemed always to be rustling up this kind of snack at odd times to fit in with their hectic social life!

ASPARAGUS AND CHEESE ON TOAST

SERVES 1–2
½ small can asparagus
125g (4oz) grated cheese
2 pieces hot toast

Drain asparagus – keep liquid for soups but put 1 tablespoon into a pan and add the cheese. Melt over gentle heat, then add asparagus and heap on to hot unbuttered toast slices. Grill until golden brown and bubbly. Serve at once.

AVOCADO TOAST

SERVES 2
1 large avocado pear
juice of ½ lemon
2–4 slices hot wholemeal toast
freshly ground black pepper

Peel, stone and thinly slice (or mash) the avocado pear; sprinkle with lemon juice. Arrange slices on toast, or spread over toast, grind some black pepper on top, warm through under the grill.

AVOCADO, TOMATO AND ALMONDS ON TOAST

SERVES 4
juice of ½ lemon
2 avocado pears
2 tomatoes
sea salt
freshly ground black pepper
4 pieces wholemeal toast
225g (8oz) curd or cottage cheese
2 tablespoons flaked almonds
lemon slices

Put lemon juice into a bowl; remove skin and stone from avocados and slice into bowl; skin and slice tomatoes, add to advocados, season with salt and pepper. Spread the toast with the cheese, put the avocados and tomatoes on top and sprinkle with almonds. Place under moderate grill just to heat through. Serve garnished with lemon slices.

MUSHROOMS ON TOAST

SERVES 2
450g (1 lb) button mushrooms
15g (½oz) butter
yeast extract, tahini or peanut butter
2–4 large slices wholemeal toast
chopped parsley

Wipe – don't peel – the mushrooms; slice and fry lightly in the butter. Serve on unbuttered toast, sprinkled with chopped parsley. Toast can be spread with yeast extract, tahini or peanut butter first if you like a more savoury taste.

MUSHROOMS AND CHEESE ON TOAST

SERVES 2–4
125g (4oz) button mushrooms
15g (½oz) butter
125g (4oz) grated cheese
4 pieces unbuttered wholemeal toast

Wash and slice mushrooms, fry lightly in the butter until tender, then add the cheese and melt over a gentle heat. Heap on toast and grill until golden brown.

PEANUT BUTTER (OR TAHINI) AND TOMATO TOASTS

SERVES 2
2 tablespoons peanut butter, or tahini
2–4 large slices wholemeal toast
3–4 large tomatoes, skinned and sliced

Spread peanut butter on the toast, top with tomato slices and heat through under the grill.

PINEAPPLE AND CHEESE ON TOAST

SERVES 2
small can pineapple pieces in own juice
125g (4oz) grated cheese
4 pieces unbuttered wholemeal toast

Make as for Asparagus and Cheese on Toast (this page).

TOMATO AND CHEESE ON TOAST

SERVES 2
3 tomatoes, skinned
15g (½oz) butter
125g (4oz) grated cheese
4 pieces unbuttered wholemeal toast

Make as for Mushrooms and Cheese on Toast, opposite.

TOMATO, NUTS AND ONION ON TOAST

SERVES 2
4 tomatoes, skinned
15g (½oz) butter
50g (2oz) very finely grated nuts
1 teaspoon grated onion
2 teaspoons lemon juice
sea salt
freshly ground black pepper
2 pieces wholemeal toast
lemon slices *or* onion slices to garnish

Chop tomatoes and cook gently in the butter for 3 minutes. Add nuts, onion, lemon juice, salt and pepper. Cook for a further few minutes to heat through thoroughly, then heap on toast and garnish with lemon or onion slices.

DRINKS

APRICOT, ORANGE AND ALMOND WHIZZ

This drink contains iron and vitamins A and C. The apricots do need soaking beforehand (this applies even to those which say they're ready for use, in fact I don't see any advantage in paying more for these). If you like this recipe, though, it might be worth soaking a larger quantity of apricots and keeping the remainder in the fridge, so they're ready when you need them.

MAKES ONE 250ML (10 FL OZ) GLASS
50g (2oz) dried apricots – unsulphured ones from
the health shop are best
200ml (7 fl oz) pure orange juice
1–2 teaspoons clear honey
25g (1 oz) blanched almonds
1 tablespoon wheat germ

Wash the apricots carefully in warm water, then put them into a bowl, covering with boiling water and leave to soak for a few hours, or overnight if possible. Then drain the apricots and put them into the blender with the orange juice, honey, almonds and wheat germ. Whizz for about 60 seconds, until smooth. Pour into a tall glass.

APRICOT AND ORANGE NECTAR

A lighter drink which, like the previous one, is also rich in vitamins A and C, and contains some iron and calcium. Brewer's yeast powder can be obtained at health food shops. It's a concentrated source of B vitamins – good for the nerves!

MAKES ONE 250ML (10 FL OZ) GLASS
50g (2oz) dried apricots – unsulphured ones from
health shop are best
200ml (7 fl oz) pure orange juice
1–2 teaspoons clear honey
1 teaspoon brewer's yeast powder

Wash and soak the apricots as in the previous recipe, then put into the blender with the orange juice, honey and yeast and whizz to a purée. Pour into a glass and serve. This is good with some ice cubes added in hot weather.

BANANA MILK SHAKE

This drink, adapted from the one Barbara Griggs gives in *The Home Herbal*, is, as she says, a palatable way to take nutritious brewer's yeast powder, and rich in iron, calcium and B vitamins.

MAKES ONE 250ML (10 FL OZ) GLASS
1 banana, peeled
200ml (7 fl oz) milk or soya milk
2 heaped tablespoons natural yoghurt *or* vegan
yoghurt (page 308)
2 teaspoons brewer's yeast powder

Peel the banana and cut into rough chunks, then put into the blender with the rest of the ingredients. Whizz until smooth and frothy; serve at once.

CAROB SHAKE

The carob gives this a deliciously rich chocolaty flavour as well as providing iron and calcium. This is another particularly good drink to have when you're feeling drained and in need of a quick boost of energy, and is a good way of taking milk or soya milk if you don't like drinking them in their natural state.

MAKES ONE 250ML (10 FL OZ) GLASS
1½ teaspoons carob powder
1 teaspoon honey
1 tablespoon skim milk powder – optional
200ml (7 fl oz) milk or soya milk
pinch cinnamon

Blend ingredients together using a whisk or in a liquidizer.

FORTIFIED MILK

This is another way of making milk palatable if you don't like drinking it plain. The addition of skim milk powder gives the milk a lovely rich taste, without adding many calories, as well as increasing the calcium. This one glass of fortified milk has double the calcium of an ordinary glass of milk. Other ingredients can be added according to taste: a little honey or a pinch of cinnamon or both, for instance.

MAKES ONE 25ML (10 FL OZ) GLASS
200ml (7 fl oz) milk
2 heaped tablespoons skim milk powder

Simply put the ingredients into a blender and whizz together. You can heat the milk first if you would prefer a hot drink.

FRUIT CUP WITH VERMOUTH

After all that serious nourishment, here's a fun one: a lovely fruit cup which a friend of mine serves as an aperitif; it is beautifully refreshing, great for drinking in the garden in the summer with friends. All you do is mix together equal quantities of apple juice, orange juice and white vermouth (Chambery is best), all well chilled. Then add a few sprigs of fresh mint and a few slices of orange, lemon and/or cucumber, as available. You can use a still apple juice or a sparkling one if you want some bubbles.

HERB TEAS

Herb teas can be very pleasant and beneficial. The herb tea bags you can get from health shops are convenient to use and come in a wide range of varieties. They contain enough herbs to make a pleasant drink rather than a herbal medicine; for a stronger effect, use two tea bags to a cupful of boiling water. Or you can make your own herb tea from dried or fresh herbs. Herb teas which are particularly useful for pregnancy and childbirth are peppermint, for digestive problems, and chamomile, which is soothing and sleep-inducing and can be cooled and given to a restless baby, too. Peppermint, chamomile, lime or meadowsweet tea, taken first thing in the morning, can be helpful for morning sickness. Raspberry-leaf tea is a traditional and well-tried herbal treatment during pregnancy and can be safely taken, unless you've been doing a great deal of physical exercise and have very well-developed muscles, in which case its muscle-toning effect might be too much. Drink a cupful of raspberry-leaf tea three times a day during pregnancy and the postnatal period.

MAKES ONE 250ML (10 FL OZ) CUP
1 teaspoon dried herbs – peppermint, raspberry leaf, lime, chamomile or meadowsweet: from health shops, or see above
275ml (10 fl oz) boiling water
a little honey to taste – optional

Put the dried herbs into a cup and pour in the boiling water. Cover and leave to infuse for 4–5 minutes. Strain if you like, and sweeten slightly to taste if necessary.

LASSI

This drink from India is refreshing in hot weather, but also nourishing because of the protein and calcium in the yoghurt. It can be made salty or sweet, according to taste.

SERVES 1
1 big tablespoon natural yoghurt or vegan yoghurt (page 308)
200ml (7 fl oz) chilled water
a pinch of salt; or 1–2 teaspoons clear honey and pinch of cinnamon; or a few drops of triple-strength rose water

Put the yoghurt into a glass and gradually stir in the water. Add the salt, or honey and cinnamon or rose water.

MILK SHAKE

If you keep a bottle of skimmed milk and some fruit yoghurt in the fridge you can make this very quickly. The children like it served in a tall glass with a straw.

MAKES 1 GLASS
200ml (7 fl oz) chilled skimmed milk
2 tablespoons fruit yoghurt, preferably the kind made without artificial colouring and flavouring and sweetened with barbados sugar

Put the skimmed milk and yoghurt into the liquidizer and blend until well mixed and frothy. Serve at once.

SOYA MILK – SUPER VERSION

This is the most delicious milk, far nicer than dairy milk! It's a fiddle to make, but rewarding when you see the beautiful white liquid. It works out at about a third of the price of bought soya milk.

MAKES ABOUT 1.2 LITRES (2 PINTS)
225g (8oz) soya beans
vanilla pod
1 tablespoon cold-pressed sunflower oil
dash of honey *or* raw sugar

Soak the beans in plenty of water for 2 days, changing the water twice a day. Liquidize beans with 1.5 litres (2½ pints) water. Pour mixture through a sieve lined with a piece of muslin, squeezing through as much liquid as possible into a large saucepan. Add the vanilla pod. Heat liquid to boiling point, then remove vanilla pod and liquidize again with the oil, and a dash of honey or sugar to taste. Strain through muslin again. (The vanilla pod can be washed, dried and used a number of times. Alternatively, you can use half a vanilla pod only and liquidize it with the milk for a strong and very delicious flavour. But since vanilla pods don't come cheap, this does put up the price of the soya-pinta.)

SOYA MILK – QUICK AND EASY VERSION

This isn't nearly as delicate as the soya milk above, but is useful for cooking.

MAKES 1.2 LITRES (2 PINTS)
75g (3oz) flour
1.2 litres (2 pints) water
1 tablespoon cold-pressed oil
dash of honey *or* raw sugar

Whisk or liquidize together. The protein in soya milk is quite similar to ordinary milk.

TIGER NUT MILK

Tiger nuts (sometimes called chufa nuts) are little chewy brown rhizones which you can sometimes get from the health shop. They're quite pricey, but make a wonderful milk for a special treat and it still works out cheaper (by about 25 per cent) than bought soya milk. It's also much easier to make than soya milk.

MAKES 1.2 LITRES (2 PINTS)
225g (8oz) tiger nuts
1.2 litres (2 pints) water

Wash the chufa nuts, then liquidize them with the water. Leave to stand 3–4 hours, then strain and use as milk. (The strained-off pulp can be eaten with muesli or incorporated into nut cutlets if you want to be really thrifty). This milk is delicious chilled as a drink (I like the flavour much better than cow's milk) or poured over cereal, fruit or puddings.

YOGHURT AND ORANGE FLIP

This is a favourite drink of mine which is calming and revitalizing.

MAKES APPROX. ONE 250ML (10 FL OZ) GLASS
1 orange, peeled
150ml (5 fl oz) natural yoghurt *or* vegan yoghurt (page 308)
a little clear honey – optional

Break the orange into segments and place in blender. Add the yoghurt, then whizz for 30–60 seconds, until fairly smooth, and add a little honey to taste, if you like. There will still be some chunky pieces of orange, but these give the drink a pleasant 'body' and provide extra fibre.

3

SAUCES

When people hear I'm vegetarian, the first thing they always ask is 'what do you have for Christmas dinner?' and the second thing is 'what do you do for gravy?'. For the answer to the first question see pages 162 and 174. As far as the second question is concerned, you can make a straightforward traditional-type gravy by browning an onion and some flour in a little oil or butter then adding vegetable stock, yeast extract, seasoning and a dash of soy sauce. If you like the flavour of gravy powder, you can add some of that, too; most of the ones on the market are vegetarian, in spite of the 'meaty' looking pictures on the packet. Sometimes when families are new to vegetarian food and perhaps a bit reluctant, I've heard that it's the sight of a familiar gravy with the nut or lentil loaf which encourages them to try – and enjoy – it.

My husband is one of the gravy-lovers of the world, but I personally think there are many more exciting ways of adding moisture to a meal. A pretty, orange purée of carrots, for instance, or a soured cream or yoghurt and green herb sauce, which is delicious with a slice of nut loaf or with crisp lentil rissoles; or a fresh tomato sauce which is quick to make, low in fat and excellent with so many dishes. I also like the German way of serving a fruit sauce, such as apple or gooseberry, with crisp potato cakes, and another favourite of mine is one of my own ideas (as far as I know), which is to make a thick lentil soup-sauce and to serve it with vegetables to make a complete main course that's great in winter made with root vegetables, very cheap and filling. Not strictly speaking sauces, but too good to leave out of this book, are two chutney recipes, one with conventional ingredients but an unconventional (and very easy) method, and the other a sugarless, almost instant one.

As far as freezing sauces is concerned, the fruit sauces and flour-based sauces freeze well, as does home-made tomato sauce. Heavily spiced sauces such as the curry sauces can develop a musty flavour, but are all right kept in the freezer for a week or so. The yoghurt, soured cream and egg yolk sauces won't freeze satisfactorily.

APPLE SAUCE

You can use cooking apples, which cook to a lovely soft fluffy purée, but if you use sweet apples you need less sugar. Either way, the result is a pleasant, fruity sauce that's ideal with nut roasts.

SERVES 4–6 F
450g (1 lb) apples
4 tablespoons water
4 tablespoons sugar
15g (½oz) butter
sea salt

Peel and core the apples, then cut them into smallish pieces. Put the apple pieces, water, sugar and butter into a medium-sized heavy-based saucepan and cook gently, with a lid on the saucepan, until the apples are soft. Season with a little sea salt, and mash the mixture slightly with a wooden spoon, if necessary, to break up the apple. (Or you can sieve or liquidize it if you prefer a smooth consistency.)

Variations

APPLE AND CRANBERRY SAUCE

For this version, cook 125g (4oz) fresh cranberries, washed and picked over, with the apples. You'll need to add more sugar, as cranberries are very sharp.

APPLE AND REDCURRANT SAUCE

This is made in the same way, using redcurrants instead of the cranberries. You can also make a pleasant sauce by just softening the apples in two rounded tablespoons of redcurrant (or cranberry jelly) and leaving out the sugar.

BLENDER BÉARNAISE SAUCE

This is a quick version of this classic, rich, creamy sauce: you first reduce the vinegar in a saucepan to concentrate the flavour, then add it to the egg yolks in the liquidizer and pour in the melted butter. It only takes a few minutes to make. It's a rich sauce, to be saved for the occasional special meal, but it's superb with dishes such as the white nutmeat with capers on page 173. A very pleasant variation is to stir 125g (4oz) *fromage blanc* into the finished sauce – this lightens it, and with this addition the quantities given below will serve eight people.

SERVES 6
125g (4oz) butter
2 tablespoons wine vinegar
1 tablespoon very finely chopped onion
8 peppercorns, lightly crushed
2 egg yolks
1 tablespoon lemon juice
sea salt
freshly ground black pepper

Melt the butter in a small saucepan. Heat the vinegar, onion and peppercorns together in a small saucepan until the vinegar has reduced by half. Put the egg yolks and lemon juice into the liquidizer goblet and blend until just creamy, then strain in the vinegar mixture and blend again. Now, with the liquidizer still going, pour the melted butter slowly in through the top of the goblet. As you do so the mixture will thicken to a beautiful creamy consistency. Season with salt and pepper and serve immediately, just warm. If you need to keep this sauce warm, the safest way is to stand the saucepan in another large saucepan or roasting tin containing very hot water.

BREAD SAUCE

I love breadsauce!

SERVES 4–6 F
1 onion, peeled
3 cloves
275ml (10fl oz) milk
1 bay leaf
50g (2oz) fresh white bread, crusts removed
15g (½oz) butter
1–2 tablespoons cream
sea salt
freshly ground black pepper
grated nutmeg

Put the onion, studded with the cloves, into a saucepan and add the milk and bay leaf. Bring to the boil, then take off the heat, add the slices of bread, cover and leave to one side for 15–30 minutes for the flavours to infuse. Then remove the onion and bay leaf, beat the mixture to break up the bread and stir in the butter, cream and salt, pepper and nutmeg to taste. If you are making the sauce in advance, once you have beaten it smooth you can put back the onion and bay leaf, so that they can continue to flavour the sauce until you're ready to serve it.

CHEESE SAUCE

Cheese sauce, is useful both for incorporating into other dishes before baking or grilling them and for serving with vegetables to make them into more of a meal. Strictly speaking, for a classic cheese sauce, this should be made with half Gruyère cheese and half Parmesan. The Gruyère makes it creamy and the Parmesan gives it a good flavour, but both are expensive and for day-to-day cooking I use a cheaper substitute plus a good seasoning of mustard, cayenne and freshly ground black pepper.

MAKES 275ML (10FL OZ) F
25g (1oz) butter
25g (1oz) plain white flour
1 bay leaf
275–425ml (10–15fl oz) skimmed milk
50g (2oz) grated cheese – Cheddar, or I like double
Gloucester as it's creamy-tasting and gives the sauce
a pretty colour
1 teaspoon mustard powder
cayenne pepper
sea salt
freshly ground black pepper

Melt the butter in a medium-sized saucepan and stir in the flour; cook for a few seconds until the flour bubbles round the edges, then add the bay leaf, turn up the heat and pour in about one-third of the milk. Stir hard until the sauce is very thick and smooth, then repeat the process twice with the remaining milk so that you finish with a smooth, medium-thick sauce. Take the saucepan off the heat and beat in the grated cheese, mustard, a tiny pinch of cayenne pepper and salt and pepper to taste. Don't let it get too hot once the cheese has been added or it may go stringy and spoil.

CRANBERRY SAUCE

Red cranberry sauce with its sweet yet slightly astringent taste is one of the most delicious parts of the traditional American Thanksgiving dinner, and of the British Christmas, of course, including a vegetarian-style one with a nut loaf or my favourite walnut pâté en croute instead of turkey! It also goes surprisingly well with vegetable dishes such as German potato pancakes and sweetcorn pudding from the USA.

SERVES 8 F
225g (8oz) cranberries
150ml (5fl oz) water
about 75g (3oz) sugar

Sort out the cranberries and remove any bruised ones; take off any little stems. Wash the berries and put them into a saucepan with the water. Cook gently until the berries begin to 'pop' and are tender – 7–10 minutes on rather a high heat. Add the sugar and simmer for a further few minutes. Taste, and add a bit more sugar if necessary – cranberries are very sharp-tasting.

Variation

GOOSEBERRY SAUCE

This, too, is delicious with nut loaves and the little potato pancakes mentioned above. Make in the same way, using just 4 tablespoons water, then liquidize. You probably won't need so much sugar. You can of course thin the sauce with more liquid if you like.

CURRY SAUCE – ENGLISH STYLE

Nothing Indian about this, but I think it's a pleasant sweet-and-sour sauce in it's own right.

SERVES 4
1 onion, peeled and chopped
1 apple, peeled and chopped
2 tablespoons olive oil
1 tablespoon curry powder
25g (1oz) flour
425ml (15fl oz) stock *or* water
1 tablespoon tomato purée
sea salt
freshly ground black pepper
lemon juice
a few sultanas – optional

Fry the onion and apple in the oil in a medium-sized saucepan for 10 minutes, without browning, then add the curry powder and fry for a further 1–2 minutes. Stir in the flour and cook for 2 minutes, then remove the saucepan from the heat and mix in the stock or water and tomato purée. Return the saucepan to the heat and bring up to the boil, stirring all the time. Let the sauce simmer gently for 15 minutes without a lid on the saucepan, then season with sea salt and freshly ground black pepper and a squeeze of lemon juice if you think it's necessary. You can serve this sauce as it is or liquidize it if you prefer it smooth. I like it with some sultanas added, for extra sweetness!

CURRY SAUCE – INDIAN STYLE

SERVES 4
4 tablespoons olive oil
1 garlic clove, crushed
1 onion, peeled and chopped
1 teaspoon grated fresh ginger
2½ teaspoons ground coriander
2½ teaspoons ground cumin
½ teaspoon curry powder
½ teaspoon turmeric
½ teaspoon white mustard seed if available
1 bay leaf
225g (8oz) canned tomatoes
425ml (15fl oz) stock
1 teaspoon garam masala
sea salt
freshly ground black pepper

Heat the oil in a medium-sized saucepan and add the crushed garlic, chopped onion and ginger. Fry gently until the onion is soft and lightly browned, about 10 minutes, then add all the spices and the bay leaf, and cook for 2 minutes longer. Mix in the tomatoes and stock and simmer gently for 15 minutes, without a lid on the saucepan. Stir in the garam masala and sea salt and freshly ground black pepper to taste. Serve the sauce as it is, or liquidize or sieve it if you prefer.

This sauce is not 'hot', but it's very flavoursome and useful for serving with pulses.

VEGETARIAN GRAVY

MAKES ABOUT 425ML (JUST OVER 15FL OZ)
1 onion, peeled and chopped
1½ tablespoons oil
25g (1oz) flour – I use 85 per cent wholemeal
1 garlic clove, crushed
425ml (15fl oz) water
1 vegetable stock cube – optional
1 teaspoon yeast extract
1–2 teaspoons Shoyu soy sauce, from health shops
sea salt
freshly ground black pepper

Fry the onion in the oil for 10 minutes. Add the flour, and let it brown over the heat, stirring all the time. Then put in all the remaining ingredients. Bring to the boil and leave to simmer for 10 minutes. Then strain and season to taste. If you like bits of onion in your gravy, there's no need to strain, of course, and in this case you could use a 100 per cent flour instead of the one suggested. (There's no point in using the 100 per cent flour if you're going to strain the gravy, because the bran will get left in the sieve anyway.)

HOLLANDAISE SAUCE

Another rich, special occasion sauce. This can also be made quickly in a blender or liquidizer, following the method given for Blender Béarnaise Sauce on page 61.

SERVES 6
1 teaspoon lemon juice
1 tablespoon cold water
sea salt
freshly ground black pepper
2 egg yolks
125g (4oz) butter

Mix together lemon juice, water, salt and pepper in top of double saucepan or a bowl set over a pan of hot water – the water must not boil. Beat in the egg yolks then whisk in a quarter of the butter, beating until butter has melted and sauce is beginning to thicken. Then add the rest of the butter in three batches; beat well. Add a little more lemon juice if liked, to taste.

LEMON MAYONNAISE SAUCE

This sauce tastes creamy yet is light and refreshing. You can serve it cold, with dishes like the walnut pâté en croûte, or use it to coat lightly cooked vegetables before topping with crumbs and grated cheese and baking, for an extra special *au gratin* dish.

SERVES 4–6
4 tablespoons mayonnaise
6 tablespoons *fromage blanc*
1 teaspoon mustard
juice of ½ lemon
sea salt
freshly ground black pepper

Just mix everything together to a smooth cream and season to taste.

LEMON LENTIL SAUCE

For a spicier version of this sauce see page 190.

SERVES 4 F
125g (4oz) red lentils
575ml (1 pint) water
1 onion
1 tablespoon oil
2 teaspoons curry powder
juice and rind of 1 lemon
sea salt
freshly ground black pepper

Soak lentils overnight in water. Next day simmer until tender. Meanwhile chop onion and sauté gently in the oil with the curry powder for 10 minutes. Add juice and grated rind of lemon and then liquidize. Season well with salt and pepper.

MINT SAUCE

Sharp-tasting yet sweet as well, mint sauce is good with many lentil and bean dishes.

SERVES 4–6
Enough fresh mint leaves to make 2 tablespoons when chopped
1 tablespoon sugar
1 tablespoon boiling water
4 tablespoons cider vinegar

If you've got a liquidizer just wash the mint leaves and take off any stalks, then put the leaves into the goblet with all the other ingredients and blend until the mint is all chopped. Pour into a jug to serve.

If you'd rather make the sauce by hand, wash and chop the mint leaves, then put them into a bowl, add the sugar, boiling water and cider vinegar and mix well.

MUSHROOM AND SOURED CREAM SAUCE

This is a creamy fresh-tasting sauce that's best served warm and is delicious with nutmeats, burgers and also with plainly cooked vegetables.

SERVES 4–6
15g (½oz) butter
125g (4oz) button mushrooms, washed and chopped
150ml (5 fl oz) soured cream
sea salt
freshly ground black pepper
paprika

Melt the butter in a medium-sized saucepan and fry the mushrooms for about 5 minutes, then stir in the soured cream and salt, pepper and a little paprika to taste. Reheat gently, but don't let the sauce get too near boiling point.

SWEET AND SOUR SAUCE

SERVES 4
1 onion
1 tablespoon oil
2 teaspoons cornflour
425ml (15fl oz) water
¼ teaspoon dry mustard
1 tablespoon wine vinegar
1 teaspoon sugar
1 teaspoon soy sauce
225g (8oz) can pineapple in own juice
½ very small green pepper
1 tomato, skinned
sea salt
freshly ground black pepper

Finely chop onion and fry gently in the oil. When tender add cornflour. Remove from heat, add water stirring all the time. Simmer gently for 5 minutes. Add mustard, vinegar, sugar, soy sauce, chopped and drained canned pineapple, chopped green pepper and tomato. Season well with salt and pepper and simmer for 2–3 minutes longer.

SOURED CREAM AND HERB SAUCE

This sauce is served cold, but I like it with hot dishes, such as the savoury loaves, as well as cold ones.

MAKES 275ML (10 FL OZ)
150ml (5 fl oz) soured cream
150ml (5 fl oz) natural yoghurt
2 tablespoons fresh herbs, chopped: parsley, chives,
tarragon, a little thyme – whatever is available
sea salt
freshly ground black pepper

Simply mix everything together and season to taste.

Variation

HORSERADISH SAUCE

Make as above, but leave out the herbs and flavour
with 2–3 teaspoons grated horseradish and 1–2
teaspoons wine vinegar. This is even nicer if you
add a little mayonnaise, or replace 2 tablespoons
yoghurt with 2 tablespoons mayonnaise.

TOMATO SAUCE

This sauce really couldn't be easier and is one of my
standbys. I find it best not to let the tomatoes cook
for very long; this way the sauce seems to have a
much fresher flavour.

SERVES 4–6
1 onion
1 tablespoon olive oil
1 garlic clove
450g (1 lb) fresh skinned tomatoes or 400g (14oz)
can tomatoes
sea salt
freshly ground black pepper

Peel and chop the onion and fry it gently in the oil
in a medium-sized saucepan until it's soft but not
browned – about 10 minutes. Peel the garlic, crush
it in a little salt with the blade of a knife and add it
to the onions along with the tomatoes.

Liquidize, mash or sieve the mixture, then put it
back in the saucepan and reheat it. Taste the sauce
and season with salt and pepper.

That's the basic recipe but you can vary it in lots
of ways. Try putting a bay leaf with the onions to
draw out its lovely flavour as the onions soften, or
add a little chopped or dried basil, thyme or powdered cinnamon to the finished sauce; or stir a
couple of tablespoons of red wine into the liquidized
mixture before you reheat it. Can be served chilled,
too.

WHITE SAUCE AND VARIATIONS

Strictly speaking a proper *sauce Béchamel* is made
from milk which has been delicately flavoured by
being heated in a saucepan with a clove, a piece of
onion, a slice of carrot and a bay leaf, covered and
left to infuse and then strained. I must admit that
for normal cookery I generally use ordinary milk
plus a bay leaf, and rely on good seasoning for the
flavouring, but if you do go to the trouble to infuse
the milk first, the sauce will be that much more
delicate and delicious.

When making a sauce I always used to let it
simmer for 10 or 15 minutes after I'd added the
milk, to cook the flour. This was a nuisance because
it was all too easy to burn it and also one had to
remember to make the sauce a bit on the thin side
to allow for it to reduce. Then one day when I
hadn't got my milk measured out properly I added it
in 2 or 3 instalments and I found the sauce had no
floury-taste and needed no extra simmering. I realized that if you add the milk in batches and let the
sauce thicken over a good heat before adding more,
by the time you've added all the milk the flour has
cooked and the process is much quicker. So I always
make sauces by this 'batch' method now.

Sauce making is easy if you can remember the
basic quantities. I find it difficult to hold figures in
my head so I remember just one quantity and relate
everything to that. 25g (1oz) each of butter and plain
(white) flour and 275ml (10 fl oz) liquid makes a
medium-thick sauce – the type you would use to
cover cauliflower or stuffed pancakes, commonly
called a coating sauce. If you want it thicker or
thinner you simply decrease or increase the quantity
of milk: 425ml (15 fl oz) milk gives a thickish
pouring sauce, 575ml (1 pint) gives a thin pouring
sauce.

MAKES 275ML (10 FL OZ) F
25g (1oz) butter or margarine
25g (1oz) plain white flour
275ml (10 fl oz) skimmed milk – ordinary skimmed
milk or milk that you have flavoured as above
1 bay leaf
sea salt
freshly ground black pepper
nutmeg

Put the butter or margarine into a medium-sized
saucepan and melt it gently over quite a low heat,
then stir in the flour and add the bay leaf. Let the
flour cook for a few seconds, then turn up the heat,
pour in one-third of the milk and stir vigorously
until you've got a very thick, smooth sauce, then add
another third of the milk. At first the sauce will look

lumpy, but don't worry, continue stirring over a high heat and soon the sauce will be beautifully smooth again.

Repeat the process with your final batch of milk, then when the sauce is smooth turn down the heat and season the sauce with salt, pepper and a grating of nutmeg. It's now ready to serve, but if you want to make it look extra good and glossy for a special occasion you can beat in about 15g (½oz) extra butter at the last minute.

If you're making the sauce in advance and want to prevent a skin forming you can dot this extra butter over the surface, then beat it in when you reheat it. Alternatively a circle of damp greaseproof paper pressed down on to the surface of the sauce also stops it getting a skin.

Variations

MUSHROOM SAUCE

This is good with vegetables and for serving with pasta and *gnocchi*. To make it, wash and finely slice 125g (4oz) button mushrooms and add them to the basic Béchamel sauce. Some people fry the mushrooms lightly in butter before adding them to the sauce but I prefer the less rich version I've given.

WHITE ONION SAUCE

Another useful variation, good when you want to add more flavour to the meal. Make it by peeling and finely chopping an onion; fry the onion in the butter before adding the flour. I think this is nice flavoured with a pinch of ground cloves.

PARSLEY SAUCE

For this fresh-tasting variation add 1 or 2 tablepoons of finely chopped parsley to the Béchamel sauce. Or, an easier way, take the stalks off a few sprigs of parsley and put the sprigs into the liquidizer with the sauce; blend for a few seconds.

CELERY SAUCE

3–4 tablespoons very finely chopped celery and ½ teaspoon celery salt can be added to sauce after the milk and simmered in it until tender.

EGG SAUCE

Made by adding 3 hardboiled eggs, very finely chopped and a pinch of mace to basic sauce.

FENNEL SAUCE

Add to the sauce 2–3 tablespoons very finely chopped fennel bulb.

GREEN HERB SAUCE

Use any fresh green herbs available, 1–2 tablespoons very finely chopped, and added just before serving.

MUSTARD SAUCE

Add 1 tablespoon French mustard and a little lemon juice.

WATERCRESS SAUCE

Add ½–1 bunch watercress, finely chopped, (or whizzed with the sauce in a blender).

LEMON SAUCE

Add some finely grated rind and juice to the basic white sauce. You can intensify the colour with a pinch of turmeric.

WHITE SAUCE QUICK BLENDER METHOD

This is the method that I use most of the time; it's so labour-saving and I find the sauce is just as good as that made by the traditional method. Parsley sauce is particularly easy when made by this method because you don't have to chop the parsley, simply pop the sprigs into the blender with everything else.

SERVES 4 [F]
25g (1oz) butter
25g (1oz) flour
275–425ml (10–15 fl oz) skimmed milk
sea salt
freshly ground black pepper

Put the butter, flour and milk into the liquidizer goblet; add about ½ teaspoon of sea salt and a good grinding of black pepper. Blend at high speed for a few seconds to break up the butter and mix everything together. There will be some lumpy bits of butter, but that doesn't matter. Turn the mixture into a medium-sized saucepan and put over a moderate heat, stir the sauce until it has thickened, then turn down the heat and leave the sauce to simmer gently for 15 minutes. The cooking is particularly important with this sauce because there has been no initial cooking of the flour, as in traditional saucemaking, and so you must allow time for this, or the sauce will have a raw, 'floury' taste.

Variations

QUICK BLENDER CHEESE SAUCE

For a quick cheese sauce, add 125g (4oz) grated cheese after the sauce has cooked.

QUICK BLENDER PARSLEY SAUCE

Put some sprigs of parsley into the liquidizer with the other ingredients at the beginning of the process.

WINE SAUCE (1)

This sauce always makes a meal taste special. You can either use a cheap wine for the sauce or buy a little extra to have with the meal and use some to make the sauce.

SERVES 6 [F]
425ml (15 fl oz) stock
425ml (15 fl oz) red wine
1 bay leaf
a piece of onion, peeled
1 garlic clove, peeled and sliced
a pinch of dried thyme
½ teaspoon black peppercorns
2–3 parsley stalks
1 tablespoon redcurrant jelly
sea salt
freshly ground black pepper
40g (1½oz) butter, softened
20g (¾oz) flour

Put the stock and red wine into a saucepan with the bay leaf, onion, garlic, thyme, peppercorns and parsley stalks and bring to the boil. Let the mixture boil vigorously for 10–15 minutes so that the amount of liquid reduces to half. Strain the liquid into a clean saucepan and mix in the redcurrant jelly and some salt and pepper. Next make a *beurre manié*: mash half the butter with the flour to make a paste and add this, in small pieces, to the still-warm sauce, mixing well after you've added each piece. Put the sauce back over the heat and stir it gently until it

has thickened slightly. Then let the sauce simmer gently for a few minutes to cook the flour. Check the seasoning again and beat the remaining butter into the sauce just before serving to make it look glossy and appetizing.

If you want to prepare the sauce in advance, after you've added the *beurre manié* and simmered the sauce for a few minutes, take it off the heat and dot the remaining butter over the top of the sauce to prevent a skin forming. When you're ready heat the sauce gently and stir the butter in.

WINE SAUCE (2)

MAKES 275ML (10 FL OZ) [F]
15g (½oz) butter
1 tablespoon oil
1 small onion, peeled and chopped
1 large garlic clove, peeled and crushed
2 large tomatoes, chopped, preferably fresh *or* canned ones, drained
425ml (15 fl oz) vegetable stock
150ml (5 fl oz) red wine *or* cider
sea salt
freshly ground black pepper

Heat the butter and oil in a medium-sized saucepan and fry the onion for 5 minutes without browning. Add the garlic and tomatoes, and cook for a further 3–4 minutes. Then pour in the stock and wine or cider and let the mixture bubble away until the liquid has reduced by about half. Strain and season with salt and freshly ground black pepper.

YOGHURT AND FRESH HERB SAUCE

I like this sauce with nut and lentil loaves and croquettes.

SERVES 4–6
275ml (10 fl oz) natural yoghurt
2 tablespoons chopped fresh herbs – parsley, chives, thyme, mint – whatever is available
sea salt
freshly ground black pepper

Simply mix everything together. An easy way to make this is to put the yoghurt into a blender or food processor with whole sprigs of fresh herbs and whizz together until the herbs are chopped. Season with salt and pepper.

Variations

YOGHURT AND SPRING ONION SAUCE

Make as above, using 275ml (10 fl oz) natural yoghurt and 3 tablespoons chopped spring onions.

YOGHURT AND CUCUMBER SAUCE

For this variation, which is delicate and refreshing, use 275ml (10 fl oz) natural yoghurt, 3–4 tablespoons finely chopped cucumber and 1 tablespoon chopped fresh fennel, dill, mint or whatever fresh herbs you fancy.

CHUTNEY IN THE RAW

The easiest chutney recipe I know and it tastes delicious.

MAKES 3 KILOS (6–7 LBS)
450g (1 lb) stoneless dates
450g (1 lb) sultanas
450g (1 lb) apples
450g (1 lb) onions
450g (1 lb) real Barbados sugar
575ml (1 pint) vinegar
1 teaspoon salt
freshly ground black pepper
dash of cayenne, allspice and ground ginger

Mince first four ingredients together and stir in sugar and vinegar. Add 1 teaspoon salt, sprinkling of pepper, dash of cayenne, a little allspice and ground ginger. Stand for 24 hours, giving the mixture a stir from time to time, then bottle. This is a quick-to-make chutney and keeps well.

SUGARLESS CHUTNEY

MAKES APPROX. 350G (12OZ)
125g (4oz dates)
125g (4oz) sultanas
1 small onion, finely chopped
1 teaspoon pickling sauce
6 tablespoons cider vinegar *or* wine vinegar

Chop the dates roughly, then put into a pan (not an aluminium one) with the rest of the ingredients. Bring to the boil, then heat gently for about 15 minutes, stirring occasionally, until the onion is tender. Keep in a container in the fridge. The chutney can be thinned, if necessary, by adding a little water, apple juice or extra vinegar.

4

SALADS AND SALAD DRESSINGS

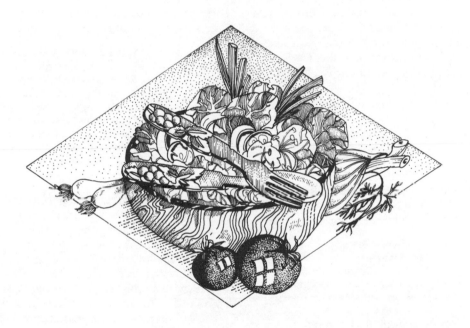

I love making salads. I find there's something very satisfying about arranging brightly coloured, fresh ingredients on a plate to create a picture which is pleasing to the senses. You can add sheen to the effect with a glossy, olive oil dressing, or you can introduce a creamy texture and a pretty pale green colour with an avocado dressing, or a flash of white with a soured cream or white cheese dressing. You can include a touch of light brown, and a crunchy texture, with a scattering of roasted, flaked almonds, cashew nuts, walnuts or hazel nuts. You can add the fragrance or pungence of fresh herbs, the warmth of spices, the tang of lemon rind or fresh ginger, the sweetness of raisins or crystallized ginger. Then you can serve your masterpiece with soft or crisp warm wholemeal rolls; wholemeal pitta bread; garlic bread or homemade cheese or raisin scones, straight from the oven; slices of bread and butter, or of a home-made fruit tea bread. There are so many variables that you could serve a salad a day for a year and never repeat yourself!

As well as the complete-meal (or, in suitably-sized portions, pretty first course) salads I've been describing, there are many salads which are useful for serving with a hot dish instead of, or as well as, a cooked vegetable. I think a green salad, or a tomato salad, for instance, is often the perfect accompaniment, especially to pasta, cereal and savoury pancake dishes, and to flans, and you'll find plenty of simple recipes for such salads in the following pages.

To make life easy for yourself, make sure you've got a large, solid wooden chopping board – 30 × 40cm (12 × 16in) and 2cm (1in) thick is a good size – a box grater that you can stand on the board, a real Sabatier knife with a blade 13cm (5¼in) long and a steel to sharpen it with. This will not be cheap but it will last you for years. Once you've got over the expense of that, buy yourself a pointed knife with a stainless steel, serrated blade the same length as that of the Sabatier knife, for cutting delicate things like avocados, tomatoes and fruits. I had one of these as a wedding present and it's still one of my top-ten kitchen utensils all these years and numerous books, demonstrations and dinner parties later!

Needless to say, few salads are suitable candidates for the freezer, though bean salads freeze beautifully as long as you leave out the garlic, for adding later. Salads made with cooked vegetables will freeze, though be careful about creamy dressings, which may separate. I've marked suitable salads for freezing with the usual freezer F symbol.

This section begins with some recipes for salad dressings and also, since they're such useful salad ingredients and used in a number of the recipes, instructions for sprouting your own beans, lentils and seeds simply at home. They're easy to do, children love helping with them, and even I, a total non-gardener, have success with them every time! After this, you'll find the salad recipes, in alphabetical order.

AVOCADO DRESSING

A luxurious and pretty dressing that I like on almost any salad! Try it on top of a red bean salad, with a base of shredded lettuce.

SERVES 4–6
1 large ripe avocado
juice of ½ lemon
1 tablespoon wine or cider vinegar
1 tablespoon best-quality olive oil
salt
freshly ground black pepper

Halve, stone and skin the avocado. Put flesh into blender or food processor with the rest of the ingredients. Whizz to a luscious pale green cream. Flavour can be perked up with a drop or two of tabasco sauce (go carefully, it's hot!) or a pinch or two of curry powder.

HONEY DRESSING

A sweet dressing that's especially good on a shredded cabbage salad.

1 tablespoon clear honey
1 tablespoon cider vinegar
3 tablespoons olive oil
¼ teaspoon salt
freshly ground black pepper

Thoroughly combine all ingredients.

Variation

HONEY AND MINT DRESSING

Made by adding 1 tablespoon chopped fresh mint or 1 teaspoon concentrated mint sauce to above.

MAYONNAISE – BLENDER METHOD

Here the use of a liquidizer makes it easy to produce creamy, successful results every time.

MAKES 200ML (7 FL OZ)
1 whole egg
¼ teaspoon salt
¼ teaspoon dry mustard
2 or 3 grindings of black pepper
2 teaspoons wine vinegar
2 teaspoons lemon juice
200ml (7 fl oz) olive oil and cold-pressed sunflower oil, mixed

Break the egg straight into the liquidizer and add the salt, mustard, pepper, vinegar and lemon juice. Blend for a minute at medium speed until everything is well mixed, then turn the speed up to high and gradually add the oil, drop by drop, through the hole in the lid of the liquidizer goblet. When you've added about half the oil you will hear the sound change to a 'glug-glug' noise and then you can add the rest of the oil more quickly, in a thin stream. If the consistency of the mayonnaise seems a bit on the thick side, you can thin it with a little boiling water or some milk.

MAYONNAISE – TRADITIONAL METHOD

It's more work to make mayonnaise by hand, but you do get a beautiful, creamy result and it's very satisfying to see the mixture gradually thicken as you whisk in the oil.

MAKES 200–275ML (7–10 FL OZ)
2–3 egg yolks
¼ teaspoon salt
¼ teaspoon dry mustard
2 or 3 grindings of black pepper
2 teaspoons wine vinegar
2 teaspoons lemon juice
200–275ml (7–10 fl oz) olive oil and cold-pressed sunflower oil, mixed

Put the egg yolks into a bowl and add the salt, mustard, pepper, vinegar and lemon juice. Whisk for a minute or two until everything is well mixed and creamy, then start to add the oil, just a drop at a time, whisking hard after each addition. When you have added about half the oil the mixture will begin to thicken and look like mayonnaise, and then you can add the oil a little more quickly, still whisking hard. Go on adding the oil until the mixture is really thick – if you use three egg yolks you will probably be able to use 275ml (10 fl oz) of oil, otherwise about 200ml (7 fl oz) will be enough. If the consistency of the mayonnaise seems a bit on the thick side, you can thin it with a little boiling water or some milk.

MAYONNAISE AND YOGHURT DRESSING

You can use either home-made mayonnaise or a good quality bought one for this.

SERVES 4
2 tablespoons mayonnaise
2 tablespoons natural yoghurt

Simpy mix everything together.

TAHINI MAYONNAISE

SERVES 2–4
1 heaped tablespoon tahini
2 tablespoons cold water
1 tablespoon lemon juice
1 garlic clove, crushed – optional
sea salt
freshly ground black pepper

Put the tahini into a bowl and gradually beat in the water and lemon juice: the mixture will be lumpy at first, but will gradually get light and fluffy, as you beat in the liquid. Add the garlic, if you're using this, and some seasoning to taste. Some chopped herbs are nice added to this, too. Use as ordinary mayonnaise.

TOFU DRESSING

This dressing, made from tofu or bean curd (page 203) is a bit like mayonnaise but considerably more nutritious, and lower in oil.

MAKES ABOUT 350ML (12 FL OZ)
300g (10½oz) packet tofu – from health shops
2 teaspoons wine vinegar
1 teaspoon dry mustard
1 teaspoon Barbados molasses sugar
2 tablespoons olive oil
sea salt
freshly ground black pepper

If you've got a liquidizer, simply put all the ingredients into the goblet and whizz together until combined. Alternatively, put the tofu into a bowl and whisk until smooth, then add the vinegar, mustard and sugar and whisk again. Then beat in the oil, a little at a time. Season with salt and pepper. This is also nice with some chopped fresh herbs or spring onions added.

VINAIGRETTE

When I'm making this to dress a salad, I usually make it straight into the salad bowl, mix quickly and put the salad in on top. But if you need it for pouring over a salad, or for serving with avocados, for instance, it's easiest to make it by shaking all the ingredients together in a clean screw-top jar, and for this you may want to double the quantities given here. (Any that's over will keep in the fridge, but I think it's very much better made fresh when you need it and it only takes a moment.)

SERVES 4–6
1 tablespoon wine vinegar – preferably red
3–4 tablespoons best quality olive oil
sea salt
freshly ground black pepper

Mix everything together, adding plenty of seasoning. Some chopped fresh herbs, also a little mustard and a dash of sugar can be added to vary the flavour.

WALNUT AND ALMOND DRESSING

This is a delicious, substantial dressing. I like it over a green salad. (It also makes a good sauce for hot pasta!)

SERVES 4
25g (1oz) walnuts
25g (1oz) almonds – whole, flaked or blanched
50g (2oz) carrot, roughly chopped
2 tablespoons cold-pressed olive oil
4 tablespoons water
1 tablespoon wine vinegar
1 teaspoon chopped fresh rosemary, thyme *or* marjoram if available
sea salt
freshly ground black pepper

Put all the ingredients into the blender or food processor and whizz to a cream.

WHITE CHEESE DRESSING

When I first evolved this dressing only cottage cheese was available in the shops and I had to sieve or liquidize it to get the smooth, creamy effect I envisaged. Now, curd cheese or a white skimmed milk cheese (like quark) make it much easier. It's still one of my favourite dressings.

SERVES 4–6
225g (8oz) curd cheese
150ml (5 fl oz) skimmed milk

Mix together the curd cheese and skimmed milk. Serve poured over almost any salad to provide not only a delicious, not-too-fattening creamy dressings, but also plentiful protein.

Variations

WHITE CHEESE AND CHIVE DRESSING

Make as above, adding 1–2 tablespoons of finely chopped chives or spring onion green.

WHITE CHEESE AND CUCUMBER DRESSING

Add ¼ cucumber and 2 sprigs of mint to above, and liquidize.

WHITE CHEESE AND COCONUT DRESSING

Add 25g (1oz) desiccated coconut and a dash of honey to the above mixture. A pleasant dressing for a fruit salad.

SOURED CREAM DRESSING

Use low-fat quark, and 150ml (5 fl oz) soured cream instead of the skimmed milk.

WHITE MAYONNAISE

My daughter Margaret invented this dressing and it's a great favourite with us all. We think it tastes very much like mayonnaise but only contains a fraction of the calories. You can vary the flavour by adding ½ teaspoon of Dijon mustard and you can also add a little liquid skimmed milk if you want a thinner consistency.

SERVES 6–8
2 tablespoons natural yoghurt
125g (4oz) curd cheese
2 teaspoons olive oil
½ teaspoon wine vinegar
sea salt
freshly ground black pepper

Simply mix everything together to a smooth cream.

YOGHURT AND GREEN HERB DRESSING

This is a fresh-tasting, slightly sharp dressing that's good with most salad mixtures.

SERVES 4–6
275ml (10 fl oz) natural yoghurt
1–2 heaped tablespoons finely chopped fresh herbs, especially parsley, also chives and mint
1 tablespoon lemon juice
sea salt
freshly ground black pepper

Put the yoghurt into a bowl and stir in the chopped herbs, lemon juice and salt and pepper to taste.

Variation

YOGHURT AND CUCUMBER DRESSING

Add some grated cucumber too, or leave out the herbs and use two tablespoons finely chopped red or green pepper, or some coarsely grated carrot and a few raisins.

CURRIED YOGHURT MAYONNAISE

My idea with this recipe was to try and make something which was a little like a rich curried mayonnaise, but without the calories. It's especially good with hardboiled eggs, bean salads and with rice or lentil fritters.

MAKES ABOUT 275ML (10 FL OZ), SERVES 6–8
1 tablespoon olive oil
1 small onion, peeled and finely chopped
2 teaspoons curry powder
1 teaspoon tomato paste
1 teaspoon honey
6 tablespoons red wine
150g (5oz) natural yoghurt
150g (5oz) *fromage blanc*
sea salt
freshly ground black pepper

Heat the oil in a small saucepan and gently fry the onion until tender – 10 minutes. Stir in the curry powder, tomato paste, honey and wine and bubble over a high heat until the liquid has reduced to a thick syrup. Remove from heat and leave to get completely cold, sieve and add the yoghurt and *fromage blanc*, or liquidize them all together to a creamy consistency. Season with salt and pepper.

HOW TO SPROUT BEANS, GRAINS AND LENTILS

Sprouted beans, grains and lentils are highly nutritious, being rich in vitamins and minerals and containing high-quality protein. It takes 9 kilos (20 lb) of vegetable protein to produce 450 g (1 lb) of animal protein; but when you sprout seeds you have a protein factory the right way round – increasing the original food value (by up to 600 per cent!).

Sprouting is easy to do. All you need is a jar (a big coffee jar is ideal), a piece of muslin or J cloth to go over the top, secured with an elastic band, and some beans or seeds. Most types are suitable, with the exception of red kidney beans (and I personally would not do large beans such as butter beans). Choose, for instance, from chickpeas, soya beans, alfalfa seeds, continental lentils, sunflower seeds, mung beans, aduki beans and wholewheat grains. Put half a cupful of chosen beans, grains or lentils into your jar, cover with cold water and leave to soak for 8–12 hours. Put your piece of muslin or J cloth over the top of the jar. Then drain off the water, fill the jar with fresh water, swish it round and then pour it all out again. All this can be done without removing the muslin or J cloth which prevents the seeds or beans falling out and blocking the sink. This rinsing has to be repeated twice a day, to keep the seeds damp (but they must on no account be left soaking in water or they'll rot rather than sprout!) I keep my seeds by the sink to remind me about the rinsing. It's really quite satisfying to see the sprouts developing day by day and in 2–4 days they're ready to use. They can be used straightaway, to add crunch and nourishment to salads and sandwiches, or they'll keep in the fridge for several days.

If you want to make long juicy beansprouts like the ones you can buy, you need to use a slightly different method. Use the little green mung beans and soak them overnight in water as usual. Then put them into a large colander or plastic draining bowl (lined with a piece of kitchen paper to prevent them falling through). Spread them out well, then put a piece of polythene and a heavy weight (like a 1.5 kilos [3 lb] bag of flour) on top. Twice a day remove these and rinse the beans as usual.

You can also use this colander method (without the weight and polythene) for all the other seeds and beans if you find it more convenient. If you get really addicted, or if you're cooking for lots of people, you might even like to invest in a gardener's large round plastic sieve, which I have found to be ideal, when lined with kitchen paper! On a smaller scale, you can buy (from many health shops) a special sprouter which consists of three sprouting trays (that means it's easy to have three lots of sprouts on the go at the same time!), with a water-collecting bowl underneath (which saves the rinsing routine).

ALFALFA SLAW

SERVES 4
450g (1 lb) grated cabbage
2 carrots, grated
225g (8oz) alfalfa sprouts
vinaigrette (page 71)

Mix together all the vegetables; add enough vinaigrette to moisten.

ANELLI AND CARROT SALAD WITH WALNUTS

A substantial salad which makes a complete light main course.

SERVES 4
175g (6oz) anelli – wholemeal pasta rings
sea salt
3 tablespoons walnut oil *or* olive oil
1 tablespoon wine vinegar
freshly ground black pepper
225g (8oz) grated carrot
125g (4oz) chopped walnuts
125g (4oz) chopped dates
small bunch watercress

Cook the anelli in plenty of boiling salted water until it's just tender; drain. Put the oil and vinegar into a bowl together with some salt and pepper; mix well, then add the pasta, carrot, walnuts and dates. Mix gently, until everything is well distributed and coated with the dressing. Heap up on a serving dish, tuck the watercress all round the edge to make a bright green border.

APPLE SALAD

This salad consists of a colourful, crunchy mixture of apples with carrots, celery, nuts and raisins, with a creamy dressing on top. It's a good salad for serving with warm wholemeal rolls and cheese for a simple meal.

SERVES 4–6
3 red apples, cored and finely diced
3 large carrots, scraped and finely diced
1 head of celery, washed and finely diced
50–125g (2–4oz) walnut pieces
50–125g (2–4oz) raisins
2 tablespoons fresh chives, chopped
juice of 1 orange
lettuce leaves
white cheese dressing (page 72) *or* coconut dressing
(page 72)

Put the apple, carrot, celery, nuts, raisins and chives into a large bowl and add the orange juice. Stir the mixture to make sure that everything is coated with the juice. Line a large dish or shallow salad bowl with lettuce and spoon the apple mixture on top. Spoon the dressing over the top of the salad, so that some of the pretty mixture still shows underneath. Serve as soon as possible.

APPLE AND GINGER SALAD

A pleasant, fruity salad. It's good with the cheese mousse on page 36 or topped with one of the white cheese dressings on page 72, to make a complete light meal.

SERVES 4
4 dessert apples
1 piece preserved stem ginger
1 orange
5cm (2in) piece cucumber
1 tablespoon syrup from ginger
lettuce, watercress *or* chicory

Peel and dice apples; finely chop ginger; remove peel and pith from orange and cut flesh into segments; dice cucumber. Mix all ingredients together and serve on a bed of watercress, lettuce or chicory.

Variation

2 tablespoons raisins plumped in a little boiling water for 10 minutes and then drained, or 2 tablespoons chopped walnuts can also be added.

MIDDLE EASTERN AVOCADO AND CARROT SALAD

This mixture of pale green buttery avocado, crisp orange carrot and sweet raisins is very pleasant. If you serve the salad with some bread and butter and soft cheese or hardboiled egg wedges it makes a good lunch or supper.

SERVES 2 AS A SALAD, 4 AS A STARTER
1 large ripe avocado pear
a little fresh lemon juice
225g (8oz) coarsely grated carrot
juice of 1 orange
50g (2oz) seedless raisins, washed
parsley sprigs

Cut the avocado pear in half, twist the halves in opposite directions to separate them, then remove the stone. Carefully peel off the outer skin of the avocado halves, using a sharp pointed knife to prise it up – it should then come away quite easily if the avocado pear is really ripe. Cut the avocado into long, thin slices and sprinkle them with lemon juice, making sure that the cut surfaces are completely coated.

Mix together the grated carrot, orange juice and raisins. Arrange the avocado slices on individual plates, top with the grated carrot mixture and garnish with parsley sprigs.

AVOCADO AND CARROT SALAD WITH RAISINS AND FRESH GINGER DRESSING

This is a luxurious salad with a rich creamy dressing and delicious citrous tang of fresh ginger. It can be served as a first course or as a light lunch, with warm wholemeal rolls.

SERVES 4
350g (12oz) carrots, scraped and coarsely grated
50g (2oz) raisins
4 tablespoons lemon juice
2 ripe avocado pears
sea salt
2 tablespoons mayonnaise
4 tablespoons natural yoghurt
1 teaspoon grated fresh ginger root
a few chopped toasted almonds

Mix together the carrot, raisins and half the lemon juice. Peel and dice the avocado; sprinkle with the remaining lemon juice and add to the carrot. Season and spoon on to a serving dish. Mix together the mayonnaise, yoghurt and ginger, and add seasoning. Spoon over the salad, and sprinkle with toasted almonds.

AVOCADO AND MUSHROOM SALAD

Make sure the avocados are really ripe; they should feel slightly soft when you cradle them in your hand.

SERVES 4
450g (1 lb) small white button mushrooms
2 tablespoons wine vinegar
4 tablespoons olive oil
sea salt
freshly ground black pepper
2 avocado pears
2 tablespoons lemon juice
1–2 tablespoons chopped fresh chives

Wash mushrooms, pat dry on kitchen paper and slice thinly. Put the slices into a bowl, add the vinegar, olive oil and some salt and pepper, and mix well. Leave on one side for 1 hour. Just before you want to serve the salad, cut the avocado pears in half then twist the two halves in opposite directions to part them and remove the stone. Peel the avocado thinly, cut the flesh into fairly large dice and sprinkle avocado with the lemon juice. Add to the mushrooms, together with the chopped chives, and mix gently.

STUFFED AVOCADO SALAD (1)

Serve this main course salad with warm wholemeal rolls and follow with fresh fruit or a fruity pudding.

SERVES 4
2 ripe avocados – they should feel pleasantly soft all over when held in the palm of your hand
juice of ½ lemon and a little of the grated rind
225g (8oz) curd cheese
1 garlic clove, peeled and crushed
50g (2oz) roughly chopped walnuts
sea salt
freshly ground black pepper
crisp leaves from half a medium-sized lettuce
4 tomatoes, sliced
4 medium-sized carrots, peeled, grated and mixed with a little lemon or orange juice
½ cucumber, coarsely grated
half a bunch watercress
2 tablespoons good quality olive oil
1 tablespoon red wine vinegar

Cut the avocados in half, twist the halves apart and remove the stones. Brush the cut surfaces of the avocados with a little of the lemon juice.

Next make the filling for the avocados. Put the cheese into a bowl and stir in the remaining lemon juice, the garlic and enough of the grated lemon rind to give a pleasant tang. Mix in the walnuts and season the mixture with salt and freshly ground black pepper. Fill the avocado cavities with the mixture, piling it up well.

Line one large dish or four individual ones with the lettuce leaves. Put the avocados on top and arrange the sliced tomato, grated carrot, cucumber and watercress around them in colourful heaps. Mix together the oil and vinegar and season very well with salt and pepper. Spoon this over the top of the avocados just before serving.

If you want to you can make the filling for the avocados in advance but I think it's best not to add the walnuts until just before serving so that they stay crisp. Don't halve the avocados until the last minute, or they might discolour.

STUFFED AVOCADO SALAD (2)

Another main-course salad. Serve with plainly dressed salad and wholemeal melba toast.

SERVES 4
2 large avocados
juice of 1 lemon
4 hardboiled eggs
2 tablespoons mayonnaise
1 tablespoon tomato purée
drop or two of tabasco
sea salt
freshly ground black pepper
1 tablespoon chopped chives
lettuce *or* watercress

Halve and stone avocados and brush with half the lemon juice. Liquidize eggs with remaining lemon juice, mayonnaise and tomato purée. Add tabasco, salt and pepper to taste. Finally stir in the chopped chives. Pile into avocado halves. Serve chilled with lettuce or watercress.

BANANA AND CARROT SALAD WITH COCONUT DRESSING

SERVES 4
50g (2oz) raisins
2 large carrots
4 large bananas
juice of ½ lemon
bunch watercress
4 oranges
coconut dressing (page 72)
toasted coconut strands to garnish, if available

Wash raisins and leave for 10 minutes in hot water to plump. Peel carrots and grate coarsely. Skin and slice bananas and toss in the lemon juice with the carrots and raisins. Place in the centre of a large serving dish or individual plates, and surround with watercress and orange slices. Serve with coconut cream dressing poured over, and a garnish of toasted coconut strands if available – otherwise use a few chopped nuts or a little finely grated orange rind. Can also be piled on to a base of crisp lettuce or chicory leaves. With its protein rich dressing this makes a complete meal served with crunchy digestive biscuits, hot wholemeal scones or slices of fruit loaf (page 330).

BANANA, RAISIN AND PEANUT SALAD

I hit on this idea one day when I wanted to serve curry and rice with extras but didn't have the time or inclination to fiddle around with lots of little bowls of different things. So I put them all in one bowl and this was the result: it's good with curries and other spicy dishes.

SERVES 4
2 bananas
2 tablespoons lemon juice
1 small red pepper, washed, deseeded and chopped
1 bunch spring onions, washed, trimmed and chopped
1–2 tablespoons desiccated coconut
2 tablespoons raisins
4 tablespoons yoghurt *or* mayonnaise *or* a mixture
sea salt
freshly ground black pepper
a dash of tabasco
125g (4oz) roasted peanuts

Peel and slice the bananas, put into a bowl and sprinkle with lemon juice. Add the chopped red pepper, spring onions, coconut, raisins, yoghurt or mayonnaise and salt, pepper and tabasco. Finally stir in the peanuts and serve at once.

BEAN AND VEGETABLE SALAD

This salad makes a filling meal. You can really use any dried beans but I prefer red kidney beans as they're nice and colourful.

SERVES 4–6
125g (4oz) frozen peas
125g (4oz) frozen green beans
125g (4oz) red kidney beans, soaked, cooked and drained *or* use a 400g (14oz) can
225g (8oz) cooked potatoes, cubed
125g (4oz) fresh firm button mushrooms
1 celery heart
225g (8oz) firm cabbage, red or white
2 tablespoons chopped chives, if available
1 garlic clove
sea salt
freshly ground black pepper
½ teaspoon mustard powder
½ teaspoon sugar
1 tablespoon wine vinegar
3 tablespoons olive oil

Cook the peas and green beans together in a little fast-boiling salted water until they're just tender, then drain them. Put them into a bowl with the kidney beans and potatoes. Wash and slice the mushrooms and celery; wash and shred the cabbage and add these all to the bowl, together with the chives.

Peel the garlic and crush it in a little salt, then put it into a small bowl and add a grinding of pepper, the mustard, sugar and vinegar. Mix well, then gradually stir in the oil. Put this dressing over the vegetables in the bowl and turn them lightly so that they all get coated with it and look glossy and appetizing. Serve the salad in a glass bowl or on a base of crisp lettuce on a flat plate.

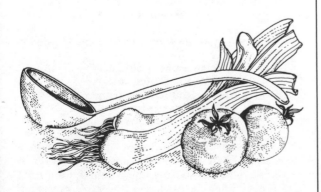

BEAN SPROUT AND CABBAGE SALAD

Cabbage is so useful for salads, particularly in the winter, but it can be a little dull without other, more exciting ingredients. In this salad bean sprouts add interest, and the pineapple gives a pleasant touch of sweetness.

SERVES 4
350g (12oz) hard white cabbage
225g (8oz) fresh bean sprouts
400g (14oz) can pineapple chunks in own juice, drained
1 tablespoon olive oil
sea salt
freshly ground black pepper
lemon juice

Wash and finely shred the cabbage and put it into a large bowl. Wash and drain the bean sprouts; lightly crush the pineapple with a fork, to break it up a bit. Add the bean sprouts and pineapple to the cabbage, together with the oil, sea salt and freshly ground black pepper and a little lemon juice to taste. Mix well.

You might feel you want to add more oil than I have suggested. Recently I have cut down rather on the amount of oil I add to salads like this, mainly out of consideration for people's figures and I find that if the salad contains moist, juicy ingredients, as in this case, the result is really just as good.

BEAN SPROUT, TOMATO AND ONION SALAD

SERVES 4
350g (12oz) bean sprouts
225g (8oz) tomatoes
1 mild onion
1 tablespoon olive oil
1 teaspoon lemon juice
1 tablespoon chopped parsley
sea salt
freshly ground black pepper

Rinse the bean sprouts; dice the tomatoes; peel and thinly slice the onion, and then put them all into a bowl. Add the oil, lemon juice, parsley and some sea salt and freshly ground black pepper to taste and mix gently but thoroughly.

BEAN SPROUT, MUSHROOM AND CELERY SALAD

A useful salad for winter when the usual vegetables are in short supply. If you want to give the salad an Oriental look, in keeping with the bean sprouts, you can slice the celery diagonally across.

SERVES 4
1 large head celery
225g (8oz) bean sprouts
175g (6oz) very fresh white button mushrooms
3 tablespoons olive oil
1 teaspoon soy sauce
½ teaspoon dry mustard
½ teaspoon sugar
1 tablespoon wine vinegar
sea salt
freshly ground black pepper

Wash the celery, discarding tough, outer stems; slice the tender stems and put them into a bowl. Rinse the bean sprouts and add them to the celery. Wash the mushrooms gently but thoroughly, then slice them and put them in the bowl with the other vegetables. Make a dressing by mixing together the oil, soy sauce, mustard, sugar, wine vinegar and some sea salt and freshly ground black pepper. Pour the dressing over the vegetables and turn them gently so that they all get coated with it.

THREE-BEAN SALAD

This attractive salad shows off the contrasting shapes and colours of three different types of beans: red kidney beans, haricot or other white beans and chick peas. Other beans could of course be used; the aim is to get as much variety as possible. It's advisable to soak and cook the red kidney beans separately as the colour can stain the others slightly pink, but you can cook them all in one saucepan if you wish.

SERVES 4 AS A MAIN MEAL, 6–8 AS A STARTER F
125g (4oz) red kidney beans
125g (4oz) haricot or other white beans
125g (4 oz) chick peas
2 tablespoons chopped fresh green herbs
2 tablespoons wine vinegar
6 tablespoons olive oil
sea salt
freshly ground black pepper

Soak the red kidney beans in water in one bowl and the other two types together in another, then drain, rinse and cook them in fresh water until they're tender, again keeping the red ones separate if possible. Drain the beans well, put them all into a bowl together and add the herbs (you don't need to cool the beans). Mix the vinegar, oil and some salt and pepper in a small bowl, then stir this dressing into the bean mixture, turning the beans until they're coated with it and all look glossy. Leave the mixture to cool, stirring it from time to time, then chill it.

Three-bean salad looks pretty served in a shallow glass bowl or white dish to show off the colours of the beans, or it can be spooned over crisp lettuce leaves and garnished with extra chopped fresh green herbs if you prefer.

THREE-BEAN SALAD WITH MUSTARD DRESSING

There are many versions of this popular salad and the best ones are made from beans which contrast well in colour, flavour and shape. I like to use green French beans as a basis because they are low in calories as well as having a lovely fresh flavour. In this recipe they're mixed with broad beans and red kidney beans in a tangy mustard dressing. To make a main course of this salad, serve it with warm wholemeal bread or rolls, or crunchy jacket potatoes and a bowl of fresh salad – carrot, apple, celery and raisin salad goes well with it.

SERVES 4 F
75–125g (3–4oz) red kidney beans, soaked and cooked, or use a 425g (15oz) can
225g (8oz) frozen broad beans
225g (8oz) French beans, frozen or fresh ones, trimmed
sea salt
1 tablespoon mild mustard – a whole-grain type is good
3 tablespoons olive oil
1 tablespoon wine vinegar
freshly ground black pepper
summer savory
fresh chopped parsley

Drain the red kidney beans and put them into a large bowl. Cook the broad beans and the French beans in a little fast-boiling lightly salted water until just tender. They can be done in the same saucepan, but if the French beans are fresh and very thin and tender, add them after the others have been cooking for 4 minutes, then cook for a further 3 minutes.

Drain the beans and add them to the bowl with the red kidney beans. Next mix up the dressing. Put the mustard into a small bowl and stir in the oil, vinegar, some salt and pepper and a pinch or two of summer savory if you have it. Mix well, then pour into the bowl with the beans. Turn the beans with a spoon so that they all get covered with the dressing. If possible let the salad stand for half an hour or so, to let the flavours blend. Spoon the salad into a serving dish – a glass one looks good – and sprinkle with chopped parsley.

BEANY SALAD BOWL

A colourful, glossy, protein-rich mixture. Serve with warm wholemeal pitta bread or rolls for a complete light meal.

SERVES 4
6 tablespoons olive oil
2 tablespoons wine vinegar
½ teaspoon dry mustard
1 teaspoon sugar
sea salt
freshly ground black pepper
125g (4oz) beans – any type, chick peas, butter beans
or some of the more unusual ones, soaked and
cooked until tender, then drained
2 tablespoons chopped fresh green herbs
1 heart of celery
1 green pepper, de-seeded and sliced
2 large carrots, scraped and coarsely grated
10cm (4in) cucumber, diced
1 apple, diced

Into a salad bowl put the oil, vinegar, mustard, sugar, some sea salt and a good grinding of black pepper. Give it a good stir, so that it's all blended, then add the beans, green herbs and the rest of the ingredients and mix well so that everything gets coated with the dressing.

BEETROOT, APPLE AND CELERY SALAD WITH CREAMY TOPPING AND WALNUTS

This pleasant mixture of flavours and textures goes well with a cold nut pâté or nut roast.

SERVES 4–6
350g (12oz) cooked beetroot – the kind with the skin
still on, not the sort that has been prepared in vinegar
2 crisp, sweet, eating apples
1 heart of celery
white cheese dressing (page 72)
50g (2oz) walnuts, chopped

Rub the skins off the beetroots, then rinse under the tap. Cut the beetroot into chunky dice. Peel, core and dice the apples; slice the celery. Mix the beetroot with the apple and celery and put on a serving dish or into a salad bowl. Pour the topping over the beetroot mixture and sprinkle with chopped walnuts.

BEETROOT AND HORSERADISH SALAD

A curiously pleasant mixture of flavours and textures, this salad makes a good accompaniment to cold savoury dishes.

SERVES 4
700g (1½ lb) cooked beetroot
1 eating apple
1 teaspoon caraway seeds
1 tablespoon sugar
2 tablespoons wine vinegar
1–2 tablespoons horseradish sauce

Peel and dice the beetroot and the apple. Put them into a bowl with the caraway seeds, sugar, vinegar and horseradish sauce and mix them all together lightly. Chill before serving.

RAW BEETROOT SALAD

Raw beetroot is said to contain enzymes which are particularly valuable for health, and features in many natural cancer cures. It is also said to contain a substance which helps to break up fat deposits in the body and thus aid slimming! In any case, I like the flavour and vibrant ruby colour of it; try it in this tasty main-course salad.

SERVES 4
225–350g (8–12oz) raw beetroot
4 apples
4 sticks of celery
4 tablespoons raisins
6 tablespoons olive oil
2 tablespoons red wine vinegar *or* cider vinegar
peel of ½ well-scrubbed lemon
1 lettuce
1 bunch watercress
lemon slices
white cheese dressing (page 72) *or* sour cream dressing (page 72)
1 tablespoon chopped chives

Peel and coarsely grate raw beetroot and apple, add finely sliced celery, raisins, oil and vinegar. Remove peel from lemon using a potato peeler, then snip into 1cm (½in) slivers using scissors; add to mixture. Allow to marinate for an hour or so if possible. Serve on bed of lettuce, bordered by lemon slices and topped with white cheese dressing or sour cream dressing. Finish with a sprinkling of chopped chives. The suggested dressings also provide protein for this meal.

BLACK AND WHITE BEAN SALAD WITH LEMON THYME

Bean salads are especially attractive when made from two or more contrasting beans and this is a particularly pleasant combination.

SERVES 4–6 F
125g (4oz) black beans
125g (4oz) cannellini beans
½ teaspoon dry mustard
½ teaspoon soft brown sugar
4 teaspoons wine vinegar
4 tablespoons olive oil
1 tablespoon chopped lemon thyme (or other fresh herbs as available)
sea salt
freshly ground black pepper

Soak, rinse and cook the beans as described on page 178, keeping the two types separate. Don't let them overcook: they are best when they still have a little 'bite' to them. Put the mustard, sugar and vinegar into a large bowl and mix together, then add the oil, herbs, hot beans and seasoning. Mix gently, then leave until cool, stirring occasionally. Serve cold, in a shallow bowl.

BLACK-EYED PEAS WITH APPLES, SULTANAS, BRAZIL NUTS AND CURRIED MAYONNAISE

A complete-meal salad with a delightful mixture of flavours and textures. Serve with warm wholemeal rolls.

SERVES 4
175g (6oz) black-eyed peas, cooked and drained
1 large sweet apple, diced
1 tablespoon lemon juice
75g (3oz) sultanas
75g (3oz) Brazil nuts, roughly chopped
2 tablespoons mayonnaise
2 tablespoons natural yoghurt
1–2 teaspoons curry paste
sea salt
freshly ground black pepper
crisp lettuce leaves
chopped chives

Put the beans into a large bowl. Sprinkle the apple with lemon juice, then add to the beans, together with the sultanas and nuts. Mix mayonnaise and yoghurt together in a separate small bowl, adding curry paste to taste. Gently stir this dressing into the bean mixture; season. Serve on a base of crisp lettuce leaves with some chives snipped on top.

BROAD BEAN AND YOGHURT SALAD

SERVES 4
450g (1 lb) tender broad beans in pod *or* 450g (1 lb) shelled broad beans
vinaigrette (page 71)
sea salt
freshly ground black pepper
sugar
1 lettuce
150ml (5 fl oz) natural yoghurt
lemon slices
1 tablespoon chopped chives

Wash beans and if tender enough, top and tail and slice in their pods into 1cm (½in) lengths, otherwise remove beans from pods; cook in a little boiling water until tender. Drain and toss hot beans in lemon dressing; allow to get quite cold, basting from time to time. Serve piled up on lettuce, topped with natural yoghurt, with a garnish of lemon slices and a sprinkling of chopped chives.

BRUSSELS SPROUT MAYONNAISE

SERVES 4
450g (1 lb) brussels sprouts
4 carrots, grated
2 tablespoons lemon juice
4 tablespoons mayonnaise
4 tablespoons chopped dates
1 bunch watercress
snipped slivers of lemon and orange rind

Wash and coarsely grate sprouts; peel and finely grate carrots. Mix together with lemon juice, mayonnaise and dates. Serve with watercress, and garnish with the lemon and orange rind.

BULGUR WHEAT, TOMATO AND PARSLEY SALAD

In this Middle Eastern salad, *tabbouleh*, parsley is used rather like a vegetable to provide the basis of the dish, and it's surprising what a big bunch you'll need to weigh 125g (4oz). If you haven't got enough I find you can use a bunch of watercress or some tender young spinach leaves instead. The bulgur wheat is quite easy to get in health shops.

SERVES 4
225g (8oz) bulgur wheat
125g (4oz) parsley
25g (1oz) mint leaves
1 onion
3 tomatoes
2 tablespoons olive oil
juice of 1 lemon
1 garlic clove, peeled and crushed in a little salt
sea salt
freshly ground black pepper

Cover the wheat with boiling water and leave it to soak for 15 minutes, then drain it thoroughly and put it into a bowl. Meanwhile wash the parsley and mint and chop them up fairly finely; peel and chop the onion and tomatoes, then add them to the wheat, together with the oil, lemon juice and garlic. Mix everything together and season with salt and pepper to taste.

Spoon the mixture on to a flat serving dish and press it down with the back of a spoon. Serve it chilled. You can sprinkle a little extra olive oil over the top if you like to make it look shiny. Or serve it simply, in a salad bowl or heaped up on crisp lettuce leaves.

BUTTER BEAN SALAD

Serve this substantial, protein-rich dish with a fresh vegetable salad such as the Middle Eastern cabbage salad or a platter of lettuce and juicy sliced tomato for a complete meal, along with soft wholemeal bread rolls or pitta bread.

SERVES 4 [F]
175g (6oz) butter beans, soaked, cooked and drained as usual *or* 2 × 400g cans, drained
6 spring onions
2 tablespoons chopped fresh parsley
1 tablespoon lemon juice
3 tablespoons olive oil
sea salt
freshly ground black pepper

Cover the butter beans with water and leave them to soak for several hours if possible. Then drain and rinse the beans and simmer them gently in plenty of water until they're tender; drain them thoroughly (the liquid makes good stock). Put the beans into a bowl.

Wash and trim the spring onions, retaining as much of the green part as seems reasonable, then chop them up and add them to the butter beans, along with the parsley, lemon juice, oil and a seasoning of salt and pepper. Stir the mixture gently, being careful not to break up the beans, then leave it to cool. I think the salad is nicest served really cold. If you're freezing this salad, don't add the onions and parsley until just before serving.

BUTTER BEAN, APPLE AND BEETROOT SALAD

SERVES 2–3

125g (4oz) butter beans, soaked cooked and drained
as usual, *or* 400g (14oz) can, drained
1 teaspoon honey
3 tablespoons oil
1 tablespoon red wine vinegar
sea salt
freshly ground black pepper
1 large, cooked beetroot
2 sweet eating apples
a little chopped fresh mint

Soak and then cook the butter beans as in previous recipe; drain them well. Make a dressing by mixing together the honey, oil, vinegar and some sea salt and freshly ground black pepper and pour this over the butter beans, turning them gently in it. Peel and dice the beetroot; wash, core and slice the apples, and add them to the beans. Mix gently, then chill the salad and serve it garnished with chopped mint.

CREAMY BUTTER BEAN AND AVOCADO SALAD

I had a delicious curried egg mayonnaise at a friend's house and I wanted to make something similar using a low-fat mayonnaise and something other than eggs, as my family aren't too keen on them. I decided on butter beans to replace the eggs, with avocados to give some richness, and although the result is certainly rather different from the original, it's creamy and delicious. You can serve this salad on a base of crisp lettuce or, if you want to make it more substantial, cold cooked rice.

SERVES 4

75–125g (3–4oz) butter beans, soaked, cooked and
drained *or* a 400g (14oz) can, drained
1 large ripe avocado
lemon juice
1 tablespoon olive oil
1 small onion, peeled and chopped
2 teaspoons curry powder
1 teaspoon tomato paste
6 tablespoons wine – red *or* white
1 teaspoon clear honey
150g (5oz) natural yoghurt
150g (5oz) *fromage blanc or* smooth low-fat white
cheese
sea salt
freshly ground black pepper
crisp lettuce *or* cold cooked rice, paprika pepper,
sprigs of watercress

Put the beans into a large bowl. Cut the avocado in half, twist the two halves in opposite directions to separate and remove stone. Peel the avocado and cut the flesh into chunky dice. Sprinkle the avocado with lemon juice and add to the bowl with the beans.

To make the sauce, heat the oil in a medium-sized saucepan and fry the onion for 10 minutes, until it is soft but not brown. Stir in the curry powder, tomato paste, wine and honey and bubble over a high heat for 2 or 3 minutes until reduced to a thick syrup. Cool. Put the yoghurt and *fromage blanc* into a bowl and sieve in the onion mixture – or liquidize them all together. Season with salt and pepper.

Pour the yoghurt mixture over the beans and avocado and mix gently. Serve on a bed of lettuce or rice, sprinkled with a little paprika pepper and decorated with sprigs of watercress.

BUTTER BEANS AND MUSHROOMS WITH CORIANDER

This is one of my favourite bean salads, succulent and spicy. It makes an excellent starter. Serve it with soft rolls to mop up the delicious juices.

SERVES 4 AS A STARTER, 2 AS A MAIN SALAD DISH

125g (4oz) butter beans
225g (8oz) small white button mushrooms
8 tablespoons vegetable oil
3–4 teaspoons ground coriander
2 garlic cloves, crushed
juice of 1 lemon
sea salt
freshly ground black pepper
crisp lettuce leaves
chopped parsley

Soak the butter beans for several hours in cold water, then drain and rinse them, cover them with fresh water, simmer them gently until they're tender, then drain them. Wash the mushrooms and halve or quarter them if necessary. Heat the oil in a saucepan and add the mushrooms and coriander. Fry the mushrooms for 1–2 minutes, just to tenderize them, but don't let them get soggy. Remove the pan from the heat and add the butter beans, garlic and lemon juice. Mix gently, adding sea salt and freshly ground black pepper to taste. Let the mixture cool, then chill it, and serve it on a base of crisp lettuce, garnished with chopped parsley.

BUTTER BEAN, TOMATO AND OLIVE SALAD

This succulent mixture of flavours makes a very good protein-rich side salad, and it also makes a lovely light lunch or supper, served with warm wholemeal rolls or French bread to mop up the juices.

SERVES 4
3 tablespoons olive oil
1 tablespoon wine vinegar
sea salt
freshly ground black pepper
1 medium-sized mild onion, peeled and sliced
450g (1 lb) tomatoes, skinned and sliced
425g (15oz) can butter beans, drained *or* 125g (4oz) dried butter beans, soaked, cooked and drained
8–10 black olives

Put the oil and vinegar into the base of a wooden salad bowl and add a little salt and freshly ground black pepper. Then put in the onion, tomatoes, butter beans and olives, and turn everything gently to mix the ingredients, making sure that all the flavours blend.

CABBAGE AND APPLE SALAD

SERVES 4
450g (1 lb) cabbage
4 rosy apples
50g (2oz) sultanas
honey dressing (page 70)
chicory *or* lettuce

Wash and finely shred cabbage; wipe apples and chop without peeling. Plump sultanas in boiling water for 10 minutes; drain, and mix with cabbage. Serve on a bed of chicory or lettuce, with a protein savoury, grated cheese or hardboiled eggs.

Variations

RED CABBAGE AND APPLE SALAD

Make as above, but use 450g (1 lb) red cabbage. Garnish with chopped walnuts.

CAULIFLOWER AND APPLE SALAD

Make as above, but use 450g (1 lb) cauliflower (1 medium cauliflower) instead of cabbage.

CABBAGE AND PINEAPPLE SALAD

Is delicious; use 450g (1 lb) shredded white cabbage; mix with the drained contents of a 400g (14oz) can of pineapple pieces canned in juice or, if fresh pineapple is available, use 225g (8oz) of this, chopped.

CABBAGE AND BEAN SALAD

SERVES 4
1 tablespoon wine vinegar
3 tablespoons olive oil
1 teaspoon sugar
½ teaspoon dry mustard
sea salt
freshly ground black pepper
1 tablespoon chopped fresh herbs
350g (12oz) white cabbage, finely shredded
2 sticks celery, chopped
½ green pepper, de-seeded and chopped
2 carrots, grated
2–3 tablespoons sultanas, washed and drained
125g (4oz) beans, any firm type, soaked, cooked and drained *or* 400g (14oz) can, drained

Put the vinegar, oil, sugar, mustard and some sea salt and freshly ground black pepper into a bowl and mix them together, then add all the other ingredients and stir them gently, so that they all get coated with the dressing. This is nice served with wholemeal rolls and some curd cheese.

CABBAGE SALAD WITH RED PEPPERS AND RAISINS

This colourful salad is excellent with jacket potatoes or a cheese flan.

SERVES 4
3 tablespoons olive oil
1 tablespoon wine vinegar
sea salt
freshly ground black pepper
350g (12oz) white cabbage, washed and shredded
175g (6oz) carrot, scraped and chopped or coarsely grated
175g (6oz) red pepper, de-seeded and chopped
2 heaped tablespoons chopped parsley, chives *or* spring onions
50g (2oz) raisins
50g (2oz) roasted peanuts

First make the dressing, straight into the bowl: put the oil and vinegar into the base of a wooden salad bowl, add some salt and pepper and mix. Then put in the cabbage, carrot, red pepper, parsley, chives or spring onions and raisins and turn everything over a few times with a spoon so that they all get covered with the dressing. If possible leave for 1 hour or so: this softens the cabbage and gives the flavours a chance to blend. Stir in the peanuts just before serving.

SWEET CABBAGE SALAD WITH LOVAGE

It's the pungent, aromatic flavour of lovage and the sweet dressing which makes this salad different and delicious. If you can grow lovage (and it's easy once you've got it as it comes up every year but needs a good deal of room) try to freeze some for the winter; otherwise use mint or mint sauce concentrate instead. This gives a completely different flavour but is still good!

SERVES 4
1 tablespoon chopped fresh lovage *or* mint, *or* 1 teaspoon mint sauce concentrate
1 tablespoon honey
1 tablespoon wine vinegar
3 tablespoons olive oil
sea salt
freshly ground black pepper
450g (1 lb) white cabbage, coarsely grated

Put the chopped herbs, honey, vinegar, oil and some salt and pepper into a large bowl and mix together to form a dressing. Add the cabbage and mix thoroughly, so that it gets well coated with the sweet herb dressing. Leave for at least 1 hour, so that the cabbage softens a little and absorbs all the flavurs.

Variation

CABBAGE SALAD WITH MINT AND POMEGRANATE

For this Middle Eastern version, guaranteed to be a talking-point, top the salad with the juicy red seeds from a pomegranate, eased out with the point of a sharp knife or a pointed skewer or cocktail stick – catch the juice on a plate as you work. Garnish with a few sprigs of fresh mint if available.

CANNELLINI, APPLE AND CELERY SALAD

Actually you could use any white beans for this salad, but cannellini are nice because of their size and shape.

SERVES 2–3
125g (4oz) cannellini beans, soaked, cooked and drained as usual, *or* 400g (14oz) can, drained
3 tablespoons oil
1 tablespoon lemon juice
sea salt
freshly ground black pepper
1 celery heart
2 eating apples
2 tablespoons raisins, washed and drained

Put the beans into a large bowl. Mix together the oil, lemon juice and some sea salt and freshly ground black pepper and add this to the beans, mixing gently. Wash and slice the celery; wash the apples and peel them if the skin is tough, then cut them into dice, discarding the core. Add the celery and apples to the beans, along with the raisins. Turn it gently with a spoon before serving so that everything gets mixed together and coated with the dressing.

CARROT AND ALMOND SALAD

SERVES 4
450g (1 lb) carrots
1 small apple
½ green pepper – optional
150ml (5 fl oz) natural yoghurt *or* mayonnaise
1 lettuce
50g (2oz) toasted almonds

Scrape and finely grate carrots and apple; chop pepper if using. Add enough mayonnaise or natural yoghurt – or a mixture – to moisten. Serve on a bed of crisp lettuce and top with a generous scattering of toasted almonds.

CARROT, APPLE AND LOVAGE SALAD

The lovage gives this salad a curiously sweet, aromatic flavour which I find delicious. It is especially good with cheese dishes.

SERVES 4
3 tablespoons olive oil
1 tablespoon wine vinegar
sea salt
freshly ground black pepper
350g (12oz) carrots
225g (8oz) white cabbage
3 sweet eating apples
2 heaped tablespoons fresh chives, chopped
2 heaped tablespoons fresh lovage, chopped

First make the dressing very simply by putting the oil and vinegar into the base of a wooden salad bowl and mixing with a little salt and freshly ground black pepper. Next, scrape the carrots and dice finely; wash and shred the cabbage, dice the apples, discarding the cores. Put the carrots, cabbage and apples into the bowl, together with the chopped chives and lovage and mix well.

CARROT, APPLE AND SPROUTED CHICKPEA SALAD

For this salad you need your own sprouted chick peas, started 3–4 days beforehand. It's a super, crunchy, vitality-mix.

SERVES 2–4
juice of 1 orange
2 medium-sized carrots, coarsely grated
2 apples, diced
175–225g (6–8oz) sprouted chickpeas

Mix everything together; serve immediately. Some chopped mint or other fresh herbs can be added, also a spoonful of natural yoghurt, if liked.

CAULIFLOWER AND APPLE IN CURRIED MAYONNAISE

Serve this salad as a first course or as a light meal, with hot wholemeal cheese scones or crisp warm poppadums.

SERVES 4–6
1 medium-sized cauliflower, chopped or coarsely grated
1 carrot, coarsely grated
2 sweet eating apples, finely diced
2 tablespoons raisins
1 tablespoon chopped chives
1 tablespoon lemon juice
a few crisp lettuce leaves
curried yoghurt mayonnaise (page 73)
paprika pepper

Put the cauliflower, carrot and apple into a bowl with the raisins, chives and lemon juice and mix. Put some crisp lettuce leaves on a shallow serving dish and spoon the cauliflower mixture on top. Pour the dressing over the salad, sprinkle with paprika pepper.

CELERIAC SALAD

Celeriac, that knobbly root with the delicious celery flavour, makes a good salad. Done this way, with a mustardy vinaigrette, it makes a pleasant side salad to accompany either a hot or cold protein dish.

SERVES 4
1 smallish celeriac – about 450g (1 lb)
½ teaspoon mustard powder
½ teaspoon sugar
¼ teaspoon sea salt
freshly ground black pepper
1 tablespoon wine vinegar
3 tablespoons olive oil
1 bunch of watercress, washed and trimmed
paprika pepper

Peel the celeriac and cut into quarters. Keep the pieces under cold water while you make the dressing as celeriac quickly discolours. Put the mustard, sugar and salt into a shallow dish with a good grinding of black pepper and add the vinegar. Mix to a paste then gradually stir in the oil. Grate the celeriac straight into the dish, turning it over in the dressing as you do so to coat it well and prevent it from discolouring. I think it's best to use a fairly coarse grater as it gives the salad a nice texture. Taste the mixture and add a little more seasoning if you think it needs it. If possible leave it for 30 minutes or so to give the celeriac a chance to soak up the flavour of the dressing, then pile it into a serving dish, arrange the watercress round the edge and sprinkle the top with a little red paprika pepper.

CELERY AND CUCUMBER SALAD

This is a nice quick salad to make and lovely with pasta and rice dishes. You could use fennel instead of celery for a change.

SERVES 4
1 good-sized head of celery *or* 1–2 heads fennel
1 cucumber
sea salt
freshly ground black pepper
1 tablespoon lemon juice

Slice the celery; dice the cucumber. Mix them together, add salt and pepper to taste and the lemon juice.

CHEESE AND TOMATO SALAD

SERVES 4
8 large tomatoes
honey dressing (page 70)
1 head chicory *or* half lettuce
225g (8oz) grated cheese
1 tablespoon chopped parsley, chives *or* mint
1 teaspoon chopped onion
1 bunch watercress

Skin tomatoes only if necessary – slice and toss in a little honey dressing. Arrange on a base of chicory or lettuce leaves. Finely grate cheese and mix with chopped herbs and onion, and sprinkle over tomatoes. Garnish with watercress.

CHICK PEA SALAD

This Middle Eastern salad is good served with crisp lettuce leaves or warm wholemeal pitta bread and some chilled natural yoghurt.

SERVES 4 F
175g (6oz) chick peas
2 garlic cloves
2 tablespoons olive oil
2 tablespoons lemon juice
sea salt
freshly ground black pepper
1 small onion, peeled and sliced into rings
3 tablespoons chopped parsley

Cover the chick peas with plenty of cold water and leave them to soak for 4–5 hours or overnight. Then drain them and rinse thoroughly under cold water. Cook the chick peas gently in fresh cold water until they're tender; drain them thoroughly.

Meanwhile, peel and crush the garlic, put it into a medium-sized bowl and mix in the olive oil, lemon juice and some sea salt and freshly ground black pepper; add the drained chick peas (which can still be hot) and turn them in the dressing. Add the onion and parsley and leave the mixture to get cold. Check seasoning; serve cold or chilled.

CHICK PEA, APPLE AND LEEK SALAD

SERVES 3
125g (4oz) chick peas, soaked, cooked and drained as usual *or* 400g (14oz) can, drained
2 eating apples
1 tablespoon lemon juice
1 tablespoon oil
1 medium leek
1 tomato
sea salt
freshly ground black pepper
crisp lettuce leaves

Put the chick peas into a large bowl. Wash the apples and peel them if they look as if they need it; then cut them into smallish dice, discarding the core. Add the apples to the chick peas, together with the lemon juice and oil. Wash the leek carefully, then cut it into thin rings, using the white part and as much of the green as possible; dice the tomato. Add the leek and tomato to the chick pea mixture. Season with sea salt and freshly ground black pepper. Serve the salad on a base of crisp lettuce leaves.

CHICK PEA AND SPINACH SALAD WITH YOGHURT

Another chick pea salad but quite different from the previous one. I like the contrast of texture and colour; firm, golden chick peas against soft, bright green spinach, and smooth, creamy white yoghurt.

SERVES 4–6 AS A STARTER, 2–3 AS A SALAD MEAL
450g (1 lb) spinach
175g (6oz) chick peas, cooked and drained *or*
2 × 400g (14oz) cans, drained
6 tablespoons olive oil
2 tablespoons wine vinegar
sea salt
freshly ground black pepper
150ml (5 fl oz) thick natural yoghurt
1–2 tablespoons chopped parsley

Thoroughly wash the spinach; cook it without extra water until it's tender, then cool, drain and chop it. Add the chick peas to the cooled spinach, together with the olive oil, vinegar and a good seasoning of sea salt and freshly ground black pepper. Mix well together, being careful not to break up the chick peas, then chill the salad until required.

To serve, arrange the spinach and chick pea mixture on a plate and spoon the natural yoghurt on top. Sprinkle with chopped parsley. Some thin buttered brown bread goes well with this.

If you want a crunchier texture, try adding some raw onion rings to the salad mixture; it's also nice with a flavouring of crushed garlic.

CHICK PEA AND VEGETABLE MAYONNAISE

I love this French salad, but with its creamy mayonnaise dressing it's too high in fat and calories to enjoy very often. So I've gradually evolved ways of reducing the calories. Even slimmers can enjoy this latest version, yet I think you'll agree it's still very luxurious-tasting. It's lovely with warm wholemeal rolls. I must say I do love artichoke hearts, but if you don't approve of using canned ones, use 225g (8oz) very fresh button mushrooms, just washed and sliced, instead.

SERVES 4–6
125g (4oz) chick peas, soaked overnight in cold water then rinsed and simmered in plenty of water until tender *or* 425g (15oz) can, drained
350g (12oz) each of cooked carrots and cooked cut green beans
400g (14oz) can artichoke hearts, drained
150ml (5fl oz) natural yoghurt
125g (4oz) *fromage blanc or* other low-fat soft white cheese
2 large garlic cloves, peeled and crushed
1 tablespoon mayonnaise
1 tablespoon wine vinegar
sea salt
freshly ground black pepper
crisp lettuce and watercress, chopped fresh parsley

Drain the chick peas and put them into a large bowl with the carrots and beans. Drain and quarter the artichoke hearts and add them to the bowl. To make the dressing, put the yoghurt, *fromage blanc*, garlic, mayonnaise and vinegar into a small bowl and mix well together until creamy. Season with salt and pepper. Pour the dressing over the vegetables and mix carefully until everything is well covered. Line a serving dish with lettuce and watercress, spoon the vegetable mixture on top and sprinkle with chopped parsley.

An alternative, richer dressing can be made using 6 rounded tablespoons each of mayonnaise and natural yoghurt, instead of the yoghurt and fromage blanc.

CHICORY SALAD

SERVES 4
4 heads chicory
4 large carrots
50g (2oz) sultanas
150ml (5 fl oz) mayonnaise (page 70) *or* natural yoghurt *or* a mixture
a few lettuce leaves
25g (1oz) toasted almonds

Cut chicory into rings; finely grate carrots. Plump sultanas in boiling water for 10 minutes, then drain and add to chicory and carrot, and mix with mayonnaise or yoghurt. Serve on lettuce leaves, garnished with toasted almonds. This goes well with a crisp textured rather simple savoury dish.

CHICORY FLOWER SALAD

This looks like a daisy, with its golden centre and white petals. The centre consists of a creamy cheese dip decorated with carrot rings, and the petals are crisp leaves of chicory stuck around the edge of the dip in two layers. You can eat the salad with your fingers, using the chicory to scoop up the dip.

SERVES 4
225g (8oz) curd cheese
125g (4oz) finely grated orange-coloured cheese
1 tablespoon tomato ketchup *or* purée
½ teaspoon paprika pepper
a little milk
sea salt
freshly ground black pepper
3 heads of chicory, washed and broken into leaves
2 carrots, scraped and cut into rings
juice of 1 lemon
2 tablespoons olive oil

Mix together the curd cheese, grated cheese, tomato ketchup or purée and paprika pepper. Add a little milk if necessary to make a soft consistency which just holds its shape; season. Heap this mixture up in the centre of a flat serving dish. Stick the chicory all round the edge of this, in two layers, like petals. Toss the carrot slices in lemon juice and arrange over the top of the cheese mixture; spoon the oil over the carrot.

CHICORY, ORANGE AND GRAPE SALAD

In this salad the sweetness of the fruit and the honey dressing contrast well with the slight bitterness of the chicory.

SERVES 4
4 large oranges
125g (4oz) black grapes
50g (2oz) chopped walnuts
honey dressing (page 70)
sea salt
freshly ground black pepper
4 heads chicory
175g (6oz) firm cheese, cubed

Cut peel from oranges and slice into segments; mix with halved and pitted grapes and walnuts. Moisten with honey dressing, season and serve on a base of chicory leaves with the cubes of cheese.

STUFFED CHICORY SALAD

SERVES 4
4 heads chicory
125g (4oz) raisins or sultanas
225g (8oz) cottage cheese
50g (2oz) chopped Brazil nuts
1 bunch watercress
2 oranges

Cut chicory in half lengthwise; remove heart from each half, leaving a 'boat'. Finely chop hearts. Plump raisins or sultanas by steeping them in boiling water for 10 minutes; drain. Chop, and mix with cottage cheese, chopped Brazil nuts and chopped chicory centres. Pile chicory boats with this mixture; serve on a bed of watercress, surrounded by rings of peeled and pithed oranges.

CHICORY AND TOMATO SALAD

SERVES 4
8 tomatoes
4 heads chicory
french dressing
sea salt
freshly ground black pepper
½ teaspoon brown sugar
1 bunch watercress or mustard and cress

Skin and quarter tomatoes. Wash and slice chicory. Put both into a bowl with enough vinaigrette dressing to moisten. Season with salt, pepper and sugar as necessary. Serve with watercress or cress. A few black olives make a very good addition to this salad. It goes well with cheese dishes – cheese mousse (page 36) for instance, or a savoury cheese flan, or simply bread and a good cheese board, or baked potatoes and grated cheese.

CHICORY AND WALNUT SALAD

If you can get red chicory, this salad is lovely made with half red and half white: otherwise use all white chicory, or a mixture of white chicory and Chinese leaves.

SERVES 4–6
350g (12oz) white chicory
350g (12oz) red chicory
3 tablespoons olive oil or if you can get it, half walnut oil and half olive oil
1 tablespoon wine vinegar
sea salt
freshly ground black pepper
50g (2oz) fresh walnut pieces, roughly chopped

Wash the chicory, dry carefully, then slice. Put the oil and vinegar into a salad bowl, add some salt and pepper and mix together, then add the chicory and walnuts and turn them in the oil until everything is shiny with the dressing. Serve at once.

Variation

SALAD OF CHINESE LEAVES WITH SPRING ONIONS

This salad is made in the same way as the previous chicory one, using 700g (1½ lb) Chinese leaves and adding a bunch of chopped spring onions instead of (or, if you prefer, as well as) the walnuts. I also rather like it with some raisins added too; they give a pleasant touch of sweetness.

SALAD OF CHINESE LEAVES WITH BEANSPROUTS AND A SWEET AND SOUR DRESSING

In this recipe, I have emphasized the Chinese theme by mixing Chinese leaves with crunchy beansprouts and a soy sauce and sesame oil dressing, rather like a salad version of Chinese fried vegetables.

SERVES 4
175g (6oz) fresh beansprouts
1 tablespoon clear honey
3 tablespoons sesame oil *or* olive oil
2 tablespoons soy sauce
freshly ground black pepper
2.5cm (1in) fresh ginger root, peeled and finely grated
350g (12oz) Chinese cabbage, shredded
2 carrots, scraped and coarsely grated

Cover the beansprouts with cold water and leave them to soak and crispen while you make the dressing and prepare the other ingredients. Put the honey, oil and soy sauce into the base of a large bowl with a grating of pepper and the ginger, and mix together. Add the Chinese cabbage and carrots, turn them well with a spoon, then drain the beansprouts and add these. Mix well and serve.

COLESLAW

Mayonnaise gives the creamiest, most delicious result in this salad, though for a less calorific version it is also good made with some natural yoghurt instead of mayonnaise, or a mixture.

SERVES 4
350g (12oz) white cabbage
1 large carrot
1 small onion
50g (2oz) sultanas
3 rounded tablespoons mayonnaise
sea salt
freshly ground black pepper

Wash and shred the cabbage; scrape and coarsely grate the carrot, peel and finely slice the onion. Put them into a large bowl with the sultanas, mayonnaise and some salt and pepper to taste and mix well. Cover and leave for 2–3 hours before serving if possible: this allows the vegetables to soften and the flavours to blend.

CONCHIGLIE SALAD WITH CUCUMBER, NUTS AND RAISINS IN CURRIED MAYONNAISE

A delicious blend of flavours and textures.

SERVES 4
½ cucumber
sea salt
225g (8oz) conchiglie – pasta shells
2 tablespoons mayonnaise
4 tablespoons natural yoghurt
1 teaspoon curry paste
50g (2oz) raisins
freshly ground black pepper
50g (2oz) flaked almonds, toasted
crisp lettuce leaves

Cut cucumber into 6mm (¼in) dice, sprinkle with salt, put into a colander under a weight and leave for 30 minutes, to draw off excess liquid, then pat dry with kitchen paper. Cook pasta in plenty of boiling salted water until just tender; drain thoroughly. In a large bowl mix together the mayonnaise, yoghurt and curry paste; add pasta, cucumber and raisins. Mix well, season to taste. Just before serving stir in most of the almonds; arrange lettuce leaves on serving dish, spoon salad on top, sprinkle with remaining nuts.

CUCUMBER, APPLE AND RAISIN SALAD

A friend of mine had this salad at, of all places, a motorway restaurant. It sounded good so I tried making a low-calorie version and it is a pleasant, easy-to-make combination.

SERVES 4
1 cucumber
2 large eating apples
1 tablespoon natural yoghurt
50g (2oz) curd cheese
1 teaspoon olive oil
a drop of wine vinegar
sea salt
freshly ground black pepper
50g (2oz) raisins

Dice the cucumber and apples, discarding the apple cores. Put the yoghurt, curd cheese and oil into a large bowl and beat until creamy, then add just a dash of vinegar and some salt and pepper to taste. Mix in the cucumber, apple and raisins.

CUCUMBER SALAD WITH SOURED CREAM AND HARDBOILED EGGS

This refreshing salad from Russia makes a useful protein-rich starter accompanied by thinly sliced brown bread and butter. Traditionally the dressing is made with soured cream, but yoghurt can also be used for a low-calorie dressing which incidently makes an excellent slimmer's substitute for mayonnaise.

SERVES 4
1 large cucumber
sea salt
whites of 4 hardboiled eggs
yolks of 4 hardboiled eggs
2 teaspoons wine vinegar
1 teaspoon caster sugar
1 teaspoon mustard powder
freshly ground black pepper
150ml (5fl oz) carton soured cream *or* natural yoghurt
1 tablespoon chopped fresh dill weed *or* ½ teaspoon dried dill and 2 teaspoons chopped parsley
4 crisp nicely shaped lettuce leaves

Wash the cucumber and remove the peel if you want to, then slice the cucumber into thin rounds, put them into a colander, sprinkle with salt and put a weight on top. Leave them for 30 minutes to draw out excess water. Meanwhile chop the egg whites and leave them on one side. Make the dressing: put the egg yolks into a medium-sized bowl with the vinegar, sugar, mustard and some salt and pepper and mash them all together. Add a little of the soured cream or yoghurt and mix well to make a smooth creamy consistency; gradually add the remainder, beating well. Taste and season. Drain the cucumber rings and mix them with the egg white and dill; chill if possible.

When ready to serve arrange a lettuce leaf on each serving dish, divide the cucumber mixture between them and spoon the dressing over the top.

STUFFED CUCUMBER SALAD

This is an unusual dish with a fresh, tangy flavour. It makes a good protein-rich starter or can be the basis of a simple lunch. It's nice served with thin slices of brown bread and butter and if you don't like onions use chopped chives or spring onion green instead.

SERVES 2 AS A SALAD MEAL, 4 AS A STARTER
1 large cucumber
150ml (5 fl oz) water
2 tablespoons wine vinegar
sea salt
freshly ground black pepper
2 hardboiled eggs
1 tablespoon olive oil
½ teaspoon mustard powder
1 small onion, peeled and chopped
sprigs of watercress
a few radishes

Trim the cucumber then cut it into 4 equal-sized chunks. Peel the chunks then halve them lengthwise and with a teaspoon scoop out the seeds to leave a cavity for the stuffing – you won't need the seeds. Put the pieces of cucumber into a saucepan with the water, wine vinegar and a little salt and pepper and bring to the boil, then put a lid on the saucepan and leave the cucumber to simmer gently for about 5–7 minutes until it feels tender when pierced with a knife. There won't be much liquid left in the saucepan so watch it towards the end of the cooking time. Drain and cool the cucumber.

To make the filling shell the eggs and mash them with a fork, then mix in the olive oil, mustard, onion and salt and pepper to taste. Arrange the cucumber in a serving dish and spoon the filling neatly into the cavities. Decorate the dish with the watercress and radishes.

CUCUMBER AND TOMATO SALAD

A refreshing late-summer salad. Serve with soft, warm wholemeal bread or rolls.

SERVES 4
1 cucumber
6 tomatoes
2 tablespoons chopped chives *or* onion green
sea salt
freshly ground black pepper
6 tablespoons olive oil
2 tablespoons wine vinegar
sugar
½ lettuce
225g (8oz) soft, creamy but sliceable cheese

Wipe and dice or coarsely grate cucumber; wash and slice tomatoes, and mix all together with chopped chives. Season with salt and pepper. Mix together oil and vinegar, add a touch of sugar, and pour over cucumber mixture. Line serving dish with lettuce; pile cucumber mixture into centre and surround with slices of a creamy textured but sliceable cheese, such as demisel, camembert or brie.

CUCUMBER AND YOGHURT SALAD

The combination of cucumber, yoghurt and herbs is very refreshing, making this a good salad to serve on a hot day, either accompanying a main dish, or as a starter.

SERVES 4–6
1 cucumber
sea salt
1 tablespoon chopped fresh parsley
1 tablespoon chopped fresh chives
2 teaspoons chopped fresh dill *or* fennel if available
275ml (10 fl oz) natural yoghurt
freshly ground black pepper
1 crisp lettuce heart, cut into 4 or 6 pieces, one for each person; or warm wholemeal rolls

Wash the cucumber and slice it finely or grate it fairly coarsely. Put the pieces into a colander, sprinkle them with salt, place a weight on top and leave for about 30 minutes to draw out the excess moisture. Then squeeze the cucumber to extract as much liquid as possible and place it in a large bowl. Stir in all the other ingredients and season with pepper and some more salt if you think it's necessary.

This salad is nicest served really cold so put it into the fridge to chill for an hour or so if you can. You can serve each portion of the salad spooned over a crisp wedge of lettuce heart, or put it into small bowls and accompany it with fresh warm wholemeal rolls.

Variation

CUCUMBER AND SOURED CREAM SALAD

Use 150ml (5 fl oz) soured cream instead of the yoghurt.

DRIED FRUIT SALAD WITH WHITE CHEESE DRESSING

An unusual iron-rich winter/salad.

SERVES 4
125g (4oz) dried apricots
125g (4oz) prunes
125g (4oz) sultanas
4 oranges
½ head celery
1 lettuce
white cheese (page 72) *or* soured cream dressing (page 72)
25g (1oz) toasted almonds

Cover apricots, prunes and sultanas with boiling water and leave to soak overnight. Cut skins from oranges and slice fruit into pieces. Slice celery; mix altogether. Arrange on a bed of lettuce with dressing poured over, and garnish with toasted almonds.

ENDIVE SALAD

SERVES 4
1 head curly endive
1 tablespoon lemon juice
6 tablespoons mayonnaise *or* natural yoghurt
4 tomatoes
50g (2oz) roasted cashewnuts

Wash endive, discarding any discoloured or damaged leaves. Chop fairly finely and toss in the lemon juice. Mix with the mayonnaise or yoghurt, perhaps adding a touch of sugar to taste, and arrange in the centre of serving dish. Slice tomatoes into thin rings and arrange round endive. Roughly chop the nuts and sprinkle over the tomatoes.

FENNEL, CARROT AND SPRING ONION SALAD

A refreshing salad that's quick to make, especially if you have an electric grater. Some raisins and roasted flaked almonds make a pleasant addition.

SERVES 4
2 tablespoons lemon juice
2 tablespoons sunflower *or* olive oil
sea salt
freshly ground pepper
1 large bulb fennel
225g (8oz) carrots, scraped and coarsely grated
4 spring onions, chopped

Put the lemon juice and oil into a large bowl with a little salt and pepper and mix to make a simple dressing. Wash and slice the fennel, trimming off any tough outer layers but keeping any feathery green top; chop these green bits and add to the dressing in the bowl, along with the sliced fennel, grated carrots and spring onions. Mix well. This salad improves with standing; leave for up to 2 hours, turning the ingredients from time to time.

FENNEL AND CUCUMBER SALAD

The mixture of fennel and cucumber is refreshing and clean-tasting, and this salad is excellent for when you're in a hurry because it's very simple to make. Good as a side salad with cheese and pasta dishes.

SERVES 4
1 tablespoon wine vinegar
2 tablespoons olive oil
sea salt
freshly ground black pepper
1 cucumber
1 large bulb fennel
a little sugar – optional

Put the vinegar, oil, salt and a grinding of pepper into a salad bowl and mix together. Peel the cucumber and cut into medium-sized dice; wash, trim and slice the fennel, discarding coarse leaves but including any tender feathery leaves. Add the cucumber and fennel to the dressing mixture in the bowl and stir well. Check the seasoning – a touch of sugar can be pleasant in this salad – then serve.

FLAGEOLET AND AVOCADO SALAD

I'm particularly fond of this salad because its colours are so pleasing; pale green flageolet beans, yellow-green avocado and lettuce, dark green chives.

SERVES 2 AS A SALAD MEAL, 4 AS A STARTER
125g (4oz) flageolet beans
3 tablespoons olive oil
1 tablespoon white wine vinegar
¼ teaspoon dry mustard
sea salt
freshly ground black pepper
1 ripe avocado pear
a few crisp lettuce leaves
2 tablespoons chopped chives

Prepare and cook the beans as usual, then drain and cool them. Mix the oil with the vinegar, mustard and some sea salt and freshly ground black pepper, and add to the beans. Halve the avocado pear and gently remove the skin and the stone, then slice the flesh and add it to the beans. Turn the mixture gently, so that everything gets coated with the dressing, then serve it spooned on top of the lettuce leaves and sprinkled with the chopped chives.

Variations

FLAGEOLET AND BUTTON MUSHROOM SALAD

Use 175g (6oz) button mushrooms, washed and sliced, instead of the avocado.

FLAGEOLET AND SPRING ONION SALAD

Use 6–8 large spring onions. trimmed and chopped, instead of the avocado.

FRENCH BEAN AND MUSHROOM SALAD WITH A CORIANDER SEED DRESSING

Here, cooked French beans are marinated, with very lightly cooked button mushrooms, in a spicy dressing of crushed coriander seeds, lemon juice and olive oil. Served with warm wholemeal rolls, this salad makes an excellent light meal or first course.

SERVES 4–6
4 tablespoons olive oil
450g (1 lb) button mushrooms, wiped and halved or quartered
1 small bay leaf
1 tablespoon coriander seed, crushed
juice of 1 small lemon
450g (1 lb) French beans, cooked and drained
1 tablespoon chopped fresh parsley
sea salt
freshly ground black pepper

Heat the oil in a large saucepan and fry the mushrooms, bay leaf and coriander seeds for 2–3 minutes, until the mushrooms are beginning to soften. Then remove from the heat and cool the mixture quickly by putting it straight into a large bowl and sprinkling with the lemon juice. Add the beans, parsley and some salt and pepper. Leave until completely cold, then chill before serving.

FRUIT AND CHEESE SALAD

SERVES 4
225g (8oz) creamy but firm cheese
125g (4oz) white grapes
125g (4oz) black grapes
1 orange
2 apples
2 pears
1 banana
juice of ½ lemon
2 heads of chicory or ½ lettuce

Cube cheese; halve and de-seed grapes; remove rind and pith from orange and cut into segments; cube apples and pears and slice banana. Toss fruits in lemon juice to keep colour, then mix with cheese and serve on chicory or lettuce leaves.

FRUIT SALAD WITH CREAMY TOPPING AND TOASTED HAZEL NUTS

Really a main course and a pudding in one, this is a favourite lunchtime salad, especially when served with wholemeal cinnamon and raisin scones straight out of the oven.

SERVES 4
3 ripe dessert apples, diced
2 ripe pears, diced
225g (8oz) grapes, halved and de-seeded
2 ripe peaches, stoned and sliced
2 large juicy oranges
white cheese dressing (page 72)
25–50g (1–2oz) roasted hazel nuts, crushed

Put the apples, pears, grapes and peaches into a bowl. Then peel the oranges thickly, holding them over the bowl, by first cutting round and round with a sharp knife, then cutting the segments away from the white membranes; add the orange to the bowl. Mix gently and spoon mixture on to a flat serving dish. Pour dressing over the fruit and sprinkle with the nuts.

GREEK SALAD

Guaranteed to evoke instant nostalgia in anyone who has happy memories of Greece, this delicious salad only needs some light-textured bread with it.

SERVES 4
1 cucumber, peeled and cut into chunky dice
450g (1 lb) firm tomatoes, cut into chunky pieces
1 medium-sized onion, peeled and cut into rings
75–125g (3–4oz) black olives
salt
freshly ground pepper
125g (4oz) white cabbage, shredded
125g (4oz) feta cheese or white Cheshire or
Wensleydale
4 tablespoons olive oil
1 tablespoon wine vinegar

Put the cucumber, tomato, onion and olives into a bowl with some salt and pepper and mix. Divide the cabbage between four plates, spreading it out in an even layer, then spoon the cucumber mixture on top and crumble the cheese over that. Combine the oil and vinegar and spoon over the salads just before serving.

GREEN SALAD

A green salad can be adapted according to the season, and is perhaps the most useful basic salad of all. I think plenty of fresh herbs make all the difference and I personally like to make it quite pungent with garlic and onion rings, but leave these out if they're not to your taste.

SERVES 4
3 tablespoons olive oil
1 tablespoon wine vinegar
sea salt
freshly ground black pepper
1 garlic clove, peeled and crushed – optional
1 medium-sized lettuce, washed, shaken dry and
shredded
other green salad as available: watercress, sliced
chicory, fennel or cucumber, finely shredded tender
spinach
2 heaped tablespoons chopped fresh herbs: parsley,
chives or spring onions, mint, tarragon, basil – as
available
1 mild onion, peeled and sliced into rings – optional

First make the dressing very simply by putting the oil and vinegar into the base of a wooden salad bowl and mix with a little salt, freshly ground black pepper and the garlic if you're using it. Add all the other ingredients and mix well, so that everything gets coated with the shiny dressing. Serve immediately.

GREEN SALAD WITH GRUYÈRE CHEESE

This delicious variation on the basic green salad makes it a useful accompaniment to a low-protein main dish such as vegetable rice or stuffed peppers. Traditionally Gruyère cheese is used, but it's also nice with other smooth, firm cheeses such as Edam or Gouda.

SERVES 4
1 lettuce
1 bunch watercress
125–175g (4–6oz) Gruyère cheese
1 garlic clove
1 tablespoon wine vinegar
3 tablespoons olive oil
sea salt
freshly ground black pepper
1 tablespoon chopped fresh summer savory if
available, otherwise use chives or tarragon

Wash the lettuce and watercress and shake them dry, then if possible put them into a polythene bag and pop it in the fridge to chill for a while. Cut the cheese into little dice and leave on one side. Peel the garlic clove, and crush it in a little salt with the blade of a knife and put it into the salad bowl together with the vinegar, oil, a little sea salt and a grinding of pepper and mix them round with the salad servers. Sprinkle the herbs on top and leave until just before the meal, then put in the lettuce and watercress, breaking them up with your fingers, and the cubes of cheese. Just before serving turn the salad over with the servers so that it all gets coated with the dressing.

GREEN SALAD, SPANISH STYLE

This Spanish-style green salad makes a useful accompaniment to dishes such as paella (page 230) and Portuguese kidney bean stew (page 199).

SERVES 4
1 large lettuce
1 bunch watercress
1 tablespoon lemon juice
1 tablespoon olive oil
sea salt
freshly ground black pepper
1 large tomato
1 large onion, preferably Spanish
A few olives

Wash the lettuce and watercress, discarding any damaged leaves and tough stems; dry the salad in a salad drier or by patting it gently in a clean tea-towel. Tear the lettuce leaves into even-sized pieces and put them into a bowl with the watercress.

Make the dressing by mixing together the lemon juice, olive oil and a seasoning of salt and pepper. Add this to the lettuce and watercress in the bowl and turn the salad gently, so that all the leaves get coated in the dressing and are glossy-looking; arrange the salad in a mound on a large plate. Slice the tomato into thin rounds; peel and thinly slice the onion; arrange these on top of the green salad, together with a few olives. Serve at once.

HARICOT BEAN SALAD, GRECIAN STYLE

This is a deliciously rich-tasting bean salad and is good with warm crusty rolls and a bowl of crisp lettuce and watercress.

SERVES 4 F
225g (8oz) haricot beans
8 tablespoons olive oil or half olive, half vegetable oil
2 garlic cloves, crushed
1 teaspoon sea salt
2 teaspoons tomato purée
2 sprigs thyme
1 bay leaf
150ml (5 fl oz) water
juice of 1 lemon
1 onion, peeled
freshly ground black pepper
chopped parsley

Soak the beans for a couple of hours or so, then drain and rinse them and cook them in plenty of water until nearly tender; drain. Heat the oil in a good-sized saucepan, add the beans and cook them very gently for about 10 minutes, then stir in the garlic, sea salt, tomato purée, thyme, bay leaf and water (you can use some of the water in which the beans were cooked) and simmer gently, without a lid, until the liquid has reduced to a thick, terracotta-coloured sauce and the beans are tender. Cool, then add the lemon juice and the onion, sliced into thin rounds. Season with more sea salt and freshly ground black pepper if necessary. Chill the salad and serve it sprinkled with chopped parsley.

HARICOT BEAN SALAD WITH GREEN HERB DRESSING

This salad is best made well in advance to allow the flavours time to blend. You can dress the salad while the beans are still hot, leave it to cool, then chill before serving. It makes a good first course or addition to a salad selection; or can be served with hot garlic bread and a green salad or tomato salad.

SERVES 4–6 F
225g (8oz) haricot beans, soaked for 2–3 hours, then
cooked in water to cover for about 1 hour, until
tender *or* use 2 × 400g (14oz) cans cannellini beans
1 teaspoon sugar
½ teaspoon dry mustard powder
1 garlic clove, peeled and crushed
sea salt
freshly ground black pepper
2 tablespoons wine vinegar
6 tablespoons olive oil
2 heaped tablespoons chopped fresh herbs: as
available

Drain the beans. Put the sugar, mustard and garlic into a bowl with a little sea salt and a grinding of pepper. Blend to a paste with the vinegar, then gradually stir in the oil to make a dressing. Add the herbs and the beans and mix well. Cool, then chill before serving.

LEEK, APPLE AND TOMATO SALAD

A mixture which sounds funny but works well, it's especially good with cheese dishes: this salad and individual cheese soufflés, for instance, would make a good combination for lunch.

SERVES 4
6 large dessert apples
4–6 tomatoes
2 small leeks
juice of ½ lemon
sea salt
freshly ground black pepper
lettuce leaves

Dice the apples, with the peel on if it is sound and attractive; cut tomatoes into small pieces and mix with the apple. Slit leeks and wash thoroughly, saving as much of the green part as possible, then slice very finely and mix with the apple and tomato, lemon juice, salt and pepper. Serve piled up on crisp lettuce leaves.

LENTIL SALAD

Combined with a good fruity olive oil, lemon juice and some crisp onion rings, continental lentils make a delicious salad. If you serve it with some bread – soft wholemeal rolls, French bread or pitta bread – and a lettuce or other green salad it makes a complete meal, good for a summer lunch in the garden.

SERVES 4 F
225g (8oz) continental lentils
1 tablespoon lemon juice
3 tablespoons olive oil
sea salt
freshly ground black pepper
1 onion

Soak the lentils in water for a couple of hours or so if possible, then drain and rinse them, put them into a saucepan with fresh water and simmer them gently until tender – about 45 minutes. Drain the lentils thoroughly (keep the cooking liquid, it makes good stock) and put them into a bowl with the lemon juice, olive oil and some salt and pepper. Peel the onion and cut it into thin rounds then add these to the lentils and mix everything gently together. Cool, then chill the salad. It looks nice in a white bowl which contrasts with the rich brown lentils.

CURRIED LENTIL AND PINEAPPLE SALAD

This salad is one of my early recipes. These days I would use a small ripe pineapple instead of the canned pineapple, slice it in half through the leaves, scoop out the flesh and use it in the salad. I'd pile the lentil and pineaple mixture back into the two halves to serve the salad.

SERVES 4
2 garlic cloves, crushed
1 medium-sized onion, peeled and chopped
6 tablespoons olive oil
1 tablespoon curry powder
225g (8oz) split red lentils
275ml (10 fl oz) water
400g (14oz) can pineapple pieces, in natural juice,
drained and chopped
1 small green pepper, de-seeded and chopped
1 tablespoon wine vinegar
sea salt
freshly ground black pepper
lettuce leaves
a few onion rings
slices of tomato

Fry the garlic and onion in half the oil in a medium-sized saucepan for 5 minutes, then add the curry powder and the split red lentils (washed and drained) and fry for a further 4–5 minutes, stirring often to prevent sticking. Mix in the water and let the mixture cook very gently for 20–30 minutes after which the lentils should be tender in texture and beige-gold in colour and all the water absorbed. Remove the saucepan from the heat and add the pineapple, green pepper, vinegar, remaining oil and sea salt and black pepper. Cool, then chill the salad and serve it piled up on lettuce leaves and garnished with slices of tomato and raw onion rings. Alternatively, it's very nice served scattered with desiccated coconut and garnished with sliced banana rings which have first been tossed in a little lemon juice to prevent them from discolouring.

SPICY LENTIL SALAD WITH FRESH GINGER

Serve this salad with the cucumber and soured cream salad on page 91, some chapaatis, rolls or poppadums and a tomato side salad, for a complete main course.

SERVES 4
4 tablespoons olive oil
1 large garlic clove, peeled and crushed
1 teaspoon grated fresh ginger root
1 onion, peeled and chopped
225g (8oz) small whole brown lentils, from health shops
575ml (1 pint) water
1 small green or red pepper, de-seeded and finely chopped
1 tablespoon wine vinegar
sea salt
freshly ground black pepper

Heat 2 tablespoons of the oil in a medium-sized saucepan and fry the garlic, ginger and half the onion for 2–3 minutes. Put in the lentils, stir, then add the water. Bring to the boil, cover and leave to cook slowly until the lentils are tender and all the water is absorbed (about 15–20 minutes). Remove from heat, add remaining oil and onion, the pepper, vinegar and seasoning. Spoon into a serving dish and leave until cool.

CHUNKY LETTUCE SALAD WITH YOGHURT AND GREEN HERB DRESSING

For this salad you need one of those firm-packed lettuces: an Iceberg or Webb's with a very solid heart. It's a quick salad to prepare and makes an excellent side dish with a cooked main course.

SERVES 4
1 Iceberg lettuce *or* very firm Webb's Wonder
1 tablespoon lemon juice
sea salt
yoghurt and green herb dressing (page 72)

Wash the lettuce as well as you can and remove the outer leaves as necessary. Then cut the lettuce down into thick slices and cut these across, so that you have chunky pieces. Put these on to a flat serving dish, or individual plates, and sprinkle with the lemon juice and some salt, if liked. Spoon some dressing over the lettuce chunks just before serving.

The soured cream dressing (page 72) and the white cheese dressing (page 72) are also delicious, instead of the yoghurt one.

LETTUCE SALAD WITH SWEET DILL DRESSING

In contrast to the previous salad, this is a way of adding interest to the soft-leaf varieties of lettuce; it works well in the winter with mediocre lettuces and dried dill weed and is wonderful in the summer with fresh lettuces and dill from the garden.

SERVES 4
1 teaspoon sugar
1 tablespoon fresh dill *or* 1 teaspoon dried dill weed
1 tablespoon wine vinegar
2 tablespoons olive oil
sea salt
freshly ground black pepper
1 large lettuce, washed and torn into pieces
1 small onion, cut into thin rings.

Put the sugar, dill, vinegar and oil into a salad bowl with a little salt and pepper and mix well. Add the lettuce and onion, turn the salad gently until all the leaves are coated with the dressing, then serve immediately.

If you want to make this salad ahead of time, prepare the dressing and onion rings and leave to one side; wash and dry the lettuce and put it into a polythene bag in the fridge. The salad can then be assembled in moments just before you want to eat.

MACARONI SALAD WITH CHEDDAR CHEESE AND TOMATOES

A colourful salad, excellent for lunch on a hot day, with some wholemeal rolls.

SERVES 4
225g (8oz) macaroni
sea salt
2 tablespoons olive oil
1 tablespoon wine vinegar
freshly ground black pepper
4 tomatoes
1 mild onion
175g (6oz) Cheddar cheese
crisp lettuce leaves
watercress

Cook pasta in plenty of boiling salted water until just tender; drain thoroughly. Put the oil and vinegar into a bowl with some salt and pepper and mix together. Add the pasta, turning it gently until coated with the dressing. Slice the tomatoes and onion, cut cheese into small dice or grate coarsely, and add these to the pasta. Mix gently to combine ingredients. Line a serving bowl or plate with lettuce leaves, spoon the pasta salad on top, then tuck some sprigs of watercress around the edge of the salad.

MEXICAN-STYLE SALAD

Serve this salad with warm pitta bread or fried Mexican corn wafers (tortilla chips).

SERVES 4
1 large ripe avocado
2 tablespoons lemon juice
1 garlic clove, peeled and crushed
1 tablespoon olive oil
1 teaspoon wine vinegar
sea salt
freshly ground black pepper
chilli powder
8 large crisp lettuce leaves
125g (4oz) red kidney beans, soaked and cooked (as
described on page 178) or 400g (14oz) can, drained
1 small onion, peeled and sliced into thin rings
4 firm tomatoes, sliced
1 green or red pepper, de-seeded and thinly sliced
125g (4oz) grated cheese or 4 hardboiled eggs, sliced
a little paprika pepper

Halve, stone, peel and mash avocado; mix with the lemon juice, garlic, oil and vinegar and season with salt, pepper and chilli powder. Lay lettuce leaves on four plates, then layer the beans, onion, tomatoes, green pepper and cheese or eggs on top, ending with a big spoonful of avocado and a sprinkling of paprika.

CHUNKY MIXED SALAD BOWL

It's best if you can find a really hearty lettuce for this salad: an iceberg or a firm Webb's or Cos, so that you can cut it into nice chunky pieces. The other ingredients are largely a matter of personal taste and can be varied according to what is available.

SERVES 4
3 tablespoons olive oil
1 tablespoon wine vinegar
1 garlic clove, peeled and crushed – optional
sea salt
freshly ground black pepper
1 good-sized hearty lettuce, washed and cut into
chunky pieces
4 firm tomatoes, cut into wedges
½ cucumber, cut into chunky dice
1 small head of celery or chicory, sliced
1 tablespoon fresh chives or spring onions, chopped
1 mild onion, peeled and sliced into rings – optional

First make the dressing very simply by putting the oil and vinegar into the base of a wooden salad bowl and mix with a little salt, freshly ground black pepper and the garlic if you're using it. Add all the other ingredients and mix well, so that everything gets coated with the shiny dressing. Serve immediately.

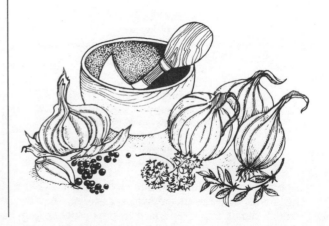

MUSHROOM, TOMATO AND AVOCADO SALAD BOWL

If you can get those small, very fresh, white mushrooms, they make a lovely salad which I especially like served with pasta tossed in a little olive oil and sprinkled with grated Parmesan.

SERVES 4
2 ripe avocado pears
juice of ½ lemon
3 tablespoons olive oil
1 tablespoon wine vinegar
sea salt
freshly ground black pepper
225g (8oz) tomatoes, skinned and sliced
225g (8oz) fresh white button mushrooms, washed and sliced
1 tablespoon fresh chives *or* spring onions, chopped

First cut the avocados in half and remove stones and skin. Cut the flesh into 1cm (½in) dice and sprinkle with the lemon juice. Put the oil and vinegar into the base of a wooden salad bowl and add a little salt and freshly ground black pepper. Then put in the tomatoes, mushrooms, avocado and chives and turn everything gently to mix the ingredients and make sure that all the flavours blend. Serve as soon as possible.

SALADE NIÇOISE

This is my vegetarian version of this classic salad, combining all the usual ingredients except the tuna fish and anchovies. It makes an excellent main lunch dish with soft warm wholemeal rolls or crunchy French bread.

SERVES 4
1 large lettuce
1 medium-sized onion, peeled
450g (1 lb) firm tomatoes
5 hardboiled eggs
450g (1 lb) cooked French beans
12 black olives
2 tablespoons chopped fresh parsley
2 tablespoons best quality olive oil
1 tablespoon red wine vinegar
sea salt
freshly ground black pepper

Line a flat serving dish with the lettuce. Thinly slice the onion, quarter the tomatoes and eggs, cut the French beans into even-sized lengths. Put the veg-

etables and eggs into a bowl and add the olives, parsley, oil and vinegar and a little salt and pepper. Mix gently so that everything gets coated with the dressing and looks glossy and appetizing. Heap the salad up on top of the lettuce and serve as soon as possible.

Variation

SALADE NIÇOISE WITH BUTTER BEANS

Make as above, adding 125g (4oz) (dry weight) butter beans, soaked, cooked and drained, or 400g (14oz) can, drained, instead of, or as well as, the eggs. Make sure the butter beans get well mixed with the dressing, to make them shiny and well-flavoured.

ONION SIDE SALAD WITH POPPY SEEDS AND PAPRIKA

If you cover onion rings with an oil and vinegar dressing and leave them for an hour or so to marinate they soften and become less hot. This salad is delicious for serving on the side with spicy lentil and rice dishes.

SERVES 4 AS A SIDE DISH
1 tablespoon wine vinegar
2 tablespoons olive oil
sea salt
freshly ground black pepper
2 large mild onions, peeled and sliced into rings
1 tablespoon poppy seeds
2 teaspoons paprika pepper

Put the vinegar and oil into a shallow container with some salt and pepper and mix together. Add the onion rings and mix again, so that they are all covered with the dressing. Sprinkle with the poppy seeds and paprika. Leave on one side for at least an hour, longer if possible: even overnight. Give the salad a stir every so often.

ORANGE, APPLE AND CELERY SALAD

A pretty, refreshing salad.

SERVES 4
4 oranges
4 apples
1 head celery
½ lettuce
50g (2oz) walnuts

Cut peel and pith from oranges and slice into segments. Chop apples and celery. Mix all together and serve on lettuce with a garnish of watercress and chopped walnuts.

Goes well with a soft-textured dish such as one of the egg pâtés, an egg mousse or cream cheese and pineapple.

ORANGE AND CUCUMBER SALAD

SERVES 4
1 hearty lettuce
4 large juicy oranges
1 cucumber
4 sprigs mint
sour cream dressing (page 72) *or* natural yoghurt

Wash lettuce, reserving the crisp, inner leaves and shredding the others. Remove skin and pith from oranges and cut into segments. Coarsely grate cucumber; chop mint. Mix together with shredded lettuce, and arrange on serving dish, surrounded by the reserved, inner lettuce leaves. Serve with sour cream dressing or natural yoghurt.

ORANGE AND RADISH SALAD

Bright red radishes and golden segments of orange make a colourful salad. Those large radishes, the size of turnips, are best if you can get them.

SERVES 4
2–4 large radishes *or* 2 bunches of radishes
6 large oranges
sea salt
1 bunch of watercress

Wash and trim the radishes then cut them into even-sized pieces. Using a sharp knife cut the skin and pith from the oranges and then cut the segments away from the white skin. Mix the oranges with the radishes and season to taste with a very little salt. Chill, then serve the salad in a border of watercress.

PASTA SALAD

Serve this complete-meal salad with grated cheese or a wedge of Brie and some good wholemeal bread.

SERVES 4
175g (6oz) wholemeal pasta rings
sea salt
1 tablespoon wine vinegar
4 tablespoons olive oil
1 garlic clove, peeled and crushed
freshly ground black pepper
1 ripe avocado
juice of 1 small lemon
125g (4oz) firm tomatoes, sliced
125g (4oz) firm white button mushrooms, wiped and sliced
6 spring onions, washed, trimmed and chopped

Cook the pasta in boiling salted water until just tender. Drain well. Mix with vinegar, oil, garlic and some salt and pepper in a large bowl, add the pasta and turn gently with a spoon. Cool, stirring from time to time.

Just before you want to eat the salad, peel and slice the avocado and mix with the lemon juice. Add to the pasta together with remaining ingredients.

STUFFED PEACH SALAD

This salad makes a delicious, light summer lunch.

SERVES 4
4 ripe peaches
juice of ½ lemon
225g (8oz) smooth soft skimmed milk cheese, such as quark
125g (4oz) black grapes, sliced and stoned
50g (2oz) chopped walnuts
lettuce leaves

Halve peaches and remove stones. Brush cut surfaces with lemon juice to prevent discolouration. Mix cheese with black grapes and walnuts. Spoon into peach halves and serve on lettuce leaves.

Can also be served as a light refreshing pudding – omitting lettuce leaves, of course!

STUFFED PEARS

The pears for this salad must be meltingly ripe, so that you can slice them easily with your fork to eat them.

SERVES 4
2 large ripe pears, preferably Comice
lemon juice
1 large piece preserved ginger in syrup
125g (4oz) carton cottage *or* curd cheese
2 tablespoons grated carrot
50g (2oz) chopped walnuts
lettuce leaves
grated carrot
watercress

Peel pears and cut in half lengthwise; using teaspoon and sharp knife remove core and any stringy bits. Brush cut surfaces with lemon juice. Crush or chop ginger; combine with cheese, grated carrot and walnuts. Pile into pears. Serve on a bed of lettuce, with a little grated carrot and watercress to garnish plate.

PINEAPPLE AND CREAM CHEESE

Some interesting ideas here for serving this classic salad combination for a special occasion.

SERVES 8
1 ripe pineapple
450g (1 lb) curd cheese
2 tablespoons whipped cream – optional

Remove skin and hard centre from pineapple, dice fruit and mix into curd cheese, lastly adding whipped cream, if using. Curd cheese rather than cottage cheese has to be used for this dish, as the latter, when combined with fresh pineapple, has a bitter taste. The resulting creamy mixture can be served in three different ways. (1) Heaped up on a dish and garnished with more pineapple or a simple salad. (2) Pressed into a simple mould – a jelly mould, or ring mould – chilled and turned out. A ring mould is particularly suitable and the centre looks attractive with grapes or strawberries when in season. (3) If the pineapple is cut carefully through the leafy green top and right down the centre and the fruit scooped out, the curd cheese mixture can be piled into the resulting pineapple 'shell' to make the centre of a large salad.

For a more usual version of this salad, simply arrange circles of fresh pineapple on lettuce-lined plates, place a spoonful of curd cheese on top of the pineapple and surround with other salad items such as sliced tomato, cucumber, grated carrot, radishes and spring onions, to make an appetizing platter.

POTATO SALAD

Potato salad is delicious if it's well made with firm chunks of potato in a creamy dressing, and makes a useful addition to a buffet party.

SERVES 6, OR MORE IF SERVED WITH OTHER SALADS
700g (1½ lb) new potatoes *or* firm-cooking old potatoes
sea salt
2 rounded tablespoons mayonnaise
2 rounded tablespoons *fromage blanc or* natural yoghurt
freshly ground black pepper
fresh chives *or* parsley, chopped

Cook the potatoes in boiling salted water until they are just tender; for the best flavour, cook them in their skins and then slip off the skins with a sharp knife afterwards. Cut the potatoes into chunky dice and put them into a bowl. Mix together the mayonnaise and *fromage blanc* or natural yoghurt, add some salt and pepper to taste. Add this to the potatoes, turning them gently with a spoon until they are all coated in the creamy dressing. Serve cold, with some fresh chives or parsley snipped over the top.

Variation

POTATO SALAD MOULD

For this buffet party variation put potato mixture into a well-oiled 850ml (1½ pint) ring mould. Press down well and leave in a cool place. Turn out on to a plate lined with lettuce leaves. Dice a 10cm (4in) piece cucumber and mix with 125g (4oz) cooked peas and a little chopped fresh mint, pile into centre of ring. Cut a red pepper into thin rings, and arrange over sides of potato ring. Cut circles of tomato and place round outside of ring and sprinkle with chopped spring onions.

HOT POTATO SALAD WITH PEANUT DRESSING

This is completely different! It's one of those dishes which sounds very strange but tastes really good. It's a mixture of hot and cold, bland and spicy, and it is rich in protein too. You can use ordinary salted peanuts but if you can get the plain roasted kind from a health shop they're better.

SERVES 4
225g (8oz) roasted peanuts
150ml (5 fl oz) milk
50g (2oz) finely grated cheese
½–1 teaspoon chilli powder *or* a small green chilli
700g (1½ lb) potatoes
1 lettuce
1 bunch of watercress
4 tomatoes
1 onion

First put the peanuts and milk into the liquidizer goblet and blend until they're thick and fairly smooth – add a little more milk if necessary to give the consistency of whipped cream. Turn the mixture into a bowl and stir in the grated cheese. Add chilli powder to taste, or, if you're using a fresh chilli remove and discard the seeds and chop the flesh very finely – add it to the mixture a little at a time, tasting to get the right degree of hotness.

Peel the potatoes and cut them into even-sized pieces, then boil them in salted water until they're just tender; drain. Wash the lettuce, watercress and tomatoes; peel the onion. Slice the onion and tomatoes into thin rounds.

To serve pile the hot potatoes into the centre of a serving dish (or individual plates) and arrange the lettuce, watercress, tomatoes and onion round the edge. Spoon the peanut sauce over the potatoes and serve at once.

RED KIDNEY BEAN SALAD

The secret of making a really good red bean salad, in my opinion, is firstly to make it in advance, so that the beans have a chance to soak up the flavour of the dressing, and secondly to include some tomato ketchup in the dressing!

SERVES 4 $\boxed{\text{F}}$
225g (8oz) red kidney beans *or* 2 × 400g (15oz) cans
2 tablespoons wine vinegar
1 tablespoon tomato ketchup
4 tablespoons olive oil
1 garlic clove, crushed
sea salt
freshly ground black pepper
1 small onion, peeled and cut into thin rings
chopped parsley

Cover beans with cold water and leave to soak overnight; or, for a quick soak, put them into a saucepan, cover with water, boil for 2 minutes, and leave to soak for 1 hour. Then drain and rinse the beans. Put the beans into a saucepan, cover with water and boil vigorously for 10 minutes, then simmer gently for about 1 hour, until beans are tender. Drain. In a large bowl combine vinegar, ketchup, oil, garlic and seasoning; add drained beans and onion, and mix well. Cool. Sprinkle with chopped parsley. If you're freezing this, add the onion and garlic just before serving.

RED KIDNEY BEAN, CARROT AND WALNUT SALAD

I'm especially fond of this version of Red Bean Salad because I find the blend of colours and texture especially pleasing. It's nourishing enough to make a light meal, with slices of wholemeal bread and butter or pitta bread and some fruit.

SERVES 4
125g (4oz) dried red kidney beans *or* 400g (14oz) can, drained
3 tablespoons olive oil
1 tablespoon wine vinegar
1 teaspoon caster sugar
½ teaspoon mustard powder
1 small garlic clove, peeled and crushed – optional
sea salt
freshly ground black pepper
1 heaped tablespoon spring onions, chopped
175g (6oz) carrot, scraped and coarsely grated
50g (2oz) fresh walnut pieces, chopped

If you're using dried red kidney beans, cover them with cold water and leave them to soak for at least 2 hours; then drain and rinse them. Put the beans into a saucepan and cover with fresh water; bring up to the boil and allow the beans to boil vigorously for at least 10 minutes. Then lower the heat and leave them to simmer, with a lid on the saucepan, until tender – about 1 hour. Drain.

Meanwhile make the dressing by putting the oil, vinegar, sugar, mustard and garlic, if you're using it, into the base of a wooden salad bowl and mix with a little salt and freshly ground black pepper. Add all the other ingredients, except the nuts, and mix well, so that everything gets coated with the shiny dressing. You can add the beans while they are still warm and the salad will be all the better for it because they will absorb the dressing and flavourings particularly well. Stir in the nuts just before serving so that they stay crisp.

RED BEAN AND ORANGE SALAD

A salad, this, for a grey winter's day, because the vivid colour is such a tonic! It's useful when conventional salad vegetables are scarce or unobtainable.

SERVES 4
175g (6oz) red kidney beans, soaked, cooked and
drained, or use 400g (14oz) can, drained
1 celery heart
4 large oranges
2 tablespoons olive oil
2 tablespoons chopped fresh mint
sea salt
freshly ground black pepper

Cover the kidney beans with water and leave to soak for several hours; then drain and rinse them. Put them into a saucepan with plenty of cold water and cook gently for about 1 hour, or until they're tender. Drain and cool them.

Wash and slice the celery; cut the peel and pith from the oranges and slice the fruit into thin rounds. Mix together the orange, celery, beans, oil and mint. Add sea salt and freshly ground black pepper to taste. Chill before serving.

RED CABBAGE SALAD WITH CARAWAY SEEDS

This is a useful winter salad and the warm mauve colour is cheerful on a cold day.

It makes a nice side salad or accompaniment to a protein-rich dish such as cheese flan. Because of its unusual colour it's also a good salad to include when you're making several for a buffet lunch or supper.

You can leave out the caraway seeds if you don't like them though they do give a pleasant spicy flavour.

SERVES 4
450g (1 lb) red cabbage
2 eating apples
50g (2oz) raisins
1 tablespoon lemon juice or red wine vinegar
2–3 tablespoons olive oil
2–3 teaspoons caraway seeds
sea salt
freshly ground black pepper

Wash the cabbage then grate or shred it as finely as you can. I think it's best grated because then it makes a nice soft mixture which blends well with the other ingredients and isn't too chewy. Cut the apples into small dice discarding the cores and wash the raisins, then add these to the cabbage together with the lemon juice or vinegar, oil, caraway seeds and a little salt and pepper. Stir well so that everything is thoroughly mixed together.

RED CABBAGE SALAD WITH CELERY, APPLES AND CHESTNUTS

The chestnuts give an unusual touch to this salad which is delicious in the autumn with the first of the red cabbage and celery. Serve it with jacket-baked potatoes split and filled with soured cream, cottage cheese or *fromage blanc* for a complete meal.

SERVES 4
450g (1 lb) red cabbage
1 tablespoon wine vinegar
2 tablespoons sunflower or olive oil
sea salt
freshly ground black pepper
2 sweet eating apples, cored and diced
1 celery heart, washed and sliced
125g (4oz) cooked chestnuts, halved or quartered
50g (2oz) raisins

Wash the cabbage and shred finely or grate coarsely. Put the vinegar and oil into a large bowl with some salt and pepper and stir together. Then add the cabbage, apples, celery, chestnuts and raisins and mix well. This salad can be made an hour or so ahead of time; it keeps well and the cabbage will become softer.

CURRIED RICE AND CHICK PEA RING

This looks very attractive when it's finished (although it's easy to do), and is a useful dish for a party.

SERVES 6
225g (8oz) brown rice
575ml (1 pint) water
1 teaspoon sea salt
2 large onions, peeled and chopped
4 tablespoons olive oil
4–6 teaspoons curry powder
2 crisp eating apples
2 bananas
juice of ½ lemon
125g (4oz) raisins
6–8 tablespoons mayonnaise (see page 70)
225g (8oz) chick peas, soaked, rinsed, cooked and drained or 2 × 400g (14oz) cans, drained
1 small red pepper, sliced into thin rings, seeds removed
a little chopped parsley
½ bunch watercress

Wash and pick over the rice, put it into a heavy-based saucepan with the water and sea salt and bring it up to the boil. Then put a lid on the saucepan, turn the heat down, and leave the rice to cook very gently for 45 minutes.

Fry the onion in the oil with the curry powder for 10 minutes until soft but not browned; add half to the cooked rice. Peel and dice the apples and bananas and toss them in the lemon juice; cover the raisins with a little boiling water and leave on one side for 10 minutes, then drain them and add to the rice with the apple and banana. Taste the rice mixture, and season it as necessary. Press the rice mixture into an oiled 1.2 litre (2 pints) ring mould and leave it to cool.

Stir the remaining onion and curry into the mayonnaise and then add the chick peas; season.

To assemble the dish, turn the rice ring out on to a large serving dish and pile the chick pea mayonnaise into the centre. Arrange the red pepper rings around the top of the rice ring, sprinkle the chick pea mayonnaise with chopped parsley, and tuck some sprigs of fresh, bright green watercress around the outside edge of the ring. A salad of bright orange grated carrots goes well with this.

RICE AND CURRY MAYONNAISE

SERVES 6
225g (8oz) brown rice
2 apples, sliced
2 bananas, peeled and sliced
lemon juice
2 heaped tablespoons raisins
2 tablespoons sunflower seeds
1 onion, grated
1 tablespoon olive oil
1 teaspoon curry powder
125ml (4 fl oz) mayonnaise
125ml (4 fl oz) natural yoghurt

Cook rice as on page 221; cool. Sprinkle apple and banana with lemon juice and add to rice. Steep raisins in a little boiling water for half an hour to plump; drain, and add to rice with sunflower seeds, mixing well. Fry onion in oil with curry powder for 10 minutes, then mix it with the mayonnaise and yoghurt and serve with the rice.

MOULDED RICE SALAD

SERVES 6
225g (8oz) long-grain brown rice
575ml (1 pint) water
sea salt
1 garlic clove, peeled and crushed
1 medium-sized onion, peeled and chopped
225g (8oz) aubergine, washed and cut into small dice
1 small red pepper, de-seeded and chopped
2 tablespoons sunflower oil
1 large tomato, skinned and chopped
2 drops tabasco sauce
freshly ground black pepper
6 small flat mushrooms, fried

Put rice into a medium-sized saucepan with the water and a teaspoonful of salt; bring to boil then cover and cook very gently for 45 minutes. Fry the garlic, onion, aubergine and pepper in the oil for 10 minutes; add the tomato and tabasco, cook for 5–10 minutes. Add to cooked rice and season. Line an 18cm (7in) cake tin or soufflé dish with foil; brush with oil. Put fried mushrooms, black side down, in base, and spoon rice mixture on top. Press down, chill. Turn out on to a flat dish and remove foil.

Variation

RICE AND BEAN SALAD

The above salad is also nice with some cooked, drained, red kidney beans added: 125g (4oz) (dry weight) or 400g (14oz) can.

MOULDED RICE AND ARTICHOKE HEART SALAD

This is a pretty salad of rice with pale green artichoke hearts, mushrooms and red pepper, made in a ring-shape with the centre filled with a glossy, golden egg mayonnaise sprinkled with toasted almonds. You could serve the salad more simply, if you prefer, just roughed-up on a plate, but for a special occasion it does look attractive like this and it's not difficult to do.

SERVES 6–8, OR MORE IF SERVED AS PART OF A
SELECTION OF SALADS
225g (8oz) long grain brown rice
575ml (1 pint) water
sea salt
4–6 tablespoons olive oil
1 large onion, peeled and chopped
225g (8oz) button mushrooms, washed and sliced
2 large garlic cloves, peeled and crushed
2 medium-sized red peppers, de-seeded and cut into
long slices about 6mm (¼in) wide
8 small, flat, open mushrooms, washed and stalks
removed
425g (15oz) can artichoke hearts, drained and
quartered
freshly ground black pepper
6 hardboiled eggs
3 tablespoons mayonnaise
3 tablespoons natural yoghurt
75g (3oz) flaked almonds, toasted
watercress

Put the rice into a medium-sized, heavy-based saucepan and add the water and a level teaspoon of sea salt. Bring to the boil, give the rice a quick stir, then cover the saucepan, turn the heat right down and leave the rice to cook very gently for 45 minutes. Then take the saucepan off the heat and leave to stand, still covered, for a further 15 minutes.

While this is happening, heat 2 tablespoons of the oil in a large saucepan and fry the onion for 5 minutes, until beginning to soften; then put in the mushrooms and garlic and cook for a further 20–25 minutes, stirring from time to time, until all the liquid has disappeared.

Heat the rest of the oil in another small saucepan or frying pan and fry the red pepper, for about 5 minutes, just to soften it a little. After you've fried the red pepper, remove it from the oil and quickly fry the eight flat mushrooms, adding a little extra oil if necessary. Drain on kitchen paper.

Oil a large (1.7 litre [3 pint]) ring mould and arrange the flat mushrooms and strips of red pepper alternately in the base. The mushrooms should be put in black-side down, and the red pepper strips should be placed so that they lie on the base of the mould and extend a bit up the sides – you won't need all the red pepper, so chop up what you don't use, also any mushrooms that are over.

Mix all the mushrooms, remaining red pepper and artichoke hearts with the cooked rice and season well. Spoon this rice mixture carefully into the ring mould, pressing it down well. Cover the ring mould with a piece of foil and chill until needed.

For the filling, chop the eggs into chunky pieces and mix them gently with the mayonnaise and yoghurt. To serve the dish, turn the rice mould out on to a large round serving dish. Quickly stir most of the almonds into the egg mayonnaise mixture and spoon this into the centre, heaping it up well. Sprinkle the rest of the almonds over the egg mixture and tuck a few sprigs of watercress round the sides of the ring.

An excellent variation is to use 450g (1 lb) small leeks, cut into 2.5cm (1in) pieces, cooked and drained, instead of the artichoke hearts.

RICE AND AVOCADO SALAD

SERVES 6
225g (8oz) natural long grain rice
575ml (1 pint) water
sea salt
1 garlic clove
3 tablespoons olive oil
1 tablespoon wine vinegar *or* cider vinegar
freshly ground black pepper
1 teaspoon sugar
2 large avocado pears
2 tablespoons lemon juice
450g (1 lb) tomatoes
1 tablespoon chopped parsley
slices of hardboiled egg

Put the rice into a saucepan with the water and a little salt; bring to the boil, then cover, turn heat down and leave to cook very gently for 40 minutes, until rice is tender and has absorbed all the water. While rice is still hot mix with the crushed garlic clove, oil and wine vinegar. Add salt, pepper and sugar. Cook, stirring from time to time. Meanwhile peel and stone avocados and slice flesh; toss in lemon juice; skin and slice tomatoes. Mix all lightly with rice and serve sprinkled with chopped parsley. This salad is good with a simple green salad and decorated with hardboiled egg slices.

MIXED ROOT SALAD

I think of this salad as a real wholefooder's salad: lots of chewing, lots of vitamins, lots of vitality! (I love it.)

SERVES 4
2 parsnips
1 turnip
2 carrots
1 small swede
1 raw beetroot
3 tablespoons mayonnaise
3 tablespoons french dressing
1 teaspoon parsley
juice of 1 orange
1 tablespoon sultanas
3 tablespoons natural yoghurt
sea salt
freshly ground black pepper
1 small onion
½ lettuce *or* 2 heads chicory
mustard and cress
tomato slices

Peel and grate root vegetables into separate bowls. Mix the parsnips with mayonnaise, the turnip with french dressing and parsley, the carrots with orange juice and sultanas, and the swede with yoghurt, salt and pepper. Slice the onion into thin rings. Arrange the lettuce or chicory on serving plates, spoon on piles of the root vegetables, garnish with slices of tomatoes and cress. A very useful salad for winter.

SALATA

Based on a Bulgarian salad, this is an interesting mixture.

SERVES 4
1 garlic clove
1 medium-sized mild onion
1 large green pepper
2 medium carrots
4 tomatoes
3 tablespoons olive oil
1 bay leaf
1 tablespoon wine vinegar
sea salt
freshly ground black pepper
2 bunches watercress

Crush the garlic; peel and slice onion; slice green pepper; scrape and coarsely grate carrots, slice tomatoes. Lightly fry in oil with a bay leaf for 5 minutes, then add wine vinegar. Chill and leave for at least 1 hour. Remove bay leaf and serve with watercress.

SERVE-YOURSELF-SALAD

This salad consists of lots of bowls of different ingredients, chosen to contrast as much as possible in colour, flavour and texture. When I serve it at home everyone makes their own selection, ending with a dollop of one of the low-fat creamy dressings. It's quite a labour-saving salad to make if you cook the wheat and beans in batches – I do a 500g (1.2lb) bag at a time, divide the beans into five boxes and store them in the freezer. It's goes well with jacket baked potatoes.

SERVES 4–6
75–125g (3–4oz) red kidney beans *or* 400g (14oz) can, drained
75–125g (3–4oz) whole grain wheat – from health shops
2 tablespoons olive oil
2 tablespoons red wine vinegar
sea salt
freshly ground black pepper
1 teaspoon tomato paste
a dash of honey
potato salad, made as described on page 100
1 small-medium lettuce, washed and shredded
3 carrots, peeled, grated and tossed in a little orange juice
2 raw beetroots, peeled, grated and tossed in a little orange juice
4 tomatoes, sliced
1 punnet of mustard and cress, cut and washed
½ cucumber, diced
white mayonnaise, page 72

Put the dried beans and wheat into separate bowls and soak them overnight in cold water. Next day drain and rinse the beans and wheat and cook them in plenty of water until tender: 1 hour for the beans (20 minutes in a pressure-cooker), 1¼ hours for the wheat (25 minutes in a pressure-cooker). Drain them both. Mix half the oil and vinegar with the beans and half with the wheat. Season both mixtures with salt and pepper and add a dash of tomato paste and just a very little honey to the beans. Leave to cool. Serve all the other ingredients separately in little bowls – soup bowls, or small wooden bowls if you have them, or put layers of the different ingredients in individual bowls, one for each person.

SOYA BEAN SALAD

Soya beans are so nutritious, being rich in iron and thiamine and containing useful amounts of calcium, that it's worth finding a number of different ways of serving them. Here they're mixed with carrots, parsley and spring onions to make a very nourishing salad.

SERVES 4 F
1 teaspoon Barbados molasses sugar
1 teaspoon dry mustard
sea salt
2 tablespoons wine *or* cider vinegar
3 tablespoons oil – olive or cold-pressed sunflower
450g (1 lb) cooked soya beans
3 large carrots, coarsely grated
small bunch spring onions, trimmed and chopped
2 heaped tablespoons chopped parsley

Put the sugar and mustard into a bowl with a little salt and mix to a paste with the vinegar. Then gradually add the oil. Stir in the soya beans, carrots, spring onions and parsley. Taste, and add a little more salt if necessary. A few drops of Shoyu soy sauce (from health shops) are nice in this, too. If you're freezing the salad, don't add the carrots, onions and parsley until just before serving.

COOKED SPINACH SALAD

I know some people find the idea of a salad made from cold cooked spinach off-putting, but I think the mixture of the soft, dark green spinach, the fruity olive oil and the sharp-tasting lemon juice is delicious. There are versions of this salad throughout the Middle East. Yoghurt can be included in the dressing or served with the salad, as in this recipe; cooked chick peas can be added, providing a pleasant contrast of colour and texture as well as protein. I also like it with a topping of slivered almonds fried golden and crisp in butter.

SERVES 4
1kg (2¼ lb) spinach
1 tablespoon lemon juice
3 tablespoons olive oil
sea salt
freshly ground black pepper
1 garlic clove
275ml (10 fl oz) natural yoghurt
fresh mint, parsley or chives: *or* 50g (2oz) slivered almonds fried in butter

Wash the spinach well then cook it in just the water clinging to it. When it's done drain it thoroughly and leave to cool. Chop the cold spinach and put it into a bowl with the lemon juice, olive oil, some salt and pepper and turn it gently so that the oil and lemon juice get well distributed.

Peel and crush the garlic then mix it with the yoghurt and add some salt and pepper. Put the spinach salad on to a flat plate and spoon some of the yoghurt mixture on top; garnish with chopped green herbs or fried almonds. Serve the rest of the yoghurt separately.

SPINACH SALAD WITH TOMATOES, MUSHROOMS AND LEEKS

Crisp raw spinach makes a good salad with a very refreshing flavour. Serve this as a side salad; it is especially good with rice and pasta dishes.

SERVES 4
450g (1 lb) fresh spinach
2 small leeks, washed and trimmed
125g (4oz) fresh white button mushrooms, washed
2 firm tomatoes
1 tablespoon wine vinegar
3 tablespoons olive oil
sea salt
freshly ground black pepper

Wash the spinach very well. Drain the spinach in a salad spinner or shaker, then shred it with a sharp knife: I generally include the stalks as well, but you can remove these if you prefer. Slice the leeks finely, discarding the green part; slice the mushrooms, and tomatoes. Put the vinegar and oil into a salad bowl with some salt and pepper; mix well, then add the spinach, mushrooms, tomatoes and leeks and turn them over so that they get coated in the dressing. Serve at once.

YELLOW AND GREEN SPLIT PEA SALAD WITH LEMON AND MINT

An attractive mixture of colours, this salad is best if you undercook the split peas a little so that they retain their shape and have a slightly chewy texture.

SERVES 4 F
125g (4oz) yellow split peas
125g (4oz) green split peas
½ teaspoon dry mustard
½ teaspoon sugar
grated rind and juice of 1 lemon
4 tablespoons olive oil
2 tablespoons chopped mint
sea salt
freshly ground black pepper

Cook the split peas in separate pans, in plenty of water, until just tender: 30–40 minutes. Drain well. Meanwhile put the mustard, sugar, lemon juice and oil into a large bowl and mix together. Add the split peas and mint, season to taste and mix gently. Cool, then transfer to a serving dish.

SWEETCORN SALAD WITH SPICY TOMATO DRESSING

With its spicy red dressing, this makes a pleasant side salad and is quick to make.

SERVES 6
450g (1 lb) fresh or frozen sweetcorn, off the cob
2 spring onions, chopped
2 tablespoons tomato ketchup
1 teaspoon paprika pepper
2 tablespoons olive oil
1 tablespoon wine vinegar
a pinch of chilli powder
2 tomatoes, peeled
sea salt
freshly ground black pepper

Cook the sweetcorn in unsalted boiling water until just tender (2–5 minutes), then drain, mix with the spring onion and leave on one side. Make the dressing by putting all the ingredients into a blender, with some salt and pepper to taste, and liquidizing until fairly smooth. Check seasoning and adjust as necessary. Pour this dressing over the sweetcorn and stir gently so that the sweetcorn all gets covered with it. Put the salad into a clean dish and serve.

Variation

SWEETCORN SALAD WITH RADISHES

Those huge radishes which you can buy these days make a pretty addition to this salad: use 2–3 big radishes, cut into dice.

TOFU, CARROT AND SULTANA SALAD

The tofu in this salad gives excellent protein, so it's really a main course salad. It's good with wholemeal bread and butter and a bowl of crisp lettuce or watercress.

SERVES 3
175g (6oz) tofu (see page 177)
2 large carrots
125g (4oz) sultanas
2 tablespoons orange juice
1 tablespoon olive oil
½ teaspoon sugar
½ teaspoon dry mustard
1 teaspoon soy sauce
sea salt
freshly ground black pepper
1 tablespoon chopped chives *or* spring onion greens

Cut the bean curd into small squares; scrape and coarsely grate the carrots. Wash the sultanas, put them into a small bowl and cover them with boiling water; leave them for 10–15 minutes to plump up, then drain them. Put the bean curd, grated carrot and sultanas into a bowl. In a small bowl beat together the orange juice, oil, sugar, mustard, soy sauce and some sea salt and freshly ground black pepper to taste. Pour this dressing over the carrot mixture and turn salad gently with a spoon until everything is coated with the dressing, but be careful not to break up the bean curd. Serve sprinkled with chopped chives or spring onion greens.

TOMATO SALAD

One of the joys of late summer is getting firm, fragrant, orange-red tomatoes and then using them extravagantly, as in this juicy salad which I like to serve with pasta dishes.

SERVES 4
700g (1½ lb) tomatoes
1 small onion
1 teaspoon red wine vinegar
1 tablespoon olive oil
sea salt
freshly ground black pepper
chopped fresh basil, if available

Wash the tomatoes and cut them into slices. Peel and finely slice the onion. Put the tomato and onion into a bowl and gently stir in the vinegar, oil and salt and pepper to taste. Sprinkle with chopped basil, if available. Serve as soon as possible.

TOMATOES AND BROAD BEANS IN BASIL DRESSING

This salad is best if you have time to pop the broad beans out of their skins, and the beautiful vivid green looks very pretty with the red tomato and chopped green basil. If you can't get fresh basil, use chopped chives or the tender part of spring onions.

SERVES 4–6
450g (1 lb) frozen broad beans
450g (1 lb) tomatoes
2 tablespoons olive oil
1 tablespoon wine vinegar
1 tablespoon fresh basil, chopped
sea salt
freshly ground black pepper
lettuce leaves

Cook the broad beans in a little fast-boiling water until just tender, then drain and cool. When the beans are cool enough to handle, pop off the grey outer skins. Peel and slice the tomatoes, removing any hard pieces from the centre. Put the oil, vinegar and basil into a bowl and mix together, then add the tomatoes, broad beans and some salt and pepper. Mix gently, so that everything gets coated with the oil and vinegar, then if possible leave for 2 hours for the beans to absorb the flavours. To serve, line a shallow bowl with a few lettuce leaves and spoon the bean mixture on top.

TOMATO, CHEESE AND OLIVE SALAD

If you serve this as a side salad with a plain pasta or rice dish it will supply the extra protein; accompanied by bread or rolls it also makes a delicious lunch, simple yet good. The type of cheese you use is up to you; the Brie or Camembert are delicious but I find a cheaper white cheese like Caerphilly is very good too.

SERVES 4 AS A SIDE SALAD, 2–3 FOR LUNCH
450g (1 lb) firm tomatoes
1 onion
8 black olives
2 tablespoons olive oil
1 tablespoon wine vinegar
sea salt
freshly ground black pepper
175g (6oz) soft white cheese such as Brie or Camembert *or* use Caerphilly

Wash the tomatoes and cut them into fairly thin slices; peel and finely slice the onion. Put them into a bowl with the olives, oil, vinegar and some salt and pepper and mix them lightly together. Just before you want to serve it cut up the cheese and add it to the salad. This looks good in a shallow glass bowl or white china dish. If possible don't make it more than about 30 minutes in advance or the juices will run and it could be a bit too wet.

STUFFED TOMATO SALAD

This refreshing stuffed tomato salad makes a good light salad after a substantial soup.

SERVES 6
6 good-sized tomatoes – about 450g (1 lb)
sea salt
2 eating apples
4 stalks of crisp, tender celery
1 tablespoon mayonnaise
1 tablespoon natural yoghurt
freshly ground black pepper
lettuce leaves

Halve the tomatoes round their middles and, using a teaspoon, scoop out the centres – you won't need them for this recipe. Sprinkle a little salt inside each tomato half and leave them upside down on a plate or in a colander to drain off any excess liquid.

Wash the apples and celery then cut them into small dice and add the mayonnaise, yoghurt and a little salt and pepper to taste. Arrange the tomatoes, right way up, on a base of lettuce. Spoon the celery and apple mixture into the tomato halves, piling it up attractively.

TOMATOES STUFFED WITH CANNELLINI BEANS, SPRING ONIONS AND MAYONNAISE

Serve this pretty dish with thinly sliced brown bread and butter as a refreshing starter, or make it the centrepiece of a cold lunch or supper, with crisp lettuce, cucumber and grated carrot. Use large tomatoes, but not the very big ones.

SERVES 2–4
4 good-sized tomatoes
sea salt
125g (4oz) cannellini beans, cooked and drained *or* use 400g (14oz) can cannellini beans, drained
2 tablespoons mayonnaise
2 tablespoons natural yoghurt
6 spring onions, chopped
freshly ground black pepper
4 crisp lettuce leaves

Slice tops off tomatoes and scoop out seeds. Sprinkle inside of tomatoes with salt and leave upside down to drain. Put beans into a bowl and add mayonnaise, yoghurt and spring onions. Mix gently; season to taste. Put a crisp lettuce leaf on each serving dish and stand a tomato on top. Spoon bean mixture into tomatoes.

Variations

TOMATOES STUFFED WITH CHICKPEAS

Use chick peas, drained, instead of cannellini beans. Some chopped basil or mint is good in this.

TOMATOES STUFFED WITH FLAGEOLET BEANS

Pale green flageolet beans make a pretty colour-contrast with the tomatoes. Use instead of the cannellini beans.

TOMATO STUFFED WITH CREAMY CHEESE

SERVES 4
4 large tomatoes
salt and pepper
225g (8oz) cottage *or* curd cheese
1 teaspoon chopped fresh basil
1 tablespoon chopped onion
dash tabasco
green salad leaves

Halve tomatoes, scoop out flesh. Sprinkle with salt; turn upside down to drain. Chop scooped-out tomato, mix with cheese, basil, onion, and a drop or two of tabasco, and salt and pepper. Pile back into tomato halves. Serve chilled on a bed of green salad.

TORTIGLIONI SALAD WITH AVOCADO

Pasta spirals with buttery avocado make a good first course or summer lunch.

SERVES 4–6
225g (8oz) tortiglioni
sea salt
2 tablespoons olive oil
1 tablespoon wine vinegar
freshly ground black pepper
2 avocado pears
2 tablespoons lemon juice
½ small red pepper, de-seeded and chopped
4 spring onions, chopped
crisp lettuce leaves

Cook pasta in plenty of boiling salted water until just tender; drain thoroughly. Put oil, vinegar and some salt and pepper into a large bowl, add pasta, turning it gently until well coated. Leave until cool. Halve avocados, remove skin and stones, dice flesh, sprinkle with lemon juice. Add avocado to pasta, together with red pepper and onions, mix gently. Serve spooned on to a base of crisp lettuce leaves.

VITALITY SALAD

SERVES 4
1 tablespoon wine *or* cider vinegar
3 tablespoons olive oil
125g (4oz) sprouted wheat grains
225g (8oz) sprouted mung beans
2 carrots, coarsely grated
50g (2oz) raisins
4 tomatoes, diced
2 sticks celery, sliced
10cm (4in) cucumber, diced
1 raw beetroot, grated
3 tablespoons natural yoghurt mixed with 1
tablespoon mayonnaise

Put vinegar and oil into a bowl and mix together. Then add wheat, mung beans, carrots, raisins, tomatoes, celery and cucumber and mix together. Divide between deep individual bowls, top with grated beetroot and a spoonful of yoghurt and mayonnaise topping.

WALDORF SALAD

Traditionally this salad consists of equal parts of diced celery and apple, bound together in mayonnaise and sprinkled with chopped walnuts. I like to make a lighter version, mixing the mayonnaise with natural yoghurt or soured cream. The salad goes well with cheese dishes and looks good served with some fresh green watercress.

SERVES 4
2 celery hearts, washed and diced
4 large ripe eating apples, diced
3 tablespoons natural yoghurt
3 tablespoons mayonnaise
sea salt
50g (2oz) shelled walnuts, roughly chopped
1 bunch watercress, washed and drained
a little paprika pepper – optional

Put the celery and apple into a bowl and add the yoghurt, mayonnaise and a little salt. Mix well. Spoon the mixture into a serving dish, scatter the walnuts on top and tuck the watercress around the edge. Sprinkle a little paprika on top for an extra touch of colour if liked.

5

VEGETABLES – FOR SERVING WITH MAIN COURSES

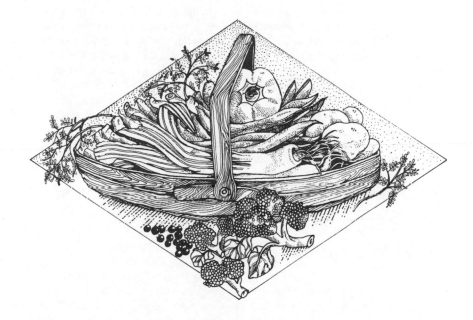

These vegetable dishes are for serving alongside the main course, rather than those which take the star-ring role, which will be found in the next chapter. Actually, sometimes the distinction between the two becomes a little blurred, because a dish like ratatou-ille, stewed red cabbage or that Italian pepper stew, peperonata, is technically an accompanying vegetable (and will be found in this section) and yet is fre-quently to be found, in our house, as a main course, with rice or jacket potatoes and a green salad. Likewise, of course, jacket potatoes themselves can form the basis of a main course and, again, are one of my favourite quick, simple every day meals.

The recipes which follow are in alphabetical order; but first, here's a brief guide to basic cooking and preparation of vegetables.

Basic Preparation

Choose small, tender vegetables which are bright and firm and look vital and full of life.

Allow 175g (6oz) vegetables per person (weighed before preparation), or 225g (8oz) where there is a lot of waste, as in leafy leeks and also spinach, and 450g (1 lb) for peas and beans in their pods.

Store vegetables in a cool place (the bottom of the fridge is ideal), and use them as soon as you can.

Cut away as little as possible when preparing the vegetables, but see that ones which will cook together are about the same size: cut larger ones if necessary.

Basic Cooking

The basic method of cooking, and the one which is suitable for nearly all vegetables is boiling (I have described other methods in the recipes and Alpha-betical Guide, pages 112–3, where they apply).

Boiling means plunging the prepared vegetables into lightly salted boiling water, letting them boil vigorously until just tender, then draining immediately.

It's important to make sure the water has reached

a rolling boil before adding the vegetables. The exception to this is root vegetables which can be started with either boiling or cold water. Root vegetables should be boiled in enough water to cover them, with a lid on the pan.

Other vegetables can either be cooked conservatively; that is, put into just enough boiling water to prevent them from boiling dry (about 1cm (½in) for 700–900g (1½–2 lb): this is how I do them; or plunged, briefly, into a large pan three-quarters full of boiling water, which is the chefs' method. The pan should be uncovered.

Whichever method you use, keep testing the vegetables by piercing them with a sharp pointed knife. The moment they feel tender but still a bit resistant, remove them from the heat immediately and drain thoroughly.

A variation of boiling is steaming. Here the vegetables are set above the water in a perforated steamer saucepan, metal colander or steaming basket so that they cook in the steam without touching the water. This is a good method for root vegetables and delicate ones such as asparagus. It's best for small quantities of vegetables because if you have too many they will not cook evenly.

An Alphabetical Guide to Preparing and Cooking Vegetables

Artichoke, globe Allow one per person; break off stem level with base. Snip off the points of the leaves. Wash artichokes well. Immerse artichokes in boiling water to cover (use an enamel or stainless steel saucepan) and boil for 30–45 minutes, until a leaf pulls off easily. Turn artichokes upside down to drain. Serve with melted butter.

Artichokes, Jerusalem Peel, then boil in an enamel or stainless steel pan for 20–40 minutes, until tender. Or cook in butter as descibed on page 114.

Asparagus Break off thick stalk ends; peel upwards to make base the same width as upper stem. Tie stems in a bundle, stand in 2 cm (1in) boiling water. Cover pan with a dome of foil if necessary. Boil for 8–12 minutes, until tender. Serve with melted butter or a creamy sauce.

Aubergines Slice or cube, with or without peeling. Sprinkle with salt and leave in a colander under a weight for 30 minutes, then rinse to remove bitter liquid. Squeeze dry, fry in oil for about 5 minutes until tender.

Beansprouts Wash, drain and stir-fry in 1–2 tablespoons oil for 1–2 minutes. Best included in a mixture of stir-fried vegetables as on page 143.

Beetroot Cut off the leaves, if still attached, 10cm (4in) above the beetroot. Do not peel or cut the beet or the colour will come out. Boil in water to cover, with a lid on the pan, for 1–3 hours. Slip off the skins, slice or cube the beetroot, re-heat in butter or a sauce (page 115).

Broad beans Prepare and cook tiny ones like French beans. Remove older beans from the pod, then boil in a large pan of unsalted boiling water for 5–10 minutes. Drain and serve with butter and chopped herbs.

Broccoli and calabrese Prepare stems as for asparagus. Boil for 5–7 minutes until just tender. Drain and serve with melted butter or a sauce.

Brussels sprouts Choose small firm ones. Trim off outer leaves and stalk ends. Cook really tiny ones whole; halve or quarter larger ones. Boil quickly until just tender: 2–5 minutes. Drain well.

Cabbage Trim off outer leaves, quarter cabbage, then shred, removing central core. Boil for 5–7 minutes; drain well, swirl with melted butter and grated black pepper.

Carrots Scrub tender carrots; scrape or peel older ones. Leave small carrots whole; halve, quarter, slice or dice larger ones. Boil in water to cover for 5–30 minutes until tender.

Cauliflower Break into florets, trim off tough stems. Boil for 3–5 minutes, drain very well. Or steam for 8–10 minutes. Serve plainly or tossed in butter or soured cream; or coat in batter, as for salsify fritters (page 41); or cover with cheese sauce, top with crumbs and bake until golden.

Celeriac Peel fairly thickly, cut into even sized chunks. Boil in a stainless steel or enamel pan for 30–40 minutes. Serve with butter or make into a purée (page 120).

Celery Choose small compact hearts and wash them well. Trim to about 15cm (6in), halve or quarter lengthwise. Or use outer stalks of celery only; trim and cut into even-sized lengths. Best braised, as on page 121.

Chicory Remove damaged leaves, trim base. Insert the point of a knife in the base and twist to remove a cone-shaped 'core'; this reduces bitterness and also ensures even cooking. Cook as described for artichokes (page 114), omitting the sauce.

Chinese cabbage, Chinese leaves Trim, shred finely and stir-fry as described on page 118.

Courgettes Top and tail finger-sized courgettes, slice, dice or coarsely grate older ones. Fry in butter; or boil until barely tender, drain well and serve with butter and herbs.

Cucumber Peel and cut into 1cm (½in) slices, cook as described on page 122.

Fennel Trim off stalk ends, base and any tough outer leaves. Boil and serve with butter or braise, as described for celery on page 121, omitting chestnuts.

French beans Top and tail; leave whole or cut large ones into shorter lengths, then boil for 2–10 minutes, depending on size.

Kale Remove stalks, pulling leaves away from stem. Boil for 5–7 minutes, drain well.

Kohlrabi Looks and sounds more exciting than it tastes. Prepare and cook as for swede.

Leeks Cut off roots and most of green part; slit down one side and rinse out grit. Leave whole, or slice. Cook as described for artichokes on page 114 or boil until tender: 1–2 minutes for sliced leeks, 8–10 minutes for thin whole leeks. Drain well.

Lettuce Prepare and cook firm, hearty lettuces as for chicory, but no need to 'core'.

Mange-tout peas Prepare as for French beans. Stir-fry or boil for 2–3 minutes: they should still be slightly crunchy.

Marrow Cut off stem, halve, peel and cut marrow into even-sized pieces. Remove seeds if tough. Cook as described for artichokes (page 114).

Mushrooms Peel wild mushrooms; wash but don't peel cultivated ones. Leave small ones whole, slice large ones. Trim stalks off flat open mushrooms. Fry in butter or oil until tender. If they give off a little liquid, increase heat and cook rapidly until it disappears; if they give off a lot, drain, reserving the liquid for stock, and start again. Flat mushrooms are good brushed with oil and grilled; baby mushrooms make good fritters: follow recipe on page 41, but no need to cook the mushrooms first.

Okra Top and tail; cook gently in oil for about 20 minutes. Good fried with onions, tomatoes and spices (page 124).

Onions Bake in skins at 200°C (400°F), gas mark 6, for about 1 hour, slit and serve with butter, salt and pepper. Or peel, cut into even-sized pieces and boil for 15–45 minutes; or fry in butter or oil for about 10 minutes. For crisp onion rings, dip raw onion rings in milk and flour then deep-fry for 1–2 minutes.

Parsnips Prepare as for swede. Mash with butter and serve or make into croquettes or bake with crumbs and butter until crisp; or roast in oil as for roast potatoes (page 130).

Peas Shell; boil for 5–10 minutes, or braise with lettuce (page 126).

Peppers Halve, remove stalk, core and seeds. Slice, fry in oil for about 15 minutes until softened. Or fill with stuffing and bake (page 159–62).

Potatoes Scrape or peel potatoes, or scrub and leave skins on. Boil in water to cover until tender and serve with butter and chopped herbs, or mash with butter and milk or cream until light and fluffy. Or cook slowly in butter as described for artichokes on page 114. To bake potatoes, see page 127. For chips, cut potatoes into slices, put one of these into a deep-frying pan one third full of fat. When it starts to sizzle add the rest and cook until golden; the longer they fry the crisper they will get. Drain and serve immediately.

Pumpkin Prepare as for marrow.

Red cabbage Prepare and cook as described on page 131.

Runner beans Top and tail; cut down the sides of beans to remove any tough strings. Cut beans into 2.5cm (1in) pieces or slice in a bean slicer. Boil for 5–10 minutes until just tender.

Salsify and scorzonera Scrape, keeping roots submerged. Cut into even-sized lengths, boil in water to cover in a stainless steel or enamel saucepan for 5–15 minutes, until tender. Serve with butter and herbs, in a creamy sauce or as fritters (page 41).

Spinach Wash very thoroughly. Remove stalks or keep them on, for added flavour and texture. Put spinach into a large saucepan with no extra water. As the spinach boils down, chop it with the end of a fish slice and turn it so that it cooks evenly. Drain and serve with butter, salt and black pepper.

Swede Peel thickly, cut into even-sized pieces, cover with water and boil for 15–20 minutes, until tender; or steam for 20 minutes. Mash with butter and seasoning. Delicious prepared like the parsnips on page 125 or the celeriac on page 120.

Sweet potatoes Scrub, cut into pieces and bake like potatoes, (page 127), or peel, boil and purée.

Sweetcorn Remove leaves and silky threads, trim off stalk. Immerse in large pan of boiling unsalted water, simmer for about 10 minutes, until yellow kernels are tender. Drain and serve with melted butter. To cook just the kernels, cut these from the husk then cook in boiling water for 2–5 minutes.

Swiss chard Strip leaves from stems and cook as for spinach. Cut stems into 10cm (4in) lengths, boil for 4–5 minutes, until just tender. Drain and serve with melted butter or a creamy sauce.

Tomatoes Remove stalks, cut a cross in the top of the tomatoes and bake at 180°C (350°F), gas mark 4, for 10–15 minutes. Or halve and fry on both sides; or halve, season, dot with butter and bake or grill for 10 minutes. Delicious stuffed (page 168–9).

Turnips Peel; leave baby turnips whole; halve or quarter larger ones. Boil for 5–10 minutes, drain well, return to pan and dry out over heat. Or steam 10–15 minutes. Serve with butter or as a purée, or diced and mixed with diced carrots.

ARTICHOKES IN FRESH TOMATO SAUCE

You can use canned tomatoes for this sauce, but it's worth using fresh ones if possible as they give the best flavour.

SERVES 4
30g (1oz) butter
1 tablespoon olive oil
450g (1 lb) tomatoes, skinned and chopped *or* 425g (15oz) can tomatoes
1 garlic clove, peeled and crushed
freshly ground black pepper
700g (1½ lb) Jerusalem artichokes
4 tablespoons water
sea salt

First make the sauce. Heat half butter with the oil in a medium-sized saucepan and add the tomatoes and garlic. Stir, then cook gently, uncovered, until reduced to a fairly thick purée: 30–40 minutes. Liquidize and season. Meanwhile peel the artichokes, and cut into even-sized chunks. Put into a heavy-based saucepan with the remaining butter, water, and some salt and cook over a very gentle heat until just tender: 20 minutes. Pour the sauce over the artichokes and serve.

STIR-FRIED BEANSPROUTS

Beansprouts are an absolute boon for a quick vegetable dish because you can cook them in the Chinese style in a matter of minutes, and they're crunchy, delicious and packed with vitamins.

SERVES 2–4
450g (1 lb) beansprouts
3 tablespoons olive oil
1 onion, peeled and very finely chopped
1 garlic clove, crushed
small piece of fresh ginger, to make about 2 teaspoons when peeled and grated
1 tablespoon sherry
1 tablespoon soy sauce
1 teaspoon sugar

Wash and drain the beansprouts. Heat the oil in a wok or large frying pan and fry the onion, garlic and ginger for 1 minute, stirring all the time. Then add the beansprouts and stir them for about 2 minutes, until they're well coated with the oil and flavourings. Mix in the sherry, soy sauce and sugar, reduce the heat and cook for a further 2–3 minutes, until everything is heated through. Serve at once.

TWO BEAN VEGETABLE DISH

I like the way the French serve dried beans with fresh green beans in such dishes as pistou and aïgroissade (see soup and salad sections). It's an idea that works well in a simple vegetable dish, too, and the contrasting shades of green make this mixture attractive to the eye, as well.

SERVES 4
175g (6oz) flageolet beans
450g (1 lb) French beans
25g (1oz) butter
1 tablespoon chopped fresh parsley
1 tablespoon chopped summer savory, if available, otherwise use other green herbs such as chives, tarragon or extra parsley.
sea salt
freshly ground black pepper

Soak, drain and rinse the flageolets, then cook them in fresh cold water until they're soft. Drain and keep them warm. Meanwhile top and tail the French beans and cut them into short lengths. Cook them in a little boiling, salted water until they're tender, then drain them and add them to the cooked flageolets, together with the butter. Check the seasoning, then add the fresh herbs just before serving.

BUTTER BEANS WITH APRICOTS, CINNAMON AND ALMONDS

An unusual sweet and sour mixture with a Middle Eastern flavour. Delicious as an accompaniment to curry or as a main dish with fluffy boiled rice and a green salad.

SERVES 2–3 AS A MAIN DISH, 4–6 AS A SIDE DISH [F]
1 onion, chopped
2 tablespoons olive oil
1½–2 teaspoons cinnamon
125g (4oz) butter beans, cooked and drained
125g (4oz) dried apricots, sliced
40g (1½oz) raisins
425ml (15 fl oz) water
25g (1oz) creamed coconut – from health shops
1 tablespoon lemon juice
sea salt
freshly ground black pepper
50g (2oz) toasted flaked almonds

Fry the onion in oil in a large saucepan for 10 minutes, then stir in the cinnamon and cook for a moment or two. Add beans, apricots, raisins and water, bring up to the boil, then turn heat down and leave to simmer, covered, for 15–20 minutes, until apricots are tender. Add coconut cream, lemon juice and seasoning. Sprinkle almonds on top before serving.

HARICOT BEANS WITH APPLES

This is an unlikely combination but it works well. The apples collapse, bathing the beans in a soft sweet-sour sauce and making this an ideal mixture for serving with a dish which would normally require an apple sauce. I like it also as a light main dish, with crisp German potato cakes (page 129) or the Swiss *rösti* (page 128).

SERVES 4
225g (8oz) haricot beans
450g (1 lb) cooking apples
25g (1oz) butter
2 tablespoons sugar
sea salt
freshly ground black pepper

Cover the beans with plenty of cold water and leave them to soak for several hours or overnight. Then drain off the water and rinse the beans under cold running water; put them into a large saucepan, cover them generously with cold water and simmer gently until they're tender – about 1 hour. Drain off the cooking liquor – it won't be needed for this recipe but as it's nutritious it's worth keeping for soups or sauces.

Peel, core and dice the apples. Melt the butter in a fairly large saucepan and fry the apples gently in it, without browning, until they're soft. Then add the beans and cook gently until they're heated through. Stir in the sugar and salt and pepper to taste.

RUNNER BEANS COOKED IN OIL WITH PAPRIKA

This is my attempt to re-create a bean dish which we ate in a little *taverna* in Greece. It was served to us just warm; it is also good chilled, as part of a salad. You can use other kinds of green beans besides runners.

SERVES 4
700g (1½ lb) runner beans
2 tablespoons olive oil
1 tablespoon paprika pepper
pinch of cayenne pepper
small garlic clove, peeled and crushed
150ml (5 fl oz) water
sea salt
freshly ground black pepper

Wash and top and tail the beans. Cut into diagonal slices. Heat the oil, paprika and cayenne pepper in a medium-sized saucepan, then stir in the beans and garlic. Pour in the water, bring up to the boil, cover, and leave over a gentle heat for 15 minutes. By this time the beans should be soft and there should be very little liquid left: if there is, bubble it away over a high heat. Check seasoning before serving.

HOT SPICED BEETROOT IN APPLE SAUCE

Beetroot makes a delicious cooked vegetable and can be very quick and easy if you buy ready-cooked beetroot (but not the kind that has been prepared in vinegar). In this recipe the beetroot is peeled, cubed and then gently heated in a lightly spiced apple sauce.

SERVES 4
450g (1 lb) cooking apples
2 tablespoons water
¼–½ teaspoon ground cloves
1–2 tablespoons sugar
450g (1 lb) cooked beetroot
sea salt

Peel, core and slice the apples; put into a medium-sized saucepan with the water and cook over a gentle heat, with a lid on the saucepan, for about 10 minutes, until soft and mushy. Mash with a spoon and mix in the ground cloves and just enough sugar to take off the sharpness. This can be all done ahead of time if convenient.

Skin the beetroot, then cut it into chunky pieces. Add these to the sauce, together with some salt, and re-heat gently.

Variation

HOT SPICED BEETROOT WITH APPLES AND CRANBERRIES

For this variation which is nice for serving with nut or lentil loaves, cook 125g (4oz) cranberries with the apples. You may need to add more sugar.

STIR-FRIED BROCCOLI WITH FRESH GINGER AND ALMONDS

This is an excellent way of preparing broccoli to make the most of its vivid green colour and crunchy texture. It's very quick to do and the ginger gives a pleasant tang; not hot, more like very aromatic lemon rind.

SERVES 4
700g (1½ lb) broccoli
piece of fresh ginger the size of a small walnut
2 tablespoons olive oil
sea salt
freshly ground black pepper
25g (1oz) flaked or slivered almonds

Wash the broccoli and cut off the thick stems – you can only use the tender part for this recipe as the cooking time is so short. Cut the broccoli into small pieces, slicing the stem pieces thinly and diagonally. Peel and finely grate the ginger. Just before you want to eat, heat the oil in a large saucepan or wok. Put in the broccoli, ginger and a little salt and pepper and stir-fry for 2–3 minutes, until the broccoli has heated through and softened a little. Sprinkle with the almonds and serve at once.

BRUSSELS SPROUTS WITH CHEESE

This is really a very simple way with Brussels sprouts but it's useful if you want to add a little extra protein to the meal. It's also good for a dinner party because it means you don't have to deal with the sprouts at the last minute.

SERVES 4
700g (1½ lb) Brussels sprouts
sea salt
a little butter
125–175g (4–6oz) finely grated Edam cheese
freshly ground black pepper

Set the oven to 160°C (325°F), gas mark 3. Wash and trim the sprouts. Leave them whole if they're tiny, otherwise halve or quarter them – that way they cook well and don't get soggy. Put 1cm (½in) water and a little salt into a saucepan and bring to the boil; add the sprouts, bring up to the boil again and cook for 2 minutes. Drain the sprouts immediately. Grease an oven-proof dish quite generously with butter and put in the sprouts; sprinkle the grated cheese over them and grind over a little pepper. Dot with a little more butter, cover with foil

or a lid and bake the sprouts in the oven for about 20 minutes until the cheese has melted and they're piping hot.

If you want to keep the sprouts warm for long I find they will stay nice and fresh-looking for quite a long time if you prepare them as above and put them in a lower oven – say 140–150°C (275–300°F), gas mark 1–2.

BRUSSELS SPROUTS WITH CHESTNUT AND WINE SAUCE

There's nothing new about the mixture of sprouts and chestnuts, but this is a different way of combining the two flavours: nutty small sprouts served with a smooth chestnut sauce. It's lovely at Christmas or for a special winter meal.

SERVES 4–6
15g (½oz) butter
1 tablespoon olive oil
1 large onion, peeled and chopped
1 small garlic clove, peeled and crushed
125g (4oz) canned chestnut purée
275ml (10 fl oz) stock *or* half stock and half red wine *or* dry cider
sea salt
freshly ground black pepper
700g (1½ lb) Brussels sprouts – small ones if possible.

First make the sauce. Heat the butter and oil in a medium-sized saucepan and fry the onion for 10 minutes until soft but not browned. Add the garlic, chestnut purée, stock or stock and wine or cider, and some salt and pepper and cook for a further few minutes, to give the flavours a chance to blend, then sieve or liquidize and adjust the seasoning with a little more stock or wine if necessary. Put the sauce back in the saucepan and keep it warm over a very low heat.

Wash and trim the sprouts. Leave them whole if they're tiny, otherwise halve or quarter them. Put 1cm (½in) water into a saucepan and bring to the boil; add the sprouts, bring up to the boil again and cook for 5–7 minutes – until they are just tender. Drain at once.

Put the sprouts into a warmed serving dish and pour a little of the sauce over them, but don't cover them completely. Serve the rest of the sauce separately.

FESTIVAL BRUSSELS SPROUTS

Here is a recipe to try if you dislike soggy, over-cooked Brussels sprouts. These could not be more different; they are stir-fried for the minimum of time, retaining all their flavour and crispness and making a cheerful vegetable mixture for a winter's day.

SERVES 4
700g (1½ lb) small, firm Brussels sprouts
175g (6oz) carrots
1 small red pepper, about 125g (4oz)
3 spring onions
1½ tablespoons olive oil
4–6 tablespoons water
sea salt
freshly ground black pepper

Wash, trim and slice the Brussels sprouts; scrape the carrots and cut into small dice; wash, de-seed and chop the red pepper; wash, trim and slice the onions. Just before you want to eat, heat the oil in a large saucepan or wok. Put in the vegetables and stir-fry for 3–4 minutes, until they have heated through and softened a little. Add the water, a little at a time, if the mixture shows signs of burning. Season with salt and pepper and serve immediately.

PURÉE OF BRUSSELS SPROUTS

A light, buttery purée is a good way of serving the larger Brussels sprouts, particularly towards the end of the season when they're cheap and plentiful but you're tired of them. For a less rich version you can use a little of the cooking liquid or some milk instead of some or all of the cream.

SERVES 4–6
700g (1½ lb) Brussels sprouts
15g (½oz) butter
150ml (5 fl oz) single cream
sea salt
freshly ground black pepper
nutmeg

Wash and trim the sprouts, then cook them in a little fast-boiling salted water for about 10 minutes, until they are tender. Drain the sprouts thoroughly, then pass the sprouts through a mouli-légumes or purée them in a food processor. Put the purée back into the saucepan and add the butter, then beat in enough cream to make a soft purée. Season with salt, freshly ground black pepper and grated nutmeg. Reheat gently.

BUTTERED CABBAGE WITH GARLIC AND CORIANDER

This is a simple way of cheering up ordinary cabbage: the garlic and coriander make it taste good enough for a special occasion.

SERVES 4
700–900g (1½–2 lb) firm cabbage, washed and shredded
sea salt
freshly ground black pepper
grated nutmeg
1–2 large garlic cloves, peeled and crushed
2 teaspoons coriander seeds, crushed
15g (½oz) butter

Put about 1cm (½in) water into a large saucepan, bring up to the boil, then add the cabbage. Let the cabbage simmer gently, with a lid on the saucepan, for about 7–10 minutes, until it is just tender. Drain the cabbage well in a colander, then put it back in the saucepan and add salt, freshly ground pepper and grated nutmeg to taste. Mix the crushed garlic, coriander and butter together, then add this to the cabbage, mixing it round well. Serve at once.

CABBAGE WITH SOURED CREAM

If you cook cabbage until it's just tender, then drain it well and stir in some soured cream you get a delicious mixture: simple, yet good enough for a special occasion.

SERVES 4
700–900g (1½–2 lb) firm cabbage, washed and shredded
sea salt
150ml (5 fl oz) soured cream
freshly ground black pepper
1 teaspoon caraway seeds – optional

Put about 2.5cm (1in) water into a large saucepan, together with a teaspoon of salt, bring up to the boil, then add the cabbage. Let the cabbage simmer gently, with a lid on the saucepan, for about 7–10 minutes, until it is just tender. Drain the cabbage well and stir in the soured cream, a good grinding of pepper and the caraway seeds if you're using them. Taste and add a little more salt if necessary. Reheat for a minute or two, just to warm through the cream, then serve.

CABBAGE WITH TURMERIC, CASHEW NUTS AND RAISINS

In this recipe, the cabbage is stir-fried with turmeric and the result is golden and spicy.

SERVES 4
700g (1½ lb) firm white cabbage
2 tablespoons olive oil
1 teaspoon turmeric
2 tablespoons desiccated coconut
15g (½oz) raisins
50g (2oz) broken cashew nuts
sea salt
freshly ground black pepper

Wash the cabbage and shred fairly finely, removing the coarse leaves and stems. Just before you want to eat the meal heat the oil and turmeric in a large saucepan or wok; put in the cabbage and stir-fry for 2½–3 minutes, until the cabbage has softened and reduced but is still crisp. Stir in the coconut, raisins and cashew nuts. Season to taste and serve immediately.

STIR-FRIED CHINESE CABBAGE WITH SPRING ONIONS

If you prepare the cabbage and spring onions in advance and keep them in a polythene bag in the fridge, this dish can be made very quickly, in about 5 minutes, just before the meal.

SERVES 4–6
1 Chinese cabbage, about 700–900g (1½–2 lb)
1 large bunch spring onions
2 tablespoons olive oil
1 tablespoon fresh parsley, chopped
sea salt
freshly ground black pepper
sugar

Wash the cabbage and shred it – not too finely. Wash, trim and chop the spring onions, keeping as much of the green part as seems reasonable. All this can be done in advance. Just before the meal, heat the oil in a fairly large saucepan and add the cabbage and spring onions. Turn them in the oil, over a fairly high heat for about 3 minutes, until the cabbage has softened just a little but is still crisp. Add the chopped parsley and some salt, pepper and perhaps a dash of sugar to taste. Serve at once.

CARROTS WITH APPLES

In this recipe, the soft slightly sharp cooking apples contrast well with the firm sweet carrots.

SERVES 4
700g (1½ lb) carrots
900g (2 lb) cooking apples
1 large onion
2 tablespoons olive oil
sea salt
freshly ground black pepper
sugar

Peel the carrots and cut them into even-sized pieces; cook them in a little boiling, salted water until they're nearly tender, then drain them, reserving the cooking liquid. While this is happening, peel and slice the apples and the onion. Add the apple to the cooked, drained carrot in the saucepan, together with 4 tablespoons of the reserved cooking liquid and cook over a gentle heat, with a lid on the saucepan, for 5–7 minutes, until the apple has reduced to a soft pulp. Meanwhile fry the onion in the oil until it's crisp and beginning to brown. Taste the carrot and apple mixture and add salt, pepper and sugar to taste.

Serve the carrot and apple with the fried onion poured over the top.

CARROTS COOKED IN BUTTER WITH LEMON AND PARSLEY

The tender young carrots of early summer are best for this recipe, but it also works well for older carrots, cut into matchsticks.

SERVES 4
700g (1½ lb) carrots, preferably small ones
15g (½oz) butter
150ml (5 fl oz) water
2–3 teaspoons sugar
a squeeze of lemon juice
sea salt
freshly ground black pepper
1 tablespoon chopped fresh parsley

Trim and scrape the carrots, halve or quarter larger ones. Put the butter, water, 2 teaspoons sugar and ½ teaspoon salt into a medium-sized saucepan and heat until the butter has melted, then add the carrots and bring up to the boil. Cover saucepan, reduce heat and leave for 25–30 minutes, until carrots are tender. Then take the lid off the saucepan, turn up the heat and let the liquid bubble away until there is hardly any left. Add lemon juice and salt, pepper and sugar to taste. Sprinkle with chopped parsley.

CARROTS IN COCONUT CREAM SAUCE WITH FRESH CORIANDER

In this recipe tender carrots are bathed in a golden sauce of coconut cream and turmeric and garnished with fresh green coriander. The flavour is spicy without being hot, making it an ideal accompaniment to curries and spiced rice dishes.

SERVES 4
700g (1½ lb) carrots, cut in rings
25g (1oz) coconut cream – from health shops
150ml (5 fl oz) water
1 teaspoon turmeric
sea salt
freshly ground black pepper
sugar
a squeeze of lemon juice
1 tablespoon chopped fresh coriander *or* parsley

Put the carrots into a medium-sized, heavy-based saucepan with the coconut cream, water and turmeric. Bring up to the boil, stir, then cover, reduce heat and leave for 10–15 minutes, until carrots are practically tender. Then turn up heat, boil uncovered, until almost all liquid has evaporated. Add sugar, lemon juice and seasoning and sprinkle with chopped coriander or parsley.

CARROT AND LEMON PURÉE

A vegetable purée is useful because it can take the place of both a cooked vegetable and a sauce or gravy. It also contrasts well with crisp dishes.

SERVES 4 [F]
450g (1 lb) carrots, scraped
225g (8oz) potatoes, peeled
7g (¼oz) butter
grated rind and juice of 1 lemon
sea salt
freshly ground black pepper

Cut the carrots and potatoes into even-sized pieces and cook them together in boiling water until tender. Drain, saving the water. Put the vegetables into the liquidizer with the butter and 150ml (5 fl oz) of the

reserved water and blend to a purée. Put the purée back into the saucepan and reheat. Just before serving add enough of the lemon to give a pleasant tang but don't let the mixture get too hot after this or it might taste slightly bitter. Season.

GOLDEN SPICED CAULIFLOWER

The cauliflower in this recipe comes out a pretty shade of gold, because of the turmeric, and it's lightly and delicately spiced.

SERVES 4
1 medium-sized cauliflower
2 tablespoons olive oil
2 teaspoons turmeric
4 cardamom pods
4 cloves
1 bay leaf
small piece cinnamon stick
1 garlic clove, peeled and crushed
sea salt
freshly ground black pepper
150ml (5 fl oz) water

Trim cauliflower and divide into florets. Heat the oil in a medium-sized saucepan and fry the spices and bay leaf for 1–2 minutes, stirring. Add cauliflower, garlic, seasoning and water. Bring up to the boil, then simmer gently, uncovered and stirring often, for 5–7 minutes, until cauliflower is just tender and most of the liquid absorbed. Check seasoning, remove bay leaf, cinnamon and cardamom, then serve.

CAULIFLOWER IN SOURED CREAM AND TARRAGON SAUCE

SERVES 4
1 medium-sized firm white cauliflower
sea salt
15g (½oz) butter
2 rounded teaspoons flour
150ml (5 fl oz) water
150ml (5 fl oz) carton soured cream
1 tablespoon chopped fresh tarragon
freshly ground black pepper

Trim cauliflower and divide into florets. Cook in 1cm (½in) boiling salted water until *just* tender when pierced with the point of a sharp knife. Drain well.

Meanwhile make the sauce. Melt the butter in a small saucepan and add the flour. Stir over a gentle heat until the flour bubbles, then add the water and stir until thick. Cook gently for 5 minutes, then remove from heat; mix in the soured cream, tarragon and seasoning to taste, and reheat. Serve the cauliflower with the sauce spooned over the top.

CAULIFLOWER IN TOMATO SAUCE

This is an easy and attractive way of cooking cauliflower and the sauce means that you don't have to serve a gravy as well.

SERVES 4
1 onion, peeled and chopped
2 tablespoons olive oil
1 garlic clove, peeled and crushed
400g (4oz) can tomatoes
275ml (10 fl oz) water
sea salt
freshly ground black pepper
1 medium cauliflower, washed and broken into florets
fresh parsley if available

Cook the onion gently in the oil for 10 minutes until it's soft but not browned, then put it into the liquidizer with the garlic, tomatoes and water and blend to a purée. Put this purée into a fairly large saucepan and add some salt and pepper. Bring the mixture up to the boil then put in the cauliflower and simmer gently, with a lid on the saucepan, for 10–15 minutes, until the cauliflower is just tender. You can take the cauliflower out of the saucepan using a perforated spoon and serve the sauce separately, but I usually serve them together with a little chopped parsley sprinkled over the top.

CELERIAC PURÉE

A purée of celeriac is useful for serving instead of a sauce with dishes which need something moist to go with them. You can make this mixture rich and creamy for serving with a fairly plain main dish; or just mash the vegetables with some of their cooking water and add plenty of butter and freshly ground black pepper.

SERVES 4 [F]
450g (1 lb) celeriac
225g (8oz) potatoes
15g (½oz) butter
up to 150ml (5 fl oz) single cream or milk – optional
sea salt
freshly ground black pepper

Peel the celeriac and potatoes, cut them into even-sized pieces and boil them in water to cover until tender. Drain thoroughly, keeping the water. Mash with a potato masher, electric hand whisk or in a food processor. Put the mixture back into the saucepan set over a low heat. Add the butter and gradually beat in enough cream, milk or reserved cooking water to make a light fluffy mixture, softer than mashed potatoes. Season with plenty of salt and freshly ground black pepper.

CELERY ALMANDINE

A lovely recipe for a special occasion. Choose small, hearty celery.

SERVES 4–6
2 celery, chopped into bite-sized pieces
sea salt
freshly ground black pepper
50g (2oz) butter
2 tablespoons chopped onion
a little flour
275ml (10 fl oz) single cream
a dash of stock
225g (8oz) toasted flaked almonds

Cook celery, seasoning, lump of butter and onion over a low flame for 20 minutes or so in a covered pan. Shake every so often. Sprinkle with flour, add cream and a dash of liquid if it's a bit too thick. Stir in almonds.

BRAISED CELERY WITH CHESTNUTS

The little celery hearts which you can sometimes buy now are ideal for this recipe, though you could use a normal-size head of celery. In this case 2 heads would be enough, sliced down into quarters.

SERVES 4
4 celery hearts
15g (½oz) butter
1 small onion, peeled and sliced
½ bay leaf
283g (10oz) can whole chestnuts in water *or* 125g (4oz) fresh cooked chestnuts
sea salt
freshly ground black pepper
a little chopped parsley

Set oven to 180°C (350°F), gas mark 4. Wash and trim celery hearts, and slice each in half lengthwise. Melt the butter in a flameproof casserole and add the onion, celery and bay leaf. Drain chestnuts, reserving liquid. If necessary make up to 125ml (4 fl oz) with water or stock; add to the celery, with the chestnuts and seasoning. Bring to the boil, cover and bake for 1–1¼ hours, until celery is tender. Sprinkle with chopped parsley.

CHICK PEAS IN TOMATO SAUCE

This spicy chick pea mixture is also good served with buttered pasta.

SERVES 4
225g (8oz) chick peas *or* 2 × 400g (14oz) cans chick peas
1 small onion
15g (½oz) butter
1 garlic clove, crushed
125g (4oz) button mushrooms, washed and sliced
450g (1 lb) skinned tomatoes *or* 400g (14oz) can tomatoes
1 bay leaf
sea salt
freshly ground black pepper
¼–½ teaspoon chilli powder
a little sugar

Soak and cook the dried chick peas as usual, then drain. Drain canned chick peas. Leave on one side while you make the sauce.

Peel and chop the onion and fry it gently in the butter in a medium-sized saucepan for 5 minutes; don't let it brown. Then stir in the garlic and mushrooms and fry for a further 5 minutes. Add the tomatoes and bay leaf and let the mixture cook over a moderate heat for 10–15 minutes, until most of the liquid has boiled away, leaving a nice thick sauce. Season with sea salt, freshly ground black pepper and chilli powder, also a dash of sugar if you think it needs it. Then mix in the chick peas and cook for a further few minutes to heat them through. Check seasoning before serving.

Variation

HARICOT BEANS IN TOMATO SAUCE WITH BASIL

Make as above, using haricot beans and 1 tablespoon olive oil instead of chick peas and butter and omitting mushrooms, bay leaf and chilli powder. Flavour with 1 teaspoon dried basil, or 1 tablespoon fresh chopped basil, for a variation with a Provençal flavour. Serve with hot buttered pasta and a green salad.

COURGETTES WITH FRESH HERBS

This is a good way to serve courgettes early in the season when they're young and tender and you want to make the most of their delicate flavour.

SERVES 4–6
700g (1½ lb) young courgettes
sea salt
25g (1oz) butter
1 tablespoon finely chopped fresh parsley
1 tablespoon finely chopped fresh chives
freshly ground black pepper

Wash the courgettes and trim the ends. Cut the courgettes into 6mm (¼in) slices then cook them in 1cm (½in) boiling salted water for 5–7 minutes, until they're just tender but not soggy. Drain the courgettes well and add the butter, parsley, chives, pepper and a little more salt to taste if necessary.

COURGETTES WITH PARMESAN CHEESE

An interesting mixture of flavours.

SERVES 4
8 courgettes
butter
1 garlic clove, crushed
finely chopped parsley
sea salt
freshly ground black pepper
grated Parmesan cheese
2 tablespoons chopped walnuts

Cut the courgettes in half lengthwise. Dot each face with butter, garlic and parsley, salt and pepper, a layer of cheese and chopped walnuts. Grill for a couple of minutes or so. The top should cook, while the courgettes stay crisp and half-raw.

BRAISED CUCUMBER WITH WALNUTS

People are sometimes surprised at the idea of cooking cucumber, but it's delicious, tender and palest green, with a delicate flavour.

SERVES 6
2 large cucumbers
sea salt
25g (1oz) butter
275ml (10 fl oz) water
1 tablespoon lemon juice
1 bay leaf
6 peppercorns
25g (1oz) walnut pieces, coarsely chopped

Peel the cucumbers, cut them into 5cm (2in) chunks, then cut each chunk down into quarters. Put the chunks into a colander, sprinkle with salt and leave under a weight for about 30 minutes to draw out the excess liquid. Drain. Melt the butter in a fairly large saucepan, then put in the cucumber chunks, water and lemon juice, bay leaf and peppercorns. Bring up to the boil, then leave to simmer for 10–15 minutes, until the cucumber is tender and looks translucent and most of the liquid has evaporated, leaving the cucumber glistening in just a little buttery stock – if there is more than two or three tablespoons of liquid, turn up the heat and let it bubble away. Put the cucumber and the liquid into a warmed, shallow casserole or serving dish and sprinkle with the chopped walnuts.

FENNEL BAKED WITH CHEESE

Fennel is widely available now, and it makes an interesting vegetable dish. It's very nice steamed and served simply with just a little butter and black pepper or you can boil it then bake it with cheese, as in this recipe, which gives a tasty golden result.

SERVES 4–6
2 large bulbs of fennel – about 700g (1½ lb) together
275ml (10 fl oz) water
sea salt
25g (1oz) butter
freshly ground black pepper
50g (2oz) grated cheese

Set the oven to 200°C (400°F), gas mark 6. Trim the fennel and slice the bulbs into quarters or eighths. Put the water and a little salt into a saucepan: bring to the boil then put in the fennel and simmer for 20–30 minutes until the fennel is tender. Take the fennel out of the saucepan with a draining spoon and put it into a shallow greased dish. While you're doing this let the water in which the fennel was cooked boil away vigorously until it has reduced to just a couple of tablespoons or so of well-flavoured liquid. Pour this liquid over the fennel, then dot with the butter, grind some pepper over the top and finally sprinkle with the grated cheese. Bake the fennel, uncovered, for 20–30 minutes, until it's heated through and golden brown on top.

The cheese in this dish adds protein of course and so makes it useful for serving when you want to increase the food value of a meal – you could use more cheese if you want to – 125g (4oz) or even 175g (6oz).

FENNEL WITH EGG SAUCE

I think this creamy egg and nutmeg sauce goes perfectly with the slightly liquorice flavour of fennel. This makes an excellent accompanying vegetable, but it also makes a very good course on its own, perhaps served in little individual ovenproof dishes.

SERVES 4–6
3 large bulbs of fennel – about 700g (1½ lb) altogether
275ml (10 fl oz) water
sea salt
1 hardboiled egg, finely chopped
2 tablespoons soured cream *or fromage blanc*
freshly ground black pepper
grated nutmeg

Trim the fennel and slice the bulbs into quarters or eighths. Put the water and a little salt into a saucepan; bring to the boil then put in the fennel and simmer for 20–30 minutes, until the fennel feels tender when pierced with the point of a sharp knife. Remove the fennel with a draining spoon, put it into a shallow, heatproof casserole dish and keep it warm. Let the water in which the fennel was cooked boil rapidly until it has reduced to just a couple of tablespoonfuls. Then take the saucepan off the heat and stir in the chopped hardboiled egg, soured cream or *fromage blanc* and add salt, pepper and grated nutmeg to taste. Spoon this sauce over the fennel and serve as soon as possible. Large, sweet onions are also very good done like this.

PURÉE OF FLAGEOLETS

A pretty pale green purée, delicate in flavour and in colour. Good served as a base for stuffed tomatoes or with jacket potatoes and a tomato salad for a light meal.

SERVES 4 [F]
225g (8oz) flageolet beans
1 small onion, peeled and chopped
25g (1oz) butter
4–6 tablespoons single cream
sea salt
freshly ground black pepper
grated nutmeg
1 tablespoon finely chopped parsley

Soak and rinse the beans, then cover them with fresh cold water and simmer them gently until tender. Drain, reserving cooking liquid.

While the beans are cooking, fry the onion gently in the butter until it is soft but not browned – about 10 minutes.

Put the beans into the liquidizer with the single cream, onion mixture, and enough of the reserved cooking liquor (if necessary) to make a smooth purée. Alternatively, pass the beans through a vegetable mill, then mix with cream and a little cooking liquor. Season with sea salt, freshly ground black pepper and grated nutmeg. Reheat gently (don't let the mixture boil) and serve garnished with chopped parsley.

LEEKS COOKED WITH TOMATOES AND CORIANDER SEEDS

This mixture of leeks and tomatoes, flavoured with aromatic coriander seeds, is really delicious, and it's good cold, as a starter, as well as hot.

SERVES 4
900g (2 lb) leeks
2 tablespoons olive oil
1 garlic clove, crushed
450g (1 lb) tomatoes, skinned and chopped
2–3 teaspoons whole coriander seeds, coarsely crushed
sea salt
freshly ground black pepper

Trim the roots and most of the leafy green tops off the leeks, then slit the leeks down one side and wash carefully under cold water. Cut into 2cm (1in) pieces. Heat the oil in a medium-sized saucepan and put in the garlic, tomatoes, leeks, coriander, half a teaspoon of salt and a grating of black pepper. Stir so that everything is well mixed, then leave to cook gently, without a lid, for 20–30 minutes, until the leeks are very tender and the tomatoes have formed a sauce around them. Stir quite often during the cooking time. Check the seasoning before serving.

BUTTERED MANGE-TOUT PEAS WITH SUGAR AND MINT

For a simple vegetable dish, I think this is hard to beat. Mange-tout peas have such a lovely, delicate flavour and are easy to cook. Like ordinary shelled peas, I think they are enhanced with a little sugar and some chopped fresh mint.

SERVES 6
700g (1½ lb) mange-tout peas
15g (½oz) butter
½–1 teaspoon caster sugar
sea salt
freshly ground black pepper
1 tablespoon fresh mint, chopped

Top and tail the peas, pulling off any stringy bits from the sides. Put about 2.5cm (1in) water into a fairly large saucepan and bring to the boil. Put in the peas and let them cook gently for 2–4 minutes until they are just tender. Drain them, then put them back in the hot saucepan and add the butter, sugar, salt and pepper to taste and the chopped mint. Mix gently, so that all the peas are coated with the butter and seasonings.

SPICY MARROW WITH GINGER

The idea for this recipe came to me when I was thinking of one of the traditional uses for marrow – marrow and ginger jam. Why not make a savoury version, I thought, which would make an interesting accompanying vegetable?

SERVES 4
1 medium-sized marrow, about 700–900g (1½–2 lb)
1 onion, peeled and chopped
2 tablespoons olive oil
1–2 teaspoons ground ginger
50g (2oz) crystallized *or* stem ginger, chopped
sea salt
freshly ground black pepper
chopped fresh coriander *or* parsley

Peel marrow, then cut into even-sized pieces about 2.5cm (1in) long and 6mm (¼in) thick: don't remove the seeds if tender. Fry the onion in oil in a medium-sized heavy based saucepan for 5 minutes. Add marrow and ground and chopped ginger. Cover and cook gently for 15–20 minutes, until marrow is nearly tender. Then take off the lid and let the mixture boil for 5–10 minutes until the liquid has evaporated. Season and sprinkle with chopped coriander or parsley.

MARROW IN TOMATO SAUCE WITH CORIANDER AND GREEN PEPPERCORNS

Here, marrow is cooked in a tomato sauce enlivened with onion, coriander seed and green peppercorns. The result is spicy and delicious.

SERVES 4
1 medium-sized marrow, about 700–900g (1½–2 lb)
1 onion, peeled and chopped
2 tablespoons olive oil
2 tablespoons tomato purée
2 teaspoons coriander seeds, coarsely crushed
1 teaspoon green peppercorns
sea salt
freshly ground black pepper
½–1 teaspoon sugar

Prepare marrow as in previous recipe. Fry the onion in the oil in a medium-sized saucepan for 5 minutes, then add the marrow, tomato purée, coriander, green peppercorns and seasoning. Stir, cover and leave over a gentle heat for 15–20 minutes, until the marrow is nearly tender. Then remove lid and boil for 5–10 minutes until the liquid has evaporated. Check seasoning, add sugar to taste.

MUSHROOMS IN SOURED CREAM

This is a simple but luxurious vegetable dish to go with a plainer main course or a special meal.

SERVES 2–3
1 medium onion
450g (1 lb) mushrooms – field ones if you have them, or else button ones
25g (1oz) butter
150ml (5 fl oz) carton soured cream
sea salt
freshly ground black pepper
fresh parsley

Peel and finely chop the onion; wash the mushrooms. If you're using wild mushrooms, remove the stalk and peel off the skin – this is not necessary with cultivated mushrooms. Cut the mushrooms into even-sized pieces. Melt the butter in a fairly large saucepan and fry the onion, without browning, for about 5 minutes, then add the prepared mushrooms and cook for a further 4–5 minutes until they are tender. If they make a lot of liquid boil them vigorously for a minute or two without a lid on the saucepan to evaporate it. Then stir in the soured cream and salt and pepper and heat through gently. Spoon at once into a warmed dish or individual containers and sprinkle with chopped parsley.

SPICY OKRA

Okra is an intriguing vegetable, a plump green pod which has a soft, glutinous texture and delicate flavour when it's cooked. Prepared like this it's nice as an accompaniment to curries or Caribbean rice dishes.

SERVES 4
225g (8oz) okra
1 medium onion, peeled and chopped
25g (1oz) butter
225g (8oz) can tomatoes
1 garlic clove, peeled and crushed
2 teaspoons ground coriander
3 teaspoons garam masala
sea salt
freshly ground black pepper
2 teaspoons lemon juice

Top and tail the okra. Fry the onion in the butter for about 10 minutes until it's soft and golden, then add the tomatoes, garlic, coriander, garam masala and a little salt – not too much if you're using canned okra. Bring to the boil then put in the okra and let it simmer gently for 15–20 minutes (until it's tender) if it's fresh, or about 5 minutes for canned. Check the seasoning and add more salt if necessary and a little lemon juice to taste.

BABY ONIONS IN A CREAM AND NUTMEG SAUCE

This is a special occasion creamy vegetable dish, delicately flavoured with nutmeg. If you can find baby onions, usually sold as 'pickling onions', they're ideal for this recipe, and worth the effort of peeling them. But you can also make it with larger onions cut into quarters or eighths. You could use thick natural yoghurt instead of the soured cream.

SERVES 4
700g (1½ lb) baby onions
sea salt
150ml (5 fl oz) carton soured cream
freshly ground black pepper
freshly grated nutmeg

Peel the onions using a sharp, pointed knife, leaving them whole if they're tiny, or cutting them into smaller sections if larger. Bring 2cm (1in) lightly salted water to the boil in a fairly large saucepan; add the onions, cover with a lid and boil for 7–10 minutes until the onions feel just tender when pierced with a sharp knife. Drain well, then put the onions back into the saucepan and stir in the soured cream and some salt, pepper and nutmeg to taste. Heat gently for a minute or two, stirring all the time, but don't let the mixture get too near boiling point or the cream may separate. Serve at once.

CREAMED ONIONS AND PEAS

An American friend gave me the recipe for this creamy vegetable dish which she serves her family at Thanksgiving.

SERVES 6
350g (12oz) baby onions – the type sold for pickling
sea salt
450g (1 lb) frozen peas
40g (1½oz) butter
40g (1½oz) flour
425ml (15 fl oz) milk
freshly ground black pepper
nutmeg
ground cloves

Peel the onions with a small sharp, pointed knife then boil them in a little salted water for 15–20 minutes until they're almost tender; drain them, reserving the liquid. De-frost the peas by putting them in a colander and rinsing them under hot water.

Melt the butter in a large saucepan and add the flour; cook for a minute or two then stir in the milk in three batches, over a high heat, stirring each time until the mixture is smooth before adding more. When all the milk has been incorporated and you have a smooth sauce taste it and season with salt, pepper, some grated nutmeg and a pinch of ground cloves. Carefully stir in the onions and peas and cook gently for 5 minutes to heat them through. Serve at once.

CURRIED PARSNIP CREAM

My original idea with this recipe was to cook and mash the parsnips then make them into a savoury bake. However they tasted so good when they'd been mashed with some curry powder and cream that I decided it would be a pity to do anything more to them!

SERVES 4
700g (1½ lb) parsnips
1 onion, peeled and chopped
15g (½oz) butter
2 teaspoons mild curry powder
150ml (5 fl oz) cream or top-of-the-milk
salt
freshly ground pepper
a few chopped walnuts

Peel the parsnips and cut them into even-sized chunks, removing any hard core. Put them into a saucepan with boiling water to cover and cook, with a lid on the saucepan, until the parsnips are tender: 15–20 minutes. Drain.

While the parsnips are cooking, fry the onion in the butter for 7–8 minutes, until nearly tender, then stir in the curry powder and cook for a further couple of minutes.

Mash the parsnips until smooth and creamy, then beat in the onion and curry mixture, the cream and salt and pepper to taste. Serve sprinkled with the chopped walnuts.

SUGAR-GLAZED PARSNIPS

This French way of cooking parsnips gently with butter, sugar and just a little liquid leaves them glistening in a buttery syrup which enhances their natural sweetness and makes a pleasant change. You can cook other root vegetables besides parsnips in this way: carrots, turnips and swedes are all good and so are sweet potatoes.

SERVES 4
700g (1½ lb) parsnips
175ml (6 fl oz) water *or* stock
25g (1oz) butter
1 tablespoon soft brown sugar
½ teaspoon sea salt
freshly ground black pepper

Peel the parsnips and cut them into small even-sized pieces, discarding the central 'core' if it is at all tough, though it should be all right if the parsnips are small. Put the parsnips into a heavy-based saucepan with the liquid, butter, sugar, salt and a grinding of black pepper, cover with a lid and simmer over a gentle heat for about 20 minutes until the pieces of parsnip are tender and the liquid reduced to a syrupy glaze.

PEAS COOKED WITH LETTUCE

This is my favourite way of cooking peas and a marvellous way of adding flavour to frozen peas.

SERVES 4
450g (1 lb) outside leaves of lettuce, such as Webb's
450g (1 lb) shelled weight of fresh or frozen peas
(this is about 1.5kg/3 lb peas weighed in the pod)
15g (½oz) butter
½ teaspoon sugar
sea salt
freshly ground black pepper

Wash the lettuce then shred it quite coarsely with a sharp knife. Put the lettuce into a heavy-based saucepan with the peas, butter, sugar and seasoning. Set the pan over a moderate heat and cook for 15–20 minutes, with the lid on the pan, until the peas are tender. Frozen peas only take about 7–10 minutes. Drain off any excess liquid which the lettuce has produced, and serve.

Variation

PURÉE OF PEAS AND LETTUCE

This mixture, liquidized, makes a good purée.

PEPERONATA

This Italian pepper stew is one of those useful dishes which can take the place of a vegetable dish and a sauce, adding moisture to a meal. It is also good with spaghetti or as a filling for pancakes, and cold, as part of a salad selection.

SERVES 4 F
3 tablespoons olive oil
1 large onion, peeled and chopped
700g (1½ lb) peppers, de-seeded and chopped: I like to use a mixture of red and green, and yellow too if available
1 garlic clove, peeled and crushed
3 tomatoes, skinned, seeded and chopped
sea salt
freshly ground black pepper

Heat the oil in a large saucepan and fry the onion for 5 minutes, until beginning to soften but not brown. Add the peppers and garlic and continue to fry for a further 10 minutes, then put in the tomatoes and leave the mixture to cook gently for 10–15 minutes, until all the vegetables are soft and the mixture is fairly thick. Stir often to prevent sticking. Check seasoning, then serve.

POTATOES ANNA

This is a useful potato dish which will cook slowly in the oven and won't spoil. It's rather like the creamy potato dish, *gratin dauphinoise*, except that it's turned out like a cake for serving. You don't have to add cheese, but I sometimes do because it improves the flavour and increases the protein content of the dish making it useful to serve with something like ratatouille, making a complete meal.

SERVES 4–6
15g (½oz) butter
700g (1½ lb) waxy potatoes such as Desirée
125–175g (4–6oz) grated cheese – optional
sea salt
freshly ground black pepper
fresh parsley

First line an 18cm (7in) cake tin by pressing a piece of foil into the base, extending it up the sides a little. Set the oven to 160°C (325°F), gas mark 3.

Melt the butter in a small saucepan, then use some of it to brush the inside of the foil-lined cake tin. Peel the potatoes, then slice them into thin rounds using a mandolin or the slicing edge of a grater. Put the rounds into a colander and rinse them thoroughly under cold water, then drain them and pat them dry with a clean cloth. Arrange a layer of potato in the base of the tin then sprinkle it with some of the grated cheese and a little salt and pepper; then add another layer of potato and continue in this way until it is all used up, ending with a generous layer of grated cheese. Pour the remaining butter over the top and cover with foil. Bake in the oven for about 2 hours, or until the potato can be pierced easily with the point of a knife. Pour off any excess butter, then slip a knife round the sides of the tin to loosen the potato. Invert the tin over a warmed plate and turn the potato out. Remove the foil. Sprinkle a little chopped parsley over the top of the potato.

POTATO AND ALMOND CROQUETTES

This mixture of creamy potato and crunchy almond is delicious and these crisp little croquettes make a good accompaniment to many dishes. They are useful for entertaining because they can be made in advance and then baked in the oven. They also make a light meal, served with a herby, green salad or tomato salad, in which case this quantity will be right for four.

SERVES 6 AS AN ACCOMPANIMENT, 4 AS A LIGHT MEAL [F]
700g (1½ lb) potatoes
25g (1oz) butter
about 4 tablespoons milk
25g (1oz) ground almonds
25g (1oz) flaked almonds
sea salt
freshly ground black pepper
extra ground almonds for coating
olive oil

Peel and boil the potatoes; when they're nearly done, set the oven to 200°C (400°F), gas mark 6. Mash the potatoes with the butter and enough milk to make a light but firm mixture. Add the ground and flaked almonds and season well with salt and pepper. Form into about twelve little sausages. Roll the potato croquettes in ground almonds, so that they are completely coated. Put the croquettes on an oiled baking sheet and bake for about 30 minutes, turning them after 15 minutes, until they are crisp and golden brown. Serve as soon as possible.

BAKED POTATOES

There are two ways of doing baked potatoes. You can rub the skins with fat or oil before you bake them, which makes the skin soft and flavoursome; or you can just wash them, prick them and bake them as they are (with the skins still wet), in a hot oven, and this way the skins will get lovely and crisp and crunchy. So you can use one method or the other depending on what people prefer and which goes best with the particular meal you're making.

SERVES 4
4 medium-sized unblemished potatoes – about 175g (6 oz) each
a little olive oil or butter if liked

Set the oven to 230°C (450°F), gas mark 8. Scrub the potatoes and cut out any blemishes if necessary. Make two or three small cuts or fork pricks on each potato to allow the steam to escape. Rub each potato in a little oil or butter if you're using this, then put them in a baking tin and place them in the oven. Bake the potatoes for 1–1¼ hours until they feel tender when squeezed slightly. Serve them at once, particularly if you want them crisp.

I find the skins get soft if you try to keep the potatoes waiting and it's no good reducing the oven heat – they have to remain at this high temperature to retain their crispness. If you're going to have to keep them waiting it's best to do the soft-skinned variety. These can be cooked at a lower temperature, too, if more convenient – anything from 160°C (325°F), gas mark 3 is all right but of course then they take longer to cook.

Baked potatoes can really make the basis of a simple meal. Of course, they're delicious split open and served with soured cream or grated cheese and a bowl of mixed salad, or you can make quite a festive meal by offering a choice of salads and several different toppings for the potatoes such as *hummus* and the soured cream dip or the goat cheese and herb spead, and bowls of different-coloured grated cheeses – a white one, such as Wensleydale, with for instance orange Leicester and golden Cheddar as well as cottage cheese.

NEW POTATOES BAKED IN BUTTER

This Norwegian way with new potatoes is easy, but it really seems to conserve their delicate flavour and the potatoes come out tender and buttery. In Norway they would probably be garnished with a sprinkling of chopped fresh dill, which is a very popular flavouring in Scandinavia, but chopped parsley or chives will do just as well.

SERVES 4
700g (1½ lb) baby new potatoes – try to choose ones that are all the same size, the smaller the better
40g (1½oz) butter
1 teaspoon sea salt
freshly ground black pepper
fresh dill, parsley *or* chives

Set the oven to 160°C (325°F), gas mark 3. Scrape the potatoes or just scrub them thoroughly and leave the skins on. Put them into an ovenproof casserole with the butter, salt and a little grinding of black pepper. Cover the casserole and place it in the oven for about 45 minutes, or until the potatoes are tender when pierced with a sharp knife. Serve the potatoes sprinkled with chopped herbs.

If you want to cook something else in the oven and need to have it hotter, I find the potatoes are all right if they're put near the bottom.

POTATOES BAKED IN CREAM

This is my version of the classic dish *gratin dauphinoise*. A favourite potato dish and one that's ideal for entertaining because it doesn't need last minute attention and will keep perfectly in a cool oven if the meal is delayed.

SERVES 4–6
40g (1½oz) butter
700g (1½ lb) firm-textured potatoes
275ml (10 fl oz) single cream
1 garlic clove, peeled and crushed
sea salt
freshly ground black pepper
a little freshly grated nutmeg – optional

Grease a shallow ovenproof dish generously with half the butter. Set oven to 160°C (325°F) gas mark 3. Peel and finely slice the potatoes. Rinse well and pat dry on kitchen paper. Mix the cream with the garlic. Arrange the potato slices in the prepared dish in layers and season with salt, pepper, and some grated nutmeg, if you like. Pour the cream and garlic mixture over them and dot with the rest of the

butter. Bake, uncovered, for 1½–2 hours, until the potatoes feel tender when pierced with the point of a knife.

BIRCHER POTATOES

In this recipe invented by Dr Bircher Benner (who also invented muesli), potatoes are scrubbed, cut in half and baked, cut-side down, on a greased baking tray. This means that the cut-side get crisp and golden, like roast potatoes, while the tops are like jacket-baked potatoes. This is a pleasant combination, and these potatoes are very popular with my children. They are also quick and easy to do, healthy and high in fibre. Leave out the caraway seeds if you don't like them.

SERVES 4
4 medium-sized potatoes
butter
sea salt
caraway seeds

Set the oven to 230°C (450°F), gas mark 8. Scrub the potatoes then cut each in half lengthwise. Grease a baking tray generously with butter. Place the potatoes, cut-side down, on the baking tray and sprinkle them with salt and caraway seeds. Bake for 40–50 minutes, until the tops of the potatoes feel soft when squeezed and the cut-sides are crisp and golden brown.

SWISS FRIED POTATO CAKE (RÖSTI)

This is made from grated potato. The cooked potato is formed into one large cake which fills the whole frying pan; it makes a good basis for a cooked supper. Protein can be introduced into the meal by serving a protein-rich side salad or by having something like yoghurt, cheese cake or biscuits and cheese for pudding.

SERVES 4
900g (2 lb) cooked potatoes
sea salt
4 tablespoons olive oil

Grate the potatoes coarsely – this is easiest to do if you chill them beforehand for a while in the fridge. Season them with salt. Heat half the oil in a large frying pan and put in all the potato, pressing it down gently with the back of a spoon. Fry the potato over a moderate heat until the underside is golden brown, then turn the cake over and cook the other side, adding the remaining oil if necessary. You may be able to turn the cake with a fish slice; alternatively you can turn it out on to a plate then tip it back into the frying pan again, crispy side uppermost. When the second side is cooked turn the potato cake out on to a hot plate and serve it in big chunky wedges.

You can vary the basic potato cake in a number of ways – it's nice with chopped herbs or spring onions added; sunflower seeds, sesame seeds and chopped hazel nuts are also good.

POTATOES WITH LEMON

Many dishes are enhanced by the taste of lemon, and one way of providing this is to flavour the accompanying potatoes with lemon. In this recipe, the potatoes are boiled until almost tender, then mixed with melted butter, lemon juice and grated rind and heated through in a fairly hot oven until they're sizzling and golden.

SERVES 6
700g (1½ lb) potatoes
25g (1oz) butter
grated rind of 1 small lemon
1 tablespoon lemon juice
sea salt
freshly ground black pepper

Set the oven to 200°C (400°F), gas mark 6. Peel the potatoes, cut them into fairly small even-sized chunks and cook them in boiling water for about 15 minutes until they are just tender – they should still have some 'bite', so don't let them get too soft. Spread the potatoes out in a shallow, ovenproof casserole dish, then dot them with the butter and sprinkle with the lemon rind and juice and some salt and pepper. Bake the potatoes for about 40 minutes, turning them several times, until they are golden. Serve at once, from the dish.

Variation

GARLIC POTATOES

This variation of lemon potatoes is also delicious. Prepare the potatoes as described, but leave out the lemon. Crush one or two large garlic cloves and mix this paste into the butter before dotting it over the potatoes. Turn the potatoes thoroughly two or three times during the cooking time to make sure that the garlic is well distributed.

POTATO PANCAKES

These crispy little German pancakes make a good quick supper dish or children's tea. It's typically German – and I think delicious – to serve them with a sharp-tasting apple or cranberry sauce or the haricot beans with apples (page 115), but children usually prefer them with tomato ketchup or baked beans!

SERVES 4
450g (1 lb) potatoes, scrubbed
1 onion, peeled
sea salt
freshly ground black pepper
2 eggs
3 tablespoons flour
olive oil for shallow-frying
cranberry *or* apple sauce

Grate the potatoes coarsely, peeled or unpeeled according to taste. Grate the onion. Mix potatoes and onion with salt and pepper, eggs and flour and stir to make a batter. Heat a little oil in a frying pan and fry tablespoons of the mixture until golden and crispy, turning them over so that both sides are cooked. Drain on kitchen paper and serve immediately with the sauce and a crunchy salad.

POTATO PURÉE

A purée of potatoes (or other vegetables) is useful for serving instead of a sauce with dishes which need something moist to go with them. You can make this mixture rich and creamy for serving with a fairly plain main dish; or just mash the potatoes with some of their cooking water and add plenty of butter and freshly ground black pepper.

SERVES 6
700g (1½ lb) potatoes
25g (1oz) butter
150ml (5 fl oz) single cream *or* milk – optional
sea salt
freshly ground black pepper

Peel the potatoes, cut them into even-sized pieces and boil them until tender. Drain the potato thoroughly, keeping the water. Pass the potatoes through a mouli-légumes or mash them by hand or in a food processor. Put the potatoes back into the saucepan set over a low heat. Add the butter and gradually beat in enough cream, milk or reserved cooking water to make a light, fluffy mixture, softer than mashed potatoes. Season with plenty of salt and freshly ground black pepper.

Variation

POTATO AND TURNIP PURÉE

Make this as above, using half potatoes and half turnips, or two thirds turnip to one of potatoes.

ROAST POTATOES

Crisp golden roast potatoes needn't be as fatty as many people think. I have carefully measured both the amount of oil I put into the tin and the amount left at the end and find that the difference is only 2 tablespoons if you do the potatoes this way.

SERVES 4
700g (1½ lb) potatoes
olive oil

Set the oven to 230°C (450°F), gas mark 8. Peel the potatoes and cut them in halves or quarters. Parboil them for 5 minutes. While the potatoes are boiling pour enough oil into a roasting tin to just cover the surface – don't make it deeper than 3mm (⅛in). Put the tin into the oven to heat.

The potatoes and the oil must both be hot. So drain the potatoes then take the tin out of the oven and put it on the hot plate or gas flame on top of your cooker while you tip the potatoes into the oil – stand back because there will be a sizzling and a spluttering. Turn the potatoes in the oil then quickly put the tin back into the oven and bake for 45–60 minutes, turning them after about 30 minutes. Drain well on kitchen paper and serve immediately.

PUMPKIN BAKED WITH BUTTER AND GARLIC

Pumpkins are a vegetable I find difficult to resist. I don't know whether it's something to do with the time of the year and the magic of Hallowe'en, or whether it's their glorious warm apricot colour and pretty rounded shape, but I always seem to end up buying one. This is my favourite way of cooking pumpkin as a vegetable (it's also good for marrow).

SERVES 4
700g (1½ lb) pumpkin *or* vegetable marrow, weighed after skin and seeds have been removed
1 large garlic clove *or* 2 small ones
sea salt
50g (2oz) butter
freshly ground black pepper

Set the oven to 180°C (350°F), gas mark 4. Cut the pumpkin or marrow into smallish, even-sized pieces. Peel the garlic and crush it into a paste with a little salt, then mix it with the butter. Use half this garlic butter to grease an ovenproof dish generously, then put in the pumpkin or marrow and top with the remaining butter and a good grinding of black pepper. Cover and bake in the oven for about 40 minutes or until the pumpkin or marrow is tender, stirring it once or twice during the cooking so that the butter gets to all the pieces.

PUMPKIN AND GARLIC PURÉE

'Is it custard?' asked one of my daughters, the first time I tried this. Used though my family are to trying strange mixtures, this was too much. I reassured them and they agreed to try this delicate mixture which is a cross between a purée and a sauce. (I did however make a mental note to try a sweet and spicy version sometime for serving with puddings.)

SERVES 4
700g (1½ lb) pumpkin
15g (½oz) butter
2 garlic cloves, peeled and crushed
sea salt
freshly ground black pepper

Peel the pumpkin and remove the seeds. Boil the pumpkin in a little water for about 10 minutes until tender. Drain very well, then return to the saucepan and mash with the butter, garlic and salt and pepper to taste. Alternatively put all these ingredients into the liquidizer and blend to a smooth cream. Check seasoning, then re-heat and serve.

RATATOUILLE

One of my favourite vegetable dishes, and a number of different versions have appeared in several of my books. This is one of the latest ones. In the late summer when courgettes, aubergines, peppers and tomatoes are cheap and plentiful, ratatouille makes the basis of delicious vegetarian meal. You can serve it with lots of plain fluffy brown rice and a crisp green salad with fresh herbs in it, with a protein starter like individual cheese soufflés or a pudding such as yoghurt or crisp wholemeal biscuits and Brie cheese. Ratatouille also makes an excellent filling for pancakes (page 276).

SERVES 6 [F]
2 large onions, peeled and chopped
450g (1 lb) red peppers, de-seeded and sliced
3 tablespoons olive oil
2–4 garlic cloves, peeled and crushed
450g (1 lb) courgettes *or* marrow, cut into small dice
450g (1 lb) aubergines, cut into small dice
700g (1½ lb) tomatoes, skinned and chopped
freshly ground black pepper
chopped parsley

Fry onions and peppers in the oil in a large saucepan for 5 minutes, without browning; add the garlic, courgettes or marrow, and aubergines; stir, then cover saucepan and cook for 20–25 minutes, until all the vegetables are tender. Add tomatoes and cook, uncovered, for a further 4–5 minutes, to heat the tomatoes through. Season and sprinkle with chopped parsley. I like to serve ratatouille as a main dish in the summer with buttered rice, pasta or new potatoes.

QUICK AND EASY RATATOUILLE

A labour-saving and economical version of the last recipe.

SERVES 4 [F]
2 large onions, peeled and chopped
2 tablespoons olive oil
1 large garlic clove, crushed
2 red peppers, de-seeded and chopped
450g (1 lb) courgettes, washed and sliced
400g (14oz) can tomatoes
sea salt
freshly ground black pepper
chopped parsley

Fry the onions gently in the oil in a large saucepan for 10 minutes without browning. Add the garlic, red peppers and courgettes and fry for a further 5 minutes, stirring often. Then stir in the tomatoes and some salt and pepper. Cook gently for 15 minutes, until vegetables are tender. Check seasoning, and serve sprinkled with lots of chopped parsley, if available. Alternatively, fork plenty of chopped parsley into the brown rice or other grains to give them a pretty green colour and add to the nourishment of the dish.

STEWED RED CABBAGE

This is a useful vegetable dish because you can more or less forget it while it cooks. It doesn't need any last minute attention; it turns out moist and juicy so you don't need gravy and it can also be reheated if necessary and still tastes good. It's a lovely warming dish for winter but it's also good cold, as a salad.

There are similar recipes for red cabbage in many other European countries and in Scandinavia. In France chestnuts are sometimes added and I've given a recipe for this delicious variation in the main course vegetables section of the book. In Russia the red cabbage might be served with soured cream which is a lovely addition and in Denmark red cabbage is part of the traditional Christmas feast.

SERVES 6 [F]
700g (1½ lb) red cabbage
2 large onions
2 large cooking apples
3 tablespoons olive oil
50g (2oz) raisins *or* sultanas
1 tablespoon sea salt
1 tablespoon brown sugar
1–2 tablespoons lemon juice
ground cinnamon, cloves *or* allspice to taste –
optional

Prepare the cabbage by shredding it fairly finely with a sharp knife, discarding the hard core. Put the cabbage into a large saucepan, cover it with cold water and bring it up to the boil then take it off the heat and turn it into a colander to drain.

Meanwhile peel and chop the onions and apples and fry them lightly in a large saucepan for 5–10 minutes. Add the cabbage together with the raisins or sultanas, salt, sugar, lemon juice and the spices (½ teaspoon of cinnamon or allspice, and a pinch of ground cloves) if you're using them. Stir well so that the cabbage gets coated with the oil and everything gets mixed together, then put a lid on the saucepan and leave the cabbage to cook very gently for 1½ hours, stirring from time to time, until it's very tender. Or you can put the cabbage into an oven-proof casserole, cover with a lid and bake it in the oven, at 160°C (325°F), gas mark 3, for about 2 hours.

Variation

RED CABBAGE WITH APPLES BAKED WITH CIDER

For this delicious variation add 275ml (10 fl oz) cider to the above mixture along with the sugar and lemon juice.

TURNIPS IN CARROT AND GINGER SAUCE

I devised this recipe without much enthusiasm one winter's day when I was working on one of my books and was extremely tired both of root vegetables and of cooking and couldn't think what to make. But as often happens when you just throw things together, it worked rather well: the orange sauce looks pretty over the white turnips and gives just the right touch of sweetness.

SERVES 4
700g (1½ lb) turnips
sea salt
1 small onion, peeled and chopped
2 teaspoons grated fresh ginger
1 tablespoon olive oil
225g (8oz) carrots, scraped and chopped
425ml (15 fl oz) water
freshly ground black pepper

Peel turnips, cut into even-sized chunks, boil in salted water until just tender and drain. Fry the onion, ginger and carrots in the oil for 5 minutes, then add the water and simmer for about 15 minutes, until carrots are tender. Liquidize and season. Serve turnips with the sauce poured over them.

ROOT VEGETABLES IN TURMERIC AND COCONUT SAUCE

This is a beautiful dish of orange and gold root vegetables, bathed in a creamy, delicately-flavoured sauce.

SERVES 6
425ml (15 fl oz) milk
125g (4oz) unsweetened desiccated coconut
225g (8oz) carrots
225g (8oz) swede
225g (8oz) parsnips
2 tablespoons olive oil
1 onion, peeled and chopped
1 garlic clove, peeled and crushed
1 teaspoon grated fresh ginger root
1 teaspoon turmeric
½ green pepper, de-seeded and sliced
sea salt
freshly ground black pepper

Heat the milk to boiling then pour it over the coconut, leaving it to infuse while you prepare the vegetables. Scrape the carrots, peel the swede and parsnips and cut them into even-sized chunky pieces. Heat the oil in a medium-sized saucepan and fry the onion for 7–10 minutes, then stir in the garlic, ginger and turmeric and cook for a further 2 minutes. Add the root vegetables, turning them with a spoon so that they all get coated with the spicy onion mixture, then strain the milk mixture over them, pressing the coconut against the sieve to extract as much flavour as possible (the coconut can now be discarded). Add the green pepper and some salt and pepper to taste, then put the saucepan over a low heat, cover and leave the vegetables to cook very gently for about 15–20 minutes, until they feel tender when pierced with the point of a knife.

CREAMED SPINACH

A Scandinavian recipe which people who don't normally like spinach might enjoy because the creamy sauce takes off the acidity and makes it less sharp-tasting. This is a useful dish for when you want to add protein to a meal; you could increase the protein content further by garnishing the creamy spinach with chopped hardboiled eggs, which is the Finnish way of serving it.

SERVES 4
450g (1 lb) spinach
25g (1oz) butter
25g (1oz) flour
275ml (10 fl oz) milk
sea salt
freshly ground black pepper
nutmeg

Wash the spinach very thoroughly: I find the easiest way to do this is to put it into a big bowl full of cold water and swish it round with my hands, then take it out and repeat the process twice with fresh water each time. Put the spinach into a large saucepan. If you have just washed it you won't need to put any water in the saucepan as the spinach will be wet enough not to burn. Cook the spinach over a moderate heat. Have a lid on the saucepan but keep pushing the spinach down into the saucepan with a fish slice, chopping it a bit as it gets softer. It will take about 10 minutes to get really tender. Drain the spinach very well – the easiest way is to turn it into a colander and press it with a spoon to squeeze out all the liquid.

While the spinach is cooking make a sauce. Melt the butter in a medium-sized saucepan and add the flour, cook for a minute or two without browning then add a third of the milk and stir over a high heat until the mixture is thick and smooth; repeat with the rest of the milk, adding it in two batches. When all the milk is in and the sauce is thick and smooth take it off the heat and season it with salt, pepper and some grated nutmeg.

Mix the sauce with the spinach and check the seasoning; you'll probably need to add some more. I think spinach needs plenty of pepper. Reheat the mixture gently, stirring all the time.

SPLIT GREEN PEAS WITH CREAM AND LEEKS

A substantial yet elegant vegetable dish: delicious with the garnish of fresh mint if you can get it.

SERVES 4
175g (6oz) split green peas
425ml (15 fl oz) water
25g (1oz) butter
sea salt
freshly ground black pepper
1kg (2¼ lb) leeks
4 tablespoons single cream
1–2 tablespoons chopped mint, if available

Put the peas into a saucepan with the water and simmer gently until very tender: 50–60 minutes. Liquidize, adding more water if necessary to make a soft consistency, like lightly whipped cream. Then add half the butter and season to taste. Meanwhile trim and wash the leeks and cut them into 2.5cm (1in) lengths. Cook leeks in a little boiling water until just tender; drain very well and add remaining butter and some seasoning. Spoon leeks into a warmed serving dish, pour the split green pea sauce on top, and the cream and chopped mint on top of that. Serve at once.

BAKED CREAMED SWEDES

This is a useful vegetable dish because you can get it ready in advance and just heat it through in the oven when you want it. The crunchy breadcrumb topping contrasts well with the soft creamy swede.

SERVES 4 [F]
900g (2 lb) swede
15g (½oz) butter
2 tablespoons creamy milk
sea salt
freshly ground black pepper
nutmeg
soft breadcrumbs
a little extra butter

Peel the swede and cut it into even-sized pieces. Put the pieces into a large saucepan, almost cover them with cold water and then cook gently, with a lid on the saucepan, until tender. Drain off all the water, then return the saucepan to the heat for a minute or two to dry the swede a little. Mash the swede until it's smooth, adding the butter, milk and seasoning and beating well. Lightly grease an ovenproof dish – a shallow one is best as it gives you plenty of crispy topping – and spoon the swede mixture into it, smoothing the surface.

Sprinkle the top fairly generously with soft breadcrumbs and dot with a few little pieces of butter. All this can be done in advance; before the meal bake the casserole in a moderate oven – 180°C (350°F), gas mark 4 – for about 40 minutes, until the inside is heated through and the top golden brown and crisp.

GLAZED SWEET POTATOES

Sweet potatoes look like ordinary rather large red-skinned potatoes and have a sweet, chestnutty flavour which I love. You can prick them and bake them in the oven like a jacket potato; par-boil and roast them as you would ordinary potatoes or glaze them as in this recipe, which was given to me by an American friend. Done like this they're good with Caribbean dishes and with the sort of dishes which you'd normally serve with redcurrant jelly or a sweet chutney. They're also very nice just on their own, with some crisp salad.

SERVES 4
700g (1½ lb) sweet potatoes – if they're very large the greengrocer may sell you a piece of potato
25g (1oz) butter
25g (1oz) brown sugar
2 tablespoons lemon juice
sea salt

Scrub the potatoes, cut them into even-sized pieces then put them in a saucepan, cover with water and boil gently until tender – about 15–20 minutes. Drain them and peel off the skins. Set the oven to 200°C (400°F), gas mark 6. Use half the butter to grease a shallow ovenproof dish generously; then arrange the potato pieces in the dish and sprinkle them with the sugar, lemon juice and a little salt, dot with the remaining butter and place them, uncovered, in the oven. Bake them for 40–50 minutes, until they're golden brown and glazed, turning them over once or twice during the cooking time.

SWEETCORN FRITTERS

Although these fritters are usually served as an accompaniment to meat they are quite filling and make a good supper or lunch dish, with tomato sauce, mashed potato and a green vegetable. They also make an interesting first course.

SERVES 3

350g (11½oz) can sweetcorn *or* 225g (8oz) frozen
sweetcorn kernels, cooked
1 egg, separated
25g (1oz) wholemeal flour
sea salt
freshly ground black pepper
olive oil for shallow-frying

Drain the sweetcorn, put it into a bowl with the egg yolk, flour and some salt and pepper and mix well. Whisk the egg white until it's standing in soft peaks, then gently fold it into the sweetcorn mixture. Heat a little oil in a frying pan and fry the sweetcorn mixture, a tablespoon at a time, on both sides, until crisp.

(Stand back as you do so because the corn tends to 'pop'.) As soon as they're ready drain the fritters on kitchen paper. Keep the first ones warm while you fry the remainder, then serve them straight away.

6

MAIN COURSE VEGETABLE AND NUT DISHES

There's something especially rewarding about taking a simple, seasonable vegetable, like red or white cabbage in the winter, aubergines or courgettes in the summer, and turning them into a main dish that's delicious and satisfying. In order to do this, some protein is usually introduced, in the form of cheese, eggs, milk, pulses or nuts. Even so, the dish generally works out very economical, though I'll admit that there are also recipes in this section which come into the 'special occasion' category.

I've included nut dishes in this chapter because they're so often combined with vegetables to turn them into main dishes; and, in their turn, the nut loaves and bakes often include vegetables, so the two categories seem to fit together naturally. Don't be put off using nuts because of the price. If you look at the recipes, and the number of people they serve, I do not think you'll find them extravagant. Nuts are concentrated, and so go a long way. They are also a rich source of nutrients, including iron and zinc. Make sure you buy really fresh nuts at a

shop which has a rapid turnover; buy in small quantities and store them carefully in an airtight container (but not for too long).

Here's a brief guide to the nuts used in the recipes:

Almonds Oval-shaped, with a ridged brown skin and well-known, distinctive flavour, almonds are useful in both sweet and savoury dishes. Grind them up and make them into nut roasts and rissoles or add them to muesli mix; or buy the flaked kind and sprinkle them over vegetable or rice mixtures, salads or trifles and fruity puddings. To remove the brown skins yourself, put the almonds into a small saucepan, cover with cold water, bring to the boil and simmer for 1 minute. Then drain. Pop the skins off the nuts using your finger and thumb. Flaked or blanched almonds can be toasted by stirring in a dry saucepan, under a grill, or as described for hazel nuts.

Brazil nuts Whitish-yellow in colour, flecked with brown, these large sausage-shaped nuts have a rich creamy flavour. They're good in nut roasts and chopped in salads.

Cashew nuts Creamy white and crescent-shaped, cashew nuts are available whole and, cheaper, in pieces. They have a pleasantly bland flavour which makes them useful in all kinds of sweet and savoury dishes. They're delicious roasted (see under hazel nuts) and also whizzed into creams.

Chestnuts These are different from the other nuts in that they are lower in oil and protein and higher in starch. They're a useful additon to stews, casseroles and savoury loaves. To prepare fresh chestnuts, nick the skins with a sharp knife, put chestnuts into a pan, cover with cold water, bring to the boil and simmer until the cuts open and the skins can be slipped off easily with a pointed knife (15–20 minutes). This is a tedious business, and I often use dried chestnuts which you can get at health shops. To use these, soak overnight, then simmer gently in water for 2–3 hours, until tender. Canned chestnut purée is also useful.

Hazel nuts It's getting more difficult to find these little round brown pointed nuts in their dark brown skins; the ones in the supermarkets are frequently sold already skinned. But for savoury recipes I prefer to use hazel nuts in their skins, and you can get these from health shops. Their flavour is enhanced by roasting. To do this, spread the hazel nuts out on a dry baking sheet and bake for 20–30 minutes in a moderate oven (190°C [375°F], gas mark 5), until the nuts under the skins are golden brown. When they have cooled the outer brown skins will rub off easily, but I generally leave them on.

Peanuts These little reddish-brown, egg-shaped nuts are familiar to most people. Buy the raw ones at the health shop and roast them in the same way as hazel nuts.

Pine nuts Sometimes called pine kernels, these are small, slim, creamy coloured nuts about 1cm (½in) long. They have a soft texture and a wonderful pine flavour. They can be roasted, as for flaked almonds, and sprinkled over vegetable, rice or fruit mixtures; they also make a superb nut roast. They're expensive but marvellous for a special occasion.

Walnuts Golden brown and with their familiar undulating shape, walnuts can be bought in halves or pieces. Their slightly bitter flavour adds intensity to savoury mixtures and they are also specially good in salads.

How to Grate Nuts

Grated nuts are often called for in vegetarian recipes. This can be done easily using a blender, electric coffee grinder or food processor; or in one of the little hand grinders, with a set of drums which grate with varying degrees of coarseness, that you can buy.

Freezing Nut and Vegetable Dishes

Most nut roasts and rissoles freeze excellently, either fully cooked or partially cooked. Vegetable stews and casseroles freeze well, too, though be careful about garlic and spices – these are better added after freezing. You'll find the freezer [F] symbol by the dishes which freeze well.

CRISPY ALMOND SLICES

One of my earliest inventions – the idea behind it was to make a protein-rich crunchy accompaniment for a creamy salad. The very finely grated onion – which should be almost liquid – is important as it helps hold the mixture together.

MAKES 12–15 [F]
125g (4oz) Weetabix
125g (4oz) ground almonds *or* other nuts, grated finely
125g (4oz) butter
125g (4oz) flaked almonds *or* chopped nuts
1 garlic clove, crushed
1 tablespoon very finely grated onion
½ teaspoon mixed herbs
sea salt
freshly ground black pepper

Set oven to 230°C (450°F), gas mark 8. Crumble Weetabix, mix with ground almonds or other ground nuts, and rub in butter as for pastry, until fine crumb stage is reached. Add flaked almonds, crushed garlic, onion, mixed herbs and seasoning. Press into buttered swiss roll tin, and bake for 15–17 minutes, until golden brown and crisp. Cut into triangles and serve hot or cold with creamy salads or hot vegetable mixtures to add protein and crisp texture to the meal.

ASPARAGUS AND ALMOND RING

This makes an attractive centrepiece for a dinner party; I created it for one of my earliest dinner parties when I was first married. These days I use a ring mould, lined with strips of non-stick paper and well-buttered.

SERVES 6

Almond Ring
1 medium onion, chopped
15g (½oz) butter
1 teaspoon mixed herbs
1 tablespoon plain flour
150ml (5 fl oz) milk
1 egg
sea salt
freshly ground black pepper
225g (8oz) grated almonds
125g (4oz) soft breadcrumbs

Asparagus stuffing
125g (4oz) button mushrooms
15g (½oz) butter
4 tomatoes
225g (8oz) fresh *or* frozen asparagus, cooked
sea salt
freshly ground black pepper
roasted almonds
parsley

Fry the onion in the butter until soft but not brown, about 10 minutes. Add mixed herbs and milk. Stir until thickened, then remove from heat and add beaten egg and the rest of the ingredients. Grease a large flat casserole dish or oven sheet, and place the almond mixture on it in the shape of a ring with a hole in the middle. Bake in a slow oven, 160°C (325°F), gas mark 3, for 1 hour. Alternatively, spoon mixture into ring mould, cover with tin foil and bake. Remove from oven and place on serving dish.

Next make the stuffing. Wash the mushrooms and cook gently in the butter for 5 minutes. Remove the skins from the tomatoes by immersing in boiling water for 1 minute and then plunging them into cold water. Cut the tomatoes into quarters and add to the mushrooms. Cut the asparagus into 2cm (1in) pieces, and add to the mushroom mixture. Keep over the heat until the tomatoes and asparagus have heated through, then season to taste.

Fill the centre of the almond ring with this asparagus mixture and garnish with roasted almonds and fresh parsley sprigs. The ring may be cooked in advance and simply filled with stuffing and heated through in a warm oven when required.

ASPARAGUS IN HOT LEMON MAYONNAISE

This is a delicious main course for the early summer when you want to make the most of the short asparagus season. The hot asparagus is coated with a lemon mayonnaise mixture, sprinkled with crumbs and heated through just enough to warm the sauce and make the crumbs go crisp. I think it's best served on it's own or just with buttered baby new potatoes, followed by a refreshing green salad before cheese or jewelled red fruit flan.

SERVES 4

1 kilo (2¼ lb) fresh *or* frozen asparagus
6 rounded tablespoons home-made *or* good quality bought mayonnaise
225g (8oz) *fromage blanc or* other smooth soft low-fat white cheese
lemon juice
Dijon mustard
sea salt
freshly ground black pepper
50g (2oz) fine wholemeal breadcrumbs
50g (2oz) cheese, grated

If you're using fresh asparagus, break off the hard stems at the base – these ends are too tough to eat but can be used to make a stock for asparagus soup. Wash the asparagus gently to remove any grit. The easiest way to cook asparagus (if, like me, you haven't got a proper asparagus steamer) is in an ordinary steamer; otherwise you can stand the asparagus up in a bunch in a saucepan containing about 1 cm (½in) water and arrange a piece of foil over the top to make a domed lid – this way the tougher ends of the stalks cook in the water and the delicate tops are steamed. Either way the asparagus will take about 10 minutes: it should be just tender. Frozen asparagus is best cooked in a steamer or in 2 cm (1 inch) boiling water, and takes 7–10 minutes.

While the asparagus is cooking, make the sauce by mixing together the mayonnaise and *fromage blanc*. Sharpen with a little lemon juice and mustard and season with salt and freshly ground black pepper. If the mixture seems a bit on the thick side, stir in a tablespoonful or two of the asparagus cooking water.

Set the oven to 200°C (400°F), gas mark 6. Put the asparagus into a large, shallow ovenproof dish and pour the sauce over the top. Cover completely with a thin layer of fine wholemeal crumbs and sprinkle with the cheese. Bake in the oven for about 30–40 minutes until heated through: the crumbs can be browned quickly under the grill after this if necessary – the dish should not be overcooked or the sauce may spoil.

CHILLED ASPARAGUS NUT LOAF

This loaf is nice served with yoghurt sauce or mayonnaise and yoghurt. It can be steamed by standing the tin in 2cm (1in) boiling water in a roasting tin, completely covered with a large piece of tin foil.

SERVES 10–12 $\boxed{\text{F}}$
225g (8oz) fresh *or* frozen asparagus cooked
1 small onion
15g (½oz) butter
1 bay leaf
6 peppercorns
1 tablespoon flour
about 150ml (5 fl oz) milk
225g (8oz) ground almonds
225g (8oz) soft white breadcrumbs
2 eggs
2 heaped tablespoons chopped parsley
grated nutmeg
sea salt
freshly ground black pepper
lettuce leaves
lemon slices

Drain asparagus, reserving liquid. Chop all but 4 best spears of asparagus; leave on one side. Peel and grate onion; cook gently in the butter with the bay leaf and peppercorns until tender but not browned. Remove bay leaf and peppercorns, add flour, then gradually pour in asparagus liquid made up to 275ml (10 fl oz) with milk, stirring until thickened. Remove from heat and add almonds, breadcrumbs, beaten eggs and chopped parsley. Season with nutmeg, salt and pepper, then lightly fold in chopped asparagus, being careful not to mash it. Line a 900g (2 lb) bread tin with a strip of non-stick paper and grease well with butter. Arrange best asparagus spears in bottom, then gently spoon in mixture. Cover with foil and steam for 2 hours. Allow loaf to cool before carefully turning out of tin. Decorate with crisp lettuce leaves and lemon slices.

This loaf can be glazed for special occasions. To do this, boil 275ml (10 fl oz) water with 1 bay leaf, 4 peppercorns, a piece of onion and some parsley sprigs. Let the mixture stand for 15 minutes, then strain mixture and bring it to the boil again. Sprinkle with 1 level teaspoon agar agar* whisking until dissolved. Mixture can then be brushed or spooned over the top of the loaf and left to set.

*vegetarian gelatine from health shops

Variations

CHILLED CELERY NUT LOAF

Replace asparagus with head of celery, very finely chopped. Garnish with red pepper or tomato slices and parsley.

CHILLED RED PEPPER NUT LOAF

De-seed, chop, and fry with the onion, one large red pepper. Season mixture with a few drops of tabasco or a pinch of chilli powder.

AUBERGINE BAKE

One of my favourite aubergine dishes, this is delicious with crusty bread or buttery brown rice and a salad.

SERVES 4 $\boxed{\text{F}}$
700g (1½ lb) aubergines
sea salt
flour
olive oil for shallow-frying
425g (15oz) can tomatoes
2 garlic cloves, peeled and crushed
175g (6oz) grated cheese
freshly ground black pepper

Cut aubergines into thin strips, sprinkle with salt and leave in a colander with a weight on top for 30 minutes. Then rinse aubergines and squeeze as dry as possible. Set the oven to 190°C (375°F) gas mark 5. Dip the aubergines in flour then shallow-fry them in the oil until crisp on both sides and soft in the middle. Drain on kitchen paper. Liquidize together the tomatoes and the garlic; season with salt and pepper. Layer the aubergine slices and cheese in a shallow ovenproof dish; pour the tomato mixture evenly on top. Bake uncovered, towards the top of the oven, for 50–60 minutes, until browned and bubbling.

AUBERGINES STUFFED WITH ALMONDS

No prizes for guessing that I like stuffed aubergines! The following recipes are all different, and I couldn't bring myself to leave any of them out.

SERVES 4 F

2 medium-sized aubergines
125g (4oz) flaked almonds, pinekernels *or* chopped nuts
2 large onions, chopped
1 garlic clove, crushed
15g (½oz) butter
1 bay leaf
125g (4oz) button mushrooms
1 egg
1 teaspoon yeast extract
1 teaspoon chopped parsley
sea salt
freshly ground black pepper
1 teaspoon lemon juice
50g (2oz) fresh soft breadcrumbs
75g (3oz) grated cheese

Wipe aubergines, score around lightly lengthwise and place on a dry baking sheet. Bake in a moderate oven, 180°C (350°F), gas mark 4, for 30 minutes, until flesh can be pierced easily through the score mark. (Leave oven on.) Insert point of knife in score mark and slice aubergines in half. Scoop out flesh leaving the skins intact. Leave skins on one side. Chop flesh finely and reserve. Flaked almonds, pinekernels or other nuts, chopped, can be toasted in the oven on a dry baking sheet while aubergines are cooking.

Fry onions and garlic in the butter with the bay leaf for 5 minutes, then add washed and chopped mushrooms and cook for a further 5 minutes. Beat the egg with the yeast extract, add aubergine pulp, parsley, flaked almonds or pinekernels and mushroom mixture. Season with salt, pepper and lemon juice. Spoon mixture into aubergine shells, top with the breadcrumbs and grated cheese mixed together and return to the oven for 20 minutes, until golden and crisp. Serve with onion, tomato, or wine sauce.

STUFFED AUBERGINES IN BÉCHAMEL SAUCE

Here is a recipe for Greek-style stuffed aubergines. Really, minced meat should be used for this recipe and you might feel that the lentils I've suggested are rather a corruption. But as lentils are used so much in Middle Eastern cookery I don't think they're too far-fetched, and they do make a tasty and satisfying dish.

SERVES 6 F

3 medium aubergines – about 700g (1½ lb) in all
salt
3–4 tablespoons olive oil
2 medium onions, peeled and chopped
3 tablespoons tomato purée
3 garlic cloves, peeled and crushed in a little salt
175g (6oz) split red lentils
225ml (8 fl oz) water
2 tablespoons chopped fresh parsley
75g (3oz) grated cheese
sea salt
freshly ground black pepper
25g (1oz) butter
25g (1oz) flour
425ml (15 fl oz) milk
1 egg
nutmeg
50g (2oz) grated cheese

Cut the aubergines in half lengthwise then scoop out the centres to leave space for the stuffing and chop up the scooped-out flesh. Sprinkle the aubergine flesh and the inside of the skins with kitchen salt; leave for half an hour, then squeeze out the bitter brown juice, rinse the aubergine flesh and skins under the tap and dry. Heat 3 tablespoons of oil in a frying pan and fry the aubergine skins for about 5 minutes on each side to soften them; drain them and put into a shallow ovenproof dish. Set the oven to 180°C (350°F), gas mark 4. Fry the onion in the same saucepan, adding a little more oil if necessary; when it is soft but not brown – about 10 minutes – add the aubergine flesh, tomato purée, garlic, lentils and water and cook for about 20–30 minutes until the lentils are done. Remove from the heat, add the parsley and grated cheese and season carefully to taste. Divide the filling between the aubergine skins, piling it up well.

Make the Béchamel sauce: melt the butter in a saucepan and stir in the flour then add a third of the milk and stir over a high heat until the mixture is smooth and thick; repeat the process twice more using the rest of the milk. Remove from the heat and beat in the egg and salt, pepper and grated nutmeg to taste. Pour the sauce over and round the aubergines, sprinkle with the grated cheese and bake in the oven for 35 minutes until they're tender and the sauce is bubbly and golden brown.

These aubergines are nice with a crisp herby green salad or a cooked green vegetable.

AUBERGINES STUFFED WITH CHEESE

This dish is based on a Yugoslavian recipe. It's a simple but delicious way of serving aubergines. I think a tomato sauce goes well with them and also something crisp – triangles of toast for instance, or crunchy roast potatoes.

SERVES 4 F
4 small/medium aubergines – about 700g (1½ lb) in all
sea salt
1 onion, peeled and finely chopped
175g (6oz) grated cheese
1 egg
1 tablespoon chopped fresh parsley
freshly ground black pepper

Set the oven to 200°C (400°F), gas mark 6. Wash the aubergines and remove the stalk ends. Half fill a good-sized saucepan with cold water, add a teaspoonful of salt and bring up to the boil. Cook the aubergines in the water for about 5 minutes, until they feel just barely tender when pierced with the point of a knife. Drain and cool the aubergines, then split them in half lengthways and scoop the flesh out into a bowl, leaving the skins intact.

Arrange the skins in a lightly greased shallow ovenproof dish. Mash the aubergine flesh with a fork, then stir in the onion, grated cheese, egg, parsley and salt and pepper to taste. Bake the aubergines for 30–40 minutes until they're golden brown.

AUBERGINES STUFFED WITH CHICK PEAS

This is a lovely mixture, reminiscent of Middle Eastern dishes, and is good served cold, as well as hot.

SERVES 4 F
2 medium-sized aubergines
sea salt
olive oil
1 large onion, peeled and sliced
1 large garlic clove, crushed
3 tablespoons olive oil
3 large tomatoes, skinned and chopped
175g (6oz) chickpeas, soaked, cooked and drained
2–3 teaspoons lemon juice
2 good tablespoons chopped parsley
freshly ground black pepper

Cut the aubergines in half and scoop out the insides. Sprinkle the insides of the aubergine skins and the scooped-out flesh with sea salt and leave on one side for about 30 minutes for the bitter juices to be drawn out. Then wash the aubergines and pat dry.

Set the oven to 180°C (350°F), gas mark 4. Put a little oil in the base of a frying pan and fry the aubergine skins on both sides to soften them a little, then place them in an oiled shallow casserole dish. Fry the onion, garlic and scooped-out aubergine flesh in 3 tablespoons of oil in a large saucepan until they're tender – about 10 minutes – then add the tomatoes and cook for a further 2–3 minutes. Remove from the heat and add the drained chickpeas, lemon juice, parsley and sea salt and freshly ground black pepper to taste. Divide the mixture between the aubergine skins, piling it up well. Bake the aubergines in the oven for 30–40 minutes. They're nice with creamy mashed potatoes and a cooked green vegetable.

AUBERGINES STUFFED WITH CONTINENTAL LENTILS AND MUSHROOMS

This is quite different from the preceding recipe. It's nice with buttered rice, a yoghurt and cucumber salad and cheesecake for pudding.

SERVES 4 F
2 medium-sized aubergines
sea salt
olive oil
1 large onion, peeled and chopped
2 garlic cloves, crushed
125g (4oz) button mushrooms, wiped and sliced
125g (4oz) continental lentils, soaked, cooked and drained as usual or 400g (14oz) can, drained
1–2 teaspoons lemon juice
2 tablespoons chopped parsley
freshly ground black pepper
a few dried crumbs
a little grated cheese

Prepare the aubergines as described in the previous recipe, salting them then frying the skins in oil. Arrange the skins in a shallow casserole.

Set the oven to 180°C (350°F), gas mark 4. Fry the onion, garlic and scooped-out aubergine flesh in 3 tablespoons of oil in a good-sized saucepan for about 10 minutes, until the onion is soft, then add the mushrooms and cook for a further 4–5 minutes. Mix in the lentils, lemon juice, parsley and some sea salt and freshly ground black pepper to taste. Pile the mixture into the aubergine skins and sprinkle with some crumbs and grated cheese. Bake them in the oven for 30–40 minutes, until the skins are completely cooked and the topping a nice golden brown.

STUFFED AUBERGINES À LA DUXELLES

Here's my adaptation of a classic French version. Duxelles is the name given to a concentrated purée of mushrooms, which is the basis of this stuffing.

This dish is nice served with a wine or tomato sauce, new potatoes or *gratin dauphinoise* and another vegetable.

SERVES 4 F
450g (1 lb) mushrooms
1 onion
25g (1oz) butter
2 medium aubergines
sea salt
olive oil
2 tablespoons chopped fresh parsley
225g (8oz) cottage cheese *or* low-fat quark
freshly ground black pepper
50g (2oz) grated cheese, preferably Parmesan *or* a
mixture of Parmesan and cheaper cooking cheese
50g (2oz) fine breadcrumbs

First prepare the *duxelles*: wash the mushrooms then chop them finely: peel and finely chop the onion. Put the chopped mushrooms and onion into a cloth and squeeze firmly to extract excess liquid – this can be saved and added to a soup or a sauce. Melt the butter in a large saucepan, then stir in the chopped mushroom and onion and fry, without a lid on the saucepan, until the mixture is thick, dry and purée-like – 15–20 minutes. Remove from the heat.

While the *duxelles* is cooking start preparing the aubergines: cut them in half lengthwise and scoop out the centres to form cavities for stuffing. Sprinkle the scooped-out aubergine and the insides of the skins with salt and leave them on one side for the bitter juices to be extracted. After about 30 minutes squeeze the liquid out of the aubergine, rinse it under cold water and pat dry.

Set the oven to 180°C (350°F), gas mark 4. Fry the aubergine skins on both sides in hot oil, then drain them and put them into a shallow ovenproof dish, ready for stuffing. Fry the scooped-out aubergine flesh in couple of tablespoons of oil for about 5 minutes, then add the *duxelles*, chopped parsley, cottage cheese or quark and most of the cheese.

Taste the mixture and season as necessary, then pile it into the prepared aubergine skins and sprinkle the tops with breadcrumbs and remaining grated cheese. Cover the dish with foil and bake for about 40 minutes, removing the foil for the last 10 minutes so that the crumbs get crisp.

AUBERGINES WITH MUSHROOM AND PARSLEY STUFFING

In this recipe, instead of salting and frying the aubergines in the usual way you will see that I reduce the fat by par-boiling them whole, first, then halving and stuffing them. I find this works very well and haven't had any problems with bitterness.

SERVES 6 F
3 medium-sized aubergines
2 onions, peeled and chopped
1 tablespoon olive oil
350g (12oz) button mushrooms, washed and chopped
2 tablespoons chopped parsley
175g (6oz) low-fat quark
125g (4oz) grated cheese
sea salt
freshly ground black pepper
1 tomato, cut into 6 slices

Wipe the aubergines and remove the leafy stalk ends. Half fill a large saucepan with water and bring to the boil. Put in the aubergines and let them simmer for 15–20 minutes, until they feel tender when pierced with the point of a knife. Cool. Cut the aubergines in half and carefully scoop out as much of the inside as you can, leaving just a shell of skin to hold the stuffing.

Set the oven to 200°C (400°F), gas mark 6. Fry the onion in the oil for 10 minutes, then add the chopped mushrooms and cook for a further 2–3 minutes. Remove from the heat and stir in the parsley, quark, grated cheese, aubergine flesh and salt and pepper to taste.

Put the aubergine skins on a lightly-greased, shallow ovenproof dish and divide the filling between them, piling it up well. Place a slice of tomato on top of each stuffed aubergine. Bake for about 45 minutes. I like these aubergines with a vegetable purée, such as potato and celeriac or carrot and lemon, and whole French beans or mange-tout peas. If you want to introduce a crisp texture, crunchy roast potatoes are good with them or some triangles of crisp wholemeal toast.

STUFFED AUBERGINES À LA PROVENÇAL

SERVES 4
2 medium-sized aubergines
2 large onions, chopped
1 garlic clove, crushed
2 tablespoons olive oil
bay leaf
4 tomatoes
8 large black olives, stoned and chopped
1 teaspoon tomato purée
50g (2oz) grated Parmesan cheese
1 beaten egg
1 teaspoon dried thyme
125g (4oz) flaked almonds
sea salt
freshly ground black pepper
a little lemon juice
25–50g (1–2oz) fresh breadcrumbs
1 tablespoon chopped parsley

Wipe aubergines, score around lightly lengthwise and place on a dry baking sheet. Bake in a moderate oven, 180°C (350°F), gas mark 4, for 30 minutes, until flesh can be pierced easily through score mark. Insert point of knife into score mark and slice aubergines in half. (Leave oven on.) Scoop out aubergine flesh, leaving the skins intact and leave on one side. Chop flesh finely and reserve.

Fry onion and garlic in the oil with the bay leaf for 10 minutes, then remove from heat and add the tomatoes skinned and sliced, the black olives, stoned and chopped, the tomato purée, half the grated cheese, the egg, thyme, aubergine pulp and the flaked almonds. Mix well together and season with salt, pepper and lemon juice. Pile into aubergine skins. Place in buttered ovenware dish, scatter with the rest of the cheese and the fresh breadcrumbs and bake for 20 minutes until golden. Scatter with chopped parsley.

STUFFED AUBERGINES IN TOMATO AND WINE SAUCE

Finally, a rich-tasting version – good with a full-bodied red wine.

SERVES 6 [F]
3 medium-sized aubergines
1 tablespoon olive oil
4 onions, peeled and chopped
3 large garlic cloves, peeled and crushed
1 green pepper, de-seeded and chopped
3 tablespoons tomato paste
8 tablespoons red wine
125g (4oz) very finely grated cashew nuts
1 heaped tablespoon finely chopped parsley
pinch each of marjoram, thyme and rosemary
sea salt
freshly ground black pepper
a little honey *or* sugar – about 1 teaspoon or less
2 × 400g (14oz) cans tomatoes

Par-boil the aubergines whole as on page 140. Cool, halve and scoop out the flesh. Place the skins in a lightly greased shallow ovenproof dish. Heat the oil in a fairly large saucepan and fry the onions for 10 minutes. Remove half the onion and put it straight into the liquidizer goblet – this is for the sauce, leave it on one side for a moment.

Add the garlic, green pepper and scooped-out aubergine pulp to the rest of the onion in the saucepan, also two tablespoons of the tomato paste, 4 tablespoons of the wine and the nuts and herbs. Season with salt and pepper and add a very little honey if you think necessary – this just seems to 'lift' the flavour without tasting at all sweet. Pile the mixture into the aubergine skins.

Finish making the sauce: add the tomatoes to the onion in the liquidizer, together with the remaining wine and tomato paste, a seasoning of salt and pepper and a little dash of honey. Blend until fairly smooth, then check seasoning, adding salt, pepper and a little honey as necessary and pour about half the sauce around the aubergines in the dish. Bake at 180°C (350°F), gas mark 4, for 1 hour. Serve the aubergines from the dish and hand round the remaining sauce separately. Very light mashed potatoes and a cooked green vegetable go well with this dish.

HOT AVOCADO WITH WINE STUFFING

Another very favourite dish of mine. Make sure that the avocados are really ripe – they should just yield to fingertip pressure all over. It's important to leave the preparation of the avocados until the last minute, and only just warm them through in the oven, though the filling can be made in advance.

SERVES 6

125g (4oz) Brazil nuts, finely grated
125g (4oz) cheese, grated
50g (2oz) fine, fresh wholemeal breadcrumbs
225g (8oz) can tomatoes
1 small garlic clove, peeled and crushed
1 tablespoon tomato purée
2 tablespoons fresh chives, chopped
4–6 tablespoons fino sherry
sea salt
freshly ground black pepper
3 ripe avocado pears
juice of 1 lemon
a little extra grated cheese and breadcrumbs for topping

First make the stuffing: put the nuts, cheese, bread-crumbs, tomatoes, garlic, tomato purée and chives into a bowl and mix together. Stir in enough sherry to make a soft mixture which will just hold its shape, then season with plenty of salt and pepper and enough tabasco to give the mixture a pleasant tang. Leave on one side until just before the meal – you can make the stuffing a few hours ahead if convenient.

Set the oven to 230°C (450°F), gas mark 8. Just before the meal, halve the avocados and remove the skin and stones. Mix the lemon juice with a good pinch of salt and a grinding of pepper and brush all over the avocados. Place the avocados in a shallow ovenproof dish. Spoon the stuffing mixture on top of the avocados, dividing it evenly between them; sprinkle a little cheese and a few breadcrumbs on top of each. Put the avocados into the oven and turn the heat down to 200°C (400°F), gas mark 6. Bake the avocados for 15 minutes. Serve immediately. (I find it best to put the avocados into the oven just as everyone sits down for their first course – it's important that they should not be overcooked.) They are delicious with puréed potatoes and a lightly-cooked vegetable such as baby carrots.

STIR-FRIED BEANSPROUTS WITH MUSHROOMS, CHINESE CABBAGE AND OMELETTE STRIPS

If you serve this with boiled rice it makes a complete meal that's quick to cook. As with all Chinese-style recipes, all the preparation of the vegetables should be done in advance; the actual cooking takes only a few minutes. If you're going to serve brown rice with this dish, remember to allow time for it to cook – it will take around 45 minutes.

SERVES 4

350g (12oz) beansprouts
350g (12oz) Chinese cabbage
225g (8oz) button mushrooms
2 onions
1 garlic clove
small piece of fresh ginger (to give about 2 teaspoons when peeled and grated)
2 tablespoons soy sauce
1 teaspoon sugar
1 tablespoon sherry
6 tablespoons oil

For omelette strips
4 eggs
sea salt
freshly ground black pepper
a little oil *or* oil and butter, for frying

Wash the beansprouts, cabbage and mushrooms; cut the cabbage and mushrooms into even-sized slices. Peel and very finely chop the onion; crush the garlic; peel and grate the ginger. Mix together the soy sauce, sugar and sherry. Whisk the eggs with some sea salt and freshly ground black pepper; have ready a small omelette pan or frying pan for making omelette strips and a wok, large frying pan or large saucepan in which to stir-fry the vegetables.

When you're ready to cook the dish, heat the oil in the wok or other pan and fry the onion, garlic and ginger for 1 minute, stirring continuously. Add the beansprouts, Chinese cabbage and mushrooms and stir-fry them for 2 minutes, turning them over so that everything gets coated with the oil, garlic and ginger. Pour in the soy sauce mixture, reduce the heat and cook for a further 3 minutes.

While this final cooking is going on, quickly make the omelette strips. Heat a little oil or oil and butter in the omelette pan and pour in half the egg; make an omelette by cooking the egg over a brisk heat, gently pushing the eggs towards the centre as they cook, tipping the pan so that the uncooked part runs towards the edges; turn it out flat on to a plate and cut it into long strips. Make another omelette in the same way.

Taste the cooked vegetable mixture and correct the seasoning with a little salt and freshly ground black pepper if necessary, then pile it into a warmed serving dish, arrange the omelette strips, lattice fashion, on top, and serve immediately with plain boiled rice.

BRAZIL NUT SAVOURY CAKE

I evolved this early recipe for serving cold with salads.

SERVES 6 F
1 medium onion
1 teaspoon mixed herbs
50g (2oz) butter
1 tablespoon plain flour
150ml (5 fl oz) milk
225g (8oz) Brazil nuts, grated
125g (4oz) soft brown breadcrumbs
2 eggs
sea salt
freshly ground black pepper
1 tablespoon chopped parsley

Set oven to 180°C (350°F), gas mark 4. Peel and chop the onion and fry with the herbs in the butter for 10 minutes without browning. Stir in the flour and the milk, allow to thicken and then add all the other ingredients, seasoning to taste. Press into a greased 20cm (8in) sandwich tin and bake for 45 minutes, until golden brown and crisp. Serve cold, with a mixed salad including tomatoes, onions, celery and green vegetables in season.

CABBAGE STUFFED WITH TOMATOES AND WALNUTS AND BAKED IN A CHEESE SAUCE

A satisfactory dish which you can put together from practically nothing. Served with potatoes baked in their jackets, it makes a warming and very economical meal.

SERVES 4 F
8 outer leaves of cabbage (savoy, Primo *or* January King)
1 onion, peeled and chopped
2 tablespoons olive oil
125g (4oz) walnuts, chopped
125g (4oz) soft breadcrumbs
425g (15oz) can tomatoes
sea salt
freshly ground black pepper
275ml (10 fl oz) cheese sauce, made from 25g (1oz) butter, 25g (1oz) flour, 275ml (10 fl oz) milk, 50g (2oz) grated cheese
50g (2oz) grated cheese

Set oven to 190°C (375°F). gas mark 5. Put the cabbage leaves into a saucepan of boiling water for 2–3 minutes, until pliable. Drain well. Fry the onion in the oil for 10 minutes, add the nuts, breadcrumbs, tomatoes and seasoning. Divide mixture between the cabbage leaves, roll them up and place in a greased shallow dish. Cover with the sauce. Sprinkle with cheese and bake for 40–45 minutes.

CASHEW NUT AND CELERY TIMBALE

This is the timbale that isn't! It was once, because originally it was baked in a loaf tin. But this is the quick version I evolved when I was first married, and the name stuck. I've kept the original name because it's one of the most popular recipes with my readers. Originally I used a can of celery hearts; today I would use fresh celery, cooked until tender.

SERVES 4 [F]
1 onion, chopped
1 bay leaf
50g (2oz) butter
1 head celery, chopped and cooked *or*
1 can celery hearts
1 tablespoon flour
1 can tomato juice
juice and rind of ½ lemon
175g (6oz) cashew nuts, grated
1 tablespoon parsley, chopped
pinch mace
sea salt
freshly ground black pepper
wholemeal toast

Fry the onion with the bay leaf in the butter, with the lid on the pan, until tender but not browned – 10 minutes. Drain and add celery (chop canned celery hearts first), then stir in the flour and tomato juice. Cook until slightly thickened, then stir in lemon rind and juice, cashew nuts, parsley and mace, and season with salt and pepper. Serve with fingers of crisp wholemeal toast.

CASHEW NUT FRITTERS

These are really nut rissoles. It was my effort to make a vegetarian fish replacement!

SERVES 4 [F]
2 medium-sized onions
50g (2oz) butter
½ teaspoon dill – optional
50g (2oz) wholemeal flour
425ml (15 fl oz) milk
1 egg
125g (4oz) finely grated cashew nuts
2 teaspoons lemon juice
sea salt
freshly ground black pepper
flour
toasted crumbs
lemon wedges

Chop the onions finely. Melt the butter over a gentle heat in a large pan, add the onions and dill and cook gently until the onions are soft but not brown (about 10 minutes). Stir in the flour and milk. Mix well, and cook very gently for 2 minutes, until thickened. Add ground cashew nuts, lemon juice, seasoning and cook for 3 minutes; when cold divide into eight portions, dip each into flour then beaten egg, and coat with toasted breadcrumbs. Flatten each piece so that it is about 8mm (⅓in) thick. Fry pieces on both sides in hot fat until golden brown. Drain well on kitchen paper and serve garnished with lemon wedges and with parsley sauce.

EASY CAULIFLOWER CHEESE

SERVES 4
1 large cauliflower
sea salt
225g (8oz) grated cheese

Preheat a moderately hot grill. Wash and trim the cauliflower, dividing it into small florets as you do so. Heat 2cm (1in) salted water in a saucepan, put in the cauliflower and cook for about 4 minutes, until just tender. Drain well and place in a lightly greased, shallow, ovenproof dish. Cover with the grated cheese and place under the grill until the cheese has melted and is beginning to brown. Serve immediately, with hot wholemeal toast or rolls, and a salad of watercress or sliced tomatoes.

CAULIFLOWER WITH SPICY PEANUT SAUCE

SERVES 4
1 large cauliflower
1 onion, peeled and chopped
1 tablespoon olive oil
1 tablespoon peanut butter
125g (4oz) roasted peanuts (see page 136) chopped
or grated
450g (1 lb) tomatoes, skinned and chopped
freshly ground black pepper

Start by making the sauce. Fry the onion in the oil for 10 minutes, then add the peanut butter, peanuts and tomatoes. Season and keep warm. Wash and trim the cauliflower, dividing it into small florets as you do so. Heat 2cm (1in) salted water in a saucepan, put in the cauliflower and cook for about 5 minutes, until tender. Serve cauliflower with the sauce spooned over it.

CHESTNUT AND MUSHROOM CASEROLE

In the original version of this recipe I said 'Any left-over red wine can be used for this – don't get any in specially'. What a picture that conjures up, just happening to have 575ml (1 pint) of 'left-over' red wine hanging around ready to go into this casserole?! But a cheap supermarket red is fine for this recipe, which is still a favourite of mine. Fresh chestnuts, yielding about 450g (1 lb) chestnuts, are even nicer than the canned ones suggested. Prepare these as described on page 136.

SERVES 4
2 large onions
1 head celery
1 tablespoon olive oil
225g (8oz) button mushrooms
4 tomatoes *or* 1 small can tomatoes
1 bay leaf
2 cans whole chestnuts
2 tablespoons flour
just under 575ml (1 pint) red wine
sea salt
freshly ground black pepper

Set oven to 180°C (350°F), gas mark 4. Finely slice onions and celery and sauté in the oil for 10 minutes, then add the mushrooms, tomatoes, peeled and quartered (drained if using canned ones), and the bay leaf. Drain chestnuts, reserving liquid. Toss chestnuts in the flour, then add to the pan together with any excess flour. I use a flame-proof casserole which can go over the hotplate as well as into the oven. Make the reserved chestnut liquid up to 575ml (1 pint) with the red wine, add to casserole. Season with salt and pepper and bake for 45 minutes.

CHESTNUT AND WINE CASSEROLE

Another, later version of a chestnut casserole, and also delicious.

SERVES 4–6 F
225g (8oz) dried chestnuts
2 large onions, chopped
450g (1 lb) carrots, cut into rings
2 tablespoons olive oil
4 garlic cloves, crushed
10 each of allspice berries, juniper berries and black peppercorns
1 teaspoon each dried thyme and rosemary
575ml (1 pint) vegetable stock (page 11)
425ml (15 fl oz) cheap red wine
1 tablespoon paprika pepper
125g (4oz) button mushrooms, sliced
sea salt

Soak chestnuts overnight; next day, cover with plenty of water and simmer for 2–3 hours, until tender. Fry the onions and carrots in the oil for 10 minutes, then add the garlic, chestnuts, crushed spices, herbs, stocks and wine. Bring to the boil, then put a lid on the pan and leave to cook gently for 30–40 minutes, until vegetables are tender, and liquid much reduced and thickened. Then add the paprika and mush-rooms. Check seasoning, simmer for a further 2–3 minutes to cook mushrooms, and serve. Jacket potatoes go well with this, and very lightly cooked Brussels sprouts, or a simple crisp green salad.

SAVOURY CHESTNUT BAKE

SERVES 6–8 F
225g (8oz) dried chestnuts
1 onion, peeled and sliced
1 celery stick, chopped
2 teaspoons ghee *or* olive oil
2 garlic cloves, peeled
125g (4oz) walnuts, grated
125g (4oz) cashew nuts, grated
grated rind and juice of ½ lemon
1 glass red wine – optional
1 free-range egg – optional
sea salt
freshly ground black pepper

Soak and cook chestnuts as in previous recipe. Set oven to 190°C (375°F), gas mark 5. Line a 900g (2 lb) loaf tin with a long strip of non-stick paper and brush with ghee or melted butter. Fry the onion and celery in the ghee or olive oil in a large saucepan for 10 minutes. Remove from heat and mix in remaining ingredients, mashing chestnuts so that mixture holds

together. Season. Put mixture into the loaf tin – it won't fill it, but is just too much for a 450g (1 lb) tin – smooth top. Cover with foil and bake for about 45 minutes, removing foil 15 minutes before end of cooking time.

CHESTNUT, SAGE AND RED WINE LOAF

A roast which I invented for the Christmas article in *The Vegetarian*. It is a moist savoury loaf which slices well either hot or cold. Served with baked red cabbage and jacket potatoes and soured cream it makes a very pleasant winter meal; it's also very good as a vegetarian alternative to Christmas turkey, with a wine sauce, bread sauce, roast potatoes and baby sprouts.

SERVES 6 F
butter and dried breadcrumbs for lining loaf tin
350g (12oz) dried chestnuts *or* 1 kilo (2¼ lb) fresh chestnuts
50g (2oz) butter
1 large onion, peeled and chopped
2 celery stalks, finely chopped
2 garlic cloves, peeled and crushed
2 tablespoons chopped fresh sage *or* 1 teaspoon dried
1 tablespoon red wine
1 egg
sea salt
freshly ground black pepper
1 fresh sage leaf if available

Set the oven to 180°C (350°F), gas mark 4. Prepare a 450g (1 lb) loaf tin by lining the base and narrow sides with a long strip of non-stick paper; brush well with butter and sprinkle lightly with the dried breadcrumbs.

If you're using dried chestnuts, cover with boiling water then leave to soak for at least 2 hours; simmer in plenty of water for about 1½ hours until tender. For fresh chestnuts, nick each with a knife then simmer in plenty of water for about 10 minutes until the cuts open. Take the chestnuts from the water one by one and strip off the skins with a sharp, pointed knife. Put the skinned chestnuts into a saucepan, cover with water and simmer for 20–30 minutes until tender. Drain and mash the chestnuts. Melt the butter in a large saucepan and fry the onion and celery for 10 minutes, without browning. Add the chestnuts, garlic, sage, wine and egg and mix together, seasoning with salt and pepper.

Lay the sage leaf, if using, in the base of the prepared loaf tin and spoon the chestnut mixture on top, smooth over the surface and cover with a piece of foil. Bake the loaf in the pre-heated oven for 1 hour. To serve, slip a knife round the sides of the loaf and turn out on to a warm dish.

CHOP SUEY

Although the list of ingredients always makes this dish look rather daunting it's actually very easy to make. You get all the preparation done in advance so you only have to cook the vegetables quickly at the last minute.

SERVES 4
1 onion
1 garlic clove
2.5cm (1in) piece of fresh root ginger
225g (8oz) beansprouts
125g (4oz) button mushrooms
1 small pepper, preferably red
432g (15½oz) can sliced pineapple in its own juice
225g (8oz) firm tofu (page 177), diced
1 teaspoon soy sauce
1 tablespoon tomato ketchup
1 teaspoon sugar
1 tablespoon cheap sherry
2 tablespoons water
1 egg
sea salt
a little olive oil

Peel and chop the onion; peel and crush the garlic, peel and grate the ginger. Wash the beansprouts. Wash and slice the mushrooms and the pepper, discarding the seeds from the pepper. Drain the pineapple, cut into small pieces. In a cup mix together the soy sauce, tomato ketchup, sugar, sherry and water. Break the egg into a bowl and whisk it with a little salt.

When you're ready to make the meal, heat 2 tablespoons of oil in a large saucepan and fry the onion for 5 minutes, then stir in the garlic and ginger and cook for a few seconds before adding the beansprouts, mushrooms, pepper, pineapple and tofu. Stir-fry over quite a high heat for about 2 minutes, then add the mixture from the cup and stir well. Leave this to cook for just a minute or so while you quickly make an omelette with the beaten egg. Keep the omelette flat. To serve the chop suey pile it up on a hot dish and lay the omelette on top.

Serve with lots of hot, well-cooked rice and some other Chinese dishes if you like.

STUFFED COURGETTES

This is a very pleasant, simple dish. Originally I used cream cheese, these days I use curd cheese or a smooth, low-fat white cheese, to reduce the fat content of the recipe. White breadcrumbs give a delicate flavour, but wholemeal can be used instead if preferred.

SERVES 4
4 large courgettes
125g (4oz) white breadcrumbs
225g (8oz) cream cheese, curd cheese *or* low-fat
white cheese
4 tablespoons flaked almonds
rind and juice of ½ lemon
sea salt
freshly ground black pepper

Set oven to 190°C (375°F), gas mark 5. Par-boil courgettes for 5 minutes, then slice in half lengthwise and scoop out centres. Place side by side in a well-buttered ovenproof dish. Mix together the breadcrumbs, cheese, flaked almonds, scooped out courgette centres, mashed, and lemon juice and rind to taste. Season with salt and pepper. Pile into prepared courgettes and bake for 45 minutes. Serve hot with lemon sauce (page 66) or parsley sauce (page 66).

STUFFED COURGETTES MORNAY

The original title of this recipe; today I'd just say 'in a cheese sauce'. It still tastes good, though.

SERVES 4
4 large courgettes
1 garlic clove
4 tomatoes
175g (6oz) button mushrooms
25g (1oz) butter
125g (4oz) breadcrumbs
1 tablespoon lemon juice
1 teaspoon lemon rind, grated
2 tablespoons parsley, choppd
sea salt
freshly ground black pepper
25–50g (1–2oz) grated cheese
425ml (15 fl oz) cheese sauce (page 62)

Set oven to 180°C (350°F), gas mark 4. Prepare courgettes as in previous recipe. Crush garlic, slice tomatoes and mushrooms, and fry lightly in the butter until tender. Mix with half the breadcrumbs, the chopped courgette centres, the lemon juice and rind, parsley, salt and pepper. Pile into prepared courgettes, place in buttered shallow ovenproof dish, sprinkle with the rest of the breadcrumbs and grated cheese. Bake for 20 minutes. Serve with cheese sauce.

Variation

STUFFED CUCUMBER MORNAY

I love cooked cucumber and this is a pleasant variation. Use 1 large cucumber instead of the courgettes.

Prepare cucumber by cutting into 8–10cm (3–4in) lengths, halving and scooping out seeds. Continue as above.

COURGETTES WITH CHICK PEA AND MUSHROOM STUFFING

In this recipe I think the firm texture of the chick peas contrasts well with the tender courgettes and mushrooms.

SERVES 4
125g (4 oz) chickpeas
4 good-sized courgettes, about 700g (1½ lb)
altogether
15g (½oz) butter
1 onion, peeled and chopped
2 garlic cloves, crushed
125g (4oz) button mushroms, wiped and sliced
1–2 teaspoons ground coriander
juice of ½ lemon
2 tablespoons chopped parsley
sea salt
freshly ground black pepper

Soak, drain, rinse and cook the chickpeas as usual. Set the oven to 180°C (350°F), gas mark 4. Wash the courgettes, then cut them in half lengthwise and scoop out the insides, leaving a 'shell'. Arrange these in a buttered, shallow casserole dish. Chop up the scooped-out courgette. Melt the butter in a saucepan and fry the onion and garlic for 5 minutes, then add the chopped courgette and the sliced mushrooms and cook for a further 5 minutes. Mix in the ground coriander, the drained chickpeas, lemon juice and parsley. Season with sea salt and freshly ground black pepper and pile the mixture into the courgette 'shells'. Bake them in the oven for 30–40 minutes, until the courgettes are tender. They're nice served with a tomato sauce and some French beans, or, Middle Eastern style, chilled, with natural yoghurt.

COURGETTES À LA POLONAISE

Another of the recipes which is in the 'top ten' most popular with readers. I got the idea for it from the 'polonaise' topping used by chefs: I thought, why not expand this egg and breadcrumb mixture to supply the protein content of the meal. This was the result.

SERVES 4
700g (1½ lb) courgettes
125g (4oz) butter
1 heaped tablespoon flour
275ml (10 fl oz) milk
juice of ½ lemon
125g (4oz) breadcrumbs
4–6 hardboiled eggs
1 tablespoon chopped parsley
1 teaspoon grated lemon rind
sea salt
freshly ground black pepper
lemon slices
fresh parsley

Wash, top and tail and slice courgettes into 6mm (¼in) slices. Sauté in a quarter of the butter, turning frequently, until tender. Meanwhile use another quarter of the butter to make a sauce, melting butter, then adding flour, cooking for a minute or two, then removing from heat and gradually adding milk. Return to heat to thicken, carefully add lemon juice and seasoning, then simmer gently over a low heat while preparing the polonaise topping. To do this, fry the breadcrumbs in the rest of the butter until golden and crisp. Finely chop hardboiled eggs and add to the breadcrumbs with the parsley, lemon rind and salt and pepper to taste.

To assemble, put courgettes on warm serving dish; pour the sauce over and top with the breadcrumb mixture. Garnish with lemon slices and fresh parsley.

Variation

CAULIFLOWER À LA POLONAISE

Break cauliflower into florets. Cook in a little fastboiling water until just tender. Drain. Make sauce and topping as above.

CREAMY CUCUMBER AND MUSHROOMS

An interesting, summery-flavoured vegetable dish. Serve with fluffy cooked rice or new potatoes.

SERVES 4
1 large cucumber
225g (8oz) button mushrooms
125g (4oz) flaked almonds
3 sprigs mint
15g (½oz) butter
squeeze lemon juice
225g (8oz) curd cheese
sea salt
freshly ground black pepper
nutmeg
2 eggs, beaten – optional
lemon slices – optional

Peel and dice cucumber; wash and slice mushrooms. Fry the almonds, cucumber, mushrooms and mint in the butter for 5 minutes. Add lemon juice, curd cheese and seasoning. Heat through gently.

For an attractive, protein-rich garnish, quickly make an omelette using the eggs, lightly seasoned. Cut the omelette across into 1cm (½in) long strips. Pour the cucumber mixture on to a hot serving dish and arrange a lattice of omelette strips across the top. Serve immediately.

Variations

Other combinations are delicious. **Creamy courgettes and mushrooms** are made in exactly the same way, using 700g (1½ lb) courgettes instead of the cucumber. Try **artichoke hearts and mushrooms**, replacing cucumber with 2 cans drained artichoke hearts. Or what about **creamy asparagus and mushrooms**, made by using 2 cans of asparagus instead of cucumber, or **creamy celery and mushrooms** in which cucumber is replaced by one very large can of celery hearts, or 2 or 3 nice fresh celery hearts, sliced and steamed, or boiled in a very little water until tender.

CREAMY ASPARAGUS AND MUSHROOMS

A delicious variation in the asparagus season! Use 1 kilo (2¼ lb) fresh asparagus. Prepare and boil or steam until tender (page 112). Then sauté gently in the butter with the mushrooms and almonds as described above.

STUFFED FENNEL (1)

If, like me, you like the fresh, aniseed flavour of fennel, you might like to try it stuffed for a change. Here, and in the next recipe, are two ways of doing it. Both make a pleasant summery main course with tender vegetables such as mange-tout peas, young carrots, new potatoes and a light sauce.

SERVES 4
4 large fennel bulbs
2 tablespoons olive oil
125g (4oz) soft breadcrumbs
125g (4oz) grated nuts
50g (2oz) chopped mushrooms
1 tablespoon grated onion
1 garlic clove, crushed
1 tomato

Set oven to 180°C (350°F), gas mark 4. Wash and trim the fennel, then cook in 2cm (1in) boiling water until tender – about 20–30 minutes. Carefully pull back the outer layers and, using a sharp knife, cut out the centre. (This can be chopped and marinated in an oil and vinegar dressing, then served with wedges of hardboiled eggs for a delicious first course or salad at another meal.)

To make the stuffing, fry the breadcrumbs and nuts in the oil for 3–4 minutes, stirring all the time, until crisp. Add a little more olive oil if necessary, but don't make it too oily: the crumbs and nuts should be golden brown and crisp. Add mushrooms, onion, garlic and tomato, and cook for a further 2–3 minutes. Spoon mixture into the fennel. Place fennel close together in an oiled casserole, and bake for 20 minutes, to heat everything through.

STUFFED FENNEL (2)

Prepare fennel as above. Fill centres with the curd cheese stuffing given for courgettes on page 148.

HAZEL NUT PIE

A simple, quick-to-make dish that children usually seem to like, although you may need to reduce the amount of onions (or leave out altogether) for some.

SERVES 4 $\boxed{\text{F}}$
700g (1½ lb) potatoes
2 large onions
1 garlic clove
25g (1oz) butter
1 teaspoon paprika
grated lemon rind and a little juice
125g (4oz) hazel nuts, grated
425ml (15 fl oz) milk
sea salt
freshly ground black pepper
cornflakes or wholemeal flakes or breadcrumbs
butter
grated cheese

Set oven to 160°C (325°F), gas mark 3. Cook potatoes until tender, then mash well with half the butter and some seasoning. Chop onions and garlic and cook gently in the remaining butter until soft but not brown – 10 minutes. Add mashed potatoes, paprika, a little lemon rind and juice to taste, the milled hazel nuts and milk. Season with salt and pepper, put into a greased casserole dish, cover with cornflakes, dot with butter and a sprinkling of grated cheese. Bake in the oven for 20 minutes to heat through.

A few halved tomatoes, put onto a baking tray and baked at the same time go well with this, and some frozen peas.

Variation

CHEESE AND POTATO PIE

Use 125–175g (4–6oz) grated hard, preferably reduced fat, cheese, instead of the hazel nuts.

STUFFED MARROW WITH BUTTER BEANS

If you can get a nice tender marrow for this recipe, it won't be necessary to peel off the skin.

SERVES 4–6
1 medium-sized marrow
15g (½oz) butter
1 large onion, peeled and chopped
2 garlic cloves, crushed
4 tomatoes, peeled and chopped (you can use canned ones)
175g (6oz) butter beans, soaked, cooked and drained *or* use 2 × 400g (14oz) cans, drained
1 tablespoon chopped parsley
125g (4oz) grated cheese
sea salt
freshly ground black pepper
a few dried crumbs
a little butter

Set the oven to 200°C (400°F), gas mark 6. Wash the marrow and cut off the stem. Cut the marrow in half lengthwise and scoop out and discard the seeds. If the marrow is a bit on the tough side, or if you want to speed up the cooking time, you can par-cook it in boiling, salted water for 5 minutes, then drain it well. This is not necessary if the marrow is young and tender. Put the marrow halves into a greased shallow baking dish. Melt the butter and fry the onion and garlic for 10 minutes, but don't brown them, then add the tomatoes and cook for a further 3–4 minutes. Stir in the butter beans, parsley, grated cheese and sea salt and freshly ground black pepper to taste. Pile the mixture into the two marrow halves, sprinkle with crumbs and dot with a little butter. Bake in the oven for about 45 minutes, or until the marrow halves are tender and the top golden brown. This is good with buttery new potatoes and a cooked green vegetable. Spicy tomato sauce goes well with it, too.

STUFFED MARROW BAKED WITH BUTTER AND THYME

A whole marrow can be hollowed out, stuffed and baked in butter and herbs, rather as you might bake a chicken. The result is delicious and one of my favourite summer dishes. Try serving it with apple and redcurrant sauce, roast potatoes and spinach.

SERVES 4–6
1 fat, medium-sized marrow weighing about 1 kilo (2¼ lb)
350g (12oz) soft, fresh breadcrumbs
225g (8oz) butter
juice and grated rind of 1 small lemon
1 teaspoon marjoram
good bunch of parsley – about 75–125g (3–4oz) – chopped
1 egg
sea salt
freshly ground black pepper
25g (1oz) butter
a small bunch of thyme, crushed

Set the oven to 200°C (400°F). gas mark 6. Cut the stalk off the marrow, then peel the marrow, keeping it whole. Cut a slice off one end and scoop out the seeds to leave a cavity for stuffing. Make the stuffing by mixing together the breadcrumbs, butter, lemon juice and rind, marjoram, parsley and egg; season with salt and pepper. Push this mixture into the cavity of the marrow, then replace the sliced-off end and secure with a skewer. Spread the butter all over the outside of the marrow and sprinkle with the crushed thyme. Put the marrow in an ovenproof dish, sprinkle with any thyme that's left over, cover loosely with a piece of greaseproof paper and bake for about an hour, or until the marrow is tender and can be pierced easily with the point of a knife. Serve with fresh tomato sauce or wine sauce.

MARROW WITH CRISPY STUFFING

SERVES 4–6
1 medium-sized marrow
175g (6oz) wholemeal breadcrumbs
175g (6oz) finely grated nuts – almonds, hazel nuts, Brazil nuts, walnuts *or* a mixture
4 tablespoons olive oil
225g (8oz) button mushrooms, sliced
4 tomatoes, skinned and sliced
1 small onion, grated
sea salt
freshly ground black pepper
parsley
tomato slices

Set oven to 200°C (400°F), gas mark 6. Prepare the marrow as described for the Stuffed Marrow with Butter Beans (page 151). Fry breadcrumbs and nuts together in the oil until crisp and golden, then add the mushrooms, tomatoes, grated onion, salt and pepper. Spoon the mixture on to the marrow pressing it together as you do so and piling it up well. Bake for about 45 minutes, or until tender. Decorate with the parsley and sliced tomato. A good vegetarian gravy goes well with this.

STUFFED MARROW WITH HAZEL NUTS

Here the stuffing is a sage-flavoured nutmeat. Vegetarian gravy, apple or cranberry sauce and roast potatoes make this into a vegetarian answer to Sunday Roast in late summer!

SERVES 4–6
1 medium-sized marrow
2 large onions, chopped
125g (4oz) mushrooms, sliced
50g (2oz) butter
1 teaspoon sage
1 tablespoon plain flour
150 ml (5 fl oz) water
1 egg
125g (4oz) hazel nuts, grated
125g (4oz) soft breadcrumbs
sea salt
freshly ground black pepper
olive oil

Set oven to 200°C (400°F), gas mark 6. Prepare the marrow as described for Stuffed Marrow with Butter Beans (page 151). Fry the onion and mushrooms in the butter for 10 minutes but do not brown. Mix in the other ingredients, cook for 2 minutes and then add salt and pepper to taste. Fill marrow halves with nut mixture and put halves together again, securing them by wrapping in greased paper. Heat a little oil in a roasting tin, place the marrow in this and bake for 45–60 minutes, until marrow is tender.

MARROW WITH RED KIDNEY BEAN STUFFING

The red stuffing looks attractive against the green and white marrow.

SERVES 4–6
1 medium-sized marrow
1 large onion, peeled and chopped
1 garlic clove, crushed
2 tablespoons olive oil
3 tomatoes, skinned and chopped
1 tablespoon tomato purée
225g (8oz) red kidney beans, soaked, cooked and
drained or use 2 × 400g (14oz) cans, drained
freshly ground black pepper
sea salt
½ teaspoon cinnamon
a few crisp breadcrumbs
a little butter
fresh parsley sprigs

Set oven to 200°C (400°F), gas mark 6. Prepare the marrow as described in the recipe for Stuffed Marrow with Butter Beans (page 151). Next, make the red kidney bean mixture. Fry the onion and garlic in the oil in a largish saucepan for about 5 minutes, then stir in the tomatoes and tomato purée and cook for a further 5 minutes or so before adding the red kidney beans, mashing them a bit with the spoon. Let the mixture simmer gently for 5–6 minutes, then season it with pepper, salt and cinnamon and spoon it carefully into the two marrow halves. Sprinkle with breadcrumbs, dot with a little butter and bake in the oven for about 45 minutes, or until the marrow is tender. Garnish with parsley sprigs and serve.

MUSHROOM BAKE

A quick and easy dish, and one which children usually like, unless they're mushroom-haters.

SERVES 4 F
225g (8oz) mushrooms
65g (2½oz) butter
450g (1 lb) tomatoes
225g (8oz) fresh soft wholemeal breadcrumbs
1 small onion
175g (6oz) grated cheese
juice and rind of ½ lemon
sea salt
freshly ground black pepper

Set oven to 190°C (375°F), gas mark 5. Wash and slice mushrooms, then fry in 15g (½oz) of the butter for 10 minutes. Skin and slice tomatoes and leave on one side. Blend together the crumbs, onion, cheese, remaining butter and lemon rind, and press half the mixture into the casserole; pour mushrooms on top of this and then the sliced tomatoes; season well with salt and pepper and the lemon juice. Press remaining crumb mixture on top. Bake for 30 minutes. Serve from the dish with a good sauce.

STUFFED MUSHROOM CAPS

Those large, flat mushrooms which you can sometimes get make a very good base for a tasty stuffing and look appetizing when garnished with lemon and parsley. If you serve the mushrooms on circles of fried bread, it makes them more substantial, as well as giving a pleasantly crisp texture. (Incidentally, if you cut the circles for the fried bread first, the excess bread can be made into crumbs for the stuffing.)

SERVES 4–6
175g (6oz) continental lentils
12 large, flat mushrooms
olive oil
1 large onion, peeled and chopped
1 large garlic clove, crushed
175g (6oz) wholemeal breadcrumbs
1 teaspoon thyme
1 tablespoon chopped parsley
grated rind and juice of ½ lemon
sea salt
freshly ground black pepper
12 slices of wholemeal bread
12 slices of lemon
12 sprigs of parsley

Wash, soak, rinse and cook the lentils as usual; drain them well. Set oven to 180°C (350°F), gas mark 4.

Wash the mushrooms and trim off any stalks level with the base. Chop up the stalks. Cover the base of a large saucepan with a thin layer of oil and heat it up. Then fry the mushroom caps for a minute or two on each side; remove them from the saucepan and put them on one side while you make the filling.

Put a little more oil in the saucepan (there should be about 6 tablespoons in all) and fry the onion, garlic and chopped mushroom stalks for 10 minutes, letting them brown lightly. Then mix in the wholemeal breadcrumbs and stir over the heat until they're brown and crunchy. Remove from the heat and add the lentils, thyme, parsley, grated lemon rind and enough of the juice to give a pleasant flavour. Season with sea salt and freshly ground black pepper.

Cut the slices of bread into circles to fit the mushroom caps. Fry the bread on both sides in a little oil until crisp. Arrange the bread circles on a flat ovenproof plate or baking tray and place a mushroom cap, black side up, on each. Divide the stuffing mixture between the mushroom caps, piling it up neatly. Bake them in the oven for about 20 minutes to heat them through. Decorate each with a slice of lemon and a sprig of parsley before serving. They go well with very light, creamy mashed potatoes, a simply cooked green vegetable such as French beans, and grilled tomatoes.

Variation

Other stuffings can be used. The crispy one given for fennel (page 150) is delicious, so is the curd cheese one in the courgette recipe on page 148.

MUSHROOM NUT FLAN

My idea in this recipe was to make a flan case which would supply the protein for the dish. I know from readers that this is one of the most popular recipes, so I'm giving it in its original form. These days, though, I'd fry the mushrooms for the filling in 15g (1oz) butter, then add a large carton of soured cream, instead of making the sauce mixture.

SERVES 6 F
1 small onion
1 teaspoon mixed herbs
½ teaspoon celery seed – optional
50g (2oz) butter
1 tablespoon plain flour
150ml (5 fl oz) milk
225g (8oz) grated almonds
125g (4oz) breadcrumbs
2 eggs
sea salt
freshly ground black pepper

Mushroom filling
1 small onion, chopped
50g (2oz) butter
225g (8oz) mushrooms
½ teaspoon marjoram
2 tablespoons plain flour
275ml (10 fl oz) milk
sea salt
freshly ground black pepper

Set oven to 180°C (350°F), gas mark 4. Chop onion finely and cook gently in the butter with the herbs and celery seed until soft but not browned, about 10 minutes. Blend in the flour and milk, stir well until thickened. Add rest of ingredients and salt and pepper to taste. Cook for 2 minutes, then allow to cool. Spread into a greased flan dish, flattening the mixture round the base and sides to resemble pastry. Bake for 20–30 minutes until golden. Meanwhile, make filling. Cook onion in the butter with the washed and chopped mushrooms and herbs for 10 minutes. Add the flour, stir well, add the milk and cook until thickened. Season to taste. Pour into the flan then serve or keep warm in a cool oven. The flan part of this can be prepared in advance and left in a cool place for filling with the mushrooms and re-heating when required.

CROUSTADE OF MUSHROOMS

This has to be my most popular recipe; I've lost count of the number of magazine articles and vegetarian cookery books I've spotted it in, but it must be nearing a dozen. Here's the original version, which I invented for one of my first dinner parties. These days, incidentally, instead of making a sauce for the mushrooms, I simply fry them in 15g (½oz) butter then add 2 large cartons of soured cream – easier and even better!

SERVES 6 F for base
125g (4oz) soft breadcrumbs
125g (4oz) ground almonds *or* other nuts, finely ground
50g (2oz) butter
125g (4oz) flaked almonds, pinekernels *or* hazel nuts
1 garlic clove
½ teaspoon mixed herbs
450g (1 lb) mushrooms
50g (2oz) butter
2 heaped tablespoons flour
425ml (15 fl oz) milk
sea salt
freshly ground black pepper
grated nutmeg
4 tomatoes
1 tablespoon chopped parsley

First make the croustade by mixing together breadcrumbs and ground almonds or other milled nuts. Rub in butter as for pastry. Add flaked almonds, or other nuts, chopped finely. If using hazel nuts, first prepare by baking on a dry baking sheet for 20–30 minutes at 180°C (350°F), gas mark 4, until skins will rub off in a clean cloth. Crush garlic and add to nut mixture with mixed herbs; mix together well and then press down very firmly in a flat ovenproof dish or swiss roll tin. Bake in a hot oven, 230°C (450°F), gas mark 8, for 15–17 minutes until crisp and golden brown. Meanwhile make topping. Wash and slice mushrooms; sauté in the butter until tender, then add the flour and when it froths, remove from heat and stir in the milk. Return to heat and stir until thickened, simmer for 10 minutes over a low heat, then season well with salt, pepper and nutmeg. Spoon mushroom mixture on top of croustade; top with tomatoes, skinned and sliced, and sprinkle with a very little salt and pepper. Return to oven for 10–15 minutes to heat through, then serve sprinkled with parsley.

This all sounds rather fiddly, but in fact it's very straightforward and the creamy topping is delicious with the crisp protein-rich croustade.

Variation

CROUSTADE OF LEEKS

Make in exactly the same way, frying 450g (1 lb) sliced leeks in the butter instead of the mushrooms.

MUSHROOM LOAF (1)

This tasty loaf is good either hot or cold. It slices well when cold and can be used as a sandwich filling.

SERVES 6 F
450g (1 lb) mushrooms
1 onion
1 tablespoon olive oil
2 tablespoons skimmed milk powder
125g (4oz) grated nuts – Brazil or cashews *or* ground almonds if you're in a hurry
225g (8oz) soft wholemeal breadcrumbs
1 teaspoon yeast extract
1 teaspoon mixed herbs
1 egg
sea salt
freshly ground black pepper
dried crumbs to coat tin

Set the oven to 180°C (350°F), gas mark 4. Wash the mushrooms and chop them roughly. Peel and chop the onion. Fry the onion in the oil in a large saucepan for 7 minutes, then add the mushrooms and fry for a further 3 minutes. Remove from the heat and liquidize. Add all the remaining ingredients and season to taste. Grease a 450g (1 lb) loaf tin generously with butter or soft margarine and coat well with dried breadcrumbs. Spoon the mushroom mixture into this and smooth the top. Bake, uncovered, for 1 hour. Slip a knife round the sides of the tin and turn the loaf out. Serve in slices, with a savoury sauce and vegetables.

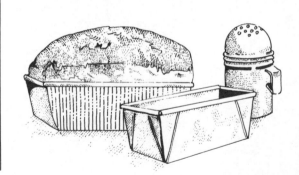

MUSHROOM LOAF (2)

I used to call this 'Mushroom Timbale' – I was rather into pretentious titles in those days! This makes a big loaf and quantities can be halved for a 450g (1 lb) loaf if you prefer.

SERVES 10 F
1 large onion
8 flat mushrooms
2 tomatoes, skinned
50g (2oz) butter
1 tablespoon flour
275ml (10 fl oz) water
1 teaspoon yeast extract
1 heaped teaspoon mixed herbs
225g (8oz) finely grated cashew nuts
225g (8oz) soft breadcrumbs
2 eggs
sea salt
freshly ground black pepper
sliced tomato
lemon slices
parsley sprigs

Set oven to 190°C (375°F), gas mark 5. Butter a 900g (2 lb) loaf tin and line with a long strip of non-stick paper, down narrow sides, and over base. Butter well. Peel onion and chop finely; wash and finely chop 4 of the mushrooms and slice tomatoes. Fry all these together gently in the butter for 10 minutes, then add the flour. Stir for 1 minute then add the water, yeast extract and herbs. Stir until thickened, then add the rest of the ingredients. Place the remaining 4 mushrooms, black side down, in bottom of the prepared tin, spoon mixture on top, and smooth over. Cover with tin foil and bake for 1½ hours. Cool for 2 minutes, then turn out of tin onto a large warm serving dish and remove paper. Garnish dish with tomato and lemon slices and some sprigs of parsley, and serve with vegetarian gravy, roast potatoes and vegetables.

MUSHROOMS AND TOFU

If you can get dried Chinese mushrooms they give this dish an excellent flavour, but you can use ordinary fresh mushrooms instead. For more about tofu see page 203.

SERVES 2
6 dried Chinese mushrooms or use 125g (4oz) fresh mushrooms
225g (8oz) firm tofu
olive oil for shallow-frying
1 onion, peeled and chopped
garlic clove, peeled and crushed
1 piece of fresh root ginger about 2.5cm (1in) long, peeled and grated
½ teaspoon soy sauce
½ teaspoon vegetarian stock powder or crumbled stock cube
2 tablespoons water or liquid drained from the dried mushrooms
50g (2oz) flaked almonds.

If you're using dried mushrooms, rinse them under the tap then put them into a small bowl, cover them with boiling water and leave them for 1 hour. Drain the mushrooms, reserving the liquid. Cut the mushrooms into pieces; if you're using fresh mushrooms wash and slice them. Cut the tofu into smallish cubes, heat a little oil in a large saucepan and fry the tofu quickly until it is lightly browned on all sides. Take it out of the oil and keep it warm. Heat a little more oil in the saucepan and fry the onions for about 7 minutes, then add the garlic, ginger and mushrooms and fry for about 2 minutes, until the mushrooms are just tender. Stir in the soy sauce, stock powder and water or mushroom liquid. Let the mixture blend for a moment or two, then put in the tofu and cook gently for about 2 minutes, just to reheat the tofu and give it a chance to absorb the flavours of the sauce. Sprinkle the almonds over the mixture just before serving it.

Serve this with fluffy cooked rice and Chinese cabbage.

MUSHROOM AND TOMATO SAVOURY

This is another very popular recipe. It's one I invented for one of my books at the last minute, when I needed one more recipe, to fill a gap! These days I have some reservations about the amount of fat used; serve with steamed vegetables and keep the rest of the day's eating low in fat.

SERVES 4 F
225g (8oz) wholemeal breadcrumbs
125g (4oz) grated nuts (any type)
8 tablespoons olive oil
225g (8oz) mushrooms, sliced
1 onion, grated
225g (8oz) tomatoes, skinned and quartered
sea salt
freshly ground black pepper
1 teaspoon marjoram – optional

Set oven to 190°C (375°F), gas mark 5. Fry the breadcrumbs and nuts in 7 tablespoons of the oil, stirring frequently until golden and crisp. Fry the mushrooms, onion and tomatoes together in the rest of the oil for 5 minutes. Grease an ovenproof dish and fill with alternate layers of the mushroom mixture and the crumb mixture, seasoning each layer with salt, pepper and marjoram (if used), and ending with the crumb mixture. Bake for 30 minutes.

BROWN NUTMEAT

This is a dark, strongly flavoured nutmeat, in contrast with the delicately flavoured white one on page 174.

SERVES 6 F
2 large onions, chopped
2 garlic cloves, crushed
50g (2oz) mushrooms, chopped
25g (1oz) butter
½ teaspoon rosemary ⎱
½ teaspoon basil ⎰ optional
½ teaspoon celery seed
1 teaspoon yeast extract
1 heaped tablespoon plain flour
150ml (5 fl oz) water or stock
2 eggs, beaten
225g (8oz) grated walnuts or hazel nuts
125g (4oz) soft wholemeal breadcrumbs
sea salt
freshly ground black pepper

Set oven to 190°C (375°F), gas mark 5. Fry the onions in the butter with the herbs and celery seed until lightly browned. Stir in the yeast extract and flour. Add the water and cook until thickened, then add the beaten eggs. Cook for 2 minutes, then add the grated nuts and breadcrumbs, and season to taste. Line a 450g (1 lb) loaf tin with a long strip of non-stick paper. Butter well. Spoon mixture in, and level the top. Cover with tin foil, and bake for 1 hour. Or the nut roast can be rolled in breadcrumbs or crushed cornflakes, dotted with butter and baked at the same temperature for 45 minutes. Serve with vegetarian gravy and redcurrant jelly.

NUTMEAT WITH MUSHROOM STUFFING

A pleasant, layered nutmeat.

SERVES 6 F
1 large onion, chopped
50g (2oz) butter
1 level teaspoon mixed herbs
1 heaped tablespoon plain flour
150ml (5 fl oz) milk
225g (8oz) grated cashew nuts, ground almonds or grated walnuts
¼ teaspoon mace
¼ teaspoon nutmeg
50g (2oz) fresh breadcrumbs
juice and rind of ½ lemon
1 egg white
sea salt
freshly ground black pepper

Mushroom stuffing
225g (8oz) mushrooms, chopped
50g (2oz) butter
1 heaped teaspoon yeast extract
175g (6oz) wholemeal breadcrumbs
1 egg yolk
sea salt
freshly ground black pepper

Set oven to 180°C (350°F), gas mark 4. Fry the onion gently in the butter with the herbs for 10 minutes, until soft but not browned. Add the flour and the milk and stir until thickened. Add the rest of the ingredients and mix well. Season to taste. Next, make the stuffing. Fry the mushrooms in the butter until tender – about 5 minutes. Stir in all the other ingredients and season to taste. Line a 450g (1 lb) loaf tin with a long strip of non-stick paper and grease with butter. Put in half the nut mixture, spread the stuffing on top, and then add the rest of the nut mixture. Cover with foil and bake for 1 hour. Turn out carefully on to a large plate and serve surrounded with roast potatoes and garnished with parsley and slices of lemon. This nutmeat can be prepared several hours beforehand and left in a cool place, covered with foil ready for baking.

NUT MINCE

My mother used to make this when I was little, it's very easy to make.

SERVES 4 [F]
1 large onion, chopped
½ teaspoon basil
50g (2oz) butter
2 × 400g (14oz) cans peeled tomatoes
sea salt
freshly ground black pepper
225g (8oz) finely ground walnuts *or* hazel nuts
125g (4oz) soft wholemeal breadcrumbs
2 tablespoons sweet chutney
triangles of fried bread or toast

Fry the onion with the herbs in the butter until brown. Add the tomatoes and all the other ingredients. Cook gently for 20 minutes. Serve garnished with small triangles of fried bread or wholemeal toast and parsley.

NUT RISSOLES

Some friends kindly made these nut rissoles for my husband and I to eat at their barbecue. They proved extremely popular with the meat eaters, too. We ate them with soft rolls and salad.

SERVES 4 [F]
50g (2oz) butter
1 small onion, chopped
1 stick celery, chopped *or* ½ teaspoon celery seed
1 teaspoon mixed herbs
1 tablespoon wholemeal flour
150ml (5 fl oz) milk
½ teaspoon yeast extract – optional
1 egg
225g (8oz) grated almonds, hazel nuts *or* walnuts
125g (4oz) fresh wholemeal breadcrumbs
sea salt
freshly ground black pepper
beaten egg
toasted crumbs
olive oil for shallow-frying

Gently cook the onion and celery or celery seed and mixed herbs in the butter. Add the flour, stir well, add the milk, yeast extract, egg, nuts and crumbs. Stir well and cook for 5 minutes. Season to taste. Make into round shapes, coat in egg and breadcrumbs, and shallow-fry in hot olive oil until crisp on both sides.

A pleasant variation is to use a tablespoon of buckwheat flour instead of wholemeal flour: this gives a dark colour and unusual flavour.

BROWN NUT RISSOLES IN TOMATO SAUCE

In this recipe, well-flavoured nut rissoles are baked in a fresh-tasting tomato sauce. These are delicious served with buttery wholemeal spaghetti, Parmesan cheese and a crisp green salad with a good olive oil dressing.

SERVES 3–4 [F]
1 tablespoon olive oil
1 onion, peeled and chopped
1 garlic clove, peeled and crushed
450g (1 lb) tomatoes, peeled and chopped *or* use
425g (15oz) can
sea salt
freshly ground black pepper
1 small onion, fried
125g (4oz) brown nuts such as unblanched almonds
or roasted hazel nuts – see page 136
50g (2oz) soft wholemeal breadcrumbs
50g (2oz) vegetarian Cheddar cheese, finely grated
2 heaped teaspoons tomato purée
1 egg
½ teaspoon dried thyme
sea salt
freshly ground black pepper

Start by making the sauce. Heat the oil in a medium-sized saucepan and fry the onion for 10 minutes, until softened but not browned. Add the garlic and tomatoes, and cook for a further 15 minutes, until the tomatoes have collapsed and reduced to a purée. Sieve or liquidize the mixture and season with salt and pepper.

Next, set the oven to 180°C (350°F), gas mark 4, and make the rissoles by simply mixing the rest of the ingredients together and seasoning to taste. Form the mixture into eight rissoles and place them in a greased, shallow, ovenproof dish. Pour the sauce over the rissoles and bake them in the pre-heated oven for 25–30 minutes, until they are puffy but firm to the touch.

Variation

NUT RISSOLES IN RATATOUILLE

Another variation is to bake the nut rissoles, either the white or brown version, in ratatouille. Prepare and cook the ratatouille, as described on page 130, and put it into a shallow ovenproof dish. Put the nut rissoles on top of the ratatouille and bake as described for nut rissoles in tomato sauce, above. These go well with fluffy brown rice and a green salad, and, if you use canned ratatouille, perhaps enlivened with a dash of wine or cider, this makes a good emergency dish.

CHUNKY NUT AND VEGETABLE ROAST

This nut roast has a pleasant, chewy texture.

SERVES 4–6 [F]
1 carrot, scraped
1 onion, peeled
1 celery stick
225g (8oz) mixed nuts, for instance, almonds, peanuts, Brazil nuts
2 teaspoons yeast extract
2 eggs
1–2 teaspoons dried mixed herbs
sea salt
freshly ground black pepper
butter and dried crumbs, wheat germ *or* oatmeal for coating tin

Set oven to 190°C (375°F), gas mark 5. Put all the ingredients into a food processor and process until vegetables and nuts are chopped into chunky pieces. Or spread the vegetables and nuts out on a large board and chop with an autochop, then put into a bowl and mix with the remaining ingredients. Line a 450g (1 lb) loaf tin with a strip of non-stick paper. Grease well and sprinkle with dry crumbs. Spoon out mixture into tin, level top. Bake, uncovered, for 45 minutes, until centre is set. Slip a knife round the edge and turn loaf out on to a warm serving dish. It's good with vegetarian gravy, mint sauce (chopped fresh mint mixed with wine vinegar and a dash of honey), potatoes and vegetables, or sliced cold, with salad.

STUFFED ONIONS (1)

This is a warming, winter dish and goes well with Bircher potatoes (page 128) which you can cook in the oven at the same time as the onions.

SERVES 4
4 large onions
75g (3oz) continental lentils, soaked and cooked as usual
1 garlic clove, crushed
2 teaspoons tomatoe purée
125g (4oz) grated cheese
½ teaspoon dried thyme
sea salt
freshly ground black pepper

Peel the onions and cook them for 15 minutes in boiling salted water, drain and cool. Preheat the oven to 200°C (400°F), gas mark 6. With a sharp knife scoop out the inside of the onions, leaving the outer layers intact. Chop up the scooped-out onion and mix it with the cooked continental lentils, the garlic, tomato purée, cheese and thyme. Season with sea salt and freshly ground black pepper. Divide the mixture between the onions, pushing it well down into the cavities. Put the onions into an oiled oven-proof casserole and, if there's any of the stuffing mixture left over, scatter that round the onions. Bake them in the preheated oven for 30–40 minutes.

ITALIAN STUFFED ONIONS (2)

I like bizarre combinations of ingredients, so this dish, with it's mixture of onions, macaroons, cheese and sultanas appeals to me! I think the mixture of sweet and savoury really works well, like cheese and chutney or curry and bananas. I like to use those big Spanish onions to make this when they come into the shops early in September.

SERVES 4
4 large Spanish onions
4 macaroons
75g (3oz) soft wholemeal breadcrumbs
¼ teaspoon ground cinnamon
¼ teaspoon ground cloves
¼ teaspoon grated nutmeg
2 eggs, beaten
50g (2oz) grated Parmesan cheese – *or* use strong cooking cheese
25–50g (1–2oz) sultanas
sea salt
freshly ground black pepper
15g (½oz) butter

Rinse the onions but don't peel them. Put them into a large saucepan of water and simmer them for about 20 minutes, until they feel tender when pierced with the point of a knife. (They should not be completely cooked through at this stage.) Drain the onions and let them get cool enough to handle, then remove the skins and root ends and cut the onions in half horizontally. Scoop out the centre of each half making a nice cavity for the stuffing and leave three or four layers of onion. Arrange the onion halves in a greased shallow oven-proof dish.

Set the oven to 180°C (350°F), gas mark 4. Now make the stuffing. Chop the scooped-out onion fairly finely and put it into a bowl. Crush the macaroons – press them with a rolling pin or pop them into the liquidizer and blend for a moment or two. Add them to the onions, also the breadcrumbs, spices, eggs, cheese and sultanas and stir until everything is well mixed to a softish consistency. You might need to add a drop or two of milk but I usually find the natural juiciness of the onions together with the eggs sufficient. Season with salt and a good grinding of pepper then spoon the mixture into the onion cavities, piling them up. Put a piece of butter on top of each and bake them uncovered, for 30 minutes.

Stuffed onions are good with a sharply flavoured cheese sauce, mashed potatoes and a cooked green vegetable.

GREEN PEPPER AND TOMATO STEW

This spicy Hungarian stew, called *lesco*, is rather similar to the Italian *peperonata* but it's made with green peppers and has a generous seasoning of paprika. You can serve it Hungarian style with a fried egg on top, but I think it's nicer with fluffy brown rice or warm crusty bread and soft cheese.

SERVES 4
450g (1 lb) green peppers, de-seeded and roughly
chopped
2 medium onions
3 tablespoons olive oil
2 garlic cloves, crushed
2 tablespoons paprika
400g (14 oz) can tomatoes
sea salt
freshly ground black pepper

Slice the peppers into even-sized pieces, discarding seeds and stalk. Peel and chop the onions, then fry them in the oil in a large saucepan for about 5 minutes until golden brown. Remove from the heat and stir in the garlic, paprika, peppers, tomatoes and a seasoning of salt and pepper. Cover and cook gently for about 30 minutes until all the vegetables are tender. Check seasoning and serve.

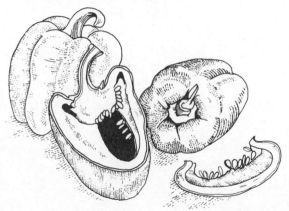

STUFFED PEPPERS (1)

My first stuffed pepper recipe, invented for a summer supper and another popular one with readers.

SERVES 4
1 medium-sized onion
1 large garlic clove
1 teaspoon basil
2 tablespoons olive oil
50g (2oz) brown rice
1 bay leaf
575ml (1 pint) tomato juice
125g (4oz) walnuts, grated
1 teaspoon lemon juice
sea salt
freshly ground black pepper
sugar
4 green peppers
cornflakes
25–50g (1–2oz) grated cheese

Set oven to 150°C (300°F), gas mark 2. Fry the onion and garlic with the basil in the oil until soft but not brown, about 10 minutes. Wash the rice and pick out any brown or hard pieces. Add rice, bay leaf, and half the tomato juice to the onion mixture, and bring to the boil. Then turn down the heat very low and cook for 40 minutes. Add walnuts and lemon juice, and season carefully with salt and pepper, adding a little more tomato juice if necessary, to make a soft consistency.

Wash the peppers and remove the tops. Scoop out all the seeds and rinse the insides of the pepper. Put 5cm (2in) water into a pan large enough to take the peppers. Bring water to boil, then add peppers and remove from heat. Leave peppers in the water with the lid on the pan for 5 minutes, then drain them and fill with stuffing. Put them on a large ovenproof dish. Add pinch salt and pinch of sugar to the remaining tomato juice and pour this round the peppers. Sprinkle cornflakes and grated cheese on top. Bake for 30–45 minutes. The peppers can be prepared in advance several hours before cooking.

STUFFED PEPPERS (2)

Stuffed peppers always seem to be popular. In this recipe I've suggested four medium-sized peppers, but you could use two large ones split in half.

SERVES 4
125g (4oz) red kidney beans
4 medium-sized green peppers
75g (3oz) long grain brown rice, washed
275ml (10 fl oz) water
1 large onion, peeled and chopped
1 large garlic clove, crushed
2 tablespoons olive oil
2 tomatoes, peeled and chopped
50 g (2oz) walnuts, chopped
¼–½ teaspoon chilli powder
sea salt
freshly ground black pepper

Wash and soak the red kidney beans as usual, then drain and rinse them and put them into a heavy-based saucepan with the water and simmer for 15 minutes. Add the brown rice, bring up to the boil, then turn the heat down and leave them to simmer gently, with a lid on the saucepan, for 45 minutes, until the rice and beans are both cooked and all the water has been absorbed.

Set the oven to 190°C (375°F), gas mark 5. Prepare the peppers by slicing off their stalk ends and removing the seeds, then put them into a large saucepan of boiling water and simmer them gently for 2–3 minutes. Drain them well and pat them dry with kitchen paper. Place the peppers in a greased shallow casserole and leave them on one side while you make the filling.

Fry the onion and garlic in the oil for 5 minutes, then add the tomatoes, the cooked rice and beans, walnuts, chilli powder and sea salt and freshly ground black pepper to taste. Spoon the filling into the peppers, replace the sliced-off tops as 'lids' and bake in the oven for about 35–40 minutes, until the peppers are completely tender. Serve them with a tasty tomato sauce and some vegetables.

PEPPERS WITH LENTIL AND TOMATO STUFFING

Another tasty dish, good with creamy potatoes and buttered baby carrots or served on a base of fluffy cooked brown rice and served with a tomato salad.

SERVES 4
4 medium-sized green peppers
1 large onion
2 garlic cloves
3 tablespoons olive oil
1 bay leaf
6 tomatoes, skinned and chopped or 400g (14oz) can, well drained
175g (6oz) continental lentils, soaked, cooked and drained
125g (4oz) wholemeal breadcrumbs
2 tablespoons chopped parsley
freshly ground black pepper
sea salt
a little grated cheese.

Preheat the oven to 180°C (350°F), gas mark 4. Slice the tops off the peppers and remove the seeds; rinse the peppers inside and out under cold water, then put them into a large saucepan of boiling, salted water and simmer them for 2–3 minutes; drain and dry them and place them in a shallow greased casserole.

Peel and slice the onion and crush the garlic; fry them together in the oil with the bay leaf for 10 minutes, then remove the bay leaf and stir in the tomatoes, lentils, wholemeal breadcrumbs, parsley and a good seasoning of freshly ground black pepper and sea salt. Mix it all together well, then divide it between the four peppers, piling them up well. Sprinkle the tops with grated cheese and bake them in the oven for 30–40 minutes, or until the peppers are tender.

PEPPERS WITH OLIVE STUFFING

A recipe with an unusual flavour.

SERVES 4
2 very large red or green peppers
1 small onion, chopped
50g (2oz) butter
225g (8oz) bread
175g (6oz) grated cheese
125g (4oz) olives, stoned
1 tablespoon chopped parsley
sea salt
freshly ground black pepper
few drops tabasco

Set oven to 180°C (350°F), gas mark 4. Halve the peppers lengthwise, remove seeds and core. Simmer in a little water for 5 minutes and drain. Meanwhile fry onion lightly in the butter until tender. Slice bread roughly, cover with warm water and leave for a minute to soften. Squeeze out water and crumble bread. Mix with the grated cheese, fried onion, stoned olives, parsley, salt, pepper and tabasco. Place pepper halves in a buttered casserole. Fill with olive stuffing and bake for 45 minutes until filling is golden brown and peppers soft.

PEPPERS STUFFED WITH PINE NUTS APRICOTS AND RAISINS

There's a Middle-Eastern flavour to this fragrantly spiced dish.

SERVES 4
1 onion, peeled and chopped
1 garlic clove, peeled and crushed
½ teaspoon powdered cinnamon
1 tablespoon olive oil
350g (12oz) cooked brown rice
50g (2oz) pine nuts or chopped cashew nuts
25–50g (1–2oz) raisins
25–50g (1–2oz) chopped dried apricots
sea salt
freshly ground black pepper
4 small squat red or green peppers, about 75–125g
(3–4oz) each
1 tablespoon tomato purée
150ml (5 fl oz) water

Fry onion, garlic and cinnamon in the oil for 4–5 minutes, then add the cooked rice, nuts, raisins and apricots; season. Set oven to 180°C (350°F), gas mark 4. Slice tops off the peppers and scoop out seeds. Stand peppers in a deep, ovenproof dish, fill them with rice mixture, and replace tops as lids. Mix tomato purée with the water, season, and pour round the peppers. Bake for 1–1½ hours.

STUFFED PEPPERS, SPANISH STYLE

In this recipe, rice, mushrooms, onions and grated cheese are used to stuff peppers, and then they're baked in a simple fresh tomato sauce. They're nice as a main course, served with a cooked vegetable and some buttery new potatoes.

SERVES 4
125g (4oz) long-grain brown rice
275ml (10 fl oz) water
sea salt
2 medium green peppers
1 large onion, peeled and chopped
1 garlic clove, peeled and crushed in a little salt
4 tablespoons olive oil
125g (4oz) button mushrooms washed and finely
sliced
1 teaspoon dried thyme
½ teaspoon mustard powder
2 teaspoons lemon juice
125g (4oz) grated cheese
freshly ground black pepper
450g (1 lb) tomatoes, peeled and chopped – or use
425g (15oz) can

First cook the rice: put it into a heavy-based saucepan with the water and a pinch of salt. Bring it up to the boil then turn the heat down and let it cook very gently, with a lid on the saucepan, for about 40 minutes, until the rice is tender and has absorbed all the liquid. (The rice can be cooked well in advance because it will keep for several days in the fridge.)

Set the oven to 180°C (350°F), gas mark 4. Halve the peppers and remove the centre and seeds; rinse them under the cold tap. Put the peppers into a saucepan half full of cold water and bring them up to the boil, then take them off the heat, drain them and leave on one side.

Fry the onion and garlic in the oil for 10 minutes. Mix half the onion and garlic with the cooked rice and add the mushrooms, thyme, mustard, lemon juice, grated cheese and a good seasoning of salt and pepper.

Mix the tomatoes with the remaining onion and garlic in the pan and add salt and pepper to taste. Pour the tomato mixture into a shallow ovenproof dish and place the peppers on top. Spoon the rice mixture into the peppers, piling it up well. Bake the peppers, uncovered for about 40 minutes, until the stuffing is golden brown and the peppers tender.

STUFFED RED PEPPERS WITH ALMONDS

And lastly a stuffed red pepper recipe. Here red peppers are stuffed with a tasty filling of mushrooms, wine, breadcrumbs, nuts and tomatoes.

SERVES 6
3 medium-sized red peppers
125g (4oz) almonds, finely grated
125g (4oz) cheese, grated
50g (2oz) fresh wholemeal breadcrumbs
225g (8oz) can tomatoes
125g (4oz) mushrooms, washed and chopped
8 tablespoons stock, red wine *or* dry cider
1 garlic clove, peeled and crushed
sea salt
freshly ground black pepper
a little extra grated cheese and breadcrumbs for topping

Set the oven to 190°C (375°F), gas mark 5. First prepare the peppers: halve them and remove the centre and seeds; rinse them under the cold tap. Put them into a saucepan half-full of cold water and bring them up to the boil, then take them off the heat, drain and place in a lightly-greased, shallow, ovenproof dish.

Next make the stuffing: put the nuts, cheese, breadcrumbs, tomatoes, mushrooms, stock (or wine or cider) and garlic into a bowl and mix together, adding plenty of salt and pepper to taste. Spoon this mixture into the peppers, dividing it between them. Sprinkle with crumbs and grated cheese. Bake, uncovered, for about 40 minutes, until the peppers are tender and the stuffing golden brown.

PINE NUTMEAT WITH HERB STUFFING

This dish consists of two layers of moist, delicately-flavoured, white nutmeat with a layer of green herb stuffing in the middle. It's a favourite vegetarian alternative to Christmas turkey and popular with my family at any time. The pine nuts are expensive and, though lovely for a special occasion, can be replaced by cheaper white nuts such as cashews or ground almonds. I would serve this loaf with golden roast potatoes and either wine sauce and a lightly cooked green vegetable or a purée of Brussels sprouts; the cranberry and apple sauce also goes very well with it.

SERVES 6 F
butter and dried breadcrumbs for lining loaf tin
25g (1oz) butter
1 onion, peeled and chopped
225g (8oz) pine nuts *or* a mixture of pine nuts,
ground almonds and cashew nuts, grated
4 tablespoons milk
125g (4oz) soft, white breadcrumbs
2 eggs
sea salt
freshly ground black pepper
grated nutmeg

Stuffing
175g (6oz) soft breadcrumbs, white *or* brown
125g (4oz) butter
grated rind and juice of ½ small lemon
½ teaspoon dried marjoram
½ teaspoon dried thyme
4 heaped tablespoons fresh parsley, chopped
sea salt
freshly ground black pepper

2 tablespoons pine nuts, lightly roasted
parsley sprigs
lemon slices

Set the oven to 180°C (350°F), gas mark 4. Line a 450g (1 lb) loaf tin with a long strip of silicon paper to cover the narrow sides and base of the tin; grease very well with butter and sprinkle with dried breadcrumbs – this helps the loaf to come out of the tin cleanly. Melt the butter in a medium-sized saucepan and fry the onion for 10 minutes until soft but not browned. Take the saucepan off the heat and mix in the rest of the ingredients, seasoning well with salt, pepper and grated nutmeg. Next make the stuffing by mixing all the ingredients together and seasoning well.

To assemble the loaf, first spoon half the nut mixture into the prepared tin, then, with your hands, press the stuffing mixture into a rectangle which is the right size to make a layer on top of the nut mixture; put it gently in place and spoon the rest of the nut mixture on top. Smooth the surface, cover with a piece of buttered foil and bake for 1 hour. After this, remove the foil and have a look at the nutmeat; if you think it needs to be a bit browner on top, pop it back into the oven, uncovered for a further 5–10 minutes. If possible, leave the loaf for 3–4 minutes after you take it out of the oven – this helps it to 'settle' and come out of the tin more easily – then slip a knife down the sides of the loaf, turn it out of the tin on to a warmed serving dish and strip off the piece of silicon paper. Garnish with the roasted nuts, parsley and lemon.

POTATO BAKE

Potatoes are an undervalued food. Yet they're cheap, popular and very nutritious, containing useful amounts of iron, vitamin C and protein, as well as fibre. I like dishes which make potatoes into a main meal. This bake makes a simple, homely supper that children love. It's good with a tomato sauce and a green vegetable. You can leave the skins on the potatoes, but I think it's better if they're peeled.

SERVES 4
450g (1 lb) potatoes, peeled
15g (½ oz) butter
1 garlic clove, crushed
sea salt
freshly ground black pepper
125g (4oz) grated cheese
4 tablespoons milk

Set oven to 160°C (325°F). gas mark 3. Slice the potatoes finely – this is quickly done with the slicing side of a grater. Mix the butter and garlic and use half to grease a shallow ovenproof dish. Put a layer of potatoes in the base of the dish, sprinkle with salt, pepper and some of the cheese. Continue like this until everything is in, ending with potatoes. Pour the milk over the top, dot with the remaining butter. Bake for 1½ hours, until the potato is tender.

POTATO CAKES

Potato cakes can be delicious, creamy on the inside, crisp on the outside. If you add a little protein, in the form of grated cheese, chopped nuts or sunflower seeds, they make a good main dish and are very popular with children.

SERVES 4
450g (1 lb) potatoes
about 150ml (5 fl oz) skimmed milk
125g (4oz) grated cheese, nuts (any type) or sunflower seeds
2 tablespoons chopped parsley
salt
freshly ground black pepper
50g (2oz) wholemeal flour
2 tablespoons olive oil

Scrub the potatoes, cover with water and boil until tender. Drain, cool slightly, then slip off the skins with a small sharp knife. Mash, adding enough skimmed milk to make a firm consistency. Stir in the cheese, nuts or sunflower seeds, the parsley and seasoning. Add some more milk if necessary – the mixture must be manageable but not too dry. Divide into eight pieces, coat in flour and fry in the oil until crisp on both sides. Drain and serve as soon as possible with salad or with a sauce and cooked vegetables.

JACKET POTATO BOATS

A dish from my childhood, which my children, too, have loved.

SERVES 4
4 large potatoes
25g (1oz) butter
175g (6oz) grated cheese
pinch cayenne pepper
150ml (5 fl oz) milk
sea salt
freshly ground black pepper

Scrub potatoes, score them horizontally round the middle and bake in a hot oven 230°C (450°F), gas mark 8, for 1 hour or until tender. Cut around the score marks and pull apart. Scoop out the potato flesh, mash it well, add the butter, cheese, a pinch cayenne, milk, salt and pepper. Pile back into the skins and brown under a hot grill, or put back into the oven for 20 minutes until browned. Serve with a 'finger salad' of lettuce, tomato, cucumber and carrot sticks.

POTATO AND MUSHROOM STEW WITH SOURED CREAM

This Hungarian stew makes a good vegetarian main dish. The protein can be supplied by serving a protein starter, side salad or pudding or by garnishing the stew with wedges of hardboiled eggs or grated cheese.

SERVES 4
900g (2 lb) potatoes
1 medium onion
1 garlic clove
175g (6oz) button mushrooms
3 tablespoons olive oil
1 tablespoon mild paprika – look for Hungarian 'rose' paprika
25g (1oz) flour
425ml (15 fl oz) stock
sea salt
freshly ground black pepper
150ml (5 fl oz) soured cream *or* natural yoghurt

Peel the potatoes and cut them into even-sized chunks, peel and chop the onion, crush the garlic, wash the mushrooms and cut them into halves or quarters if necessary. Heat the oil in a large saucepan and fry the onion for about 5 minutes until golden, then stir in the garlic, potatoes, paprika and flour and cook for a further minute or two. Add the stock and bring up to the boil. Put a lid on the saucepan and leave it over a gentle heat for about 20 minutes, until the potatoes are very nearly tender, then put in the mushrooms and cook for a further 3–4 minutes.

Put the soured cream or yoghurt into a small bowl and gradually add to it a ladleful of the liquid from the saucepan; mix well then pour this into the saucepan and heat gently until the mixture is very hot. Season to taste. Serve immediately.

RED CABBAGE AND CHESTNUT CASSEROLE

Real warming winter food this, a rich burgundy-coloured casserole of succulent red cabbage and sweet-tasting chestnuts cooked with butter, onions and red wine. It's lovely served as a main dish with jacket potatoes which have been split and filled with soured cream and chopped chives. If there's any over it's very good cold as a salad. I rather lazily tend to use dried chestnuts but you could use fresh ones. You'll need about 450g (1 lb) for this recipe. Prepare them in the way I've described on page 136 and add them to the casserole with the wine and seasoning.

SERVES 3–4
125g (4oz) dried chestnuts
1 large onion
50g (2oz) butter
700g (1½ lb) red cabbage
275ml (10 fl oz) cheap red wine
sea salt
freshly ground black pepper
sugar

Cover the chestnuts with plenty of cold water and leave them to soak for several hours. After that cook them gently until they're tender – this will take 1–1½ hours and you'll need to watch the level of the water and probably add some more so that they don't burn dry. Drain the chestnuts.

Set the oven to 150°C (300°F), gas mark 2. Peel and chop the onion and fry it in the butter for 10 minutes; while it's cooking wash and shred the cabbage, then add this to the onion and turn it so that it gets coated with the butter. Stir in the chestnuts, wine and some salt and pepper. Bring the mixture up to the boil, then transfer it to an ovenproof casserole, cover with a lid and bake slowly for 2–3 hours, until the cabbage is very tender. Check the seasoning – you'll probably need to add more salt and pepper and some sugar to bring out the flavour.

This dish can be made in advance and reheated – in fact I think this actually improves the flavour – and it can also be cooked at the bottom of a hotter oven if you want to bake jacket potatoes at the same time.

RED CABBAGE STUFFED WITH CHESTNUTS

The sweetness of chestnuts goes particularly well with red cabbage and if you add butter and red wine too you get a really rich-tasting, warming dish, just right for the winter when the chestnuts and cabbage are in season.

SERVES 6
700g (1½ lb) fresh chestnuts *or* 225g (8oz) dried chestnuts
1 small/medium red cabbage, about 1.5 kilos (3 lb)
125g (4oz) butter
2 large onions, peeled and chopped
1 tablespoon lemon juice
sea salt
freshly ground black pepper
2 carrots, peeled and sliced
1 tablespoon redcurrant jelly
275ml (10 fl oz) red wine

First prepare the chestnuts. If you're using fresh ones slash each one with a sharp knife then simmer them in boiling water for about 10 minutes until the cuts open and you can remove the skins using a small, sharp pointed knife. Keep the rest of the chestnuts in the boiling water as you work because the skins get hard again as they cool. If you've decided to save time by using dried chestnuts, as I must admit I usually do, let them soak in some cold water for a while if possible – this isn't essential but it helps as they can be very hard sometimes – then simmer them gently in plenty of water for at least an hour, until they're tender, then drain them.

Now wash and trim the cabbage, removing any tough or damaged leaves and cutting the stalk end level. Slice a lid from the top of the cabbage and using a small sharp knife and a spoon scoop out as much of the inside of the cabbage as possible, leaving a neat, good-sized cavity for stuffing. Chop the cabbage which you've scooped out fairly finely. Heat half the butter in a largish saucepan and fry half the onion for about 5 minutes, without browning, then stir in the chopped-up cabbage and cook for a further 5 minutes, with a lid on the saucepan, stirring occasionally. Add the chestnuts and half the lemon juice and season with salt and pepper. Leave on one side. Put the whole cabbage into a large saucepan half filled with cold water. Bring to the boil and simmer for 2 minutes with a lid on the saucepan. Drain and rinse the cabbage under cold water.

Melt the remaining butter in a saucepan that's large enough to hold the cabbage and fry the remaining onion and the carrots for 5 minutes. Mix the redcurrant jelly and the rest of the lemon juice with the onion and carrots, add some salt and pepper, then place the cabbage on top and carefully fill the cavity with the chestnut mixture, piling it up high. Pour the wine around the sides of the cabbage, put the saucepan over a low heat and cover with a lid. Leave it to cook very gently for about 3 hours or until the cabbage feels beautifully tender when pierced with the point of a knife.

It's easiest to serve this straight from the cooking pot and it's delicious with really light mashed potatoes.

SALSIFY WITH WHITE WINE AND MUSHROOMS

Cooked like this, in a wine-flavoured lemon mayonnaise sauce, with a topping of crisp crumbs and a garnish of fresh lemon, salsify is excellent either as a main course or starter. If you're serving this as a main course, I think it goes best with just a simply cooked green vegetable such as courgettes, spinach or mange-tout peas; or just buttered new potatoes, followed by a refreshing green salad before the cheese or pudding course.

SERVES 4
1 kilo (2¼ lb) salsify *or* scorzonera which is very similar
3 tablespoons lemon juice
sea salt
freshly ground black pepper
6 rounded tablespoons mayonnaise, home-made *or* good quality bought
225g (8oz) *fromage blanc*
4 tablespoons dry white wine *or* cider
Dijon mustard
225g (8oz) baby, white, button mushrooms, wiped and trimmed
50g (2oz) fresh wholemeal breadcrumbs
50g (2oz) cheese, grated

Peel the salsify or scorzonera roots and cut them into 2.5cm (1in) pieces. As they're prepared, put them into a saucepan containing 1 litre (1¾ pints) cold water and 2 tablespoons of the lemon juice – this will help to keep them white. When they're all prepared, put the saucepan over the heat, bring to the boil and cook for about 10 minutes, or until the salsify feels tender when pierced with the point of a knife. Drain, sprinkle with the remaining lemon juice and season with salt and pepper.

While the salsify is cooking, make the sauce by mixing together the mayonnaise, *fromage blanc*, white wine or cider and a dash of mustard if necessary. Season with salt and freshly ground black pepper. Set the oven to 200°C (400°F), gas mark 6. Put the salsify into a large, shallow, ovenproof dish and add the mushrooms; pour the sauce over the top. Cover completely with the crumbs and cheese and bake for 30–40 minutes, until heated through. (Timing will depend partly on the depth of the dish you've used, but the mixture shouldn't be overcooked or the sauce may separate.) If the top isn't crisp enough, finish it off quickly under a hot grill. Serve at once.

SALSIFY BAKED IN A LEMON SAUCE

Salsify has a delicate flavour, said to slightly resemble that of oysters. I don't know how much truth there is in this, having never tasted oysters, but I do like the flavour of salsify which I think is very pleasant and delicate.

SERVES 4–6
900g (2 lb) salsify
sea salt
freshly ground black pepper
25g (1½oz) butter
2 tablespoons flour
275ml (10 fl oz) water
2 tablespoons lemon juice
275ml (10 fl oz) soured cream
1 teaspoon Dijon mustard
fresh wholemeal crumbs and a little butter for
topping

Scrape the salsify, cut into 5cm (2in) lengths and cook in boiling salted water to cover, until just tender; drain and put into a lightly greased shallow gratin dish. Set the oven to 180°C (350°F), gas mark 4. Melt the butter in a small saucepan and stir in the flour; when it bubbles add the water and stir until smooth and thick. Then remove from the heat and mix in the lemon juice, soured cream and mustard, and salt and pepper to taste. Spoon the sauce over the salsify, sprinkle with breadcrumbs, dot with butter and bake for 40–45 minutes, until heated through and crisp on top.

SPINACH ROULADE

This is good served with buttered new potatoes or lemon potatoes, tomato sauce and baby carrots.

SERVES 4
900g (2 lb) fresh spinach *or* 450g (1 lb) chopped
frozen spinach
15g (½oz) butter
sea salt
freshly ground black pepper
4 eggs, separated
a little grated Parmesan cheese
175g (6oz) button mushrooms
15g (½oz) butter
1 rounded teaspoon cornflour *or* arrowroot
275ml (10 fl oz) single cream
grated nutmeg
sea salt
freshly ground black pepper

First prepare the spinach. If you're using fresh spinach, wash it thoroughly and put it into a large saucepan without any water. Put a lid on the saucepan and cook the spinach for 10 minutes until it's tender, pressing it down with the end of a fish slice and chopping it a bit as it gets softer. Drain thoroughly. Cook frozen spinach according to the directions on the packet, and drain well. Add the butter and seasoning and stir in the egg yolks.

Line a shallow swiss roll tin, 18 × 28cm (7 × 11in), with greased non-stick paper to cover the base of the tin and to extend 5cm (2in) up each side. Sprinkle with Parmesan cheese. Set oven to 200°C (400°F), gas mark 6. Whisk the egg whites until stiff but not dry and fold them into the spinach mixture. Pour the mixture into the prepared tin and bake for 10–15 minutes, until risen and springy to touch.

While the roulade is cooking, make the filling. Wipe and slice the mushrooms and fry them in the butter for 5 minutes until tender. Mix together the cornflour or arrowroot and cream; add this to the mushrooms and stir over the heat briefly until slightly thickened. Season with salt, pepper and nutmeg. Keep the mixture warm, but don't let it boil.

Have ready a large piece of greaseproof paper dusted with Parmesan cheese and turn the roulade out on to this; strip off the greased paper. Spread the filling over the roulade, then roll it up like a swiss roll and slide it on to a warmed serving dish. Return to the oven for 5 minutes to heat through, then serve immediately.

SWEETCORN PUDDING

Really this is another of those dishes that's supposed to be served as an accompaniment to meat, but I think you'll agree it also makes a good main dish in its own right. I like to serve it with sprouts, gravy, roast potatoes and cranberry sauce for a vegetarian Thanksgiving Day meal – rather a bizarre-sounding combination, I know, but it works.

SERVES 3–4
275ml (10 fl oz) milk
25g (1oz) butter
125g (4oz) bread, weighed with the crusts removed
330g (11½oz) can sweetcorn kernels, drained
1 egg *or* 2 egg yolks
1 tablespoon chopped fresh parsley
½ teaspoon paprika
sea salt
freshly ground black pepper
a little grated cheese

Set the oven to 190°C (375°F), gas mark 5. Put the milk and butter into a saucepan and heat gently until the butter has melted. Remove from the heat and with your fingers crumble the bread into the milk – don't worry if there are some lumpy pieces. Leave on one side for a few minutes to allow the bread to soften, then mix it round and add the sweetcorn, egg, parsley, paprika and salt and pepper to taste. Spoon the mixture into a greased ovenproof dish and sprinkle with grated cheese. Bake the pudding for 35–40 minutes until set and golden brown.

STIR-FRIED TOFU WITH CARROTS

When using bean curd in a stir-fried mixture, flavouring is all-important and that's where the Chinese are so skilled. Here the flavour is supplied by the garlic, ginger, soy sauce, bean paste, sherry and stock. It's lovely to use Chinese mushrooms if you can get them – they're available dried from Chinese grocers – but if not, ordinary mushrooms can be used instead. The miso (bean paste) can be bought from health shops. It's useful for flavouring soups, stews and casseroles, as well as Chinese-style dishes.

SERVES 2–3
225g (8oz) carrots
4 dried Chinese mushrooms *or* 225g (8oz) fresh
mushrooms
1 onion
2 garlic cloves
a piece of root ginger, peeled and grated to give
about 2 teaspoons
2 tablespoons soy sauce
½–1 teaspoon miso
1 teaspoon sugar
few drops of tabasco
4 tablespoons boiling water
1 tablespoon sherry
225g (8oz) firm bean curd (tofu)
3 tablespoons olive oil

Prepare the carrots by scraping them and then cutting them into thin diagonal slices. Parboil them for 4–5 minutes, until they're almost tender; drain. Soak the dried mushrooms in enough water just to cover them, then drain them and cut into narrow strips. Or, if you're using ordinary mushrooms, wash and slice them. Peel and very finely chop the onion; crush the garlic; peel and finely grate the ginger. Mix together the soy sauce, miso, sugar, tabasco, hot water and sherry. Cut the bean curd into smallish dice.

When ready to cook, heat the oil in a wok or large frying pan and fry the garlic, ginger and onion for a few seconds, then stir in the mushrooms and carrots; cook for 30 seconds, then pour in the soy sauce mixture and cook for a couple of minutes, so that all the flavours have a chance to blend. Mix in the bean curd and stir-fry for a further 2 minutes, so that everything is hot. Serve immediately.

TOMATO PIE

A quick and easy supper dish.

SERVES 4
450g (1 lb) creamy mashed potatoes
225g (8oz) grated cheese
1 small onion, grated
sea salt
freshly ground black pepper
grated nutmeg
450g (1 lb) tomatoes, skinned
pinch basil
15g (½oz) butter

Set oven to 200°C (400°F), gas mark 6. Add grated cheese and grated onion to the potatoes, mix well and season with salt, pepper and nutmeg. Spread half mixture in a shallow buttered casserole; smooth well to form base of pie. Slice tomatoes, mix with seasoning and basil, and spread over potato base. Season lightly, spread with rest of potato to cover. Rough-up with prongs of fork and dot with butter. Bake for 30–40 minutes, until golden brown.

Variations

MUSHROOM PIE

Use 225–350g (8–12oz) sliced and lightly fried button mushrooms.

SWEETCORN PIE

Use 225g (8oz) packet of frozen sweetcorn, cooked according to the directions on the packet.

TOMATOES STUFFED WITH CHEESE

These juicy tomatoes with their cheesy breadcrumb stuffing make a delicious hot starter or light supper dish for late sumer when tomatoes are plentiful, and they're quick and easy to do.

SERVES 4–5
8 large or 4 very large tomatoes – about 700g (1½ lb) in all
sea salt
125g (4oz) wholemeal breadcrumbs
225g (8oz) grated cheese
1 garlic clove, peeled and crushed
freshly ground black pepper
1 tablespoon olive oil

Set the oven to 190°C (375°F), gas mark 5. Halve the tomatoes and scoop out the centres. Sprinkle a little salt inside each tomato and put them upside down on a plate to drain off any excess liquid while you make the filling. Chop the tomato centres and mix them with the breadcrumbs, grated cheese and garlic. Season with salt and pepper to taste. Arrange the tomato halves in a shallow greased dish. Pile the stuffing mixture into the tomato halves and sprinkle the olive oil on top. Bake the tomatoes for 20–30 minutes until they're tender and the filling is golden brown. Serve with buttered noodles and a crisp green salad.

TOMATOES STUFFED WITH CHICK PEAS

Served on crisp circles of fried bread these make an excellent starter, or, with brown rice or buttered noodles and a green vegetable or salad, they're excellent for a light main course.

SERVES 8 AS A STARTER OR 4 AS A MAIN DISH
8 large or 4 very large tomatoes
sea salt
2 large onions, peeled and chopped
3 garlic cloves, crushed
8 tablespoons olive oil
225g (8oz) chickpeas, cooked and drained or 2 × 400g (14oz) cans, drained
2 teaspoons dried basil
freshly ground black pepper
2 tablespoons lemon juice
fresh parsley sprigs
8 circles of fried bread, if serving the tomatoes as a starter

Cut a small slice from the top of each tomato, then, using a teaspoon, carefully scoop out the inside – this will not be needed in the recipe but can be used in tomato soups and sauces, etc. Sprinkle the insides of the tomatoes with a little sea salt; place the tomatoes upside down on a plate and leave for 30 minutes to draw out any excess liquid.

Preheat the oven to 180°C (350°F), gas mark 4. Fry the onions and garlic in 3 tablespoons of the olive oil in a medium-sized saucepan for 10 minutes, until soft but not browned, then mix in the cooked chickpeas, mashing them a bit as you do so. Add the basil, some sea salt and freshly ground black pepper and the lemon juice.

Use a little of the remaining olive oil to grease a shallow ovenproof dish. Place the tomatoes in the dish and fill each with some of the chickpea mixture, piling it up well. Put any remaining mixture around the edges of the dish. Replace the sliced-off tomato tops as 'lids'. Pour the remaining oil over the tops of the tomatoes and bake them in the oven for 30–40 minutes. Serve them from the dish, garnished with some fresh parsley sprigs. Or, if serving them as a starter, place each tomato on a circle of crisp fried bread and serve on individual plates.

TOMATOES STUFFED WITH PINE NUTS

I cannot make this dish without thinking of summer holidays in France because it's something I've made so often at the end of a hot sunny day there, with big tomatoes and fragrant thyme from the market. These tomatoes are delicious with onion rice or buttered noodles and a green salad. You should be able to get pine nuts at a health shop; if not, or if you think they're too extravagant, use chopped cashew nuts instead.

SERVES 4
4 large tomatoes, weighing about 225g (8oz) each
sea salt
2 tablespoons olive oil
1 onion, peeled and finely chopped
125g (4oz) pine nuts
125g (4oz) soft wholemeal breadcrumbs
1 garlic clove, peeled and crushed
2 tablespoons fresh parsley, chopped
1 tablespoon fresh thyme or 1 teaspoon dried
freshly ground black pepper

Set the oven to 190°C (375°F), gas mark 5. Wash the tomatoes, slice off the tops and scoop out the seeds with a spoon – they will not be needed for this recipe, although they can be made into a good sauce to serve with it, following the recipe for tomato sauce (page 65). Sprinkle the inside of the tomatoes with a little salt and place them upside down in a colander to drain while you prepare the stuffing. To do this, heat the oil in a saucepan and fry the onion for about 7 minutes, until softening, then remove from the heat and stir in the pine nuts, breadcrumbs, garlic, parsley and thyme; season. Arrange the tomatoes in a lightly-greased, shallow, ovenproof dish and fill each with some of the nut mixture, dividing it between them. Then replace the sliced-off tops, if you like, and bake, uncovered, for 20–30 minutes until they're tender.

STUFFED TOMATOES À LA PROVENÇALE

These tomatoes, with their herby, garlicky stuffing, make a very good first course but if you serve them with some buttery noodles or rice and a sharp-flavoured cheese sauce they also make an excellent lunch or supper, with a crisp green salad to accompany them.

SERVES 4
8 large tomatoes – about 700g (1½ lb) in all
sea salt
1 large onion
150ml (5 fl oz) olive oil
4 garlic cloves, peeled and crushed
75g (3oz) fine fresh wholemeal breadcrumbs
4 tablespoons chopped fresh parley
½ teaspoon dried thyme
freshly ground black pepper

Cut a thin slice off the top of each tomato and leave these slices on one side to use as lids later. Using a teaspoon scoop out the tomato pulp to leave a cavity for stuffing (you won't need the pulp for this recipe but it can be used to flavour sauces and soups). Sprinkle the inside of each tomato with a little salt then turn them upside down on a large plate and leave them while you prepare the filling.

Peel and finely chop the onion. Heat the olive oil in a large saucepan and fry the onion until it's golden, then take it off the heat and add the garlic, breadcrumbs, herbs and a good seasoning of salt and pepper.

Set the oven to 200°C (400°F), gas mark 6. Place the tomatoes in a lightly greased baking dish; fill each with some of the stuffing mixture and arrange the reserved lids on top.

Bake them in the oven for 15–20 minutes, to heat them right through, then serve them at once.

TOMATOES STUFFED WITH RICE

Like the stuffed tomatoes in the previous recipes this Grecian-style dish can be served either as a starter or as a main course. If you're making it a main course I think it's a good idea to begin with a starter like *hummus* and finish with the yoghurt tart or special ground rice, all of which add protein to the meal and continue the Middle Eastern theme.

SERVES 4
125g (4oz) long-grain brown rice
275ml (10 fl oz) water
sea salt
8 large tomatoes – about 700g (1½ lb) in all
2 tablespoons olive oil
1 medium onion, peeled and chopped
2 garlic cloves, peeled and crushed
6 tablespoons tomato purée
6 tablespoons chopped fresh parsley
2 tablespoons chopped fresh mint
pinch of oregano
freshly ground black pepper
150ml (5 fl oz) stock – or red wine is delicious

Put the rice into a heavy-based saucepan with the water and half a teaspoon of salt; bring it up to the boil then turn the heat right down, put a lid on the saucepan and cook the rice very gently for about 40 minutes until it's tender and all the water has been absorbed.

While the rice is cooking prepare the tomatoes. Cut a small piece off the top of each and hollow out the centre, using a teaspoon – keep the sliced-off tomato tops to use as lids later. Sprinkle some salt inside each tomato then leave them upside down to drain.

Set the oven to 180°C (350°F), gas mark 4. Next make the stuffing. Heat the oil in a fairly large saucepan and fry the onion until beginning to soften – about 5 minutes – then add the garlic, rice, scooped-out tomato pulp, half the purée, the herbs and seasoning. Cook over a highish heat until the mixture is fairly dry. Arrange the tomatoes in a greased ovenproof dish, fill with the stuffing and put the slices back as lids. Mix the remaining tomato purée with the stock or red wine and a little salt and pepper and pour it round the tomatoes, then bake them for about 20 minutes until they're tender.

A cheesy sauce goes well with these, and a crisp green salad.

VEGETABLE CASSEROLE

You can use all kinds of vegetables for this casserole, as available. It's good served just as it is, or with an extra cooked green vegetable such as sprouts, and grated cheese or roasted nuts for protein if you wish.

SERVES 4
1 tablespoon olive oil
3 onions, peeled and sliced
450g (1 lb) carrots, scraped and sliced
450g (1 lb) potatoes, peeled and cut into even-sized
pieces
2 sticks of celery, washed and sliced
125–225g (4–8oz) button mushrooms, wiped and
sliced
2 tablespoons flour
575ml (1 pint) water
2 vegetable stock cubes
1 tablespoon tomato paste
2 bay leaves
sea salt
freshly ground black pepper
dash of honey – optional

Set oven to 190°C (375°F), gas mark 5. Heat the oil in a large saucepan and fry the onions for 5 minutes. Add the rest of the vegetables and fry for a further couple of minutes, stirring often. Then mix in the flour; when it is well distributed add the water, stock cubes, tomato paste, bay leaves and a little salt and pepper – you won't need much because of the stock cubes. Bring mixture up to the boil, then transfer to a heatproof casserole and bake for 1 hour. Check the seasoning and add a very little honey if you think it needs it.

CHINESE VEGETABLES WITH ALMONDS

A Chinese-style vegetable dish is pleasant for a change and, served with some brown rice, makes a surprisingly substantial main dish. If you get all the basic preparation done in advance, the actual cooking takes only a few minutes, just before you want to serve the meal. Some tinned pineapple pieces – the kind canned in their own juice – are also good added to this mixture if you like a touch of sweetness.

SERVES 4
450g (1 lb) white salad cabbage, finely shredded
1 large onion, peeled and finely sliced
1 large carrot, scraped and finely diced
1 turnip, peeled and finely diced
225g (8oz) button mushrooms, washed and sliced
300g (10oz) bean sprouts, washed
1 garlic clove, peeled and crushed
2 tablespoons arrowroot or cornflour
1 tablespoon soy sauce
2 teaspoons clear honey
4 tablespoons cheap sherry
1–2 teaspoons salt
1 tablespoon olive oil
salt
freshly ground black pepper
125g (4oz) flaked almonds, toasted under a moderate
grill until crisp and golden

Have all the vegetables prepared ready to cook. Put the cornflour or arrowroot into a small bowl or cup and mix to a smooth paste with the soy sauce, honey, sherry and salt. Heat the oil in a large saucepan (or a wok, if you have one) and add the cabbage, onion, carrot and turnip. Fry, stirring often, for 3 minutes, then add the rest of the vegetables, including the garlic, and fry for a further 1–2 minutes. Give the sherry mixture a quick stir, then pour it in with the vegetables, stirring for a moment or two until thickened. Add the almonds then serve immediately, with the rice.

VEGETABLE PIE

A dear friend, who had thriftily brought up six children on a very limited income, gave me this economical recipe.

SERVES 4
450g (1 lb) potatoes
2 onions
450g (1 lb) can tomatoes
275ml (10 fl oz) cheese sauce
sea salt
freshly ground black pepper
basil
celery salt
50g (2oz) butter or margarine
2 tablespoons grated cheese

Set oven to 180°C (350°F), gas mark 4. Peel and thinly slice potatoes and cook in boiling water until tender. Peel and slice onions and tomatoes and arrange in layers with potato in a well greased shallow dish with cheese sauce and seasoning of salt and pepper, basil and celery salt between each layer. Finish with layer of potato. Sprinkle with grated cheese and butter (or margarine), cover and bake for 45 minutes.

MIXED VEGETABLE PLATTER

I think a huge platter of different coloured vegetables makes a delightful vegetarian meal. The problem is having enough saucepans to cook everything in, and getting all the vegetables ready at the same time.

SERVES 4
450g (1 lb) courgettes
225g (8oz) French beans
225g (8oz) small carrots
225g (8oz) button onions
225g (8oz) frozen sweetcorn kernels
6 tomatoes
225g (8oz) button mushrooms
25g (1oz) butter
6 hardboiled eggs
juice of ½ lemon
fresh parsley sprigs
575ml (1 pint) lemon mayonnaise sauce (page 63),
hollandaise sauce (page 63) *or* yoghurt and fresh
herb sauce (page 67)

Wash and top and tail courgettes and beans; scrape carrots, leave whole; peel onions. Cook vegetables in separate pans in a little boiling water until tender. Cook sweetcorn according to directions on packet. Halve tomatoes widthwise; scoop out pulp, and chop. Wash and chop mushrooms and fry gently in one-third of the butter with the tomato pulp for 5 minutes, then heap into tomato halves. Place under a moderate grill for 5–10 minutes to cook tomatoes. Slice eggs and keep warm. When ready to serve, arrange the vegetables and hardboiled eggs attractively on a large warmed plate or individual plates. Melt rest of butter, mix with lemon juice and pour over vegetables. Garnish each tomato half with a parsley sprig. Serve with the sauce of your choice.

Many other combinations of vegetables can of course be used, aiming for as colourful and varied a mixture as possible. Aubergines, sliced, salted, drained and then fried are good, also peppers, sliced and lightly fried; small new potatoes, steamed or boiled, are also nice included in this. Also, any of the stuffed vegetables in this section can form the centrepiece and source of protein. The hard-boiled eggs can then be omitted and the whole dish served with a suitable sauce.

Variations

MIXED VEGETABLE PLATTER WITH CRISPY ALMOND SLICES

The hardboiled eggs can be omitted, and the dish garnished with the crispy almond slices on page 136.

MIXED VEGETABLE PLATTER WITH CHEESE OR EGG SAUCE

Omit hardboiled eggs from recipe, and serve with egg or cheese sauce.

SPICED VEGETABLES WITH DAL

This is a lovely dish, not hot but lightly spiced. The dal sauce supplies the protein and it's nice served with spiced rice (page 236), poppadums, mango chutney and banana, raisin and peanut salad (page 76).

SERVES 4
3 tablespoons olive oil
1 onion, peeled and chopped
1 large garlic clove, peeled and crushed
1 teaspoon turmeric
1 teaspoon ground coriander
1 teaspoon ground cumin
1 bay leaf
2 carrots, total 225g (8oz) weight in all, scraped and
thinly sliced
450g (1 lb) potatoes, peeled and cubed
2 leeks, washed and sliced
150ml (5 fl oz) water
sea salt
freshly ground black pepper
dal (page 190)

Heat the oil in a fairly large saucepan and fry the onion for 5 minutes, then add the garlic, spices and bay leaf and stir over the heat for 1–2 minutes. Put in the remaining vegetables and stir over the heat for a further 1–2 minutes so that they are all coated with the oil and spices. Add the water and a little salt and pepper. Cover and leave to simmer for 15–20 minutes, until the vegetables are all tender, stirring from time to time and checking towards the end to make sure they do not burn dry – there will be very little water left. Alternatively, the spiced vegetables can be put into an ovenproof casserole and baked at 160°C (325°F), gas mark 3, for about 1–1½ hours, until tender when pierced with the point of a knife.

Serve the vegetables with the dal.

VEGETABLE STEW

Although aubergine isn't usually the cheapest of vegetables, this stew can make quite an economical main course if you serve it with some cooked grains: millet or bulgur wheat go well with it, and some cooked pulses can be added, too.

SERVES 4
1 large aubergine
sea salt
1 large onion, peeled and chopped
3 tablespoons olive oil
2 garlic cloves, crushed
425g (15oz) can tomatoes
freshly ground black pepper
2 sticks celery, sliced
350g (12oz) carrots, scraped and sliced
50g (2oz) button mushrooms, washed and sliced
chopped parsley

Trim stalk from aubergine. Cut aubergine into 1cm (½in) dice, put into a colander, sprinkle with salt and leave under a weight for about 30 minutes. Then rinse under cold water and squeeze as dry as possible in your hands. Fry the onion in 1 tablespoon of the oil for 10 minutes. Add the garlic and tomatoes, liquidize and season. Heat the rest of the oil in a large saucepan and fry the aubergine, celery, carrots and mushrooms for 10 minutes. Add the tomato mixture. Cook over a gentle heat until the vegetables are tender. Serve with hot, cooked, brown rice, wholemeal rolls or jacket potatoes.

RUMANIAN VEGETABLE STEW

This stew, can be a gloriously colourful mixture of every sort of vegetable you can find. You can really use whatever is available.

In the early autumn I make it with the first of the parsnips, celery and leeks and the last of the marrow and serve it with jacket potatoes, baked in a hot oven so they've got crunchy skins. As the season progresses I replace the marrow with swede or turnip and at the end of the cooking time I may stir in some cooked butter beans, kidney beans or even some baked beans to make it more filling for the cold weather.

When preparing the vegetables try to cut them up into the sort of sizes which will make them all cook in about the same amount of time.

SERVES 4
2 tablespoons olive oil
2 large onions, peeled and sliced
2 celery stalks, washed and chopped
225g (8oz) carrots, scraped and sliced
225g (8oz) parsnips, peeled and diced
225g (8oz) marrow, de-seeded, peeled if necessary
and cut into chunks
450g (1 lb) leeks, washed, trimmed and cut into
2.5cm (1in) pieces
3 large tomatoes, skinned and quartered
450g (1 lb) potatoes, peeled and cut into chunks
25g (1oz) flour
575ml (1 pint) water *or* stock
2 tablespoons tomato purée
2 bay leaves
1 garlic clove, peeled and crushed
sea salt
freshly ground black pepper

Heat the oil in a large saucepan and fry the onion for 5 minutes, then put in the celery, carrots, parsnips, marrow, leeks, tomatoes and potatoes and cook for a further 4–5 minutes, turning them often to prevent sticking. Then sprinkle the flour over the vegetables and mix gently to distribute it. Pour in the water or stock, stirring, and add the tomato purée, bay leaves, garlic and a seasoning of salt and pepper. Bring the mixture up to the boil then turn the heat down and leave the stew to simmer very gently, with a lid on the saucepan, for about 25–30 minutes or until the potatoes and other vegetables are tender. Taste the mixture and add more seasoning if necessary.

I often serve this with a bowl of grated cheese or roasted sunflower seeds (just sunflower seeds spread on a baking sheet and baked for about 10 minutes in a moderate oven) for people to help themselves and sprinkle over the top of their portion – but really it's very nice just as it is because it's delicately flavoured with all the vegetables. If you don't serve the cheese or sunflower seeds, though, you need to add protein to the meal, and I think the best way is to serve a pudding such as yoghurt, cheese cake or even *pashka* – or just finish with biscuits and cheese.

STUFFED VINE LEAVES

These dolmades, or little leafy parcels of rice with nuts and raisins make an excellent first course, or can be served for a light meal with some warm bread, crisp green salad and some dry white wine. The green salad with Gruyère cheese goes well with them and supplies some extra protein.

SERVES 3–4 AS A MAIN MEAL, 4–6 AS A STARTER
36 fresh vine leaves if available *or* a package of preserved vine leaves
225g (8oz) long-grain brown rice
1 large onion, chopped
2 tablespoons chopped parsley
2 tomatoes, skinned and chopped
50g (2oz) pine kernels
50g (2oz) raisins
½ teaspoon cinnamon
2 garlic cloves, crushed
sea salt
freshly ground black pepper
6 tablespoons olive oil
150ml (5 fl oz) water
lemon juice
lemon wedges

If you're using fresh vine leaves, half fill a large saucepan with water and bring it to the boil. Trim the leaves and put into the boiling water, cover and simmer for 2 minutes. Then drain them and run them under the cold tap to refresh them. Drain well. With preserved vine leaves just drain them and rinse them well under the cold tap. Half fill a large saucepan with water; put in the rice and boil for 10 minutes, then drain.

Mix together the rice, onion, parsley, tomatoes, pine kernels, raisins, cinnamon, garlic and seasoning. Place a spoonful of this filling on each leaf, fold the edges over and place the little bundles side by side in a frying pan. If there are some leaves left over use them to fill in any gaps. Mix together the oil and water and pour over the vine leaves. Sprinkle a little lemon juice on top.

Cook over a very gentle heat for 2–2½ hours until the rice and leaves are tender. Keep an eye on the water level, and add a little more from time to time if necessary. Serve garnished with lemon wedges.

WHITE NUTMEAT WITH CAPERS

My original idea with this nutmeat was to use green peppercorns; when it was sliced I wanted to get the effect of white flecked with green. But the number of peppercorns needed to get that effect made the loaf far too hot! So then I hit on the idea of using capers instead and I must say I was pleased with the result: the slices look just as I envisaged them and the capers give the loaf a lovely tangy flavour. The loaf is good served hot with a rich sauce – Béarnaise is lovely – or cold, with mayonnaise and salad.

SERVES 6 F
butter and dried breadcrumbs for lining loaf tin
25g (1oz) butter
1 onion, peeled and chopped
225g (8oz) cashew nuts, grated *or* half cashew nuts and half ground almonds
4 tablespoons milk
125g (4oz) soft white breadcrumbs
2 eggs
sea salt
freshly ground black pepper
75g (3oz) capers
a few extra capers
whole cashew nuts, lightly roasted

Set the oven to 180°C (350°F), gas mark 4. Line a 450g (1 lb) loaf tin with a long strip of non-stick paper to cover the narrow sides and base of the tin; grease very well with butter and sprinkle with dried breadcrumbs – this helps the loaf to come out of the tin cleanly. Melt the butter in a medium-sized saucepan and fry the onion for 10 minutes until soft but not browned. Take the saucepan off the heat and mix in the nuts, milk, breadcrumbs, egg and a good seasoning of salt and pepper. Lastly, carefully fold in the capers, being careful not to mash them.

Spoon the mixture into the prepared tin, smooth the surface, cover with a piece of buttered foil and bake for 1 hour. After this, remove the foil and have a look at the nutmeat; if you think it needs to be a bit browner on top, pop it back into the oven, uncovered, for a further 5–10 minutes. If possible, leave the loaf for 3–4 minutes after you take it out of the oven – this helps it to 'settle' and come out of the tin more easily – then slip a knife down the sides of the loaf, turn it out of the tin on to a warmed serving dish and strip off the piece of non-stick paper. Decorate with a row of capers down the centre and some roasted cashew nuts either side.

WHITE NUTMEAT WITH PARSLEY STUFFING

SERVES 8–10
575ml (1 pint) milk
1 bay leaf
1 onion
1 clove
75g (3oz) semolina
125g (4oz) finely ground cashew nuts
pinch mace
2 eggs
sea salt
freshly ground black pepper
lemon slices
parsley sprigs

Stuffing
125g (4oz) soft wholemeal bread
50g (2oz) butter
1 good tablespoon chopped parsley
½ teaspoon mixed herbs
1 teaspoon lemon juice
2 teaspoons lemon rind

Set oven to 200°C (400°F), gas mark 6. Make the basic nut mixture by heating together the milk, bay leaf and onion (with the clove stuck into it). Bring to the boil, remove from heat and leave for 15 minutes, then remove bay leaf and onion. Reheat milk to boiling point, then gradually sprinkle in the semolina, stirring vigorously all the time to avoid lumps. Cook gently for 5 minutes until very thick, still stirring well. Add cashew nuts, ground in a liquidizer, fine electric grater or electric coffee mill, the mace, eggs – beat them in well – and salt and pepper. Make a good stuffing by blending together all the other ingredients as listed. Line a 900g (2 lb) loaf tin with foil and butter generously, then place a layer of half the white mixture in the bottom; spread the stuffing evenly over this and finish with the rest of the white mixture. Cover with foil, and bake for 45 minutes to 1 hour, until nicely set. Cool for a minute or two, then loosen edges of roast and turn out on to a warm plate. Garnish with parsley and lemon slices and surround with roast potatoes.

WHITE NUTMEAT WITH STUFFING BALLS

This is a delicately-flavoured nutmeat in contrast to the brown nutmeat on page 156. The stuffing balls are optional – my mother always made them when serving this roast at Christmas.

SERVES 6 F
1 onion, chopped
50g (2oz) butter
1 teaspoon mixed herbs
1 tablespoon plain flour
150ml (5 fl oz) milk *or* water
2 eggs
225g (8oz) grated nuts, (almonds, Brazils *or* cashews)
125g (4oz) soft wholemeal breadcrumbs
sea salt
freshly ground black pepper

Stuffing Balls
125g (4oz) butter
225g (8oz) soft brown breadcrumbs
2 good tablespoons chopped parsley
1 teaspoon mixed herbs
grated rind of ½ lemon and 1–2 teaspoons juice
½ small onion, grated
½ egg, beaten

Set oven to 180°C (350°F), gas mark 4. Fry the onion in the butter with the herbs. Cook gently with the lid on the pan for 10 minutes but do not allow the onion to brown. Add the flour and stir well; add the milk and cook gently until thickened. Beat in the eggs, cook for 2 minutes, then add the nuts, breadcrumbs and seasoning. Put the mixture into a well-greased and non-stick, paper-lined 450g (1 lb) loaf tin or casserole dish. Cover with greased paper or tin foil and bake for 1 hour. Or the nut roast can be rolled in breadcrumbs or crushed cornflakes, dotted with cooking fat, and baked at 190°C (375°F). gas mark 5 for 45 minutes.

Meanwhile make the stuffing balls. Mix all ingredients together and form into little balls. Fry until golden brown or roast in hot fat in the top of the oven while the nutroast is cooking.

Turn out the nutroast on to a large plate and serve with gooseberry sauce (page 62), or with vegetarian gravy and stuffing balls.

WHITE NUT RISSOLES BAKED WITH MUSHROOMS

In this recipe, delicately-flavoured nut rissoles are baked on a moist base of fried button mushrooms and onions. It's delicious with a light vegetable dish or fluffy brown rice and a green salad.

SERVES 3–4 [F]
15g (½ oz) butter
1 tablespoon olive oil
1 large onion, peeled and chopped
2 garlic cloves, peeled and crushed
225g (8oz) button mushrooms, washed and sliced
2 tablespoons white wine *or* cider
125g (4oz) cashew nuts, grated
50g (2oz) soft white breadcrumbs
50g (2oz) white cheese, finely grated
2 tablespoons single cream – optional
½ teaspoon dried thyme
sea salt
freshly ground black pepper
1 egg
fresh parsley, chopped

First prepare the mushroom mixture. Heat the butter and oil in a medium-sized saucepan and fry the onion for 5 minutes, until beginning to soften, then add the garlic and mushrooms and fry for a further 5 minutes. Add the wine or cider, let the mixture bubble and scrape down the crusty bits from the sides of the pan. Remove from the heat and season to taste. Pour the mixture into a shallow casserole dish.

Set the oven to 180°C (350°F), gas mark 4. Make the rissoles by mixing together all the remaining ingredients except the cream and parsley; season with salt and plenty of pepper. Form the mixture into eight rissoles and put them on top of the mushroom mixture. Bake, uncovered, for 25–30 minutes, until the rissoles are puffed up a little and firm but not hard. Pour the cream into the casserole dish, around the rissoles, sprinkle with chopped parsley and serve.

A pleasant variation is to put a cooked chestnut (or a well-drained canned chestnut) into the centre of each nut rissole, moulding the white nut mixture gently round it.

7

PULSE DISHES

When I started writing about vegetarian cookery, people were still talking about first class and second class protein, and pulses – that strangely-named group consisting of dried beans, peas and lentils – were firmly in the second class group. Added to that, they also had the reputation of being both indigestible and fattening. So, as you can imagine, it was quite an uphill struggle, sometimes, persuading people to give them a try! Who could have thought that they were destined to become one of the 'wonder foods' of the 1980s, featured in just about every slimming diet and almost any magazine you open, or so it seems.

One of the reasons I've always liked them is that they appeal to my aesthetic sense. They're such an attractive ingredient to buy and use, with their shiny colours and varied shapes. They also appeal to me because they're such an ancient food. I like to feel I'm using the same ingredients as my counterpart in

Egypt used 2,000 or more years ago, and, as I prepare a pan of golden lentil soup or sprinkle olive oil over a plate of creamy hummus, this thought gives me a satisfactory feeling of well-being and continuity.

But, enough of these fanciful thoughts. The recipes in this chapter are for main course pulse dishes – you'll find recipes for using them in first courses, soups, salads and accompanying vegetables elsewhere in this book – and they're arranged in alphabetical order. But first, here's a guide to identifying and using the basic types, followed by general information on soaking and cooking. Don't let 'all that soaking and cooking' as some people put it, deter you; it's all very simple and straightforward. On the other hand, if you're really short of time, some excellent canned beans are available, and I've given these as alternatives in the recipes where possible.

TYPES OF PULSES AVAILABLE

Aduki beans Small, reddish brown beans, round with a small point at one end. Have a pleasant, slightly sweet flavour. Good in vegetable stews and stir-fries.

Black beans A type of kidney bean, a little larger than red kidney beans, shiny black in colour. Have a rich flavour and pleasant, mealy texture. Delicious in vegetable casseroles and salads; can be used instead of red kidney beans in any recipe.

Black-eyed peas Sometimes called black-eyed beans or cowpeas. About the same size as haricot beans, beige-coloured with a black spot or 'eye'. They cook quickly and have a pleasant, slightly sweet flavour.

Field beans One of the cheapest beans, which can be grown in gardens and allotments in temperate climates. They have a tough outer skin so need chopping in a food processor or strong blender to break this down and release the pleasant, earthy flavour. Excellent in a dip and as burgers.

Brown lentils Sometimes called continental lentils, these are dark brown or reddish brown lentils, smaller than continental lentils and with a more intense flavour.

Butter beans One of the largest beans, flattish, kidney-shaped and creamy white in colour. They absorb flavours particularly well and are useful for making pâtés, or combined with tasty vegetables and spices.

Cannellini beans White kidney-shaped beans, a little larger than red kidney beans, and a member of the same family. Pleasant flavour and texture; can be used in place of haricot, butter or red kidney beans.

Chick peas Look like small hazel nuts, beige in colour, cooking to a darker gold. Have a particularly delicious flavour and are excellent in salads and casseroles, also in dips, such as *hummus* and in crisp croquettes.

Continental lentils Sometimes called whole green lentils, these are large, flat and lens-shaped, and vary in colour from light greenish beige to brown. They retain their shape after cooking and are excellent with spices and warm bread or rice, or made into tasty non-meat burgers. They're bigger than the brown lentils.

Flageolet beans Have an attractive pale green colour, slim shape and delicate flavour when cooked. They make an excellent salad, particularly when combined with other pale green vegetables such as avocado; they also make a pretty pale green soup.

Haricot beans These small, oval white beans belong to the kidney bean family. Probably best known in the form of 'baked beans', they have a delicious slightly sweet flavour and mealy texture. Try them as Boston baked beans, in a tasty flan, or as a salad.

Mung beans Are the small, round green beans from which bean sprouts are produced. Delicious cooked with rice and spices in the traditional Indian dish, khitchari.

Peas These are whole dried peas and look like wizened versions of fresh peas. They cook to the familiar 'mushy peas' and make a cheap and filling winter vegetable or soup: follow the recipe for lentil soup on page 21, but leave out the apple and spices and flavour with some chopped mint.

Pinto beans Pinto means 'speckled' and these beans are creamy coloured with brown specks. They are a type of kidney bean and can be used in any recipe calling for red kidney beans or haricot beans. They have a delicate, slightly sweet flavour and can be used in place of red kidney beans in any recipe.

Red kidney beans Rich red in colour and with the characteristic kidney shape, these have a delicious mealy texture and an excellent flavour. They make an excellent salad, combine well with rice, and can be used in many tasty main-course dishes.

Split red lentils These are lentils which have had the outer skin removed and are bright orange-red in colour. Easy to buy at any supermarket, they have a pleasant savoury flavour and cook quickly to a purée. Excellent made into soup, rissoles, savoury spread, spicy dal, croquettes or loaves.

Soya beans Small, round and yellowish in colour. The most protein-rich pulse, but take a long time to cook and need careful flavouring. They can be made into an excellent milk and this, in turn, can be made into tofu, a firm or firmish creamy-coloured curd. You can buy a soft tofu in health shops in a vacuum pack, and some sell a firmer one which slices well. To make it yourself, see page 203.

Split peas Bright green or yellow in colour, these, like split red lentils, have had their outer skin removed. Undercook them slightly so that they still hold their shape and mix them with dressing to make an unusual salad, or cook them to a purée and make traditional and comforting pease pudding, or tasty split peas with fennel seeds.

Choosing Pulses

Although pulses will keep for many years, they become harder and drier with time. So for best results buy fresh stock from a shop with a rapid turnover and store carefully in a screwtop jar or airtight cannister, using up each batch before topping up with the next. There is a new season of pulses every autumn.

Equipment

The equipment required for cooking pulses is simple and basic. A large sieve or colander is useful for washing the pulses and a large saucepan in which to soak and cook them. As most pulses take quite a long time to cook, a pressure cooker saves time and fuel and a slow cooker can also be used. A food mill, liquidizer or food processor is needed for puréeing the pulses to make soups and dips, and essential for preparing field beans.

Preparation, Cooking and Using

Washing Many pulses are cleaned before packing, but they are sometimes dusty and occasionally there are small pieces of grit or wood with them. I have found this especially with brown lentils and chick peas and it's a wise precaution to spread these out on a large white plate or tray and sort them through carefully, removing any foreign bodies. Then put the pulses into a large colander or sieve and wash them under cold water, moving them about with your fingers as you do so.

Soaking Most pulses need soaking before cooking. This is unnecessary for split red lentils, and optional for the other types of lentils, small green mung beans, split peas and black-eyed peas, although soaking these does reduce their cooking time and helps them to cook more evenly.

Put the pulses into a large saucepan and cover them with their height again in cold water. Either leave them to soak for 6–8 hours, or bring them to the boil, boil for 2 minutes, then remove from heat and soak for 45–60 minutes.

Rinsing Next, whether you've done the long cold soak or the short hot soak, the pulses should be turned into a colander and rinsed thoroughly under cold water. This helps to remove some of the sugars, called oligosaccharides, which can make pulses indigestible.

Basic Cooking Put the rinsed pulses into a large saucepan with a generous covering of fresh water. A homemade unsalted stock can be used instead of water, but do not use a salty stock or add salt, as this can toughen the outside of the beans and prevent them from cooking properly. Bring the water to the boil and allow to boil rapidly for 10 minutes. This destroys any toxins which may be present in some types of bean (especially red kidney beans), making them perfectly safe to eat. After this initial boiling the pulses can be incorporated with other ingredients and cooked slowly, or they can be gently simmered on their own until tender and then mixed with other ingredients. See the table for cooking times, but remember that these can vary a little from batch to batch (particularly chick peas).

Using a Pressure Cooker

This reduces the cooking time by about two-thirds. Boil the pulses for 10 minutes as usual, then cook at 6.7kg (15 lb) pressure for a third of the usual time given in the chart. Some of the pulses, particularly lentils, tend to 'froth up' when they come to the boil, and this can clog the valve of the pressure cooker. You can avoid this by adding 2 tablespoons of oil to the cooking water.

Using a Slow Cooker

This is an economical way to cook pulses but it is important to boil the pulses vigorously for 10 minutes before transferring them to the slow cooker. Pulses which normally take 1–1½ hours to cook need 2–3 hours in a slow cooker with the heat set at 'low'.

Soaking and Cooking Times

	cold soak	hot soak	average cooking time
Aduki beans	6–8 hours	45–60 minutes	1–1½ hours
Black Beans	6–8 hours	45–60 minutes	1–1½ hours
Black-eyed peas	6–8 hours	45–60 minutes	25–30 minutes
	unsoaked	unsoaked	35–45 minutes
Butter beans	6–8 hours	45–60 minutes	45–60 minutes
Cannellini beans	6–8 hours	45–60 minutes	1–1½ hours
Chick peas	6–8 hours	45–60 minutes	1–2 hours
Field beans	6–8 hours	45–60 minutes	30–60 minutes
Flageolet beans	6–8 hours	45–60 minutes	30–60 minutes
Haricot beans	6–8 hours	45–60 minutes	1–1½ hours
Lentils			
Continental	6–8 hours	45–60 minutes	25–30 minutes
	unsoaked	unsoaked	1–1½ hours
Brown	6–8 hours	45–60 minutes	25–30 minutes
	unsoaked	unsoaked	1–1½ hours
Split red	unsoaked	unsoaked	20–30 minutes
Mung beans	6–8 hours	45–60 minutes	25–30 minutes
	unsoaked	unsoaked	30–40 minutes
Peas, whole	6–8 hours	45–60 minutes	45–60 minutes
Pinto beans	6–8 hours	45–60 minutes	1–1½ hours
Red kidney			
beans	6–8 hours	45–60 minutes	1–1¼ hours
Soya beans	6–8 hours	45–60 minutes	1–3 hours
Split peas	6–8 hours	45–60 minutes	25–30 minutes
	unsoaked	unsoaked	45–60 minutes

FLAVOURING AND SERVING

Pulses are simple to cook, but it's the flavouring and presentation which make all the difference to the attractiveness of the finished dish. Butter and well-flavoured vegetable oils – in particular olive oil – enhance them greatly, as do small quantities of cream. Strongly flavoured vegetables, such as onions, garlic, celery, mushrooms and tomatoes, also go particularly well with pulses and so do some fruits, particularly sharp apples, pineapple, dried apricots, raisins or sultanas and also lemon juice. Do not add acid fruits, or tomatoes, until after the pulses have softened – the pulses may toughen.

Perhaps more than anything else, herbs and spices make all the difference to the appeal of the finished dish. It is surprising what the addition of a bay leaf or bouquet garni to the cooking water of any of the pulses will do for the flavour. The bouquet garni herbs are bay leaf, thyme, parsley and marjoram, and these can be used together or individually. Other useful herbs are mint and oregano, while of the spices, fennel, cumin, coriander, cinnamon and cadamom seeds are particularly good ones to have; also chilli powder, paprika, cloves, curry powder or paste and turmeric. Grated fresh ginger root, with its delicious citrus-like flavour, also comes in handy.

Pulse dishes look attractive served simply, in chunky pottery, with garnishes such as triangles of crisp toast or fried bread, raw onion or tomato rings, lemon wedges or chopped parsley.

Storing cooked pulses Drained, cooked pulses will keep for several days in a covered container in the fridge and they also freeze well. It is often worth cooking a double batch, using half and freezing the rest.

Many made-up pulse dishes also freeze well and these recipes are marked [F]. Freeze the dishes after cooking unless stated otherwise and thaw before reheating. If possible, garlic and spices are best added after freezing, before you use the dish. Rissoles and fritters should be frozen uncovered on a baking sheet then packed in polythene bags. They can be fried while still frozen.

ADUKI BEAN, CARROT AND GINGER STIR-FRY

The beans for this stir-fry are cooked in advance – and if you do an extra batch they can be kept in the freezer for another occasion. Serve with fluffy brown rice and a side salad.

SERVES 4
1 onion, sliced
4 tablespoons olive oil
700g (1½ lb) carrots, thinly sliced
1 tablespoon grated fresh ginger
125g (4oz) aduki beans, soaked, cooked and drained
(page 178)
275ml (10 fl oz) water *or* stock
bunch of spring onions, chopped
sea salt
freshly ground black pepper
sugar

Fry the onion in a large saucepan for 4–5 minutes, until beginning to soften, then add the carrots and ginger and stir-fry for a further 3–4 minutes. Add the aduki beans and water, cover and leave to simmer gently for 10–15 minutes, until the carrots are just tender. Stir in the spring onions. Season with salt and pepper and a dash of sugar if necessary.

BEAN RATATOUILLE

The addition of some beans to ratatouille turns this delectable dish into a main meal, and if you use rather bland beans, such as haricot or cannellini, they will soak up the flavour of olive oil and garlic.

SERVES 4 [F]
175g (6oz) haricot beans *or* 2 × 400g (14oz) cans
cannellini *or* butter beans
450g (1 lb) courgettes
450g (1 lb) aubergines
sea salt
2 large onions, peeled and chopped
2 tablespoons olive oil
3 large garlic cloves, crushed
2 red peppers, de-seeded and chopped
4 tomatoes, skinned and chopped (you can use
canned ones)
freshly ground black pepper
a little chopped parsley

If you're using haricot beans, soak, rinse and cook in the usual way (page 178) until tender, then drain. Drain canned beans. Cut the courgettes and aubergines into small dice and put them into a colander with a good sprinkling of sea salt. Place a plate with a weight on it on top and leave for at least half an hour for any bitter liquids to be drawn out of the aubergines and excess moisture out of the courgettes. Rinse them and pat dry.

Fry the onion in the oil in a large saucepan for about 10 minutes, then add the garlic, peppers and the courgettes and aubergines. Cook gently with a lid on the saucepan for about 30 minutes, then add the tomatoes and cook for a further 30 minutes. Then stir in the beans and allow them to heat through. Season the mixture with sea salt and freshly ground black pepper and sprinkle it with parsley just before serving.

I like this with hot garlic bread, wholemeal rolls or fluffy brown rice, a green salad, fragrant with fresh herbs and a glass of chilled wine, for a simple summer supper.

BEANY GOULASH

I like this served with a dollop of thick natural yoghurt or soured cream, some rice and a green salad. Incidentally, if you want the best flavoured paprika pepper it's worth looking out for a 'Hungarian' or 'rose' one, and buying only a small quantity at a time.

SERVES 4 F
225g (8oz) cannellini or haricot beans or 2 × 400g
(14oz) cans cannellini beans
4 garlic cloves, crushed
450g (1 lb) onions, peeled and sliced
2 tablespoons olive oil
2 large green peppers, de-seeded and sliced
2 × 400g (14oz) cans tomatoes
4 tablespoons tomato purée
2–4 teaspoons paprika
sea salt
freshly ground black pepper
a little sugar
150ml (5 fl oz) thick natural yoghurt or soured cream
if liked

Soak and cook dried beans in the usual way (page 178), then drain. Drain canned beans. Fry the garlic and onions in the oil in a large saucepan for about 10 minutes, until the onion is soft, then add the green pepper and fry for a further 4–5 minutes. Mix in the tomatoes, tomato purée, the drained beans and paprika pepper, sea salt, freshly ground black pepper and perhaps a little sugar to taste. Simmer the mixture for about 15 minutes, without a lid on the saucepan, to heat everything through and to reduce the liquid a little. Serve with the yoghurt or soured cream if liked.

BEANS WITH MARROW AND CORN

For this Latin American dish you can use any white beans; I like it with black eyed beans, but haricot or cannellini beans are also good. Choose if possible a marrow that's tender enough for the skin to be left on or use courgettes, as the stripey green looks attractive against the red tomato and yellow sweetcorn. Pumpkin, that very popular ingredient in Latin American cookery, can be used when in season, but this of course needs the skin removing.

SERVES 4
3 tablespoons olive oil
1 large onion, peeled and chopped
1 large garlic clove, crushed
400g (14oz) can tomatoes
1 teaspoon dried basil
1 teaspoon dried oregano
225g (8oz) black eyed beans, soaked and cooked until
very nearly tender or 2 × 400g (14oz) cans cannellini
beans, butter beans or red kidney beans
450g (1 lb) marrow or courgettes, cut into largish
dice
125g (4oz) frozen sweetcorn kernels
sea salt
freshly ground black pepper

Heat the oil in a good-sized saucepan and fry the onion for 5 minutes, until beginning to soften, then add the garlic, tomatoes, basil and oregano, and cook fairly fast for about 10 minutes, without a lid on the saucepan, to make a thickish sauce. Stir in the drained beans and marrow or courgettes and simmer gently for about 10 minutes, until the marrow or courgettes are nearly cooked, then mix in the sweetcorn and continue to cook until everything is tender and the mixture piping hot. Season with sea salt and freshly ground black pepper and serve at once.

SHEPHERDS' BEANY PIE

It's not essential to purée the cooked beans, but personally I think it gives a better result.

SERVES 4 |F|
225g (8oz) black eyed beans
2 tablespoons olive oil
1 large onion, peeled and chopped
1 garlic clove, crushed
50g (2oz) mushrooms, wiped and chopped
225g (8oz) canned tomatoes
1 tablespoon tomato purée
1 tablespoon chopped parsley
1 teaspoon mixed herbs
sea salt
freshly ground black pepper
700g (1½ lb) creamy mashed potatoes
50g (2oz) grated cheese

Soak the black eyed beans, then drain and rinse them. Put them into a saucepan, cover with water and cook until tender, then drain and purée in a food processor or liquidizer, or pass them through a vegetable mill.

Meanwhile, heat the oil in a medium-sized saucepan and fry the onion and garlic for about 5 minutes, then put in the mushrooms and go on cooking for another 4–5 minutes. Add the tomatoes, tomato purée, the sieved beans, parsley and mixed herbs and cook over a gentle heat for 10 minutes. Then season with sea salt and freshly ground black pepper.

Set the oven to 200°C (400°F), gas mark 6. Grease a shallow ovenproof dish and put the bean mixture in the base. Spread the mashed potato evenly over the top, rough up the surface with a fork and sprinkle with grated cheese. Bake in the oven for 35–40 minutes, until golden brown and crispy.

BEORIJCH

An unusual mixture of black eyed beans and nuts, this is an Armenian dish that's rich in protein and quick to make. It's also surprisingly tasty.

SERVES 4 |F|
225g (8oz) black eyed beans
1 large onion, peeled and chopped
2 tablespoons olive oil
1 garlic clove, crushed
2 tomatoes, skinned and chopped (canned are fine)
1 tablespoon tomato purée
125g (4oz) mixed nuts, roughly chopped
2 tablespoons chopped fresh parsley
sea salt
freshly ground black pepper
a little sugar

Soak and cook the black eyed beans as usual; drain them well. Fry the onion in the olive oil in a good-sized saucepan for 10 minutes, then stir in the garlic, tomatoes and tomato purée and cook for a further 10 minutes to make a thick purée. Add the nuts, parsley and the beans, mashing them slightly as you do so. Taste the mixture and season with sea salt, freshly ground black pepper and a dash of sugar if you think it's necessary. Put over a gentle heat for about 10 minutes, stirring often to prevent sticking. Serve piping hot, with buttered new potatoes or creamy mashed potatoes and a cooked green vegetable or crisp green salad.

BLACK EYED BEAN BAKE

A simple dish, but one that's popular with children, I find. A nice spicy tomato sauce goes well with it, or a tasty gravy.

SERVES 4 |F|
350g (12oz) black eyed beans
2 large onions, peeled and sliced
3 garlic cloves, crushed
2 tablespoons olive oil
½ teaspoon thyme
1 teaspoon marjoram
sea salt
freshly ground black pepper
wholemeal breadcrumbs
50g (2oz) grated cheese

Drain and rinse the beans. Fry the onions and garlic in the oil for 10 minutes, until the onion is tender, then add the beans, herbs and water to cover. Simmer gently, until the beans are tender (about 40–45 minutes). Preheat the oven to 180°C (350°F), gas mark 4. Purée the bean mixture in a liquidizer or food processor or pass it through a vegetable mill, then season to taste with sea salt and freshly ground black pepper. Spoon mixture into a greased, shallow ovenproof dish, sprinkle with the wholemeal breadcrumbs and grated cheese and bake in the oven for about 30 minutes, until the top is golden and crunchy.

BLACK EYED BEAN AND VEGETABLE STEW

This is a colourful stew, with black eyed beans peeping out of a rich red tomato sauce and a garnish of fresh green parsley. It goes well with baked or creamy mashed potatoes and some buttery spinach or green beans.

SERVES 4 [F]
225g (8oz) black eyed beans
1 large onion
3 sticks celery
3 carrots
1 green pepper
2 garlic cloves
25g (1oz) butter
400g (14oz) can tomatoes
1 tablespoon tomato purée
2–3 tablespoons red wine if available
sea salt
freshly ground black pepper
2 tablespoons chopped parsley

Put beans into a saucepan, cover with cold water and simmer gently until tender, about 40 minutes. Drain.

Peel and chop the onion; slice the celery thinly, scrape and dice the carrots. Remove seeds from the pepper, then slice it fairly thinly; crush the garlic. Melt the butter in a good-sized saucepan and add all the prepared vegetables; fry them gently, without browning, for about 10 minutes, then mix in the beans, tomatoes, tomato purée and the wine if you're using it. Season the mixture with sea salt and freshly ground black pepper and let it cook gently for 10–15 minutes, until all the vegetables are tender. Check seasoning. Serve sprinkled with the parsley.

BOSTON BAKED BEANS

'Boston runs to brains as well as beans and brown bread' noted William Cowper Brann in the *Iconoclast, Beans and Blood*. Well, here's a recipe for the beans.

SERVES 4 [F]
350g (12oz) haricot beans
1 large onion
1 tablespoon olive oil
1 teaspoon dry mustard
2 teaspoons black treacle
150ml (5 fl oz) tomato juice (you can use the liquid from a can of tomatoes)
2 tablespoons tomato purée
2 teaspoons brown sugar
275ml (10 fl oz) unsalted stock

Soak, drain and rinse the beans, then cook them in fresh water until they're almost tender, and drain them again.

Set the oven to 140°C (275°F), gas mark 1. Peel and slice the onion. Heat the oil in a flameproof casserole and fry the onion for about 5 minutes, then add the rest of the ingredients and bring the mixture up to the boil. Cover the casserole and put it into the oven; cook for about 4 hours, stirring occasionally. These beans are lovely served with hunks of hot wholemeal bread or garlic bread.

BUTTER BEAN AND CIDER CASSEROLE

This is lovely served with hot crusty rolls or potatoes baked in their jackets and grated cheese. If you've got a large, flameproof casserole dish, that's ideal for making this; otherwise you will need to fry the vegetables in a saucepan first and then transfer them to an ovenproof dish to finish cooking. A variation is to put medium-large peeled potatoes, one for each person, into the pot with the butter beans and vegetables and cook them together. Done like this, the potatoes soak up the flavours and are delicious, but you need a large casserole.

SERVES 4 [F]
15g (½oz) butter
1 tablespoon olive oil
3 large onions, peeled and sliced
2 garlic cloves, peeled and crushed
450g (1 lb) carrots, scraped and sliced
225g (8oz) dried butter beans, soaked, cooked and drained *or* 2 × 400g (14oz) cans, drained
275ml (10 fl oz) stock
150ml (5 fl oz) cider
bouquet garni *or* ½ teaspoon mixed herbs
sea salt
freshly ground black pepper

Set the oven to 160°C (325°F), gas mark 3. Heat the butter and oil in a large saucepan and add the onions and garlic; fry for 5 minutes, browning them slightly, then stir in the carrots and cook for a further 4–5 minutes, stirring frequently to prevent sticking. Add the butter beans, stock, cider, bouquet garni or mixed herbs and a little salt and pepper. Bring up to the boil, then cover and transfer to the oven to cook for 1½–2 hours. If you want a slightly thicker gravy, stir in a teaspoon of cornflour or arrowroot blended with a little stock and let the mixture boil for a minute or two to thicken. Remove bouquet garni before serving.

BUTTER BEAN AND TOMATO CUTLETS

A friend gave me this tasty recipe which I think may have been developed from a wartime one. The crumbs are made by drying out slices of wholemeal bread on a baking sheet, then crushing with a rolling pin or in a food processor. They keep well in an airtight tin or in the freezer.

SERVES 2–3 F
125g (4oz) butter beans *or* 1 × 400g (14oz) can
1 medium onion, peeled and chopped
15g (½oz) butter
50g (2oz) dried wholemeal breadcrumbs
2 tablespoons tomato chutney
1 teaspoon lemon juice
1 egg
sea salt
freshly ground black pepper
beaten egg
dried crumbs to coat
oil for shallow-frying

Soak and cook the dried butter beans until they're tender, then drain; drain canned beans. Mash the beans. Fry the onion in the butter until it's tender, but not browned, then add it to the butter beans with all the other ingredients, seasoning the mixture with sea salt and freshly ground black pepper. Shape into cutlets and coat in egg and wholemeal bread-crumbs. Fry the cutlets in hot shallow oil, then drain them well on kitchen paper. Serve with a tasty gravy, tomato sauce or with yoghurt sauce and crisp green salad.

BUTTER BEANS AND MUSHROOMS

The original version of this recipe included double cream. These days I make it using thick natural yoghurt (the Greek sheep's milk type, preferably) or a soft, smooth, white cheese like *fromage blanc* or quark.

SERVES 4
175g (6oz) butter beans, *or* 2 × 400g (14oz) cans
225g (8oz) young white button mushrooms
15g (½oz) butter
1 tablespoon lemon juice
150ml (5 fl oz) thick natural yoghurt or low-fat soft white cheese
sea salt
freshly ground black pepper
grated nutmeg
1 tablespoon chopped parsley

If you're using dried butter beans, soak and cook them in the usual way (page 178). Keep butter beans warm; heat canned beans in their liquid.

Wash the mushrooms and halve or quarter them if necessary. Fry them gently in the butter in a medium-sized saucepan for 2–3 minutes until they're just tender, then drain the butter beans and add, together with the lemon juice, yoghurt or white cheese. Season to taste with the salt, pepper and nutmeg. Heat gently, but don't allow the mixture to become too hot or the yoghurt will separate. Serve sprinkled with chopped parsley.

BUTTER BEANS WITH TOMATOES, MINT AND OLIVE OIL

This is a Greek recipe for butter beans and the result is moist and flavoursome. The beans can be served as a vegetable, or with fluffy brown rice. I think they make a pleasant supper dish, with home-made wholemeal rolls and green salad. They're also very good cold, especially if you throw in a few black olives too. It will freeze, but add the garlic later.

SERVES 4–6 AS A MAIN PROTEIN DISH, 8 AS A VEGETABLE F
225g (8oz) butter beans *or* 2 × 400g (14oz) cans
2 large onions
2 garlic cloves
4 tablespoons olive oil
450g (1 lb) tomatoes, skinned *or* 400g (14oz) can
2 tablespoons fresh chopped mint
sea salt
freshly ground black pepper
a little sugar

Cover the butter beans with a good layer of cold water and leave them to soak for several hours. Then rinse them and put them into a saucepan of fresh cold water. Bring the butter beans up to the boil and simmer them until tender, then drain them.

While all this is happening, peel the onions and chop them finely; crush the garlic. Fry the onions in the olive oil in a good-sized saucepan for 10 minutes, allowing them to brown lightly, then stir in the garlic. Chop the tomatoes and add these to the saucepan, together with the cooked beans, the mint and some sea salt and freshly ground black pepper. Let the mixture simmer gently, covered, for about 20 minutes, to allow all the flavours to blend. Taste and add more sea salt and freshly ground black pepper and a dash of sugar if you think it's necessary.

BUTTER BEANS WITH TOMATOES AND GREEN PEPPER

This is a simple dish which is good served as a vegetable, or, with just a tossed green salad and some warm rolls and butter, for a simple meal, with fruit and yoghurt to follow. It's also delicious cold, particularly if you can stir in a few black olives and some extra olive oil.

SERVES 4 F
225g (8oz) butter beans *or* chick peas *or* 2 × 400g
(14oz) cans
2 large onions
2 large garlic cloves
2 tablespoons olive oil
2 green peppers
450g (1 lb) tomatoes, skinned and chopped *or* 400g
(14oz) can
1 tablespoon tomato purée
½ teaspoon chilli powder
sea salt
freshly ground black pepper
a little sugar to taste
2 tablespoons chopped parsley

Soak, rinse and cook the butter beans or chick peas as usual (see page 178), then drain them. Drain canned beans, if using. Meanwhile peel and slice the onions and crush the garlic; fry them gently in the olive oil until they're tender, about 10 minutes. Halve the green peppers and remove the seeds, then slice the peppers thinly and add them to the onions and garlic; cook for 5 minutes, then stir in the tomatoes, tomato purée and chilli powder and cook gently for 10 minutes. Add the butter beans or chick peas and heat through gently. Season with sea salt, freshly ground black pepper and a little sugar if you think the mixture needs it. Serve sprinkled with chopped parsley.

Variation

CHICK PEAS WITH TOMATOES AND GREEN PEPPER

This is equally delicious made exactly as above but using chick peas instead of butter beans.

BUTTER BEAN AND VEGETABLE AU GRATIN

I tend to think of this as a warming winter dish, made with root vegetables, but in fact there's no reason why it shouldn't work equally well with some of the tender early summer vegetables such as young carrots, courgettes and French beans. A variation which I like is to use a 400g (14oz) can tomatoes, whizzed to a purée or mashed and seasoned, instead of the cheese sauce.

SERVES 4–6 F
175g (6oz) butter beans *or* 2 × 400g (14oz) cans
150–275ml (5–10 fl oz) milk
225g (8oz) carrots
225g (8oz) swede
225g (8oz) leeks
4 sticks celery
4 onions
40g (1½oz) butter
40g (1½oz) flour
125g (4oz) grated cheese
sea salt
freshly ground black pepper
wholemeal breadcrumbs

If you're using dried beans, soak, rinse and cook them as usual (page 178). Drain beans, reserving liquid. Make the liquid up to 425ml (15 fl oz) with milk.

Peel and dice the carrots and swede; clean and slice the leeks and celery; peel and slice the onions. Cook all the vegetables together in boiling water until they're just tender, then drain them.

Melt the butter in a good-sized saucepan and stir in the flour; when it 'froths', draw the saucepan off the heat and stir in the milk mixture, then return the saucepan to the heat and stir until the sauce thickens. Let the sauce simmer gently for about 10 minutes, to cook the flour, then stir in half the cheese, the butter beans and cooked vegetables. Season with sea salt and freshly ground black pepper. Turn the mixture into a shallow heatproof casserole, sprinkle with the crumbs and remaining cheese and brown under the grill.

CANNELLINI BEANS WITH MUSHROOMS AND SOURED CREAM

This is very simple and quick to do and can be served as an accompanying vegetable or as a main course in its own right, with buttered noodles, warm bread or rice. It also works well with thick natural yoghurt instead of the soured cream.

SERVES 4
225g (8oz) cannellini beans, soaked and cooked *or* 2 × 425g (15oz) cans
175g (6oz) button mushrooms, wiped and sliced
25g (1oz) butter
½ teaspoon cornflour
300ml (11 fl oz) soured cream
sea salt
freshly ground black pepper
grated nutmeg

Drain beans. Fry mushrooms in the butter for 3–4 minutes without browning, then add the cornflour. Cook for a few seconds, then add the soured cream or yoghurt, beans and salt, pepper and nutmeg to taste. Heat gently, stirring all the time. Serve as soon as possible.

CREAMED CHICK PEAS WITH GARLIC

This is very easy to make, especially if you use canned chick peas. A tomato salad goes well with it.

SERVES 4
250g (8oz) chick peas *or* 2× 400g (14oz) cans
3 large garlic cloves, crushed
2 tablespoons lemon juice
sea salt
freshly ground black pepper
2 tablespoons olive oil
paprika pepper
lemon wedges
wholemeal toast

Soak the chick peas, then rinse them and cook in fresh water as usual. Drain and reserve the cooking liquid. Mash or purée the chick peas, adding some of the liquid if necessary, to make a smooth, fairly thick consistency. Flavour this purée with the garlic, lemon juice, salt, pepper and the olive oil. Put into a saucepan and stir until heated through. Sprinkle the chick pea purée with paprika and serve with lemon wedges and wholemeal toast.

Variation

CHICK PEA PURÉE WITH TOMATOES AND ONIONS

For a delicious Greek variation, add 2 onions, fried in olive oil until tender, 225g (8oz) skinned, chopped tomatoes (or 225g [8oz] can) and a good tablespoon each of chopped parsley and mint to the above mixture. Heat through and serve as above.

MIDDLE EASTERN CHICK PEA AND AUBERGINE CASSEROLE

This colourful chick pea and aubergine casserole from the Middle East is good with fluffy brown rice or jacket-baked potatoes and a green salad. If there's any over, it's splendid served chilled, with crusty bread and some green salad.

SERVES 4 F
150g (5oz) chick peas *or* 400g (14oz) can
1kg (2 lb) aubergine
sea salt
2 large onions
6 tablespoons olive oil
450g (1 lb) tomatoes, skinned, *or* 400g (14oz) can
freshly ground black pepper

Soak the chick peas in cold water for several hours, then drain and rinse them, cover with fresh water, cook gently until they're tender, then drain them. Drain canned chick peas. Wash the aubergines and cut them into chunky pieces; put them in a colander, sprinkle with sea salt and place a plate and a weight on top. Leave for about 30 minutes to give the sea salt time to draw out any bitterness, then rinse the pieces and pat them dry on kitchen paper.

Set the oven for 200°C (400°F), gas mark 6. Peel and slice the onions and fry them in the oil in a large saucepan, then remove them with a draining spoon and fry the aubergine chunks in the oil until they're crisp and lightly browned. Put the aubergine pieces into a casserole dish, together with the oil in which they were cooked, the onion, chick peas, tomatoes and a good seasoning of sea salt and freshly ground black pepper. Cover the casserole and bake it in the oven for 40–60 minutes.

CHICK PEA AND POTATO CROQUETTES

These creamy croquettes are good served with a tomato sauce and a green vegetable, or with yoghurt sauce and some salad, or curry sauce and spiced rice.

SERVES 4 [F]
175g (6oz) chick peas, soaked and cooked *or* 2 ×
400g (14oz) cans
450g (1 lb) potatoes, cooked, drained and mashed
(not too wet)
1 garlic clove, crushed
½ teaspoon paprika pepper
2 tablespoons chopped parsley
sea salt
freshly ground black pepper
wholemeal flour
1 egg, beaten with 1 tablespoon water
dry crumbs
olive oil for shallow-frying

Drain the chick peas, and mash roughly with a fork, then mix them with the mashed potato, crushed garlic, paprika pepper and parsley. Season with sea salt and freshly ground black pepper. Form the mixture into small croquettes and roll them in wholemeal flour. Then dip the croquettes first into beaten egg and then into dry crumbs; fry them in hot, shallow oil; drain well on kitchen paper. Alternatively, place croquettes on an oiled baking sheet, bake for 30–40 minutes, at 200°C (400°F), gas mark 6, turning them over after about 20 minutes, to brown both sides evenly.

SPANISH CHICK PEA STEW

There are many versions of this Spanish stew, cocido, containing varying quantities of meat. This is one of the more modest ones and, as a vegetarian, I prefer to make it without meat, although strictly speaking, a piece of salted pork or bacon should be included – about 125–175g (4–6oz). Some of the more complicated cocidos are served as three courses; first the liquid is strained off, mixed with vermicelli and served as soup; then the chick peas and vegetables are removed from the saucepan for the next course, and finally the meat. This simple cocido is best served in one bowl, however, as a stew, with some bread or croûtons.

SERVES 4
350g (12oz) chick peas
unsalted stock
3 potatoes
2 onions
2 carrots
1 turnip
2 leeks
1 small cabbage
2 garlic cloves
1 tablespoon paprika pepper
bouquet garni – a couple of sprigs of parsley, a sprig
of thyme and a bay leaf, tied together
2 tablespoons olive oil
sea salt
freshly ground black pepper

Soak the chick peas for several hours, then drain and rinse them. Put the chick peas into a large saucepan, cover them generously with unsalted stock and simmer them for about 1 hour, until they're almost tender. Meanwhile, peel the potatoes, and cut them into even-sized chunks; peel and slice the onions, carrots and turnip. Wash the leeks thoroughly and cut into slices; wash and quarter the cabbage and crush the garlic. Add the vegetables to the chick peas in the saucepan, together with the paprika pepper, *bouquet garni*, oil and a little more stock if you think it necessry. Simmer gently for a further 30 minutes or so until everything is done. Remove the *bouquet garni*; season the mixture with sea salt and freshly ground black pepper.

FELAFEL

In the Middle East, chickpeas are used for these spicy little fritters, and very good they are too. Serve with warm pitta bread, thick Greek yoghurt and a tomato, onion and black olive salad.

SERVES 4 [F]
225g (8oz) chick peas *or* 2 × 400g (14oz) cans)
1 large onion
1 teaspoon ground coriander
1 teaspoon ground cumin
good pinch of chilli powder
1 garlic clove, crushed
sea salt
freshly ground black pepper
wholemeal flour to coat
olive oil to shallow-fry

Soak and cook dried chick peas as usual; make sure they're really tender, then drain. Drain canned chick peas. Purée or mash thoroughly.

Peel and finely grate the onion and add it to the chick peas, together with the spices, garlic and sea salt and freshly ground black pepper to taste. If the mixture is rather soft, put it into the refrigerator for half an hour or so to firm up.

Form tablespoons of the mixture into small, flat cakes, coat them well in wholemeal flour and then shallow-fry them in hot olive oil until they're brown on both sides.

FIELD BEAN BURGERS

These are made from the beans you can grow yourself in a garden or vegetable patch. They cost practically nothing and are chewy, filling and delicious. But you do need a food processor or strong blender to break down the skins of the beans.

SERVES 4 F
1 onion, chopped
2 tablespoons olive oil
2 garlic cloves, crushed
350g (12oz) field beans, soaked and cooked
4 tablespoons chopped parsley
1 tablespoon lemon juice
sea salt
freshly ground black pepper
flour to coat
olive oil for shallow-frying

Fry the onion in the oil for 5 minutes, then add the garlic and fry for a further 5 minutes. Chop beans in food processor until reduced to a coarse purée. Add onion, parsley, lemon juice and salt and pepper to taste. Coat with flour, then shallow-fry on both sides until crisp and browned. Drain on kitchen paper and serve immediately.

HARICOT AND ONION CASSEROLE

This is a wartime recipe which I've adapted slightly. It's very thrifty but surprisingly good to eat.

SERVES 4 F
225g (8oz) haricot beans
sea salt
freshly ground black pepper
450g (1 lb) onions
425ml (15 fl oz) water
about 275ml (10 fl oz) milk
50g (2oz) butter
50g (2oz) flour
50g (2oz) grated cheese
½ teaspoon dry mustard
225g (8oz) canned tomatoes, chopped
a few dried crumbs
a little butter

Soak, drain and rinse the beans, then cover them with water and let them simmer gently for about 1 hour, or until tender. Drain; season with sea salt and freshly ground black pepper.

Preheat oven to 190°C (375°F), gas mark 5. Peel and slice the onions and cook them gently in the water until they're tender, then drain them, reserving the water and making it up to 575ml (1 pint) with the milk. Melt the butter in a saucepan and add the flour; when it 'froths' remove the saucepan from the heat and stir in the milk and onion water. Return the saucepan to the heat, stirring all the time for 3 minutes, until the sauce has thickened. Add the grated cheese, dry mustard, sea salt and freshly ground black pepper to taste.

Put the beans into a shallow greased casserole dish and arrange the tomatoes on top; season with sea salt and freshly ground black pepper. Put the onions on top of the tomatoes and season again; finally pour the sauce evenly over the onions. Scatter a few crumbs over the top, dot with butter and bake for 30–40 minutes. Serve with potatoes and a green vegetable.

HARICOT BEAN AND VEGETABLE PIE

An economical family dish consisting of a tasty bean and vegetable mixture topped with mashed potatoes and cheese and baked until golden brown.

SERVES 4 F
175g (6oz) haricot beans
15g (½oz) butter
1 large onion, peeled and chopped
1 large garlic clove, crushed
425ml (15 fl oz) water or unsalted stock
2 tablespoons tomato purée
½ teaspoon dried basil
sea salt
freshly ground black pepper
a little sugar
700g (1½ lb) potatoes, peeled
450g (1 lb) carrots, scraped and diced
450g (1 lb) leeks, cleaned and sliced
a little milk
125g (4oz) grated cheese

Soak the beans as usual, then drain and rinse them. Melt two-thirds of the butter in a medium-sized saucepan and fry the onion for about 10 minutes, then add the drained beans, garlic and water or stock. Bring up to the boil, then let it simmer gently for about 1 hour, until the beans are soft and the liquid reduced to a thick sauce. Stir in the tomato purée and season with basil, sea salt, freshly ground black pepper and a little sugar if necessary.

Meanwhile, cook the potatoes, carrots and leeks; drain. (The carrots and leeks can be cooked in the same saucepan.) Preheat oven to 190°C (375°F), gas mark 5. Mash the potatoes, using the remaining butter, a drop of milk and sea salt and freshly ground black pepper to taste.

Grease a shallow, ovenproof casserole dish and put the leeks and carrots in the base; pour the bean mixture on top, sprinkle with most of the grated cheese, then spread the mashed potato on top. Fork over the top of the potato and sprinkle with the remaining cheese. Bake for 30–40 minutes, until piping hot and crispy and golden on top. It's nice served with a green vegetable like spinach or broccoli.

EASY CHEESY LENTILS

This is cheap, nourishing and very easy to make! Serve with a salad of sliced tomatoes and onions.

SERVES 4 F
1 onion, peeled and chopped
2 tablespoons olive oil
1 garlic clove, crushed
225g (8oz) split red lentils
750ml (1¼ pints) water
125g (4oz) grated cheese
sea salt
freshly ground black pepper

Fry the onion in the oil in a large saucepan for 10 minutes. Add the garlic, lentils and water. Bring to the boil, then cover, turn down the heat and cook gently for 15–20 minutes, until lentils are pale and soft. Beat in the grated cheese and season with salt and pepper. Serve at once.

LENTIL AND CHEESE SLICE

A simple, quick-to-make supper dish which children like: crisp golden lentil and cheese slices. Serve with parsley sauce, new potatoes and a green vegetable. They're also good cold, with pickles and salad.

SERVES 4 F
225g (8oz) split red lentils
1 onion, sliced
1 bay leaf
450ml (16 fl oz) water
50g (2oz) grated cheese
sea salt
freshly ground black pepper
1 tomato, thinly sliced
a little butter

Put lentils, onion and bay leaf into a saucepan with the water and cook gently, without a lid, for 20–25 minutes, until lentils are tender. Remove bay leaf. Set oven to 220°C (425°F), gas mark 7. Beat half the cheese into the cooked lentils and season. Grease a 20cm (8in) square tin, spoon in lentil mixture, spreading to corners. Top with remaining cheese and tomato slices, dot with butter. Bake for 20–25 minutes.

LENTILS WITH CORIANDER AND FRESH GINGER

This spicy lentil mixture is lovely with plain boiled brown rice and a tomato and onion or cucumber and yoghurt side salad.

SERVES 3
225g (8oz) continental lentils
2 large onions, peeled and chopped
2 garlic cloves, crushed
40g (1½oz) butter
2 teaspoons grated fresh ginger
2 teaspoons ground coriander
2 teaspoons ground cumin
lemon juice
sea salt
freshly ground black pepper

If possible soak the lentils for a few hours in cold water, then rinse them and put them into a saucepan with water just to cover them; simmer them for about 40 minutes, or until they're tender. If there isn't time to soak them, either do the quick, hot soak (page 178) and then cook them, or put the washed lentils into a saucepan with plenty of water and simmer them until they're tender – about 1¼ hours or so. In any case, drain the lentils well.

Fry the onion and garlic in the butter for about 5 minutes, then add the ginger, ground coriander, and cumin and cook for a further 5 minutes. Stir the onion and spices into the cooked lentils and flavour with lemon juice, sea salt and freshly ground black pepper.

That's the basic, simple curry, but you can jazz it up by adding other vegetables such as sliced green pepper or button mushrooms; simply fry them with the onions.

LENTIL CROQUETTES

I find these crisp croquettes appeal even to those who don't think they like lentils. They're good with mint sauce, gravy and cooked vegetables, or with chilled natural yoghurt, brown rice and a tomato salad. Mango chutney goes well with them, too.

SERVES 4 F
225g (8oz) split red lentils
425ml (15 fl oz) water
1 onion, peeled and finely chopped
2 tablespoons olive oil
1 tablespoon lemon juice
sea salt
freshly ground black pepper
wholemeal flour
olive oil for shallow-frying

Put the lentils and water into a medium-sized saucepan and cook them for 20–30 minutes, until the lentils are pale and soft and the water has been absorbed.

Fry the onion in the oil for about 10 minutes, until it's soft, then add to the lentils, together with the lemon juice and seasoning to taste. Mix it all together well, then form it into 8 croquettes and coat each one with wholemeal flour.

Heat a little oil in a frying pan and fry the croquettes until they're crisp, then drain them on kitchen paper and keep them warm. For a crisper coating the croquettes can be dipped first in flour, as described, then in beaten egg and dried breadcrumbs.

Variations

SPICED LENTIL CROQUETTES WITH YOGHURT SAUCE

Make as above, adding ½ teaspoon each of ground cumin, ground coriander and turmeric to the onions after they have been frying for 5 minutes. Serve with one of the yoghurt sauces on page 67 and some spiced rice (page 236).

LENTIL AND CHEESE CROQUETTES IN CHILLI-TOMATO SAUCE

Add 125g (4oz) grated cheese and ½ teaspoon each of paprika pepper and dry mustard to the above mixture. Add ¼–½ teaspoon chilli powder to tomato sauce on page 65 and serve with the croquettes.

LENTIL AND EGG CUTLETS

Continental lentils and hardboiled eggs are one of those great combinations, like basil and tomatoes and sage and onion. I particularly like them together in these crisp cutlets. They are lovely served with some plain or garlic mayonnaise or with yoghurt and a crunchy cabbage, carrot, green pepper and pineapple salad. Or serve them with creamy mashed potatoes, cooked vegetables and a good gravy. The eggs help to bind the lentils in this recipe.

SERVES 4 F
225g (8oz) continental lentils or 2 × 400g (14oz) cans
1 large onion
1 tablespoon olive oil
4 hardboiled eggs
2 tablespoons finely chopped parsley
½ teaspoon powdered mace or a little grated nutmeg
sea salt
freshly ground black pepper
wholemeal flour to coat
oil for shallow-frying

Cook dried lentils in plenty of water until very tender, then drain well. Drain canned lentils. Meanwhile, peel and finely chop the onion and fry it in the oil for about 10 minutes until it's tender and golden brown. Peel and chop the hardboiled eggs and mix them in with the cooked lentils, together with the onion, parsley, mace or nutmeg and sea salt and freshly ground black pepper to taste. Mash mixture well, so that it holds together. Let the mixture cool, then shape it into eight round cutlets and roll them in wholemeal flour. Fry the cutlets in hot, shallow fat until they're crisp on both sides; drain them on kitchen paper.

LENTIL DAL (1)

Dal makes a good side dish with curries and is also good poured over lightly cooked root vegetables, turning them into a complete winter meal.

SERVES 4 F
225g (8oz) red lentils
850ml (1½ pints) water
1 bay leaf
5cm (2in) piece cinnamon stick
4 cardamoms
2 teaspoons ground coriander
2 teaspoons ground cumin
4 tablespoons olive oil
2 onions, chopped
2 garlic cloves, crushed
1 tablespoon lemon juice
50g (2 oz) coconut cream (from health shops, Indian stores or large supermarkets)
sea salt
freshly ground black pepper

Put lentils, water, bay leaf and cinnamon into a saucepan. Cook gently until lentils are tender: 20–25 minutes. Meanwhile fry spices in oil for 1-2 minutes, then add onion and garlic and fry for 10 minutes, until tender. Add this mixture, including the oil, to the cooked lentils, then stir in lemon juice, coconut cream and seasoning. Cook gently until coconut cream has dissolved, then remove spices and liquidize dal. (This liquidizing isn't essential, but I prefer the smoother, creamy texture which it produces.)

LENTIL DAL (2)

This makes a hotter tasting dal than the previous recipe; pleasant for serving with a mild curry or, with some mango chutney, to add interest to winter root vegetables and turn them into a meal.

SERVES 4
1 onion, chopped
15g (½oz) butter
1 garlic clove, crushed
1 green chilli
1 teaspoon ground cumin
1 teaspoon ground coriander
¼ teaspoon turmeric
225g (8oz) split red lentils
700 ml (1¼ pints) water
50g (2oz) creamed coconut – from health shops
1–2 tablespoons lemon juice
sea salt
freshly ground black pepper

Fry the onion in the butter for 7–8 minutes, until it is nearly soft but not browned. Add the garlic. Halve, de-seed and finely chop the chilli and add to the onions, being careful not to touch your face or eyes with your hands while preparing the chilli, and washing your hands well afterwards. Stir in the spices, then the lentils, mixing well. Then pour in the water, bring it up to the boil, half cover and leave to simmer gently for 15–20 minutes, when the lentils should be soft and pale golden-beige. Add the coconut cream and stir until melted, then flavour with the lemon juice and some salt and pepper to taste. This dal can be served as it is, or puréed in a liquidizer or food processor; I like it best puréed.

LENTIL DAL WITH VEGETABLES

As the split red lentils used in this recipe cook in half an hour without soaking, this dish is quickly made. In fact if you want to serve it with brown rice, it's best to get the rice cooking before you start making the dal.

SERVES 3–4
225g (8oz) split red lentils
425ml (15 fl oz) water
1 bay leaf
3 tablespoons olive oil
1 large onion, peeled and chopped
1 garlic clove, crushed
1 teaspoon turmeric
1 teaspoon ground cumin
1 teaspoon ground coriander
½ teaspoon ground ginger
2 tomatoes, skinned and chopped
1 large carrot, scraped and diced
1 large green pepper, de-seeded and sliced
1 leek, washed and sliced
sea salt
freshly ground black pepper

Put the lentils, water and bay leaf into a saucepan and cook gently for about 30 minutes, until the lentils are tender and have absorbed all the water.

Meanwhile, heat the oil in a saucepan and fry the onion and garlic with the turmeric, cumin, coriander and ginger for 10 minutes, stirring from time to time, then add the tomatoes and cook for a further minute or two before putting in the carrot, pepper and leek. Mix well, so that all the vegetables are coated with the spices, then put a lid on the saucepan, turn down the heat and cook gently for about 15 minutes or until the vegetables are all tender. Stir the vegetables into the cooked lentils; season with sea salt and freshly ground black pepper and serve with plain boiled or fried brown rice.

SPICY LENTIL DAL WITH SAMBALS

This is a surprisingly quick dish to make and always seems popular with its accompanying 'sambals' or little bowls of colourful ingredients. If you're planning to serve it with brown rice, it's a good idea to get this on to cook before starting on the dal, so that they're ready at the same time.

SERVES 4

225g (8oz) split red lentils
1 bay leaf
575ml (1 pint) water
1 large onion, peeled and chopped
1 small cooking apple, peeled and chopped
1 garlic clove, peeled and crushed
1 tablespoon oil
½–1 teaspoon sea salt
¼ teaspoon pepper
1–2 teaspoons curry paste *or* powder
1 tablespoon lemon juice

For the sambals:

Some or all of the following, in little bowls – diced cucumber, grated carrot, chopped cabbage and raisins, sliced banana, sliced tomato and onion, flaked almonds, desiccated coconut, mango chutney

Put lentils, bay leaf and water into a medium-sized saucepan and simmer gently until tender – about 20 minutes. Remove bay leaf. Meanwhile fry the onion, apple and garlic in the oil for 10 minutes. Add the onion mixture to the lentils, together with the remaining ingredients. You can liquidize the mixture at this point if you want to, or leave it as it is. I prefer it liquidized. Reheat the dal gently and serve with fluffy brown rice and sambals.

LENTIL LOAF

A friend of mine has almost converted her meat-loving in-laws to vegetarianism with the aid of this loaf. It's good either hot or cold, and slices well, especially when cold. If you're serving it hot, a savoury sauce, Bircher or roast potatoes and a green vegetable go well with it. Chutney or one of the low-fat mayonnaises are pleasant accompaniments if you want to have the loaf cold. Slices of the cold loaf make an excellent open sandwich topped with the mayonnaise, circles of tomato and onion, and some chutney or pickles.

SERVES 4–6 F

175g (6oz) split red lentils
225g (8 fl oz) water
1 bay leaf
125g (4oz) grated cheese
1 medium-sized onion, peeled and finely chopped
50g (2oz) button mushrooms, washed and finely chopped
40g (1½oz) fine fresh wholemeal breadcrumbs
1 tablespoon chopped parsley
1 tablespoon lemon juice
1 egg
sea salt
freshly ground black pepper
butter and dried crumbs for coating tin

Put the lentils, water and bay leaf into a medium-sized saucepan and simmer very gently, uncovered, until the lentils are tender and all the liquid absorbed – about 20 minutes. Remove bay leaf.

Set the oven to 190°C (375°F), gas mark 5. Prepare a 450g (1 lb) loaf tin by putting a long narrow strip of non-stick paper on the base and up the narrow sides. Grease the tin well with butter or margarine – I find the loaf comes out of the tin best if I use butter – and sprinkle generously with dried crumbs.

Add the grated cheese, onion, mushrooms, breadcrumbs, chopped parsley, lemon juice and egg to the lentils, mixing well. Season with plenty of salt and pepper. Spoon the mixture into the tin and level the top. Bake, uncovered, for 45–60 minutes, until firm and golden-brown on top.

LENTIL AND CIDER LOAF

The cider gives this loaf a lovely rich, fruity flavour, though you could leave it out and use a good vegetable stock if you prefer, or try a cheapish red wine instead which is also delicious and better if you want to drink red wine with the meal. The loaf is rich in protein and very good hot, perhaps with fresh tomato sauce and lemon potatoes; or cold, with salad and home-made mayonnaise. It can also be used as a sandwich filling, cut in thin slices and spread with mild mustard or chutney.

SERVES 6–8 F

175g (6oz) split red lentils
425ml (15 fl oz) cider
butter and dried breadcrumbs for lining loaf tin
1 large onion, peeled and chopped
1 carrot, about 50 g (2oz), scraped and chopped
1 stick of celery, chopped
1 garlic clove, peeled and crushed
25g (1oz) butter
1 teaspoon dried thyme
50g (2oz) hazel nuts, roasted for about 20 minutes in a moderate oven until nuts are golden beneath the skins, then ground in a liquidizer
50g (2 oz) cheese, grated
1 tablespoon fresh parsley, chopped
1 egg
sea salt
freshly ground black pepper
parsley sprigs

Put the lentils and cider into a saucepan and bring to the boil; turn the heat down, half-cover the saucepan and leave to simmer over a fairly low heat for 20 minutes, until the lentils are tender and all the water absorbed.

When the lentils are nearly cooked, set the oven to 180°C (350°F), gas mark 4. Prepare a 450g (1 lb) loaf tin by lining the base and narrow sides with a long strip of non-stick paper; brush well with butter and sprinkle lightly with dried breadcrumbs. Next, fry the onion, carrot, celery and garlic in the butter for 10 minutes, until they are softened and lightly browned. Add the fried vegetables to the lentils, together with the thyme, nuts, cheese, parsley and egg. Mix everything together thoroughly and add salt and plenty of pepper to taste.

Spoon the mixture into the prepared tin, smooth over the surface and cover with a piece of foil. Bake the loaf in the pre-heated oven for 1 hour, then remove the foil and cook for a further 10–15 minutes, uncovered if necessary, to brown the top. To serve, slip a knife round the sides of the loaf and turn out on to a warm dish. Decorate the top with some sprigs of fresh green parsley.

TASTY CONTINENTAL LENTIL LOAF WITH PINEAPPLE

This lentil loaf is different from the preceding one because it uses those big brown continental lentils that you can get at health shops. These stay intact when they're cooked, giving a pleasantly chewy texture. The pineapple adds interest and gives just the right touch of sweetness.

SERVES 4 F

175g (6oz) continental lentils or 400g (14oz) can
2 large onions, peeled and finely chopped
2 tablespoons chopped parsley
1 teaspoon mixed herbs
1 teaspoon yeast extract
1 tablespoon lemon juice
75g (3oz) soft wholemeal breadcrumbs
sea salt
freshly ground black pepper
1 tablespoon olive oil
225g (8oz) can pineapple rings in juice

Put the dried lentils into a medium-sized saucepan and cover with plenty of water. Simmer gently for about 45 minutes, until lentils are soft. Drain. Just drain canned lentils, if you're using these. Set the oven to 200°C (400°F), gas mark 6. Add the onion, parsley, herbs, yeast extract, lemon juice and two-thirds of the crumbs to the lentils and mix well. The mixture should be firm enough to hold its shape – add a few more crumbs if necessary. Season with salt and pepper. Form lentil mixture into a loaf shape and coat with the remaining crumbs. Brush a baking tin with the oil and lift the loaf on to the tin, using a fish slice to help if needed. Bake for 40–45 minutes, turning the loaf over, again with the aid of a fish slice, after about 30 minutes. Put the pineapple, together with its juice, into a small heatproof container and place in the oven to heat through about 15 minutes before the loaf is ready. Serve the lentil loaf in slices, with the pineapple, a tasty sauce, potatoes and a lightly-cooked green vegetable.

LENTILS AND MUSHROOMS AU GRATIN

This is another of the 'top twenty' recipes, judging by the letters and comments I've received over the years. It consists of mushrooms covered with a smooth lentil purée and topped with crunchy bread-crumbs and grated cheese.

SERVES 4 F
175g (6oz) lentils
575ml (1 pint) milk and water mixed
25g (1oz) butter
1 large onion, peeled and sliced
1 teaspoon grated lemon rind
2 tablespoons lemon juice
sea salt
freshly ground black pepper
1 teaspoon yeast extract
225g (8oz) mushrooms
25g (1oz) fresh breadcrumbs
25g (1oz) grated cheese

Put lentils into a saucepan with the milk and water and simmer for 20–30 minutes, until golden and tender.

Set oven to 180°C (350°F), gas mark 4. Meanwhile, melt half the butter, add the onion and cook until tender but not brown. Add to the lentils with the lemon rind and juice, salt, pepper and yeast extract. Liquidize this mixture to make a smooth, thick purée. Wash and slice mushrooms and fry in the rest of the butter until just tender. Place fried mushrooms in a shallow casserole, top with the lentil mixture, breadcrumbs and cheese. Bake for 40–45 minutes, until golden and bubbly.

Variations

LENTILS AND CELERY AU GRATIN

Use the outside stalks of one large head of celery, chopped and cooked, instead of mushrooms.

LENTILS AND COURGETTES AU GRATIN

Make this using 450g (1 lb) courgettes, sliced, instead of the mushrooms.

LENTILS AND TOMATOES AU GRATIN

Use 6 tomatoes, skinned and sliced, and ½ teaspoon dried, or ½ tablespoon fresh, chopped basil, instead of mushrooms. No need to fry the tomatoes, put them straight into the casserole.

LENTILS AND FENNEL AU GRATIN

Use 450g (1 lb) fennel, sliced and cooked in a little fast-boiling water until tender, instead of the mushrooms. Drain, and use the water with the milk for the lentil sauce.

CONTINENTAL LENTIL AND WALNUT LOAF

People usually find it difficult to guess what this loaf is made from: the result is tasty and 'chewy' and of course it's packed with protein. It's nice served hot with roast potatoes, gravy and vegetables – a vegetarian-style Sunday lunch – or cold, with some mayonnaise, thick natural yoghurt, or chutney.

SERVES 4–6 F
175g (6oz) continental lentils
1 onion, peeled and chopped up small
1 large garlic clove, crushed
2 tablespoons olive oil
1 teaspoon dried thyme
125g (4oz) walnuts, grated
125g (4oz) wholemeal breadcrumbs
1 tablespoon tomato purée
1 tablespoon chopped fresh parsley
1 egg
sea salt
freshly ground black pepper
1 tomato, sliced
a few sprigs of parsley

Soak the lentils for a few hours, then rinse them and put them into a saucepan with enough cold water to cover. Simmer gently for about 40 minutes, until they're tender, then drain off any liquid.

Prepare a 450g (1 lb) loaf tin by putting a long strip of non-stick paper across the bottom and up the two narrow sides; grease it generously with butter. Set oven to 190°C (375°F) gas mark 5.

Fry the onion and garlic in the oil in a good-sized saucepan for 10 minutes until tender and lightly browned; stir in the thyme and fry for a few seconds, then remove the saucepan from the heat and add the lentils, walnuts, wholemeal breadcrumbs, tomato purée, parsley and egg. Mix well, then season with sea salt and freshly ground black pepper. Spoon the mixture into the prepared loaf tin and smooth the top. Cover with a piece of greased foil and bake in the oven for 1 hour. Leave the loaf to stand in its tin for a minute or two after removing it from the oven, then slip a knife round the edges of the loaf to loosen it and turn it out; strip off the paper. Garnish the top of the loaf with slices of tomato and a sprig of parsley.

LENTIL AND MUSHROOM BURGERS

The mushrooms make these burgers moist while the lentils add texture and protein. The burgers hold together well and can be cooked in the oven on an oiled baking sheet, fried on top of the stove or grilled over a barbecue. I like them with a dollop of creamy Béarnaise sauce – or mayonnaise – and fresh watercress; but they are also lovely when eaten in a soft roll with lots of mustard or chutney.

SERVES 4
15g (½oz) butter
1 tablespoon olive oil
1 onion, peeled and chopped
450g (1 lb) mushrooms, washed and chopped
2 large garlic cloves, peeled and crushed
125g (4oz) (dry weight) continental lentils, cooked and very well drained
2 tablespoons fresh parsley, chopped
sea salt
freshly ground black pepper
flour for coating
olive oil for shallow-frying – optional

If you're going to bake the burgers in the oven, set it to 200°C (400°F), gas mark 6. Heat the butter and oil in a large saucepan and fry the onion for 5 minutes, until beginning to soften, then put in the mushrooms and garlic. Fry over a moderate heat for 20–25 minutes, until all the liquid has evaporated and the mushrooms are reduced to a thick purée. Stir them from time to time while they are cooking. Then take the saucepan off the heat and mix in all the other ingredients, seasoning to taste with salt and pepper. Form the mixture into burger shapes and roll the burgers lightly in flour. Place them on a greased baking sheet and bake for about 30 minutes, turning them over half way through the cooking time. Alternatively, fry the burgers quickly in a little hot oil, or brush them with oil and grill on both sides.

LENTIL PIE

An economical wartime dish which I find is very popular with children, especially if they have it with fried potatoes and are allowed a free hand with the tomato ketchup! It's also nice with parsley sauce and slices of lemon.

SERVES 4 F
175g (6oz) split red lentils
1 large onion
350g (12oz) mashed potatoes
1 tablespoon chopped parsley
1 tablespoon chutney
sea salt
freshly ground black pepper
15g (½oz) butter

Wash the lentils; peel and chop the onion. Put them into a saucepan with enough water to cover and cook gently until the lentils are tender and the water absorbed (20–30 minutes), then mash them lightly with a fork or potato masher. (The original recipe says 'pass through a sieve', but I think this is unnecessary.) Preheat oven to 200°C (400°F), gas mark 6. Beat the mashed potatoes into the cooked lentils, together with the parsley, chutney and sea salt and freshly ground black pepper to taste. Put the mixture into a shallow greased dish, smoothing then forking over the top. Melt the butter and pour it over the top of the lentil mixture. Bake in the oven for about 20 minutes, until crisp and browned. (Alternatively, this can be cooked under a moderate grill if more convenient.)

LENTIL AND RED PEPPER STEW

You can make this stew with all lentils or all beans but I think with this half-and-half mixture you get the best of both; the lentils thicken the sauce and give it body while the beans supply extra interest and texture. One of the nicest things about this is its colour – it comes out a heart-warming vivid red and is really welcoming on a chilly day. Serve it with a dollop of thick natural yoghurt or soured cream, some crunchy jacket potatoes and a green salad; or try creamy mashed potatoes and a cooked green vegetable.

SERVES 4 F
125g (4oz) red lentils
125g (4oz) haricot beans
2 large onions
700g (1½ lb) red peppers – about 4 large ones
25g (1oz) butter
1 litre (2 pints) unsalted stock *or* water
4 tablespoons tomato purée
sea salt
sugar

Put the lentils and beans into a bowl and cover generously with cold water; leave them to soak for several hours or overnight, then drain and rinse them.

Peel and chop the onions; slice the peppers, discarding the cores and seeds. Melt the butter in a large saucepan and fry the onion for about 10 minutes to soften it, then add the red peppers and cook for a further 4–5 minutes before stirring in the drained lentils and beans and the stock or water. Bring the mixture up to the boil and let it simmer gently, with a lid half on the saucepan, until the beans are tender – 1–1¼ hours.

Then mix in the tomato purée, and some salt and sugar to taste, as necessary. If the stew seems a bit runny, turn up the heat and boil it for a few minutes without the lid on until it's the right consistency.

SPICY ROOT VEGETABLE AND LENTIL STEW

Real warming winter food, this; root vegetables with pulses, and very filling and satisfying, too. You can add whatever herbs and spices you fancy; my suggestion of ground coriander and cumin makes it spicy without being 'hot'.

SERVES 3–4 F
3 tablespoons olive oil
700g (1½ lb) mixed root vegetables – swede, parsnip, carrot, turnip – peeled and diced
2 large onions, peeled and chopped
2 sticks celery, sliced
175g (6oz) split red lentils
2 garlic cloves, crushed
225g (8oz) canned tomatoes
700ml (1¼ pints) unsalted stock
1 onion, peeled and chopped
1–2 teaspoons ground coriander
1–2 teaspoons ground cumin
sea salt
freshly ground black pepper
2 tablespoons lemon juice
a little chopped parsley

Heat the oil in a large saucepan and put in the root vegetables, two-thirds of the onion and the celery. Fry the vegetables in 2 tablespoons of the oil, without browning them, for about 5 minutes, then add the lentils and garlic and cook them all gently for a further 4–5 minutes, stirring often. Mix in the tomatoes and stock, put a lid on the saucepan and leave it to simmer away gently for about 30 minutes, until all the vegetables are tender and the lentils pale golden and soft. Meanwhile, fry the extra onion in the remaining oil for 10 minutes, then add the ground coriander and cumin and fry for a further minute or two to draw out the flavour of the spices. Stir this mixture into the cooked lentils and add sea salt and freshly ground black pepper to taste and the lemon juice. Scatter with a little chopped parsley before serving.

If you prefer to cook this in the oven, it takes about an hour towards the bottom at 200°C (400°F), gas mark 6.

SHEPHERD'S LENTIL PIE

Continental lentils also make a tasty moist filling for a shepherd's pie. I find this a quick dish to make, if I can remember to save some mashed potatoes from a previous meal, and it only needs some savoury gravy (page 63) and a quickly cooked green vegetable such as baby sprouts or spinach to go with it. Leave out the wine, by the way, if you think it's extravagant, but if you can spare a little it does give a lovely flavour.

SERVES 4–6 F

175g (6oz) brown lentils
575ml (1 pint) water
1 bay leaf
1 onion, peeled and finely chopped
1 tablespoon olive oil
1 small carrot, peeled and chopped
1 stick of celery, finely chopped
1 garlic clove, crushed
4 tablespoons wine – optional, but any cheap kind will do
425g (15oz) can tomatoes
sea salt
freshly ground black pepper
700g (1½ lb) mashed potato
25g (1oz) grated cheese

Put the lentils, water and bay leaf into a medium-sized saucepan and leave to simmer gently until the lentils are tender – 45–60 minutes. Set the oven to 200°C (400°F), gas mark 6. Fry the onion in the oil for 10 minutes, then add the carrot, celery and garlic and cook for a further couple of minutes, stirring from time to time. Remove from the heat and stir in the wine and tomatoes; season to taste with salt and pepper. Spoon the mixture into a lightly greased, shallow ovenproof dish and cover with the mashed potato. Level the surface, then rough it up with the prongs of a fork and sprinkle with the grated cheese. Bake for 45 minutes.

SPICY LENTILS AND POTATOES

This is quick, easy and cheap; it's good with slices of firm raw tomato and some mango chutney.

SERVES 4

1 onion, peeled and chopped
2 tablespoons olive oil
1 garlic clove, crushed
1 teaspoon whole cumin seeds
walnut-sized piece of fresh ginger, peeled and finely grated
3 medium-sized potatoes, peeled and cut into 2cm (1in) cubes
225g (8oz) split red lentils
750ml (1¼ pints) water
sea salt
freshly ground black pepper

Fry the onion in the oil for 10 minutes in a large saucepan or large, deep, frying pan. Add the garlic, cumin and ginger; stir-fry for 1–2 minutes, then put in the potatoes and stir for a further minute or two. Add the lentils, water and a little seasoning, bring to the boil, then cover, turn down the heat and cook gently for 15–20 minutes, until lentils are pale and soft and potatoes just tender when pierced with a knife. Check seasoning, serve at once.

LENTIL AND SPINACH CASSEROLE

The marriage of lentils and spinach is a particularly pleasing one, and this is a nice easy casserole to make.

SERVES 4

225g (8oz) split red lentils
575ml (1 pint) water
1kg (2 lb) spinach
15g (½oz) butter
225g (8oz) tomatoes, peeled and sliced
sea salt
freshly ground black pepper
75–125g (3–4oz) grated cheese

Cook the lentils in the water for about 20 minutes, until they're soft, and pale in colour. Meanwhile wash the spinach carefully, then cook it in a dry saucepan for 7–10 minutes, until it's tender. Drain off the excess liquid and chop the spinach, then season it with sea salt and freshly ground black pepper. Preheat the oven to 190°C (375°F), gas mark 5.

Use the butter to grease a shallow ovenproof dish generously, then put the spinach in the base and arrange the tomatoes on top. Sprinkle with sea salt and freshly ground black pepper. Season the lentils and then pour them over the tomatoes and spread them to the edges of the dish; top with a layer of grated cheese. Bake in the oven for about 40 minutes. It's good with buttery noodles or new potatoes.

LENTILS AND SPINACH

You might think this is a most unpromising combination, but it works well; it's so soothing to eat.

SERVES 4
450g (1 lb) spinach
225g (8oz) continental lentils, soaked and cooked until tender, then drained
1 onion, peeled and chopped
2 garlic cloves, crushed
15g (½oz) butter
good pinch each of ground cumin and ground coriander
sea salt
freshly ground black pepper
juice ½ lemon

Wash the spinach carefully by putting it into a big bowl of cold water and swishing it round, then draining it and repeating twice more. Shred it roughly, then put it into a dry saucepan and cook over a moderate heat, with a lid on the saucepan, until it's tender – about 10 minutes. Drain off the liquid. Add the cooked drained lentils to the spinach and have the saucepan over a gentle heat to keep the spinach hot and heat the lentils through.

Fry the onion and garlic in the butter for 10 minutes, until tender, then stir in the spices and cook for a minute or two longer. Add this mixture to the spinach and lentils, together with sea salt and freshly ground black pepper to taste, and the lemon juice. Serve at once.

This dish looks attractive garnished with some wedges of hardboiled egg, yellow and white against bright green, but it's also very good served just as it is, perhaps with some slices of brown bread and butter.

MOCK GOOSE

This is a wartime recipe (slightly adapted) for a layered lentil loaf which no self-respecting goose would own! But it's quite good and tasty in its own right, especially if served with a well-flavoured gravy and some apple sauce.

SERVES 2–3
175g (6oz) split red lentils
275ml (10 fl oz) water
15g (½oz) butter
1 tablespoon lemon juice
sea salt
freshly ground black pepper
1 large onion, peeled and chopped
2 tablespoons olive oil
50g (2oz) soft wholemeal breadcrumbs
1½ teaspoons dried sage
a little butter

Wash the lentils and put them into a saucepan with the water; simmer them gently until they're cooked and all the water has been absorbed, then beat in the butter, lemon juice and seasoning. Set oven for 200°C (400°F), gas mark 6.

For the stuffing, fry the onion in the oil for about 10 minutes, then take it off the heat and add the wholemeal breadcrumbs, sage and a seasoning of sea salt and freshly ground black pepper.

Put a layer of half the lentils into a greased 450g (1 lb) loaf tin or casserole dish; spread the stuffing on top and then spoon in the remaining lentils and smooth the top. Dot with butter and bake in the oven for 30–40 minutes, until the top is browned and crisp. It's good served with some crisp golden roast potatoes and cooked cauliflower.

PEASE PUDDING

Pease pudding is one of the few traditional British dishes which are vegetarian. Mrs Beeton describes it as 'an exceedingly nice accompaniment to boiled beef' but I think it also makes a very good main dish in its own right, with crisp roast potatoes, a vegetable such as sprouts, a savoury brown gravy and some mint or apple sauce which gives a pleasant sharpness that's just right with the sweet-tasting peas.

SERVES 4
225g (8oz) yellow split peas
1 large onion
25g (1oz) butter
sea salt
freshly ground black pepper

If possible soak the peas in cold water for a couple of hours or so – this speeds up the cooking time – then drain and rinse them, put them into a large saucepan with a good covering of cold water and simmer them gently, with the lid half on the saucepan, until they're tender. I find the cooking time of split peas seems to vary quite a bit; sometimes they're done in 30 minutes, other times they can take as long as an hour. Watch the water level and add more if necessary as they cook; when they're done drain off any excess – they should be soft but not soggy.

While this is happening, peel and chop the onion and fry gently in the butter until soft and golden – 10 minutes. Add the onion to the split peas and season with salt and pepper. You can serve the mixture straight away or keep it warm in a covered casserole in a low oven.

You can vary pease pudding in quite a few ways. It's nice with some grated lemon rind added, or some chopped marjoram or sage. Caraway, cumin and fennel seeds also go well with it – add them to the onion when it's nearly done – and a pinch of ground cloves is nice, too. You can also add an egg to the mixture and bake it on a greased casserole dish in a moderate oven 180°C (350°F), gas mark 4 for 30–40 minutes.

RED BEAN MOUSSAKA

For a simpler version of this dish, leave out the aubergine, sprinkle the bean mixture with crumbs and bake as it is. It's also good made with black kidney beans.

SERVES 6
2 medium-sized aubergines (about 450g/1 lb) sliced into 6mm (¼in) circles
1 large onion, peeled and chopped
1 garlic clove, crushed
5 tablespoons olive oil
225g (8oz) red beans, cooked or 2 × 400g (14oz) cans
4 tomatoes
1 tablespoon tomato purée
3–4 tablespoons red wine – optional
½ teaspoon allspice or cinnamon
sea salt
freshly ground black pepper
sugar
1 egg
425ml (15 fl oz) cheese sauce (page 62)
50g (2oz) grated cheese

Sprinkle aubergine circles with salt, place in a colander with a plate and a weight on top and leave for 30 minutes. Then rinse under the cold tap and squeeze dry. Set oven to 180°C (350°F), gas mark 4. Fry the onion in 1 tablespoon of the oil for 10 minutes, then add garlic, drained beans, tomatoes, purée and wine, mashing the beans a little. Add allspice or cinnamon and season with salt, pepper and a dash of sugar if necessary. Fry the aubergine slices in the remaining oil and pat on kitchen paper to remove excess oil. Beat the egg into the cheese sauce. Grease a shallow ovenproof dish; put half the aubergine slices into base of dish, cover with half the red bean mixture and then half the sauce. Repeat layers, ending with the sauce, then sprinkle the top with grated cheese. Bake for 1 hour.

QUICK AND EASY RED BEAN AND TOMATO PIE

An 'emergency meal' that the children like. Serve with a green vegetable.

SERVES 4
750g (1½ lb) potatoes, peeled and cut into chunks
sea salt
40g (1½oz) butter
a little milk
125g (4oz) grated cheese
freshly ground black pepper
1 onion, chopped
400g (14oz) can tomatoes
400g (14oz) can red kidney beans, drained, or 125g (4oz) red kidney beans, soaked, cooked and drained

Set oven to 200°C (400°F), gas mark 6, or prepare a hot grill. Cook potatoes in salted water to cover until tender, then drain and mash with half the butter or margarine, cheese and milk to make a soft consistency. Season. While potatoes are cooking, fry the onion in remaining butter or margarine, then add tomatoes and beans, mashing them a little. Spoon red bean mixture into a shallow, greased, ovenproof dish, spread potato on top and sprinkle with remaining cheese. Bake for 25–30 minutes. Or have bean mixture and potatoes piping hot when you put them in the dish, then just brown the top under the grill.

REFRIED RED BEANS

This traditional South American dish, *frijoles refritos*, is good with crisp toast triangles and a lettuce salad, perhaps with an avocado cut up in it, to continue the South American theme. If you use canned beans, it makes a good 'emergency meal'.

SERVES 4 F
2 onions, chopped
2 garlic cloves, crushed
3 tablespoons olive oil
40g (1½oz) butter
225g (8oz) red kidney beans, soaked and cooked *or* 2 × 400g (14oz) cans
¼–½ teaspoon chilli powder
sea salt
freshly ground black pepper
triangles of toast to serve

Fry the onions and garlic in half the oil and butter for 10 minutes. Then add the remaining oil and butter and the beans, mashing them with a fork and mixing them with the onions and garlic, and the chilli powder, salt and pepper to taste. Continue to fry the beans for 10–15 minutes, until they form a 'cake' with a crisp base, rather like a large potato cake. Then flip over one side to form a roll. Serve immediately.

RUSSIAN RED BEANS WITH DAMSON SAUCE

This Russian dish has an unusual, sweet flavour which goes well with a crunchy salad of white cabbage. If you haven't any damson jam, you could use plum jam or redcurrant jelly.

SERVES 4
225g (8oz) red beans
2 tablespoons damson jam
½ teaspoon red wine vinegar
1 garlic clove, crushed
sea salt
½ teaspoon dried basil
½ teaspoon ground coriander

Soak and cook the beans as usual, then drain them. Sieve the jam and put it into a small saucepan with the vinegar; cook them gently over a low heat until the jam has melted, then add the crushed garlic, a little sea salt and the basil and coriander. Remove from heat and add to the beans, stirring well so that all the beans get coated. Leave the beans for 2–3 hours, so that the flavours can blend, then serve them very cold.

RED KIDNEY BEAN STEW

This warm-coloured stew is good with buttery brown rice, baked potatoes or creamy mashed potatoes and a lightly cooked green vegetable. If you use canned beans, it is very quick to make.

SERVES 4 F
175g (6oz) dried red kidney beans *or* 2 × 400g (14oz) cans
450g (1 lb) onions, peeled and chopped
25g (1oz) butter
2 × 400g (14oz) cans tomatoes
sea salt
freshly ground black pepper
sugar

Soak, rinse and cook the beans as usual; drain. Or drain canned beans. Fry the onions in the butter in a good-sized saucepan for about 10 minutes until they're soft but not browned. Add the tomatoes and beans and season with salt, pepper and a little sugar if necessary. Let the mixture simmer gently for 10–15 minutes, then serve.

Variations

RED KIDNEY BEANS WITH TOMATOES, ONIONS AND CUMIN

For this Portuguese version of the above, use 2 tablespoons of olive oil instead of the butter and add 2 teaspoons of whole cumin seeds to the onions after about 5 minutes. Continue as above.

CHILLI RED BEANS

Make as above, adding chilli powder to taste: ½–1 teaspoon, depending on your taste and how hot it is!

WEST INDIAN RED BEANS

This recipe was told to a friend of mine, as she was buying vegetables in a market, by a West Indian woman. The creamed coconut gives the touch of sweetness so characteristic of Caribbean cookery. It also thickens the sauce. You should be able to buy it at a health shop or Indian store.

Incidentally, this dish is always very strongly seasoned with thyme, but if you think the amount given will be too powerful, start with less. West Indian red beans are nice served with lots of plain boiled brown rice.

SERVES 4
225g (8oz) red kidney beans
1 large onion, peeled and sliced
1 large carrot, scraped and sliced
1 large garlic clove, crushed
1 tablespoon dried thyme
75g (3oz) creamed coconut
sea salt
freshly ground black pepper

Soak the beans for several hours in cold water, then drain and rinse them. Put the beans, onion, carrot and garlic into a large saucepan and cover them with cold water; simmer gently for 45 minutes, until the beans are nearly cooked, then add the thyme and continue cooking for another 15–30 minutes to finish cooking the beans. Cut the creamed coconut into pieces and add to the bean mixture; heat gently, stirring occasionally, until all the creamed coconut has melted. Season carefully with sea salt and freshly ground black pepper.

SOYA BEAN AND EGG CROQUETTES

There's no problem about protein here: these tasty little croquettes are as nutritious as any beef steak!

SERVES 3–4 F
125g (4oz) soya beans, soaked, well rinsed, cooked
until very tender and drained
1 onion, peeled and finely chopped
1 garlic clove, crushed
15g (½oz) butter
4 hardboiled eggs
50g (2oz) soft wholemeal breadcrumbs
1 tablespoon tomato purée
2 tablespoons chopped parsley
½ teaspoon ground mace
1 egg, beaten
sea salt
freshly ground black pepper
wholemeal flour
beaten egg
dried crumbs
olive oil for shallow-frying

Mash the beans with a fork, just to break them up. Fry the onion and garlic in the butter for 10 minutes, then remove from the heat and stir in the beans. Shell the hardboiled eggs, then chop them fairly finely and add them to the beans, together with the wholemeal breadcrumbs, tomato purée, chopped parsley, mace and beaten egg. Mix well, then taste and season. Form mixture into little croquettes, roll them in wholemeal flour, then dip them into beaten egg and roll them in dried crumbs. Fry the cro-

quettes in hot, shallow oil and drain them well on kitchen paper. They're nice with a spicy tomato sauce.

Variations

SOYA BEAN AND WALNUT CROQUETTES

These are good, too. Omit the egg and use instead 125g (4oz) grated walnuts, and a ½ teaspoon dried thyme. You may need to add a little more liquid to the mixture (or don't use all the wholemeal breadcrumbs).

SOYA SAUSAGES

Omit hardboiled eggs, beaten egg and mace. Add 125g (4oz) peanuts, roasted, as described on page 136, and grated, 1 tablespoon each soy sauce and lemon juice and a teaspoon mixed herbs. Form into sausage shapes, coat with wholemeal flour.

SOYA AND WALNUT LOAF

A tasty loaf, rich in protein. It's good with vegetarian gravy or parsley sauce and cooked vegetables, or cold with pickles, and it makes a good filling for a soft wholmeal roll or pitta bread.

SERVES 4–6
175g (6oz) soya beans
butter and dried crumbs for coating tin
1 onion, peeled and finely chopped
2 sticks of celery, finely chopped
2 tablespoons olive oil
100g (3½oz) chopped walnuts
2 tomatoes, skinned and chopped
1 tablespoon tomato purée
1 tablespoon lemon juice
1 teaspoon mixed herbs
2 eggs
sea salt
freshly ground black pepper

Soak, rinse and cook soya beans as usual – they will take about 4 hours to get really soft. Set oven to 180°C (375°F), gas mark 5. Grease a 450g (1 lb) loaf tin with butter and line base and short narrow sides with a piece of well-buttered, non-stick paper; sprinkle with dried crumbs. Fry the onion and celery in the oil for 10 minutes, browning lightly. Remove from the heat and mix with the soya beans, walnuts, tomatoes, tomato purée, lemon juice, herbs, eggs, and seasoning to taste. Mix well, mashing the soya beans a bit to help bind mixture together. Spoon into prepared tin, press down well. Bake for 45 minutes until firm in the centre. Slip a knife round the edge and turn loaf out on to a warm serving dish.

SPLIT PEA CUTLETS WITH APPLE RINGS

Fruit goes surprisingly well with pulses; here, there is also a pleasant contrast of texture, soft apple rings against crisp cutlets.

SERVES 4–6 F
350g (12oz) yellow split peas
425ml (15 fl oz) water
1 large onion, peeled and chopped
15g (½oz) butter
½ teaspoon sage
pinch of ground cloves
1 egg
sea salt
freshly ground black pepper
a little lemon juice
wholemeal flour
1 egg, beaten with 1 tablespoon water
dry crumbs
olive oil for shallow-frying
2 medium-sized cooking apples
25g (1oz) butter
2 tablespoons olive oil

Soak the split peas in water, then rinse them. Put them into a saucepan with the water and cook them until they're tender; drain if necessary and dry by stirring over a moderate heat for a minute or two.

Fry the onion in the butter in a large saucepan for 10 minutes, then add the sage, split peas, ground cloves and egg. Mix well, mashing the split peas a bit with the spoon, then season with sea salt and freshly ground black pepper and add a little lemon juice if you think the mixture needs it.

Shape the split pea mixture into 12 small cutlets on a floured board, then dip each in egg and dry crumbs; coat well. Fry the cutlets in hot shallow oil until they're crisp on both sides; drain them on kitchen paper and keep them warm.

To make the apple rings, peel the apples and remove the core using an apple-corer, keeping the apple whole. Then slice the apples into thin rings.

Heat the butter and oil in a clean frying pan and fry the apple rings for a minute or two on each side to cook them through and brown them lightly. Serve the cutlets with the apple rings.

GREEN SPLIT PEA LOAF WITH CARROT AND MINT

A cheap and tasty non-meat loaf, this is prettily flecked with pieces of orange carrot and dark green mint. Serve with a gravy or sauce and cooked vegetables.

SERVES 4 F
225g (8oz) green split peas
1 onion, chopped
1 carrot, chopped
1 garlic clove, crushed
15g (½oz) butter
½ teaspoon marjoram
2 tablespoons chopped mint
1 egg, beaten
sea salt
freshly ground black pepper

Put split peas into a pan, cover with water and boil gently until tender: 40–60 minutes. Drain. Set oven to 190°C (375°F), gas mark 5. Grease a 450g (1 lb) loaf tin and line with a strip of greased non-stick paper. Fry onion, carrot and garlic in the butter for 10 minutes. Add to drained peas, together with marjoram, mint, egg and plenty of seasoning. Spoon into tin, cover with foil and bake for 40–45 minutes. To serve, turn out on to a warmed dish and cut into thick slices.

SPLIT PEA DAL WITH HARDBOILED EGGS

This is a pretty dish, yellow split pea dal against white and yellow hardboiled eggs with a garnish of fresh green parsley. It's nice with plain fluffy brown rice.

SERVES 4
225g (8oz) yellow split peas
2 tablespoons olive oil
2 large onions, peeled and chopped
2 large garlic cloves, crushed
3 teaspoons ground cumin
3 teaspoons turmeric
1 tablespoon lemon juice
sea salt
freshly ground black pepper
4 hardboiled eggs, cut into quarters
1–2 tablespoons chopped parsley

Soak the split peas in cold water for several hours, then rinse them and cook them in fresh cold water until they're tender. Drain off any excess liquid.

Meanwhile, heat the olive oil in a good-sized saucepan and fry the onion and garlic for 5 minutes, then add the ground cumin and turmeric and fry for a further 5 minutes. Mix in the cooked split peas and heat gently, stirring often to prevent sticking. When it's piping hot, add the lemon juice and sea salt and freshly ground black pepper to taste and serve it heaped up on a warm serving dish with the hardboiled egg quarters round the edge and the parsley sprinkled on top.

Variation

SPLIT PEAS WITH FENNEL SEEDS AND HARDBOILED EGGS

Make as above, omitting cumin and turmeric. After putting split pea mixture into serving dish, fry 1 tablespoon of fennel seed in 15g (½oz) butter for 1–2 minutes, until seeds start to pop, then pour over split peas, arrange hardboiled eggs around edge and serve.

YELLOW SPLIT PEA PURÉE WITH VEGETABLES

This recipe from Germany, is not unlike our pease pudding. I think some triangles of crisp wholemeal toast or jacket potatoes go well with it.

SERVES 4
225g (8oz) yellow split peas
575ml (1 pint) water
2 medium onions, peeled and sliced
1 medium carrot, scraped and sliced
1 small leek, cleaned and sliced
1 stick celery, sliced
good pinch of dried mint or marjoram
1 tablespoon lemon juice
sea salt
freshly ground black pepper
40g (1½oz) butter
triangles of crisp wholemeal toast

Soak the split peas in the water for an hour or two, then drain and rinse them and put them into a saucepan with the water, half the sliced onion and all the other vegetables and herbs and let them simmer gently until the split peas are soft and the vegetables tender – about 30 minutes. Sieve or liquidize the mixture, then season it with lemon juice, sea salt and freshly ground black pepper. Spoon the mixture into a shallow heatproof dish. Fry the remaining onion in the butter until it's beginning to soften, then pour the onion and the butter over the top of the purée. Put the purée under a fairly hot grill until the top is slightly crusted looking and the onion very crisp and brown. (Alternatively, this can be done in the oven, if it's on, but I don't think it's worth heating it up specially.)

WARTIME BEAN ROAST

This is one of those abstemious wartime recipes which works very well, though I think the roast does need to be served with a good tasty sauce – a spicy tomato one, or a really well-flavoured gravy, and some apple sauce goes well with it, too.

SERVES 4
225g (8oz) butter beans, soaked, rinsed and cooked
as usual, or 2 × 400g (14oz) cans
15g (½oz) butter
1 onion, peeled and chopped
125g (4oz) fresh wholemeal breadcrumbs
4–6 tablespoons strongly flavoured tomato or curry
sauce
sea salt
freshly ground black pepper
beaten egg and dried crumbs to coat
a little butter

Preheat the oven to 200°C (400°F), gas mark 6. Drain and mash the butter beans, but don't make them too smooth. Melt the butter in a saucepan and fry the onion for about 10 minutes, until it's soft, then add it to the butter beans, together with the breadcrumbs and enough of the sauce to flavour and bind the mixture; season with sea salt and freshly ground black pepper. Then form the mixture into a roll and dip it first in beaten egg and then into the crumbs. Put the roll on to a well-greased baking sheet and dot it with a little extra butter. Bake for about 45 minutes in the oven, until the roll is browned and crisp.

TOFU

I'm grateful to Leah Leneman for permission to use this recipe, which I've adapted from the book *Vegan Cooking* published by Thorsons. This makes a firm textured tofu. Nigari can be bought from some health shops and gives a better result than the Epsom salts if you can get it.

MAKES APPROX. 125g (4oz)
575ml (1 pint) super soya milk (page 59)
½ teaspoon Epsom salts *or* Nigari
4 tablespoons hot water

Put soya milk into a pan and bring to the boil. Dissolve the Epsom salts or Nigari in the hot water and add to the milk. Leave for 5 minutes for mixture to curdle. Line a sieve with a piece of muslin. Pour curdled mixture through, separating curds from liquid (liquid will not be needed). Fold muslin over to cover curds and place weight on top. Leave for 1 hour. Remove curds – the tofu – from muslin and store in a bowl of cold water in the fridge.

TOFU FRITTERS WITH LEMON

Meat-eaters compare this to fried fish. Delicious with the yoghurt sauce (page 67), or parsley sauce (page 66) and a salad or quickly-cooked vegetable. You need to allow time for the tofu to drain.

SERVES 4
2 × 300g (10oz) packets tofu – from health shops
sea salt
freshly ground black pepper
lemon juice
wholemeal flour
olive oil *or* ghee for shallow-frying
lemon wedges

Drain the tofu carefully, being careful not to break it up. Then wrap each block of tofu in a clean absorbent cloth, place in a colander and arrange a weight on top. Leave for several hours – overnight and during the following day if possible – to drain and firm up. Then cut into slices, sprinkle each with salt, pepper and a few drops of lemon juice and coat in flour. Shallow-fry until crisp and golden brown on both sides. Drain on kitchen paper. Serve at once, with the lemon wedges.

8

PASTA DISHES

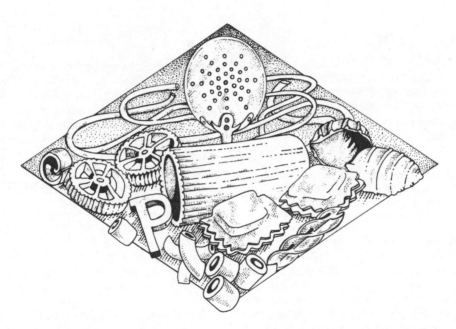

Pasta is a wonderful convenience food for vegetarians, just as it is for meat-eaters. The only difference is that we serve it with sauces made from vegetables or pulses instead of meat or fish, and very tasty and warming they can be, too. (Try the spaghetti with brown lentil bolognese, or the spaghetti with lentil and tomato sauce, to mention but two, and see for yourself.)

Many vegetarians prefer to use wholemeal pasta and this is becoming available in a growing range of shapes. If you haven't tried wholemeal pasta before, I suggest you start with the wholemeal pasta rings, which, in my opinion, are the best and lightest. There is a school of thought which says that as vegetarians get so much phytic acid (a substance present in the outer layers of cereals, nuts and pulses which inhibits the body's ability to absorb nutrients such as zinc and iron) from the pulses and nuts they eat, they should use white pasta and flour for cakes. On the other hand, there's evidence to show that, given a diet high in phytic acid, the body quite quickly adapts, breaking down the phytic acid lower in the digestive process, after the nutrients have been extracted. So, you pays your money and you takes your choice! And that is what I personally do regarding white and wholemeal pasta; sometimes I use one, sometimes the other, depending on how the mood takes me. All the following recipes work with either, so the choice is yours.

TYPES OF PASTA AVAILABLE

There are many different types of pasta; here's a list of some of the most popular and widely available:

Anelli Pasta rings, especially good in salads and savoury bakes. The wholemeal version is particularly good and my favourite type of wholemeal pasta.

Cannelloni Large pasta tubes. Par-boiled, then filled with stuffing, such as the curd cheese stuffing on page 148 or the walnut and tomato stuffing on page 144 and baked in a tasty sauce, these make a delicious dish.

Conchiglie Shells, available in various shapes and sizes. Delicious with olive oil, garlic and fresh herbs, or mixed with colourful vegetables as in the recipe for hot conchiglie with avocado and mozzarella cheese (page 207); conchiglie with red and white beans in parsley butter (page 208); and conchiglie salad with cucumber, nuts and raisins in curried mayonnaise (page 89).

Farfalle Butterflies. Good as above, with butter or olive oil and grated cheese, or mixed with vegetables as in the recipe for farfalle with courgettes, peas and mint (page 208), or farfalle with mushrooms and parsley (page 208).

Fettucce A wide, ribbon-like egg noodle. Fettuccine is a narrower version. Both are excellent with creamy sauces.

Lasagne Broad strips of pasta which are cooked and then rolled round tasty ingredients, or layered with them in an ovenproof dish and baked, as in lasagne with aubergine, onions and tomatoes (page 209); lasagne, red kidney bean and wine bake (page 209), and lasagne with spinach and curd cheese (page 212). Some people do not cook lasagne first and add extra liquid to the dish to compensate, and you can buy lasagne specially prepared for using like this which saves time.

Linguini Flat spaghetti; use like spaghetti (see below).

Maccheroni Macaroni. Can be bought in straight or curved 'elbow' versions, and in varying thicknesses, some with ridges. Serve with tasty sauces, like the very easy one in the recipe for macaroni with four cheeses on page 212, with cooked vegetables (see recipe for macaroni with butter beans, tomatoes and black olives, page 212) or in salad mixtures, like the one on page 97.

Penne Straight macaroni with diagonally cut ends, like the nib of a pen. Use like macaroni.

Ravioli Little cushions of pasta containing a filling; they are cooked and served with butter and grated cheese, or with a sauce. Specially good when home-made, with your own choice of filling, as in the recipes on page 214.

Rigatone Large, ridged pasta tubes, generally served in a sauce or in baked dishes. The ridges help the sauce to cling to the pasta.

Ruote di carro Cartwheels, good with a sauce, popular with children, especially when served with the tomato sauce on page 65 and sprinkled with grated cheese.

Spaghetti Probably the best known and most popular type of pasta. Makes an excellent quick meal when served with a tasty sauce, such as the mushroom cream sauce (page 217); the lentil sauces, or the classic rich green pesto (page 217).

Tagliatelle Ribbon-like egg noodles, usually coiled into bundles before packing. Can be used like spaghetti; particularly good with creamy sauces.

Tortiglioni Pasta spirals, like little corkscrews. Look pretty when mixed with colourful vegetables and in salads, as in tortiglioni salad with avocado (page 109).

Vermicelli Thin spaghetti, usually packed in coils. Cooks very quickly; ideal in delicate vegetable mixtures, such as the recipe for vermicelli with young carrots, broad beans and summer savory on page 219, or the classic dish *tuoni e lampo*, vermicelli with chick peas and garlic (page 219).

Wholemeal pasta Many of the above shapes can now be bought in a wholemeal version, and the range is expanding. Wholemeal pasta looks quite dark in the packet, but is lighter after cooking.

HOW TO MAKE YOUR OWN PASTA

If you enjoy pasta and eat a fair amount of it, you might find it worthwhile making your own at home. Using one of the new pasta machines makes it a surprisingly quick and easy process; it's fun to do – one of my young daughter Claire's favourite occupations on a wet afternoon – and the results are very good.

Equipment

You'll need a large bowl for mixing the dough, a pastry wheel if you want to make ravioli (see page 214), and a pasta-making machine. You can buy electric pasta machines, also fitments for some electric mixers, but I think the little hand machines are best for normal domestic use. These consist of rollers which are turned by a handle, like an old fashioned mangle, and are easy both to use and to clean.

Ingredients

To make 175g (6oz) pasta you will need:
100g (3½oz) plain flour: wholemeal, wheatmeal, unbleached white, or a mixture. Bread flour, made from hard wheat, is best.
¼ teaspoon salt
1 egg, size 3

Method

Put the flour and salt into a bowl and crack in the egg. Using your hands, mix the flour, little by little, into the egg, until you have a fairly smooth dough.

Set the rollers of your pasta machine to their widest position. Take a piece of pasta dough about the size of an egg, flatten it roughly with your hands, then feed it through the rollers. Fold the piece of dough in three, then feed it through again.

Do this six or seven times, until the dough is smooth and pliable then lay it on one side and repeat the process with the rest of the dough, keeping the pieces in the right order.

Next, tighten the rollers a notch and put the pieces of pasta through again, once only this time, and without folding. Repeat three times, tightening the rollers a notch each time. Cut the pieces of pasta in half if they become too long to handle, and support them as they come through the machine so that they don't fall in folds and stick together.

If you want to make a lasagne, cannelloni or ravioli, feed the pasta through the machine again with the rollers on the tightest setting but one. The pasta can then be cut to the required size and used straight away in savoury bakes, without further drying or cooking. For ravioli, see page 214. If you want to make noodles, pass the sheets of pasta through one of the cutting rollers, then spread it out on a clean, lightly floured cloth, or drape it over the edge of a saucepan or clean piece of dowelling or broom handle, and leave it to dry for 1 hour. It can then be cooked as described below, allowing 2–3 minutes only.

Guide to Quantities

Fresh pasta can replace the same quantity of dried pasta in any recipe. Like dried pasta, fresh pasta will swell and expand as it cooks.

HOW TO COOK PASTA

Allow 25–50g (1–2oz) uncooked pasta for each person for a first course; 75–125g (3–4oz) per person for a main course. The main thing to remember when cooking pasta is that it needs plenty of water to enable it to move around, so allow 1.2 litres (2 pints) water for every 125g (4oz) pasta, or 4 litres (6 pints) for 450g (1 lb) and use your largest saucepan, or two smaller ones if necessary, and add a teaspoon of salt. You can also add a tablespoon of oil, if you like: this helps prevent the pasta from sticking together. Bring the water to the boil.

When the water reaches boiling point, add the pasta. Long types like spaghetti need to be eased into the water. Hold the spaghetti like a bunch of flowers, stand it upright in the water and gradually let it all down into the water as it softens and bends. Drop other types of pasta into the water a few at a time, then give them a stir once they're all in. Let the pasta boil gently, without a lid on the pan.

It's important not to overcook pasta. It should be tender but not soggy. Most packets state a cooking time, but it's best to treat this as a guide only, and to start testing the pasta well before that time is up. To see if pasta is cooked, take a piece out of the water and bite it. It should be tender yet still have a little resistance: *al dente* – 'to the tooth' as Italians say. If it's not quite ready, cook it for a bit longer, but keep testing. Here is a rough guide to the cooking times of various types of pasta:

very thin pasta, small shapes	5–9 minutes
larger shapes, long tubes	10–20 minutes
fresh pasta	2–3 minutes

As soon as the pasta is done, tip it into a colander to drain. Give it a shake, then put it back into the saucepan or into a heated serving dish with a knob of butter or some olive oil and salt and freshly ground black pepper to taste.

SERVING PASTA

Cooked pasta can be served simply, just with butter or olive oil and seasoning, and perhaps the addition of some crushed garlic or chopped fresh herbs, or a sprinkling of grated Parmesan cheese. Like this it's delicious as a first course, or even, with a colourful salad and extra grated cheese, as a simple main course: a great favourite with my young daughter Claire and her friends. Or serve the pasta with a tasty sauce, or make it into a savoury bake. I hope the following pages will give you some useful ideas.

CANNELLONI FILLED WITH CURD CHEESE AND BAKED IN TOMATO SAUCE

You can use cannelloni or large squares of lasagne or homemade pasta for this recipe, which is good served with buttered spinach or broccoli or a watercress salad for a pretty colour contrast.

SERVES 4 [F]
12 cannelloni tubes or large squares of pasta
sea salt
225g (8oz) curd cheese
1 garlic clove, crushed
2 tablespoons milk
freshly ground black pepper
tomato sauce (page 65)

Plunge pasta into boiling salted water: cook cannelloni for 4–5 minutes only, until pliable but not collapsed, lasagne or pasta squares until just tender. Drain well, spread out on clean cloth. Set oven to 200°C (400°F), gas mark 6. Mix curd cheese with garlic, milk and seasoning. Spoon curd cheese mixture into cannelloni, or spoon on top of pasta squares then make into rolls. Place in a greased shallow ovenproof dish, cover with sauce and bake for 45 minutes.

CANNELLONI WITH MUSHROOM STUFFING BAKED IN SOURED CREAM

SERVES 4
12 cannelloni tubes or squares of pasta – see previous recipe
sea salt
1 onion, chopped
25g (1oz) butter
350g (12oz) mushrooms, chopped
1 garlic clove, crushed
50g (2oz) fine breadcrumbs
2 tablespoons chopped parsley
freshly ground black pepper
300ml (11 fl oz) soured cream

Cook pasta as described in previous recipe, drain, spread out on a clean cloth and leave on one side. Set oven to 200°C (400°F), gas mark 6. Fry the onion in butter for 5 minutes; add mushrooms and garlic and fry for 5 minutes more. If mushrooms make much liquid, increase heat and boil hard until this has gone. Remove from heat, add breadcrumbs, parsley and seasoning. Spoon into cannelloni, or on top of pasta squares then make into rolls. Place in a greased shallow ovenproof dish, cover with soured cream. Bake for 45 minutes.

CANNELLONI WITH WALNUTS, TOMATOES AND RED WINE

Serve with the remaining wine for an excellent supper.

SERVES 4 [F]
12 cannelloni tubes or large squares of pasta
sea salt
1 onion, peeled and chopped
1 garlic clove, crushed
2 tablespoons olive oil
225g (8oz) tomatoes, skinned and chopped
175g (6oz) walnuts, chopped
175g (6oz) fine wholemeal breadcrumbs
1 teaspoon basil
150ml (5 fl oz) red wine
freshly ground black pepper
575ml (1 pint) cheese sauce (page 62)

Plunge pasta into boiling salted water: cook cannelloni for 4–5 minutes only, so that it's pliable but not collapsed, lasagne or pasta squares until just tender. Set oven to 200°C (400°F), gas mark 6. Fry onion and garlic in oil for 10 minutes, remove from heat, add tomatoes, walnuts, breadcrumbs, basil, wine and seasoning. Spoon mixture into cannelloni, or put on top of pasta squares then make into rolls. Place in a greased shallow ovenproof dish, cover with cheese sauce. Bake for 45 minutes.

HOT CONCHIGLIE WITH AVOCADO AND MOZZARELLA CHEESE

Excellent as a hot first course or a light supper dish.

SERVES 4–6
225–350g (8–12oz) conchiglie – pasta shells
sea salt
2 large avocado pears
2 tablespoons lemon juice
175g (6oz) mozzarella cheese
2 tablespoons olive oil
2 garlic cloves, crushed
2 tablespoons chopped parsley
freshly ground black pepper
grated Parmesan cheese

Cook pasta in plenty of boiling salted water until just tender, drain thoroughly. While pasta is cooking, halve avocados, remove stones and skins, dice flesh, sprinkle with lemon juice. Dice cheese. Add oil, garlic, parsley, avocado and cheese to hot drained pasta, stirring gently over the heat to distribute the ingredients and warm through the avocado and cheese. Grind in some black pepper to taste, then serve immediately. It's good with some grated Parmesan sprinkled over the top.

CONCHIGLIE WITH RED AND WHITE BEANS IN PARSLEY BUTTER

This complements a salad with a creamy dressing, such as equal parts chopped celery and sweet apple bound with mayonnaise and natural yoghurt.

SERVES 4–6
225–350g (8–12oz) conchiglie – pasta shells
sea salt
40g (1½oz) butter
3 tablespoons chopped parsley
2 tablespoons lemon juice
125g (4oz) red kidney beans, soaked and cooked *or*
400g (14oz) can
125g (4oz) cannellini beans, soaked and cooked *or*
400g (14oz) can
freshly ground black pepper

Cook pasta in plenty of boiling salted water until just tender, drain thoroughly. While pasta is cooking, beat butter with parsley and lemon juice until well blended; leave on one side. Drain beans. Add parsley butter and beans to hot drained pasta and season. Stir gently over the heat until ingredients are well distributed and beans heated through. Serve immediately.

FARFALLE WITH COURGETTES, PEAS AND MINT

Fresh flavours and pretty colours are combined in this summery dish.

SERVES 4–6
225–350g (8–12oz) farfalle – butterflies
sea salt
25g (1oz) butter
1 tablespoon olive oil
450g (1 lb) courgettes, thinly sliced
175g (6oz) shelled peas
2 tablespoons chopped mint
freshly ground black pepper
grated Parmesan cheese

Cook pasta in plenty of boiling salted water until just tender, drain thoroughly. While pasta is cooking, melt butter and oil in a large saucepan and cook the courgettes and peas over a gentle heat until tender: 5–8 minutes. Add courgettes and peas to hot drained pasta, together with fat from pan and chopped mint. Stir gently, add salt and pepper to taste. Spoon on to a hot dish, sprinkle with grated Parmesan cheese and serve at once.

FARFALLE WITH MUSHROOMS AND PARSLEY

Serve with a tomato and watercress salad for a light supper dish.

SERVES 4–6
225–350g (8–12oz) farfalle – butterflies
sea salt
25g (1oz) butter
1 tablespoon olive oil
350g (12oz) button mushrooms, sliced
1 garlic clove, crushed
2 tablespoons chopped parsley
1 tablespoon lemon juice
freshly ground black pepper
grated Parmesan cheese – optional

Cook pasta in boiling salted water until just tender, drain well. Meanwhile, heat butter and oil in a large saucepan and fry the mushrooms and garlic for 4–5 minutes, until mushrooms are just tender. Remove from heat, stir in parsley, lemon juice and seasoning, then add this mixture to the hot drained pasta. Stir gently, to distribute ingredients, check seasoning. Transfer mixture to a hot dish and serve at once, sprinkled with grated Parmesan cheese if liked.

QUICK LASAGNE BAKE

A quick and easy lasagne, excellent with a green salad.

SERVES 4
175g (6oz) lasagne
sea salt
450g (1 lb) onions, sliced
2 tablespoons olive oil
450g (1 lb) tomatoes, peeled and sliced *or* 425g (15oz) can, chopped
freshly ground black pepper
300ml (11 fl oz) soured cream, natural yoghurt *or* cheese sauce (page 62)
125g (4oz) grated cheese

Cook lasagne in plenty of boiling salted water until tender, then drape the pasta pieces over the sides of the colander to prevent them sticking together. Or use the 'no cook' type of lasagne and add 150ml (5fl oz) milk to the soured cream. Set oven to 200°C (400°F), gas mark 6. Fry onions in the oil until tender: 10 minutes. Put a layer of lasagne in the base of a greased shallow ovenproof dish. Top with half the onion and tomato, season with salt and pepper, then sprinkle with a third of the grated cheese. Repeat these layers, then cover with lasagne. Spread soured cream, yoghurt or cheese sauce over the top, so lasagne is completely covered, sprinkle with remaining cheese and bake for 45 minutes.

LASAGNE BAKED WITH AUBERGINES, ONIONS AND TOMATOES

A delicious colourful and welcoming dish that can be prepared in advance, then baked and served with a green salad or lightly cooked broccoli.

SERVES 4 F
350g (12oz) aubergines
sea salt
4–6 tablespoons olive oil
2 onions, sliced
175g (6oz) lasagne
350g (12oz) tomatoes, peeled and sliced
125g (4oz) grated cheese
575ml (1 pint) cheese sauce (page 62)

Peel aubergines, cut into thin rings, place in colander, sprinkle with salt. Leave for 30 minutes, then rinse, pat dry and fry in the oil until tender and lightly browned on both sides. Drain well on kitchen paper. Fry onions in remaining oil for 10 minutes. Cook lasagne in plenty of boiling salted water until just tender. Drain well, and drape pieces over the sides of the colander to prevent them sticking together. Or use 'no cook' lasagne, and make cheese sauce using usual quantity butter and flour with an extra 150ml (5 fl oz) milk. Set oven to 200°C (400°F), gas mark 6. Cover base of greased shallow ovenproof dish with lasagne, top with half the aubergine, onion and tomato, some grated cheese and cheese sauce. Repeat layers, then cover with lasagne, the rest of the cheese sauce and grated cheese. Bake for 45 minutes.

LASAGNE AND BROWN LENTIL BAKE

This dish is tasty, filling and very cheap to make.

SERVES 4 F
175g (6oz) lasagne
sea salt
2 onions, chopped
1 stick of celery, chopped
1 carrot, finely chopped
2 tablespoons olive oil
225g (8oz) brown lentils, cooked or 2 × 400g (14oz) cans
freshly ground black pepper
575ml (1 pint) cheese sauce (page 62)
50g (2oz) grated cheese – optional

Cook lasagne in plenty of boiling water until just tender. Drain thoroughly, then drape the pieces over the sides of the colander to prevent them from sticking together. Or use 'no cook' lasagne and make cheese sauce with usual amount of butter and flour and an extra 150ml (5 fl oz) milk. Set oven to 200°C (400°F), gas mark 6. Fry onions, celery and carrot in the oil for 10–15 minutes, until tender and lightly browned. Drain lentils and add to vegetables, together with salt and pepper to taste. Put a layer of lasagne in a greased shallow ovenproof dish, cover with half lentils and a quarter of the sauce. Repeat layers, then cover with lasagne, remaining sauce and cheese if using. Bake for 45 minutes.

LASAGNE, RED KIDNEY BEAN AND WINE BAKE

Cheap to make, yet tasty enough for an informal supper party, served with remaining wine.

SERVES 4 F
175g (6oz) lasagne
sea salt
2 onions, chopped
2 tablespoons olive oil
225g (8oz) red kidney beans, soaked and cooked, or 2 × 425g (15oz) cans
225g (8oz) tomatoes, skinned or 225g (8oz) can
2 tablespoons tomato purée
1 teaspoon ground cinnamon
2 tablespoons red wine
freshly ground black pepper
575ml (1 pint) cheese sauce (page 62)

Cook lasagne in plenty of boiling salted water until just tender. Drain thoroughly, then drape the pieces over the edges of the colander to prevent them from sticking together. Or use 'no cook' lasagne and make cheese sauce using an extra 150ml (5 fl oz) milk to usual quantity of butter and flour. Set oven to 200°C (400°F), gas mark 6. Fry onions in oil for 10 minutes. Drain kidney beans, chop tomatoes. Mix with onions, mashing beans. Add tomato purée, cinnamon, wine and seasoning. Put a layer of lasagne in a greased shallow ovenproof dish, cover with half red bean mixture and a quarter of the sauce. Repeat, then top with lasagne and remaining sauce. Bake for 45 minutes.

LENTIL LASAGNE (1)

This dish consists of layers of lasagne and a tasty mixture of lentils, tomatoes and wine, topped with cheese sauce. I must admit that, contrary to my wholefood principles, I prefer this dish made with white lasagne rather than the wholemeal type, although it works with either. If you use white lasagne you won't be short of fibre, because there's so much in the lentils! The lasagne can be made in advance and only needs a crisp green salad and perhaps some red wine or cider to go with it.

SERVES 4–6
2 tablespoons olive oil
1 onion, peeled and chopped
2 garlic cloves, peeled and crushed
1 medium-large red *or* green pepper, de-seeded and chopped
175g (6oz) split red lentils
400g (14oz) can tomatoes
1 bay leaf
275ml (10 fl oz) vegetable stock *or* water
2 tablespoons tomato purée
150ml (5 fl oz) red wine *or* dry cider
¼ teaspoon each of dried oregano, thyme and basil
½ teaspoon cinnamon
15g (½oz) butter
1 tablespoon fresh parsley, chopped
sea salt
freshly ground black pepper
sugar
175g (6oz) lasagne
2 eggs
150ml (5 fl oz) milk
225g (8oz) *fromage blanc*
125g (4oz) cheese, grated

Heat the oil in a medium-sized saucepan and fry the onion for 10 minutes, then add the garlic, pepper, lentils, tomatoes, bay leaf, stock or water and tomato purée. Bring to the boil and simmer gently for 20–30 minutes, until the lentils are tender and most of the water absorbed. Remove the bay leaf, and stir in the wine or cider, herbs, cinnamon, butter and chopped parsley. Mix well, then add salt, pepper and a little sugar to taste.

While the lentil mixture is cooking, prepare the lasagne. Half fill a large saucepan with lightly salted water and bring to the boil. Ease the pieces of lasagne into the boiling water and cook them for about 8 minutes, until they are just tender, then drain and drape the pieces of lasagne round the edge of the colander so they don't stick together.

Set the oven to 200°C (400°F), gas mark 6. Put a layer of lasagne in the base of a shallow ovenproof dish and cover with half the lentil mixture; follow this with another layer of lasagne, followed by the rest of the lentils, finishing with a layer of lasagne. Whisk together the eggs, milk and *fromage blanc*, season lightly and pour this over the top. Sprinkle with the grated cheese. Bake for about 45 minutes, until golden brown and bubbling.

LENTIL LASAGNE (2)

This dish consists of layers of lasagne with a tasty mixture of onion, mushroom and lentil, and cottage and cheddar cheese. It's not much bother to make and only needs a salad to accompany it.

SERVES 4–6 F
175g (6oz) lasagne
1 onion, peeled and chopped
1 tablespoon olive oil
125g (4oz) mushrooms, wiped and chopped
400g (14oz) can tomatoes
125g (4oz) split red lentils
150ml (5 fl oz) stock *or* red wine
3 large garlic cloves, peeled and crushed
½ teaspoon each dried basil, thyme, oregano and marjoram
sea salt
freshly ground black pepper
225g (8oz) cottage cheese
125g (4oz) grated Cheddar cheese
a few breadcrumbs
Parmesan cheese

Cook the lasagne in a large saucepan half filled with boiling salted water; drain and drape the lasagne over the sides of the colander so they don't stick together while you prepare the filling. Fry the onion in the oil for 7 minutes, add the mushrooms and cook for a further 3 minutes, then stir in the tomatoes, lentils, water or wine and crushed garlic. Cook gently for 20–30 minutes, until the lentils are very tender. Add the herbs and season to taste. Set oven to 200°C (400°F), gas mark 6.

Put a layer of the lentil mixture in the base of a lightly-greased shallow casserole dish, cover this with some pieces of lasagne followed by another layer of lentils, some cottage cheese, some grated cheese then lasagne; continue in layers like this until everything is used. Sprinkle the top with some crumbs and grated Parmesan cheese and bake in the oven for 1 hour.

LENTIL LASAGNE (3)

This one is different from the preceding two in that it uses continental lentils and is delicately spiced. Serve it with buttery French beans or broccoli, or a green salad.

SERVES 6–8 [F]
350g (12oz) continental lentils
1 large onion, peeled and chopped
2 garlic cloves, crushed
25g (1oz) butter
2 tablespoons olive oil
575ml (1 pint) water or unsalted stock
1 teaspoon ground coriander
sea salt
freshly ground black pepper
225g (8oz) lasagne
2 eggs
575ml (1 pint) well-flavoured white sauce
125g (4oz) grated cheese

Wash and pick over the lentils, then cover them with cold water and leave them to soak for several hours. Fry the onion and garlic in the butter and oil in a medium-sized saucepan for 10 minutes, then add the lentils and stir for a minute or two so that the lentils are coated with the garlic and fat. Mix in the water, bring up to the boil and simmer gently, uncovered for about 45 minutes, when the lentils should be tender and the mixture thick. Mix in the coriander and season with salt and freshly ground black pepper.

Set the oven for 200°C (400°F), gas mark 6. Cook the lasagne in boiling salted water until it's tender, then drain it well. Beat the eggs into the white sauce.

Put half the lentil mixture into the base of a well-greased shallow ovenproof casserole dish and arrange half the lasagne slices on top, then pour in half the sauce mixture. Repeat the layers, ending with the sauce, and sprinkle the top with grated cheese. Bake in the centre of the oven for 40–50 minutes, until it's all bubbling and golden brown.

LASAGNE WITH MIXED VEGETABLES AND BASIL

SERVES 4 [F]
175g (6oz) lasagne
sea salt
225g (8oz) onions, chopped
225g (8oz) carrots, finely diced
225g (8oz) leeks, shredded
225g (8oz) courgettes, thinly sliced
2 tablespoons olive oil
3 tomatoes, skinned and chopped
125g (4oz) button mushrooms, sliced
1 tablespoon fresh basil or 1 teaspoon dried
freshly ground black pepper
575ml (1 pint) cheese sauce (page 62)
25g (1oz) grated cheese

Cook lasagne in plenty of boiling water until just tender, then drain. Drape the pieces over the sides of the colander to prevent them from sticking together. Or use 'no cook' lasagne, and make the cheese sauce using 150ml (5 fl oz) extra milk to usual quantity of butter and flour. Set oven to 200°C (400°F), gas mark 6. Fry onions, carrots, leeks and courgettes gently in the oil, covered, for 20 minutes, stirring occasionally. Add tomatoes, mushrooms and basil, cook for 5 minutes. Season. Put a layer of lasagne in a greased shallow ovenproof dish, top with half vegetable mixture and a quarter of the sauce. Repeat, then cover with lasagne, rest of sauce and cheese. Bake for 45 minutes.

Quick Spinach and Curd Cheese Lasagne

This is one of those dishes you can put together in moments, using frozen spinach (which needs to thaw) and the kind of lasagne which doesn't need precooking. The result is very tasty. A tomato salad goes well with it.

SERVES 4
40g (1½oz) butter
40g (1½oz) flour
575ml (1 pint) skimmed milk
125g (4oz) grated cheese
sea salt
freshly ground black pepper
450g (1 lb) frozen spinach, thawed
225g (8oz) curd or cottage cheese
grated nutmeg
125–175g (4–6oz) no-cook lasagne

Set the oven to 200°C (400°F). gas mark 6. Make a thin cheese sauce: melt the butter in a saucepan and stir in the flour, then add the milk, stirring over the heat, until the mixture thickens. Add half the cheese and salt and pepper to taste. Remove from heat. Next, prepare the spinach mixture. Put the thawed spinach into a bowl, add the curd or cottage cheese and mix well; season with salt, pepper and freshly grated nutmeg. Put a layer of half this mixture into the base of a shallow casserole; cover with pieces of lasagne, breaking them to fit if necessary, then pour some sauce over, to cover. Repeat the layers, ending with all the sauce. Sprinkle with the rest of the cheese. Bake for 30–40 minutes until golden and bubbling.

Macaroni with Butter Beans, Tomatoes and Black Olives

SERVES 4–6
225–350g (8–12oz) macaroni
sea salt
225g (8oz) butter beans, soaked and cooked or 2 ×
400g (14oz) cans
2 tablespoons olive oil
2 tablespoons lemon juice
350g (12oz) tomatoes, skinned and sliced
8–12 black olives
freshly ground black pepper
grated cheese

Cook pasta in plenty of boiling salted water until just tender, drain thoroughly. While pasta is cooking, heat butter beans in their liquid. Drain beans, add

to hot drained pasta together with olive oil, lemon juice, tomatoes, black olives and salt and pepper to taste. Stir gently over the heat until ingredients are well distributed and piping hot, then serve immediately and hand round grated cheese separately.

Macaroni Cheese

This homely dish has the reputation of being stodgy and the reason, in my opinion, is that most recipes for it contain too much macaroni and too little sauce. This one is light and delicious.

SERVES 4 F
125g (4oz) macaroni
sea salt
40g (1½oz) butter
40g (1½oz) flour
575ml (1 pint) milk
175g (6oz) grated cheese
freshly ground black pepper
50g (2oz) wholemeal breadcrumbs

Set oven to 200°C (400°F), gas mark 6. Cook macaroni in boiling, salted water until just tender, drain. Make sauce: melt butter in a saucepan, add flour, cook for a few seconds, then stir in a third of the milk. Bring to boil, stirring, then add another third of the milk and repeat until all milk has been added. Remove from heat, add macaroni, two-thirds of grated cheese and seasoning. Spoon into greased ovenproof dish, top with breadcrumbs and remaining cheese and bake for 40 minutes.

Macaroni with Four Cheeses

A classic dish that's really a sophisticated version of macaroni cheese. The point of interest is the inclusion of four different cheeses, each with it's distinctive flavour and texture. I like this served with hot wholemeal toast and a green salad.

SERVES 4
125g (4oz) macaroni
sea salt
15g (½oz) butter
275ml (10 fl oz) single cream
50g (2oz) grated Parmesan cheese
75g (3oz) Gruyère cheese, cubed
75g (3oz) provolone cheese, cubed
75g (3oz) mozzarella cheese, cubed
freshly ground black pepper

Cook macaroni in boiling, salted water until just tender, drain, return to saucepan and add the butter and cream. Turn mixture gently over the heat, then stir in half the Parmesan and all the other cheeses, season, and stir gently until the cheeses are heated through and beginning to melt. Sprinkle with remaining Parmesan and serve at once.

MACARONI AND CURD CHEESE MOULD

This is an all-time favourite with my youngest daughter, especially if she can have a free hand with the tomato ketchup.

SERVES 4 [F]
125g (4oz) macaroni
sea salt
225g (8oz) curd cheese
125g (4oz) grated cheese
1 egg, beaten
freshly ground black pepper
wholemeal breadcrumbs

Set oven to 200°C (400°F), gas mark 6. Cook macaroni in boiling, salted water until just tender, drain and put into a bowl with the curd cheese, grated cheese and egg. Mix well, season to taste. Line a 450g (1 lb) loaf tin with a strip of non-stick paper, grease generously with butter, sprinkle with wholemeal breadcrumbs. Spoon macaroni mixture into tin, smooth top. Bake for 45–50 minutes, until set and golden brown. Turn mould out on to warmed plate, and cut into slices to serve.

MACARONI MOULD

This recipe turns out rather like a savoury nut loaf.

SERVES 4 [F]
125g (4oz) macaroni
1 small onion, chopped
25g (1oz) butter
1 teaspoon mixed herbs
1 egg
2 tablespoons chopped fresh parsley
225g (8oz) hazel nuts, grated
sea salt
freshly ground black pepper

Cook macaroni in boiling water until tender then drain. Fry the onion in the butter until tender but not brown. Mix in all the other ingredients, turn into a buttered basin or mould, and steam for 1 hour. Serve cold in slices, with a green salad and some mayonnaise or natural yoghurt.

MACARONI WITH PEPPERS

SERVES 4
2 large onions, chopped
1 tablespoon olive oil
1 large green pepper, de-seeded and sliced
1 large red pepper, sliced
4 tomatoes, sliced
1 garlic clove, crushed
225g (8oz) macaroni
sea salt
freshly ground black pepper
a few black olives
chopped parsley
grated cheese

Cook the onions and peppers gently in the oil with the lid on the pan for 10–15 minutes, then add tomatoes and garlic. Meanwhile, cook the macaroni in plenty of fast-boiling water until just tender. Drain, add to the vegetable mixture, season and heat through. Serve topped with a few black olives and sprinkled with chopped parsley. Hand round grated cheese.

PASTA AND BEANS

You can serve this mixture as soon as it's ready or you can spoon it into a shallow ovenproof dish, sprinkle the top with breadcrumbs and grated cheese and bake until it's crisp and golden. Whichever you do I think you'll agree it's a tasty, satisfying and economical dish.

SERVES 3–4 [F]
125g (4oz) red kidney beans
125g (4oz) split red lentils
1 large onion
2 tablespoons olive oil
1 garlic clove, crushed
2 tomatoes, skinned
1 litre (1¾ pints) water
125g (4oz) cut wholemeal macaroni
1 tablespoon tomato ketchup
2 tablespoons chopped parsley
1 teaspoon cinnamon powder
1 teaspoon lemon juice
sea salt
freshly ground black pepper
dry crumbs ⎫
50g (2oz) grated cheese ⎬ optional

Put the beans and lentils into a big bowl, cover with plenty of cold water and leave for several hours if possible, then drain and rinse them. Peel and chop the onion and fry it in a large saucepan in the oil for

10 minutes. Add the garlic, tomatoes, beans and lentils and the water. Bring up to the boil, put a lid on the saucepan and leave it to simmer for 1–1¼ hours until the beans are tender. At this stage the mixture will look more like soup than anything else, but don't worry. Add the macaroni, tomato ketchup and parsley to the saucepan and let it simmer for about 10 minutes until the macaroni is tender. The mixture should still be quite moist – add a little liquid if necessary (red wine if you've got any). Then stir in the cinnamon, lemon juice and salt and pepper to taste. Serve immediately or spoon the mixture into a lightly greased shallow casserole, sprinkle with the crumbs and grated cheese and bake in a moderate oven (180°C [350°F], gas mark 4) for 30–40 minutes until golden brown.

This is lovely served with a fresh juicy salad with a good dressing.

PASTA WITH LENTILS

You can use either spaghetti or tagliatelle for this, and either the little red split lentils or continental lentils.

SERVES 4

225g (8oz) split red lentils *or* continental lentils
1 large onion
2 tablespoons olive oil
2 garlic cloves
1 small green pepper *or* 125g (4oz) mushrooms
575ml (1 pint) water
1 tablespoon tomato ketchup
1 tablespoon chopped parsley
½ teaspoon cinnamon
sea salt
freshly ground black pepper
225g (8oz) tagliatelle *or* spaghetti
2 tablespoons olive oil

Wash the lentils. Peel and chop the onion and fry it in the oil in a large saucepan for 5 minutes. While this is happening peel and crush the garlic and wash, de-seed and chop the pepper or wash and chop the mushrooms. Add the garlic and pepper or mushrooms to the saucepan and cook for a further 2–3 minutes, then put in the lentils and stir them so that they get coated with the oil. Mix in the water, tomato ketchup, parsley and cinnamon; bring up to the boil then cover the saucepan and leave it to simmer gently until the lentils are cooked – from 30 minutes to an hour, depending on the type. Season with salt and pepper.

When the lentils are nearly done cook the taglia-

telle or spaghetti in plenty of boiling salted water for about 10 minutes. Drain the pasta and turn it in the oil. Serve the pasta with the lentils. A green salad goes well with this.

RAVIOLI WITH CHEESE FILLING IN TOMATO SAUCE

SERVES 4 F

double quantity homemade pasta dough (page 205)
225g (8oz) curd cheese
75g (3oz) grated cheese
25g (1oz) grated Parmesan cheese
sea salt
freshly ground black pepper
1 egg, beaten
tomato sauce (page 65)

Make pasta dough as described on page 205, roll it into long pieces, place on lightly floured surface to prevent sticking. Mix together the curd cheese and grated cheeses and season to taste. Place small mounds of cheese mixture about 3cm (1½in) apart on half the pieces of pasta, brush around each mound with beaten egg. Cover with rest of pasta, pressing down round edges and trying to exclude as much air as possible. Cut between the mounds with a pastry wheel. Put ravioli on a lightly floured surface and leave to dry for 30 minutes. Then put ravioli into a large panful of boiling salted water and cook for 4–6 minutes. Drain well, put on hot serving dish, pour hot tomato sauce on top.

RAVIOLI WITH CURD CHEESE AND HAZEL NUT FILLING IN GREEN HERB SAUCE

The cooked ravioli will freeze, but add the cream and herbs later.

SERVES 4

double quantity homemade pasta dough (page 205)
225g (8oz) curd cheese
1 garlic clove, crushed
125g (4oz) skinned hazel nuts, grated
sea salt
freshly ground black pepper
1 egg, beaten
150ml (5 fl oz) single cream
2 tablespoons chopped mixed fresh herbs

Make pasta dough as described on page 205, roll it into long pieces as in previous recipe and place on lightly floured surface. Mix together curd cheese, garlic, nuts and seasoning to taste. Place small mounds of curd cheese mixture about 3cm (1½in) apart on half the pieces of pasta, brush around each mound with beaten egg. Cover with rest of pasta, pressing down round edges and trying to exclude as much air as possible. Cut between the mounds with a pastry wheel. Leave ravioli for 30 minutes, then cook and drain as in previous recipe. Meanwhile heat cream and herbs in small pan, then pour over ravioli and serve.

SPAGHETTI WITH AUBERGINE AND WINE SAUCE

A delicious quick supper dish: spaghetti in a colourful and rich-tasting sauce. I like to make it with, for example, an inexpensive Italian red wine and drink the remaining wine with the meal. The sauce will freeze.

SERVES 4 F
1 large aubergine
sea salt
1 onion, chopped
2 tablespoons olive oil
1 garlic clove, crushed
1 green pepper, de-seeded and chopped
1 tablespoon chopped fresh basil *or* 1 teaspoon dried
225g (8oz) tomatoes, skinned and chopped
4 tablespoons red *or* white wine, whichever is available
freshly ground black pepper
225–350g (8–12oz) spaghetti
15g (½oz) butter
grated Parmesan cheese

Dice aubergine, sprinkle with salt, leave for 30 minutes to extract bitter juices, then rinse. Lightly brown onion and aubergine in the oil, then add the garlic, green pepper, basil, tomatoes and wine and cook gently for 25 minutes; season. Cook spaghetti in plenty of boiling, salted water until just tender, then drain thoroughly into a colander. Tip drained spaghetti back into the still-hot saucepan, and add a knob of butter and some freshly ground black pepper. Turn spaghetti out onto a hot serving dish, pour the sauce on top and sprinkle with grated Parmesan cheese.

SPAGHETTI AND BEAN BAKE

Tasty, filling and full of protein, this really only needs a green salad to go with it.

SERVES 6 F
175g (6oz) haricot *or* butter beans *or* 2 × 400g (14oz) cans cannellini beans
2 large onions, peeled and chopped
2 large garlic cloves, crushed
4 tablespoons olive oil
1 teaspoon oregano *or* basil
1 teaspoon cinnamon
2–3 tablespoons chopped parsley
½ teaspoon chilli powder
sea salt
freshly ground black pepper
sugar
125g (4oz) mushrooms, washed and chopped
2 × 400g (14oz) cans tomatoes
3 tablespoons tomato purée
2 tablespoons red wine if available
175g (6oz) thin spaghetti
dry crumbs
a little grated cheese
a little butter

If you're using dried beans, soak, rinse and cook them as usual, then drain. Drain canned beans. Next, make a tomato sauce: fry the onion and garlic in the olive oil in a largish saucepan for 10 minutes, then stir in the mushrooms and cook for a further 4–5 minutes. Add the tomatoes, tomato purée, the red wine if you're using it, and the oregano or basil, cinnamon, parsley and chilli powder. Let the sauce simmer, without a lid on the saucepan, for 10 minutes or so, until the vegetables are all cooked and the liquid has reduced to a thickish purée. Season with sea salt, freshly ground black pepper and a little sugar to taste.

Preheat the oven to 180°C (350°F), gas mark 4. Cook the spaghetti in plenty of boiling salted water until it's just tender, then drain it well. Grease a 1.7 litre (3 pint) shallow ovenproof casserole and spread a layer of half the spaghetti in the base; arrange half the beans on top and pour in half the sauce. Repeat the layers, ending with a layer of sauce and sprinkle generously with dry crumbs and grated cheese; dot with butter. Bake in the oven for 45–50 minutes, until golden and crisp on top.

SPAGHETTI WITH BROWN LENTIL BOLOGNESE

A very tasty vegetarian version of this classic dish. The sauce freezes well.

SERVES 4 F
225g (8oz) brown lentils *or* 2 × 400g (14oz) cans
2 onions, chopped
2 tablespoons oil
2 garlic cloves, crushed
2 celery sticks, chopped
2 carrots, finely diced
2 tablespoons tomato purée
sea salt
freshly ground black pepper
225–350g (8–12oz) spaghetti
15g (½oz) butter
grated Parmesan cheese

Cook dried lentils in plenty of water until tender: 45–50 minutes, then drain; or drain canned lentils. In either case, keep liquid. Brown onions in the oil, add garlic, celery and carrot; cover and cook gently for about 15 minutes, until tender. Add lentils, tomato purée, seasoning and a little reserved liquid to make thick soft consistency. Cook the spaghetti as in previous recipe, drain, add butter, salt and pepper. Serve spaghetti with sauce on top, sprinkled with Parmesan cheese.

SPAGHETTI WITH LENTIL AND TOMATO SAUCE

As split red lentils cook in under half an hour without soaking, this dish is useful for those times when you suddenly find yourself having to produce a meal quickly, particularly as the ingredients are basic store-cupboard ones. The protein content of this recipe is excellent, because the pulse and wholemeal complement each other. The sauce freezes well.

SERVES 4 F
2 tablespoons olive oil
1 large onion, peeled and chopped
1 large garlic clove, crushed
400g (14oz) can tomatoes
½ teaspoon dried basil *or* oregano
½ teaspoon powdered cinnamon
225g (8oz) split red lentils, washed
425ml (15 fl oz) water
2 tablespoons red wine (if possible)
sea salt
freshly ground black pepper
225g (8oz) wholemeal *or* buckwheat spaghetti
15g (½oz) butter
a little grated cheese

Heat the oil in a largish saucepan and fry the onion and garlic until they're tender – about 10 minutes; then add the tomatoes, herbs, cinnamon, lentils, water and wine and bring up to the boil. Simmer mixture with a lid on the saucepan for about 25 minutes, until the lentils are tender. Taste, and season with sea salt and freshly ground black pepper.

About 10 minutes before the lentils are done, start cooking the spaghetti. Half-fill a large saucepan with water, add some sea salt and bring to the boil. Add the spaghetti to the saucepan by holding it upright in the boiling water and gradually pushing it down into the water as it softens. Simmer the spaghetti until it's just tender, or 'al dente', as the Italians say, then drain it and add the butter and a good grinding of black pepper. Pile the spaghetti on to a warm serving dish, pour the sauce on top and sprinkle with grated cheese. Serve with a nice crisp green salad.

SPAGHETTI WITH LENTIL AND WINE SAUCE

This is a delicious spaghetti dish with a rich-tasting lentil and tomato sauce. The protein in the spaghetti complements that of the lentils, with a bit more from the cheese besides, so this dish represents excellent nourishment. The lentil sauce can be made in advance, if convenient, and reheated when you need it. Serve with a green salad with a good garlicky dressing and some robust red wine and finish with fruit or some good cheese – or ice cream if you're in the mood and want to keep the Italian theme – for a lovely cheap and comforting meal. The sauce will freeze.

SERVES 2–3 F
1 tablespoon olive oil
1 onion, peeled and chopped
1 large garlic clove, peeled and crushed
1 teaspoon basil
225g (8oz) tomatoes, peeled and chopped *or* use a small can, drained
125g (4oz) continental 'brown' *or* 'green' lentils
1 tablespoon tomato purée
275ml (10 fl oz) cheap red wine *or* dry cider
275ml (10 fl oz) vegetable stock
sea salt
freshly ground black pepper
225g (8oz) spaghetti
butter
grated Parmesan cheese

Heat the oil in a medium-sized saucepan and fry the onion for 10 minutes, until softened and lightly browned. Add the garlic, basil, tomatoes, lentils, tomato purée, wine or cider and stock. Bring to the boil, then put a lid on the saucepan, turn down the heat and leave to cook gently for about 45 minutes, stirring from time to time, until the lentils are tender and the mixture is reduced to a thick purée. Season with sea salt and plenty of freshly ground black pepper. Just before the lentil mixture is done, cook the spaghetti in plenty of boiling salted water (page 206); drain well, return the spaghetti to the hot saucepan with a knob of butter and turn the spaghetti so that it all gets coated with the melted butter and looks glossy and appetizing. Put the spaghetti on a large, heated dish, pour the lentil sauce on top and sprinkle with grated Parmesan cheese.

SPAGHETTI WITH MUSHROOM SAUCE

This classic dish is usually made with double cream, but I prefer to make this lighter version using soured cream which has a third of the calories in double cream yet still gives a rich, smooth result.

SERVES 4
1 onion, chopped
40g (1½oz) butter
1 garlic clove, crushed
350g (12oz) button mushrooms, sliced
275ml (10 fl oz) soured cream
sea salt
freshly ground black pepper
freshly grated nutmeg
225–350g (8–12oz) spaghetti
chopped parsley

Fry the onion gently in 25g (1oz) butter until softened: 10 minutes. Add garlic and mushrooms and cook gently for 4–5 minutes, then add soured cream. Remove from heat, season with salt, pepper and nutmeg, then leave on one side. Cook spaghetti in plenty of fast-boiling salted water until just tender, then drain, put back in still-hot saucepan, add rest of butter and some freshly ground black pepper. Keep spaghetti warm while you reheat sauce gently, stirring often. Tip spaghetti on to a hot dish, spoon sauce on top, sprinkle with parsley.

SPAGHETTI WITH PESTO

The classic way to serve spaghetti, bathed in this delectable green pesto sauce, wonderful as a first course or, with extra grated cheese and a salad, as a light main meal. If you can use freshly grated Parmesan, that gives the best flavour of all.

SERVES 4–6
2–3 garlic cloves, peeled
75g (3oz) fresh basil
75g (3oz) grated Parmesan cheese
25g (1oz) pine nuts
4 tablespoons olive oil
sea salt
freshly ground black pepper
225–350g (8–12oz) spaghetti
grated Parmesan cheese to serve

The easiest way to make the pesto is to blend all the ingredients (except the spaghetti!) to a purée in a blender or food processor. Otherwise crush the garlic to a paste with a little salt, using a pestle and mortar, then gradually add the rest of the ingredients, crushing and mixing to make a thick, smooth sauce. Cook spaghetti in plenty of fast-boiling water until just tender, then drain. Put the spaghetti back into the still-hot saucepan. Add 2 tablespoons of boiling water to pesto, then add to spaghetti, stirring gently until spaghetti is green and glossy. Serve at once, with more Parmesan.

SPAGHETTI WITH FRESH TOMATO SAUCE AND BASIL

A delicious summer supper dish, made with well-flavoured tomatoes and fresh basil. Serve with grated cheese and a green salad with a good olive oil dressing. The sauce will freeze.

SERVES 4 F
1 onion, chopped
25g (1oz) butter
1 tablespoon olive oil
1 garlic clove, crushed
700g (1½ lb) tomatoes, skinned and chopped
sea salt
freshly ground black pepper
225–350g (8–12oz) spaghetti
sea salt
15g (½oz) butter
1–2 tablespoons chopped fresh basil

First make the sauce: fry onion gently in 25g (1oz) butter and the oil until softened (about 10 minutes). Add garlic and tomatoes, cook gently for 10–15 minutes, until pulpy. Season. Cook spaghetti in plenty of boiling salted water for 7–10 minutes, until just tender. Drain well, put back in pan with 15g (½oz) butter and some salt and pepper. Spoon spaghetti on to hot dish, top with sauce, sprinkle with basil and serve at once.

TAGLIATELLE WITH EASY CHEESE SAUCE

Another example of a special pasta dish that you can rustle up in a moment; serve with a tomato and black olive side salad for an excellent quick supper.

SERVES 4–6
350g (12oz) tagliatelle
sea salt
15g (½oz) butter
150ml (5 fl oz) single cream
175–225g (6–8oz) dolcelatte *or* Gorgonzola cheese, cut into rough dice
freshly ground black pepper
grated Parmesan cheese

Cook the tagliatelle until just tender in plenty of boiling salted water; drain well and put back in saucepan. Add butter, cream, cheese and a grinding of black pepper. Stir over a gentle heat until cheese has melted. Spoon on to a hot serving dish, or individual plates, sprinkle with Parmesan, and serve at once.

TAGLIATELLE WITH ROASTED PEANUT SAUCE

Here's one to try out on your more adventurous friends! The sauce has a South American flavour and is very quick to make.

SERVES 4–6
350g (12oz) tagliatelle
sea salt
15g (½oz) butter
225g (8oz) raw peanuts
4 tomatoes, skinned
125g (4oz) green pepper, de-seeded
125g (4oz) grated cheese
1 teaspoon chilli powder
275ml (10 fl oz) milk
freshly ground black pepper

Cook tagliatelle, drain and add butter as described on page 206. Meanwhile roast peanuts by putting on dry baking sheet and placing under hot grill for a few minutes until nuts under skins are golden brown. Do not remove skins; put nuts into liquidizer or food processor with tomatoes, green pepper, cheese, chilli powder and milk and blend to a thick purée – you may need to do this in two batches. Transfer mixture to saucepan and heat gently, stirring. Thin with a little hot water if mixture seems too thick. Pile tagliatelle on to heated dish, pour sauce over and serve at once.

TAGLIATELLE VERDE WITH SWEET PEPPER SAUCE

A pretty blend of colours: green tagliatelle with a vivid orange-red sauce. Serve with a watercress salad to complete the colour scheme. The sauce will freeze.

SERVES 4–6
1 onion, chopped
2 tablespoons oil
1 garlic clove, crushed
3 large red peppers, de-seeded and chopped
225g (8oz) tomatoes, skinned and chopped
2 tablespoons tomato purée
4 tablespoons dry sherry
sea salt
freshly ground black pepper
350g (12oz) tagliatelle
15g (½oz) butter
grated Parmesan cheese

First make the sauce; fry onion gently in oil for 5 minutes, then add garlic and red pepper and cook for 10 minutes. Add tomatoes, tomato purée, sherry and seasoning and cook for a further 10–15 minutes. Cook tagliatelle in plenty of boiling salted water until tender; drain well and add the butter and some black pepper. Put tagliatelle on to a hot serving dish, spoon pepper mixture into the centre and sprinkle with grated Parmesan.

TORTIGLIONI WITH GARLIC, OLIVE OIL AND FRESH HERBS

Pasta spirals cook quickly and are excellent served simply like this, as a first course, or, with extra grated cheese and a juicy tomato and watercress salad, as a quick supper.

SERVES 4–6
350g (12oz) tortiglioni
sea salt
4 tablespoons olive oil
2 garlic cloves, crushed
3 tablespoons chopped fresh herbs
freshly ground black pepper
grated Parmesan cheese – optional

Cook the tortiglioni in plenty of boiling salted water until just tender; drain into a colander. Put the olive oil into the pan in which the pasta was cooked, add the garlic and stir over the heat for a few seconds. Then add the drained pasta and stir gently until pasta is piping hot and the garlic and oil well distributed. Finally put in the herbs, stir again, and serve immediately, on hot plates, sprinkled with grated Parmesan if liked.

VERMICELLI WITH YOUNG CARROTS, BROAD BEANS AND SUMMER SAVORY

A delectable and pretty summer pasta dish. If summer savory isn't available, use other chopped fresh herbs or even chopped spring onions instead.

SERVES 4–6
1 onion, chopped
40g (1½oz) butter
1 tablespoon olive oil
225g (8oz) young carrots, finely diced
350g (12oz) shelled broad beans
sea salt
freshly ground black pepper
225–350g (8–12oz) vermicelli
2 tablespoons chopped summer savory
grated Parmesan cheese – optional

Fry the onion in the butter and oil for 5 minutes, then add the carrots and beans and cook gently, covered, for 10–15 minutes, until vegetables are tender. Season. Cook pasta in plenty of boiling salted water until just tender, drain thoroughly. Add the cooked vegetables to the cooked pasta, together with the savory. Mix gently, check seasoning. Serve at once, sprinkled with grated Parmesan, if you're using it.

VERMICELLI WITH CHICK PEAS AND GARLIC

This traditional Italian dish, often called *tuoni e lampo* – 'thunder and lightning' – to describe the different textures of the pasta (soft) and the chick peas (firm), is also good made with wholemeal pasta rings.

SERVES 4–6
225–350g (8–12 oz) vermicelli
sea salt
225g (8oz) chick peas, soaked and cooked *or* 2 ×
400g (14oz) cans
3 tablespoons olive oil
2 garlic cloves, crushed
freshly ground black pepper
grated Parmesan cheese – optional

Cook pasta in plenty of boiling salted water until just tender, drain thoroughly. While pasta is cooking, heat chick peas in their cooking liquid. When pasta is ready, drain peas and add to pasta, together with oil and garlic. Stir gently over the heat until ingredients are well mixed, check seasoning, grinding in some black pepper, then spoon on to a heated serving dish, or individual plates, sprinkle with grated Parmesan, if you're using it, and serve immediately.

EASY WHOLEMEAL PASTA RING AND CHEESE BAKE

This is a real stand-by because it only takes about 10 minutes to prepare and can be left in a pre-set oven to cook so that its savoury aroma will greet you on your return. If you also leave some green salad washed and ready in the fridge you can have a complete meal on the table in a few minutes.

SERVES 4 F
4 large onions, chopped
2 teaspoons butter
175g (6oz) wholemeal pasta rings
700g (1½ lb) tomatoes, skinned and chopped *or*
2 × 400g (14oz) cans
125g (4oz) grated cheese

Set oven to 150°C (300°F), gas mark 3. (If pre-setting it, time it for 2 hours.) Peel and slice onions. Using a pan or flameproof casserole, fry in the butter for 5 minutes. If necessary transfer to an oven dish. Put uncooked pasta rings in an even layer on top and then tomatoes on top of that, making sure that the pasta is covered. Sprinkle with the grated cheese. Cover and bake for 2 hours. Serve with a green salad.

WHOLEMEAL PASTA RING SAVOURY BAKE

A quick, cheap and tasty dish that's good served with a cooked green vegetable.

SERVES 4 [F]
125g (4oz) wholemeal pasta rings
sea salt
2 onions, chopped
2 tablespoons olive oil
125g (4oz) mushrooms, chopped
225g (8oz) tomatoes, peeled and chopped
1 egg, beaten
125g (4oz) grated cheese
freshly ground black pepper
wholemeal breadcrumbs for topping

Set oven to 190°C (375°F), gas mark 5. Cook pasta in plenty of boiling salted water until just tender, drain and leave on one side. Fry onions in oil for 7 minutes, add mushrooms and tomatoes and fry for a further 3 minutes. Add egg and stir for a moment or two longer. Then remove from heat, add pasta rings, two-thirds of grated cheese and seasoning to taste. Put mixture into a lightly greased shallow ovenproof dish, sprinkle with breadcrumbs and rest of cheese and bake for 25–30 minutes.

WHOLEMEAL PASTA RING AND AUBERGINE MOULD

An attractive and unusual first course or light lunch or supper dish.

SERVES 4–6 [F]
450g (1 lb) aubergines
sea salt
4–6 tablespoons olive oil
2 onions, chopped
75g (3oz) wholemeal pasta rings
3 tomatoes, peeled and chopped
1 tablespoon tomato ketchup
1 teaspoon oregano
1 egg, beaten
freshly ground black pepper
grated Parmesan cheese
parsley sprig

Peel, slice, salt, rinse, fry and drain the aubergines as on page 112. Fry onions in 2 tablespoons of the oil for 10 minutes. Cook pasta in plenty of boiling salted water until just tender, drain and mix with onion, tomatoes, ketchup, oregano, egg and season-ing. Set oven to 200°C (400°F), gas mark 6. Put aubergine slices in base and sides of a well-buttered 450g (1 lb) loaf tin. Spoon pasta mixture on top. Bake for 40–45 minutes. Turn out on to a warmed plate, sprinkle with Parmesan, top with parsley.

WHOLEMEAL PASTA RINGS WITH TOMATO SAUCE

A beautifully quick dish; serve with watercress or a watercress-based salad. The sauce freezes well.

SERVES 4 [F]
1 onion, peeled and chopped
2 tablespoons olive oil
400g (14oz) can tomatoes
sea salt
freshly ground black pepper
350g (12oz) wholemeal pasta rings
15g (½oz) butter
grated cheese

Fry the onion in the oil in a medium-sized saucepan for 10 minutes, until softened, then add the tom-atoes, liquidize, return to pan, season, keep warm. Meanwhile cook the pasta in a large saucepan half-filled with boiling, salted water: it will take 8–10 minutes. Drain it when it is just tender, then return the pasta to the pan with the butter and seasoning. Serve the pasta rings with the sauce and hand round grated cheese.

9

CEREALS, CURRY AND RICE DISHES

By 'cereals' I mean brown rice, and the less-well known millet, bulgur wheat, buckwheat and couscous, which can make the basis of some delicious vegetarian main courses or complete a curry or spiced vegetable dish. Although we usually think of cereals as starchy ingredients, they are in fact a useful source of protein in their own right and even better when combined with small quantities of other proteins such as nuts, pulses, eggs or cheese.

Cereal-based dishes usually freeze well, but watch the spices and garlic if you intend storing them for more than a week or two. These flavourings are best added later, just before serving. Dishes which will freeze (with this proviso) are marked [F].

GUIDE TO USING CEREALS

Brown rice When I started demonstrating vegetarian cookery, brown rice was always a talking-point at demonstrations, since most people had never seen it before. Now brown rice can be found in almost any supermarket and and it's no longer a novelty, but I find people are still unsure how to cook it. In fact, it couldn't be simpler as long as you don't try to hurry it! You need to allow a good 45–50 minutes from start to finish.

To cook brown rice, put one cup of rice into a saucepan with 2 cups of water (or 225g [8oz] rice to 575ml [1 pint] water.) Add a little salt. Bring to the boil, then put a lid on the pan, turn down the heat and leave rice to cook very gently for 40–45 minutes, when rice should be tender and have absorbed all the water. If there's still some water left, take the pan off the heat and let it stand, still covered, for a further 10–15 minutes, for the rice to go on cooking in its own heat.

You can save time by using a pressure-cooker which will cook brown rice in about 15 minutes from start to finish. Put the rice into the pressure-cooker pan using the same proportions as above.

Bring up to pressure and cook for 10 minutes at full pressure. Then allow pressure to reduce naturally. After that, the rice should be perfectly cooked.

Bulgur wheat Sometimes called burghul wheat, or referred to as 'cracked wheat' in Middle Eastern recipes, this is wheat which has been cracked and steamed. It consists of little golden-brown grains and, in the packet, looks a bit like demerara sugar! You soak it in water for 15–20 minutes, then use it as the basis of salads (see page 81); or you cook it like rice, as described above, except that it will only take 15–20 minutes.

Buckwheat This isn't really a grain at all, though it's always classified as one. It's actually the seed of a plant which belongs to the sorrel family. The grains are larger than rice and are triangular-shaped. You can buy buckwheat either toasted or untoasted. The toasted one – which is dark brown – has the best flavour. Again, you cook it as described for rice, and it takes only about 15 minutes. It has an unusual taste which goes well with strongly-flavoured vegetables.

Couscous This is made from semolina and looks golden and granular in the packet, rather similar to bulgur wheat. It has a delicious flavour. To use couscous, you soak it in water for 10–15 minutes, using 1 cup of couscous to 2 cups of water, then steam it. This is usually done in a steamer above the stew which you're going to serve with it – see recipe on page 227.

Millet Or 'budgie-food', as people say at demonstrations when I introduce them to this one! Millet has small, round pale golden grains. Again, you cook it as described for rice, except that it only takes 15–20 minutes to cook. It's got a pleasant flavour and makes a nice change from rice.

BUCKWHEAT BAKE

SERVES 4 [F]
175g (6oz) toasted buckwheat: buy this, already toasted, from the health shop
425ml (15 fl oz) hot water
1 teaspoon yeast extract
sea salt
15g (½oz) butter
1 large onion, peeled and chopped
3 carrots, scraped and sliced
2 leeks, washed and sliced
125g (4oz) button mushrooms, washed and sliced
225g (8oz) tomatoes, skinned and sliced
freshly ground black pepper
1 teaspoon cornflour
275ml (10 fl oz) natural yoghurt
1 egg

Set oven to 190°C (375°F), gas mark 5. Grease a shallow ovenproof dish. Put the buckwheat into a saucepan with the hot water, yeast extract and a little salt; bring to the boil, stir, then put a lid on the saucepan, turn the heat right down and leave to cook for 10 minutes, until the buckwheat is fluffy and all the water absorbed. Meanwhile, melt the butter in a saucepan and fry the onion, carrot and leek gently, with a lid on the pan, for 7 minutes. Add the mushrooms and tomatoes and cook for a further 3 minutes. Season. Put half the buckwheat into the casserole dish, spoon the vegetables over and top with the rest of the buckwheat. Whisk together the cornflour, yoghurt and egg. Season and pour over the top of the bake. Bake for 30 minutes.

BUCKWHEAT AND MUSHROOMS

Buckwheat has a strong flavour which I think goes well with dark mushrooms (field ones, if you can get them), garlic and onions, as in this recipe. Buckwheat is a natural source of rutin, by the way, which naturopaths prescribe for high blood pressure and varicose veins!

SERVES 4
225g (8oz) roasted buckwheat
275g (10 fl oz) water
2 tablespoons yeast extract
1 tablespoon tomato purée
2 large onions, chopped
2 sticks celery, sliced
1 tablespoon olive oil
4 garlic cloves, crushed
350g (12oz) dark, open mushrooms, washed and sliced
soy sauce – tamari
sea salt
freshly ground black pepper

Put the buckwheat into a saucepan with the water, yeast extract and tomato purée and bring to the boil. Cover with a lid, turn the heat right down and leave for 15 minutes, until buckwheat is fluffy and all the water has been absorbed. Meanwhile fry the onions and celery in the oil for 10 minutes, until soft, then add the garlic and mushrooms and fry for a further 3–4 minutes. Then fork the cooked buckwheat gently into the mixture. Season with some soy sauce, salt and pepper as necessary – buckwheat is rather bland and needs plenty of flavour; the cooked buckwheat is also nice with a well-flavoured garlicky tomato sauce.

Variation

BUCKWHEAT WITH MUSHROOMS AND TOMATOES

Use 225g (8oz) mushrooms and 225g (8oz) skinned, sliced tomatoes. Make as above, adding the tomatoes to the onions with the mushrooms.

BULGUR WHEAT AND BEAN CASSEROLE

It's quite easy to get the crushed, pre-cooked wheat, called 'bulgur wheat', at health shops these days, and it makes a pleasant casserole with beans and vegetables.

SERVES 4 [F]
225g (8oz) any beans: red kidney, cannellini *or* butter beans *or* 2 × 400 (14oz) cans
1 large onion, chopped
1 large green pepper, sliced
3 carrots, scraped and sliced
1 large garlic clove, crushed
3 sticks celery, chopped
2 tablespoons olive oil
1 bay leaf
150g (5oz) bulgur wheat
400g (14oz) can tomatoes
1 tablespoon tomato purée
½ teaspoon chilli powder
sea salt
freshly ground black pepper
a few dried breadcrumbs
a little butter

Soak, drain and rinse the beans as usual, then cover them with cold water and cook them gently until they're all tender and drain. Drain canned beans. Set oven to 190°C (375°F), gas mark 5.

Heat the oil in a saucepan and fry the vegetables gently with the bay leaf for about 15 minutes, but don't let them brown. Remove the bay leaf. Add the bulgur wheat, tomatoes, purée and seasonings to the mixture, together with the drained beans. Spoon the mixture into a greased shallow casserole dish and sprinkle with breadcrumbs. Dot a few small pieces of butter over the top of the casserole, then bake it for about 30 minutes. Serve with a short-cooked green vegetable or green salad.

BULGUR WHEAT WITH PEACH AND RAISIN SAUCE

I like the sweetness of dried fruit with bulgur wheat and especially like the flavour of the dried peaches in this recipe. Again, for economy, roasted peanuts can be used instead of flaked almonds.

SERVES 4 [F]
225g (8oz) bulgur wheat
575ml (1 pint) boiling water
½ teaspoon sea salt
125g (4oz) dried peaches, from health shops
275ml (10 fl oz) boiling water
1 onion, peeled and chopped
2 tablespoons olive oil
1 garlic clove, crushed
1 teaspoon cinnamon
50g (2oz) raisins
125g (4oz) flaked almonds, toasted under a grill

Put the bulgur wheat into a large saucepan with the boiling water and salt. Cover and leave for 15 minutes. Meanwhile make the sauce. Put the peaches into a bowl, cover with boiling water and leave on one side. Fry the onion in the oil for 10 minutes, then add the garlic and cinnamon. Liquidize the peaches together with their soaking water and add to the onion mixture together with the raisins. Heat gently. Heat the bulgur wheat gently for 10 minutes, then drain off any water and add the almonds. Serve immediately, with the sauce.

BULGUR WHEAT PILAF

This pilaf is delicious as the basis of a Middle Eastern-style meal, starting with hummus or chilled cucumber soup and ending with oranges in orange-flavoured sauce. I find you can make the pilaf in advance and heat it through in a covered casserole in a moderate oven for about 30 minutes, but it's best to add the nuts just before serving so that they retain their crispness.

SERVES 3–4 [F]
225g (8oz) bulgur wheat
575ml (1 pint) boiling water
2 large onions, chopped
1–2 garlic cloves, crushed
1 red pepper, chopped
25g (1oz) butter
50g (2oz) raisins
sea salt
freshly ground black pepper
50–125g (2–4oz) cashew nuts, almonds *or* pine kernels, roasted on a dry baking sheet in a moderate oven

Put the bulgur wheat and boiling water into a large bowl or saucepan, cover and leave on one side for 15 minutes; it will absorb the water and swell up.

Meanwhile, heat the butter in a large saucepan and fry the onions for 5 minutes, without browning them, then put in the garlic and pepper and fry gently for another 5 minutes. Add the bulgur wheat together with the raisins, stirring over the heat until they're well coated with butter. Season with salt and pepper to taste. Cook over a low heat for 5–10 minutes to heat through.

Serve sprinkled with nuts. A juicy tomato salad goes well with this.

Variations

BULGUR WHEAT AND CHEESE PILAF

This mixture of chewy, garlic-flavoured bulgur wheat and soft melted cheese is very good. Make as above, omitting nuts. Then, just before serving, fork 175–225g (6–8oz) diced white cheese (such as Lancashire) into the pilaf. Serve at once, with a tomato salad.

BULGUR WHEAT PILAF WITH CARROTS, NUTS AND RAISINS

Make as above, frying 225g (8oz) scraped, diced carrots with the onions, and 1 teaspoon cinnamon. Increase quantity of raisins to 125g (4oz) and add full quantity (125g [4oz]) of nuts.

BUTTER BEAN AND VEGETABLE CURRY

This is a mild curry with a lovely spicy flavour. I usually serve it with fried rice, but it's also good with plain boiled brown rice and some mango chutney. Don't forget to allow time for the rice to cook – it takes 45 minutes.

SERVES 4
175g (6oz) butter beans or 2 × 400g (14oz) cans
3 tablespoons olive oil
1 onion, peeled and chopped
1 garlic clove, crushed
1 teaspoon ground cumin
1 teaspoon turmeric
¼ teaspoon chilli powder
2 tomatoes, peeled and roughly chopped (you can use canned ones)
450g (1 lb) potatoes, peeled and cut into chunky cubes
1½ teaspoons sea salt
2 bay leaves
125g (4oz) frozen peas

If you're using dried butter beans, soak and cook them as usual. Drain butter beans, reserving the liquid and making it up to 275ml (10 fl oz) with extra water if necessary.

Heat the oil in a good-sized saucepan and add the onion and garlic; fry them for 5 minutes, but don't brown them, then stir in the spices and cook for 1 minute, before adding the tomatoes. Let them simmer together, with a lid on the saucepan, for about 5 minutes, then add the potatoes and mix well so that they are coated with the spice mixture. Stir in the reserved 275ml (10 fl oz) of liquid and the sea salt and bay leaves. Put a lid on the saucepan and let everything simmer gently until the potatoes are nearly cooked, then add the butter beans and peas and cook for a further 5–6 minutes.

CASHEW NUT AND TOMATO RISOTTO

This recipe appeared in my first book and is a family one which I was brought up on. A reader wrote to me to say she thought the recipe must be wrong because it had turned out 'a disgusting brick red colour'. I had to write back and tell her that it's supposed to be that colour, which I personally like!

SERVES 3–4 F
125g (4oz) brown rice
400g (14oz) can tomatoes, chopped
125g (4oz) cashew nuts, grated
2 eggs, hardboiled
2 tablespoons fresh chopped parsley
1 teaspoon grated lemon rind
1–2 tablespoons lemon juice
sea salt
freshly ground black pepper
cornflakes or wholemeal flakes
butter
grated cheese

Put the rice into a pan with 275ml (10 fl oz) cold water. Bring to the boil, then cover and cook very gently for 40 minutes until tender. Set oven to 180°C (350°F), gas mark 4. Fork through the rice, then add the tomatoes, cashew nuts, hardboiled eggs, parsley, lemon rind and juice. Season, then put into an ovenproof dish, cover top with cornflakes, a little butter and a scattering of grated cheese. Bake for 20–30 minutes. Serve with a green salad or lightly-cooked vegetables.

CELERY RICE

A tasty way of using up those outer stalks of celery! You'll need a large saucepan for this recipe. It makes quite a lot, but if there's any over, it's excellent as a filling for green or red peppers or cold, as a salad, perhaps decorated with black olives.

SERVES 5–6 F
2 tablespoons olive oil
2 large onions, chopped
8 sticks of celery, sliced
2 red peppers, de-seeded and chopped
2 garlic cloves, crushed
225g (8oz) can tomatoes
350g (12oz) brown rice
1.2 litres (2 pints) water
sea salt
freshly ground black pepper
2 tablespoons chopped parsley

Fry the onions gently in the oil for 5 minutes, without browning them. Then put in the celery and peppers, and fry for a further 5 minutes. Add the garlic, tomatoes, rice, water and some salt. Bring up to the boil, then let mixture simmer away, uncovered, for 40 minutes, until the rice is just about tender and nearly all the water has been absorbed. Take the pan off the heat, cover, and leave to stand, so that the rice can finish cooking in its own steam, for a further 10–15 minutes. Fluff up mixture with a fork, check seasoning, and serve sprinkled with the chopped parsley.

CHEESE CURRY

In India the cheese for this curry would probably be made at home from yoghurt. As this is rather a laborious process I use white Lancashire cheese instead. You may feel my method is cheating a bit but I think you'll agree the spicy sauce and melting, creamy cheese make a delicious combination.

SERVES 3–4
1 large onion
2 tablespoons olive oil, butter or ghee
1–2 garlic cloves, peeled and crushed
225g (8oz) can tomatoes
1 teaspoon grated fresh ginger
1 teaspoon ground cumin
2 teaspoons ground coriander
1 bay leaf
275ml (10 fl oz) water
225g (8oz) frozen peas
sea salt
freshly ground black pepper
175–225g (6–8oz) firm white cheese, such as
Lancashire or white Cheshire
hot cooked rice and mango chutney

Peel or chop the onion then fry it in the oil, butter or ghee in a large saucepan for 10 minutes, until it's tender but not browned. Add the garlic, tomatoes, spices and bay leaf to the onions, mixing them around so that they all get coated with the fat. Pour in the water and bring up to the boil, then turn the heat down, partially cover the saucepan and leave the mixture to simmer for about 20 minutes. Then add the peas and cook for a further 3–4 minutes, just to heat them through. Season with salt and pepper. Cut the cheese into smallish dice – about 6mm (¼in) – and stir them into the curry just as you are about to serve it. Don't add them too soon or they will melt too much and spoil the curry. Serve with hot cooked rice and mango chutney.

CHEESE KEDGEREE

A simple, comforting dish. Serve with something brightly-coloured, like a tomato salad and some watercress.

SERVES 4
4 onions, chopped
25g (1oz) butter
225g (8oz) brown rice
575ml (1 pint) water
275ml (10 fl oz) milk
pinch dry mustard
pinch nutmeg
175g (6oz) grated cheese
sea salt
freshly ground black pepper
chopped parsley

Cook onions in the butter until soft but not brown – about 10 minutes. Add the rice and water. Bring to the boil, put a lid on the pan and simmer very gently for 40 minutes until rice is tender. Stir in the milk, mustard, nutmeg and grated cheese – the mixture will be creamy. Season, sprinkle with chopped parsley and serve immediately.

CHICKPEA CURRY

Chopped fresh coriander is the authentic garnish for this spicy curry – and coriander is not difficult to grow – but I find chopped parsley will substitute quite happily if necessary. Serve with fluffy brown rice (see page 221) and allow time for this to cook: 45 minutes.

SERVES 3–4
225g (8oz) chickpeas or 2 × 400g (14oz) cans
3 tablespoons olive oil
1 teaspoon cumin seeds
1 small onion, finely chopped
1 teaspoon grated fresh ginger
½ teaspoon turmeric
½ teaspoon ground cumin
½ teaspoon ground coriander
½ teaspoon garam masala
1 tablespoon chopped fresh coriander or parsley
sea salt

If you're using dried chickpeas, soak and cook them as usual. Drain canned chickpeas, keeping the liquid.

Heat the oil in a medium-sized saucepan and fry the cumin seeds for 1 minute, then add the onion, ginger, turmeric, ground cumin, ground coriander and garam masala and fry for 2 minutes, stirring all the time. Mix in the cooked chickpeas and 275ml

(10 fl oz) of the reserved cooking liquid and bring to the boil. Put a lid on the saucepan and let everything simmer gently for 10–15 minutes. Season to taste and sprinkle with the chopped coriander or parsley; serve with plenty of brown rice and a side salad of grated carrot, banana and yoghurt, garnished with chopped walnuts.

CHINESE-STYLE FRIED RICE

SERVES 3
1 large onion, chopped
1 green pepper, chopped
1 garlic clove, crushed
1 tablespoon grated stem ginger
2 tablespoons olive oil
¼ fresh pineapple or 225g (8oz) can pineapple chunks in natural juice
225g (8oz) mushrooms
225g (8oz) bean sprouts
350g (12oz) cooked rice (this is about 125g (4oz) uncooked rice)
1 tablespoon soy sauce
sea salt
freshly ground black pepper
125–175g (4–6oz) blanched almonds

Fry the onion, pepper, garlic and ginger in the oil for 5 minutes, then add the pineapple, mushrooms, beansprouts and rice. Fry over a high heat for 3–4 minutes, stirring all the time, then add soy sauce, salt and pepper. Pile rice mixture on heated serving dish; scatter with almonds and serve.

COURGETTE RICE

A beautiful recipe for the summer when courgettes are plentiful. You can get this dish started, then go and enjoy the sunshine while it cooks! Serve it with a green salad and some warm crunchy bread. If there's any of the rice over, it's also delicious cold, as a salad.

SERVES 4 [F]
2 onions, chopped
2 tablespoons olive oil
1 large red pepper, de-seeded and chopped
700g (1½ lb) courgettes, washed and sliced
1 large garlic clove, crushed
175g (6oz) brown rice
400g (14oz) and 200g (7oz) can tomatoes
sea salt
freshly ground black pepper
2 tablespoons chopped parsley

Fry the onions in the oil for 5 minutes, without browning them, then add the pepper and fry for a further 3–4 minutes. Add the courgettes, garlic and rice, turning them with the spoon so that they all get coated with the oil. Then add the tomatoes and a little salt and pepper. Bring mixure up to the boil, then cover, turn heat right down, and leave to cook gently for 40 minutes. (The rice cooks in the liquid produced by the vegetables; no extra water is added.) After this, take the pan off the heat, give the mixture a stir with a fork, then leave the pan to stand, covered, for 10–15 minutes, so that the rice can go on cooking in its own steam. Check seasoning; sprinkle with parsley and serve.

COUSCOUS

Couscous looks rather like tiny grains of rice but it's actually made from semolina formed into little pellets. You sprinkle the pellets with water then steam them and serve them with a spicy vegetable stew. In Morocco couscous is cooked in a steamer called a *couscousier* but you don't really need any special equipment – I cook mine in a steamer with the vegetable stew cooking in the saucepan below. You could equally well put the couscous into a metal colander, put it on top of the saucepan of vegetables and cover with a lid or some foil.

SERVES 3–4
225g (8oz) couscous
275ml (10 fl oz) water
1 large onion, chopped
3 tablespoons olive oil
2 large carrots, diced
2 tomatoes, skinned and chopped
125g (4oz) chick peas, soaked, cooked until tender *or* use 400g (14oz) can
1 teaspoon cinnamon
1 teaspoon ground cumin
1 teaspoon ground coriander
2 tablespoons tomato purée
75g (3oz) raisins
425ml (15 fl oz) water
1 tablespoon chopped parsley
2 teaspoons lemon juice
sea salt
freshly ground black pepper
a little butter or olive oil

Put the couscous into a bowl with the water and leave to stand for 10 minutes or so until the water has been absorbed.

Meanwhile, begin the stew. Fry the onions in the oil in a large saucepan for 10 minutes until they're tender. Peel and dice the carrots and add them to the onions together with the tomatoes, chick peas, spices, tomato purée, raisins and water. Bring the mixture to the boil.

Line a steamer or metal colander with a piece of clean muslin or a double layer of kitchen paper. Gently separate the grains of couscous with your fingers, then put them into the steamer over the saucepan containing the stew and cover with a lid or a piece of foil. Let it simmer gently for about 30 minutes, until the vegetables are cooked. Add some more water to the vegetable mixture if it is too thick and stir in the parsley, lemon juice and salt and pepper to taste.

Stir the couscous gently with a fork to make sure the grains are separate and fluffy and mix in a little butter or olive oil just to add flavour and make the couscous look shiny and appetizing.

To serve, spoon the couscous on to a large, warmed dish and pour the stew in the centre. Couscous makes a pleasant change from curry and rice. It shouldn't be too hot-tasting, just warmly and fragrantly spiced.

EGG CURRY

SERVES 4
6 eggs
1 large onion
8 tablespoons olive oil
2 teaspoons white mustard seed
2 teaspoons ground coriander
2 teaspoons ground cumin seed
2 teaspoons turmeric
2 tablespoons flour
575ml (1 pint) water
4 tablespoons tomato purée
½ oz coconut cream, from health shops and some supermarkets
sea salt
freshly ground black pepper
cooked rice to serve

Hardboil the eggs, shell and slice and keep warm and covered in the ovenproof serving dish you will be using for the curry. Peel and chop onion and fry gently in the oil until tender, then add the spices and cook for a further minute or two until the mustard seeds start to 'pop'. Stir in the flour, add the water and tomato purée and simmer gently for 10 minutes, then add the coconut cream, salt and pepper. Pour over the hardboiled eggs. Serve with cooked rice.

LEFT-OVER RICE DISH

A friend of mine gave me this recipe for her tasty, thrifty standby.

350–450g (12oz–1 lb) left-over cooked rice
6 hardboiled eggs, sliced
50g (2oz) butter
2 heaped tablespoons flour
575ml (1 pint) skimmed milk
1–2 teaspoons curry powder
sea salt
freshly ground black pepper
a drop or two of tabasco

Arrange rice and eggs in a casserole. Make a sauce with the butter, flour and milk. Flavour with the curry powder, salt, pepper and tabasco. Pour sauce over the eggs and rice; serve piping hot. (And if there is any of that over, it makes excellent croquettes!)

QUICK LENTIL CURRY

This is a simple, English-style curry; serve it with some fluffy brown rice and plenty of mango chutney.

SERVES 4
2 onions, peeled and chopped
1 apple, peeled and chopped
2 tablespoons olive oil
1 bay leaf
1 large garlic clove, crushed
1–1½ tablespoons curry powder
350g (12oz) split red lentils, washed but not soaked
850ml (1½ pints) water
sea salt
freshly ground black pepper
a little lemon juice to taste

Fry the onion and apple in the oil in a medium-sized saucepan for 5 minutes, then add the bay leaf, garlic and curry powder and continue to cook for a further 3–4 minutes. Stir in the lentils and mix them round so that they get coated in the oil and curry powder, then add the water and bring the mixture up to the boil. Put a lid on the saucepan, turn the heat down and leave the mixture to simmer gently for about 30 minutes, or until the lentils are cooked. Season with sea salt, freshly ground black pepper, and lemon juice; remove bay leaf before serving. It's also nice with some diced, peeled cucumber stirred in just before serving.

LENTIL AND PINEAPPLE CURRY

Many of the pulses are enhanced by being served with something sweet and I particularly like this mixture of split red lentils and pineapple. It's an English-style curry and nice with a garnish of desiccated coconut and sliced tomato. Serve it with some fluffy brown rice and lime pickle. Put the rice on to cook (see page 221) before you start making the curry, as the rice will take 45 minutes.

SERVES 4
1 large onion, chopped
1 garlic clove, crushed
2 tablespoons olive oil
4 teaspoons curry powder
350g (12oz) split red lentils, washed
400g (14oz) can pineapple pieces in juice
850ml (1½ pints) water
sea salt
freshly ground black pepper
a little desiccated coconut
1 tomato, sliced

Fry the onion in the oil in a large saucepan for about 10 minutes, then mix in the garlic, curry powder and lentils and stir for a minute or two so that they get well coated with the oil and curry powder. Drain and roughly mash the pineapple and add it to the saucepan, together with the water. Bring the mixture up to the boil, then cover the saucepan with a lid and cook over a low heat for 20–30 minutes, until the lentils are soft. Season with sea salt and freshly ground black pepper. Pile on a warm serving dish, sprinkle with the desiccated coconut and garnish with the sliced tomato.

MILLET AND COURGETTE RISOTTO

Millet cooks in 20 minutes and has an attractive pale golden colour and a pleasant flavour which makes a change from rice.

SERVES 4
225g (8oz) millet
2 onions, peeled and chopped
1 red pepper, de-seeded and chopped
450g (1 lb) courgettes, sliced
2 garlic cloves, crushed
2 teaspoons olive oil
575ml (1 pint) water
seasoning

First toast the millet by stirring it in a dry saucepan over a moderate heat for about 5 minutes until the grains are lightly browned, smell 'toasted' and some start to 'pop'. Leave on one side. Fry the onions, pepper, courgettes and garlic in the oil in a medium-sized saucepan for 10 minutes. Then add the millet and water and bring to the boil. Cover, turn the heat down and leave to cook for 20 minutes, when the millet should be fluffy and the water absorbed. Season to taste.

MUSHROOM RICE WITH ALMOND AND RED PEPPER

The secret of this recipe is to use plenty of mushrooms and to cook them thoroughly, separately from the rice, so that you get a really rich flavour and a tender moist texture. This is a nice easy-going dish because if necessary you can cover it with foil and keep it warm for a while in a cool oven. It only really needs some grated Parmesan and a well-dressed salad to go with it, though I must admit that for a special occasion I also like it with some rich-tasting Béarnaise sauce!

SERVES 4–6
225g (8oz) long grain brown rice
575ml (1 pint) dry cider or good vegetable stock or a mixture
sea salt
25g (1oz) butter
3 tablespoons olive oil
1 large onion, peeled and chopped
900g (2 lb) button mushrooms, washed and sliced
2 large garlic cloves, peeled and crushed
50g (2oz) blanched almonds, cut lengthwise into slivers
1 medium-sized red pepper, de-seeded and chopped
freshly ground black pepper
fresh parsley, chopped
grated Parmesan cheese

Put the rice into a medium-sized, heavy-based saucepan and add the cider, stock or stock and cider and a level teaspoon of sea salt. Bring to the boil, give the rice a quick stir, then cover the saucepan, turn the heat right down and leave the rice to cook very gently for 45 minutes. Then take the saucepan off the heat and leave to stand, still covered, for a further 15 minutes.

While this is happening, heat the butter and 1 tablespoon of the oil in a large saucepan and fry the onion for 5 minutes, until beginning to soften; then put in the mushrooms and garlic and cook for a further 20–25 minutes, stirring from time to time,

until all the liquid has disappeared and the mushrooms are dark and glossy-looking.

Heat the rest of the oil in another small saucepan or frying pan and first fry the almonds until golden, then take them out and place on to a piece of kitchen paper. Quickly fry the red pepper, for about 5 minutes, just to soften it a little.

To complete the dish, add the mushrooms, red peppers and almonds to the cooked rice, using if possible a wooden fork to avoid mashing the rice. Season carefully with salt and plenty of freshly ground black pepper. Spoon the mixture on to a large, warmed plate or shallow ovenproof dish and sprinkle with freshly chopped parsley. Serve with Parmesan cheese.

NUTTY BROWN RICE WITH VEGETABLES

A dish of brown rice mixed with colourful vegetables and topped with shiny golden nuts always looks mouthwatering and inviting and isn't difficult to prepare. Leave out the ginger, chilli and coriander if you can't get them and use some basil or thyme instead. Serve the rice with a crisp salad and a sauce, too, if you like – tangy cheese sauce or sharp-tasting horseradish, lemon and mustard go well.

SERVES 4
275g (10 oz) long grain brown rice
500ml (18 fl oz) water
sea salt
1 medium-sized aubergine
2 large onions
3–4 garlic cloves
1 teaspoon coriander seed, lightly crushed
2 tomatoes, peeled and roughly chopped
freshly ground black pepper
1 tablespoon olive oil
1 red pepper
350g (12oz) button mushrooms
½–1 green chilli if available
½–1 teaspoon grated fresh ginger, if available
125g (4oz) hazel nuts, roasted on a dry baking sheet in a moderate oven for about 20 minutes, until skins loosen and the nuts are golden.

Put the rice into a medium-sized saucepan with the water and a teaspoon of salt. Bring to the boil, then cover and cook very gently for 40–45 minutes, when the rice should be tender and all the water absorbed.

Wash the aubergine and remove the stalk. Cut the aubergine into fairly small dice, put them into a colander, sprinkle with salt and place a weight on top. Leave on one side while you prepare the rest of the vegetables.

Peel and chop the onions and peel and crush the garlic. Fry together in the oil in a large saucepan for 5 minutes, stirring quite often to prevent sticking. Remove stalk and seeds from the pepper and cut the flesh into dice; wash the mushrooms, cutting any larger ones. Cut the chilli in half and remove the seeds; finely chop the flesh. (Wash your hands thoroughly after preparing the chilli as the juice can sting if you get it on your face or in your eyes.) Drain the aubergine, rinse under the cold tap and squeeze it dry with your hands. Add the mushrooms, peppers, aubergine, chilli, ginger and coriander to the onions and fry for a further 5–10 minutes, until all the vegetables are soft. When the rice is cooked, stir it gently with a fork to 'fluff' it, then mix it lightly with the vegetables. Add the tomatoes and half the nuts and season well with salt and freshly ground black pepper. Serve with the rest of the nuts on top.

PAELLA WITH ALMONDS

Paella usually consists of saffron-flavoured rice with onions, tomatoes, fish and sausages, but the composition varies enormously depending on the whim of the cook and the contents of the store cupboard so I don't think my vegetarian version too far-fetched. Anyway, people seem to enjoy this mixture of pale yellow saffron rice and tomatoes or green peas with its crunchy topping of golden brown, flaked almonds. We like it with a fresh-tasting tomato sauce and a Spanish green salad. You can use ½ teaspoon turmeric powder instead of the saffron, for economy.

SERVES 4–5
2 large onions
2 tablespoons olive oil
350g (12oz) long-grain brown rice
850ml (1½ pints) water
1 packet of saffron – or 2 packets give a more intense colour and flavour for a special occasion
2 teaspoons sea salt
freshly ground black pepper
2 large garlic cloves, crushed
4 large carrots, diced
1 large red pepper, sliced
4 tomatoes, skinned and quartered
125g (4oz) frozen peas
125g (4oz) flaked almonds toasted on a dry baking sheet in a moderate oven for 10–15 minutes

Peel and slice the onions. Heat the oil in a large saucepan and fry the onions for 10 minutes until they're soft but not browned. Wash and pick over the rice then add it to the onion together with the

water, saffron, salt, a good grinding of pepper and the garlic. Bring the water up to the boil then turn the heat down, put a lid on the saucepan and leave the rice to cook very gently for 40 minutes. While the rice is cooking scrape the carrots and cut them into chunky dice. Cut the pepper into rings, discarding the seeds, and quarter the tomatoes. After the rice has been cooking for 20 minutes add the carrot – just put it on top of the rice then put the lid back on the saucepan.

Ten minutes later add the pepper in the same way. After the rice has cooked for its 40 minutes put the tomatoes and peas into the saucepan. Put the lid back and leave the rice, off the heat, for a further 15 minutes, to finish cooking slowly in its own heat. Then gently reheat the mixture, stirring with a fork to mix the rice with all the other vegetables. Sprinkle the nuts on top of the paella just before you serve it, so that they keep nice and crisp.

PAELLA WITH BEANS

Don't be put off by the rather long list of ingredients in this recipe; it's very easy to make and tastes delicious.

SERVES 3–4
125g (4oz) red kidney beans or 400g (14oz) can
1 small aubergine, diced
225g (8oz) brown rice
425ml (15 fl oz) water
½ teaspoon turmeric
2 tablespoons olive oil
1 large onion, peeled and chopped
1 green pepper, de-seeded and chopped
1 stick celery, chopped
2 large carrots, scraped and diced
1 large garlic clove, crushed
2 large tomatoes, peeled and chopped (you can use canned ones)
125g (4oz) button mushrooms, wiped and sliced
sea salt
freshly ground black pepper
2 tablespoons chopped parsley

Wash, soak and rinse the beans, then cook them as usual until tender and drain them. Sprinkle the aubergine with sea salt and leave it for 30 minutes to draw out the bitter juices, then rinse and pat dry on kitchen paper. Meanwhile, wash the rice and put it into a large saucepan with the water, turmeric and sea salt. Bring it up to the boil, then give it a stir, put a lid on the saucepan and turn down the heat. Let the rice cook gently for 30 minutes.

Heat the oil in a saucepan and fry the prepared

onion, pepper, celery, carrots, aubergine and garlic for 10 minutes, but don't let them brown, then add the tomatoes and mushrooms and cook for a further 5 minutes. Tip all this mixture on top of the rice and add the beans as well, then put a lid on the saucepan and let it all go on cooking over a low heat for a further 15 minutes. Then turn off the heat and leave the paella to stand for another 10 minutes. After this, stir the mixture carefully with a fork and add some sea salt and freshly ground black pepper to taste and the chopped parsley. Reheat gently if necessary before serving.

OVEN-BAKED PAELLA

This is a useful dish because after you've done the initial preparation, you can put it into the oven and forget about it!

SERVES 4 F
1 medium-sized aubergine
2 tablespoons olive oil
1 red pepper, de-seeded and cut into strips
1 green pepper, de-seeded and cut into strips
2 large onions, peeled and chopped
2 garlic cloves, crushed
225g (8oz) long grain brown rice
275ml (10 fl oz) boiling water
225g (8oz) tomtocs, skinned and chopped
1 teaspoon oregano *or* basil
1 bay leaf
freshly ground black pepper
125g (4oz) blanched almonds *or* sunflower seeds

Discard stalk end from aubergine and dice. Place the pieces in a colander, sprinkle with salt, put a plate and weight on top and leave for 30 minutes. Then rinse under cold water and squeeze out moisture. Set oven to 180°C (350°F), gas mark 4. Heat the oil in a large saucepan or flame-proof casserole and fry the aubergine, peppers, onion and garlic for 5 minutes. Add the rice and stir over the heat for a further 2–3 minutes, then stir in the boiling water, oregano or basil, bay leaf and some freshly ground black pepper. Transfer mixture to an ovenproof casserole if necessary. Put into the oven and bake for 1 hour, until rice is tender and all liquid has been absorbed. Fifteen minutes before the rice is done, spread almonds or sunflower seeds on a dry baking sheet and place in oven until golden brown. Fluff up rice with a fork and sprinkle with the roasted almonds or sunflower seeds. Serve with a green salad.

RED BEAN CURRY

Serve with fluffy brown rice, some chutney and perhaps a cucumber and yoghurt salad. Don't forget to allow 45 minutes for cooking the rice.

SERVES 4
225g (8oz) red kidney beans *or* 2 × 400g (14oz) cans
1 onion, chopped
1 large garlic clove, crushed
1½ tablespoons olive oil
1–2 teaspoons grated fresh ginger
2 teaspoons ground coriander
1 teaspoon turmeric
½ teaspoon ground cumin
½ teaspoon garam masala
2 large tomatoes, peeled and chopped (canned ones are fine)
sea salt

Soak and cook dried beans as usual. Peel and chop the onion and crush the garlic; fry them in the oil in a largish saucepan, together with the grated ginger, for 6–7 minutes, stirring them from time to time, then add the ground coriander, turmeric and garam masala and cook for a further minute or two, stirring, before adding the tomatoes. Then put a lid on the saucepan and let everything cook gently for 5 minutes.

Drain the beans, reserving 150ml (5 fl oz) of the liquid, and add this to the tomato and spice mixture, together with a good teaspoon of sea salt. Let it simmer for a further 5 minutes, then add the drained beans and heat them through. Serve with some fluffy boiled brown rice and chutney.

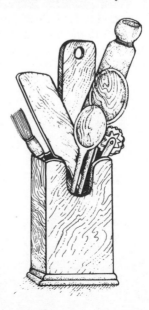

RED BEAN RICE

This rice dish is a lovely medley of reds: tomato-coloured rice, with pieces of bright red pepper and deep crimson kidney beans – warming fare indeed and with a spicy taste to match! Serve it with pumpkin soup as a starter, a well-dressed green salad as an accompaniment and exotic fruit salad to follow for a delicious Caribbean-style vegetarian meal.

SERVES 4
125g (4oz) red kidney beans, soaked and cooked *or* a
400g (14oz) can
2 large onions, peeled and chopped
3 tablespoons olive oil
2 large garlic cloves, crushed
2 large red peppers, de-seeded and sliced
400g (14oz) can tomatoes
150ml (5 fl oz) water *or* stock
225g (8oz) long-grain rice
sea salt
3 teaspoons ground coriander
½–1 teaspoon chilli powder
freshly ground black pepper

Drain the kidney beans; leave on one side. Peel and chop the onions and fry them for 10 minutes until they're tender. Stir in the garlic and red pepper and fry for a further minute or two, stirring so that everything gets coated with the oil. Add the can of tomatoes and the water or stock. Rinse the rice in cold water then put this into a saucepan together with a teaspoon of salt, the spices and a grinding of pepper. Bring the mixture up to the boil then turn the heat right down and leave it to cook very gently for 40–45 minutes, until the rice is tender. Take the saucepan off the heat and leave it to stand, with the lid still on, for 10–15 minutes. Add the red beans, mixing them in gently with a fork. Check the seasoning then reheat.

RED BEANS WITH RICE AND VEGETABLES

Golden rice flecked with red kidney beans and green, red and orange vegetables. Serve with a green salad.

SERVES 4 [F]
2 onions, chopped
2 garlic cloves, crushed
4 tablespoons olive oil
350g (12oz) brown rice
1 tablespoon turmeric powder
850ml (1½ pints) water
sea salt
freshly ground black pepper
4 carrots, diced
2 courgettes, sliced
1 red pepper, de-seeded and chopped
4 tomatoes, skinned and chopped
125g (4oz) red kidney beans, cooked and drained *or*
400g (14oz) can, drained

Fry the onion and garlic in oil for 10 minutes, then stir in rice and turmeric. Add water and seasoning, bring to boil, cover and simmer for 20 minutes. Then add carrot – don't stir in. Ten minutes later add rest of vegetables and beans; again, don't stir in. Cook for further 10 minutes (40 minutes in all), then remove from heat and leave to stand for 15 minutes. Mix gently with a fork; check seasoning.

CURRIED RICE AND CHEESE FRITTERS

If you have some cooked rice over, these fritters can be made very quickly. They are crisp on the outside, moist and tasty within. We like them with a crisp salad and natural yoghurt or one of the yoghurt/mayonnaise dressings in the sauces section, but they're also good with a tomato or curry sauce and a cooked vegetable. A pleasant variation is to add 2 chopped hardboiled eggs to the mixture.

SERVES 4
about 450g (1 lb) cooked brown rice – this is about
225g (8oz) uncooked
125g (4oz) grated cheese
2 teaspoons curry powder
2 eggs, beaten
sea salt
freshly ground black pepper
50g (2oz) soft wholemeal breadcrumbs for coating
olive oil for shallow-frying

Mix together the cooked rice, grated cheese, curry powder and half the beaten egg. Season with salt and pepper. Form into croquettes, dip each in the rest of the beaten egg then coat with the breadcrumbs. Fry the croquettes quickly on both sides in the minimum of oil; drain well and serve as soon as possible.

RICE WITH CHICK PEAS AND TOMATOES

This rice dish is good hot or cold.

SERVES 4

225g (8oz) chick peas *or* 2 × 400g (14oz) cans
225g (8oz) long grain brown rice
425ml (15 fl oz) water
sea salt
2 large onions
3 tablespoons olive oil
4 garlic cloves, crushed
450g (1 lb) tomatoes, skinned and sliced
2–3 tablespoons chopped parsley
2 tablespoons lemon juice
freshly ground black pepper

If you're using dried chick peas, soak and cook them as usual. Drain the chick peas and mash lightly to break them up a little. Wash the rice carefully, then put it into a medium-sized saucepan with the water and a little sea salt. Bring up to the boil, then put a lid on the saucepan and leave to simmer very gently for 45 minutes to cook the rice.

Meanwhile, peel and finely chop the onions and fry them in the olive oil in a large saucepan until they're soft but not browned – 10 minutes. Add the garlic, chick peas and tomatoes and cook for a further few minutes to make everything nice and hot, then stir in the cooked rice and the chopped parsley and lemon juice, using a fork so that you don't mash the rice. Add more sea salt to taste and a good grinding of black pepper and serve immediately, or let the mixture cool and then serve it as part of a salad meal.

RICE CROQUETTES

These crisp croquettes are good for a first course if you serve them on small plates with a tomato or mushroom sauce: or with vegetables they make a tasty supper – I like them with a tomato salad. They're an excellent way of using up leftover risotto and I sometimes make an extra large batch specially with this in mind – you simply form the risotto into little rounds and coat them in beaten egg and dried crumbs. But if you're making the croquettes from scratch, this is the way to do them.

SERVES 4

225g (8oz) brown rice
425ml (15 fl oz) water
sea salt
1 large onion, peeled and finely chopped
25g (1oz) butter
125g (4oz) grated cheese
½–1 teaspoon mustard powder
1 egg
freshly ground black pepper
1 egg, beaten with 1 tablespoon of cold water
dried crumbs
olive oil for shallow-frying

Wash the rice and put it into a saucepan with the water and a little sea salt. Bring up to the boil, then turn the heat down low, put a lid on the saucepan and leave it to simmer for 40 minutes until the rice is cooked. Then take it off the heat and leave it to stand, with the lid still on the saucepan, for a further 10 minutes.

While the rice is cooking fry the onion gently in butter for 10 minutes until it's golden and soft. Stir the onion into the cooked rice together with the grated cheese, mustard and egg. Mix well and season to taste with salt and plenty of pepper. It's easier to shape the mixture into croquettes if it's cool and better still if there's time to chill it in the fridge. Dip tablespoons of the mixture first into the beaten egg then into the dried crumbs, shaping them into rounds with your hands. Fry the croquettes in a little olive oil until they're crisp all over. Drain them on kitchen paper and serve them as soon as possible.

RICE AND PEAS WITH TOMATO SAUCE, GERMAN-STYLE

This German dish, *Schoten*, is made from ingredients similar to those used for the Italian *risi e bisi* (see next recipe) but the result is different. The rice and pea mixture is drier, more like a pilaf, and it's served with a tomato sauce which provides moisture and colour.

SERVES 4
350g (12oz) long grain brown rice
850ml (1½ pints) water
sea salt
350g (12oz) frozen peas
25g (1oz) butter
1 onion, peeled and chopped
400g (14oz) can tomatoes
freshly ground black pepper

Wash the rice and put it into a heavy-based saucepan with the water and a little salt. Bring it up to the boil then turn the heat down, put a lid on the saucepan and let the rice cook very gently for 40 minutes. If the peas are very frozen tip them into a sieve and run hot water over them for a minute, then put them on top of the rice 5 minutes before it's ready.

When the rice is cooked take it off the heat and leave it, with the lid still on the saucepan, for 10 minutes to finish steaming in its own heat. While this is happening make the sauce. Melt half the butter in a medium-sized saucepan and fry the onion for 10 minutes until it's tender. Stir in the tomatoes and cook for 2–3 minutes, then liquidize the mixture. Season with salt and pepper and reheat gently.

To finish the dish add the remaining butter to the peas and rice and stir gently with a fork. Season carefully and serve with the tomato sauce.

RICE AND PEAS, ITALIAN-STYLE

This Italian dish, *risi e bisi*, is really halfway between a risotto and a soup, with a creamy consistency. It's easy to make and good served with a tomato salad and some triangles of crisp toast.

SERVES 4
2 large onions
25g (1oz) butter
350g (12oz) brown rice
1.2 litres (2 pints) water
sea salt
350g (12oz) frozen peas
175g (6oz) finely grated cheese
1 teaspoon dry mustard
freshly ground black pepper
grated nutmeg

Peel and chop the onions. Melt the butter in a large saucepan and add the onions; fry them gently for about 10 minutes until they're soft and buttery but not browned. Wash the rice and put it into the saucepan with the onion; stir in the water and a little salt. Bring the mixture up to the boil then put a lid on the saucepan, turn the heat down and leave the rice to cook gently for 40 minutes.

If the peas are very icy put them into a sieve and rinse them under hot water, then put them into the saucepan on top of the rice 5 minutes before it's cooked. At the end of the cooking time take the rice off the heat and leave it, with a lid on the saucepan, for 10 minutes, to finish cooking in its own heat. After this you should find that the rice and peas are both cooked but that there is still some liquid left in the saucepan.

Stir the mixture with a fork, mixing in the cheese, dry mustard and salt, pepper and nutmeg to taste. Reheat very gently then serve at once.

RICE AND PEAS, CARIBBEAN-STYLE

The 'peas' in this dish are actually red kidney beans, but this recipe was given to me by a friend who lives in the Caribbean, and I've kept the original name. She tells me it's a popular dish out there and they generally use immature or 'water coconuts', as they call them, for the coconut milk. Here, I've found the best way to make the coconut milk is to put some pieces of fresh coconut into a liquidizer, together with the liquid in the coconut (if present) and some water, blend to a purée, then strain and use the resulting liquid. Alternatively, you could soak about 125g (4oz) of desiccated coconut in boiling water for 10 minutes, then drain through a sieve, pressing out as much liquid as you can.

SERVES 4
2 tablespoons olive oil
1 medium onion, peeled and chopped
1 red pepper, de-seeded and chopped
350g (12oz) long grain brown rice
425ml (15 fl oz) coconut milk
½ teaspoon dried thyme
sea salt
freshly ground black pepper
275ml (10 fl oz) cold water
175g (6oz) red kidney beans, soaked, cooked and
drained *or* 2 × 400g (14oz) cans, drained

Heat the oil in a large saucepan and fry the onion until golden. Add the pepper, rice, coconut milk, thyme, sea salt, freshly ground black pepper and water and bring up to the boil, then cover the saucepan, turn the heat right down and leave to cook very slowly for 45 minutes, until the rice is tender and all the liquid absorbed. Stir in the cooked red beans, using a fork so that you don't mash the rice, and cook for a further few minutes to heat the beans through. Serve with a nice crisp green salad with a herby dresing.

RICE AND SPINACH BAKE

This dish from France, called 'Tian', is a baked vegetable casserole, rather like a savoury loaf except that it is served from the dish. It takes it's name from the earthenware casserole dish in which it is cooked in Provence and it can be made from any green vegetable, although spinach or chard are the most usual, with courgettes sometimes added too. It can be served hot or cold. If you're having it hot, try it with crunchy roast potatoes, tomato sauce and a colourful vegetable such as carrots. Cold it's nice with some garlic mayonnaise or thick natural yoghurt, tomato salad and hot French bread.

SERVES 4 F
175g (6oz) brown rice
just under 575ml (1 pint) water
sea salt
450g (1 lb) spinach
2 tablespoons olive oil
2–3 garlic cloves, peeled and crushed
1 tablespoon chopped fresh parsley
125g (4oz) grated cheese
2 eggs
freshly ground black pepper
2–3 tablespoons dried crumbs
2–3 tablespoons grated Parmesan cheese
2 tablespoons olive oil

Wash the rice then put it into the saucepan with the water and a teaspoon of salt, bring it up to the boil then turn the heat down and leave the rice to cook very slowly, with a lid on the saucepan, for 40–45 minutes, until it's tender and all the liquid has been absorbed. (If there's still some water left in the saucepan just leave it to stand off the heat but with the lid on for 10–15 minutes, after which you should find it has been absorbed.)

Set the oven to 200°C (400°F), gas mark 6. Wash the spinach thoroughly in three changes of water, then chop it up – you can use the stalks too. Heat the olive oil in a large saucepan and put in the spinach; turn it in the hot oil for 2–3 minutes until it has softened slightly and is all glossy-looking from the oil. Take it off the heat and add the rice, garlic, parsley and grated cheese. Beat in the eggs and mix everything together, seasoning it with salt and a good grinding of pepper. Spoon the mixture into a shallow ovenproof dish and sprinkle the crumbs, Parmesan and olive oil on top. Bake without a lid for 30–40 minutes until its puffed up and golden brown and crispy on top.

RISOTTO

A creamy risotto makes a delicious supper dish and is easy to prepare. If you can spare a little dry cider or wine for this it really does make all the difference to the flavour.

SERVES 4
25g (1oz) butter
2 large onions, peeled and chopped
275g (10oz) brown rice
275ml (10 fl oz) dry cider *or* dry white wine
575ml (1 pint) water
sea salt
225g (8oz) button mushrooms
125g (4oz) grated cheese
freshly ground black pepper

Heat half the butter in a large saucepan and fry the onion gently for 10 minutes, without browning. Add the rice, cider or wine, water and a teaspoon of sea salt. Bring to the boil, cover and leave to cook gently for 40 minutes. Towards the end of the cooking time, lightly fry the mushrooms in the remaining oil, then add them to the cooked rice, mixing lightly with a fork. Stir in the cheese and check the seasoning. Serve with a crisp green salad with a good olive oil and wine vinegar dressing, or with a tomato and onion salad, and some chilled white wine or cider.

SPICED RICE

This is a basic recipe for a spicy rice to eat with curries. It comes out a pretty bright yellow colour because of the turmeric. You can vary it by stirring in some nuts, sesame seeds or poppy seeds at the end to make it more crunchy and nutritious or you can add raisins or currants for sweetness, or chopped red or green peppers for extra colour.

SERVES 4
225g (8oz) long-grain brown rice
1 tablespoon *ghee or* olive oil
575ml (1 pint) boiling water
1 teaspoon turmeric
3 cloves
1 bay leaf
sea salt
freshly ground black pepper

Wash the rice thoroughly, then drain it and, if possible, leave it for half an hour or so to dry off a little.

Heat the *ghee* or oil in a heavy-based saucepan and add the drained rice. Fry the rice over a gentle heat until it has become opaque – this will take about 5 minutes and it's best to stir the rice all the time so that it doesn't brown – then put in the boiling water, turmeric, cloves and bay leaf and a seasoning of salt and pepper. When the mixture is boiling vigorously, turn down the heat and put a lid on the saucepan. Leave the rice to cook very gently for about 45 minutes, after which it should be tender and have absorbed all the liquid. Take out the cloves and bay leaf before serving the rice. (If there is still a little water left in the saucepan let the rice stand, still covered with the lid, for a further 10–15 minutes, after which you should find all is well.)

Variation

SPICED ONION RICE

Made as above, but fry one chopped onion and a crushed garlic clove in the *ghee* or oil for 5 minutes before putting in the rice.

TOO-TIRED-TO-COOK RICE

This is one of the things I make when the last thing I feel like doing is cooking! I put the rice on to cook, then go away and do something else for about 30 minutes. Then, 10 minutes before the rice is due to be cooked, I prepare the mushroom mixture and a green salad. The whole meal is ready in about 45 minutes, with biscuits and cheese, fruit or yoghurt for pudding.

SERVES 4
225g (8oz) long grain brown rice
575ml (1 pint) water
1 level teaspoon sea salt
225g (8oz) button mushrooms
15g (½oz) butter
50g (2oz) sunflower seeds
Shoyu soy sauce – from health shops

Put the rice, water and salt into a pan (with a lid) and bring to the boil. Boil hard for 5 minutes, then put the lid on and turn heat right down. Leave for 40 minutes. Meanwhile fry the mushrooms in the butter. Fork up the rice when cooked, add sunflower seeds and serve with the mushrooms and their liquid poured over, and a sprinkling of Shoyu.

VEGETABLE BIRIANI

This is a lovely curry dish: spicy golden rice garnished with slices of tomato and hardboiled egg and served with a tasty curry sauce. I love the strange, glutinous texture of okra, or ladies' fingers (which Indians call *bhindi*). This is quite often available fresh, but if you can't get it you could use the same quantity of French beans or courgettes and add with the peas.

SERVES 4
1 onion, peeled and chopped
1 large garlic clove, peeled and crushed
1 tablespoon olive oil
1 bay leaf
2 teaspoons turmeric
4–5 cardamom pods
piece of cinnamon stick
pinch of ground cloves
1–2 teaspoons sea salt
275g (10oz) long grain brown rice
125g (4oz) okra, washed and trimmed if necessary
500ml (18 fl oz) water
125g (4oz) frozen peas
1 tomato, sliced
1 hardboiled egg, sliced
½ punnet mustard and cress, washed

Fry the onion and garlic in the oil for 10 minutes, then stir in the bay leaf, spices and salt. Add the rice, okra, turmeric and water and bring up to the boil. Put a lid on the saucepan, turn the heat right down and leave to cook very gently for 40 minutes. Alternatively the biriani can be cooked in the oven for 40 minutes at 200°C (400°F), gas mark 6. 10 minutes before the rice is ready, add the peas – just tip them on top without stirring. When the rice is ready remove the saucepan from the heat and leave it to stand, still covered, for 10 minutes. Then fork the rice through lightly and serve it piled up on a warmed serving dish garnished with the slices of tomato and egg, and the cress. Serve it with mango chutney, poppadums and the following sauce.

VEGETABLE CURRY SAUCE FOR BIRIANI

Don't be put off by the long list of spices in this recipe; the method is very quick and easy.

SERVES 4
2 medium-sized onions, peeled and chopped
4 garlic cloves, peeled and crushed
1 tablespoon olive oil
2 teaspoons curry paste *or* powder
1 teaspoon paprika pepper
½ teaspoon turmeric
1 teaspoon garam masala
225g (8oz) can tomatoes
1 tablespoon tomato paste
275ml (10 fl oz) water
sea salt
freshly ground black pepper
a drop of honey
125g (4oz) okra, washed and trimmed as necessary
450g (1 lb) potatoes, peeled and cut into even-sized chunks

Fry the onion and garlic in the oil for 10 minutes, then add all the spices. Cook for 1 minute, then stir in the tomatoes, tomato paste, water and a little salt and pepper. Taste and add a very little honey if necessary. Bring up to the boil, then put in the vegetables and simmer gently for about 25 minutes, until the potatoes are cooked. Check seasoning. Serve with the biriani.

VEGETABLE CURRY (1)

This vegetable curry is spicy but not 'hot'. If you want to you can make it 'hotter' by increasing the amount of chilli powder. It's lovely with plain boiled rice, or the spicy fried rice, some mango chutney and crunchy golden poppadums or chapaatis. I usually serve it with a juicy side salad, too, which is cooling and refreshing. It's best to get the rice on to cook before starting to make this, as brown rice takes so long!

SERVES 4
25g (1oz) *ghee or* butter
1 large onion, peeled and chopped
2 garlic cloves, peeled and crushed
1 bay leaf
3 teaspoons ground coriander
3 teaspoons ground cumin
1 teaspoon ground ginger
¼ teaspoon chilli powder
225g (8oz) can tomatoes
1 teaspoon sea salt
freshly ground black pepper
575ml (1 pint) water
350g (12oz) carrots
350g (12oz) potatoes
125g (4oz) peas

Heat the *ghee* or butter in a large saucepan and fry the onion for 7–8 minutes, then add the garlic, bay leaf and spices and stir over the heat for 2–3 minutes. Mix in the tomatoes, salt, a grinding of pepper and the water. Simmer for 5–10 minutes while you prepare the vegetables. Scrape and slice the carrots, peel the potatoes and cut them into even-sized chunks. Add the potatoes and carrots to the tomato mixture and simmer gently for 15–25 minutes, until the vegetables are almost tender, then put in the peas and simmer for a further 5 minutes. Check the seasoning before serving.

VEGETABLE CURRY (2)

Not such an authentic-tasting curry as the previous one, but one I like. Serve it with fluffy brown rice, or spiced brown rice, and any of the following: chopped, hardboiled eggs, mango chutney, salted almonds or cashew nuts, sliced, skinned tomatoes, sliced bananas, desiccated coconut, onion rings.

SERVES 4
225g (8oz) leeks
1 small cauliflower
2 small onions, sliced
1 small cooking apple, cored and chopped
225g (8oz) peeled potatoes
225g (8oz) tomatoes, chopped
2 tablespoons plain flour
1 level tablespoon turmeric powder
4 tablespoons olive oil or ghee
2 teaspoons curry powder
275ml (10 fl oz) water
pinch coriander seed
3 rounded tablespoons mango chutney
sea salt
freshly ground black pepper

Trim roots and leaves off leeks, and discard. Clean leeks thoroughly by slitting lengthways down one side and washing under running water. Cut into pieces. Wash cauliflower and divide into pieces. Cut potato into equal pieces. Mix flour and turmeric in a large bowl, add all vegetables and fruits and turn them gently until coated. Heat the oil or ghee in a large pan, add vegetables and fry lightly. Add curry powder, water, coriander seed and chutney. Cook for 30 minutes. Season to taste. Serve with boiled rice.

Variation

OKRA CURRY

Add 225g (8oz) fresh okra, trimmed, to the above, coating it with the flour and spice mixture along with the other vegetables.

10

SAVOURY FLANS
AND PIES

There's something very satisfying, I always think, about a main course based on a pie or pastry roll, while quiches – or flans, as I prefer to call them – turn a salad into a main meal, and are almost indispensable for parties, picnics and fork suppers. The only problem with them is that from the health point of view they are rather heavy on fat, both on account of the pastry and, usually, the filling, too. That doesn't mean that you can't have them if you're health conscious; it just means you need to plan for them. Keep the rest of the meal and of your day's eating low in fat to compensate, and save the creamy flans and the richer flaky and puff pastries for special occasions.

BASIC PASTRY RECIPES

I use plain wholemeal flour for all pastry; 100% wholemeal, generally, for shortcrust, and 85% for flaky or cream cheese pastry. The only pastry which you cannot make satisfactorily with these flours is real puff pastry, for which you need unbleached white bread flour. Personally, though, I rarely make my own puff pastry; if I need to use this kind of pastry, which I reserve for special occasions, I prefer to save time by buying an all-vegetable fat, frozen puff pastry. The fat which I normally use is unsalted butter, though I have also had very good results with an unsaturated soft vegetable margarine.

HOW TO MAKE WHOLEMEAL SHORTCRUST PASTRY

And I know, from the letters I get, and the questions I'm asked at demonstrations, that this is one of the things many people find most difficult! I think the main problem is that they're expecting the pastry to handle and behave in the same way as pastry made from white flour – but it just doesn't! In fact, it might comfort you to know that if wholemeal pastry is easy to handle, then something has gone wrong, and it's not going to be at all good to eat. But, before you put down this book in disgust, let me reassure you that it does become easier with practice, and there are ways to make it easier for yourself from the beginning, so read on!

First of all, you might find it best to start by using an 85% wholemeal flour, or a mixture of half that and half 100%, so that you can get used to the crumblier texture gradually. Use the same proportions of ingredients as you would for ordinary white pastry, that is half as much fat as flour, with a little cold water to bind. I find 3 tablespoons of cold water to 225g (8oz) flour gives best results. When it comes to rolling the pastry out, I strongly recommend that you use a pastry board or a large chopping board, well-sprinkled with flour. The reason for this is that you can use this to convey the pastry easily to your flan tin or pie dish without the pastry disintegrating on the way! Hold the board at an angle 1cm (½in) above the container in or on which you want your pastry, then increase the angle of the board so that the pastry slides off the board and into position. All you have to do then is gently press the pastry into place and trim it in the usual way.

Here is the basic recipe for wholemeal shortcrust:

SHORTCRUST PASTRY

This is the easiest pastry to make and the most useful.

MAKES 225G (8OZ) PASTRY
225g (8oz) plain flour
½ teaspoon salt
125g (4oz) butter
3 tablespoons water

Sift the flour and salt into a bowl. If you're using wholemeal flour, sift through as much flour as you can, then add the residue of bran from the sieve (the purpose of the sifting is to aerate the flour, not to remove the bran). Add the butter then rub it into the flour with your fingertips, lifting the mixture high out of the bowl to incorporate as much air as possible and make the pastry light. Continue until the mixture looks like fine breadcrumbs, then add the water a little at a time and use your fingertips to press the mixture together and form a dough. Put the dough on a lightly floured surface and knead lightly for a minute or two until smooth. Before rolling out the dough, use your hands to press it roughly into whatever shape you want – a round, oval or rectangle – then roll out using light, even strokes and bake in a hot oven, 200–220°C (400–425°F), gas mark 6–7.

CHEESE SHORTCRUST

Make this as shortcrust above, sifting ½ teaspoon mustard powder with the flour and adding up to 50–150g (2–5oz) grated cheese after rubbing the fat into the flour.

CREAM CHEESE PASTRY

This is the easiest way I know of making a pastry with a flaky texture; it is a most delicious pastry, at its best when made with an 81% or 85% wholemeal flour, although it is the one flaky pastry which also works with 100% flour. Suitable for pie crusts, savoury rolls and tartlets.

MAKES 225G (8OZ) PASTRY
225g (8oz) plain flour
½ teaspoon salt
125g (4oz) butter
125g (4oz) full fat cream cheese
1 teaspoon lemon juice

Make as for shortcrust pastry, adding the cream cheese and lemon juice after you have rubbed the fat into the flour. Chill for 1 hour before using; bake as for shortcrust pastry.

ROUGH PUFF PASTRY

This is the quickest and easiest of the traditional flaky pastries and a good choice for savoury rolls and decorated pastries. Lightest when made with white flour, it also works well with an 85% wholemeal flour, which is what I normally use.

MAKES 225G (8OZ) PASTRY
75g (3oz) butter *or* hard margarine
75g (3oz) white cooking fat
225g (8oz) plain flour
½ teaspoon salt
2 teaspoons lemon juice
6 tablespoons cold water (approx.)

Cut the butter or margarine and fat into walnut-sized pieces and chill in the fridge. Sift flour and salt into a bowl. Add fat, cutting it in lightly with a round-bladed knife so that the fats get coated with the flour and are about the size of a pea. Then add lemon juice and water. Using your fingertips, gently gather the mixture together to form a soft pliable dough. Put the dough on to a lightly floured surface and, without kneading, shape to a rectangle. Roll out to an oblong three times as long as it is wide (about 12 × 36cm/5 × 15in). Fold the bottom third up and the top third down, then lightly press the edges together with a rolling pin. Give the dough a half turn so that the open edges are at the top and bottom, then roll out to a long strip again and repeat the folding and sealing. Wrap the dough in polythene and chill in the fridge for at least 30 minutes, then repeat the rolling, folding and sealing twice more and chill for a further 30 minutes. Rough puff pastry should be baked in a hot oven, 200–220°C (400–425°F), gas mark 6–7.

FLAKY PASTRY

This is the flakiest pastry apart from puff and ideal for making special pies. This way of making flaky pastry is based on the one described by Claudia Roden in *A Book of Middle Eastern Food*. It is a highly unconventional method but, having tried them all while testing recipes for this book, it is the one which I have found gives best results every time, rising in delicious flaky layers, even with 81% or 85% wholemeal flour.

MAKES 225G (8OZ) PASTRY
225g (8oz) plain flour
½ teaspoon salt
175g (6oz) butter, at room temperature
2 teaspoons lemon juice
8 tablespoons cold water (approx.)

Sift flour and salt into a bowl and rub in 50g (2oz) of the butter. Add the lemon juice and enough water

to make a pliable dough. Wrap in polythene and chill overnight in the fridge. Next day form the dough into a rectangular shape and roll it out as thinly as possible. You will have a very long piece of pastry and will need to fold up the part you've already rolled or allow it to hang over the pastry board while you work on the rest. Next spread the surface of the dough evenly with the rest of the butter, then roll the dough up like a swiss roll. Wrap the roll of dough in polythene and chill in the fridge for 1 hour. Then roll out the pastry and use as required. Bake in a hot oven, 200–220°C (400–425°F), gas mark 6–7.

Making a Single-crust Pie

First prepare the filling, as it needs to be completely cooled. To make the pastry lid, pat the pastry out to roughly the shape of the dish, then roll it out 6mm (¼in) thick and about 1.5cm (½in) wider all round than the top of the dish. Cut a strip from the outer edge of pastry and place on the rim of the dish. Put filling into dish and if it's moist and soft, stand an egg cup in the centre of the dish to help support the pastry. Damp the pastry strip on the rim with cold water, then place the pastry on top and press the edges together. 'Knock up' the pie and flute the edges, then insert the blade of a knife under the pastry at the sides of the pie to make a gap for the steam to escape, or make a couple of steam-holes in the top of the pie. Decorate with pastry trimmings as desired (page 242) and brush top of pie with beaten egg or milk to glaze, if you wish.

Making a Double-crust Pie

Prepare and cool the filling. Take just over half the pastry, pat into the shape of the dish and roll out about 3mm (⅛in) thick and about 2.5–4cm (1–1½in) larger than the dish. Lift pastry into dish, press into place, then spoon the filling in on top: it should fill the dish generously, piled up to the centre. Roll out remaining pastry so that it is 1cm (½in) larger than the dish, then place on top of dish to cover filling. Press pastry edges together, trim, knock up, decorate and glaze just as described for single-crust pies.

Making Quiches, Flans and Tarts

Set the oven to 200°C (400°F), gas mark 6, position oven shelf above centre and place a large baking sheet on the shelf. Lightly grease a flan tin. Roll out the pastry fairly thinly so that it is 4cm (1½in) wider all round than the diameter of the tin. Then lift it into the tin, using either the rolling pin or, and this is easier with crumbly wholemeal pastry, sliding it straight off the pastry board into the tin. Press pastry into tin, trim edges, prick base. When making an ordinary shallow flan I do not think it is necessary to weight the pastry down with baking beans; just put flan tin into oven on top of baking sheet (which helps to cook base of flan) and bake for 15–20 minutes, until pastry is set and feels crisp and firm when you touch it lightly. If you want to ensure that your flan has a lovely crisp base, just before you take the flan case out of the oven, heat 2 tablespoons of oil in a small saucepan. Tip oil into flan case as soon as it comes out of the oven so that base is covered: you probably won't need all the oil, or, if the recipe includes something like fried onions, you could fry this in the oil and add it at this point, too. You can then continue and put the filling straight in on top, or leave the flan case to get cold before proceeding. Either way this tip, which was discovered by a friend of mine, Mary, means you will never make a soggy flan again!

It's fun to experiment with different combinations of ingredients for the filling. Although cream is often used – and is wonderful for a special occasion – lower calorie versions can be made by using milk, half milk and half single or soured cream, or by substituting a low-calorie soft white cheese such as *fromage blanc* or quark.

Freezing Pastry Dishes

Double-and single-crust pies freeze well. Freeze before baking, then thaw completely and bake the usual way. You can also freeze flans after baking. Recipes which are suitable for the freezer are shown by the symbol [F].

ASPARAGUS FLAN

This is a creamy, delicious flan with a crisp pastry case. You could use all cream, if you like, but I find this lighter, half-and-half mixture of cream and *fromage blanc* works well. This is lovely for an early summer lunch, with buttered new potatoes.

SERVES 6 [F]
450g (1 lb) fresh *or* frozen asparagus
shortcrust pastry made from 175g (6oz) wholemeal flour (page 240)
sea salt
freshly ground black pepper
2 tablespoons olive oil
1 small onion, peeled and chopped
125g (4oz) Cheddar cheese, grated
150ml (5 fl oz) single cream
125g (4oz) *fromage blanc*
2 eggs
fresh parsley, chopped

First cook the asparagus for the filling. If you're using fresh asparagus, break off the hard stems at the base – these ends are too tough to eat but can be used to make a stock for asparagus soup. Wash the asparagus gently to remove any grit, then place it in a steamer and cook for about 10 minutes: it should be just tender when pierced with a pointed knife. Cook frozen asparagus according to the directions on the packet. Drain asparagus and season with salt and pepper.

Set the oven to 200°C (400°F), gas mark 6, and if possible place a heavy baking sheet on the top shelf to heat up with the oven. Roll out the pastry and ease it into an 20cm (8in) flan tin which has been lightly greased. Trim the edges and prick the base. Put the flan case into the oven on top of the baking sheet and bake for 15 minutes, until the pastry is lightly browned and the base feels set and crisp to touch.

While the flan case is in the oven, heat the 2 tablespoons of oil in a large saucepan and fry the onion for 10 minutes, until the onion has softened and browned lightly. Have the fried onion piping hot when you take the flan out of the oven and pour this, oil and all, over the base of the hot flan case, making sure that the oil spreads over the whole of the base. This makes the pastry crisp (and ensures that it will stay crisp after the filling is added) but you must put the hot oil and onion into the flan case as soon as it comes out of the oven. After that the flan case can be cooled and the rest of the filling added later if more convenient.

To finish the flan, reduce the oven setting to 180°C (350°F), gas mark 4. Arrange the cooked asparagus in the base of the flan and sprinkle with half the cheese. Whisk the cream, *fromage blanc* and eggs together until smooth; season with salt and freshly ground black pepper. Pour this mixture over the asparagus and cheese and sprinkle with the remaining cheese. Bake the flan for 30 minutes, until the filling is puffed up, golden and set. Sprinkle with chopped parsley before serving.

INDIVIDUAL ASPARAGUS TARTS

These light, creamy little tarts make a very good starter for a dinner party; they're also nice with salad for lunch. They would be lovely made in individual flan dishes if you've got them. Otherwise use patty tins or any small ovenproof containers.

SERVES 6 F
shortcrust pastry made from 175g (6oz) plain
wholemeal flour (page 240)
2 tablespoons olive oil – optional
1 onion, peeled and finely chopped
1 small garlic clove, peeled and crushed
25g (1oz) butter
2 eggs
275ml (10 fl oz) milk *or* single cream
sea salt
freshly ground black pepper
grated nutmeg
225g (8oz) fresh or frozen asparagus, cooked and cut
into 2cm (1in) lengths.

Place a baking sheet in the centre of the oven and set the temperature to 200°C (400°F), gas mark 6. Roll out the pastry on a lightly floured board and use it to line 6 individual patty tins. Prick the bases all over and place the tins on the baking sheet in the oven. Bake for 10–15 minutes until crisp and golden brown. To 'waterproof' the tartlet cases, and prevent any possibility of soggy bottoms, have the 2 tablespoons of oil very hot and brush this over the tarts as soon as you take them out of the oven. Turn the oven setting down to 180°C (350°F), gas mark 4.

Fry the onion and garlic in the butter over a gentle heat for 10 minutes, but don't let them brown. Take the saucepan off the heat and add the eggs and milk or cream. Season with salt and pepper and add some grated nutmeg to taste. Arrange the asparagus in the flans and then pour in the egg mixture, dividing it equally between them.

Bake the flans in the preheated oven for about 20 minutes until the filling is set. Serve them hot or warm.

AUBERGINE, RED PEPPER AND CHEESE FLAN

This is a pretty flan with a chunky, aubergine filling set in a light custard. I think the nutty flavour of the wholemeal pastry goes well with the onion and aubergine filling. This flan is best served hot, with new potatoes and French beans.

SERVES 6 F
1 medium-sized aubergine, about 225g (8oz)
sea salt
shortcrust pastry made from 175g (6oz) wholemeal
flour (page 240)
1½ tablespoons water
3 tablespoons olive oil
2 large onions, peeled and chopped
1 red pepper, about 175g (6oz)
1 fat garlic clove, peeled and crushed in a little salt
freshly ground black pepper
125g (4oz) Cheddar cheese, grated
2 eggs
150ml (5 fl oz) milk

First make the filling. Wash the aubergine and remove the stem, then cut the aubergine down into 1 cm (½in) cubes. Put these into a colander, sprinkle them with salt and then place a plate and a weight on top and leave for at least 30 minutes. After that rinse the pieces of aubergine under the cold tap and squeeze them to remove excess water.

Set the oven to 200°C (400°F), gas mark 6. Make the pastry flan case as described for the asparagus flan (page 242) and bake for 15 minutes.

While the flan case is in the oven, heat 2 tablespoons of the oil in a large saucepan and fry the onion for 10 minutes until the onion has softened and browned lightly. Have the fried onion piping hot when you take the flan out of the oven and pour this, oil and all, over the base of the hot flan case, making sure that the oil spreads over the whole of the base.

To finish the flan, reduce the oven setting to 180°C (350°F), gas mark 4. Heat the remaining tablespoon of oil in a medium-sized saucepan and fry the aubergine, red pepper and garlic for about 10 minutes, until they are tender but not too soft. Season with salt and freshly ground black pepper. Put two thirds of the grated cheese in the base of the flan case, then spoon the aubergine mixture on top and sprinkle with the rest of the cheese. Whisk together the eggs and milk and pour evenly over the top of the flan. Bake towards the top of the oven for 50–60 minutes, until the filling is set and golden.

HOT AVOCADO TARTLETS (1)

To make these tartlets, chunks of avocado pear are mixed with soured cream (or *fromage blanc* or yoghurt for a less rich version) and heated through in crisp pastry cases. I think it's a delicious mixture of flavours and textures, but it's important not to let the avocados overheat or you will spoil the flavour. However, the pastry cases can be made several hours in advance and just reheated and assembled, with the avocado, at the last minute. I use little Pyrex tartlet dishes measuring 10cm (4in) across and 1cm (½in) deep; alternatively you could use metal flan tins of the same size. This dish can also be made in a 20cm (8in) flan tin and served either as a starter or a light main course.

SERVES 6
cheesy shortcrust pastry made from 125g (4oz)
wholemeal flour (page 240)
2 tablespoons olive oil – optional
2 fairly large avocado pears
juice of ½ small lemon
sea salt
freshly ground black pepper
150ml (5 fl oz) soured cream *or fromage blanc or*
natural yoghurt
2 tablespoons fresh chives, chopped

Set the oven to 200°C (400°F), gas mark 6, and if possible place a heavy baking sheet on the top shelf to heat up with the oven. Divide the pastry into six pieces and roll each out fairly thinly to fit the little flan dishes; press the pastry on to the dishes, trim the edges and prick the bases. Put the flan cases into the oven on top of the baking sheet and bake for 15 minutes, until the pastry is lightly browned and the pastry feels set and crisp to touch. To ensure crisp bottoms to the tartlets, immediately they come out of the oven brush them with hot oil as described in the previous recipe.

To finish the tartlets, reduce the oven setting to 180°C (350°F), gas mark 4. Cut the avocados in half and remove stones and skin. Cut flesh into 1cm (½in) dice, sprinkle with lemon juice and salt and pepper. Mix the soured cream with a spoon to make it creamy, then gently add it to the avocado, turning the avocado with a spoon so that it all gets coated with the cream, but don't mash it. Spoon the avocado mixture into the flan cases, dividing it between them. Pop them into the oven for about 15–20 minutes to heat through, then sprinkle with chives and serve at once.

HOT AVOCADO TARTLETS (2)

Here is another version of hot avocado tartlets (as you may gather, I love avocado!), this time filled with avocado and coated with lemon juice and a light, mustardy, cheese sauce. With their melt-in-the-mouth pastry and delicate avocado topping, these make a delectable first course.

SERVES 6
shortcrust pastry made from 175g (6oz) wholemeal
flour (page 240)
2 tablespoons olive oil – optional
25g (1oz) butter
25g (1oz) flour
275ml (10 fl oz) milk
1 teaspoon mild wholegrain mustard
50g (2oz) grated cheese
sea salt
freshly ground black pepper
2 avocado pears
3 tablespoons lemon juice

Set oven to 200°C (400°F), gas mark 6. Roll out pastry and line six 10cm (4in) tartlet dishes. Bake for 15 minutes. To ensure crisp bottoms, brush the tartlets with hot oil as described on page 242 when they come out of the oven. Melt butter in a saucepan, add flour, cook for a moment then pour in milk, stirring until thick. Add mustard and most of cheese; season to taste. Peel and dice avocados, sprinkle with lemon juice, gently stir into sauce. Divide between flans, sprinkle with rest of cheese. Bake for 15–20 minutes.

LITTLE FLAKY BRIE, WALNUT AND SORREL PIES

Serve these hot from the oven as a delicious first course; or accompanied by salad, made from diced eating apples and tomatoes, watercress and a little finely shredded leek, for a light lunch.

MAKES 12
flaky, rough puff *or* cream cheese pastry made from
175g (6oz) wholemeal flour (page 240)
125g (4oz) Brie, finely diced
25g (1oz) walnuts, chopped
25g (1oz) sorrel or spinach, finely shredded
sea salt
freshly ground black pepper

Set oven to 220°C (425°F) gas mark 7. Roll out pastry and cut out 24 circles with a 6cm (2½in) round cutter. Place 12 of these in a lightly greased tartlet tin. Mix together Brie, walnuts and sorrel or spinach; season lightly. Divide mixture between tartlets, cover with remaining circles, press edges together. Make a steam-hole in the centre of each little pie, then bake for 15 minutes, until crisp, golden brown and flaky looking. Serve at once.

BUTTER BEAN AND CHUTNEY ROLL

Melt-in-the-mouth wholemeal pastry, onions, butter beans and sweet chutney make a tasty savoury roll that's good hot or cold, and useful for packed lunches.

SERVES 4 [F]
2 onions, sliced
2 tablespoons olive oil
125g (4oz) butter beans, soaked and cooked, *or* a 439g (15½oz) can
sea salt
freshly ground black pepper
225g (8oz) shortcrust pastry
2–3 tablespoons chutney
beaten egg to glaze

Fry onions in the oil for 10 minutes, until soft. Drain butter beans; add beans to onions, together with salt and pepper. Leave on one side to cool. Set oven to 200°C (400°F), gas mark 6. Divide pastry in half; roll out each half to a rectangle about 26 × 22cm (10 × 9in). Place one rectangle on a baking tray, spread with the chutney, spoon bean mixture on top. Dampen edges with water, cover with second rectangle, press edges together. Brush with glaze, prick with a fork. Bake for 25–30 minutes.

BUTTER BEAN AND ONION FLAN

This is a lovely tasty flan, packed with protein.

SERVES 4–6 [F]
shortcrust pastry made from 125g (4oz) wholemeal flour (page 240)
2 tablespoons olive oil – optional
1 large onion, chopped
15g (½oz) butter
125g (4oz) grated cheese
1 teaspoon dry mustard
1 egg
150ml (15 fl oz) milk
sea salt
freshly ground black pepper
125g (4oz) butter beans, soaked, cooked and then drained
1 tablespoon chopped parsley

Set oven to 200°C (400°F), gas mark 6. Roll out the pastry and use it to line a 20cm (8in) flan dish. Prick the base of the flan, then bake it in the oven for about 15 minutes, until firm and crisp. Heat the 2 tablespoons of oil and brush this over the base of the flan case as soon as it comes out of the oven. This will keep it crisp. Turn oven heat down to 180°C (350°F), gas mark 4.

Peel and slice the onion and fry it in the butter for about 10 minutes, until it's soft but not browned. Mix together the cheese and mustard; beat the egg with the milk and season with sea salt and freshly ground black pepper. Put the hot cooked onion straight into the hot flan case and arrange the butter beans on top. Sprinkle with the cheese and mustard mixture, then pour in the egg and milk and scatter with the chopped parsley. Bake for 40–50 minutes, until set and golden brown. I think it's nicest served hot or warm, but you can also serve it cold. You can freeze it, too, but the pastry is never as crisp afterwards, I find.

BUTTER BEAN AND TOMATO PIE

The wholemeal crust gives this pie a lovely country look, but it's also good made with the puff pastry, like the butter bean and vegetable pie.

SERVES 4 [F]
175g (6oz) butter beans *or* 400 g (14oz) can
1 large onion, chopped
15g (½oz) butter
1 tablespoon tomato purée
400g (14oz) can tomatoes
½ teaspoon dried basil
sea salt
freshly ground black pepper
a little sugar
shortcrust pastry made from 125g (4oz) wholemeal flour (page 240)
beaten egg to glaze, if liked

Soak the butter beans for several hours, then drain and rinse them, cover with cold water and cook until tender, then drain.

Preheat the oven to 200°C (400°F), gas mark 6. Fry the onion in the butter for 10 minutes, then add the tomato purée, tomatoes, basil and a seasoning of sea salt, freshly ground black pepper and a dash of sugar (if you think it needs it), and simmer gently for 10 minutes. Mix in the butter beans, check seasoning and pour into a 1.2 litre (2 pint) pie dish.

Roll out the pastry and use it to cover the top of the pie. Crimp the edges and decorate the top as required. Bake the pie in the preheated oven for 20 minutes, then turn the heat down to 190°C (375°F), gas mark 5 and cook for a further 10–15 minutes.

FLAKY CABBAGE, RICE AND HARDBOILED EGG ROLL

Based on a Russian recipe, this is good served with a sauce made by stirring chopped herbs into soured cream or thick natural yoghurt.

SERVES 6
1 onion, chopped
15g (½oz) butter
350g (12oz) cabbage, shredded
125g (4oz) button mushrooms, washed and sliced
350g (12oz) cooked brown rice
4 tablespoons chopped parsley
2 hardboiled eggs, chopped
sea salt
freshly ground black pepper
rough puff, cream cheese *or* shortcrust pastry made from 225g (8oz) wholemeal flour (page 240)
beaten egg to glaze

Fry onion in the butter for 5 minutes; add cabbage and mushrooms, cook for a further 10 minutes, until cabbage is tender, then add rice, parsley, hardboiled eggs and seasoning. Cool. Set oven to 220°C (425°F), gas mark 7. Roll half pastry into an oblong 26 × 22cm (10 × 9in). Spoon rice mixture on top, dampen edges. Roll out second half, cut as described on page 257, place on top, press edges together. Brush with glaze. Bake for 35 minutes.

CARROT, COURGETTE AND PARSLEY FLAN

A pretty mixture of colours in this summery flan.

SERVES 4–6 F
shortcrust pastry made from 125g (4oz) wholemeal flour (page 240)
2 tablespoons olive oil
1 onion, chopped
175g (6oz) carrots, diced
25g (1oz) butter
175g (6oz) courgettes, sliced
150ml (5 fl oz) single cream *or* milk
1 egg
2 tablespoons chopped parsley
sea salt
freshly ground black pepper

Set oven to 200°C (400°F), gas mark 6. Roll out pastry, put into a 20cm (8in) flan tin, trim edges, prick base and bake for 15–20 minutes, until the pastry is set and firm to the touch. As soon as the flan case comes out of the oven, brush it with the oil which you've heated in a small saucepan. This will 'waterproof' the base and make sure the pastry stays crisp. Meanwhile fry onion and carrot in the butter, without browning, for 10 minutes, then add courgettes and cook gently for a further 5–7 minutes, until vegetables are tender. Spoon into flan case. Whisk cream with egg, parsley and seasoning. Pour into flan case. Reduce oven setting to 190°C (375°F), gas mark 5. Bake for 30–35 minutes.

CAULIFLOWER, STILTON AND WALNUT FLAN (1)

This flan consists of a crisp wholemeal pastry base with a filling of cauliflower with Stilton cheese and walnuts. Serve with a crisp salad, and new potatoes with parsley for a more substantial meal.

SERVES 4–6
shortcrust pastry made from 125g (4oz) wholemeal flour (page 240)
2 tablespoons olive oil
1 small cauliflower
25g (1oz) butter
25g (1oz) flour
275ml (10 fl oz) milk
125g (4oz) Stilton cheese, grated
sea salt
freshly ground black pepper
50g (2oz) chopped walnuts

Set oven to 200°C (400°F), gas mark 6. Make a flan case as described in previous recipe. Break cauliflower into florets, boil or steam for 5–7 minutes until just tender, drain. Melt butter in a saucepan, add flour, cook for a few seconds, then pour in milk and stir over heat to make a smooth sauce. Simmer gently for 5–10 minutes, to cook flour, then remove from heat, mix in 75g (3oz) of the cheese and season. Add cauliflower, stirring gently to coat. Spoon into flan case, sprinkle with rest of cheese and the walnuts. Return flan to oven for 30 minutes, until golden brown. Serve at once.

Variation

CAULIFLOWER, STILTON AND WALNUT FLAN (2)

For an alternative filling using eggs instead of the sauce, put the cooked cauliflower into the cooked flan case with the grated cheese and walnuts. Whisk together 2 eggs and 150ml (5 fl oz) milk, season, and pour evenly over the top of the flan. Bake at 190°C (375°F), gas mark 5 for about 50 minutes, until the filling is set. Serve at once if possible.

CHEESE, APPLE AND SAGE TURNOVERS

These are quick to make and have a moist filling with a pleasant combination of flavours. They are delicious made with wholemeal pastry.

SERVES 4 F
shortcrust pastry made from 225g (8oz) wholemeal
flour (page 240)
125g (4oz) eating apple, finely chopped
125g (4oz) grated cheese
1 tablespoon chopped fresh sage *or* 1 teaspoon dried
beaten egg to glaze

Set oven to 200°C (400°F), gas mark 6. Divide pastry into four, roll each into a circle 15cm (6in) across. Mix together apple, cheese and sage. Place a quarter of the cheese mixture on one side of each piece of pastry, fold rest of pastry over and seal edges. Brush with glaze, prick. Place turnovers on baking sheet and bake for 20–25 minutes, until golden brown and crisp.

CHEESE AND ONION FLAN

This is a good flan, a tasty mixture of cheese, mustard and onion on a crisp wholemeal pastry base. It's quite quick to make and popular with all the family. It's good served hot with a cooked vegetable such as French beans and frozen peas and some tomato sauce, or with one of the mixtures from the salads and vegetables section – the carrot, apple, celery and raisin one goes well with it.

SERVES 6 F
shortcrust pastry made from 175g (6oz) wholemeal
flour (page 240)
2 large onions, peeled and finely chopped
125g (4oz) *fromage blanc or* other soft white low-fat
cheese such as quark
1 teaspoon Dijon mustard
2 eggs
1–2 tablespoons chopped parsley
sea salt
freshly ground black pepper
25g (1oz) grated cheese
chopped fresh or dried basil
1 tomato, sliced

Preheat the oven to 200°C (400°F), gas mark 6. Roll out the pastry on a lightly floured board and use to line a 20cm (8in) flan dish. Prick the base and bake in the oven for 15 minutes, until well set and lightly browned. Turn the heat down to 190°C (375°F), gas mark 5.

While the flan case is cooking, make the filling. Put the onions, *fromage blanc*, mustard, eggs and parsley into a bowl and mix well together. Season with salt and pepper. Spoon the mixture into the cooked flan case – it doesn't matter if the flan case is still hot. Sprinkle with the grated cheese and a little basil and arrange the slices of tomato attractively on top. Bake for 30 minutes.

SWISS CHEESE AND ONION TART

This is a good tart and the layer of little cubes of cheese seems to help keep the pastry nice and crisp. The proper cheeses, Gruyère and Emmenthal, are expensive and Edam can be used instead – it gives a very similar result. This makes a good lunch with a juicy tomato salad and some fresh fruit to follow.

SERVES 4–5 F
shortcrust pastry made from 125g (4oz) wholemeal
flour (page 240)
1 tablespoon olive oil
1 medium onion, chopped
15g (½oz) butter
75g (3oz) Gruyère cheese and 75g (3oz) Emmenthal
cheese *or* use all Edam cheese
2 eggs
150ml (5 fl oz) single cream *or* milk
sea salt
freshly ground black pepper
grated nutmeg

Put a baking sheet in the centre of the oven, then set the temperature to 200°C (400°F), gas mark 6. On a lightly floured board roll the pastry out to fit a

20cm (8in) flan dish or tin. Press the pastry gently into place, trim the edges and prick the base. Cook the flan case on the baking sheet in the preheated oven for 15 minutes until it's crisp, then take the flan out of the oven. Have the tablespoon of oil smoking hot in a saucepan and as soon as you take the flan out of the oven brush it all over with the very hot oil – this will help to keep the pastry crisp.

While the flan case is cooking make the filling. Fry the onion gently in the butter for 10 minutes until it's soft but not browned. Cut the cheeses into 6mm (¼in) dice. In a small bowl beat together the eggs and cream or milk and season them with salt, pepper and nutmeg. Scatter half the cheese over the base of the cooked flan, put the onions on top and then the rest of the cheese; finally gently pour in the egg mixture. Bake the flan for 30–35 minutes until it's puffed up and golden. Serve hot.

QUICK CHEESE AND TOMATO FLAN

If you put a simple filling straight into an unbaked pastry case, the flan can be on the table in an hour and although the pastry isn't as crisp as when it's pre-baked, the flan is tasty and delicious eaten hot with a cooked vegetable or salad. I think this is best with pastry made slightly richer than usual.

SERVES 4–6 F
125g (4oz) self-raising 85 per cent wholemeal flour
pinch of sea salt
65g (2½oz) butter
50g (2oz) grated cheese
6 spring onions, chopped
2 tomatoes, skinned and sliced
sea salt
freshly ground black pepper
1 egg
150ml (5 fl oz) milk

Set the oven to 190°C (375°F), gas mark 5. Put a baking tray into the oven to heat up: standing the flan on this helps the base to cook crisply. Grease a 20cm (8in) round flan tin or dish. Sift the flour and salt into a bowl. Add the butter and rub in with your fingertips until the mixture looks like fine breadcrumbs. Gently press the mixture together to make a dough: you won't need any water. Put dough on to a lightly floured board and knead into a smooth circle. Then roll out thinly and lift gently into flan tin or dish. Press down, trim edges. Do not prick. Sprinkle cheese and spring onions over pastry, then arrange tomatoes on top and sprinkle with salt and pepper. Whisk egg and milk in a bowl with a

little seasoning, then pour over tomatoes. Put the flan into the oven and bake for 40 minutes, until pastry is crisp and golden brown and centre is set and puffed up. Serve immediately.

LITTLE RUSSIAN CHEESE TARTLETS

In Russia these little tartlets, *vatrushki*, are usually served either on their own as a first course or as an accompaniment to beetroot soup. I think they make a lovely first course if you serve them hot from the oven and offer a bowl of soured cream and chopped dill for people to spoon over the tartlets. They are also very good with the beetroot soup, turning it into a meal, but it's quite an unusual combination, one for your adventurous friends!

SERVES 4 FOR LUNCH OR SUPPER – 4–6 AS A
STARTER F
225g (8oz) cottage cheese, curd cheese *or* quark
1 egg
sea salt
freshly ground black pepper
shortcrust pastry made from 225g (8oz) wholemeal
flour (page 240)
1 egg beaten with ½ teaspoon salt

Set the oven to 220°C (425°F), gas mark 7. Make the filling by mixing the cottage cheese, curd cheese or quark with the egg and seasoning with salt and pepper.

Roll the pastry out fairly thinly on a lightly floured board and cut into 16 or 18 7.5cm (3in) rounds. Put a heaped teaspoonful of the cheese mixture on to each round. Press the edges of the rounds up towards the centre to make a rim. Brush the tartlets over with the beaten egg glaze then bake them for about 20 minutes until set, puffed up and golden brown. They're best served immediately.

GREEK CHEESE PIE

This is a beautiful flaky golden pie with a creamy mild-tasting cheese filling. In Greece the crust would be made from phyllo pastry and the filling from feta and mitzithra cheeses but you can also make it with a quick flaky pastry, and a mixture of cottage cheese, curd cheese or quark and Lancashire cheese for the filling. I also sometimes add some lightly fried onion which gives extra flavour. You might think all this is very unauthentic but it still makes a lovely pie! It's nice as a hot starter or as a main meal with a cooked vegetable, such as the cauliflower in tomato sauce.

SERVES 6–8 F
quick flaky pastry *or* cream cheese pastry made from
225g (8oz) wholemeal flour (page 240)
450g (1 lb) cottage cheese, curd cheese *or* quark
225g (8oz) Lancashire cheese, grated
50g (2oz) flour
150ml (5 fl oz) natural yoghurt
3 eggs
sea salt
freshly ground black pepper

First make the pastry as described on page 240–1 – you need to do this an hour or so in advance to give it a chance to chill before you use it.

Meanwhile you can make the filling for the pie. Put the cottage cheese, curd cheese or quark into a large bowl and stir in all the other ingredients, beating them together until you've got a nice creamy mixture. Season with salt and pepper. (If you want to add some onion to the pie chop 1 or 2 onions, fry them in a little butter and add them to the mixture when they're tender.)

Set the oven to 200°C (400°F), gas mark 6. Roll out two-thirds of the pastry and use it to line a pie dish. Dampen the edges with cold water. Fill with the cheese mixture then roll out the remaining pastry and put that on top, pressing the edges together. Trim and decorate the pie, making two or three holes in the top to allow the steam to escape. Bake the pie for 35 minutes, until it's golden brown. Serve it while it's all hot and light and flaky.

CHEESE AND ONION PIE

This – very English – pie makes a warming family meal, served with a homemade tomato sauce and vegetables.

SERVES 6 F
450g (1 lb) onions, sliced
sea salt
shortcrust, flaky *or* cream cheese pastry made from
225g (8oz) wholemeal flour (page 240)
225g (8oz) grated cheese
freshly ground black pepper
milk *or* beaten egg to glaze

Cook the onions in boiling salted water until just tender: about 10 minutes. Drain well, cool. Set oven to 220°C (425°F), gas mark 7. Roll out half the pastry and place in 1 litre (1½–1¾ pint) pie dish. Mix onions with cheese and seasoning, spoon on top of pastry. Moisten edges of pastry with cold water. Roll out rest of pastry to cover pie, press edges together, knock up edges and trim if liked. Brush with glaze if you want a shiny finish, then bake for 30–35 minutes until pastry is crisp.

Variation

CHEESE AND ONION ROLL

My mother always used to make this in the form of a roll and it was a great favourite with me and my sister. For this variation, roll the pastry into a large oval, put onions and grated cheese on one half and fold over. Press edges together, prick top, glaze with milk or beaten egg if you like, and bake for 25–30 minutes.

CHICK PEA AND MUSHROOM FLAN

I think this flan is best served hot, with a crisp salad or cooked green vegetable. As with the other flans, different beans can be used according to your inclination and store-cupboard.

SERVES 6 F
shortcrust pastry made from 225g (4oz) wholemeal
flour (page 240)
2 tablespoons olive oil – optional
15g (½oz) butter
1 onion, sliced
1 large garlic clove, crushed
125g (4oz) button mushrooms, wiped and sliced
125g (4oz) chick peas, soaked, cooked and drained *or*
400g (14oz) can, drained
1 tablespoon chopped parsley
sea salt
freshly ground black pepper
1 egg
150ml (5 fl oz) milk
75g (3oz) grated cheese

Preheat the oven to 200°C (400°F), gas mark 6. Roll out the pastry and line a 20cm (8in) flan dish; prick the base and bake in the oven for 15 minutes.

While the flan case is cooking, make the filling by melting the butter in a saucepan and frying the onion and garlic for about 10 minutes, until tender but not browned; then add the mushrooms and cook for a further 3–4 minutes. Stir in the cooked chick peas and the chopped parsley and season with sea salt and freshly ground black pepper. Put the mixture straight into the hot flan case. Beat together the egg and top of the milk, season with sea salt and freshly ground black pepper, and pour into the flan case; scatter the grated cheese over the top. Bake the flan in the preheated oven for 40–50 minutes until it's set and golden brown.

LITTLE CURD CHEESE PIES WITH SPICY TOMATO SAUCE

These little pies with their creamy white filling, crisp wholemeal pastry and tangy tomato sauce, make a wonderful first course.

SERVES 6 F
shortcrust pastry made from 225g (8oz) wholemeal
flour (page 240)
250g (9oz) curd cheese
garlic clove, crushed
sea salt
freshly ground black pepper
1 onion, chopped
2 tablespoons olive oil
450g (1 lb) tomatoes, skinned and chopped
¼–½ teaspoon chilli powder

Set oven to 220°C (425°F), gas mark 7. Roll out pastry, stamp into 24 6cm (2½in) rounds, place half in shallow bun tin. Mix curd cheese with garlic and seasoning, then divide between tartlets. Place remaining circles on top, press together. Make a steam-hole in the top of each pie, then bake for 15 minutes, until crisp and golden brown. Meanwhile make the sauce; fry the onion in the oil for 10 minutes, add the tomatoes and chilli powder. Liquidize, season and reheat. Serve with the pies.

SPICED CHICK PEA AND POTATO PASTIES

These are delicious hot or cold.

MAKES 4 F
1 onion, chopped
2 tablespoons olive oil
225g (8oz) potato, peeled and cut into 6mm (¼in)
dice
1 tablespoon ground coriander
1 teaspoon ground cumin
125g (4oz) chick peas, soaked and cooked or 400g
(14oz) can
sea salt
freshly ground black pepper
shortcrust pastry made from 225g (8oz) wholemeal
flour, page 240
beaten egg to glaze

Fry onion in oil for 5 minutes, then add potato and spices. Cook gently, covered, for 10–15 minutes, until potatoes are just tender, stirring often. Drain chick peas and add to potato mixture, season to taste. Leave on one side until cool. Set oven to 200°C (400°F), gas mark 6. Divide pastry into four pieces; roll each into a circle 15cm (6in) across. Spoon a quarter of chick pea mixture into centre, fold up pastry and press together edges. Brush with glaze, then place on baking sheet; bake for 20–25 minutes.

HARICOT BEAN FLAN

Serve this tasty and filling flan hot with a crisp salad or lightly cooked vegetables.

SERVES 4 F
shortcrust pastry made from 125g (4oz) wholemeal
flour (page 240)
1 onion, chopped
25g (1oz) butter
125g (4oz) haricot beans, soaked and cooked or 400g
(14oz) can cannellini beans, drained
125g (4oz) well-flavoured Cheddar cheese
1 egg
150ml (5 fl oz) creamy milk
1 teaspoon dry mustard
sea salt
freshly ground black pepper
2 tomatoes, sliced

Set oven to 200°C (400°F), gas mark 6. Roll out pastry and line a 20cm (8in) flan tin. Prick base and bake for 15–20 minutes. Fry onion in butter for 10 minutes then pour into hot flan case. Reduce oven setting to 180°C (350°F), gas mark 4. Drain beans thoroughly. Arrange beans and cheese evenly in flan. Whisk together the egg, milk, mustard and seasoning. Pour into flan, then arrange tomato slices on top. Bake for 35–40 minutes, until set.

HARICOT, PEPPER AND TOMATO FLAN

This is another tasty mixture. It's lovely with a bowl of crisp, mixed salad or with cooked green beans or buttery young carrots. Other types of beans can also be used for this flan – cannellini beans, butter beans, flageolet beans and red kidney beans are all suitable.

SERVES 6 F
shortcrust pastry made from 125g (4oz) wholemeal flour (page 240)
25g (1oz) butter
1 onion, peeled and sliced
1 garlic clove, crushed
1 medium-sized green pepper, de-seeded and sliced
2 tomatoes, skinned and sliced
½ teaspoon dried basil
125g (4oz) haricot beans, soaked, cooked and drained or use 400g (14oz) can cannellini beans, drained
sea salt
freshly ground black pepper
1 egg
150ml (5 fl oz) top of the milk

Preheat oven to 220°C (425°F), gas mark 7. Roll out the pastry and line an 20cm (8in) flan dish. Prick the base and bake the flan in the oven for about 15 minutes, until crisp. Reduce heat to 180°C (350°F), gas mark 4.

Meanwhile make the filling. Melt the butter in a medium-sized saucepan and fry the onion, garlic and green pepper for 10 minutes. Remove from the heat and add the tomatoes, basil and haricot beans. Season with sea salt and freshly ground black pepper and pour this mixture into the hot flan case.

Beat together the egg and the top of the milk, season it with sea salt and freshly ground black pepper and then pour it carefully into the flan case. Bake for 40–50 minutes, until set and golden. Serve hot or cold.

LEEK LATTICE FLAN

This is made in a square tin, to accommodate the shape of the leeks; the flan can be cut before serving and the squares arranged on a warmed plate.

SERVES 6 F
Shortcrust pastry made from 225g (8oz) wholemeal flour (page 240)
3 tablespoons olive oil – optional
8 thin leeks, washed and trimmed
sea salt
freshly ground black pepper
300ml (11 fl oz) soured cream or thick natural yoghurt
2 egg yolks or 1 egg
1 tablespoon chopped parsley

Set oven to 200°C (400°F), gas mark 6. Roll out pastry and line a 20cm (8in) square tin. Cut trimmings into long strips, wrap in foil. Bake flan in oven for 15–20 minutes, until pastry feels firm to a light touch. Brush pastry with very hot oil when it comes out of the oven as described on page 242, to 'waterproof' it if desired.

Trim leeks to fit flan, then cook them whole in boiling salted water until tender: 15–20 minutes. Drain well, arrange side by side in flan case, sprinkle with salt and pepper. Whisk cream or yoghurt with egg yolks, parsley and seasoning, and pour over leeks. Arrange reserved pastry strips in lattice over top. Reduce oven setting to 190°C (375°F), gas mark 5. Bake flan in centre of oven for 35–40 minutes, until set.

LEEK PIE (1)

Thick cream is traditionally used for this delicious Cornish pie. Thinking of all those calories, I make a lighter version, which is also excellent.

SERVES 4–6 F
1kg (2¼ lb) leeks
sea salt
freshly ground black pepper
flaky or puff pastry made from 175g (6oz) wholemeal flour (page 240)
150ml (5 fl oz) single cream
2 egg yolks
milk or beaten egg to glaze

Wash and trim leeks, cut into 1cm (½in) lengths. Boil in salted water until just tender: 20–30 minutes. Drain well, season with salt and pepper, place in a 1 litre (1½–1¾ pint) pie dish and leave to cool. Set oven to 220°C (425°F), gas mark 7. Roll pastry, place on top of pie dish but do not dampen edges. Trim and finish as described on page 241. Bake pie for 25 minutes until crust is golden brown and crisp. Reduce oven setting to 170°C (325°F), gas mark 3. Remove pie from oven, slip knife under crust and carefully remove. Whisk cream with egg yolks and seasoning, pour over leeks. Replace crust and bake for further 25 minutes.

LEEK PIE (2)

Here is another version of this traditional pie, made with wholemeal shortcrust pastry. In this recipe the method of making the pie differs a little from the traditional one. Instead of baking the leeks under the pie crust then carefully removing it and pouring in the cream, which is a bit tricky with light, crumbly, wholemeal pastry, I find it best to boil the leeks first, then mix them with the cream, cover with pastry and bake for about 20–25 minutes until the pastry is golden and the filling set. If you're using cream, serve with a fresh salad or steamed vegetables and fruit for pudding, and keep the rest of the day's eating low in fat.

SERVES 4 [F]
1 kilo (2¼ lb) leeks
25g (1oz) grated Parmesan cheese
150ml (5 fl oz) Cornish cream (*or* use double cream for an extra special treat, *or* low-fat quark *or* thick natural yoghurt for a less rich, healthier dish)
2 eggs, beaten
sea salt
freshly ground black pepper
shortcrust pastry made from 175g (6oz) wholemeal flour (page 240)
a little beaten egg – optional

Wash the leeks and cut them into 2.5cm (1in) pieces. Put them into a large saucepan, cover them with cold water and bring to the boil. Simmer the leeks gently for 5–10 minutes, until they're tender, then drain them very well in a colander, using a spoon to press out all the water. On a lightly floured board roll the pastry out big enough to fit your pie dish. Set oven to 200°C (400°F), gas mark 6.

Mix the leeks with the Parmesan cheese, the cream, low-fat quark or yoghurt, eggs, and salt and pepper to taste. Put the mixture into the pie dish and cover with the pastry, trimming it to fit and decorating it as you fancy. Brush it over with a little beaten egg for a shiny finish. Bake the pie for 20–25 minutes until the pastry is golden brown and cooked. Serve immediately.

LENTIL AND GREEN PEPPER FLAN

Apart from its pleasant flavour, the green pepper looks attractive in this flan because it contrasts well with the colour of the lentils.

SERVES 6 [F]
shortcrust pastry made from 125g (4oz) wholemeal flour (page 240)
2 tablespoons olive oil – optional
175g (6oz) split red lentils
350ml (12 fl oz) water *or* unsalted stock
1 onion, peeled and chopped
1 garlic clove, crushed
15g (½oz) butter
1 green pepper
125g (4oz) grated cheese
1 tablespoon tomato purée
1 egg
sea salt
freshly ground black pepper

Set the oven to 200°C (400°F), gas mark 6. Roll out the pastry and line a 20cm (8in) flan dish; prick the base and bake in the oven for 15–20 minutes, or until set and golden brown. Brush it with hot oil as soon as you take it out of the oven to prevent it getting soggy, as described on page 242, if you like. Turn the oven down to 180°C (350°F), gas mark 4.

Wash and pick over the lentils, then put them into a saucepan with the water or stock and simmer gently until tender – 20–30 minutes. Fry the onion and garlic in the butter, without browning, for about 5 minutes. While that's happening, wash the green pepper and slice it into thin rings, discarding the seeds. Add it to the onions and garlic in the saucepan and cook for about 5 minutes, then add the onion and pepper mixture to the cooked lentils, together with the grated cheese, tomato purée, egg and sea salt and freshly ground black pepper to taste. Spread the mixture into the prepared flan case and bake in the oven for about 40 minutes.

LENTIL, TOMATO AND MUSHROOM FLAN

This flan is nice hot or cold; if we're having it hot I sometimes serve a parsley sauce which seems to go well with it.

SERVES 6 [F]
shortcrust pastry made from 125g (4oz) wholemeal flour (page 240)
2 tablespoons olive oil – optional
175g (6oz) split red lentils
350ml (12 fl oz) unsalted stock *or* water
1 large onion, peeled and chopped
15g (½oz) butter
125g (4oz) mushrooms, wiped and sliced
1 tablespoon chopped parsley
125g (4oz) grated cheese
1 egg
sea salt
freshly ground black pepper
2 tomatoes

Preheat the oven to 200°C (400°F), gas mark 7. Make and bake flan case as described in previous recipe. Turn the oven down to 180°C (350°F), gas mark 4.

Wash and pick over the lentils, then put them into a saucepan with the stock or water and cook until they're tender and have absorbed all the water – 20–30 minutes.

Fry the onion in the butter in a medium-sized saucepan for 10 minutes, but don't brown it, then add the mushrooms and cook for another 3–4 minutes. Stir in the cooked lentils, parsley, grated cheese, egg and plenty of seasoning. Spoon the mixture into the cooked flan case and smooth the top. Slice the tomatoes and arrange them on the top of the flan. Bake in the oven for about 40 minutes – watch it towards the end so that it doesn't get too dry.

LENTIL AND TOMATO PIE

SERVES 4–6 [F]
1 large onion, chopped
15g (½oz) butter
1 large garlic clove, crushed
175g (6oz) split red lentils, washed
350ml (12 fl oz) unsalted stock *or* water
2 tomatoes, skinned and chopped
75g (3oz) grated cheese
1 teaspoon dried basil
1 tablespoon lemon juice
1 egg
sea salt
freshly ground black pepper
shortcrust pastry made from 225g (8oz) wholemeal flour (page 240)
beaten egg

First make the filling: fry the onion in the butter in a good-sized saucepan until it's golden and beginning to soften, about 5–6 minutes, then add the split red lentils and garlic and stir for a moment or two before adding the stock or water. Bring the mixture up to the boil, half-cover with a lid and simmer for about 20 minutes, until the lentils are soft and pale golden. Remove the saucepan from the heat and add the tomatoes, cheese, basil, lemon juice, egg and sea salt and freshly ground black pepper to taste. Leave the mixture to cool.

Preheat the oven to 200°C (400°F), gas mark 6. Roll out about two-thirds of the pastry and use to line a 20cm (8in) flan dish or sandwich tin. Roll the remainder into a circle to fit the top of the dish.

Spread the lentil mixture into the pastry case. Dampen the edges of the pastry with a little cold water, then put the circle of pastry on top and press down lightly, crimping the edges. Prick the top and brush with a little beaten egg if you want a shiny finish. Bake the pie in the oven for about 40 minutes, until the pastry is golden brown and crisp.

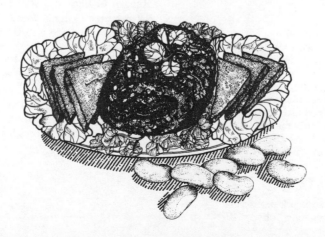

LETTUCE, PEA AND SPRING ONION FLAN

A most delicious blend of flavours and textures; serve with a fresh tomato salad for a light summer lunch.

SERVES 4–6 F
shortcrust pastry made from 125g (4oz) wholemeal flour (page 240)
2 tablespoons olive oil – optional
6 spring onions, chopped
½ lettuce, shredded
125g (4oz) shelled fresh peas or frozen *petit pois*
25g (1oz) butter
6 sprigs mint, chopped'
150ml (5 fl oz) single cream or milk
1 egg yolk
sea salt
freshly ground black pepper

Set oven to 200°C (400°F), gas mark 6. Roll out pastry, line a 20cm (8in) flan tin, prick base and trim edges. Bake for 15–20 minutes, until pastry is set and feels firm to a light touch. Brush base of flan with hot oil (as described on page 242) when it comes out of the oven to keep it crisp.

While flan case is cooking, fry the spring onions, lettuce and peas gently in the butter for 2–3 minutes. Remove from heat, mix in mint, cream, egg and seasoning; pour into flan case. Reduce oven setting to 190°C (375°F), gas mark 5 and bake for 30–35 minutes.

MARROW, GINGER AND CASHEW NUT FLAN

An unusual late-summer flan with a pleasant tang. Nice with jacket potatoes and a salad for an early autumn lunch.

SERVES 4–6
shortcrust pastry made from 125g (4oz) wholemeal flour (page 240)
2 tablespoons olive oil – optional
1 onion, chopped
15g (½oz) butter
450g (1 lb) marrow, weighed after peeling and dicing
1 garlic clove, crushed
walnut-sized piece fresh ginger, grated
¼–½ teaspoon chilli powder
150ml (5 fl oz) milk
1 egg
sea salt
freshly ground black pepper
50g (2oz) cashew nuts, chopped

Set oven to 200°C (400°F), gas mark 6. Roll out pastry and line a 20cm (8in) flan tin, trim edges, prick base. Bake for 15–20 minutes, until pastry feels firm. Brush base of flan with hot oil to seal base and keep it crisp, as described on page 242, if liked. To make filling, fry onion in butter for 5 minutes. Add marrow, garlic, ginger and chilli and fry for 5–6 minutes. Spoon into flan case. Whisk milk and egg, add seasoning. Pour into flan, sprinkle with cashew nuts. Reduce oven setting to 190°C (375°F), gas mark 5. Bake for 35–40 minutes.

MUSHROOM AND EGG PASTIES

The wholemeal pastry used for these pasties has a nutty flavour and texture which contrasts well with the creamy filling and makes white pastry taste like old cardboard by comparison.

MAKES 8
50g (2oz) butter
125g (4oz) mushrooms, sliced
50g (2oz) 85 per cent wholemeal flour
425ml (15 fl oz) skimmed milk
4 hardboiled eggs, finely chopped
sea salt
freshly ground black pepper
mace
1 tablespoon chopped parsley
shortcrust pastry made from 350g (12oz) wholemeal flour (page 240)
beaten eggs to glaze

Start by making the filling. Melt the butter and fry the mushrooms until tender, then add the flour. When mixture froths, draw off heat and add milk. Return to heat and stir until thickened; simmer for 10 minutes to cook flour, then add hardboiled eggs, salt, pepper, mace to taste and parsley. Leave to get quite cold.

Set oven to 200°C (400°F), gas mark 6. Divide pastry into 8 pieces, roll each into a circle 15cm (6 in) across. Place a good heap of the filling on each, damp edges and gather up sides to centre, Cornish pasty style. Brush with the beaten egg and bake for 20–25 minutes until golden and crisp.

ASPARAGUS AND EGG PASTIES

Omit mushrooms. Make sauce as above, then add 125–225g (4–8oz) cooked, chopped asparagus to the sauce, together with the eggs.

LEEK AND EGG PASTIES

Omit mushrooms. Make sauce using the butter and flour, as above. Add 125–225g (4–8oz) cooked, chopped leeks to the sauce along with the eggs.

MUSHROOM FLAN

Creamy, light and delicately flavoured, I think this is my favourite flan. It is delicious for a special lunch or supper. As it is rich I try to plan the rest of the meal accordingly: a simple cooked vegetable or salad to accompany the flan and a fresh-tasting fruity pudding to follow it.

SERVES 4–6 F
wholemeal pastry made from 125g (4oz) wholemeal
flour (page 240)
1 onion, chopped
1 garlic clove, crushed
50g (2oz) butter
225g (8oz) button mushrooms
1 heaped tablespoon chopped parsley
2 eggs
150ml (5 fl oz) single cream *or* milk for everyday
sea salt
freshly ground black pepper
grated nutmeg

Place a baking sheet in the centre of the oven and set the temperature to 200°C (400°F), gas mark 6. Roll out the pastry and use to line a 20cm (8in) flan tin. Prick the base then put the flan into the oven on the baking sheet and bake for 15–20 minutes, until it's firm and golden. Reduce the oven heat to 180°C (350°F), gas mark 4.

While the flan is cooking make the filling. Peel and chop the onion, peel and crush the garlic and cook them together in the butter for 10 minutes, until the onion is soft but not browned. Meanwhile wash and slice the mushrooms: add these to the onion and garlic and fry for a further 3 minutes or so without a lid on the saucepan. Pour this hot mixture straight into the flan case when it comes out

of the oven, so that the hot fat 'seals' the base and keeps it crisp (page 242). Sprinkle with chopped parsley. Put the egg yolks into a medium-sized bowl and whisk them with the cream or milk. Season with salt and pepper to taste, then pour into the flan case. Bake in the oven for about 30 minutes, until the creamy mixture is set. Serve hot or warm.

MUSHROOM FLAN WITH TOFU

The custard part of this is made from tofu (soya bean curd, page 203) yet it is almost identical to a light custard made from eggs and cream. It's good served with new potatoes and a salad of watercress and lettuce or frozen peas.

SERVES 4 AS A MAIN DISH
shortcrust pastry made from 125g (4oz) wholemeal
flour
1 onion, peeled and finely chopped
15g (½oz) butter
1 garlic clove, crushed – optional
125g (4oz) white button mushrooms, washed and
thinly sliced
300g (10½oz) packet soft tofu
sea salt
freshly ground black pepper
25g (1oz) ground almonds

Set the oven to 200°C (400°F), gas mark 6. Roll out pastry to fit a 20cm (8in) round flan tin; prick base, trim edges. Bake for 15–20 minutes.

Meanwhile, fry the onion gently in the butter for 7 minutes, then put in the garlic and mushrooms and cook for a further 3 minutes. Remove from the heat, then stir in the tofu. Season with salt and pepper. Spoon into flan case, level top, sprinkle with the ground almonds. Put the flan into the oven, reduce heat to 190°C (375°F), gas mark 5. Bake for 25–30 minutes until the filling is set and puffed up. Serve immediately.

MUSHROOM PATTIES WITH YOGHURT AND SPRING ONION SAUCE

I make these in shallow bun tins – the kind with a rounded base that you make jam tarts or mince pies in. They are lovely as a starter, served warm with the chilled creamy sauce, or for a party, without the sauce.

SERVES 6 F
15g (½oz) butter
1 tablespoon olive oil
1 medium-size onion, peeled and chopped
1 large garlic clove, peeled and crushed
450g (1 lb) button mushrooms, washed and sliced
1 tablespoon fresh parsley, chopped
sea salt
freshly ground black pepper
cheese shortcrust pastry made from 225g (8oz)
wholemeal flour (page 240)
275ml (10 fl oz) natural yoghurt
3 tablespoons single cream
3 tablespoons finely chopped spring onions
sea salt
freshly ground black pepper

First prepare the filling. Heat the butter and oil in a large saucepan and fry the onion for about 5 minutes, until it is beginning to soften, then put in the garlic and mushrooms and fry for a further 20–25 minutes, until the mushrooms are very tender and all the liquid has boiled away, leaving them dry. Add the parsley and salt and pepper to taste. Leave them on one side to cool.

Meanwhile make the pastry, roll out, and use a round cutter to stamp out twenty-four circles to fit the twelve shallow tartlets. Grease the tin very well. Use half the pastry circles to line the tartlets. Set the oven to 200°C (400°F), gas mark 6.

Put a heaped teaspoon of fried mushrooms into each pastry case and put one of the remaining pastry circles on top, pressing down lightly; make a hole in the top of each to let the steam out. Bake the patties for about 15 minutes, until they are golden-brown.

While the patties are cooking, make the sauce by mixing the yoghurt with the cream and spring onions and seasoning with salt and pepper.

When the patties are done, carefully remove them from the tin and serve hot, with the sauce.

The patties will freeze, but not the sauce.

DEEP DISH MUSHROOM PIE

My aim with this was to make a pie which could be cut into slices for a party or buffet, as you might cut up a long meat pie. It looks very attractive, especially if you can make it in a long, thin loaf tin. I have one with collapsible sides which is 7.5cm (3in) deep with an inside base measurement of 25 × 8cm (9¾ × 3¼in) and a top measurement of 27.5 × 10.5cm (10¾ × 4¼in), and that is ideal, but the capacity is the same as that of a standard 900g (2 lb) loaf tin, so you could use that instead, lined with greased foil to help ease the pie out after baking.

SERVES 10
25g (1oz) butter
1 large onion, peeled and chopped
2 large garlic cloves, peeled and crushed
350g (12oz) button mushrooms, wiped
275g (10oz) ground almonds
125g (4oz) cheese, grated
2 eggs, beaten
1 tablespoon lemon juice
3 tablespoons fresh parsley, chopped
1 teaspoon ground mace
freshly ground black pepper
shortcrust pastry made from 350g (12oz) wholemeal
flour (page 240)
3 or 4 hardboiled eggs – optional: these go down the
centre of the loaf and the number needed depends
on the length of both the tin and the eggs, so try
them first
beaten egg to glaze

To make the filling, melt the butter in a large saucepan and fry the onion for 10 minutes until soft but not browned; add the garlic and fry for a further minute or two. Then take the saucepan off the heat and stir in all the remaining ingredients except the hardboiled eggs. Season with salt and pepper. Cool.

Set the oven to 200°C (400°F), gas mark 6, and if possible place a heavy baking sheet on the top shelf to heat up with the oven. Roll out three quarters of the pastry and ease it into the loaf tin which has been well greased if it's a collapsible one or lined with well-greased foil if not. This is not an easy process as the pastry is fragile, and I find it usually breaks and has to go in in several separate pieces – this doesn't matter; just patch it up and press it together. Spoon in half the filling, then put the hardboiled eggs on top of this, if you're using them, and cover with the remaining mixture. Roll the last piece of pastry into a rectangle to fit the top of the pie and press into position. Neaten and trim the edges, decorate with the pastry trimmings, brush with beaten egg and make several holes in the top to allow the steam to escape.

Bake the pie for 30 minutes in the pre-heated oven, then turn the oven setting down to 180°C (350°F), gas mark 4, and bake for a further 30 minutes. Leave the pie to cool in the tin, then remove it carefully. It slices best when chilled a little.

MUSHROOM PUDDING

This is a steamed pudding, rather like a vegetarian steak and kidney pudding. It's very easy to do and makes a warming meal in winter. I like to serve it with mashed potatoes and the red cabbage on page 131.

SERVES 4 F
cheese shortcrust pastry made from 175g (6oz)
wholemeal flour (page 240)
350g (12oz) dark mushrooms, wiped and sliced
1 onion, peeled and chopped
1 teaspoon tomato purée
1 small garlic clove, peeled and crushed
sea salt
freshly ground black pepper
1 teaspoon yeast extract
2 tablespoons hot water

First make the pastry as described on page 240. Leave to chill while you grease an 850ml (1½ pint) pudding basin and make the filling. Put the mushrooms into a bowl and mix with the remaining ingredients, softening the yeast extract in the hot water. Roll out two thirds of the pastry and use to line the pudding basin; spoon the mushroom mixture into this, then cover with the rest of the pastry, rolled out to fit the top. Trim edges and prick the top with a fork. Cover with a piece of foil, secured with string. Steam the pudding for 2½ hours (or 1 hour in a pressure cooker). When it's done, slip a knife down the sides of the bowl to loosen the pudding, then turn out onto a warmed serving dish.

MUSHROOM VOL AU VENTS

Serve these as a first course, or as a light lunch or supper, with ratatouille and a green salad.

MAKES 8, SERVES 4
500g (1 lb 2oz) packet frozen puff pastry
450g (1 lb) button mushrooms, washed and chopped
25g (1oz) butter
2 teaspoons cornflour
275ml (10 fl oz) milk or single cream
sea salt
freshly ground black pepper
grated nutmeg

Set oven to 200°C (400°F), gas mark 6. Using short strokes, in one direction only, roll pastry out 1cm (½in) thick. Cut into rounds with a lightly floured 5cm (2in) cutter. With a cutter one size smaller, mark each circle with another, inner circle. Place on a damp baking sheet; bake at top of oven for 30 minutes. Meanwhile fry mushrooms in butter for 5 minutes; add cornflour and cream, stir until thickened. Remove from heat; season. Remove tops of vol au vents, scoop out and discard inner pastry layers; fill with mushroom mixture. Reheat for 10–15 minutes before eating, but do not fill in advance or cases will go soggy.

FLAKY MUSHROOM ROLL

This is good served with the yoghurt and fresh herb sauce described on page 67.

SERVES 6 F
15g (½oz) butter
1 onion, chopped
1 garlic clove, crushed
225g (8oz) mushrooms, washed and chopped
2 tablespoons chopped parsley
125g (4oz) (raw weight) brown rice, cooked
sea salt
freshly ground black pepper
rough puff or cream cheese pastry made from 225g
(8oz) flour (page 240)
milk or beaten egg to glaze

Heat butter in a large saucepan and fry onion for 5 minutes; add garlic and mushrooms, cook for a further 20–35 minutes, until all liquid has boiled away. Remove from heat, add parsley, rice and seasoning. Cool. Set oven to 220°C (425°F), gas mark 7. Divide pastry in half, roll each into a rectangle 30 × 26cm (12 × 10in). Spoon mushroom mixture on to one half, dampen pastry edges. Fold second piece in half lengthwise. Make diagonal slashes about 1cm (½in) apart to within 1cm (½in) of fold; open out and place on top of mixture, press down. Place on baking sheet. Brush with glaze, bake for 30 minutes.

MUSHROOM, TOMATO AND HARICOT VOL AU VENTS

SERVES 4

500g (1 lb 2oz) frozen puff pastry
1 large onion, chopped
1 rounded tablespoon flour
4 tablespoons double cream
125g (4oz) haricot beans, cooked and drained
2 garlic cloves, crushed
15g (½oz) butter
225g (8oz) button mushrooms, wiped and sliced
225g (8oz) canned tomatoes
a little cold water or stock
1 tablespoon chopped parsley
sea salt
freshly ground black pepper

Set oven to 200°C (400°F), gas mark 6. Make the vol au vent cases as described in the previous recipe.

While the vol au vent cases are cooking, make the filling. Fry the onion and garlic gently in the oil in a large saucepan for 10 minutes, then add the mushrooms and cook for a further 4–5 minutes. Drain the tomatoes; measure the liquid and make it up to 275ml (10 fl oz) with some cold water or stock. Add the tomatoes and liquid to the mushrooms and onion in the saucepan and simmer for 15 minutes, without a lid on the saucepan. Blend the flour smoothly with the cream and add to the onion mixture, together with the beans, parsley and sea salt and freshly ground black pepper to taste. Cook gently for 10 minutes, stirring often. Check seasoning.

Remove tops of vol au vent cases; spoon the bean mixture into the vol au vent cases and replace lids. Serve warm.

NUTTY SLICE

This quick-to-make, nourishing, savoury pastry is good for picnics and lunch boxes.

SERVES 4 F

shortcrust pastry made from 125g (4oz) wholemeal
flour (page 240)
2 tablespoons chutney or pickle
125g (4oz) raw peanuts or hazel nuts, roasted in their
skins for 10 minutes at 200°C (400°F), gas mark 6
1 onion, peeled
3 tomatoes, skinned
sea salt
freshly ground black pepper

Set oven to 220°C (425°F), gas mark 7. Roll pastry into a rectangle, spread with chutney. Blend peanuts, onion and tomatoes together in food processor; or grate or very finely chop peanuts and onion, chop tomato and mix together to make a paste. Spread mixture over half pastry, cover with other half. Press edges together, prick top. Place on baking sheet, bake for 30 minutes. Serve hot or cold, in slices.

ONION FLAN

This is a good flan with a creamy onion filling and crisp pastry base.

SERVES 4–6 F

shortcrust pastry made from 125g (4oz) wholemeal
flour (page 240)
450g (1 lb) onions, peeled and thinly sliced
25g (1oz) butter
50g (2oz) grated cheese
4 egg yolks or 2 whole eggs
150ml (5 fl oz) milk or single cream
½ teaspoon mustard powder
sea salt
freshly ground black pepper
1 tomato, sliced, to decorate the top

Put a baking sheet in the centre of the oven and set the temperature to 200°C (400°F), gas mark 6. Roll the pastry out on a lightly floured board and use it to line a 20cm (8in) flan tin. Trim the edges, prick the base, put the flan on the baking sheet in the oven and bake it for 15–20 minutes, until it's crisp and golden brown. Turn the oven down to 180°C (350°F), gas mark 4.

To make the filling fry the onions lightly in the butter until they're soft and golden – about 10 minutes. Put hot onions and their fat straight into the flan case when it comes out of the oven. The hot fat will 'seal' the pastry and keep it crisp. Sprinkle the grated cheese on top. Whisk together the eggs or egg yolks and the milk or cream, mustard and seasoning. Pour this mixture into the flan case. Arrange the tomato slices on top. Put the flan into the oven on the baking sheet and bake for about 30 minutes, until the filling is set.

This flan is delicious served hot with some tender French beans, courgettes or a crisp salad. It also makes a good first course before a vegetable-based meal.

PEANUT, GINGER AND GREEN PEPPER FLAN

I admit this is an unusual combination of ingredients, but it does work, resulting in a delicious flan.

SERVES 4–6
shortcrust pastry made from 125g (4oz) wholemeal
flour (page 240)
4 tablespoons olive oil
1 onion, chopped
50g (2oz) green pepper, de-seeded and chopped
1 garlic clove, crushed
walnut-sized piece fresh ginger, grated
1 tomato, skinned, seeded and chopped
175g (6oz) crunchy peanut butter
1 egg
sea salt
freshly ground black pepper

Make a 20cm (8in) flan case as described in previous recipe. Heat 2 tablespoons of the oil and add it to the baked flan case as it comes out of the oven to keep pastry crisp (page 242). Fry onion in the butter and remaining oil for 5 minutes, then add pepper, garlic, ginger and tomato and fry for a further 5–6 minutes. Remove from heat, mix in peanut butter, egg and seasoning. Spoon into flan case. Reduce oven setting to 190°C (375°F), gas mark 5. Bake for 25–30 minutes, until set.

QUICK NON-YEAST PIZZA

A very useful recipe for those emergencies when you find yourself having to rustle up food unexpectedly, because it's quick to make and uses basic store-cupboard ingredients. Serve with a green salad, which you can prepare while the pizza is cooking, and fresh fruit to follow.

SERVES 4 F
225g (8oz) self-raising 85% wholemeal flour
2 teaspoons baking powder
½ teaspoon salt
50g (2oz) butter
25g (1oz) grated cheese
8 tablespoons milk
2 onions, chopped
2 tablespoons olive oil
1 garlic clove, crushed
2 tablespoons tomato purée
1 teaspoon oregano
sea salt
freshly ground black pepper
50g (2oz) cheese, grated

Set oven to 220°C (425°F), gas mark 7. Sift the flour, baking powder and salt into a bowl. Rub in the butter, then add the grated cheeese and the milk to make a soft but not sticky dough. Knead the dough lightly on a floured board then leave it to rest for a minute or two while you make the pizza topping.

Peel and chop the onion and fry it in the oil in a large saucepan for 10 minutes, until it's soft but not browned, then remove from the heat and stir in the garlic and tomato purée.

Roll the dough into a piece to fit a swiss roll tin. Press down and prick with a fork. Spread the tomato mixture over the pizza. Sprinkle with oregano, salt and pepper and the cheese. Bake for 20–25 minutes.

RATATOUILLE FLAN

This is good made with a shortcrust pastry flavoured with grated cheese: use 50–125g (2–4oz) cheese.

SERVES 4–6 F
shortcrust pastry made from 125g (4oz) wholemeal
flour (page 240)
4 tablespoons olive oil
1 onion, chopped
125g (4oz) aubergine, diced
125g (4oz) courgette, diced
1 small red pepper, de-seeded and chopped
1 garlic clove, crushed
2 tomatoes, skinned, de-seeded and chopped
150ml (5 fl oz) soured cream
1 egg
sea salt
freshly ground black pepper

Make a 20cm (8in) flan case as in previous recipe, adding hot oil to baked flan case as described. While flan case is cooking, fry onion in the oil for 5 minutes, then add aubergine, courgette, pepper and garlic and fry for a further 10 minutes. Add tomato, cream, egg and seasoning; spoon into flan case. Reduce oven setting to 190°C (375°F), gas mark 5. Bake flan in centre of oven for 35–40 minutes, until set.

RED BEAN AND TOMATO FLAN

The red beans, tomatoes and parsley make this a colourful flan. I think it's nice made with soured cream, but you could use single cream or top-of-the-milk. This flan is lovely warm, with a green salad.

SERVES 6 F

shortcrust pastry made from 125g (4oz) wholemeal
flour (page 240)
2 tablespoons oil – optional
1 onion, peeled and chopped
1 garlic clove, crushed
2 tablespoons olive oil
3 tomatoes, skinned and chopped
125g (4oz) red kidney beans, soaked, cooked and
drained or 400g (14oz) can, drained
150ml (5 fl oz) soured cream
1 egg
½ teaspoon paprika pepper
pinch chilli powder
sea salt
freshly ground black pepper
1 tablespoon chopped parsley

Preheat the oven to 200°C (400°F), gas mark 6. Use the pastry to line a 20cm (8in) flan dish. Prick the base of the flan and bake in the oven for 15 minutes. Remove the flan from the oven, have the 2 tablespoons of oil smoking hot, brush over base of flan case to 'seal' base and keep it crisp. Turn the oven down to 180°C (350°F), gas mark 4.

Next, make the filling. Fry the onion and garlic in the oil in a medium-sized saucepan for 10 minutes. Remove the saucepan from the heat and add the tomatoes and beans. You can mash the beans a little as you mix them in, or leave them whole, whichever you prefer. In a small bowl, beat together the soured cream and the egg, then stir them into the bean mixture, together with the paprika, a good pinch of chilli powder and sea salt and freshly ground black pepper to taste. Pour the mixture into the flan case and sprinkle with the chopped parsley. Bake the flan in the oven for 35–40 minutes, until it's set.

SAMOSAS

These little Indian pasties with their spicy vegetable filling are delicious as a first course, or for a main meal with some Indian curry sauce and perhaps a curried vegetable or side salad. They are also nice cold with some yoghurt or mayonnaise to dip them into and a crisp salad.

SERVES 6
1 large onion
1 large garlic clove
25g (1oz) *ghee or* butter
1 teaspoon mustard seed
1 teaspoon ground ginger
1 teaspoon ground cumin
1 teaspoon ground coriander
900g (2 lb) cooked mixed vegetables: potatoes, carrots
and frozen peas, or whatever is available
sea salt
freshly ground black pepper
225g (8oz) plain wholemeal flour
½ teaspoon sea salt
½ teaspoon baking powder
50g (2oz) *ghee or* butter
6–7 tablespoons cold water
oil for deep *or* shallow-frying

First make the filling. Peel and chop the onion, peel and crush the garlic. Fry them gently in the fat for 10 minutes then stir in the spices. Mix well, then add the cooked vegetables and turn these gently with a spoon so that they all get coated with the spicy onion and oil. Season with salt and pepper then let the mixture cool.

To make the pastry sift the flour, salt and baking powder into a bowl, together with any residue of bran, and rub in the *ghee* or butter and enough water to make a soft but not sticky dough. Knead the dough for 5 minutes, then divide it into 16 pieces. Roll each piece into a ball then use a rolling pin to roll each into a circle about 15cm (6in) in diameter. Cut the circles in half to get 32 half circles. Put a heaped teaspoonful of the filling on to each half circle of pastry, dampen the edges with a pastry brush dipped in cold water and fold the corners over to make a little triangle-shaped packet, pressing the edges well together. When all the *samosas* are ready, deep or shallow fry them a few at a time until they are golden and crisp. Drain them well and serve them hot or cold.

SAUSAGE ROLLS

This recipe, one of my earliest inventions, was (is) one of the most popular recipes with my readers. These days I have reservations about the amount of fat used in the pastry, but I'm giving the recipe as it stands; keep the rest of the meal and day's eating low in fat, or save the recipe for a special occasion.

SERVES 4 [F]
125g (4oz) ground nuts (hazel nuts, almonds, walnuts or a mixture)
50g (2oz) cooked, mashed potato
2 medium onions, peeled, finely chopped and fried
1 teaspoon yeast extract
1 teaspoon basil
1 egg, beaten
sea salt
freshly ground black pepper

Special cheese pastry
125g (4oz) butter *or* margarine and vegetable fat, mixed
175g (5oz) plain wholemeal flour
1 teaspoon baking powder
75g (3oz) grated cheese
a little sweet chutney

To make the sausages, mix all the ingredients to a fairly stiff consistency. Place small rolls of the mixture on a greased baking sheet and bake in oven at 160°C (325°F), gas mark 3, for 20 minutes.

Meanwhile make the pastry by rubbing the fat into the flour and baking powder and adding the cheese. Roll out carefully (it will be rather tacky) and brush with sweet chutney. Put sausages on the pastry and wrap it round each to form rolls. Increase oven setting to 230°C (450°F), gas mark 8, and bake rolls for 10 minutes. Serve hot or cold, with mixed salad including grated raw carrot, beetroot, turnip or swede and green vegetables available.

SPINACH TART

Chopped green spinach and creamy *fromage blanc* make a lovely, low-fat filling for a flan and go particularly well with the nutty flavour of wholemeal pastry. It's best served hot and is good with tomato and onion salad.

SERVES 4–6 [F]
shortcrust pastry made from 125g (4oz) wholemeal flour (page 240)
2 tablespoons olive oil
300g (11oz) packet frozen, chopped spinach *or* 450g (1 lb) fresh spinach, washed, cooked and finely chopped
75g (3oz) *fromage blanc or* low fat, smooth white cheese
grated nutmeg
sea salt
freshly ground black pepper
25g (1oz) finely grated cheese
1 small tomato

Set oven to 200°C (400°F), gas mark 6. Roll pastry out thinly and line an 18–20cm (7–8in) flan dish or tin; prick base. Bake the flan in the oven for about 15 minutes, until golden and crisp. Give the flan the hot-oil 'waterproofing' treatment (page 242) if desired.

While the flan case is cooking, make the filling. Mix together the spinach, *fromage blanc* or other soft white cheese, a good grating of nutmeg, and some salt and pepper. Spoon the spinach mixture into the flan and smooth the surface; finish with the grated cheese and decorate with the slices of tomato. Return the flan to the oven, reduce setting to 190°C (375°F), gas mark 5, and bake for a further 30 minutes.

SPINACH, ALMOND AND CHEESE FLAN

SERVES 4–6 F
shortcrust pastry made from 125g (4oz) wholemeal
flour (page 240)
2 tablespoons olive oil – optional
450g (1 lb) spinach
15g (½oz) butter
125g (4oz) split blanched almonds, toasted
75g (3oz) grated cheese
1 egg
sea salt
freshly ground black pepper

Set oven to 200°C (400°F), gas mark 6. Use pastry
to make a 20cm (8in) flan case, prick base, bake for
15–20 minutes until base is set and feels firm to a
light touch. Brush with hot oil, as described on page
242, to 'waterproof' base of flan, if liked. Meanwhile
cook spinach in a large saucepan without extra water
for about 10 minutes. Drain and chop, then add
butter, half almonds, half cheese, egg and seasoning.
Mix well, then pour into flan case, spread top level
and sprinkle with remaining cheese and almonds.
Reduce oven setting to 190°C (375°F), gas mark 5.
Bake flan in centre of oven for 35–40 minutes, until
set.

SPINACH PIE

This flaky golden pie makes a delicious first course
or light lunch or supper dish, with a soured cream
sauce (page 64) and salad or cooked vegetables.

SERVES 4–6 F
900g (2 lb) fresh spinach or 450g (1 lb) frozen
bunch spring onions, chopped
125g (4oz) feta or white Cheshire cheese, crumbled
sea salt
freshly ground black pepper
flaky pastry made from 350g (12oz) wholemeal flour
(page 240)
milk or beaten egg to glaze

Wash fresh spinach, cook in a large saucepan without
extra water for about 10 minutes; cook frozen spinach according to instructions on packet. Drain and
chop, add spring onions, cheese and seasoning, then
leave until cold. Set oven to 200°C (400°F), gas
mark 6. Roll out just over half of the pastry and
place in pie tin or dish. Put spinach mixture on top,
moisten edges of pastry with cold water. Roll out
rest of pastry to cover pie, press edges together,
knock up and trim. Brush with glaze if liked. Bake
for 40 minutes.

QUICK SPRING ONION FLAN

Here is another speedily made flan, using spring
onions which are quick to prepare and need no precooking. If you've time to bake the flan case before
adding the filling, of course it's crisper; but either
way this flan is delicious served hot.

SERVES 4–6
shortcrust pastry made from 125g (4oz) wholemeal
flour (page 240)
large bunch spring onions
300ml (11 fl oz) single or soured cream
2 egg yolks
sea salt
freshly ground black pepper

Set oven to 190°C (375°F), gas mark 5. Make pastry
as described on page 240, roll out pastry, line a
20cm (8in) flan tin. Wash, trim and chop spring
onions, place in flan. Whisk cream and egg yolks,
add seasoning. Pour over spring onions. Bake flan
in centre of oven for 45–50 minutes, until set. Serve
at once.

SLIMMER'S FLAN

Although pastry dishes are not normally considered
'slimming', this flan, cut into six pieces, contains
only 270 calories a slice.

SERVES 4–6 F
shortcrust pastry made from 125g (4oz) wholemeal
flour (page 240)
2 tablespoons olive oil – optional
50g (2oz) chopped spring onion
125g (4oz) carrots, coarsely grated
1 tablespoon chopped parsley
50g (2oz) grated cheese
6 tablespoons single cream
1 egg
sea salt
freshly ground black pepper

Set oven to 200°C (400°F), gas mark 6. Make a
20cm (8in) flan case as described in previous recipe.
Mix together spring onion, carrot, parsley and
cheese; spoon into flan case. Whisk cream and egg,
add seasoning. Pour into flan case. Reduce oven
setting to 190°C (375°F), gas mark 5. Bake flan in
centre of oven for 30–35 minutes, until set.

SWEETCORN SOUFFLÉ FLAN

SERVES 4–6
shortcrust pastry made from 125g (4oz) wholemeal
flour (page 240)
300g (11oz) can sweetcorn
just under 275ml (10 fl oz) milk
25g (1oz) butter
25g (1oz) flour
2 eggs, separated
sea salt
freshly ground black pepper
paprika
25–50g (1–2oz) grated cheese

Set oven to 200°C (400°F), gas mark 6. Roll out pastry, line a 20cm (8in) flan tin, trim edges, prick base. Bake for 15–20 minutes, until firm. Reduce oven setting to 190°C (375°F), gas mark 5.

Drain sweetcorn and make the liquid up to 275ml (10 fl oz) with milk. Make a roux by melting the butter and stirring in the flour to make a smooth paste. Remove from heat to stir in the milk, then stir over a gentle heat until thickened. Add egg yolks, sweetcorn and seasoning. Whisk egg whites stiffly and fold into the mixture. Spoon into flan case, scatter with grated cheese and bake for 25 minutes until risen and golden. Serve immediately.

TOMATO FLAN WITH SOURED CREAM AND BASIL

If you're using yoghurt for this, the thick strained, Greek sheep's milk type is best.

SERVES 4–6
450g (1 lb) tomatoes, skinned de-seeded and sliced
sea salt
freshly ground black pepper
shortcrust pastry made from 125g (4oz) wholemeal
flour (page 240)
2 tablespoons olive oil
1 tablespoon chopped basil
300ml (11 fl oz) soured cream *or* thick natural
yoghurt
2 egg yolks

Put the tomatoes into a sieve or colander, sprinkle with salt and pepper and leave on one side. Set oven to 200°C (400°F), gas mark 6. Roll out pastry, line a 20cm (8in) flan tin, prick base. Bake at top of oven for 20 minutes. Heat oil in a small saucepan and as soon as flan case comes out of oven pour hot oil into base. Arrange tomato slices in flan case, sprinkle

with basil. Whisk cream and egg yolks, add seasoning, then pour over tomatoes. Reduce oven setting to 190°C (375°F), gas mark 5. Bake flan in centre of oven for 35–40 minutes, until set.

VEGETABLE FLAN

A favourite flan of my daughter Margaret and her boyfriend!

SERVES 4–6 F
shortcrust pastry made from 125g (4oz) wholemeal
flour (page 240)
2 tablespoons olive oil
600g (1¼ lb) mixed vegetables: carrot, courgette,
onion, cauliflower, leek, as available, sliced
sea salt
25g (1oz) butter
25g (1oz) flour
275ml (10 fl oz) skimmed milk
125g (4oz) grated cheese
½ teaspoon mustard powder
125g (4oz) button mushrooms, sliced
freshly ground black pepper

Set oven to 200°C (400°F), gas mark 6. Make a 20cm (8in) flan case as described in previous recipe. Cook vegetables in a little boiling, salted water until just tender; drain. Melt butter in a pan, add flour, cook for 1–2 minutes, then add milk and stir over heat until thickened. Add half grated cheese, mustard, vegetables and mushrooms. Season, pile into flan case, sprinkle with rest of cheese. Bake for 20–25 minutes, until golden brown.

VEGETABLE AND BUTTER BEAN PIE WITH FLAKY CRUST

Serve this pie with mashed potatoes and a cooked green vegetable for an economical and delicious family meal.

SERVES 4–6 [F]
1 onion, chopped
25g (1oz) butter
450g (1 lb) tomatoes, skinned and chopped
225g (8oz) carrots, scraped and sliced
350g (12oz) leeks, trimmed and sliced
125g (4oz) mushrooms
125g (4oz) butter beans, soaked and cooked *or* 400g (14oz) can
sea salt
freshly ground black pepper
flaky pastry made from 175g (6oz) wholemeal flour (page 240)

Fry the onion in the butter for 5 minutes, then add the tomatoes, carrots, leeks and mushrooms and fry very gently for about 30 minutes, until vegetables are tender. Drain butter beans, add to mixture, together with seasoning. Spoon into 1 litre (1¾ pint) pie dish, cool. Set oven to 220°C (425°F), gas mark 7. Roll pastry, place on top of pie dish, trim and finish as described on page 241. Bake pie for 30 minutes.

DEEP DISH STRIPY VEGETABLE PIE

This idea came to me when I was telling a friend about the deep dish mushroom pie, I'd invented (page 256), and she said why didn't I try a variation of a Cornish pasty, as these, traditionally, are made from root vegetables and do not contain meat. So I used the same deep tin and, so that the pie would look good when sliced, I put the thinly-sliced vegetables into the tin in layers. I was very pleased with the result; the pie looks good and slices well. Other variations are possible; you can add some thin layers of different coloured grated cheeses or some chopped parsley to give a green layer. It's delicious served hot, with some yoghurt and spring onion sauce or lemon mayonnaise.

SERVES 10 [F]
wholemeal pastry made from 350g (12oz) wholemeal flour (page 240)
225g (8oz) swede *or* parsnip, peeled
450g (1 lb) carrots, scraped
225g (8oz) potatoes *or* turnips, peeled
freshly ground black pepper
grated nutmeg

First make the pastry and leave it to chill while you prepare the filling.

To do this, slice the vegetables as thinly as possible, preferably on an electric grater or food processor. Keep the different types separate, covered with water if necessary, until you're ready to use them.

Set the oven to 200°C (400°F), gas mark 6. Roll out the pastry and line the loaf tin as described for the deep dish mushroom pie. Put the sliced swede or parsnip in an even layer in the base of the pie, pressing it down well. Season well with salt, pepper and grated nutmeg. Follow this with a layer of half the carrot, then the potato or turnip, followed by the rest of the carrot, seasoning each layer. Roll the last piece of pastry into a rectangle to fit the top of the pie and press into position. Neaten and trim the edges, decorate with the pastry trimmings, brush with beaten egg and make several holes in the top to allow the steam to escape. Bake the pie for 30 minutes in the pre-heated oven, then turn the oven setting down to 160°C (325°F), gas mark 3, and bake for a further hour, covering the pastry with foil for the last half hour or so if it is getting too brown. Remove the pie from the tin and serve hot; or, if you are going to serve it cold, let it cool in the tin, then remove it carefully. I like it best hot.

WALNUT PÂTÉ EN CROÛTE

I think of this dish now as my Woman's Hour one; it's the one I made in the studio for Christmas and which provoked a record number of requests for the recipe! It makes a delicious main course for a special meal; a moist wine-flavoured pâté in a crisp crust of golden pastry. This can be made in advance (but don't brush with beaten egg) and frozen for up to 4 weeks. It's best to allow to de-frost completely, then brush with the beaten egg just before baking.

SERVES 8–10
15g (½oz) butter
1 onion, peeled and chopped
1 small stick celery, chopped
1 large garlic clove, crushed
1 tomato, skinned and chopped
225g (8oz) unsweetened chestnut purée
175g (6oz) grated cashew nuts
50g (2oz) grated walnuts
125g (4oz) baby button mushrooms, washed and chopped
1 tablespoon brandy
½ teaspoon each paprika, thyme and basil
1 egg *or* 2 egg yolks
sea salt
freshly ground black pepper
225g (8oz) flaky pastry made from 225g (8oz) wholemeal flour (page 240) *or* 450g (1 lb) frozen puff pastry
beaten egg to glaze

Set oven to 220°C (425°F), gas mark 7. To make the filling, melt the butter in a large saucepan and fry the onion, celery and garlic for 10 minutes, until soft. Remove from heat and add the rest of the ingredients, mixing well. Season. Cool. Roll out one third of the pastry to a rectangle 15 × 30cm (6 × 12in). Put filling on top of strip, piling it up into a loaf shape and leaving edges clear. Moisten edges with cold water. Roll out rest of pastry to an oblong to fit on top. Place over filling, press down gently, trim edges. Decorate with pastry trimmings, brush with beaten egg. Bake for about 30 minutes. Serve with vegetarian gravy or wine sauce, Brussels sprouts, bread sauce, cranberry sauce, new potatoes. It's also delicious cold, with a sauce made by adding chopped fresh herbs to natural yoghurt or soured cream.

11

CHEESE, EGG AND PANCAKE DISHES

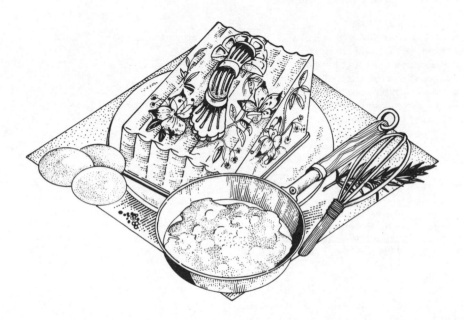

These are useful sources of protein for lacto-veg-etarians, though we do not use cheese and eggs nearly as extensively as many non-vegetarians think we do. In spite of what I say in my introduction, when a vegetarian has a meal at a restaurant and asks for a non-meat alternative to the main course, the chances are we'll be offered either a cheese salad or an omelette, unless the restaurant has been given warning, or has an exceptional chef. These dishes may be all right in their way, but when you're being offered them for the umpteenth time, and your carnivorous companions are having difficulty deciding between various mouthwatering (to them, if not to you) alternatives, the pleasure can pall.

However, having said that, there are many delicious dishes which can be made from these ingredients, and they're often quick and easy to prepare. One of my favourites, for instance, is cheese fondue, which is perfect for impromptu entertaining; gougère, a puffy choux ring with a delicious filling, is another, as is a golden cheese soufflé. The cheese

fritters and gnocchi recipes, too, are other ones which I know are very popular with many people, and the Glamorgan sausage is one which children like.

I find savoury, pancake-based dishes very useful and, again, popular with most people. The pancakes can be made in advance and stored in the freezer, or the whole dish can be made and frozen. A savoury pancake gateau is always a successful dinner party dish.

One of the many positive developments which has taken place since I started out as a vegetarian cook is the arrival on the market of good cheeses made with vegetarian rennet. These can be bought at supermarkets and health shops; I find the health shop ones especially good. Now I'd like to see some vegetarian versions of the reduced-fat hard cheeses which I think are so useful for reducing one's overall fat intake (is this woman never satisfied?!).

I also always use free range eggs; 'farm eggs', 'new-laid eggs', 'brown eggs' and 'farm-fresh eggs' are not the same thing. Make sure you get genuine free range eggs and let's hope that, soon, they'll be the only ones there are.

Recipes which are suitable for freezing are marked [F].

ASPARAGUS PUDDING

This Italian savoury pudding is a cross between a soufflé and a savoury loaf. I think it's best to serve it straight from the dish with hot garlic bread and a crisp green salad.

SERVES 4 AS A MAIN DISH, 6 AS A STARTER
450g (1 lb) asparagus
50g (2oz) butter
50g (2oz) flour
275ml (10 fl oz) milk
2–3 tablespoons grated Parmesan cheese
sea salt
freshly ground black pepper
3 eggs
1 tablespoon chopped fresh parsley
triangles of fried bread

Set the oven to 180°C (350°F), gas mark 4. Trim asparagus, cutting off tough ends. Cook in 2.5cm (1in) fast-boiling water until tender; drain. (Keep liquid for making soup.) Cut asparagus into 2.5cm (1in) pieces. Make a sauce: melt the butter and stir in the flour; when it's blended add the milk in three batches, keeping the heat up high and stirring well each time until the mixture thickens before adding any more. Take the saucepan off the heat and add the grated Parmesan cheese and salt and pepper to taste.

Whisk the eggs and mix into the sauce, then gently stir in the drained asparagus and parsley. Check the seasoning, then pour the mixture into a lightly greased shallow ovenproof dish. Put the dish into a baking tin containing about 2.5cm (1in) of very hot water and place it in the centre of the oven. Bake for about 1 hour or until the mixture is set.

CHEESE, GREEN PEPPER AND TOMATO BAKE

This is an economical family bake that's quick to make and low in calories. I like it best with a tomato sauce and Bircher potatoes – see sections on sauces and vegetables – and cauliflower or a lightly-cooked green vegetable. This dish freezes well, either cooked or par-cooked.

SERVES 4 [F]
1 large onion, peeled and chopped
1 small/medium green pepper, de-seeded and chopped
225g (8oz) can tomatoes
125g (4oz) wholemeal bread
175g (6oz) grated cheese
2 tablespoons chopped parsley
1 egg
½–1 teaspoon tabasco sauce
sea salt
freshly ground black pepper

Set the oven to 200°C (400°F), gas mark 6. Put the onion, pepper and tomatoes into a bowl and crumble in the bread with your fingers. Mix well to break up the bread. Add most of the grated cheese, the parsley, the beaten egg and enough tabasco sauce to give a pleasant 'lift'. Season with salt and pepper. Spoon mixture into a shallow, lightly-greased oven-proof dish, sprinkle with the remaining cheese and bake for 40–50 minutes, until set and golden brown.

CAULIFLOWER, EGG AND POTATO BAKE

This is a filling dish rather like a substantial cauliflower cheese. If you don't like eggs you could put in a layer of sliced mushrooms instead – you'll need about 225g (8oz). All this needs as an accompaniment is some lightly cooked greens – little firm sprouts are ideal, or some buttered cabbage or spinach.

SERVES 4–6
700g (1½ lb) even-sized smallish potatoes
sea salt
1 medium-sized cauliflower
850ml (1½ pints) cheese sauce
6 hardboiled eggs, sliced
dried crumbs
a little butter for topping

Scrub the potatoes then cook them in their skins in boiling salted water until they're tender; drain and cool them, then slip off the skins with a sharp knife. (Cooking the potatoes in their skins like this makes a big difference to the flavour.) Cut the potatoes into slices. Wash the cauliflower, break it into even-sized sprigs and cook these in a little boiling salted water for about 7 minutes until they're just tender; drain well. Set the oven to 190°C (375°F), gas mark 5.

Grease a large shallow ovenproof dish with butter, then place a layer of the potato slices in the base, followed by some of the sauce, then the cauliflower and the egg slices, then some more sauce. Continue like this until everything has been used, ending if possible with layers of potato and sauce. Sprinkle the top with dried crumbs, dot with a little butter and bake for about 50 minutes, until heated through and golden brown on top.

BAKED CHEESE SOUFFLÉ PUDDING

A quick and easy dish.

SERVES 4
175g (6oz) grated cheese
1 garlic clove, crushed
125g (4oz) soft brown breadcrumbs
pinch cayenne pepper
sea salt
freshly ground black pepper
3 eggs, separated
275ml (10 fl oz) milk
25g (1oz) butter, melted

Mix all the dry ingredients together and add the well-beaten egg yolks, milk and melted butter. Beat the egg whites until a stiff froth. Fold this into the other ingredients; put the mixture into a greased soufflé dish, and bake in a moderate oven 220°C (425°F), gas mark 7, for 30 minutes. Serve with a tomato sauce.

CHEESE EGG PIE

Another family recipe, which my mother evolved as a vegetarian version of fish pie. It's a very soothing dish.

2 tablespoons potato flour or cornflour
575ml (1 pint) milk
1 bay leaf or pinch of mace
15g (½oz) butter
50g (2oz) grated cheese
6 hardboiled eggs
700g (1½ lb) creamy mashed potatoes

Set oven to 190°C (375°F), gas mark 5. Mix the cornflour with a little of the milk to make a thin creamy consistency. Put the rest of the milk in a pan with the bay leaf or mace and bring to the boil, then remove bay leaf and pour the milk over the cornflour mixture, stirring all the time. Tip back into pan, add the knob of butter and cook gently till thickened, still stirring, then beat in the cheese and remove

from the heat. Season to taste. Chop the eggs and stir into the sauce. Turn into an ovenproof dish and top with the creamy mashed potatoes. Rough up the surface with a fork or pipe some decorative whirls of potato on top. Bake for 30–40 minutes. Serve with grilled tomatoes and a lightly-cooked green vegetable.

Variation

LEEK PIE

Use 700g (1½ lb) leeks instead of the hardboiled eggs. Trim, wash and slice the leek, cook in a little boiling water until tender, drain well, then add to sauce, as above. Some chopped parsley is nice in this.

CHEESE FONDUE

This is such a useful dish for those occasions when you have to make something delicious and a bit special on the spur of the moment. As fondues are rich, I like to start with a light, fruity first course such as pineapple wedges or melon with strawberries and then have a refreshing salad after the fondue. If you want to serve a pudding course, a tart such as the blackcurrant lattice or Bakewell tart go well, or, for something lighter, a fruit sorbet.

SERVES 4–6
1 garlic clove
275ml (10 fl oz) dry white wine or cider
225g (8oz) Gruyère cheese and 225g (8oz) Emmenthal cheese, grated; or use 450g (1 lb) vegetarian Cheddar cheese, grated
1 tablespoon cornflour
1–2 tablespoons kirsch – optional
sea salt
freshly ground black pepper
grated nutmeg
1 large French loaf or crusty wholemeal loaf – or half of each – cut into bite-sized pieces and warmed in the oven

Halve the garlic and rub the cut surfaces over the inside of a medium-sized saucepan (or special fondue pan). Put the wine or cider and cheese into the saucepan and heat gently, stirring all the time until the cheese has melted. Mix the cornflour to a paste with the kirsch if you're using it, or use a drop more wine or cider; pour this paste into the cheese mixture, stirring all the time until you have a lovely creamy consistency. Occasionally, the cheese goes all lumpy and stringy at this point. Don't despair; if you beat it vigorously for a moment or two with a rotary whisk all will be well. Season the fondue then place the saucepan over the lighted burner and let everyone start dipping their bread into the delicious mixture.

CHEESE FRITTERS

This is another all-time favourite recipe. It's a fried version of the Italian dish gnocchi, and sounds unpromising, but results in crisp, tasty fritters which everyone loves. I serve them with lemon slices and a parsley sauce. They freeze excellently and can be used from frozen.

SERVES 4 F
575ml (1 pint) milk
1 small whole onion, peeled
1 bay leaf
1 clove
125g (4oz) semolina
125g (4oz) finely grated cheese
½ level teaspoon mustard powder
sea salt
freshly ground black pepper
beaten egg
toasted crumbs
olive oil for shallow-frying

Put milk, onion, bay leaf and clove in saucepan and bring to the boil. Then remove from heat, cover and leave for 10–15 minutes. Then take out the onion, bay leaf and clove. Reboil the milk and sprinkle in semolina, stirring all the time. Simmer until very thick – about 5 minutes. Remove from the heat and beat in the cheese, mustard and some salt and pepper. Spread the mixture over an oiled plate or baking tray to a depth of about 1cm (½in). Smooth top and leave until quite cold. Cut into pieces, coat with egg, then breadcrumbs, and fry in hot oil until crisp and golden. Drain well.

BAKED EGGS

SERVES 4
125g (4oz) mushrooms *or* tomatoes
4 eggs
a little butter
4 tablespoons cream *or* milk

Chop the mushrooms or tomatoes and fry lightly in the butter. Put a little of this mixture in the bottom of four ramekin dishes, then add an egg, and lastly 1 tablespoon of cream or milk to each. Sprinkle the tops with salt and a grinding of black pepper, place the dishes in a tin containing some boiling water, cover, and simmer gently for 20–30 minutes until the eggs are set. Serve at once, with hot toast and lettuce or endive (when in season), tomatoes, cucumber and chicory.

BANANA EGGS

An unusual recipe given to me originally by a friend who lived for a number of years in India.

SERVES 6
2 medium onions, sliced
1 garlic clove, crushed
15g (½oz) butter
6 bananas, skinned and chopped
1 green pepper, chopped
1 tablespoon chopped parsley
2 tomatoes, skinned and sliced
½ teaspoon turmeric
sea salt
freshly ground black pepper
6 eggs

Set oven to 180°C (350°F), gas mark 4. Fry onions and garlic in the butter until brown, then add the rest of the ingredients, except for the eggs, and cook all together until soft. Put into a largish shallow ovenproof dish and make six hollows. Break eggs into the hollows and bake for about 15 minutes until eggs are set.

EGG CROQUETTES (1)

Potato flour could be used instead of the cornflour.

SERVES 4
50g (2oz) butter
1 heaped tablespoon cornflour
275ml (10 fl oz) milk
sea salt
freshly ground black pepper
pinch mace *or* grated nutmeg
2 tablespoons grated cheese
4 hardboiled eggs
2 tablespoons chopped parsley
flour for coating
olive oil for shallow-frying

Melt butter in a pan; blend in the cornflour. Remove from heat and add the milk slowly, stirring. Bring to the boil, stirring all the time till the mixture thickens. (It will be thick.) Add the seasoning and grated cheese and allow the cheese to melt before adding the well-chopped eggs and parsley. When the mixture has cooled a little, shape into croquettes. Coat with flour and shallow-fry both sides in very hot fat until golden brown. Serve at once with grilled tomatoes and other vegetables in season.

EGG CROQUETTES (2)

SERVES 4
4 hardboiled eggs
15g (½oz) butter
125g (4oz) soft wholemeal breadcrumbs
½ teaspoon yeast extract
1 tablespoon chopped parsley
sea salt
freshly ground black pepper
2 eggs, beaten
crumbs for coating
olive oil for shallow-frying

Chop the eggs finely and mix with the butter. Add breadcrumbs, yeast extract, chopped parsley, salt and pepper, and half the beaten egg to make a stiff paste. Mould into croquettes, dip in remaining egg, coat with breadcrumbs and fry in the hot oil. Drain and serve garnished with parsley sprigs. Tomato sauce goes well with these.

EGGS FLORENTINE

SERVES 4
4 eggs
450g (1 lb) spinach
sea salt
freshly ground black pepper
grated nutmeg
15g (½oz) butter
275ml (10 fl oz) cheese sauce
50g (2oz) grated cheese
25g (1oz) crumbs

Poach eggs in boiling water until just cooked. Meanwhile, wash spinach and cook in a pan without any water; drain very well and add salt, pepper, nutmeg and almost half the butter. Butter a shallow casserole, or four individual ones, and spread a layer of spinach in the base. Place eggs on top and cover with the cheese sauce. Sprinkle with the grated cheese and crumbs, and dot with the rest of the butter. Brown under a moderately hot grill.

BAKED STUFFED EGGS

These stuffed eggs are good as a first course baked in individual dishes and served with hot toast or as a main course, with fluffy boiled rice and perhaps a buttery spinach purée.

SERVES 4 AS A MAIN COURSE, 8 AS A STARTER
8 hardboiled eggs
2 large onions
50g (2oz) butter
1 tablespoon chopped fresh parsley
sea salt
freshly ground black pepper

Set the oven to 180°C (350°F), gas mark 4. Cut the hardboiled eggs in half and take out the yolks; put the whites to one side. Peel and finely chop the onions. Melt the butter in a medium-sized saucepan and use some of it to brush a shallow oblong ovenproof dish which is big enough to hold all the egg whites in a single layer. Add the onion to the rest of the butter in the saucepan and fry it gently for 10 minutes, without letting it brown. Take the saucepan off the heat and add the egg yolks, mashing them into the onions until they're fairly creamy and smooth then stir in the parsley, salt and pepper. Spoon the mixture into the egg white cavities, piling it up neatly, then put the egg whites into the greased dish. Cover the dish with foil and bake in the oven for about 30 minutes, until the eggs are heated through.

These are also good with ½–1 teaspoon of dried dill, fennel or caraway seeds added to the mixture, if you like the taste.

CURRIED STUFFED EGGS

This is a tasty dish, hardboiled eggs stuffed with a curry mixture and baked in a spicy sauce. Serve with hot boiled rice or spiced rice, some mango chutney and crisp poppadums.

SERVES 4
8 hardboiled eggs
1 large onion
3 tablespoons *ghee*, oil *or* butter
1 garlic clove
225g (8oz) can tomatoes
1 teaspoon ground cumin
1 teaspoon ground coriander
1 teaspoon ground ginger
½ teaspoon turmeric
275ml (10 fl oz) water
sea salt
freshly ground black pepper

Halve the eggs, take out the yolks and put them into a bowl. Leave the whites on one side for the moment. Peel and finely chop the onion and fry it gently in the *ghee* for 10 minutes. Peel and crush the garlic and add it to the onion, together with the tomatoes, spices, water and some salt and pepper. Let the mixture simmer, with a lid on the saucepan, for 20 minutes, then sieve or liquidize this sauce. Check the seasoning. Set oven to 180°C (350°F), gas mark 4. Mash the egg yolks and stir in 2 or 3 tablespoons of sauce, enough to make a soft but not sloppy mixture.

Spoon the yolk mixture into the egg whites. Pour the curry sauce into a shallow ovenproof dish that's big enough to hold all the eggs in one layer, then put the eggs in on top of the sauce. Cover with foil and bake for 30 minutes just to heat the eggs through.

STUFFED EGGS WITH SAVOURY SAUCE

This is an equally tasty stuffed eggs recipe. Serve with boiled rice.

SERVES 3–4
6 eggs, hardboiled
15g (½oz) butter
1 tablespoon grated onion
½–1 teaspoon curry powder
1 tablespoon tomato ketchup
sea salt
freshly ground black pepper
½ teaspoon lemon juice
425ml (15 fl oz) white sauce
150ml (5 fl oz) mayonnaise
juice 1 lemon
¼ teaspoon paprika
curry powder – optional
chopped parsley
lemon slices

Set oven to 180°C (350°F), gas mark 4. Slice hardboiled eggs in half lengthwise. Carefully remove yolks. Leave whites on one side. Mash yolks finely. Melt butter and lightly fry onion and curry powder to taste, then mix in all the other ingredients (except egg whites) and blend to a smooth paste. Spoon into egg whites, arrange in a casserole and keep warm.

Make a good white sauce and add mayonnaise, lemon juice, paprika and maybe a little curry powder. Pour most of the sauce over the eggs and bake for 15 minutes. Garnish with a little chopped parsley and lemon slices and serve with rest of sauce separately.

Variation

STUFFED EGGS MORNAY

Stuff eggs exactly as above, but cover with 425ml (15 fl oz) cheese sauce, top with 25–50g (1–2oz) breadcrumbs and grated cheese, and brown under a moderate grill.

TOMATO BAKED EGGS

A quick-to-make supper dish. Serve with green salad or cooked spinach. Some fluffy rice or hot toast are also good with this.

SERVES 4
4 large tomatoes
4 eggs
sea salt
freshly ground black pepper
275ml (10 fl oz) cheese sauce

Set oven to 180°C (350°F), gas mark 4. Remove top of tomatoes and scoop out pulp – this will not be needed but can be used up in salads, soups or sauces. Place tomato 'cups' in a buttered casserole and break an egg into each. Top with cheese sauce and bake eggs or 20 minutes until set. Serve immediately.

GLAMORGAN SAUSAGE

These little cheesy sausages are delicious with salad and some chutney or with parsley or tomato sauce and cooked vegetables. If you make the sausages tiny they're good as a nibble with drinks. I'm going to try them out on my youngest daughter's friends at her next birthday party to solve, I hope, the sausage problem.

SERVES 4
350g (12oz) Caerphilly cheese, grated
125g (4oz) soft wholemeal breadcrumbs
1 teaspoon mustard powder
6 tablespoons cold water
freshly ground black pepper
a little flour
1 egg, beaten with 1 tablespoon of cold water
dried crumbs for cooking
oil for shallow-frying

Mix together the cheese, soft breadcrumbs, mustard, cold water and some pepper to taste. Gather the mixture into a ball then divide it into 8 pieces and roll each into a sausage shape on a floured board. Dip each little sausage into the beaten egg and then into dried crumbs. Heat a little oil in a frying pan and fry the sausages quickly until they're crisp, then drain them and serve immediately.

Variation

GLAMORGAN SAUSAGE, NUTTY VERSION

I've found that you can also make a delicious nut version of this recipe which I'm sure a Welshman wouldn't own but which we prefer. Use 225g (8oz) grated cheese and 125g (4oz) grated cashew nuts or hazel nuts with the breadcrumbs and water as above. It's nice flavoured with a little chopped rosemary.

Both this mixture and the proper version are good baked instead of fried – press the mixture into a greased ovenproof dish and bake it at 200°C (400°F), gas mark 6 for about 45 minutes. The result is rather a crisp savoury cake which can be cut up and served with a parsley or tomato sauce; it's also nice cold with chutney and salad.

LAZY GNOCCHI

This is a quick, lazy version of gnocchi. You make a thick cheesy semolina mixture as usual but instead of spreading it out on a plate to cool then cutting it into shapes, you just pour the hot mixture into a shallow ovenproof dish, sprinkle the surface with cheese and grill or bake until crisp and golden. It looks and tastes almost the same and is delicious with just a well-dressed green salad or with tomato sauce and a lightly-cooked green vegetable.

SERVES 4–6
575ml (1 pint) skimmed milk
1 bay leaf
1 onion stuck with a clove
175g (6oz) semolina
150g (6oz) grated cheese
1 teaspoon mustard powder
sea salt
freshly ground black pepper
1 tomato, sliced

Put the milk into a large saucepan with the bay leaf and the onion and bring to the boil. Remove from the heat, cover and leave for at least 10 minutes. Remove the bay leaf and onion. Bring milk up to the boil again then gradually sprinkle the semolina over the surface, stirring all the time, until you have a smooth, thick sauce. Let it cook over a gentle heat for 5 minutes, stirring often. Remove from the heat and stir in two-thirds of the cheese, the mustard and some salt and pepper. Pour the thick mixture into a shallow ovenproof dish so that it makes a layer not more than 1 cm (½in) deep. Top with the rest of the cheese and the slices of tomato. Put under a hot grill for 10–15 minutes until bubbling underneath and golden brown and crisp on top. Serve at once.

GNOCCHI ALLA ROMANA

When this is brought from the oven, sizzling and golden brown, people find it difficult to believe it's made from semolina which they associate with dull school puddings. It's delicious and though you've got to allow time for the semolina mixture to get completely cold, it's not a difficult dish to make and one which you can do in stages and get ready in advance. It also freezes well.

SERVES 4
175g (6oz) semolina
1½ teaspoons sea salt
a good grinding of black pepper and nutmeg
850ml (1½ pints) milk
175g (6oz) grated cheese – including some Parmesan
2 eggs
olive oil

Put the semolina into a large bowl with the salt, pepper and nutmeg and mix it to a cream with some of the milk. Bring the rest of the milk to the boil, then pour it into the semolina mixture, stirring all the time. Tip the semolina and milk mixture back into the saucepan and stir over a fairly high heat until it thickens. Then let the mixture simmer gently until it's very thick and has lost its very granular appearance, stirring from time to time. In Italy they say that the mixture is ready when a spoon will stand up in it unsupported. In practice I find you can only achieve this if you've happened to use a small, deep saucepan, and that 10 minutes simmering is about right. Remove the saucepan from the heat and stir in two-thirds of the cheese and the eggs which will cook in the heat of the mixture. Taste and add more seasoning if necessary. Lightly oil a large plate, tray or other suitable flat surface and turn out the semolina mixture on to this, spreading it to a thickness of about 6mm (¼in). Leave it to get completely cold – overnight if possible.

When the mixture is cold it should be firm enough to cut into shapes. Traditionally it should be cut into circles with a pastry cutter which makes the finished dish look very attractive and doesn't really take a moment, but squares will do if you're in a hurry. Brush a large flat ovenproof dish with oil – I use one of those big white pizza plates which is ideal – and arrange the *gnocchi* in slightly overlapping circles, like roof tiles. Brush the top of the *gnocchi* with some oil and sprinkle with the remaining grated cheese, then either bake for about 15 minutes in a fairly hot oven 200°C (400°F), gas mark 6, or put the whole dish under a hot grill for about 20 minutes, if you have a grill which is big enough. Get the *gnocchi* really crisp and golden, then serve at once.

GOUGÈRE WITH MUSHROOMS, ONIONS AND RED WINE SAUCE

This is an impressive and delicious dish, a big puffed-up ring of golden choux pastry, the centre filled with button mushrooms and onions in red wine sauce. It's lovely served with baby Brussels sprouts and creamy mashed potatoes. *Gougère* is not difficult to make but it's best eaten as soon as it's ready, so you need to be able to get everyone to the table on time. Don't be put off by the long list of ingredients for the sauce; it's really quite easy to do.

SERVES 6

For the gougère
125g (4oz) butter or margarine
275ml (10 fl oz) water
150g (5oz) plain wholemeal flour – or half wholemeal and half unbleached white flour
1 teaspoon sea salt
4 eggs, beaten
175g (6oz) grated cheese
a good pinch of cayenne pepper

For the filling
3 onions, peeled and sliced
15g (½oz) butter
225g (8oz) baby button mushrooms, washed and left whole

For the sauce
425ml (15 fl oz) stock *or* water and a good teaspoon of vegetarian stock powder
425ml (15 fl oz) red wine
1 bay leaf
1 piece of onion, peeled
1 garlic clove, peeled and sliced
a good pinch of thyme
½ teaspoon black peppercorns
1–2 parsley stalks if available
1 tablespoon redcurrant jelly
sea salt
freshly ground black pepper
sugar
40g (1½oz) soft butter
20g (¾oz) flour

You can make the main preparations for the various parts of this dish in advance if that is most convenient for you. To make the *gougère*, put the butter or margarine and water into a medium-sized saucepan and heat gently until the butter has melted, then turn up the heat and bring the mixture to the boil. Mix the flour with the salt and quickly pour into the saucepan all at once. Stir over the heat with a wooden spoon for 1 minute, by which time the mixture will have formed a glossy ball of dough, then take the saucepan off the heat and tip the dough into a clean bowl.

Add about a quarter of the beaten egg and beat vigorously with a wooden spoon until the dough has absorbed the egg and become smooth and glossy again, then add another quarter and beat again. Repeat until all the egg has been used. I sometimes find when I'm using all wholemeal flour that the mixture will only take three-quarters of the egg; by then it is quite soft and any more would make it sloppy – it must hold its shape softly. If this happens to you don't worry; just use the extra to glaze the top before sprinkling on the cheese and baking. The reason is that wholemeal flour is not as absorbent as white and varies quite a bit from batch to batch. Stir in about two-thirds of the grated cheese, and the cayenne pepper. You can cover the mixture with a plate and leave it at this point for several hours if you wish.

To make the filling, fry the onions in the butter for 10 minutes until they're soft, then put in the mushrooms and fry for a further 3–4 minutes until they too are tender. Season with salt and pepper and leave on one side. If the mushrooms produce a great deal of liquid drain it off and use it as part of the stock for the sauce.

For the sauce put the stock and red wine into a good-sized saucepan with the bay leaf, onion, garlic, thyme, peppercorns and parsley stalks if you've got them and bring up to the boil. Let the mixture bubble away furiously without a lid for 10–15 minutes until it has reduced by half and you're left with 425ml (15 fl oz) of liquid. Strain this liquid into a clean saucepan and stir in the redcurrant jelly and salt, pepper and sugar to taste. Make a *beurre manié*: put half the butter on a plate with the flour and mash them together with the back of a spoon to make a paste. Add this *beurre manié* to the wine mixture in several pieces, beating well after each, then put the sauce back on the heat and stir it for a minute or two until it's slightly thickened. Let it simmer for a further 4–5 minutes to cook the flour, then take the saucepan off the heat and dot the remaining butter over the surface of the sauce to prevent a skin forming. Leave on one side until you're ready to serve the *gougère*.

To finish the *gougère* preheat the oven to 200°C (400°F), gas mark 6. Oil a large ovenproof dish – one of those big white pizza plates is ideal if you have one but any large shallow ovenproof dish will do – and spoon the *gougère* mixture all round the edge, heaping it up into as neat a ring as possible but leaving the centre free. Sprinkle the top of the ring with the rest of the grated cheese then bake the *gougère* for 40 minutes until it is puffed up and golden brown. When the *gougère* is nearly done reheat the onions and mushrooms gently, also the sauce.

Take the *gougère* out of the oven, spoon the mushroom mixture into the centre and pour a little sauce over the mushrooms and onions – serve the rest of the sauce separately in a jug. Serve the *gougère* immediately.

You can put other things into the centre of the *gougère*; it's nice with a buttery purée of spinach in the middle and cheese sauce served separately.

COLD GOUGÈRE WITH CREAM CHEESE FILLING

If you make a *gougère* as in the previous recipe and bake it for longer so that it's really firm, you can split it round the middle and serve it cold, sandwiched with soft white cheese and its centre filled with crisp lettuce, tomato, watercress and spring onion salad. It makes an attractive buffet dish.

SERVES 8–12
gougère mixture as in the previous recipe
700g (1½ lb) curd cheese
sea salt
freshly ground black pepper
1 crisp lettuce
½ bunch watercress
4 tomatoes, sliced
6 spring onions, trimmed

Make the *gougère* as described in the preceding recipe but bake it for a good hour until it is well-risen and very firm – all 'sizzling' should have ceased in the choux pastry. If it's not really firm it will collapse and be soggy inside.

Take the *gougère* out of the oven, slit it horizontally with a sharp knife and leave it on the dish to get completely cold.

It's best not to fill the *gougère* until just before you're going to serve it so that it stays as crisp as possible. Put the cheese into a bowl and mash it with a fork to break it up, then beat it until it's soft and light. Season the cheese with salt and pepper –

a touch of garlic is nice too, if you like it. Carefully remove the top half of the *gougère* and spread the cheese over the bottom layer, then replace the top half. Arrange the salad in the middle of the circle. An alternative is to put the salad inside the *gougère* on top of the cheese.

OMELETTE

A well-made omelette should be light and golden brown on the outside, creamy and moist within. It's versatile, because you can serve it with all sorts of different fillings. The important thing is to have the filling all ready to pop into the omelette and everyone sitting at the table before you start to cook the omelette because it's speed that's the essence of success.

SERVES 1
2 eggs
2 teaspoons cold water
sea salt
freshly ground black pepper
1 teaspoon olive oil
15g (½oz) butter

Filling suggestions:
50g (2oz) finely grated cheese
50g (2oz) button mushrooms, sliced
and lightly fried
50g (2oz) canned cut green asparagus, heated in its
own liquid and drained just before using
50g (2oz) canned artichoke hearts, sliced, heated and
drained just before using
1 tablespoon chopped fresh green herbs – parsley,
chives, chervil, tarragon – whatever is available

Beat the eggs in a bowl with the water, a pinch of salt and a grinding of pepper. Put the frying pan – a 15–18cm (6–7in) one is best if you've got one as it makes a nice thick omelette – over a high heat for about one minute, then turn the heat down and put in first the oil and then the butter. When the butter has melted turn up the heat again and put in the beaten egg. Immediately start moving the egg using a palette knife to push the edges of the omelette towards the centre, tipping the pan as you do so to make the liquid egg in the middle run to the edges – keep the heat up high. All this happens very quickly – the omelette should be done in under a minute. Loosen the edges of the omelette quickly with the palette knife, spoon one of the above fillings on top then tip the pan away from you so that the omelette folds over itself, then gently tip it on to a warmed plate. Serve immediately.

BASIC PANCAKE BATTER

I usually make this batter in a liquidizer, which is very labour-saving, but you can equally well use the traditional method. I never let my batter stand, by the way, without any dire results! For best results you do need a small frying pan: mine measures 18cm (7in) across the top.

MAKES ABOUT 12 PANCAKES
125g (4oz) plain 85 per cent wholemeal flour
¼ teaspoon sea salt
2 eggs
2 tablespoons melted butter
275ml (10 fl oz) skimmed milk
butter for frying

If you're using the quick liquidizer method to make the batter, simply put the flour, salt, eggs, melted butter and 200ml (7 fl oz) milk into the goblet and blend at medium speed for 1–2 minutes, to make a smooth, creamy batter. Or, for the traditional method, sift the flour and salt into a bowl, make a well in the centre and add the eggs, oil and about a third of the milk. Mix to a smooth consistency, gradually adding the remaining milk, then beat well for 1–2 minutes. The batter should be the consistency of thin cream.

To fry the pancakes, set a small frying pan over a low heat and add a small knob of butter. When the pan is hot and the butter melted pour excess butter into an old cup; the frying pan should be just 'greased', with no excess fat. Then pour in about 2 tablespoons of batter – enough to coat the bottom of the frying pan thinly – and swirl it round so that the base of the frying pan is covered. Fry for a minute or two, until the top is set, then, using a palette knife, quickly flip the pancake over to cook the other side for a second or two. Lift out the pancake and put it on a plate while you make the rest. Brush the frying pan with oil before making each pancake, and pile them up on top of each other on the plate as they're done. I don't find there's any need to put pieces of greaseproof paper between the pancakes, as some people suggest, by the way: they don't seem to stick together. It is a good idea to keep an old pastry brush specially for oiling the frying pan, though, as the heat of the pan makes the bristles curl.

Pancakes freeze very well: simply wrap the pile of cooled pancakes in foil and put them in the freezer. When you want to use them, loosen the foil and let them thaw out naturally, or put the foil parcel in a low oven if you want to speed up the process. They will also keep for several days in an ordinary refrigerator.

Variations

BUCKWHEAT PANCAKE BATTER

Make as above but replace half the flour with buckwheat flour, for dark, nutty-tasting pancakes. These are nice filled with tomato-based mixtures such as ratatouille.

MIXED VEGETABLE PANCAKE BATTER

Add 2 tablespoons finely chopped spring onion or leek and 2 tablespoons finely diced raw carrot to the basic batter mixture for interesting flecked pancakes with a slightly chewy texture.

SPINACH PANCAKE BATTER

Stir 3 tablespoons sieved cooked spinach into the batter for green pancakes.

PANCAKES STUFFED WITH ASPARAGUS

I'm afraid this is rather an extravagant dish, using 1 kilo (2¼ lbs) of asparagus, but for a special occasion it really makes a wonderful main course that's no more expensive (when asparagus is in season!) than good meat or fish would be. An alternative to the sauce topping is to use 2 large cartons of soured cream.

SERVES 6
basic pancake batter (page 275)
1 kilo (2¼ lb) asparagus
2 tablespoons chopped parsley
50g (2oz) butter
50g (2oz) flour
575ml (1 pint) milk
1 bay leaf
1 teaspoon mustard powder
125g (4oz) grated cheese, preferably double Gloucester
sea salt
freshly ground black pepper
50g (2oz) grated cheese

First make the pancake batter and cook 12–15 thin pancakes.

To make the filling, break off the hard stems at the base of the asparagus – these ends are too tough to eat but can be used to make a stock for asparagus soup. Wash the asparagus gently to remove any grit. The easiest way to cook asparagus (if, like me, you haven't got a proper asparagus steamer) is in an ordinary steamer; otherwise you can stand the asparagus up in a bunch in a saucepan containing about 1 cm (½in) water, and arrange a piece of foil over the top to make a domed lid – this way the tougher ends of the stalks cook in the water and the delicate tops are steamed. Either way the asparagus will take about 10 minutes: it should be just tender. Add the chopped parsley.

While the asparagus is cooking, make the sauce. Melt the butter in a large saucepan and stir in the flour, cook for a moment or two then add about a fifth of the milk and the bay leaf and stir over a good heat until the mixture is smooth and very thick. Then add another lot of milk and repeat the process until it has all been incorporated and you've got a smooth sauce. Take the saucepan off the heat, stir in the mustard and grated cheese and season the sauce carefully. If you're having some white wine with the meal a couple of tablespoons of it will make a delicious addition.

To assemble the dish put a heaped tablespoon of asparagus on each pancake, roll the pancake neatly and place it in a large shallow, greased casserole. These pancakes look best arranged in a single layer but you will need a big dish to accommodate them. When the pancakes are all in the dish pour the sauce evenly over them, removing the bay leaf. Sprinkle the grated cheese over the top and cover the dish with a piece of foil.

When you're ready to bake the pancakes set the oven to 180°C (350°F), gas mark 4. Bake them for about 1 hour, removing the foil about 15 minutes before the end of that cooking time to brown the cheese on top.

Variations

BUCKWHEAT PANCAKES FILLED WITH RATATOUILLE

Use buckwheat batter to make pancakes as described above. Fill with ratatouille made according to recipe on page 130. Top with cheese sauce as above or use soured cream variation. Sprinkle with grated cheese and finish as above.

PANCAKES STUFFED WITH FLAGEOLET, MUSHROOM AND ARTICHOKE HEART FILLING

Make pancakes as on page 275. To make filling, mix together 450g (1 lb) cooked flageolet beans, 350g (12oz) button mushrooms (lightly fried in butter), 2 × 400g (14oz) cans artichoke hearts, drained and sliced, 175g (6oz) curd cheese and a garlic clove, crushed. Season. Fill pancakes with this mixture, cover with cheese sauce and bake as described.

PANCAKES STUFFED WITH LEEKS

For this variation, make pancakes as on page 275, then for the filling wash and slice 900g (2 lb) leeks and cook them in a little fast-boiling salted water for about 10 minutes, until just tender. Drain well and add 15g (½oz) butter, 1 tablespoon chopped parsley, salt and pepper to taste.

Fill the pancakes with leek mixture, then finish recipe as described above, using cheese sauce or soured cream.

PANCAKES STUFFED WITH LENTIL AND MUSHROOM FILLING

For this variation use the basic pancake batter (page 275) to make 10–12 thin pancakes, then leave them on one side to cool while you make the filling.

Fry a large onion and garlic clove in 15g (½oz) butter in a medium-sized saucepan for 5 minutes, then stir in 175g (6oz) red lentils, 275ml (10 fl oz) water or stock, 400g (14oz) can tomatoes, ½ teaspoon cumin and 2 tablespoons wine. Let the mixture simmer gently, uncovered, for 30 minutes. Add 225g (8oz) washed and sliced mushrooms and cook for a further 5–6 minutes, then season with sea salt and freshly ground black pepper. Spread a little of the lentil mixture on each pancake; roll the pancakes up neatly and arrange them side by side in a well-greased, shallow ovenproof dish. Pour the sauce over the pancake rolls, sprinkle with grated cheese and bake as described above.

PANCAKES STUFFED WITH MUSHROOMS AND ARTICHOKE HEARTS

First make the basic pancake batter (page 275) and cook 12–15 thin pancakes.

To make the filling, fry 1 finely chopped onion in 25g (1oz) butter for 10 minutes but don't let it brown. Add 700g (1½ lb) halved or quartered mushrooms and cook for a further 5 minutes. If the mushrooms produce much water let them boil vigorously until the mixture is fairly dry. Take the saucepan off the heat and stir in the 2 garlic cloves (crushed), 400g (14oz) artichoke hearts, drained and sliced, 2 tablespoons chopped parsley and 4 tablespoons cream. Sharpen the mixture with a little lemon juice and add sea salt and freshly ground black pepper to taste.

Divide the filling between the pancakes, roll up neatly and place them side by side in a shallow ovenproof dish. Cover with cheese and bake as described above.

PANCAKES STUFFED WITH SPICY RED BEANS

First make basic pancake batter (page 275) and cook 12–15 thin pancakes.

Then make the Mexican-style filling. Fry a large, chopped onion in 1 tablespoon olive oil in a large saucepan for 10 minutes, until it's soft but not browned. Then stir in 2 crushed garlic cloves, 780g (1 lb 11½oz) can tomatoes, 450g (1 lb) cooked red kidney beans, and enough chilli powder, sea salt and freshly ground black pepper to give a good flavour. Mash the beans and tomatoes a bit with the spoon to break them up.

Fill pancakes with this mixture, cover with cheese sauce or soured cream and bake as described above.

PANCAKES WITH SPINACH AND CONTINENTAL LENTIL FILLING

Make basic pancake batter (page 275) and cook 10–12 thin pancakes.

Soak and cook 125g (4oz) continental lentils as usual, then drain and add a fried onion, 175g (6oz) fried, sliced mushrooms, 1 garlic clove, crushed, 1 tablespoon tomato purée, sea salt and freshly ground black pepper. Fill half the pancakes with the mixture and place in a shallow, ovenproof dish, allowing room to alternate these pancakes with spinach-filled ones.

To make the spinach filling, wash 450g (1 lb) spinach thoroughly then cook it as usual in a dry saucepan over rather a high heat for about 7–10 minutes, until it's tender. Drain and chop the spinach, then add 15g (½oz) butter, and a good seasoning of salt, pepper and nutmeg. Fill remaining pancakes with this mixture, cover with cheese sauce and bake as described above.

PANCAKES STUFFED WITH SPINACH AND CURD CHEESE

Make basic pancake batter (page 275) and cook 12–15 thin pancakes.

Cook 900g (2 lb) fresh spinach as described in last recipe, or use 2 × 300g (11oz) packets frozen spinach. Add 225g (8oz) curd cheese. Season with sea salt, freshly ground black pepper and grated nutmeg. Fill pancakes with this mixture, cover with cheese sauce and bake as described above.

PANCAKES STUFFED WITH TOMATOES AND HAZEL NUTS

Make basic pancake batter (page 275) and cook 12–15 thin pancakes.

To make the filling, chop 6 skinned tomatoes and put into a bowl with 175g (6oz) soft wholemeal bread; mash the bread into the tomatoes with a fork and leave for 10 minutes to allow the bread to soften, mashing it with a fork once or twice more. Add 1 large fried onion, 1 garlic clove, crushed, and 125g (4oz) hazel nuts, ground, 1 teaspoon thyme, 1 tablespoon tomato purée and 3 tablespoons red wine. Season with salt, pepper and a little honey. Divide this mixture between pancakes, cover with cheese sauce and bake as described above.

PANCAKES STUFFED WITH CHEESE AND BAKED IN SPICY TOMATO SAUCE

When you put the spoon into this dish the creamy white filling oozes out and looks very appetizing against the golden pancakes and tomato sauce.

SERVES 6–8

12–15 pancakes made as described on page 275
700g (1½ lb) cottage cheese, curd cheese *or* quark
350g (12oz) grated cheese
1½ teaspoons mustard powder
2 garlic cloves, peeled and crushed
sea salt
freshly ground black pepper
1 large onion, peeled and chopped
1 tablespoon olive oil
1 garlic clove, peeled and crushed
792g (1 lb 12oz) can tomatoes
½–1 teaspoon chilli powder
125g (4oz) grated cheese

Make the filling by mixing together the cottage cheese, curd cheese or quark, the grated cheese, mustard powder and garlic; add salt and pepper to tate.

Fry the onion in the oil for 10 minutes, then stir in the garlic, tomatoes, chilli powder and salt and pepper to taste. Sieve or liquidize the sauce.

Heat the oven to 190°C (375°F), gas mark 5. Grease a large shallow ovenproof dish. Spoon the filling on to the tortillas, rolling them neatly round and dividing the mixture evenly between them. Place the plump rolls side by side in the dish and pour the tomato sauce over them. Sprinkle the grated cheese on top.

Cover the dish with foil and bake the pancakes for 45 minutes, then take off the foil and leave them in the oven for a further 15 minutes or so to brown the top.

PANCAKE GÂTEAU (1)

This is quite a spectacular-looking dish, a 'gâteau' of light pancakes layered with three different mixtures, spinach, continental lentil, and tomato, topped with a creamy sauce. You can use different fillings if you like, but aim for contrasting colours, as they look so attractive when the 'gâteau' is sliced. You can make all the parts of the 'gâteau' separately in advance and the actual assembly only takes a matter of minutes. It's nice served with a contrasting vegetable such as buttered carrots.

SERVES 4–6

For the pancakes
basic pancake batter (see page 275)
butter for frying

Continental lentil filling
125g (4oz) continental lentils, soaked in cold water overnight

1 large onion, peeled and chopped
1 large garlic clove, crushed
1 tablespoon olive oil
sea salt
freshly ground black pepper

Tomato filling
1 large onion, peeled and chopped
1 garlic clove, crushed
1 tablespoon olive oil
400g (14oz) can tomatoes
½ teaspoon oregano

Spinach filling
700g (1½ lb) spinach
15g (½oz) butter
grated nutmeg

Topping
425ml (15 fl oz) well-flavoured cheese sauce (see page 62)

1 tomato, sliced
a few sprigs of parsley

Use the basic batter mixture to make 10 thin pancakes (page 275) piling them up on a plate as they're ready, then leaving them on one side while you make the fillings.

For the lentil filling, drain and rinse the lentils, then put them into a saucepan, just cover with warm water and cook gently until they're tender – 30–40 minutes. Drain off any excess liquid. Meanwhile fry the onion and garlic in the oil until they're soft, then add them to the lentils and season the mixture with sea salt and freshly ground black pepper to taste.

To make the tomato filling, fry the onion and garlic in the oil (I usually do this with the onion and garlic for the lentil mixture, then take out half to mix with the lentils, leaving the rest in the saucepan), then add the tomatoes and boil fairly rapidly for about 10 minutes, until most of the liquid has evaporated and the mixture is thick. Add the oregano and season with sea salt and freshly ground black pepper.

Next prepare the spinach filling. Wash the spinach thoroughly in three changes of cold water, then cook it in a dry saucepan over a fairly high heat, with a lid on the saucepan, until it's tender – 7–10 minutes. Chop the spinach in the saucepan using the end of a fish slice, then drain off all the liquid and add the butter, plenty of sea salt and freshly ground black pepper and some grated nutmeg.

Now, to assemble and finish the 'gâteau'. First of all set the oven to 180°C (350°F), gas mark 4. Put one of the pancakes on a flat ovenproof plate and spread it with a third of the lentil mixture. Place another pancake on top and cover with a third of the tomato sauce, then lay another pancake on that,

followed by a third of the spinach. Continue in layers in this way until all the pancakes have been used. Pour the sauce over the top of the 'gâteau'; sprinkle with grated cheese. Put it into the oven for about 40 minutes to heat through. Garnish with the tomato slices and parsley.

PANCAKE GÂTEAU (2)

In this 'gâteau', which is a delicious dish to serve for a special occasion, light pancakes are layered with a rich-tasting mixture of mushrooms, chestnuts, walnuts and red wine, and the whole mixture is topped with cheese sauce.

SERVES 8
basic pancake batter (page 275)
butter for frying
1 onion, finely chopped
1 celery stick, finely chopped
15g (½oz) butter
2 garlic cloves, crushed
225g (8oz) button mushrooms, sliced
50g (2oz) grated cheese
225g (8oz) unsweetened canned chestnut purée
350g (12oz) cashew nuts, grated
125g (4oz) walnuts, grated
150ml (5 fl oz) red wine
2 tablespoons chopped parsley
sea salt
freshly ground black pepper
425ml (15 fl oz) well-flavoured cheese sauce
(page 62)
1 tomato, sliced
parsley

Use the pancake mixture to make 10 thin pancakes as described on page 275. To make the filling, fry the onion and celery in the butter for 7–8 minutes, then add the garlic and mushrooms, and fry for a further 2–3 minutes. Remove from the heat and add the cheese, chestnut purée, cashew nuts, walnuts, wine and parsley. Season with salt and pepper. Set oven to 190°C (375°F), gas mark 5. To assemble the gâteau, put one pancake on a flat ovenproof dish and spread with some of the filling mixture. Put another pancake on top, followed by more filling, and continue in this way, until all the pancakes and filling are used, ending with a pancake. Pour the cheese sauce over the top of the 'gâteau', and bake for 30–40 minutes, to heat through and brown top. Garnish with tomato slices and parsley; serve at once.

CHILLI RED BEAN PANCAKES

In this recipe pancakes are filled with red beans and baked in a tomato sauce.

SERVES 4
basic pancake batter (page 275)
butter for frying
175g (6oz) red kidney beans, soaked for several hours
in cold water, then drained and rinsed
575ml (1 pint) water
2 tablespoons olive oil
2 onions, peeled and chopped
2 garlic cloves, crushed
1 bay leaf
½ teaspoon oregano
400g (14oz) can tomatoes
1 tablespoon tomato purée
¼–1 teaspoon chilli powder
sea salt
freshly ground black pepper
125g (4oz) grated cheese

Use the pancake batter to make 10–12 thin pancakes (page 275); these can be made in advance if it's more convenient. Put the beans into a saucepan with the water and cook them gently until they're tender – about 1 hour – then drain them, reserving the cooking liquid.

Preheat the oven to 180°C (350°F), gas mark 4. Heat the oil in a medium-sized saucepan and fry the onion for 10 minutes, but don't let it get brown, then add the garlic, bay leaf, oregano, tomatoes, tomato purée and chilli powder and let it all simmer gently, uncovered, for about 15 minutes. Add half of this tomato mixture to the cooked beans, mashing them roughly, and seasoning with sea salt, freshly ground black pepper and, if necessary, more chilli powder to taste. Spread about 2 tablespoons of this bean mixture on each pancake, roll them up and place them side by side in a well-greased shallow ovenproof dish.

Mix the rest of the tomato mixture with the reserved bean liquor – there should be just under 150ml (5 fl oz). Season to taste, then pour this over the pancakes and sprinkle the top with grated cheese. Put the dish into the oven for about 30 minutes, to heat it through and brown the top.

PARMESAN ROULADE

A rich but delicious dish for a special occasion

SERVES 4
4 eggs, separated
3 tablespoons Parmesan cheese, grated
2 tablespoons soft breadcrumbs
a few drops tabasco *or* some cayenne
15g (½oz) butter
175g (6oz) cooked, chopped asparagus
½ teaspoon cornflour
150ml (5 fl oz) double cream
1 teaspoon chopped parsley
1 tablespoon lemon juice
sea salt
freshly ground black pepper

Set oven to 220°C (425°F), gas mark 7. Beat egg yolks to make them smooth, then add cheese, bread-crumbs, tabasco or cayenne. Whisk egg white stiffly and fold in to the mixture. Turn into a swiss roll tin which has been lined with foil and well brushed with oil or melted butter. Bake for 8–10 minutes until the mixture springs back when touched lightly.

While roulade is cooking, make the filling. Melt the butter in a medium-sized saucepan, add the asparagus and stir over a gentle heat, then add cornflour and cream and heat until thickened; stir in parsley and lemon juice and season to taste.

Turn roulade out on to a piece of greaseproof paper, peel off foil, spread with filling, and using the greaseproof underneath to help, roll up and slide on to a warming dish. Decorate with parsley and serve immediately.

PIPÉRADE

This tasty mixture of tomatoes, peppers and onions in creamy, lightly-set, scrambled egg makes a good quick supper dish, served with warm crisp French bread or wholemeal rolls.

SERVES 4
2 onions
2 garlic cloves
1 green pepper
1 red pepper
4 tomatoes
50g (2oz) butter
6 eggs
sea salt
freshly ground black pepper
chopped fresh parsley

Peel and chop the onions, peel and crush the garlic; wash, de-seed and chop the peppers, skin and chop the tomatoes. Melt the butter in a large saucepan, put in the onion and fry it for about 5 minutes without letting it brown, then mix in the garlic, peppers and tomatoes and cook for a further 5 minutes over a low heat with the lid on the saucepan.

Meanwhile beat the eggs in a small bowl with some salt and pepper. When the vegetables are tender pour the egg into the saucepan and stir gently over a low heat until the egg is lightly scrambled, but don't let it get too dry – it's best to keep the heat low all the time and take the *pipérade* off the stove while it's still runny. Check seasoning, then serve at once, sprinkled with chopped parsley and accompanied by the warm bread. Follow with fresh fruit.

PORTUGUESE EGGS

I don't know where this name originated, but it's basically hardboiled eggs in a sauce flavoured with onion, tomatoes and mushrooms. It's quick to make. Serve with fingers of crisp wholemeal toast.

SERVES 4
6 eggs
50g (2oz) butter
1 small onion, chopped
4 tomatoes, peeled and chopped
50g (2oz) mushrooms, chopped
50g (2oz) plain flour
575ml (1 pint) milk
sea salt
freshly ground black pepper
1 tablespoon chopped parsley
1 teaspoon grated lemon rind
1 tablespoon lemon juice

Hardboil the eggs. Meanwhile, melt the butter in a saucepan, add the onion and cook for 7 minutes, then add the tomatoes and mushrooms, and cook for 3–4 minutes. Stir in the flour, then gradually add the milk, bring to the boil and simmer for 10 minutes. Add the parsley, lemon rind and juice, salt and pepper to taste. Cut the eggs into quarters, arrange in a dish and pour the sauce over them.

QUICK SOUFFLÉ OMELETTE

Another almost instant supper recipe. A green salad or a tomato salad go well with it.

SERVES 4
6 eggs, separated
25g (1oz) flour
sea salt
freshly ground black pepper
50g (2oz) grated cheese
15g (½oz) butter

Preheat the grill. Separate eggs and whisk whites until stiff; leave on one side while beating yolks with flour until smooth and creamy, then fold in egg whites, seasoning and grated cheese. Melt butter in a frying pan or shallow casserole. Pour egg mixture into the piping hot butter and fry quickly until underneath is cooked; then place under the hot grill to cook the top and finish the soufflé. Serve immediately.

VEGETARIAN SCOTCH EGGS

Scotch eggs look attractive when they're sliced, and are useful for picnics and buffets. The secret of getting the outside to stick to the eggs is to dip the hardboiled egg into beaten egg before putting the coating on. The protein content of these Scotch eggs is excellent and they're good for lunch boxes, with some nice crisp salad.

MAKES 4
1 onion, peeled and grated
50g (2oz) roasted hazel nuts, grated
50g (2oz) ground almonds
50g (2oz) cheese, grated
2 heaped teaspoons tomato purée
1 egg
1 tablespoon fresh thyme, chopped *or* 1 teaspoon dried
sea salt
freshly ground black pepper
4 hardboiled eggs, shelled
beaten egg and crisp wholemeal crumbs to coat
fat for deep-frying

First make the outside coating for the Scotch eggs; simply mix the onion, nuts, cheese, tomato purée, egg and thyme together to a fairly firm paste and season, adding a tablespoonful of stock, water or cider to soften the consistency a little if necessary.

To finish the eggs, dip the whole hardboiled eggs in beaten egg and then press the nut mixture round to cover them completely. Coat the Scotch eggs in egg and breadcrumbs. Heat the oil in a deep frying pan to a temperature of 190°C (375°F), then deep-fry the Scotch eggs for 2–3 minutes, until golden brown and crisp, and drain on crumpled kitchen paper. Leave the Scotch eggs until they are cool, then cut each in half or into quarters and serve with salad.

Variation

BEANY SCOTCH EGGS

Use the lentil and walnut loaf mixture on page 193 to encase the hardboiled eggs. This gives that very successful partnership of lentils and hardboiled eggs in a particularly attractive form.

WELSH RABBIT

Some people say that this dish derives its name from the fact that it was served instead of rabbit when times were hard; anyway it's one of my husband's favourite quick supper dishes.

SERVES 2–4
4 large slices wholemeal bread
225g (8oz) grated Cheddar *or* Caerphilly cheese
3 tablespoons milk *or* beer
cayenne pepper
freshly ground black pepper

Toast the bread; arrange the slices in a grill pan or on a baking sheet which will fit under the grill. Put the grated cheese and milk or beer into a saucepan and heat them together, stirring all the time until the cheese has melted. Remove from the heat and add a pinch of cayenne pepper and a grating of black pepper. Pour this cheese mixture over the toast and pop it under a moderately hot grill for about 5 minutes, until the cheese is bubbly and lightly browned. Serve immediately.

This goes well with a tomato and onion salad or a nice crisp lettuce salad with fresh green herbs in it; alternatively serve the Welsh rabbit on its own and follow with some fresh fruit.

CHEESE SOUFFLÉ

I think this is perhaps the best soufflé of all with it's satisfying savoury flavour and lovely golden colour. The classic cheese to use is Gruyère but I find Cheddar is fine for everyday cooking whilst a red cheese such Leicestershire or double Gloucester makes the soufflé a beautiful rich golden colour which looks very appetizing. Cheese soufflé is lovely with a green salad or simply cooked vegetables such as new potatoes and French beans; it also makes an excellent first course, followed by a vegetable-based main course such as ratatouille and garlic bread or stuffed tomatoes à la Provençale and courgettes, with a fruity pudding to follow.

SERVES 4
40g (1½oz) butter
40g (1½oz) flour
275ml (10 fl oz) milk
125g (4oz) grated cheese
4 egg yolks
1 teaspoon mustard powder
sea salt
freshly ground black pepper
5 egg whites

Grease a 1¾ litre (3 pint) soufflé dish or tin with a little butter or oil. Melt the butter in a large saucepan and stir in the flour; cook for a few seconds then add a third of the milk. Stir the mixture over a high heat until it first goes lumpy then smooth and very thick, then add another third of the milk and repeat until you've used all the milk. Stir for a minute or two then draw the saucepan off the heat and pour the sauce into a large bowl. Let the mixture cool slightly then mix in the grated cheese, egg yolks, mustard and a good seasoning of salt and pepper. (You can cover the mixture and leave it for several hours at this stage if necessary.)

Set the oven to 190°C (375°F), gas mark 5. If you have a baking sheet place this on the shelf above the centre – it will get hot and when you put your soufflé dish on it there will be a nice blast of heat from the base to get things off to a good start. Whisk the egg whites. They should be stiff enough for you to be able to turn the bowl over without them coming out, but not so stiff that you could almost slice them with a knife, so stop in time. Mix a rounded tablespoonful of egg white in to the cheese mixture to soften it then tip the rest of the egg white on top of the mixture and using the side of a flattish metal spoon cut and fold the egg whites into the cheese mixture until the egg white has all been incorporated and you have a very light airy mixture. Pour the soufflé gently into the prepared dish – ideally the mixture should come up level with the rim; it doesn't matter if it's lower but don't pile it up above the rim. Bake the soufflé for 30–35 minutes until it looks firm when you shake it slightly – you can test it if you like with a fine skewer which should come out clean.

If you want to make a soufflé feed 6 people, use a 2 litre (3½–4 pint) dish and increase the quantities like this: 50g (2oz) each of butter and flour; 425ml (15 fl oz) milk; 175g (6oz) grated cheese; 5 egg yolks and 6 egg whites. You will need to cook it for just a little longer, too.

INDIVIDUAL CHEESE SOUFFLÉS

Puffy, golden, individual, cheese soufflés look impressive and make a marvellous first course or lunch dish. They're also very practical because they only take 15–20 minutes to cook so you can get the initial preparation done in advance, receive your visitors or round up the family, then add the egg whites and put the soufflés to cook 15 or 20 minutes before you want to eat. As a starter these soufflés are ideal before one of the low-protein vegetable dishes. Or for an easy-going lunch for a friend, serve them after avocados, with a tasty green salad and fruity pudding.

MAKES 3 INDIVIDUAL SOUFFLÉS
25g (1oz) butter
25g (1oz) flour
150ml (5 fl oz) milk
pinch each of mustard powder and cayenne pepper
125g (4oz) grated cheese
2 eggs, separated

Prepare 3 individual soufflé dishes – those little white porcelain ones are ideal – by greasing lightly with oil or butter. Place a baking sheet in the centre of the oven.

Melt the butter in a medium-sized saucepan and stir in the flour; when it froths add the milk mixing well over a gentle heat for a few minutes until smooth and thick. Remove from the heat, cool slightly then add the seasoning, grated cheese and the egg yolks. (The mixture can be prepared in advance up to this stage.)

Set the oven to 190°C (375°F), gas mark 5. Whisk the egg whites until they are very stiff and able to hold their shape but not dry. Mix a heaped tablespoon of egg white into the cheese mixture to loosen it, then add the rest and carefully incorporate it by folding the cheese mixture gently over it with a metal spoon, so that you don't flatten the egg white.

Divide the mixture between the little dishes and place them in the oven on the baking sheet. Bake for 15–20 minutes until risen and golden brown. Serve immediately; they will keep in the oven for a further few minutes if you turn off the heat but the sooner they are served the better they are.

These quantities will double satisfactorily to serve 6. To serve 4 use the basic mixture with an extra egg.

LEEK SOUFFLÉ

The chunky pieces of leek in this soufflé give it a delicate flavour and interesting texture. Try to find really thin leeks if you can then they can be sliced into nice neat pieces which will stay firm when they're cooked.

SERVES 4
3–4 thin leeks, weighing 350g (12oz) before you trim them
sea salt
40g (1½oz) butter
40g (1½oz) flour
275ml (10 fl oz) milk
4 egg yolks
freshly ground black pepper
nutmeg
5 egg whites

First of all prepare a 1¾ litre (3 pint) soufflé dish or tin by greasing generously. Then cut the roots and leafy green part off the leeks. Slit the leeks down one side and wash them carefully under running water, then cut them into 2.5cm (1in) lengths. Cook the leeks in 1cm (½in) boiling salted water until they're just tender – about 7–10 minutes. Drain the leeks and keep them on one side.

Melt the butter in a medium-sized saucepan and put in the flour; cook for a few moments then add a third of the milk. Stir all the time over a high heat until the mixture has thickened, then add another third of the milk and repeat the process until all the milk has been added and you've got a nice smooth, thickish sauce. Transfer the sauce to a large bowl – this cools it slightly ready for adding the egg yolks and is more convenient later when you want to fold in the egg white. Beat in the egg yolks one by one then gently stir in the leeks. Season the mixture with salt, pepper and nutmeg – be fairly generous because the egg whites will 'dilute' the mixture. Now you can leave this mixture until just before you want to cook the soufflé – I have kept it for several hours in the fridge and it has been perfect.

When you're ready to cook the soufflé place a baking sheet on the middle shelf of the oven. Set the oven to 190°C (375°F), gas mark 5. Whisk the egg whites until they're thick and standing in soft peaks but don't let them get hard and dry. Stir a generous heaped tablespoon of egg white into the leek sauce mixture to loosen it then tip all the egg white on top of it and gently fold it in with a metal spoon. When it has all been incorporated pour the mixture gently into your prepared dish – it should come just up to the rim. If it is lower it will still taste good even though it won't look so impressively high and puffy but if it is piled above the rim it will overflow.

Put the soufflé on the baking sheet and bake for 30–35 minutes until it looks firm when you move the dish slightly and a skewer pushed gently down into the soufflé comes out clean. If it's done before you're quite ready turn off the oven and the soufflé will keep for 4–5 minutes longer although it won't be quite so puffy. I think this soufflé is nicest served with just one well-cooked vegetable such as buttered baby carrots, sprouts or peas.

If you want to make this soufflé serve 6 people grease a 2 litre (3½–4 pint) dish and use 50g (2oz) butter and flour and 425ml (15 fl oz) milk for the sauce with 5 egg yolks and 6 egg whites – cook the soufflé for a little longer.

Variation

SPRING ONION SOUFFLÉ

Use 350g (12oz) of those thick spring onions which you can get now. Cut into 1cm (½in) lengths. No need to cook before adding to the mixture.

MUSHROOM SOUFFLÉ

This is a delicious soufflé – when you cut it open the chunks of mushroom look most appetizing. It's nicest made with those firm white button mushrooms.

SERVES 4
175g (6oz) firm white button mushrooms
50g (2oz) butter
1 garlic clove, peeled and crushed
40g (1½oz) flour
275ml (10 fl oz) milk
4 egg yolks
sea salt
freshly ground black pepper
5 egg whites

Prepare a 1¾ litre (3 pint) soufflé dish or tin by greasing with a little butter. Wash the mushrooms then cut them into halves or quarters so that the pieces are all roughly the same size. Melt a quarter of the butter in a medium-sized saucepan and put in the mushrooms. Cook them gently without a lid on the saucepan for about 5 minutes, then stir in the garlic.

Melt the rest of the butter in another medium-sized saucepan and stir in the flour, then add about a third of the milk, stirring over a high heat until the mixture has thickened, then add another third and continue like this until it has all been added. Take the saucepan off the heat and pour the sauce into a large bowl. Let it cool a bit then mix in the mushrooms (drain off any excess liquid), egg yolks and seasoning to taste. Leave on one side (for several hours or overnight in the fridge if necessary) until you're ready to cook the soufflé.

Put a baking sheet on the shelf above the centre of the oven and heat to 190°C (375°F), gas mark 5. Whisk the egg whites until they're stiff but not dry and fold them carefully into the mushroom mixture. Spoon the soufflé into the prepared dish – ideally it should come to the top but no higher – and bake it for 30–35 minutes, until it's golden brown, well risen and it looks firm when moved slightly. A skewer inserted should come out clean. Serve at once. This soufflé is nice with some green beans, baked tomatoes and creamy mashed potatoes.

If you want to expand this soufflé to serve 6 people, here are the quantities. Use a 2 litre (3½–4 pint) dish and 60g (2½oz) butter, 225g (8oz) mushrooms, 50g (2oz) flour, 425ml (15 fl oz) milk, 5 egg yolks and 6 egg whites. You will need to allow a few minutes longer for the soufflé to cook.

CONTINENTAL LENTIL TOAD-IN-THE-HOLE

SERVES 4–6
125g (4oz) continental lentils
4 tablespoons olive oil
1 onion, peeled and chopped
1 garlic clove, crushed
125g (4oz) mushrooms, washed and sliced
1 teaspoon thyme
sea salt
freshly ground black pepper
125g (4oz) self-raising wholemeal flour
½ teaspoon sea salt
2 eggs
275ml (10 fl oz) milk

Wash, soak, rinse and cook the lentils, then drain them.

Preheat the oven to 220°C (425°F), gas mark 7. Heat 2 tablespoons of the oil in a good-sized saucepan and fry the onion and garlic for 5 minutes, letting them brown lightly, then add the mushrooms and fry for another 5 minutes. Stir in the continental lentils, thyme and sea salt and freshly ground black pepper to season; keep the mixture hot.

Put the remaining oil into the shallow baking tin in which you are going to cook the toad-in-the-hole, and heat in the oven.

Next, make the batter. Sift the wholemeal flour and sea salt into a bowl and tip in the residue of bran left in the sieve. Make a well in the middle and add the eggs and about a third of the milk; beat vigorously with a wooden spoon, gradually incorporating the rest of the milk; beat well.

Pour the batter straight into the sizzling hot fat, then quickly spoon the lentil mixture on top. Bake for 20–25 minutes, until risen and golden. With gravy, potatoes and vegetables, this makes a good cheap family meal.

Variation

NUTMEAT AND MUSHROOM BATTER PUDDING

The above recipe comes from The Bean Book. For this simply delicious variation, just make the batter and add 225g (8oz) sliced left-over nut loaf, a fried onion, 125g (4oz) sliced, fried onions and, if you like, a teaspoon of mixed herbs.

12

PUDDINGS
HOT AND COLD

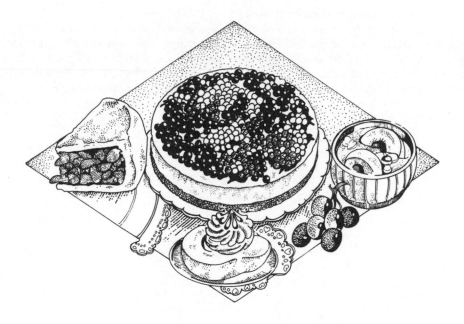

A pudding, even if it is only a piece of fresh fruit – which is the one served most frequently in our house – rounds off a meal pleasantly. Probably the most useful pudding most of the time is something which looks pretty and tastes good without being too high in fat or sugar. You'll find quite a few here which come into that category, as well as some more substantial ones for when something more filling is called for. Also, although I like to eat healthily most of the time, I love cream, chocolate and ice cream and, just occasionally, I like to have a pudding made from these (though perhaps not all at the same time!) and so, in case you feel the same, I've included one or two of my favourite sweet indulgences.

This chapter is divided into the following sections. First, since fruit features in so many of the puddings, there's a note on the basic preparation of all the common (and some of the not-so-common) fruits; this is followed by two useful non-dairy creams for serving with puddings. Then you'll find all the hot

puddings; after that you'll find the cold puddings, followed by a section of ice creams and sorbets. As before, puddings which will freeze are marked F.

Guide to Preparing Fruit

Apple Use dessert apples with or without the skin; slice, core and add to salads or fruit salad mixtures, or grate to make a real fruit muesli (page 303). Stew apples as described on page 298, serve with cream and shortbread biscuits or as a sauce with savoury dishes, or make into a crumble (page 295), or ice cream (page 308). For baked apples, see page 289, and for apple pie, see recipes on page 290 using uncooked apples in place of the fruits given.

Apricot Ripe apricots are delicious raw; less perfect apricots are best cooked. Poach in a vanilla-flavoured sugar syrup or put into a casserole with 3 tablespoons sugar and 1–2 tablespoons water to 450g (1 lb) apricots and bake for 30–60 minutes at 180°C

(350°F), gas mark 4. Cooked apricots can be made into a crumble, served on a crisp pastry base or puréed and made into fools, ices or sorbets.

Banana Top sliced banana with a dollop of yoghurt or *fromage blanc* and some maple syrup or runny honey and chopped nuts; or, for a treat, peel and cut lengthwise, put a scoop of vanilla ice cream between the halves, top with melted chocolate and chopped nuts. Also good cooked in a crumble (page 295). Or make a slit down the top of a banana and bake whole in the oven, 190°C (375°F), gas mark 5, for about 20 minutes until soft, then serve with cream, yoghurt or rum butter.

Bilberry Known as blueberry in the USA, can be eaten raw with sugar and cream if very ripe and soft, but is usually best cooked. Wash and pick over berries, make into a pie (page 290) or stew as described on page 288.

Blackberry Wash, pick over and serve with sugar and cream; or stew as described on page 288 and eat with cream or yoghurt, topped with crumble (page 295), or puréed and made into sorbets, sauces and fools. For blackberry ice cream follow the recipe on page 309 using cooked blackberries instead of raspberries.

Blackcurrant Wash and remove the stems or, for a purée leave the stems on. Stew as described on page 288. Blackcurrant purée is delicious with ice cream or made into a sorbet (page 310). Blackcurrants also make an excellent plate pie (page 290).

Cherry Wash sweet cherries and serve them as they are, or remove stalks and stones and add to a fruit salad. Also delicious made into a compôte. Stew cherries with a little water until tender, add sugar to taste.

Date Shiny plump fresh dates can quite often be found at good supermarkets and greengrocers now and are delicious. Serve as they are or slice and stone and add to fruit salads; or remove the stones and fill the centres with nuts or almond paste.

Fig Serve ripe figs Greek-style with a bowl of thick creamy yoghurt and runny honey, or slice and add to fruit salads.

Gooseberry Wash and leave as they are if you're going to purée them, otherwise 'top and tail', then cook in a sugar syrup as described on page 288. Add a few sprigs of elderflowers for a delicious muscat flavour. Can be puréed and made into a fool, or a sauce, see page 62. Also make excellent pies; follow recipes on page 290.

Grape Just wash gently and arrange in a fruit bowl or on a cheese-board; or halve, remove seeds and add grapes to a fruit salad or arrange on top of a sponge cake and glaze with jam.

Grapefruit Halve across, loosen sections with a sharp knife, carefully ease out white skin and membranes. Can be sprinkled with sherry and a little sugar or topped with brown sugar and dots of butter and grilled. Or cut out the segments as described for oranges (below).

Greengage Prepare as for plums.

Kiwi fruit, Chinese gooseberry Should feel just soft to the touch. Use raw, peeled and sliced, in fruit salads and to decorate cheesecakes, fools and creams.

Lemon To use the skin, scrub well in warm water to remove residue of sprays, then grate finely, or pare off thinly. Use both the juice and the rind to flavour ice creams, fools and sorbets as well as cakes and pastries.

Lime Gives a delicious flavour to fools and creams and makes an unusual garnish for fruit fritters or pancakes.

Loganberry Prepare and use as for blackberries.

Lychee Looks like a small horsechestnut, with a reddish prickly shell. Inside is translucent white fragrant flesh and a large shiny brown stone. Serve raw, or peel, stone and add to an exotic fruit salad.

Mango Large oval fruits, green or gold, often splashed with red. They are ripe when soft to the touch. To prepare, first cut in half and remove the stone: make two downward cuts, each about 6mm (¼in) from the stalk at the top. As you cut down you will feel the large flat stone, and the two halves will fall apart. Serve the halves as they are and scoop out the juicy golden flesh with a teaspoon; or cut off the skin, slice flesh and add to fruit salad. Mango also makes an excellent sorbet or ice cream (melon sorbet, page 310, raspberry ice, page 309).

Melon *Cantaloupe melon* has a rough, wart-like skin and deep grooves, as if ready for slicing; the flesh is orange, fragrant and juicy, *Charantais melons* are smaller versions. *Musk melons* have a netted skin and green or yellow aromatic flesh; delicious little *ogen melons* belong to this group as do *winter melons* which have smooth, green, yellow or white skins but very little flavour. *Honeydew melons* have ridged green or yellow skins and sweet white or pale green flesh. *Watermelons* have smooth green skin, scarlet flesh and shiny brown pips. Melons should feel heavy and yield to slight pressure at the stalk end. Serve large melons cut in slices, the smaller ones halved and maybe filled with sweet sherry or port, ripe strawberries or a scoop of ice cream (page 309). They can also be made into a sorbet (page 310).

Nectarine Prepare as for peaches.

Orange Scrub skins, if using, to remove residue of sprays. Use the rind, either grated or thinly pared, for flavouring; the juice is good instead of sugar syrup in fruit salads. Oranges can be peeled and divided into segments; but the best way is to cut round and round with a sharp knife and a sawing action, removing both the peel and the white skin. Then insert the knife and cut each segment away from the inner skin. Hold the orange over a bowl to catch the juice. Good in fruit salad, or served on their own, as described on page 303.

Passion fruit *Granadilla* has a wrinkled brown skin, sweet fragrant greenish flesh and quite a number of seeds. Halve the fruits, scoop out the flesh and add to fruit salads or use to top ice cream.

Pawpaw Also called papaya and custard apple. Large, pear-shaped fruits, green or greenish yellow. Smell fragrant and feel soft when ripe; flesh inside is pink with tiny black seeds. Halve, scoop out seeds and eat flesh with a teaspoon; or peel, slice and add to fruit salads, see page 301.

Peach To skin peaches, put into a bowl, cover with boiling water and leave for 2 minutes; drain and slip off skins with a sharp knife. Slice and cover with sweet white wine, add to fruit salads or make into peach brulée (page 304).

Pear Wash thin-skinned dessert pears and serve simply, or peel, core and slice and serve with cream, a raspberry purée, or as part of a fruit salad. Both dessert and cooking pears are delicious poached (see below).

Persimmon Also called a sharon fruit, looks like a ripe tomato and is ready for eating when it feels very soft. Flesh is very sweet and tastes like fresh dates. Peel, slice and add to fruit salad.

Pineapple Should be dark golden brown in colour, have a pronounced sweet smell and feel slightly soft to the touch. Serve like melon as a starter; or in fruit salads, compôtes and sorbets.

Plum Slice and stone sweet plums and add to fruit salad; poach sharper plums in syrup as described below, make into pies (page 295), or crumble.

Pomegranate Halve, scoop out the scarlet flesh, add to fruit salad or use as a topping for a pale creamy pudding or coleslaw.

Quince Peel, core and slice, then stew or add to pies. Makes an excellent jelly preserve. The fruits of the scarlet-flowered Japanese quince are edible and can be used in this way.

Raspberry Eat raw with cream and sugar, or make into ice cream (page 309), sorbet or a fresh purée for serving with ice cream or other fruits (page 305).

Redcurrant Prepare as described for blackcurrants; mix with raspberries and strawberries to make traditional dishes such as rødgrød from Denmark (page 306), summer pudding (page 307), or raspberry and redcurrant tart (page 297).

Rhubarb Cut off the leaves (don't eat, they're poisonous) and pull off any strings from the sides of the rhubarb. Cut rhubarb into even-sized pieces, stew as described below; make into a fool (page 298), or crumble (page 295). Best not to serve rhubarb more than once a week because, like spinach, its high oxalic content prevents the absorption of magnesium and calcium.

Strawberry Wash gently, remove stems and serve strawberries with sugar and cream; or, French-style, with little cream cheese hearts (page 306), or in little sweet pastry tartlets with a glaze of red jam. For strawberries cardinal, hull and slice the strawberries and cover with a raspberry sauce (page 304).

Tangerine, satsuma, clementine and mandarin Peel and eat as they are, or divide into segments and add to fruit salads.

Basic Preparation and Cooking

Buy ripe, firm fruit; prepare quickly, cutting with a sharp stainless steel knife and use as soon as possible. Coat cut surfaces of fruit which you're going to serve raw with lemon or orange juice to prevent discoloration.

The method of cooking fruit most frequently used, and one which is suitable for almost all types, is poaching. To poach fruit, first make a sugar syrup. For 450–700g (1–1½ lb) fruit you need 275ml (10 fl oz) water (or other liquid such as wine or cider) and 75g (3oz) granulated sugar or mild honey. Put the sugar or honey and water into a heavy-based saucepan and heat gently until dissolved. Then turn up the heat and boil rapidly for 2 minutes. Put in the prepared fruit, bring back to the boil, then leave to simmer gently until the fruit feels tender when pierced with the point of a sharp knife.

It's important to give large fruits like whole or halved pears and peaches time to cook right through to the centre or they may discolour. Allow at least 20–30 minutes for whole pears and 15–20 minutes for the others.

The syrup can be flavoured with thin slices of lemon or orange peel, a cinnamon stick, vanilla pod or a few heads of fresh elderflowers: add when making the syrup and remove before serving the fruit. (The vanilla pod can be rinsed, dried and used several times.)

Let the fruits cool in the syrup, or remove with a draining spoon and thicken the syrup by boiling rapidly until reduced in quantity.

Soft, juicy fruits are best poached in the minimum of water, or none at all. Put red and black currants, bilberries, cranberries and blackberries into a heavy-based saucepan with 2 tablespoons of water to 450–700g (1–1½lb) fruit and heat gently until the juices run and the fruit is tender. Instead of the water use butter for apples, redcurrant or mild jelly for rhubarb. When fruit is soft, add sugar or mild honey to taste: do not put this in sooner or the outside of the fruits may toughen.

Cooked fruit, as well as uncooked soft fruits such as raspberries and strawberries, can be puréed. Simply push through a sieve or mouli légumes, or, to make it easier, liquidize first then sieve. Serve as a sauce or make into ice cream, fools or sorbets.

CASHEW NUT CREAM

A delicious, thick non-dairy cream.

MAKES ABOUT 250ML (8 FL OZ)
125g (4oz) cashew nuts
150ml (5 fl oz) water
dash of honey *or* raw sugar
real vanilla extract *or* a piece of vanilla pod

Simply put everything into a liquidizer or food processor and whizz to a cream. If you're using the vanilla pod, your cream will have some black specks in it, but will taste superb. (Any larger pieces of vanilla pod which don't get broken down by the blender can be removed and used again.) If you want a thinner cream, simply add more water.

TOFU 'WHIPPED' CREAM

For this you need firm tofu – homemade or bought from a health shop or Chinese shop. You could use the vacuum-packed tofu which you can buy, but that will not give such a thick effect.

MAKES 225G (8OZ)
225g (8oz) tofu
2 teaspoons honey *or* raw sugar
real vanilla extract *or* a piece of vanilla pod

Drain water from tofu. Break tofu into rough pieces and place in blender or food processor with the honey or sugar and the vanilla extract or pod and whizz to a thick cream. As with the nut cream above, using a vanilla pod will result in a wonderful flavour but slightly speckled appearance. This is also delicious flavoured with some triple distilled rose water or orange flower water (Langdales), some grated orange or lemon rind, or 25g (1oz) ground almonds and a few drops of real almond essence.

HOT PUDDINGS, TARTS, PIES AND CRUMBLES

BAKED APPLES WITH RAISINS

These are nice served just as they are, or with natural yoghurt or one of the low-fat toppings. Other fillings can be used instead of the raisins; dates are good and so is a spoonful of the healthy mincemeat (page 293).

SERVES 4
4 large cooking apples
50g (2oz) raisins

Wash the apples and remove cores, using an apple corer or by cutting them out neatly with a sharp pointed knife. Score round the middle of the apples, just cutting the skin. Place the apples in a shallow ovenproof dish. Fill the cavities of the apples with raisins, pressing them down well. Bake the apples, uncovered, at 180°C (350°F), gas mark 4, for 45–60 minutes, until the apples are tender, but not collapsed.

OPEN APPLE TART

This is mouthwatering with its topping of glazed apple slices, moist filling of apple purée and crisp pastry base.

SERVES 4–6
20cm (8in) pastry flan case, baked as on page 242
900g (2 lb) cooking apples, peeled, cored and sliced
25g (1oz) butter
75g (3oz) sugar
2 large Cox apples
3 tablespoons warmed sieved apricot jam

Put the cooking apples, butter and sugar into a heavy-based saucepan and cook gently, uncovered, for about 15 minutes. The mixture should be able to hold its shape, so if necessary turn up heat and cook until this stage is reached, stirring often. Cool. Set the oven to 200°C (400°F), gas mark 6. Spoon apple purée into flan case. Peel Cox apples and slice thinly, arrange on top of purée, then spoon the jam over them. Bake for 20–30 minutes, until the apple slices are tender. Serve warm or cold.

BAKEWELL TART

This traditional tart, with its crisp pastry covered with jam and a light almond sponge, makes a very satisfactory pudding after a vegetable-based main course.

SERVES 6
175g (6oz) plain wholemeal flour
75g (3oz) butter
1½ tablespoons cold water
3 tablespoons raspberry jam
125g (4oz) soft butter
125g (4oz) caster sugar
2 eggs
25g (1 oz) plain flour
50g (2oz) ground almonds
a few flaked almonds

First make the pastry: sift the flour into a large bowl, and just tip in the bran which will be left in the sieve. Rub the fat into the flour using your fingertips or a fork until the mixture resembles fine breadcrumbs – if the fat is soft you might find it easiest to start this process with a fork – then add the cold water and press the mixture together to form a dough. If there's time, leave this dough to rest for 30 minutes (this makes it easier to roll out but isn't essential).

Set the oven to 220°C (425°F), gas mark 7, and if possible place a heavy baking sheet on the top shelf to heat up with the oven. Roll out pastry and ease it into a 20cm (8in) lightly greased flan tin; trim edges. Spread with the jam. Put the butter, sugar, eggs, flour and ground almonds into a bowl and beat for 2 minutes, until light and creamy. Spoon this mixture over the jam and sprinkle with a few flaked almonds. Bake in the pre-heated oven for 5 minutes, then turn the oven down to 180°C (350°F), gas mark 4, and bake for a further 30–35 minutes, until golden and firm to the touch. Serve hot or cold with single cream if liked.

BILBERRY PLATE PIE

I use wholemeal flour as I like its flavour and wholesome appearance, but white flour or a half-and-half mixture could be used instead.

SERVES 4–6
225g (8oz) plain wholemeal flour
125g (4oz) butter
25g (1oz) caster sugar
3 tablespoons cold water
450g (1 lb) bilberries, stalks removed
50g (2oz) sugar
15g (½oz) butter
milk to glaze

Set oven to 200°C (400°F), gas mark 6. Sift flour into a bowl, adding bran from sieve. Rub in the butter, add sugar and water, mix to a dough. Roll out a third of pastry, use to line a 20–22cm (8–9in) pie plate. Put bilberries on top, sprinkle with sugar, dot with butter. Roll out rest of pastry and put over top of fruit. Trim, decorate, and make two or three steam holes. Brush with milk. Bake for about 30 minutes.

BLACKBERRY AND APPLE PIE

This is a deep-dish pie with a top-crust. For a plate pie, see Bilberry Plate Pie (above).

SERVES 4–6
225g (8oz) wholemeal flour
2 teaspoons baking powder
125g (4oz) butter
3 tablespoons cold water
450g (1 lb) blackberries, washed
450g (1 lb) apples, peeled, cored and sliced
75–125g (3–4oz) sugar
2–3 tablespoons water
milk to glaze
caster sugar

Set oven to 200°C (400°F), gas mark 6. Make pastry as in previous recipe, roll out quite thickly, and cut out so that it is about 2.5cm (1in) larger all round than pie dish. Cut 1 cm (½in) strips of pastry from trimmings, brush with cold water, press round rim of pie dish. Mix fruit with sugar and put in dish; sprinkle with water. Ease pastry on top of fruit, moulding it over. Trim, decorate, and make steam holes. Brush with milk, bake for 15 minutes, then reduce the heat to 180°C (350°F), gas mark 4, for 15–20 minutes. Sprinkle with caster sugar.

BLACKCURRANT LATTICE TART WITH LEMON PASTRY

You could use a good quality blackcurrant jam (I like the Bulgarian ones) or one of the lovely no-added-sugar jams from health shops instead of the fruit, if you prefer: the tart is sweeter if you use jam.

SERVES 6
175g (6oz) plain wholemeal flour
finely grated rind of 1 lemon
75g (3oz) butter
1½ tablespoons cold water
2 × 350g (12oz) jars bottled blackcurrants *or* about
350g (12oz) fresh ones, topped and tailed
50–125g (2–4 oz) sugar
1 tablespoon cornflour
milk and extra sugar to glaze

First make the pastry: sift the flour into a large bowl, and just tip in the bran which will be left in the sieve. Add the lemon rind, then rub the fat into the flour using your fingertips or a fork until the mixture resembles fine breadcrumbs – if the fat is soft you might find it easiest to start this process with a fork – then add the cold water and press the mixture together to form a dough. If there's time, leave this dough to rest for 30 minutes (this makes it easier to roll out but isn't essential).

Set the oven to 220°C (425°F), gas mark 7, and if possible place a heavy baking sheet on the top shelf to heat up with the oven. Roll out the pastry and ease it into a 20cm (8in) lightly greased flan tin; trim edges.

Put the blackcurrants into a bowl and sprinkle with the sugar and cornflour. You will probably need the full amount of sugar for fresh blackcurrants but less for ones which have been bottled in a light syrup. Gently turn the blackcurrants so that they all get coated with the sugar and cornflour.

Spread the blackcurrants evenly in the flan case. Gather up and re-roll the pastry trimmings, cut into thin strips and arrange in a lattice on top of the blackcurrants. Brush the strips with milk and sprinkle with a little sugar. Bake in the pre-heated oven for 5 minutes, then turn the oven down to 180°C (350°F), gas mark 4, and bake for a further 30–35 minutes, until the pastry is golden brown. Serve hot or cold, with single cream if liked.

CHRISTMAS PUDDING – SUGARLESS

This is a beautiful dark, glossy Christmas pudding which is sweet and spicy, even though it contains no sugar. It's my healthy, sugarless version of our traditional family pudding, but the dried fruits are so sweet in themselves that no one can tell the difference between this one and a 'normal' pudding! In fact it makes me wonder why we ever put sugar into Christmas puddings at all.

MAKES 1 LARGE PUDDING WHICH SERVES 8–10 AT LEAST
225g (8oz) cooking dates
150ml (5 fl oz) rum or milk
225g (8oz) butter
2 eggs, beaten
1 tablespoon black treacle
grated rind and juice of 1 lemon
125g (4oz) stoned raisins, chopped
125g (4oz) whole candied peel, chopped
25g (1oz) blanched almonds, chopped
225g (8oz) currants
125g (4oz) sultanas
125g (4oz) plain wholemeal flour
125g (4oz) soft wholemeal breadcrumbs
½ teaspoon grated nutmeg
½ teaspoon ground ginger
1½ teaspoons mixed spice

Cut up the cooking dates, being careful to remove any stones and hard pieces of stem. Put the dates into a small saucepan with the milk or rum and heat gently until mushy. Remove from heat and cool. Cream together the butter and dates in a large mixing bowl, then beat in the eggs, treacle, lemon rind and juice. Add all the remaining ingredients, stirring well to make a soft mixture which will fall heavily from the spoon when shaken. Put the mixture into a well greased 900ml (2 pint) pudding basin or two 575ml (1 pint) basins, filling to 2.5cm (1in) from the top. Cover with greased greaseproof paper and piece of foil, tying down well. Steam for 4 hours, topping up the water with more boiling water as necessary. Store in a cool dry place; steam for another 3 hours before serving. It's lovely with some brandy butter, single cream or thick Greek strained yoghurt.

CHRISTMAS PUDDING – TRADITIONAL

When we have a family Christmas with my parents, my father always makes the pudding. This is the recipe he uses, and has done for as long as I can remember, and very good it is, too.

SERVES 8–12
225g (8oz) currants
125g (4oz) sultanas
125g (4oz) raisins
125g (4oz) candied peel
25g (1oz) blanched almonds
125g (4oz) plain flour
½ teaspoon salt
½ teaspoon nutmeg, grated
½ teaspoon ground ginger
1½ teaspoon mixed spice
225g (8oz) Barbados sugar
125g (4oz) soft brown breadcrumbs
225g (8oz) vegetable suenut, shredded – from health shops (I would use unsalted butter)
rind and juice of 1 lemon
2 eggs
1 tablespoon treacle
approx 4 tablespoons milk *or* milk and rum

Wash and dry fruit; stone and chop raisins, finely chop peel and blanched almonds. Sieve flour with salt and spices. Mix all dry ingredients, add fruits nuts and peel, lemon rind and strained juice. Beat eggs and stir into mixture, then mix in treacle. Add sufficient milk and rum mixture, or plain milk, to make a soft mixture which will fall heavily from the spoon when shaken. Stir all well together. Put mixture into well-greased 1.2 litre (2 pint) basin, or two 575ml (1 pint) basins, and fill to 2.5cm (1in) from top. Cover with greased greaseproof paper and tie on a pudding cloth, or cover with greased tinfoil. Steam for 4 hours. Store in a dry place; steam for another 3 hours before serving. This pudding serves 8 people – at least!

DATE TART WITH ORANGE PASTRY

The dates make a lovely moist sweet filling for this flan. Serve it warm with a dollop of chilled natural yoghurt, or *fromage blanc*; their smooth cool sharpness provides a perfect contrast to the sweet crunchy pie.

SERVES 6–8 F
225g (8oz) cooking dates
150ml (5 fl oz) orange juice
225g (8oz) wholemeal flour
125g (4oz) butter
grated rind of 1 orange and 2 tablespoons of the juice

Chop the dates coarsely, removing any stones or hard bits. Put the dates into a small saucepan with the orange juice and heat gently until mushy. Cool.

Make the pastry; sift the flour into a bowl, adding also the residue of bran from the sieve. Using a fork, mix in the butter, orange rind and the 2 tablespoons orange juice to make a dough. Roll out the dough and use to line a 22cm (8in) flan dish; spoon in the date mixture, smoothing it level with the back of the spoon. Trim the pastry. Re-roll the trimmings and cut into thin strips; arrange these in a lattice on top of the tart. Bake the tart in the oven for 30 minutes. Serve hot, or warm.

LINZERTORTE

This light, crumbly Austrian tart is delicately flavoured with spices and lemon rind and melts in your mouth. I experimented many times with this recipe until I came up with this version which we think is just right. With one of my later efforts my husband said he liked the flavour but the tart wasn't thick enough to get his teeth into, so I increased the amount of pastry to the present quantity. If you'd like to make a thinner tart you could try using only 125g (4oz) of flour, almonds and butter and 25g (1oz) sugar or alternatively use a larger tin. A good pudding to serve after a vegetable-based meal, or to offer as an alternative to a fruit or ice cream pudding at a dinner party.

SERVES 6 F
175g (6oz) plain wholemeal flour
1 teaspoon powdered cinnamon
pinch of ground cloves
175g (6oz) ground almonds – or whole unblanched almonds pulverized in a liquidizer
grated rind of ½ lemon
40g (1½oz) sugar
175g (6oz) butter
1 egg yolk
175–225g (6–8oz) raspberry, cherry or blackcurrant jam – the raw sugar conserves from health shops are ideal
a little icing sugar

Sift the flour, cinnamon and cloves into a bowl; add also the residue of bran left in the sieve. Mix in the almonds, lemon rind and sugar then rub the butter into the dry ingredients as if you were making pastry. Gently mix in the egg yolk to make a soft dough. If possible wrap the dough in a piece of foil or polythene and chill it in the refrigerator for 30 minutes or so. If you have time for this the dough will be easier to roll out but it isn't essential if you're in a hurry.

Set oven to 200°C (400°F), gas mark 6. On a lightly floured board roll out three-quarters of the dough to fit a 20–23cm (8–9in) fluted flan dish – one of those pretty porcelain ones is ideal for this recipe. Spread the jam evenly over the pastry. Roll out the rest of the pastry and cut into long strips; arrange these strips in a lattice over the jam, then fold the edges of the pastry down and press them in to make a sort of rim round the edge of the tart. Bake the tart for 25–30 minutes, until it's slightly risen and golden brown.

You can serve the tart hot, cold or, my choice, warm. Sieve a little icing sugar over the top of the tart before taking it to the table; the red jam looks very appetizing glistening underneath this snowy topping. It's nice with single cream.

MINCEMEAT – SUGARLESS, FATLESS VERSION

I suddenly thought why put extra sugar and fat into mincemeat? The fat is only a hang-over from the days when it was made with minced meat, and the sugar isn't necessary, because the dried fruit is very sweet. So I made this version, and it was a great success. Make the mincemeat fresh, just before you want to use it.

ENOUGH FOR 3 DOZEN MINCE PIES
125g (4oz) currants
125g (4oz) raisins
125g (4oz) sultanas
50g (2oz) cooking dates
50g (2oz) candied peel
50g (2oz) glacé cherries
50g (2oz) flaked almonds
1 ripe banana
4 tablespoons brandy *or* whisky
½ teaspoon each ground ginger, grated nutmeg, mixed spice

Simply mix everything together. This can be done in a food processor to make a smoothish texture.

This mincemeat will keep for a week in a covered bowl in the fridge, but doesn't keep in the same way as ordinary mincemeat because of the lack of sugar.

MINCE PIES

WILL MAKE 1 DOZEN PIES F
shortcrust pastry made from 225g (8oz) flour (page 240)
mincemeat from previous recipe

Set oven to 220°C (425°F), gas mark 7. Roll the pastry out thinly. Cut circles to fit small tartlet tins; fill with a good spoonful of mincemeat. Cover with a smaller pastry circle to fit top, press down lightly and prick. Bake for about 10 minutes. Cool slightly, then carefully remove from tin using a palette knife.

MINCEMEAT – TRADITIONAL

MAKES APPROX. 3 KILOS (7 LB)
450g (1 lb) currants
450g (1 lb) sultanas
450g (1 lb) raisins
450g (1 lb) cooking apples
50g (2oz) glacé cherries
50g (2oz) dates
50g (2oz) blanched almonds
175g (6oz) candied peel
450g (1 lb) shredded vegetable suenut – from health shops
350g (12oz) Barbados sugar
½ teaspoon salt
½ teaspoon nutmeg (grated)
½ teaspoon ground ginger
1 teaspoon mixed spice
2 lemons
2 tangerines
150ml (5 fl oz) rum *or* brandy

Clean and dry fruit. Stone and chop raisins. Peel, core and chop or mince apples finely. Chop peel, cherries, dates and blanched almonds. Mix all together in a large basin with shredded suenut. Stir in sugar, spices and salt. Grate in rind of 1 lemon and 1 tangerine, and add juice of 2 lemons and 2 tangerines. Add spirit. Mix thoroughly with wooden spoon. Put into clean jars and store in a cool, dry place. Make into mince pies.

PANCAKES

Pancakes make a super, quick family pudding and, health-conscious slimmers, the good news is, they're quite low in calories (about 70 for each pancake) if you make them as they should be made, thin and cooked in a pan with just enough fat to prevent them from sticking: see recipe and method on page 275. The batter can be varied by adding grated orange or lemon rind, or by using orange juice to make the batter instead of milk. You can also make chocolate or carob pancakes by replacing a tablespoon of the flour in the batter with a tablespoon of cocoa or carob powder. Add a teaspoon of sugar to this batter and serve the pancakes with whipped cream (slimmers, forget this one!).

The traditional way to serve pancakes, is, of course, with caster sugar and slices of lemon; real maple syrup or clear honey are delicious alternatives. Pancakes are also delicious filled with the apple and raisin compôte mixture on page 298 and served with thick natural yoghurt; or with a compôte made by simmering fresh or frozen pitted black cherries with a little water and sugar – this one is nice with soured cream. Another delicious filling for pancakes is a mixture of curd cheese, chopped dried and glacé fruits and a little grated orange or lemon rind and sugar to taste.

Variation

CRÊPES SUZETTE

Crêpes suzette aren't difficult to make – you do all the preparation well in advance – and are delicious for a treat, especially after a light main course.

SERVES 4–6
14–15 thin pancakes, made according to recipe on page 275
125g (4oz) butter
150g (5oz) caster sugar
grated rind and juice of 3 small-medium oranges
grated rind and juice of 1 lemon
2 tablespoons orange liqueur such as Curaçao if available
4 tablespoons brandy

First of all make the pancakes as described on page 275, so that you have a pile of about 14 thin pancakes. Cover them and keep them in a cool place until needed.

When you're ready to serve the pancakes, put the butter, sugar, grated rinds, and juices, and the orange liqueur if you're using it, into a large frying pan or shallow flameproof dish that you can take to the table, and heat gently to melt the butter and sugar. Turn off the heat, then dip the pancakes in this mixture, one by one, coating each side of the pancake then folding it in half and in half again, so that it's a triangle shape. As each pancake is done push it to the side of the frying pan. When all the pancakes have been dipped leave them in the frying pan or dish until you're almost ready to eat them then put the frying pan over the heat to warm through the sauce and the pancakes. When they're ready, turn up the heat high for about 1 minute to make the sauce very hot, quickly pour in the brandy and set it alight with a taper or by tilting the frying pan down towards the gas flame. You can take it to the table at this point, burning away. The flame will die out in a few seconds, when all the fat has been burnt. Serve immediately.

PANCAKES WITH MAPLE SYRUP

Although you might think of pancakes as being greasy, they're not because they're only cooked in a very little oil. They therefore make a good, substantial pudding and one that's always popular with my children. If I've got time I like to make a double batch, and keep half of them in the freezer. Just wrap the pile of pancakes in foil, label and freeze. There is no need to put pieces of greaseproof paper between them. To use, loosen the foil, thaw or half thaw and put the pancakes in a slow oven to defrost and heat through. They make a useful weekend pudding when life is hectic.

MAKES 12 PANCAKES
125g (4oz) wholemeal flour
2 eggs
1 tablespoon olive oil
225ml (8 fl oz) liquid skimmed milk
oil for frying
Maple syrup (or clear honey)
slices of lemon

If you've got a liquidizer, simply put the flour, eggs, oil and milk into the goblet and blend until smooth. Otherwise put the flour into a bowl, break in the eggs and add the oil and milk gradually, beating to a smooth consistency. If you're making the batter ahead of time, leave it to stand, but if not, don't worry as it doesn't seem to make much difference, especially if you use the liquidizer method.

Brush a small frying pan with oil and set over a moderate heat. When hot, put in two tablespoons or so of the batter. Tip and swirl the frying pan so that the batter runs all over the base and covers it thinly. When the top has set, use a spatula and your fingers to flip the pancake over and cook the other side, which will do very quickly. Remove from the frying pan and put on to a plate. Cover with foil and keep warm in a low oven while you make the rest. Serve the pancakes with maple syrup and slices of lemon.

WHOLEMEAL PLUM CRUMBLE

This is just a wholemeal version of an old favourite that always seems to be popular. It's good with a dollop of thick natural yoghurt.

SERVES 4–6
700g (1½ lb) plums
75–125g (3–4oz) sugar
225g (8oz) plain wholemeal flour
1 teaspoon baking powder
1 teaspoon allspice
125g (4oz) real demerara sugar
75g (3oz) butter

Set the oven to 180°C (350°F), gas mark 4. Halve the plums and take out the stones. Put the plums into a shallow pie dish and sprinkle with the sugar. To make the topping, sift the flour, baking powder and allspice into a bowl, adding the bran left in the sieve too. Mix in the sugar and then blend in the butter – it may be easiest to use a fork for this – until the mixture looks like fine breadcrumbs. Sprinkle this over the top of the plums in an even layer and press down lightly. Bake for 40 minutes, until crumble is crisp and the plums tender. Serve hot or warm.

Variations

RHUBARB CRUMBLE

Make this as above, using 700g (1½ lb) trimmed rhubarb cut into 1cm (½in) pieces.

APPLE AND RAISIN CRUMBLE

For this first make the apple and raisin compôte (page 298). Top with crumble and bake for 25–30 minutes.

BANANA CRUMBLE WITH ALMONDS

For this unusual variation (which I love but which some people think is strange) replace 50g (2oz) of the flour with ground almonds. Slice 4–6 large bananas into a shallow, greased baking dish. Cover with crumble, sprinkle with 25g (1oz) flaked almonds and bake for 25–30 minutes.

PUMPKIN PIE

An American friend gave me this recipe which I've adapted to give the right quantity for a 20–22cm (8–9in) flan dish. It makes a lovely autumn pudding, smooth and warmly spiced. I think it's best when it's hot but you can also serve it cold; it's nicest with cream. Sometimes I scatter some roughly chopped walnuts over the top of the pie which makes it look specially interesting and is a pleasant variation.

SERVES 6
175g (6oz) plain wholemeal flour
1½ teaspoons baking powder
125g (4oz) butter
1 tablespoon cold water
1 kilo (2¼ lb) pumpkin, weighed in the shop with skin and pips
4 tablespoons water
125g (4oz) soft brown sugar
½ teaspoon ground ginger
½ teaspoon powdered cinnamon
a little grated nutmeg
pinch of cloves
150ml (5 fl oz) single cream
2 eggs

Set the oven to 200°C (400°F), gas mark 6. Sift the flour and baking powder into a bowl and add the residue of bran left in the sieve. Rub in the butter until the mixture looks like fine breadcrumbs then add the water and mix to a dough. Roll the pastry out on a lightly floured board and put into a 20–23cm (8–9in) diameter flan dish. Prick the base, then bake the flan in the oven for about 15 minutes until it's browned and crisp. Take it out of the oven and let it cool slightly while you make the filling. Reduce the oven setting to 180°C (350°F), gas mark 4.

Peel the pumpkin and remove the pips. Cut the pumpkin into even-sized pieces, put them into a heavy-based saucepan with the water and cook gently, with a lid on the saucepan, until the pumpkin is tender – about 10 minutes. Put the pumpkin into a colander and drain it very well indeed, pressing gently with a spoon to extract as much water as possible. Put the pumpkin into a bowl and add the sugar, spices, cream and eggs. Mix well, then pour into the flan case and bake in the preheated oven for about 50 minutes, until it's set.

RAISIN SOUR CREAM PIE

The friend in the USA who kindly gave me this recipe serves it as an alternative to pumpkin pie at Thanksgiving. I think it also makes an excellent alternative to mincemeat pie at Christmas because it's got a spicy, festive flavour. It's a nourishing, protein-rich pudding with the wholemeal flour, eggs and nuts. If you can't get pecan nuts you can use walnuts instead, or flaked almonds which I like best of all; and an alternative to the soured cream is natural yoghurt.

SERVES 6
225g (8oz) seedless raisins – or use sultanas
150ml (5 fl oz) soured cream
¼ teaspoon ground cloves
¼ teaspoon grated nutmeg
1 teaspoon powdered cinnamon
2 eggs
50g (2oz) soft brown sugar
50g (2oz) pecan nuts or walnuts, chopped or flaked almonds
125g (4oz) plain wholemeal flour
1 teaspoon baking powder
50g (2oz) butter
1 tablespoon cold water

First start making the filling by putting the raisins or sultanas into a bowl with the soured cream and the spices: mix well, then leave on one side while you make the flan case.

Set the oven to 200°C (400°F), gas mark 6. To make the pastry sift the flour and baking powder into a bowl and also add the residue of bran left in the sieve. Rub in the fat until the mixture looks like breadcrumbs, then mix in the water and gently press the mixture together to form a dough. Roll out the dough on a lightly floured board and use to line a 20–23cm (8–9in) flan dish. Trim the edges and prick the base of the flan, then bake in the oven for about 15 minutes, until it is set and golden brown. Take the flan out of the oven and reduce the temperature to 180°C (350°F), gas mark 4.

Finish making the filling: beat the eggs, then add them to the soured cream and fruit mixture, together with the sugar and nuts. Mix everything together well, then pour the filling evenly into the flan case –

it doesn't matter if this is still warm – and smooth the top gently with a knife or the back of a spoon. Bake the flan in the oven for 35–40 minutes, until the filling is set. You can serve the flan hot or cold but I think it's nicest hot.

RAISIN AND NUT TART WITH SPICY PASTRY

This is a lovely flan, crisp cinnamon-flavoured pastry filled with a moist, lightly spiced mixture of raisins and creamy cheese. I find the pastry keeps crisp even after the flan has been in the fridge overnight. It's quick to make as the filling is uncooked. You could use firm tofu to make the filling instead of the white cheese.

SERVES 8
150g (6oz) raisins
150g (6oz) wholemeal flour
½ teaspoon allspice or ground cloves
1 teaspoon ground cinnamon
75g (3oz) butter
1 tablespoon cold water
250g (8¾oz) quark or other soft white skimmed milk cheese
2–3 tablespoons liquid skimmed milk
1 teaspoon thick honey
50g (2oz) flaked almonds

Set the oven to 200°C (400°F), gas mark 6. Put the raisins into a small bowl and cover with boiling water. Leave for 10 minutes to plump, then drain. Meanwhile make the pastry. Sift the flour, allspice, and half the cinnamon into a bowl, adding also the residue of bran left in the sieve. Using a fork blend in the margarine until the mixture looks like coarse breadcrumbs then add the water and mix to a dough. Roll out on a lightly floured board and use to line a 20cm (8in) flan dish. Prick the pastry all over then bake in the oven for 15 minutes, until lightly browned and crisp. Leave to cool while you make the filling.

Mix together the quark, raisins, skimmed milk and remaining half a teaspoon of cinnamon. When it's creamy, stir in half the nuts. Spoon the filling into the cooked flan case and smooth the top. Sprinkle with a little more cinnamon and the remaining almonds. Chill before serving – it will get firmer, but you will need a sharp knife to cut it cleanly.

RASPBERRY AND REDCURRANT TART

A pretty, jewelled tart to make from ripe fruit at the height of summer.

SERVES 4–6
125g (4oz) plain wholemeal flour
50g (2oz) butter
25g (1oz) caster sugar
1 egg yolk
350g (12oz) raspberries
125g (4oz) redcurrants, washed and stems removed
225g (8oz) redcurrant jelly, warmed

Sift the flour into a bowl and rub in the butter until the mixture looks like breadcrumbs. Add sugar and egg yolk; mix to form a dough. Cover with polythene and chill for 30 minutes. Set the oven to 200°C (400°F), gas mark 6. Roll out pastry and line a 20cm (8in) flan tin with a removable base. Prick base, trim sides. Bake for 15 minutes. Cool, arrange circles of raspberries and redcurrants in the flan. Pour redcurrant jelly over fruit; cool.

STRAWBERRY TARTLETS

Delicious, fragile tartlets of early summer which melt in your mouth. Serve them as they are, or with pouring cream.

SERVES 4
175g (6oz) plain wholemeal flour
125g (4oz) butter
2 teaspoons caster sugar
1–2 tablespoons cold water
4 rounded tablespoons redcurrant jelly, warmed
225g (8oz) small strawberries, hulled

Make pastry as on page 240; cover with polythene and chill for 30 minutes. Set the oven to 190°C (375°F), gas mark 5. Roll out pastry and use a cutter to stamp out circles to fit small tartlets. Prick lightly, bake for about 8 minutes, then cool. Brush a little redcurrant jelly over each tartlet case, then arrange about three or four strawberries in each and spoon some redcurrant jelly over them so that they glisten. Cool before serving.

YOGHURT TART

In this tart the combination of creamy, fresh-tasting filling and crisp wholemeal pastry is delicious, and it couldn't be simpler to make as the filling is uncooked.

SERVES 6
125g (4oz) plain wholemeal flour
1 teaspoon baking powder
50g (2oz) butter
1 tablespoon cold water
225g (8oz) low-fat quark or curd cheese
150ml (5 fl oz) thick natural yoghurt
1 tablespoon honey
1 tablespoon sugar
a few chopped walnuts

Set the oven to 200°C (400°F), gas mark 6. Sift the flour and baking powder into a bowl, adding the bran in the sieve too. Rub the fat into the flour then mix to a dough with the cold water. Roll the pastry out on a lightly floured board then put the pastry into a 20–23cm (8–9in) flan dish; trim edges and prick the base. Bake the flan for about 15 minutes until it's set and golden brown. Leave on one side while you make the filling.

Put the quark or curd cheese into a bowl and break it up with a fork, then gradually beat in the yoghurt, honey and sugar until you've got a light, creamy mixture. Spoon the mixture into the flan case and smooth the top. Chill the flan for 1–2 hours, then scatter a few chopped nuts over the top just before serving. The filling will be fairly soft at first but it will firm up as it chills.

COLD PUDDINGS

APRICOT FOOL

This smooth, golden cream looks and tastes too rich and luxurious to be good for you – but it is! It's made from that favourite ingredient of mine, smooth low-fat white cheese – *fromage blanc*. If the apricots are nice and sweet they will provide all the sweetening necessary, otherwise you can use a little honey. This fool freezes well for 4–6 weeks.

SERVES 4 F
175g (6oz) dried apricots
350g (12oz) *fromage blanc or* quark
1 tablespoon honey – optional
a few toasted flaked almonds *or* sesame seeds

Wash the apricots well in hot water. Put them into a medium-sized saucepan and cover with cold water. Leave to soak for an hour or so if possible, then simmer them over a low heat for 20–30 minutes, until they're very tender and the water is reduced to just a little syrupy glaze. (It's best to let them soak first, but I have found that you can get away with just simmering them if you're rushed for time.) Cool, then liquidize to a thick purée. Mix the apricot purée with the *fromage blanc*, beating well until smooth and creamy and add honey if liked. Spoon the mixture into four dishes – it looks lovely in glass ones – and chill. Serve sprinkled with a few toasted flaked almonds or sesame seeds.

APPLE AND RAISIN COMPÔTE WITH ORANGE

I am particularly fond of this compôte because it relies on the natural sweetness of the apples and raisins without added sugar. It's at its best and most luscious when made with Cox or other sweet apples, though it also works well with cooking apples, and they're what I normally use.

SERVES 4–6
900g (2 lb) apples
25g (1oz) butter
225g (8oz) raisins
juice and grated rind of 1 orange

Peel, core and slice the apples, then put them into a heavy-based saucepan with the butter, raisins and orange juice and rind. Cook gently, with a lid on the pan, for about 10 minutes, stirring frequently, until the apples look pulpy. Serve hot or cold – with *fromage blanc*, thick natural yoghurt or whipped cream. Some crunchy shortbread biscuits go well with it.

CHOCOLATE AND ORANGE MOUSSE

Serve in small glasses, after a plainish vegetable- or cereal-based main course.

SERVES 6
225g (8oz) dark chocolate
2 tablespoons orange juice
grated rind of 1 orange
1 tablespoon orange liqueur such as Curaçao – *or* use brandy
4 eggs, separated
a little whipped cream
a few toasted almonds *or* chocolate curls

Break up the chocolate and put it into a bowl. Set the bowl over a saucepan of boiling water, or pop it into a moderate oven for about 10 minutes until the chocolate has melted. Stir the orange juice and rind into the melted chocolate, then the liqueur or brandy and the egg yolks. Whisk the egg whites until they're standing in soft peaks then gently fold them into the chocolate mixture using a metal spoon and a cutting and folding motion. Spoon the mixture into six little dishes – it looks very nice in those little white individual soufflé dishes. You can leave it overnight if this is convenient.

It's lovely served just as it is, or you can garnish it with some whipped cream and toasted flaked almonds or chocolate curls. To make the chocolate curls just run a potato peeler down the flat side of a bar of chocolate.

REFRIGERATOR CHOCOLATE CAKE

This is one of those unsophisticated puddings – and non-wholefood, to boot – that I have to admit a liking for! It's a good one for a party as it can be made in advance.

SERVES 6–8
225g (8oz) unsalted butter
1 tablespoon Barbados sugar
2 eggs, separated
225g (8oz) plain chocolate
2 tablespoons sherry *or* rum – optional
225g (8oz) semisweet, preferably wholemeal, biscuits,
lightly crushed
15ml (5 fl oz) whipping cream
50g (2oz) flaked almonds

Cream together butter and sugar; when light and fluffy beat in the egg yolks. Melt chocolate and beat in with the sherry or rum if using, then add broken biscuits. Whip egg whites until stiff but not dry and fold into chocolate mixture. Line a square cake tin with foil and spoon in mixture. Smooth top and chill in fridge until firm. To serve, turn out of tin, and spread with whipped cream. Scatter with the nuts.

CHEESECAKE ON A CHOCOLATE BASE

Another favourite, special-occasion one; a delicious smooth cheesecake swirled with sharp-tasting blackcurrant purée on a crisp base of chocolate and nuts. It's easy to make and needs no cooking.

SERVES 6
125g (4oz) digestive biscuits, crushed
125g (4oz) plain chocolate, melted
50g (2oz) chopped mixed nuts
225g (8oz) curd cheese
275ml (10 fl oz) whipping cream
25g (1oz) sugar
3 tablespoons thick blackcurrant purée made by
liquidizing then sieving the drained contents of a
375g (13oz) jar of blackcurrants *or* 225g (8oz) fresh
or frozen blackcurrants, cooked and sweetened to
taste
a little grated chocolate

First make the base: put the biscuits, chocolate and nuts into a bowl and mix together, then spread evenly in a 20cm (8in) springclip tin or cake tin with a loose base. Leave in a cool place while you make the filling.

To make the filling, whip the curd cheese, cream and sugar together. Lightly mix in the blackcurrant purée, just swirling it. Don't mix it in too much. Pour the topping over the biscuit base. Chill for at least 2 hours, preferably overnight. Remove the sides of the tin; sprinkle with grated chocolate to serve.

HEALTHY CHEESECAKE

I invented this one for a mid-summer cookery demonstration; since then it's become a favourite.

SERVES 6–8
225g (8oz) rolled oats
25g (1oz) flaked almonds
grated rind of a well-scrubbed orange
4 tablespoons clear honey
175g (6oz) quark *or* firm tofu, drained
225g (8oz) firm yoghurt, preferably strained Greek
225g (8oz) ripe strawberries *or* raspberries, *or* black
grapes, halved and pipped *or* orange segments *or*
peach slices sprinkled with lemon juice

To make the base, mix the oats, almonds, orange rind and 3 tablespoons honey together, press into a 20–22cm (8–9in) flan dish. Chill while you make the filling. Put quark or tofu into a bowl and mix in the yoghurt and 1 tablespoon honey. Spoon into flan case, level top. Arrange fruit on top. Chill for 2–3 hours.

This flan can be varied in many ways. For a carob-banana flan, replace 25g (1oz) of the oats with 25g (1oz) carob powder and top the cheesecake with sliced bananas sprinkled with lemon juice. Or for a continental-style cheesecake, add 125g (4oz) raisins to the cheese mixture and finish cheesecake by sprinkling top with cinnamon instead of the fruit.

STRAWBERRY CHEESECAKE

This recipe makes a big, luscious cheesecake with a shiny strawberry topping. It makes a wonderful pudding for a summer party.

SERVES 8–10
175g (6oz) digestive biscuits
75g (3oz) soft butter
350g (12oz) curd cheese
3 eggs
1 teaspoon vanilla essence
125g (4oz) caster sugar
150ml (5 fl oz) soured cream

Topping
150ml (5 fl oz) soured cream
450g (1 lb) small ripe strawberries, washed and hulled
6–8 tablespoons redcurrant jelly

Set the oven to 150°C (300°F), gas mark 2. Put the digestive biscuits on a board and crush them with a rolling pin, then mix them with the butter. Press the biscuit mixture evenly into the base of a 20cm (8in) springclip tin or cake tin with a removable base. Leave in a cool place while you make the filling.

To do this, if you've got a liquidizer, just put everything into that and blend for a minute until smooth. Alternatively, put the curd cheese into a large bowl, then add the eggs, vanilla, caster sugar and soured cream and beat thoroughly to a smooth consistency. Pour the mixture into the tin on top of the crumbs.

Bake the cheesecake towards the bottom of the oven for 1½ hours, until it looks set and feels firm to a very light touch. Cool, then lightly beat the second carton of soured cream and spread over the top of the cheesecake. Chill for 2–3 hours.

To finish the cheesecake, arrange the strawberries evenly over the top. Melt the redcurrant jelly in a small, heavy-based saucepan over a gentle heat, then pour over the strawberries in a thin layer to glaze. Leave to cool, then carefully remove the cheesecake from the tin to serve.

UNCOOKED LEMON CHEESE CAKE

I devised this easy-to-make cheesecake to use up some lemon curd which I had been given.

SERVES 6
175g (6oz) digestive biscuits
75g (3oz) butter
225g (8oz) curd cheese or quark
6 tablespoons lemon curd
150ml (5 fl oz) double cream, whipped

Crush digestive biscuits between 2 pieces of grease-proof paper with rolling pin. Melt butter and mix with biscuit crumbs. Press into fluted flan tin or flan ring on a flat dish; leave in a cool place to become firm. Meanwhile mix curd cheese or quark with 4 tablespoons of the lemon curd, and fold in the cream. Smooth into prepared flan and leave to set. Glaze top by spreading with rest of lemon curd, slightly warmed if necessary, before serving.

Variation

UNCOOKED STRAWBERRY CHEESECAKE

Leave out the lemon curd and use 50g (2oz) caster sugar instead. Top with 225g (8oz) ripe strawberries, hulled and halved if necessary.

COFFEE RICOTTA PUDDING

This Italian pudding is very easy to make and good served after one of the vegetable casseroles or cereal main dishes, or after a low-protein pasta dish.

SERVES 4
2 teaspoons best quality instant coffee, continental type
1 tablespoon water, rum or Tia Maria
450g (1 lb) curd cheese or quark
50g (2oz) caster sugar or mild honey

Dissolve the coffee by mixing it with the water, rum or Tia Maria. If the cheese is very lumpy it might be best to push it through a sieve, otherwise put it straight into a bowl. Add the coffee mixture and sugar or honey to the cheese, stirring until everything is combined. Spoon into small dishes; serve chilled. It's nice with macaroons or other small crunchy biscuits.

DRIED FRUIT COMPÔTE IN GINGER WINE

You can buy dried fruit salad mixture at health shops and in some supermarkets and it makes a lovely pudding, especially if you stew it and then marinade it in ginger wine, as in this recipe. (An alternative, if you don't want to use the wine, is to add some ground ginger or chopped crystallized ginger to the water.) Top it with a generous dollop of sharp-tasting thick natural yoghurt or *fromage blanc* for a delicious blend of flavours and textures.

SERVES 4–6
450g (1 lb) mixed dried fruit salad – apricots, peaches, pears, prunes and apple rings
water to cover
150 ml (5 fl oz) green ginger wine

Put the dried fruit into a medium-sized saucepan, cover generously with cold water and if possible leave to soak for a couple of hours or so. Then simmer the fruit over a gentle heat, without a lid on the saucepan, for about 30 minutes, until it is very tender and the liquid has reduced to just a little glossy-looking syrup. Remove from the heat and pour in the wine. Leave to cool, then chill before serving. It looks good in a pretty glass bowl, or in individual glasses, topped with a swirl of low-fat cream.

FRUIT PLATTER

SERVES 4
1 ripe mango
150ml (5 fl oz) water
2 kiwi fruits
2 ripe figs
125g (4oz) strawberries
4 sprigs of fresh mint

To make the sauce, first remove the stone from the mango. The easiest way to do this is to stand the mango up with the stalk end at the top. Then, using a sharp knife, cut down, right through the mango, about 6mm (¼in) away from the stalk. The piece of mango should fall away, revealing the stone. Make another similar cut the other side. Then peel off the skin and cut the extra pieces of mango flesh away from the stone. Put all the mango flesh into a liquidizer or blender with the water and whizz to a smooth purée. Add a little more water if necessary to get the right consistency. Chill until ready to assemble the dish. To do this, peel the kiwi fruit and slice into thin rings; cut the figs downwards into quarters or eighths; hull the strawberries and halve if necessary. Pour some of the mango sauce over the base of four flat serving plates. Arrange the kiwi slices, figs and strawberries on top. Garnish with a sprig of fresh mint and serve as soon as possible.

FRUIT SALAD – EXOTIC

In this fruit salad, fresh orange juice is used instead of sugar syrup for a lighter, fresher result.

SERVES 4–6
1 small ripe pineapple
1 ripe mango
4 kiwi fruit
1 pawpaw
150ml (5 fl oz) orange juice

Cut the leafy top and prickly skin from the pineapple and remove the 'eyes' with a sharp pointed knife. Cut the pineapple into even-sized pieces and put into a bowl. Halve the mango and remove the stone and peel. Cut the flesh into dice and add to the bowl. Peel and slice the kiwi fruit, peel, de-seed and slice the pawpaw. Add these to the bowl, together with the orange juice. Chill before serving.

FRUIT SALAD – SUMMER

Apricots, peaches and strawberries, soaked in orange juice (to which you can add a dash of orange liqueur, if you like, for special occasions) and chilled to make a luscious fruit salad. I can't think of a nicer pudding for a hot summer's day.

SERVES 4
225g (8oz) ripe apricots
2–3 ripe peaches
225g (8oz) strawberries
150ml (5 fl oz) orange juice
thinly pared rind from ½ orange
1–2 tablespoons Cointreau or other orange liqueur – optional

Wash the apricots and peaches, halve and remove stones. Slice flesh fairly thinly. Wash and hull the strawberries; halve or quarter any large ones so that they are all about the same size. Put all the fruits into a pretty bowl and pour in the orange juice. Snip the rind into thin slivers and add these to the fruit, together with the liqueur if you're using it. Chill for 1 hour or so before serving if possible.

FRUIT SALAD – WINTER

Winter is, surprisingly, a very good time for making a fruit salad: excellent apples such as Cox and Russet are easy to come by and there are plenty of good citrus fruits, and grapes. This is a simple refreshing salad, made with fruit juice instead of sugar syrup and is very good after you've eaten too many rich things at Christmas!

SERVES 4–6
2 large oranges
4 tangerines or similar
2 large apples, preferably Cox
225g (8oz) black or green grapes
150ml (5 fl oz) orange juice

Cut the peel and pith off the oranges, cutting right into the flesh and holding them over a bowl to catch the juice. Then cut the segments away from the inner white skin. Put these into the bowl. Peel the tangerines and divide into segments; peel, core and slice the apples; wash, halve and de-seed the grapes. Add all these to the bowl, together with the orange juice, and mix well. Chill before serving.

RASPBERRIES IN REDCURRANT JELLY

This is a refreshing pudding: raspberries set in a clear jelly which is made from redcurrant juice. You can buy this at large supermarkets, and you can get a powdered vegetarian jelling agent, at health shops. These make a jelly set very quickly, and if you're using frozen raspberries which haven't thawed, the jelly will set almost immediately, making this a good emergency dish!

SERVES 6–8
350g (12oz) fresh *or* frozen raspberries
700ml (25 fl oz) carton redcurrant juice
2 tablespoons sugar
2 level teaspoons vegetarian jelling agent (agar agar *or* gelozone)
whipped cream
pistachio nuts, shelled and coarsely chopped

Divide the raspberries between six or eight dishes. Follow the packet directions for using the jelling agent, either heat the redcurrant juice and sugar in a large saucepan, bring to the boil then sprinkle the jelling agent over the top, a little at a time, whisking after each addition to help the powder dissolve; or blend the jelling agent with a little of the redcurrant juice, heat the rest, then add the hot juice to the blended jelling agent and return the whole lot to the saucepan, stirring over the heat for 1–2 minutes. Remove mixture from the heat and strain over the raspberries. Leave to cool, then chill. Top the jellies with whipped cream and a few green pistachio nuts, shelled and chopped, to show their pretty green colour.

APRICOT JELLY WITH FRESH APRICOTS AND STRAWBERRIES

For this jelly you need apricot juice, called 'apricot nectar' and available in a carton from large supermarkets and delicatessens; or you can make your own by soaking 175g (6oz) dried apricots in water overnight then whizzing to a purée in a blender and adding extra water if necessary to make up to 575ml (1 pint).

SERVES 6–8
8 ripe apricots
700ml (25 fl oz) carton apricot nectar
2 tablespoons sugar
2 level teaspoons vegetarian jelling agent
whipped cream
6–8 ripe strawberries to garnish

Skin the apricots by plunging them into boiling water for 2 minutes, then drain and slip off the skins with a sharp knife. Halve the apricots, remove the stones, then slice the flesh. Make the jelly exactly as in the last recipe. Put the apricots into the individual bowls, pour the apricot juice over and leave to set. Garnish with a swirl of whipped cream and some ripe strawberries.

KIWI FRUIT IN GRAPE JELLY

Kiwi fruit is so pretty and this dish makes the most of its flower-like appearance.

SERVES 6–8
4 kiwi fruit
700ml (25 fl oz) still, white grape juice
2 tablespoons sugar
2 level teaspoons agar agar
whipped cream
pistachio nuts, shelled and coarsely chopped

Make the jelly exactly as for raspberries in redcurrant jelly above, arranging the slices of kiwi fruit attractively in the bowls.

FRESH MANGO COMPÔTE

If you can find some really ripe medium-sized mangoes, they make a wonderful pudding that's very simple to do. The mangoes should feel really soft to the touch; like avocados they will ripen in the airing cupboard if put into a paper bag and left for two or three days.

SERVES 4–6
5 medium-sized mangoes

Stand the mangoes on a board with the stalk end at the top. Slice each mango down from the top, cutting about 6mm (¼in) each side of the stalk. The object of this is to make the cuts each side of the large flat stone in the centre. Then cut skin from the two halves and from the flesh around the stone. Cut as much of the flesh away from around the stone as you can. Then dice all the flesh. Put a cupful of mango pieces into the liquidizer or food processor with 1–2 cupfuls of water or orange juice and whizz to a purée. Add this to the rest of the mango pieces. Chill before serving in glass bowls.

MUESLI WITH APPLES, HONEY AND ALMONDS

As I've explained below, muesli needn't be just a cereal dish eaten at breakfast. I often make a fruity version and serve it as a pudding.

SERVES 4
3 large apples, washed and grated, skin, core and all
150ml (5 fl oz) orange juice
125g (4oz) rolled oats, *or* a mixture of oats and barley flakes from the health shop
1 tablespoon clear honey
50g (2oz) raisins
50g (2oz) flaked almonds

Put all the ingredients except the almonds into a bowl and mix together. Spoon into bowls, sprinkle with the nuts. This is lovely, if you want to spoil yourself, with some single cream on top.

MUESLI – ORIGINAL VERSION

Most people think of this as a breakfast dish consisting mainly of oats and other cereals. But when Dr Bircher-Benner invented it for his patients in his clinic in Zurich at the turn of the century it was really a fruit dish and as such it makes a delicious pudding, light and nourishing. If you use condensed milk, which is the type Dr Bircher-Benner used, it gives the muesli a delectable almost jellied consistency and sweet taste.

SERVES 4
4 tablespoons sweetened condensed milk
4 tablespoons lemon juice
4 level tablespoons rolled oats
4 large eating apples
4 tablespoons chopped or grated hazel nuts *or* almonds

Put the condensed milk and lemon juice into a large bowl and mix them until they're smooth, then stir in the oats. Wash the apples and grate them fairly coarsely then add them to the bowl. If the mixture seems rather stiff add a little cold water or orange juice. Spoon the muesli into individual bowls and sprinkle the nuts over the top.

For a less sweet version of the pudding you can use natural yoghurt instead of the condensed milk but the consistency will not be quite the same.

FRESH ORANGE SALAD WITH HONEY AND ORANGE FLOWER WATER

One of the most refreshing puddings I know, this is delicious served well-chilled. The orange flower water is optional; it can be bought at chemists and gives a fragrant, honeyed flavour to this dish.

SERVES 4–6
1 tablespoon honey, preferably orange blossom
2 tablespoons boiling water
6 large oranges
150ml (5 fl oz) orange juice
2 tablespoons orange flower water – optional

Put the honey into a large bowl and mix with the boiling water until dissolved. Scrub one of the oranges in warm water and pare off the peel with a potato peeler. Cut the peel into fine shreds and add to the honey and water. Then cut the peel and pith from the oranges, holding them over the bowl as you do so to catch any juice. Cut the segments away from the inner skin and put them into the bowl. Squeeze the remaining skin over the bowl to extract any extra juice. Add the 150ml (5 fl oz) orange juice to the oranges in the bowl, together with the orange flower water. Stir well, then chill before serving.

PASHKA

This traditional Easter dish from Russia makes a beautiful pudding and it's useful when you're planning a cereal or vegetable meal because it's rich in protein. In Russia it's made in a special tall pyramid-shaped mould and decorated with the initials 'XB' for 'Christ is Risen'. I use a 15cm (6in) clay flower pot which I scrubbed and baked in a hot oven and now keep in my kitchen cupboard. *Pashka* needs to be prepared several hours before you want to eat it to allow time for liquid to drain away through the hole in the flower pot leaving the mixture firm enough to turn out. It's nice served with macaroons or slices of Madeira cake.

This is *Pashka* as traditionally made. These days however, I often make a lighter version of it, simply mixing the curd cheese with chopped candied fruits, chopped almonds and a little honey to taste.

SERVES 6
2 egg yolks
75g (3oz) vanilla sugar: or caster sugar and a drop or
two of vanilla essence
4 tablespoons single cream or creamy milk
700g (1½ lb) curd cheese or quark
125g (4oz) unsalted butter, softened
50g (2oz) chopped candied fruits
50g (2oz) chopped blanched almonds
a little chopped glacé fruit

Beat the egg yolks and sugar together until they're pale and foamy. Put the cream or creamy milk into a small saucepan and bring it just to the boil, then pour it over the egg yolks and sugar. Tip the whole lot back into the saucepan and stir over a gentle heat until it has thickened – this won't take a moment, so watch it carefully. Leave on one side to cool.

Beat together the cheese and butter; add the candied fruits and nuts and finally the cooled custard. Line your 15cm (6in) flower pot with a double layer of dampened muslin or fine net curtain, spoon in the *pashka* mixture and smooth the top. Fold the ends of the muslin over the top, cover with a saucer and a weight and leave in a cool place or the fridge for several hours, preferably overnight. Some moisture will seep out of the hole in the base of the flower pot so stand it on a plate.

To serve the pudding invert the flower pot on to a serving dish, turn out the *pashka* and carefully peel off the muslin or net. Decorate with the glacé fruit.

PEACH BRULÉE

One of my favourite fruit dishes and always popular for a dinner party, yet very quick and simple to prepare, and convenient because it is best made in advance. You can make a healthier, slimmer's version by replacing the whipped cream with *fromage blanc* or thick strained Greek yoghurt or using half cream and half *fromage blanc* or thick yoghurt.

SERVES 6
6 large ripe peaches
2–3 tablespoons orange, peach or apricot liqueur –
optional
275ml (10 fl oz) double cream or fromage blanc
demerara sugar

Put the peaches into a bowl and cover with boiling water. Leave for 2 minutes, then drain the peaches and slip off the skins with a sharp pointed knife. Halve, stone and thinly slice the peaches. Put the slices into a shallow dish that's suitable for putting under the grill. Sprinkle with the liquer if you're

using it. Whip the cream until it stands in soft peaks, then spoon this on top of the peaches, smoothing it evenly over them. Cover with an even layer of demerara sugar. Heat the grill to moderate; put the peach mixture under the grill until the sugar melts. Remove from the heat; cool, then chill for several hours before serving.

PEACHES IN STRAWBERRY PURÉE

This dish consists of juicy, ripe peach slices bathed in a pink strawberry purée. It's another pudding that's very simple to do and a perfect way of using frozen strawberries. It's also delicious made with ripe comice pears instead of peaches and raspberries instead of strawberries.

SERVES 6
6 large, ripe peaches – white ones are best if they're
available
2 tablespoons lemon juice
450g (1 lb) ripe strawberries
50g (2oz) sugar

Cover the peaches with boiling water; leave for 2 minutes, then drain. Slip the skins off using a sharp knife. Halve the peaches and remove the stones, then slice the flesh. Put the slices into a pretty glass bowl or six individual ones and sprinkle with half the lemon juice to preserve the colour.

Wash and hull the strawberries, then put them into a liquidizer with the rest of the lemon juice and reduce to a purée. Press the mixture through a sieve, to make it really smooth, then add the sugar gradually – taste the mixture, as you may not need it all. Pour the strawberry purée over the peaches, or pour a pool of purée on to individual serving plates and arrange peach slices on top.

PEACHES IN WHITE WINE

This is a simple yet very delicious pudding. Make it in the summer when peaches are cheap and good. You can also make this successfully using red grape juice instead of wine.

SERVES 6
6 ripe peaches
275ml (10 fl oz) sweet white wine
2 teaspoons honey

Put the peaches into a bowl and cover with boiling water. Leave for 1 minute, then drain. Remove the skins with a sharp knife and cut the peaches into thin slices, discarding the stones. Put the slices into a glass serving bowl. Mix the wine with the honey and pour over the peaches. Chill before serving.

PEARS IN RED WINE

These pears, cooked whole and deeply stained by the red wine, make a most attractive pudding. Serve them hot or cold, with whipped cream that's been lightly flavoured with cinnamon, and the almond biscuits on page 324.

SERVES 6
125g (4oz) sugar *or* mild honey
275ml (10 fl oz) water
275ml (10 fl oz) red wine
6 ripe pears
whipped cream flavoured with a little sugar and cinnamon

Put the sugar, water and wine into a heavy-based saucepan and heat gently until the sugar has dissolved. Then boil rapidly for 2 minutes. Peel the pears, keeping them whole and leaving the stalks on. Put them into the syrup and let them cook gently, with a lid on the pan, for 30 minutes (or longer if necessary) – they must be really tender right through. Remove the pears to a shallow serving dish. Thicken the cooking liquid if necessary by boiling rapidly without a lid until reduced to 3–4 tablespoons; spoon over the pears.

PINEAPPLE AND GRAPE COMPÔTE

SERVES 6
1 large ripe pineapple
125g (4oz) white grapes
125g (4oz) black grapes
2 tablespoons clear honey
2 tablespoons orange juice, Grand Marnier *or* other orange liqueur

Remove prickly skin and top from pineapple. Cut flesh into neat dice, removing hard core. Halve grapes and remove pips. Arrange fruit in a large glass bowl, pour over honey and orange juice, or Grand Marnier, and turn once or twice to mix. Leave for at least 2 hours in a cool place. Serve as it is, or with cream.

STUFFED PINEAPPLE HALVES

For this, small pineapples, one between two people, are halved right through the centre, including the leafy green top, then the flesh is cut and scooped out, mixed with black grapes or ripe strawberries and piled back in again. The stuffed pineapples look very pretty arranged like the spokes of a wheel on a large round plate.

SERVES 6
3 small pineapples with attractive leafy tops
225g (8oz) small, ripe strawberries *or* black grapes

Wash and dry the pineapples, then slice each in half right through the green top. Using a sharp knife and a spoon, scoop out the flesh and cut into small pieces, discarding any hard core. Wash the strawberries or grapes. Halve and stone the grapes; hull the strawberries and cut them as necessary. Mix the pineapple pieces with the strawberries or grapes and pile the mixture back into the skins. Arrange the stuffed pineapples on a large, flat plate.

RASPBERRY MERINGUE GÂTEAU

This is a superbly rich and indulgent pudding which nobody ought to eat but which everyone loves for a special occasion. It's also delicious made with sweet ripe blackberries, either freshly picked or frozen.

SERVES 6
3 egg whites
175g (6oz) caster sugar
275ml (10 fl oz) whipping cream *or* if you want to make it healthier, half whipping cream and half *fromage blanc*
350g (12oz) fresh *or* frozen raspberries, thawed icing sugar

First make the meringue. Whisk the egg whites until stiff and dry, then whisk in half the sugar to make a smooth, glossy mixture. Fold in the rest of the sugar using a metal spoon. Draw two circles, 20cm (8in) in diameter, on greaseproof, foil or non-stick paper and brush with oil. Spoon the meringue to cover the circles in an even layer. Bake in a very cool oven, 120°C (250°F), gas mark ½, for 2–3 hours, until crisp and dry but not brown. Leave the meringue circles to cool completely, then peel off the paper. Store in an airtight tin until required for filling.

To fill the meringue, put one of the layers on a flat serving dish. Whip the cream, or cream and *fromage blanc*, until standing in soft peaks. Spread half this mixture over the meringue and top with half the raspberries. Cover with the other meringue circle and the rest of the cream and raspberries, and sieve a little icing sugar over the top. Serve as soon as possible.

Variation

CHESTNUT MERINGUE GÂTEAU

Use half a 400g (14oz) can chestnut purée, beaten until smooth (warming the mixture helps) and sweetened to taste, instead of the raspberries. Decorate with some *marrons glacés* if you can get them.

RED FRUIT PUDDING

I think this is one of the most delicious puddings and it makes a little fruit go a long way. My version is unusual in that I hardly cook the fruit; I think this gives a particularly fresh-tasting result. Serve the pudding in individual glass bowls if possible to show off its rich ruby red colouring.

SERVES 6
450g (1 lb) fresh ripe red fruit: raspberries, redcurrants, strawberries, *or* a mixture
125g (4oz) caster sugar
575ml (1 pint) water
50g (2oz) cornflour *or* arrowroot
a little lemon juice
whipped cream to serve

Put the fruit into a liquidizer with the sugar and water and blend to a purée; sieve. Mix the cornflour or arrowroot to a paste with a little of this purée; put the rest into a saucepan and heat to boiling point. Pour the boiling purée over the cornflour or arrowroot paste, then return to the pan and stir until the mixture thickens. Taste and sharpen with a little lemon juice if necessary. Pour the mixture into 4 individual bowls and leave to cool. It looks pretty with some whipped cream on top and goes well with the almond biscuits on page 324.

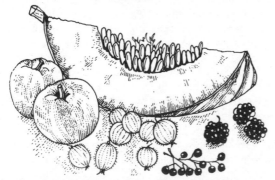

STRAWBERRIES WITH COEURS À LA CRÈME

Hearts of creamy white cheese surrounded by shiny red strawberries make a beautiful summer pudding that's rich in protein and ideal for serving after something like ratatouille and rice. You need to start making the hearts the night before you want to serve the pudding. The quantities I've given are right for five of those white heart-shaped china dishes you can get with little holes in the base. Alternatively you can make some holes in the base of cream, yoghurt or small cottage cheese cartons and use these; I've also used a colander successfully. And if you can't get muslin to line the moulds, kitchen paper or pieces of medical gauze from the chemist make good substitutes.

SERVES 6
600g (1¼ lb) curd cheese *or* quark
150ml (5 fl oz) double cream
3 tablespoons caster sugar
450g (1 lb) strawberries
a little extra caster sugar

Put the cheese into a large bowl, mix it with the cream and sugar and beat with a wooden spoon until the mixture thickens and holds its shape. Line your white china dishes, yoghurt, cream or cottage cheese pots, or colander, with muslin, then spoon in the creamy mixture and smooth the surface. Stand the containers or the colander on a plate to catch the liquid which will drain off and place them in the fridge overnight.

Next day wash and hull the strawberries, halving or quartering any larger ones as necessary. Then sprinkle them lightly with sugar and leave on one side.

To serve, turn the creamy cheese mixture out on to a large plate and carefully peel off the muslin. Arrange the strawberries round the cheese or cheeses.

Don't assemble this dish until just before you need it or the juice from the strawberries can spoil the look of it. It's a good way of making a few strawberries go further when they're expensive.

If you're slimming I've found you can make this dish equally well using natural yoghurt instead of cream. The result is very similar though not so creamy-tasting, and I find if I use 450g (1 lb) low-fat quark, 150ml (5 fl oz) natural yoghurt and 3–4 tablespoons caster sugar, the mixture fills four white china hearts. The yoghurt version gives off a little more liquid than the richer version as it drains and settles in the fridge.

SUMMER PUDDING

Use a light-textured bread for this recipe.

SERVES 4–6
700g (1½ lb) red fruit: raspberries, redcurrants,
blackcurrants and strawberries, as available
125g (4oz) caster sugar *or* mild honey
8–10 thin slices of bread, crusts removed

Wash the fruit and remove stems and stalks as necessary. Put the fruit into a large heavy-based saucepan with the sugar or honey and heat gently until the sugar has dissolved and the juices are running. Remove from the heat. Lightly grease a 1 litre (1¾ pint) pudding basin. Soak pieces of bread in the juice from the fruit, then arrange in the pudding basin so that it is completely covered. Pour the fruit in on top of the bread and cover with more bread to make a lid. Place a plate and a weight on top and leave in a cool place for several hours, or overnight if possible. To serve, dip the basin in very hot water, slip a knife around the edge of the pudding, then invert over a plate. Serve with whipped cream.

TRIFLE

Proper trifle, made with egg custard and topped with whipped cream, is a delicious pudding, light, not too sweet and excellent served after a cereal or vegetable-based main course or to round off a salady buffet meal.

SERVES 6–8
1 small sponge cake
3 tablespoons raspberry jam
4 tablespoons cheap sherry
3 eggs
50g (2oz) caster sugar – vanilla sugar if you have it,
otherwise add a few drops of vanilla essence
575ml (1 pint) milk
250ml (10 fl oz) whipping cream
25g (1oz) toasted flaked almonds

Split the sponge cake and sandwich with the jam or sandwich the fingers together in pairs then cut them up into smaller pieces. Put the pieces of sponge into the base of a serving dish – a pretty glass one is nice – and pour the sherry over them. Leave on one side while you make the custard.

Whisk the eggs and sugar together in a bowl; put the milk into a saucepan and bring it just to the boil, then pour it over the egg mixture and whisk again.

Strain the mixture back into the saucepan and stir over a gentle heat for just a minute or two until it thickens. Don't let it over-cook or it will separate. (If this does happen I've found if I put it in the liquidizer for a moment and blend it at a high speed, amazingly, it seems to be all right again.) Pour the custard over the sponge pieces and leave on one side to cool. To finish the trifle whisk the cream until it's softly thickened, then spoon it over the top of the trifle. Chill the trifle then sprinkle the almonds over the top just before you serve it, so that they're still crisp.

YOGHURT

You can certainly save money if you make your own yogurt and it is really very easy to do. I find I need to buy a fresh pot every three or four times I make it, otherwise I just save a little from the previous batch to start the next. When you're making yoghurt you can make a very simple pudding by putting some of the mixture into those little individual ramekins; it will set beautifully and get firm as it chills. Then all you have to do is top it with some maple syrup, clear honey, chopped nuts, Jordan's original crunchy, preserved ginger or sugar free jam before serving. Make sure your yoghurt 'starter' really is live; most of the yoghurt sold in supermarkets isn't. Read the carton carefully, or go to your health shop.

MAKES 575ML (1 PINT)
575ml (1 pint) liquid skimmed milk
2 rounded tablespoons skimmed milk powder
1 teaspoon fresh natural yoghurt – from a carton or
from your last batch

Put the milk into a saucepan and bring up to the boil, then leave to simmer gently without a lid for 10 minutes. This reduces the milk slightly and helps to make the yoghurt thick and creamy. Remove the saucepan from the heat and leave until the milk is luke-warm. Meanwhile wash a couple of jars and sterilize them by swishing them out with warm water with some household bleach added, then rinse thoroughly in hot water.

Whisk the skimmed milk powder and the yoghurt into the milk then pour it into your clean jars, cover with foil and leave in a warm place for a few hours or overnight until it's firm. By the pilot light on a gas cooker is a good place, or in an airing cupboard. Cool the yoghurt, then put it into the fridge to chill and firm up.

VEGAN YOGHURT

MAKES 575ML (1 PINT)
575ml (1 pint) soya milk
yoghurt starter culture – from health shops

Any yoghurt culture will work as well on soya milk as it does on dairy milk. Put the soya milk into a saucepan and bring to the boil, then cool to luke-warm. Add the starter as directed on the packet, stir well. Pour the mixture into a thermos flask or large jar or bowl which has been sterilized by being rinsed out with boiling water. Cover the jar or bowl with clingfilm or foil and wrap in a warm towel. Leave in a warm place for 5–8 hours, until set, then chill in the fridge. This first batch will not be 100 per cent vegan, but a tablespoon of this can be used to start the next batch, which will be. The yoghurt gets thicker and better each time.

YOGHURT GLORY

If you like yoghurt, this is a mouthwatering way of serving it in a tall glass to look like a pink and white striped knickerbocker glory. It looks far more calorific than it really is and makes a good treat for slimmers.

SERVES 2
1 medium-sized banana
125ml (4 fl oz) raspberry, blackcurrant *or* strawberry yoghurt – preferably without artificial flavouring or colouring.
125ml (4 fl oz) low-fat natural yoghurt
15g (½oz) toasted hazel nuts, chopped

Peel the banana and slice thinly. Spoon a little of the flavoured yoghurt into the base of two tall glasses, then add some banana slices. Top with a layer of natural yoghurt followed by more of the fruit yoghurt. Continue in this way until all the ingredients are used up. Sprinkle the nuts on top and serve at once.

APPLE AND HONEY ICE CREAM WITH BLACKBERRY SAUCE

At our old house, we had a wonderful Bramley apple tree, and I was always thinking of ways to use the apples. Here's one solution, which includes another late-summer flavour, blackberries. The pale green ice looks pretty with the vivid deep red sauce.

SERVES 4
225g (8oz) cooking apples, peeled, cored and sliced
3 tablespoons clear honey
275ml (10 fl oz) whipping cream, whipped
1 tablespoon grated lemon rind
225g (8oz) blackberries
1 tablespoon sugar

Put apples and honey into a heavy-based saucepan and cook gently until pulpy. Then liquidize and cool. Fold cream and lemon rind into cooled purée. Pour into suitable container and freeze until firm, beating once or twice during freezing. To make sauce, put blackberries into a heavy-based saucepan, cook gently for 10 minutes until pulpy, then add sugar, liquidize and sieve. Chill.

Remove ice cream from freezer 30 minutes before serving; spoon into individual glasses and pour sauce on top.

CHESTNUT ICE CREAM

This is a beautiful ice cream with a delicate flavour. These quantities make a generous amount of ice cream and you could halve them if you prefer; half this would be enough for four people but I don't think it's quite enough for six. If you want to make a less-rich, healthier version, half whipping cream and half *fromage blanc* works quite well, and honey can be used for sweetening instead of sugar.

SERVES 8
425g (15oz) can chestnut purée
575ml (1 pint) whipping cream
175g (6oz) caster sugar
4 tablespoons brandy

Put the chestnut purée into a bowl or the bowl of your mixer and beat until smooth. Then add the cream, sugar and brandy and beat everything together until thick, smooth and standing in peaks. Turn mixture into a plastic container and freeze until solid. There is no need to stir this mixture during freezing, but do take it out of the fridge at the beginning of the meal and beat if before serving as it is much nicer if it is not too solid.

CHOCOLATE ICE CREAM

I use this ice cream to make an iced Christmas 'bombe' which my daughters prefer to traditional Christmas pudding. To make the 'bombe', spoon this ice cream (which should be frozen but not too hard) into the base and up the sides of a foil-lined pudding basin or mould and freeze. Then fill centre with raspberry ice cream (below) and freeze again.

Another Christmas variation is to soak some sultanas and chopped glacé fruit in sweet sherry, then fold into the ice cream together with some flaked almonds and freeze in a pudding basin, for an iced 'Christmas pudding'.

SERVES 4–6
125g (4oz) plain chocolate
275ml (10 fl oz) single cream
275ml (10 fl oz) double cream
1 teaspoon instant coffee dissolved in 1 tablespoon boiling water
1 tablespoon clear honey

Break up the chocolate and melt in a bowl set over a pan of gently steaming water. Meanwhile whip creams together. Add coffee dissolved in the water, honey and melted chocolate. Turn into a polythene container and freeze until set.

MELON FILLED WITH GINGER ICE CREAM

A very attractive pudding for a special occasion.

SERVES 6
125g (4oz) granulated sugar or 175g (5oz) honey
150ml (5 fl oz) water
3 eggs
275ml (10 fl oz) whipping cream, whipped
6 pieces of stem ginger, chopped
a little syrup from the jar of ginger
3 small ripe melons, preferably ogen, halved and de-seeded

Put sugar and water into a heavy-based saucepan and heat gently until dissolved. Turn up heat and boil steadily for about 5 minutes until the syrup thickens and will form a thread between your finger and thumb. Keep testing, removing the pan from the heat as you do so. Meanwhile put eggs into a bowl and whisk until light and frothy. Pour sugar syrup over beaten eggs, whisking all the time, until mixture is very light and pale. Cool, then fold in cream and ginger. Pour into container and freeze until solid, beating once. Serve melons with a scoop of ice cream in the centre and a spoonful of ginger syrup on top.

RASPBERRY ICE CREAM

This is a favourite ice cream with all my daughters.

SERVES 6
225g (8oz) fresh or frozen raspberries, thawed
125g (4oz) sugar or honey
275ml (10 fl oz) whipping cream

Liquidize, then sieve the raspberries to remove the pips and make a smooth purée. Add the sugar or honey. Whisk the cream until soft peaks are formed. Fold gently but thoroughly into the raspberry purée. Turn the mixture into a plastic container and put in the coldest part of the fridge. Leave until half frozen, then remove from the container and beat well. Return mixture to the freezing compartment and leave until completely frozen.

This ice cream is best if it's not too hard; put it into the normal part of the fridge for about an hour before you need it to let it 'come to' before serving.

STRAWBERRY AND CASHEW NUT ICE CREAM

In my opinion, this is an amazingly good, totally non-dairy, ice cream!

SERVES 4–6
225g (8oz) cashew nut pieces
300ml (11 fl oz) water
225g (8oz) strawberries, stalks removed
1 tablespoon clear honey

Put the cashew nuts and water in the food processor or liquidizer and whizz to a cream. Then add the strawberries and honey and whizz again. Pour into a polythene container and freeze until solid. Remove from the deep freeze a good 30 minutes before you want to eat it.

VANILLA ICE CREAM WITH HOT CHESTNUT AND BRANDY SAUCE

In this recipe, smooth, creamy, vanilla ice cream is topped with a hot sauce made from chestnut purée with wine and brandy. It is a wonderful pudding for special occasions. You could use honey instead of sugar, but it changes the flavour.

SERVES 4–6
2 eggs *or* 4 egg yolks
275ml (10 fl oz) milk
75g (3oz) vanilla sugar *or* caster sugar plus a few drops of vanilla essence
275ml (10 fl oz) whipping cream
125g (4oz) canned, unsweetened chestnut purée
200ml (7 fl oz) white wine *or* cider
25g (1oz) sugar
3 tablespoons brandy

Whisk the eggs in a medium-sized bowl. Put the milk and sugar into a heavy-based saucepan and bring just up to the boil, then slowly add it to the eggs, stirring all the time. Strain the eggs and milk back into the saucepan, put back on the heat and stir for just a minute or two until the mixture thickens; this happens very quickly, so watch it and stir all the time. Leave this custard to cool.

Whisk the cream until it has thickened and is standing in soft peaks, then fold this gently but thoroughly into the cooled egg custard. Pour the mixture into a plastic container and freeze until it's setting well round the edges. Then scrape the ice cream into a bowl and whisk it thoroughly. Put the ice cream back into the container and freeze until it's firm. Take the ice cream out of the fridge at the beginning of the meal and beat it before serving as it is much nicer if it is not too solid.

To make the sauce, put the chestnut purée into a saucepan and break it up with a fork; then gradually stir in the wine or cider and the sugar. Set the pan over a gentle heat and stir until you have a thick, creamy consistency; this can all be done well in advance. Just before you want to serve the ice cream, reheat the chestnut mixture, beating it smooth, and add the brandy.

You can make this ice cream with half cream and half *fromage blanc* if preferred, and the results are very good.

BLACKCURRANT SORBET WITH CASSIS

It's the Cassis – that blackcurrant liqueur which you can mix with dry white wine to make the pretty pink drink, kir – which gives this recipe a pleasant 'kick', but you could leave it out!

SERVES 4–6
450g (1 lb) fresh *or* frozen blackcurrants
150ml (5 fl oz) water
125g (4oz) sugar
1 egg white
6 tablespoons cassis
a little lightly whipped cream – optional

Put the blackcurrants and water into a saucepan, cook gently for 10–15 minutes until soft, then add sugar. Liquidize, then sieve. Reserve 3 tablespoonfuls. Pour the rest into suitable container and freeze until solid round edges. Whisk egg white until stiff, add the frozen backcurrant purée, still whisking, to make a fluffy mixture. Pour back into container and freeze again until solid. Make a simple sauce by mixing reserved purée with the cassis.

Take the sorbet out of fridge 30 minutes before eating. Serve in individual glasses with sauce on top and cream if liked.

MELON SORBET WITH CRYSTALLIZED MINT LEAVES

This is prettiest if you can find two small melons with flesh of contrasting colours, orange and pale green. Make the sorbet in two separate containers and put a spoonful of both in each bowl. Leave out the mint leaves if you haven't time to do them; but they are pretty for a special occasion and can be made in advance and stored in an airtight tin.

SERVES 6
2 small ripe melons, if possible one with orange flesh and one with green, each weighing about 700g (1½ lb)
2 tablespoons fresh lemon juice
50g (2oz) sugar *or* honey
2 egg whites
20 fresh mint leaves
1 egg white
granulated sugar

Halve the melons, take out the seeds and then scoop all the flesh from the skins, keeping the two colours separate. Liquidize the chunks of scooped out melon, add half the lemon juice and half the sugar or honey to each, taste and add a little more sweetener if necessary. Turn the two mixtures into separate containers, then freeze and finish as for blackcurrant sorbet, adding half the egg white to each bowl.

About an hour before you want to eat the sorbet, take the containers of sorbet out of the coldest part of the fridge and stand them on a shelf in the fridge to give them time to soften a little. Put alternate spoonfuls of each colour in individual glasses and garnish with the mint leaves.

To make the mint leaves, first wash the leaves and pat dry with kitchen paper. Beat the egg white lightly, just to break it up. Have a saucer of sugar ready. Brush the mint leaves all over with egg white then dip them into the sugar, coating them on both sides. Lay the leaves on a piece of greaseproof or silicon paper on a dry baking sheet and put them into a very cool oven, 120°C (250°F), gas mark ½, for about 2 hours to dry out, until they are crisp and brittle. Cool, then store in an airtight tin until needed.

ORANGE SORBET SERVED IN ORANGE SKINS

This makes an attractive pudding and once assembled it can be stored in the freezer until just before you want to eat it. I like to serve the oranges on a base of fresh green leaves: bay leaves if available, or rose leaves.

SERVES 4
275ml (10 fl oz) water
125g (4oz) sugar *or* honey
4 large oranges
juice of half a lemon
extra orange juice: see recipe
2 egg whites

Put water and sugar or honey into a heavy-based saucepan and heat gently until sugar has dissolved; then simmer gently for 10 minutes. Cool. Slice tops off oranges and scoop out the flesh, keeping skins whole. Liquidize then sieve orange flesh, add lemon juice and extra orange juice if necessary to make 275ml (10 fl oz). Add this to the cooled syrup, then pour mixture into suitable containers and freeze until solid round the edges. Whisk the egg whites until stiff, then beat in the orange mixture. Freeze until firm, then spoon into the orange skins and put back tops as 'lids'. Wrap oranges in clingfilm and freeze until 15 minutes before eating.

PINEAPPLE SORBET

Here, a pineapple is halved and the flesh made into a sorbet, served in the skins and decorated with fresh strawberries.

SERVES 6
1 large ripe pineapple
125g (4oz) sugar *or* 175g (5oz) honey
575ml (1 pint) water
1 egg white
225g (8oz) small, ripe strawberries

Halve the pineapple from top to bottom, cutting right through the leaves. Scoop out flesh, discarding hard core. Heat sugar or honey and water gently in a pan until sugar has dissolved, then boil for 2 minutes. Liquidize pineapple with this sugar syrup. Put the mixture into a shallow container and freeze until solid around the edges. Whisk egg white, then add pineapple mixture, and whisk until well blended. Freeze mixture until solid. About 30 minutes before you want to eat the sorbet take it out of the fridge. Spoon the sorbet into the pineapple skins and decorate with strawberries.

STRAWBERRY SORBET WITH KIWI FRUIT

I think this sorbet is one way of getting the best from frozen strawberries, because for this their mushiness is actually an advantage! The sorbet looks pretty served in a border of sliced green kiwi fruit.

SERVES 6
450g (1 lb) fresh *or* frozen strawberries, thawed
1 tablespoon fresh lemon juice
125g (4oz) sugar *or* 175g (5oz) mild honey
2 egg whites
3 kiwi fruit

Liquidize and sieve the strawberries, adding the lemon juice to bring out the flavour and enough sugar to sweeten, then make the sorbet exactly as for blackcurrant sorbet (page 310).

About an hour before you want to eat the sorbet, take it out of the coldest part of the fridge and stand it on a shelf in the fridge to give it time to soften a little. Peel the kiwi fruits and cut them into thin slices. Put spoonfuls of the sorbet in individual glasses and tuck the kiwi fruit round the edge.

13

BAKING: CAKES, BISCUITS, SCONES AND TEABREADS

My husband has a sweet tooth. His mother is a wonderful cook, so he was brought up on excellent traditional tea-time favourites such as Dundee cake, Victoria sandwich cake and flapjacks. Then he went and married me, with all my reservations about sugar and fat, not to mention white flour, and full of ideas for experimenting with healthy, sugarless, fatless mixtures most unlike anything mother ever made. 'What hasn't this got in it?' he said about one of my cakes the other day 'or is it a real cake?' The situation is further complicated by the fact that one of my daughters is a non-egg-eating vegetarian, so any cake which she is going to share has to be made without eggs. Actually, some of my sugarless/fatless/eggless cakes have been very good, as I hope you'll agree if you try some of the recipes, even if they don't have my husband's unqualified recommendation. This section contains a mixture of what I consider to be the best versions of conventional cakes and biscuits, together with some unconventional

inventions of my own which are popular with readers, friends and family.

Note on Ingredients

Flour When I first started cooking, and at the time I wrote *Simply Delicious* and *Not Just a Load of Old Lentils*, full of the enthusiasm and crusading zeal of youth, I used 100% wholemeal flour for absolutely everything. I still use this for bread and for some types of pastry and scones, but these days I find I more often use an 85% wholemeal for cakes. It's a flour which has had some of the coarsest bran removed but retains the wheatgerm and a little of the bran. Cakes and pastry baked with this flour look browner than those made with white flour, but are beautifully light. You can buy both plain and self-raising 85% flour at health shops and some supermarkets.

Fat Most cakes and biscuits contain a fair proportion of fat and so (with the exception of some of the sugarless/fatless ones in this section) they should really be considered as occasional treats rather than everyday eating in a health-conscious diet. Bearing this in mind, my own preference is for unsalted butter or for a soft margarine that is high in unsaturated fat.

Sweetenings I was brought up on real Barbados molasses sugar (which my father used to bring back to Hampshire from London, such was the lack of health shops in those days!). I continued to use this when I was cooking at the retreat centre, believing it to be better than white sugar. Then as a result of reading various articles I realized that all sugar is basically unhealthy, being just a source of calories with no nutritional value. So I started using date purée instead (as you will see in some of the following recipes – and very good it is too). Yes, I know that dates, too, are high in sugar, but at least it's still wrapped up in the natural fibre of the fruit (therefore more chewy and able to be absorbed more slowly by your body) and contains iron, calcium an B vitamins, too. Sometimes I used honey instead of sugar. The only scientific basis for this was the fact that honey is slightly lower in calories than sugar, but my instincts told me that honey felt right.

I thought I'd got it all sorted out, then about eighteen months ago I read about some Russian experiments (by Professor I. I. Brekkman) which clearly showed the value of real Barbados molasses sugar in improving the body's ability to resist illness and to counter stress. So I looked again at this old friend, and, having dismissed it as being virtually the same thing as white sugar, was surprised to find how much iron, calcium and thiamin it contains (white sugar and light brown sugars contain no trace minerals). But it has to be the real thing: Barbados molasses sugar, dark and sticky in the packet.

So now I use this or my date purée for dark cakes; also honey, which I still believe to be good and am hoping my intuition here will be backed up by scientific evidence – I have heard some amazing tales of the healing qualities of honey when applied to wounds and bed-sores; and I use caster sugar and icing sugar occasionally when I feel in the mood, but this isn't often!

This chapter is divided into four sections. First there is a selection of icings, fillings and toppings. next are cakes; followed by biscuits and tray bakes; then scones, teabreads and unleavened breads; and finally there's a small section of healthy sweets. Recipes which are suitable for the freezer are shown by the symbol ⌷.

ICINGS, FILLINGS AND TOPPINGS

ALMOND PASTE – TRADITIONAL

ENOUGH TO COVER A 20–22CM (8–9IN) CAKE ⌷
450g (1 lb) ground almonds
225g (8oz) caster sugar
225g (8oz) icing sugar
1 teasoon lemon juice
few drops almond essence
2 eggs, beaten

Put the ground almonds and caster sugar into a bowl, then sift in the icing sugar and mix together. Add lemon juice, essence and enough egg (you may not need it all) to make a smooth, firm paste. Knead lightly; use immediately.

HONEY ALMOND PASTE (1)

Although this doesn't contain sugar, it tastes like conventional almond paste and can be used similarly.

MAKES 350g (12oz) ⌷
50g (2oz) unsalted butter or margarine
1 tablespoon thick honey
2 teaspoons lemon juice
125g (4oz) rice flour
125g (4oz) ground almonds
a few drops of almond extract

Mix all the ingredients together, flavouring with a little almond extract. Handle the mixture lightly to avoid the almonds becoming oily.

HONEY ALMOND PASTE (2)

MAKES 250g (9oz) ⌷
200g (7oz) ground almonds
4 tablespoons clear honey
1 tablespoon lemon juice

Put all the ingredients into a bowl and mix gently together to form a firm dough.

SUGARLESS APRICOT CONSERVE

This is simple to make and tastes wonderful. It makes an excellent filling for a cake or a healthy substitute for either jam or marmalade, but it doesn't keep in the same way, so make it in small quantities.

MAKES ABOUT 225G (8OZ)
125g (4oz) dried apricots – the unsulphured ones from health shops are best
275ml (10 fl oz) water
grated rind and juice of 1 small well-scrubbed orange

Soak the apricots in the water overnight. Next day put them into a saucepan with their soaking water and the orange juice and rind. Bring to the boil then simmer gently, with a lid on the pan, for 40–45 minutes, until the mixture is thick, soft and jam-like. Stir mixture occasionally and add a little extra water if necessary to prevent sticking. Cool, then transfer to a jar and store in the fridge.

CURD CHEESE ICING

You can use honey instead of the caster sugar; this will make a creamy dressing, whereas the icing sugar version will firm up a little more. I sometimes make it without the butter, and this, too, gives a softer result.

ENOUGH TO FILL AND TOP ONE 18CM (7IN) CAKE
125g (4oz) curd cheese
25g (1oz) icing sugar
few drops vanilla essence
25g (1oz) unsalted butter

Beat together until smooth and creamy.

DATE FILLING

This is popular with the children, and the carob version is a good healthy substitute for a chocolate filling.

MAKES ABOUT 225G (8OZ)
250g (8oz) dates
orange or apple juice

If you have a food processor, you can simply put the dates into that, with enough juice to make a soft, spreadable mixture. Alternatively, put the dates into a saucepan with 150ml (5 fl oz) water and heat gently until dates are soft. Then mash to a purée.

For the 'chocolate' variation, simply stir in a tablespoon of carob powder and a few drops of real vanilla extract (or add a piece of vanilla pod to the dates when you whizz them in the food processor).

Another version is to add a few almonds: whizz these up in the food processor with the dates, or powder them in a liquidizer or electric coffee grinder, before adding them.

FRESH FRUIT 'JAM' FILLING

In the summer, when fresh soft fruits are at their peak, you can make a wonderful raw 'jam' by simply mashing raspberries, strawberries or redcurrants with a little clear honey. Delicious also on homemade wholemeal bread (you don't even need butter). Or try it on homemade wholemeal scones with a dollop of quark, homemade soft cheese or thick natural yoghurt for a marvellous and healthy cream tea!

FUDGE ICING

ENOUGH TO TOP AND FILL, OR COAT 18CM (7IN) CAKE
40g (1½oz) butter
2 tablespoons water
175g (6oz) icing sugar
few drops vanilla essence

Heat butter and water gently until melted. Remove from heat and sift in the icing sugar. Add vanilla essence, beat well. The icing will thicken up as it cools.

Flavour can be varied as for simple buttercream.

GLACÉ ICING

ENOUGH TO COAT THE TOP OF 18CM (7IN) CAKE
125g (4oz) sifted icing sugar
1–2 tablespoons warm water

Sift icing sugar into a bowl, then add water and beat until smooth and glossy. Use at once.

SIMPLE BUTTERCREAM

ENOUGH TO TOP AND FILL, OR COAT 18CM (7IN)
CAKE
125g (4oz) icing sugar or soft brown sugar
50g (2oz) softened butter
1–2 tablespoons hot water

Sift icing sugar. Beat butter until light, then add icing sugar or soft brown sugar and beat again, adding enough liquid to make a light consistency.

Variations

CHOCOLATE BUTTERCREAM
Add 50g (2oz) melted chocolate or 1 tablespoon cocoa dissolved in the hot water.
COFFEE BUTTERCREAM, 2 teaspoons instant coffee dissolved in the hot water. For **ORANGE** or **LEMON BUTTERCREAM**, add the grated rind and mix with orange or lemon juice instead of water.
REDUCED SUGAR BUTTERCREAM, replace 50g (2oz) of the icing sugar with 50g (2oz) dried skim milk powder or granules; beat well until smooth.

NO SUGAR ICING

ENOUGH TO COAT ONE 20 × 30CM (8 × 12IN)
OBLONG CAKE OR TOP OF ONE 18–20CM (7–8IN)
ROUND CAKE
125g (4oz) coconut cream, from health shops
2 tablespoons boiling water
a dash of honey or raw sugar

Grate the coconut cream, add boiling water and honey or sugar and stir until creamy. Smooth cake with a knife dipped in boiling water, and leave to set. Orange icing can be made with the addition of a little grated orange rind.

For a chococlaty icing, stir in a teaspoon of carob powder.

For lemon icing, use grated lemon rind.

PINEAPPLE FILLING

MAKES JUST UNDER 225G (8OZ)
225g (8oz) can pineapple rings in their own juice
2 teaspoons arrowroot

Liquidize the pineapple with the arrowroot. Pour into a saucepan and heat, stirring, until the mixture thickens and looks translucent. Cool.

ROYAL ICING

ENOUGH TO ICE TOP AND SIDES OF ONE 20–22CM
(8–9IN) ROUND CAKE
900g (2 lb) icing sugar
4 egg whites
1 tablespoon lemon juice
2 teaspoons glycerine

Sift icing sugar. Put egg whites into a bowl and whisk until just frothy. Then add the icing sugar a little at a time, beating well after each addition. When about half has been added, beat in the lemon juice. When all the icing sugar has been added beat in the glycerine.

CAKES

ALMOND AND CHERRY RING

A pretty cake baked in the shape of a ring and flavoured with almonds and cherries; a favourite with my daughter Katy.

MAKES ONE 20CM (8IN) CAKE $\boxed{F}$
150g (5oz) self-raising flour 85% wholemeal
50g (2oz) glacé cherries
175g (6oz) butter
175g (6oz) caster sugar
3 eggs, beaten
50g (2oz) ground almonds
few drops almond essence
1 quantity glacé icing (page 314)
25g (1oz) toasted flaked almonds

Set oven to 180°C (350°F), gas mark 4. Line and grease a 20cm (8in) ring tin (see illustration). Sift

flour. Rinse cherries, slice half and keep on one side. Chop remainder. Cream butter and sugar until light, gradually beat in the egg. Fold in flour, ground almonds, chopped cherries and essence. Spoon into tin, smooth top, bake for 55–60 minutes. Remove from tin, strip off paper, cool. Spoon icing over top of cake, decorate with the reserved sliced cherries and toasted almonds.

Variation

ROSE RING

Make as above, but leave out the cherries. Make the glacé icing using triple-distilled rose water instead of water, or a few drops of rose essence, and colour it pale pink. Spoon icing over the cake and arrange a bunch of tiny pink garnet roses in the cake. A nice cake to celebrate a February birthday!

LITTLE BUNS

MAKES 15 F
175g (6oz) self-raising 85% wholemeal flour
1 teaspoon baking powder
125g (4oz) soft butter
125g (4oz) caster *or* real Barbados sugar
2 eggs
1–2 tablespoons water

Set oven to 190°C (375°F), gas mark 5. Make an all-in-one sponge mix as described on page 322 and put a heaped teaspoonful in each cake case. Bake just below centre of oven for 20–25 minutes, until golden brown. Cool on a wire rack.

Variation

BUTTERFLY CAKES

Make buns as above. When they are cold, cut a thin slice, horizontally, from the top of each, then cut slice in half and leave on one side. Spoon or pipe a dollop of buttercream on top of each cake, then

press the two cut pieces on top like butterfly wings. Pipe or spoon any remaining buttercream decoratively between the 'wings'. Dredge with icing sugar.

CHRISTMAS CAKE – TRADITIONAL

MAKES ONE 20CM (8IN) CAKE F
175g (6oz) plain 85% or 100% wholemeal flour
1 teaspoon mixed spice
175g (6oz) soft butter
175g (6oz) soft brown sugar
5 eggs, beaten
1 tablespoon treacle
grated rind and juice of 1 lemon
700g (1½ lb) mixed dried fruit
75g (3oz) chopped glacé pineapple
125g (4oz) glacé cherries, halved
75g (3oz) ground almonds
40g (1½oz) chopped blanched almonds
1 tablespoon brandy

Set oven to 140°C (275°F), gas mark 1. Grease a 20cm (8in) round cake tin; line with greased greaseproof paper. Sift flour and spice. Cream butter and sugar; gradually beat in eggs. Stir in treacle, then fold in flour. Gently mix in lemon juice and rind, dried and glacé fruit and nuts. Turn into tin, hollow centre slightly. Bake for 4½–5 hours. Cool on wire rack. Prick top of cake and sprinkle with

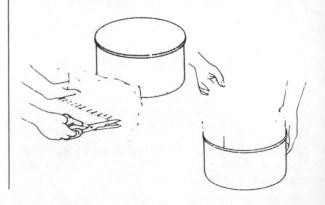

brandy. Wrap in greaseproof paper, store in tin until ready for icing. This cake improves with keeping: I usually try and make it at the end of October, ready for Christmas. Put on the almond paste 7–10 days before Christmas.

To coat cake with almond paste (see drawing below)

Make sure the cake is level: trim with a sharp knife if necessary. Sieve about 3 tablespoons apricot jam and melt gently in a small saucepan. Use a piece of string to measure all round the outside of the cake, and another to measure its depth. Roll two thirds of the almond paste into a rectangle half the length of the cake and twice the depth, then cut in half lengthwise. Brush each piece with melted apricot jam. Roll the cake on to the strips to cover the sides and press together the joins. Roll out remaining almond paste to fit the top. Brush with jam, place on top of cake and roll gently with a rolling pin. Roll a straight-sided jam jar around the outside of the cake to help the almond paste to stick. Leave in a cool airy place to dry before applying the icing: ideally 2–3 days if you're going to eat the cake quickly, 6–7 days for one you're going to keep longer.

To rough-ice a fruit cake

Put all the icing on top of the cake and roll it backwards and forwards with a palette knife a few times to remove air bubbles. Then spread evenly over the cake. Finally use the blade of the knife to rough up the icing into peaks (see drawing). The cake can be decorated with silver balls, bought decorations or shapes cut or moulded from coloured

almond paste. A winter birthday cake looks pretty with a candle in the middle surrounded by almond paste leaves and fruits. An alternative is to decorate the cake with the glacé fruit topping (page 319) either with or without almond paste.

CHRISTMAS CAKE – SUGARLESS

There is no added sugar or honey in this cake: it is sweetened entirely by dried fruit yet, as I think you'll agree if you try it, it's certainly sweet and isn't at all strange either in taste or looks! If you're very health conscious you may not approve of my using candied peel and glacé cherries, but I like them for this once-a-year special cake. You could use chopped dried apricots and dates instead, though.

MAKES ONE 20CM (8IN) ROUND CAKE ☐F☐
175g (6oz) cooking dates, from a block
4 tablespoons water
175g (6oz) soft butter
5 eggs
175g (6oz) plain 85% *or* 100% wholemeal flour
1 teaspoon mixed spice
75g (3oz) ground almonds
grated rind and juice of 1 lemon
225g (8oz) currants
175g (6oz) raisins
175g (6oz) sultanas
125g (4oz) candied peel, chopped
125g (4oz) glacé cherries
50g (2oz) flaked almonds
1–2 tablespoons brandy

Break up the dates with your fingers, being careful to remove any stones and hard pieces of stalk. Put the dates into a small saucepan with the water and stir over a moderate heat until mushy. Remove from the heat and cool. Set the oven to 150°C (300°F), gas mark 2. Line a 20cm (8in) cake tin with two layers of greaseproof paper and tie a piece of brown paper around the outside.

Put the cooled dates into a large bowl with the butter and beat until light and creamy – like creaming fat and sugar together – then beat in the eggs, one by one. Sift in the flour and spice and beat again. Add all the remaining ingredients except the brandy and mix well together. Spoon the mixture into the prepared tin and bake in the oven for 4½–5 hours – a skewer should come out clean when pushed into the centre. Cool cake on a wire rack. When the cake is cold, remove the paper, prick the cake with a skewer and pour the brandy all over it. It will keep for 4–5 weeks, wrapped in greaseproof paper and foil, in a tin. It can then be decorated with one of the honey almond pastes and conventional icing, or honey almond paste and a glacé fruit topping, or just a glacé fruit topping and a red ribbon. To do the glacé fruit topping brush the top of the cake with warmed, clear honey, cover with circles of halved glacé cherries, nuts and dates, and brush with more honey.

CHRISTMAS CAKE – UNCONVENTIONAL

This is very much an alternative-style Christmas cake that I wouldn't dare present before my husband, but I like it. It's uncooked, more a kind of rich meusli-mix, bound together with dates and grated apples, than a cake. It can be served as it is, or covered with honey almond paste and sugarless icing or some dried fruits and nuts and a brushing of honey to glaze.

MAKES ONE 450G (1 LB) LOAF-SIZE CAKE [F]
225g (8oz) chopped dates
225g (8oz) Brazils
225g (8oz) rolled oats
125g (4oz) mixed dried fruit
2 tablespoons honey
2 tablespoons carob
2 grated apples
grated rind of 2 oranges
2 tablespoons brandy or orange juice
50g (2oz) ground almonds
2 teaspoons mixed spice

Line a 450g (1 lb) loaf tin with non-stick paper. If you've got a food processor, simply put everything into that and process until mixture holds together. Otherwise, heat the dates gently in a saucepan with a very little water until soft enough to mash, then transfer to a bowl. Chop or grind the Brazil nuts and add to the date purée, together with the rest of the ingredients. Mix until well combined. Either way, press mixture into tin, put weight on top and leave in fridge for several hours. Turn out and serve in small slices; or coat with honey marzipan (page 313) and/or sugarless icing, as described above.

WHOLEMEAL DUNDEE CAKE

This is my original recipe with one or two small amendments which I've added over the years! It's a delicious, crumbly, fruity cake.

MAKES ONE 20CM (8IN) ROUND CAKE [F]
300g (10oz) plain 85% *or* 100% wholemeal flour
1 teaspoon baking powder (or use half self-raising and half plain flour)
175g (6oz) butter
175g (6oz) Barbados sugar
3 large eggs, beaten
225g (8oz) sultanas
175g (6oz) currants
50g (2oz) candied peel
50g (2oz) glacé cherries, halved
1 teaspoon grated orange rind
50g (2oz) ground almonds
25g (1oz) blanched split almonds
about 6 tablespoons cold water

Set oven to 160°C (350°F), gas mark 3. Sift the flour with the baking powder and mix in any bran which is left in the sieve. Cream the butter and sugar until light and fluffy, then add the beaten eggs, one at a time, slowly, beating all the time, adding a little flour if the mixture starts to curdle. (It curdles because the egg is being added too quickly.) Fold in the flour and all the other ingredients, adding the water to give a soft mixture which drops easily from the spoon. Put into a 20cm (8in) tin which has been lined with two layers of greased greaseproof paper, and arrange the split almonds on top. Bake for 2–2½ hours, or until a warmed knife inserted into the cake comes out clean. Cool the cake in the tin.

WHOLEMEAL DUNDEE CAKE – SUGARLESS

In this cake a purée of dates is used instead of sugar: it's rich in vitamins, minerals and fibre and lower in calories than sugar. But the taste is excellent: no one ever guesses that there's any difference.

MAKES ONE 20CM (8IN) CAKE F
225g (8oz) self-raising 85% *or* 100% wholemeal flour
1 teaspoon mixed spice
175g (6oz) cooking dates, chopped
150ml (5 fl oz) water
125g (4oz) soft butter
grated rind of 1 lemon *or* orange
3 large eggs
450g (1 lb) mixed dried fruit
25g (1oz) ground almonds
25g (1oz) flaked almonds

Set oven to 160°C (325°F), gas mark 3. Grease and line a 20cm (8in) deep cake tin. Sift flour with spice. Put dates into a pan with the water and heat until reduced to a purée. Cool. Put all ingredients except flaked almonds into a bowl and beat until thick and fluffy: 3–5 minutes. The mixture should be soft enough to drop easily from the spoon: add a bit more water, if necessary, to achieve this. Turn into tin, sprinkle with almonds, bake for 2–2½ hours. Cool on a wire rack.

FRUIT CAKE – EGGLESS

A fruit cake for non-egg eating vegetarians like my daughter Margaret. The cake is light and delicious.

MAKES ONE 18CM (7IN) CAKE F
225g (8oz) plain 85% *or* 100% wholemeal flour
2 teaspoons baking powder
1 teaspoon mixed spice
175g (6oz) Barbados molasses sugar – from health shops
6 tablespoons melted butter
450g (1 lb) mixed dried fruit
50g (2oz) glacé cherries, washed and quartered – optional
25g (1oz) soya flour
25g (1oz) ground almonds
225ml (8 fl oz) water
25g (1oz) flaked almonds

Set oven to 160°C (325°F), gas mark 3. Grease an 18cm (7in) round cake tin and line with greased greaseproof paper. Sift the flour, baking powder and spice into a large bowl, tipping in the bran from the sieve too. Then put in all the remaining ingredients except for the flaked almonds. Beat together with a wooden spoon (or in a mixer) for 2 minutes, then spoon mixture into tin and sprinkle with flaked almonds. Bake for about 2¼ hours, until a skewer inserted in the centre comes out clean. Let cake cool for 15 minutes in the tin, then turn out on to a wire rack, strip off paper and leave until completely cold. Store in an airtight tin. This cake will keep for 3 months in the freezer.

FRUIT CAKE – EVERYTHING-LESS

This is my *amazing eggless, sugarless, fatless cake*. My husband wasn't very impressed with this invention of mine – see page 312 – but I was thrilled with it and other friends – male and female – have also liked it (and asked for the recipe!). It comes out just like a moist, rich fruit cake, yet contains none of the 'baddies'.

MAKES ONE 900G (2 LB) LOAF-SIZE CAKE F
225g (8oz) cooking dates (not sugar-rolled)
275 ml (10 fl oz) water
450g (1 lb) mixed dried fruit
175g (6oz) plain 100% wholemeal flour
1 tablespoon carob powder – optional
3 teaspoons baking powder
1 teaspoon mixed spice
grated rind of 1 orange *or* lemon
40g (1½oz) ground almonds
4 tablespoons orange juice
few flaked almonds for top

Set oven to 160°C (325°F), gas mark 3. Grease a 900g (2 lb) loaf tin and line with a strip of greaseproof or non-stick paper. Put dates and water into a saucepan and heat gently until dates are soft, then remove from heat and mash to break up dates. Add dried fruit, flour, carob powder, baking powder, spice, grated rind, ground almonds and orange juice. Spoon mixture into tin, level top. Sprinkle with almonds and bake for about 1½ hours, until a skewer inserted into centre comes out clean. Cool a little in tin, then turn cake out and finish cooling on a wire rack.

GINGERBREAD – TRADITIONAL

This is my mother's recipe which she made when I was a child. When she was well-organized, she'd make a double batch and let one get sticky in a tin; mostly she'd rustle it up quickly when visitors were coming for tea.

MAKES 20 PIECES
50g (2oz) golden syrup
175g (6oz) black treacle
125g (4oz) butter
225g (8oz) plain 85% *or* 100% wholemeal flour
2 level teaspoons baking powder
½ teaspoon ground ginger
75g (3oz) real Barbados sugar
2 eggs
50g (2oz) chopped walnuts, candied peel *or*
crystallized ginger – optional
½ teaspoon bicarbonate of soda
150ml (5 fl oz) milk

Set oven to 160°C (325°F) gas mark 3. Grease a square tin and line with layers of greased greaseproof paper. Melt and blend the syrup, treacle and butter in a pan over a moderate heat. Sieve flour with ginger and baking powder, add sugar and nuts or peel. Make a well in the centre and pour in warmed treacle mixture and the beaten eggs. Quickly beat in the milk with the bicarbonate of soda dissolved in it, and pour mixture into tin. Bake for 1¼ hours or until well risen and firm to touch.

GINGERBREAD – HONEY

A nice, not-too-sweet gingerbread and it will get sticky if you wrap it in foil and keep in a tin for a week before eating. You could use sultanas or raisins in this gingerbread instead of the chopped ginger – or you could simply leave it out – though I must say I like it best with some chunky pieces of ginger in it.

MAKES ONE 20CM (8IN) SQUARE GINGERBREAD
WHICH CUTS INTO 20 PIECES
125g (4oz) soft butter
125g (4oz) clear honey
125g (4oz) black treacle
225g (8oz) plain 100% wholemeal flour
1 teaspoon bicarbonate of soda
1 teaspoon ground ginger
1 teaspoon mixed spice
150ml (5 fl oz) milk
1 egg
50–125g (2–4oz) crystallized ginger, roughly chopped
or sultanas

Line a 20cm (8in) square tin with a piece of greaseproof paper, folded and eased into the tin so that it fits into the corners. Set the oven to 160°C (325°F), gas mark 3.

Put the butter, honey and treacle into a medium-sized saucepan and melt over a gentle heat. Sift the flour, bicarbonate of soda and spices into a large bowl, adding the bran left behind in the sieve, too. Pour the hot melted ingredients into the flour mixture and add the milk; mix well, then beat in the egg and chopped ginger or sultanas and mix again. The mixture will be quite runny and you will have to pour it into the tin. Bake for about 50–60 minutes, until the gingerbread is well-risen and springs back when pressed lightly in the centre. Cool for 5 minutes or so in the tin, then transfer to a wire rack. Remove the greaseproof paper when the gingerbread is cool.

MADEIRA CAKE

This traditional golden cake – a great favourite of my daughter Katy, and base for many of her childhood birthday cakes – has a deliciously tender texture and buttery flavour.

MAKES ONE 18CM (7IN) ROUND CAKE [F]
125g (4oz) plain 85% wholemeal flour
125g (4oz) self-raising 85% wholemeal flour
175g (6oz) softened butter
175g (6oz) caster sugar
4 eggs
2 thin slices of citron peel

Set oven to 180°C (350°F), gas mark 4. Grease and line an 18cm (7in) deep round cake tin. Sift flours together. Cream the butter and sugar until very light and fluffy, then gradually add the eggs, beating well after each addition. Fold in the sifted flour. Spoon mixture into tin, smooth top. Bake for 30 minutes, then carefully open oven and place peel on top of cake, without removing cake from oven. Bake for a further 1–1¼ hours, until a skewer inserted into the centre comes out clean. Turn out on a wire rack to cool.

ORANGE AND ALMOND CAKE

This comes out like a madeira cake, with a light, close texture and delicate flavour. It is very good baked in a deep tin and just finished with a sprinkling of ground almonds, or you can make it shiny by spooning warmed, clear honey on top and sticking some flaked almonds on to it. You can use two sandwich tins instead of the deep one and bake for 25–30 minutes, and that also works well. This way it's nice filled with the healthy butter cream in the toppings section.

MAKES ONE 18–20CM (7–8IN) CAKE F
175g (6oz) soft butter
175g (6oz) clear honey
2 large eggs
grated rind of 1 orange and 4 tablespoons juice
225g (8oz) plain 85% *or* 100% wholemeal flour
3 teaspoons baking powder
25g (1oz) ground almonds – *or* you could use semolina *or* rice flour and a few drops of almond extract if you want to economize

Line the base and sides of an 18 or 20cm (7 or 8in) deep cake tin with greaseproof paper, or if you're using shallower tins just put a circle of greaseproof paper in the base. Set the oven to 160°C (325°F), gas mark 3.

Put the butter, honey, eggs, orange rind and juice into a large bowl – or the bowl of an electric mixer – and sift the flour and baking powder on top, adding also the bran which will be left in the sieve. Stir in the ground almonds, then beat everything vigorously together until smooth, thick and creamy. This takes about 3 minutes electrically, 5 minutes by hand. Spoon the mixture into the tin or tins, level the top and bake for 25–30 minutes for sandwich cakes or 1–1¼ hours for one deep cake. The cake is done when it springs back when pressed lightly in the centre with a finger. Cool on a wire rack.

Variation

CHOCOLATE AND ALMOND CAKE

Leave out the orange rind and juice. Use 200g (7oz) flour; add 25g (1oz) cocoa (or carob powder from the health shop, if you prefer). Use 4 tablespoons milk or water instead of the orange juice, and a teaspoon of vanilla to flavour.

EGGLESS ORANGE SPONGE SLICES

Another variation on the eggless theme.

MAKES ONE 20 × 30CM (8 × 12IN) OBLONG, CUTTING INTO 14–16 PIECES
175g (6oz) 85% *or* 100% plain wholemeal flour
1 teaspoon baking powder
125g (4oz) butter
125g (4oz) light muscovado sugar
rind and juice of ½ orange
150ml (5 fl oz) milk
no-sugar icing (page 315)

Set oven to 180°C (350°F), gas mark 4. Grease and line a 20 × 30cm (8 × 12in) swiss roll tin. Sift together the flour and baking powder, adding the residue of bran from the sieve too. Cream butter and sugar, then gently fold in sifted ingredients and orange rind alternately with the milk and orange juice. If the mixture looks a bit lumpy, beat it well and it will smooth out again. Spread in the prepared tin and bake for 25 minutes, until it springs back when touched. Cool in the tin, then pour over the icing. Cut into fingers when icing has set.

For chocolaty flavoured slices, leave out the orange and add 1 tablespoon carob powder and 3–4 tablespoons extra milk or water to the mixture. Cover with the carob version of the sugarless icing.

PARKIN

A simple recipe (eggless) for a sticky, well-flavoured parkin. It gets stickier if wrapped in foil and stored for 2–7 days, and is a favourite with everyone in our family, especially my daughter Margaret and her boyfriend.

MAKES ONE 20CM (8IN) SQUARE CUTTING INTO 12 PIECES F
125g (4oz) plain 100% wholemeal flour
2 teaspoons baking powder
2 teaspoons ground ginger
125g (4oz) medium oatmeal
75g (3oz) soft brown sugar
125g (4oz) black treacle
125g (4oz) golden syrup *or* honey
125g (4oz) butter
175ml (6 fl oz) milk

Set oven to 180°C (350°F), gas mark 4. Grease and line a 20cm (8in) square tin. Sift flour, baking powder and ginger into a bowl and add the oatmeal. Put the sugar, treacle, syrup and butter into a pan and heat gently until melted. Cool until you can comfortably place your hand against the pan, then stir in the milk. Add this mixture to the dry ingredients and mix well. Pour into tin, bake for 50–60 minutes, until firm to the touch. Cool on a wire rack. Cut into squares when cold.

ROCK CAKES

These spicy buns are quick to make and delicious eaten warm from the oven.

MAKES 8 CAKES ☐F
225g (8oz) plain 85% or 100% wholemeal flour
2 teaspoons baking powder
1 teaspoon mixed spice
125g (4oz) butter, cut in pieces
75g (3oz) soft brown sugar
125g (4oz) mixed dried fruit
1 egg, beaten
1–2 tablespoons milk

Set oven to 220°C (425°F), gas mark 7. Grease a baking sheet. Sift the flour, baking powder and spice into a large bowl. Add the butter and rub in with your fingertips until the mixture looks like fine breadcrumbs, then use a fork to stir in the sugar, dried fruit and egg. The mixture should be fairly stiff and just hold together: add milk only if necessary to achieve this. Place tablespoons of the mixture about 4cm (1½in) apart on baking tray. Bake for 15 minutes, until golden brown and firm. Cool on tray for 5 minutes then transfer to wire rack.

Variation

ROCK CAKES – SUGARLESS

Make these exactly in the same way, but instead of the sugar, use a purée made by heating 125g (4oz) cooking dates gently with 2 tablespoons of water until soft. Mash and cool.

ALL-IN-ONE SPONGE

The quick, modern version of the traditional Victoria sponge. I find it works just as well with butter as with soft margarine, as long as the butter is soft.

MAKES ONE 18CM (7IN) CAKE ☐F
125g (4oz) 85% or 100% self-raising wholemeal flour
1 teaspoon baking powder
125g (4oz) soft margarine or butter
125g (4oz) caster sugar or soft brown sugar
2 eggs
1–2 tablespoons water
3 tablespoons jam
caster sugar or icing sugar

Set oven to 160°C (325°F), gas mark 3. Grease and base-line two 18cm (7in) sandwich tins. Sift flour and baking powder into a large mixing bowl, add margarine or butter, sugar and eggs. Beat for 2–3 minutes, until mixture is light and glossy. Add water a little at a time, if necessary, to make a soft, dropping consistency. Divide mixture between the two tins, smooth tops. Bake for 35 minutes, until centre of cake springs back when touched lightly. Cool for 30 seconds, then turn cakes on to a wire rack, strip off paper and leave to cool. Sandwich cakes with jam and sift a little icing sugar on top or sprinkle with caster sugar.

Variations

CHOCOLATE CAKE

Sift 1 tablespoon cocoa with the flour. You may need to add a little extra water to make a soft dropping consistency. When the cake is cool it can be sandwiched and iced with one of the fillings/toppings on pages 313–5.

LEMON DAISY CAKE

Make the cake as described above, adding the grated rind of a lemon before the eggs. Bake and cool. Fill and ice with a lemon-flavoured buttercream; decorate with mimosa balls and blanched almonds on top to resemble daisies.

ROSE CAKE

For a pretty pink, rose-flavoured cake, make as described above for basic all-in-one sponge, using triple-distilled rosewater (from the chemist) or a few drops rose essence. Sandwich cooled cake with a red jam and/or a little whipped cream. Cover the top with glacé icing, made as described on page 314 but coloured pale pink and made with triple-distilled rosewater instead of water. Then decorate with some crystallized rose petals.

COFFEE AND WALNUT CAKE

Make cake exactly as described above, adding 1 tablespoon good quality instant coffee, dissolved in 1 tablespoon warm water along with the eggs. Bake and cool. Make up double quantity of buttercream (page 315). Put two tablespoons buttercream into a piping bag fitted with a medium-sized nozzle. Sandwich cake with a third of remaining buttercream. Spread sides of cake with half rest of buttercream then coat in chopped walnuts: see drawing below. Cover top of cake with remaining buttercream, decorate with swirls of piping and walnuts as shown below.

SPONGE CAKE FOR CYNICAL FRIENDS

MAKES ONE 18CM (7IN) SPONGE SANDWICH CAKE
125g (4oz) wholemeal flour
4 free-range eggs
125g (4oz) light muscovado sugar (not the very dark one, as it's too treacly for this)
for filling suggestions, see below

Set oven to 190°C (375°F), gas mark 5. Grease two 18cm (7in) tins and line with a circle of greased greaseproof paper. Sift wholemeal flour on to a plate, adding the residue of bran from the sieve too. Whisk together eggs and sugar in an electric mixer, or with a hand whisk over a pan of boiling water, until thick and pale, and mixture leaves a tail on itself (about 5 minutes with the mixer, 15–20 minutes by hand). Fold in flour. Pour into the tins. Bake for about 10 minutes, until cakes have shrunken away from the edge of the tins and spring back when touched lightly. Cool on a wire rack that has been covered with a clean tea towel. When cool, sandwich with your choice of filling. Some ideas are:

the no-sugar icing on page 315;

reduced-sugar or sugarless jam from the health shop, or some fresh raspberries or strawberries with or without a little whipped cream, whipped tofu, page 289, or quark;

homemade sugarless conserve, page 314;

honey mixed with almonds which have been powdered in the blender of an electric coffee mill;

the date filling on page 314;

a raw-sugar butter icing made by beating 50g (2oz) unsalted butter and 50g (2oz) light Barbados sugar together until light. A tablespoon of carob powder can be added to this (plus a little hot water) for a chocolaty flavour.

SPONGE CAKE WITHOUT EGGS

Needless to say, this is one I make a lot for my daughter who doesn't eat eggs. The first time I made it I was amazed what a good cake it was possible to make without eggs.

MAKES ONE 18CM (7IN) CAKE [F]
225g (8oz) self-raising 81 per cent wholemeal flour
2 teaspoons baking powder
175g (6oz) caster sugar or soft brown sugar
6 tablespoons oil or melted butter
225ml (8 fl oz) water
1 teaspoon vanilla essence
2 heaped tablespoons jam and caster sugar to dredge, or 1 quantity of fudge icing (page 314) or buttercream (page 315)

Set oven to 180°C (350°F), gas mark 4. Grease and base-line two 18cm (7in) sandwich tins. Sift flour and baking powder into a bowl. Add caster sugar, then stir in oil, water and vanilla essence. Mix to a smooth batter-like consistency; pour into the tins. Bake for 25–30 minutes, until centre springs back to a light touch. Turn out on to a wire rack, strip off paper. Sandwich with the jam and sprinkle with caster sugar, or fill and top with fudge icing or buttercream.

SWISS ROLL

MAKES ONE SWISS ROLL, 8 SLICES [F]
65g (2½oz) plain flour
3 eggs
125g (4oz) caster sugar
125g (4oz) warmed raspberry jam
caster sugar to dredge

Set oven to 200°C (400°F), gas mark 6. Grease and line a 33 × 23cm (13 × 9in) swiss roll tin. Sift flour. Half fill a large saucepan with water and bring to the boil. Break eggs into a large bowl and place over pan. Whisk eggs lightly; add sugar. Whisk for 10–15 minutes until very thick and fluffy and mixture will hold trail of whisk for 3 seconds. Remove bowl from saucepan. (It is not necessary to whisk eggs over hot water if using a table mixer, and this only takes 5 minutes.) Gently fold in a quarter of the flour; repeat with remaining flour. Pour into tin, bake for 8–10 minutes. Turn out on to a piece of greaseproof which has been sprinkled with flour. Leave to cool. When completely cold, trim crisp edges of swiss roll, spread with jam and roll up. Sprinkle with caster sugar.

TRADITIONAL VICTORIA SANDWICH CAKE

One of my husband's favourites!

MAKES ONE 18CM (7IN) CAKE [F]
175g (6oz) 85% *or* 100% wholemeal self-raising flour
175g (6oz) softened butter
175g (6oz) caster sugar
3 eggs, beaten
1–2 tablespoons water
3 tablespoons raspberry jam
icing *or* caster sugar to dredge

Set oven to 180°C (350°F), gas mark 4. Grease and line two 18cm (7in) sandwich tins. Sift flour. Cream butter and sugar until very light and fluffy, then gradually add the eggs, beating well after each addition. Fold in the flour. Divide mixture between

the tins, smooth tops. Bake for 25–30 minutes: the cake should spring back when pressed lightly. Cool on wire rack, then sandwich with jam and dredge with caster or icing sugar, or fill with whipped cream and sliced strawberries in the summer; or any of the fillings on page 314, or the suggestions given for varying the basic All-in-One Sponge on page 322.

BISCUITS

CRISP ALMOND TUILES

These are useful for serving with fruit salads and creams for a special occasion.

MAKES 18
75g (3oz) butter
75g (3oz) caster sugar
a few drops almond essence
50g (2oz) plain flour
50g (2oz) flaked almonds

To make biscuits, set oven to 200°C (400°F), gas mark 6. Beat butter and sugar until light, stir in essence, flour and almonds. Put teaspoonfuls on to a greased baking sheet and flatten with a fork, allowing plenty of room to spread. Bake until browned at the edges; 6–8 minutes. Leave to stand for 1–2 minutes until firm enough to lift from tin, but not brittle, then place over a rolling pin to curl as they cool.

BRANDY SNAPS

Crisp brandy snaps are delicious, with or without the filling of whipped cream. They're really quite easy to make and lovely for serving for a special occasion, perhaps to accompany a fruit salad or purée.

MAKES APPROXIMATELY 14
50g (2oz) butter
50g (2oz) Barbados sugar
50g (2oz) golden syrup
50g (2oz) plain 85% wholemeal flour
½ teaspoon ground ginger
a litte grated lemon rind
150ml (5 fl oz) double cream
few drops brandy – optional

Heat oven to 160°C (325°F), gas mark 3. Stir the butter, brown sugar and golden syrup together in a pan over a gentle heat until melted. Remove from heat and sift in the flour, ground ginger and a little grated lemon rind to taste. Drop teaspoonfuls of mixture on to greased baking sheets; flatten lightly with palette knife; leave plenty of room for them to spread. Bake for 8–10 minutes, until golden. Cool for 1–2 minutes, until just firm enough to handle, then loosen with a knife and quickly roll snaps round the greased handle of a wooden spoon, or I use the thicker handle of a fish slice, then slide off and leave to cool. This process must be done quickly or the brandy snaps will harden. Should this happen, pop them back into the oven for a few minutes to soften. When quite cold use piping bag with star nozzle to fill the brandy snaps with whipped cream (flavoured with a touch of brandy if liked). Brandy snaps can be made a day or two in advance and stored in a tin ready for filling with cream when desired.

CHEESE BISCUITS

You can get round the sugar problem sometimes, I've found, by simply avoiding it and offering crisp home-made cheese biscuits instead of sweet ones. Many people in fact prefer savoury things, and these biscuits always seem to disappear fast. It's fun to experiment with different flours – they're lovely made with half wholemeal, half barley, rye or buck-wheat flour, and sometimes I add some dried herbs, chopped nuts, sesame, cumin or caraway seeds, too.

MAKES ABOUT 32 BISCUITS [F]
225g (8oz) plain wholemeal flour, or half wholemeal and half one of the other flours
175g (6oz) soft polyunsaturated margarine or butter
175g (6oz) grated cheese
good pinch each of dry mustard and cayenne pepper

Set the oven to 230°C (450°F), gas mark 8. Put the flour into a bowl and mix in the margarine or butter with a fork. Add the grated cheese, cayenne pepper and mustard. Form into a dough, roll out 6mm (¼in) thick, cut into 5cm (2in) rounds, prick each several times with a fork and bake for 15–20 minutes, until golden brown. The biscuits will get crisp as they cool. Store in an airtight tin. These biscuits will freeze. Cool the biscuits then put them into a rigid container and freeze. To use, spread them out on a wire rack to de-frost at room temperature – this will only take about 40 minutes.

Variation

WHOLEMEAL CHEESE STRAWS

Make mixture as above, roll out and cut into straws about 3mm (⅛in) wide and 5cm (2in) long. Put the straws on a floured baking sheet and bake in the pre-heated oven for about 7–10 minutes until they are crisp and golden-brown. ...ol on a wire rack – they will get crisper as they co...

CHOCOLATE SHORTBREAD

Another favourite with readers. You can also make this using that chocolaty-flavoured powder, carob, from health shops, instead of the cocoa, and carob bar instead of the chocolate. These biscuits will freeze, see cheese biscuits (above).

MAKES 15 [F]
125g (4oz) butter
50g (2oz) dark brown sugar
100g (3½oz) plain wholemeal flour
65g (2½oz) desiccated coconut
2 tablespoons cocoa powder
50g (2oz) plain chocolate

Set oven to 180°C (350°F), gas mark 4. Cream together the butter and sugar until well blended, then add flour, coconut and cocoa and mix well. Press mixture firmly into a greased swiss roll tin (a palette knife helps here) and bake for 30 minutes.

While shortbread is cooking, break chocolate into small pieces or grate coarsely. When shortbread is cooked, scatter chocolate over the top, and return shortbread to oven for a minute or two, until chocolate has melted. Remove from oven and spread chocolate evenly over top. Cool in tin, then cut into slices.

CRUNCHY BARS

MAKES 16 [F]
125g (4oz) rolled oats
125g (4oz) plain wholemeal flour
125g (4oz) real demerara sugar – from health shops
1 tablespoon clear honey
150ml (5 fl oz) oil – sunflower *or* corn oil, *or* 150g (5oz) soft butter
40g (1½oz) flaked almonds *or* roasted peanuts (see page 136) lightly chopped
2 teaspoons vanilla essence
2 tablespoons sesame seeds

Set oven to 200°C (400°F), gas mark 6. Grease a 20 × 30cm (7¾ × 12in) swiss roll tin. Put all the ingredients into a bowl and mix together. Spread in tin. Bake for 15–17 minutes, until golden brown. Mark into slices, cool in tin. When completely cold, store in an airtight tin. These biscuits freeze well: follow instructions as given for cheese biscuits (page 325).

CRUNCHY BISCUITS

These are quick to make, popular with most people, and useful for offering with coffee or tea.

MAKES 18 [F]
50g (2oz) butter
50g (2oz) real Barbados sugar
25g (1oz) golden syrup or treacle
½ teaspoon bicarbonate of soda
75g (3oz) rolled oats
50g (2oz) plain wholemeal flour

Set oven to 180°C (350°F), gas mark 4. Grease one or two large baking sheets. Melt the butter, sugar and syrup together in a saucepan over a gentle heat. Remove from the heat, cool slightly, then stir in the bicarbonate of soda. Mix well, then add the oats and flour. Put heaped teaspoons of the mixture in little heaps on the baking sheet. Bake for 10–15 minutes, until golden brown. Cool on the tray, lift off carefully with a spatula. These biscuits freeze well and thaw quickly.

SPICY CURRANT BISCUITS

The sweetness in these crisp biscuits comes from the currants, almonds and spice.

MAKES 22 BISCUITS [F]
125g (4oz) plain wholemeal flour
½ teaspoon baking powder
½ teaspoon allspice
50g (2oz) butter *or* polyunsaturated margarine
15g (½oz) ground almonds
50g (2oz) currants
1 tablespoon water

Set the oven to 200°C (400°F), gas mark 6. Sift the flour, baking powder and spice into a large bowl; add the residue of bran from the sieve and the butter or margarine, almonds and currants. Mix everything together with a fork, then stir in the water to make a dough. On a lightly-floured board roll the dough out to a thickness of about 6mm (¼in). Stamp into rounds with a 5cm (2in) cutter, prick the top of each biscuit with a fork. Put the biscuits on floured baking sheets and bake for 10 minutes. Lift them on to wire rack to cool. These biscuits will freeze. See instructions given for the cheese biscuits (page 325).

DATE SLICES

These also make a good pudding, eaten warm from the oven with some milk, cream, nut cream or a dollop of natural yoghurt over them.

MAKES 16 [F]
225g (8oz) cheapest dates – not the 'sugar-rolled' type
150ml (5 fl oz) water
175g (6oz) plain wholemeal flour
175g (6oz) porridge oats
175g (6oz) butter
75g (3oz) real demerara sugar
2 tablespoons cold water

Set oven to 190°C (375°F), gas mark 5. Grease a 20 × 30cm (7¾ × 12in) swiss roll tin. Put the dates into a saucepan with the water and heat gently for 5–10 minutes, until the dates are mushy. Remove from the heat and mash with a spoon to make a thick purée, looking out for and removing any stones as you do so. Then leave on one side to cool. Meanwhile sift the flour into a bowl, adding also the residue of bran from the sieve and the oats. Rub in the butter with your fingertips, then add the sugar and water, and press mixture together to form a dough. Press half this mixture into the greased tin, spread the cooled date purée on top, then cover evenly with the remaining oat mixture and press down gently but firmly. Bake for 30 minutes. Cool in tin, then mark into sections and remove with a spatula. Date slices freeze well and defrost very quickly; can be eaten almost immediately.

I think this is the best version of these, though for a sugarless recipe, make as above, just omitting the sugar. Handle carefully, as the mixture is rather crumbly.

FLAPJACKS

If you use ordinary rolled oats for these, the flapjacks are crisp; if you use jumbo oats or cereal muesli base from the health shop, they come out gooey and toffee-like.

MAKES 15 PIECES [F]
125g (4oz) Barbados sugar
125g (4oz) butter
1 slightly rounded tablespoon golden syrup
175g (6oz) rolled oats

Set oven to 190°C (375°F), gas mark 5. Melt together the brown sugar, butter and golden syrup, then stir in the rolled oats. Spread into a greased swiss roll tin, and bake for 10–15 minutes until golden brown. Cool a little, then mark into slices. Remove from tin when quite cold. With the jumbo oat version, it's a good idea to get them out of the tin before they are completely cold because they're inclined to stick.

FRUIT SLICES

Easy to make, with a delicious topping of crunchy almonds.

MAKES 10–12 [F]
50g (2oz) butter
50g (2oz) Barbados molasses sugar – from health shops
1 egg
125g (4oz) wholemeal flour
225g (8oz) mixed dried fruit
4 tablespoons water
40g (1½oz) flaked almonds

Set oven to 160°C (325°F), gas mark 3. Line a 20cm (8in) square tin with non-stick or greaseproof paper and grease. Put the butter and sugar into a bowl and cream together, then beat in the egg. Add the flour, dried fruit and water. Mix to a firm consistency which will drop heavily from the spoon when it's tapped against the side of the bowl. If necessary, add a little more water. Spoon mixture into the tin, level the top, sprinkle with flaked almonds. Bake for about 45 minutes, until the cake feels firm in the centre. Cool on a wire rack. Cut into ten or twelve pieces when cold. Fruit slices freeze well for up to 2 months.

HAZEL NUT SHORTBREAD

This is one of those useful recipes that really seems made for wholemeal flour and Barbados sugar. The shortbread has a rich caramelly, nutty flavour.

MAKES 15 PIECES [F]
75g (3oz) hazel nuts
125g (4oz) butter
50g (2oz) real Barbados sugar
175g (6oz) plain 85% wholemeal flour

Set oven to 180°C (350°F), gas mark 4. If the nuts are the kind still in their brown outer skins, spread them out on a dry baking sheet and bake in the oven for about 20 minutes, until the nuts under the skins are a golden brown. Then either rub off the outer skins, or leave them on. If the nuts have already had their outer skins removed, you could just roast them for a few minutes in the oven to improve the flavour, or use them as they are. In either case, grind them quite finely in a nutmill, liquidizer or food processor. Turn oven setting down to 160°C (325°F), gas mark 3. Cream the butter and sugar until they're light and fluffy, then beat in the flour and hazel nuts, to make a dough. Press this dough into a lightly-greased 18 × 28cm (7 × 11in) swiss roll tin. Prick top thoroughly with a fork. Bake for 1 hour. Mark into slices while still hot, then leave to cool in tin. This shortbread freezes well.

JAM AND ALMOND FINGERS

The 'jam' in these is one of the beautiful 'no-added sugar' ones now available from health shops. My favourites are the pear and apple, a lovely deep red colour with a very fruity flavour, and the apricot and damson ones, which are lower in calories. In this recipe the jam is melted over a light, crisp wholemeal shortcrust base, to make a shiny glaze, which is topped with crunchy flaked almonds. It's good with other nuts, too: chopped roasted hazel nuts and also chopped Brazils.

MAKES 20 F
175g (6oz) plain wholemeal flour
75g (3oz) soft butter
4 teaspoons cold water
225g (8oz) sugarless jam – preferably pear and apple,
apricot *or* damson
25g (1oz) flaked almonds

Set the oven to 200°C (400°F), gas mark 6. Put the flour into a large bowl and use a fork to blend in the butter. Add the water and mix to a dough. On a lightly-floured board roll out the dough to fit a 30 × 20cm (12 × 8in) swiss roll tin. The easiest way to transfer the crumbly wholemeal pastry is to tip it straight from the board to the tin. Prick the base and bake the pastry for 15–20 minutes, until golden and crisp. Put the jam into a medium-sized saucepan and melt over a fairly gentle heat, then pour it evenly over the pastry and sprinkle with the almonds. Leave to cool. The pastry will crisp and the glaze will set. The pear and apple jam sets better than the others, which may need to go in the fridge to become really firm. Cut into slices. These fingers will freeze.

MACAROONS

A favourite with my daughter Katy, crisp macaroons are useful for serving with cold, creamy puddings for a special occasion.

MAKES 12
1 egg white
125g (4oz) ground almonds
125g (4oz) caster sugar
rice paper
12 whole blanched almonds

Set the oven to 180°C (350°F), gas mark 4. Put the egg white into a good-sized bowl and whisk lightly, just to break it up. Stir in the ground almonds and caster sugar and mix to a paste. Lay the rice paper on baking sheets and put spoonfuls of the macaroon mixture on it, leaving room for them to spread a little. Smooth the macaroons with the back of a spoon dipped in cold water and place an almond in the centre of each. Bake for 15–25 minutes.

Transfer the macaroons to a wire rack, tearing the rice paper roughly; trim off the remaining paper when the macaroons have cooled.

OATCAKES

Oatcakes are easy to make and crisp and nutty-tasting to eat. Try them for breakfast or tea with butter and clear honey, or serve them with a creamy dip or Scottish cream cheese.

MAKES 24–28 F
225g (8oz) medium oatmeal
½ teaspoon baking powder
½ teaspoon salt
25g (1oz) butter *or* margarine, melted
6 teaspoons hot water
a little extra oatmeal to finish

Set the oven to 200°C (400°F), gas mark 6. Put the oatmeal into a bowl with the baking powder, salt and butter or margarine. Mix them together lightly, then stir in enough warm water to make a dough – you'll need about 6 teaspoons.

Sprinkle some oatmeal on a board and turn the dough out on to this, kneading lightly, then roll it out to a thickness of about 3mm (⅛in), sprinkling the surface with a little extra oatmeal if necessary to prevent it from sticking. You can either roll the mixture into a circle and then cut it into wedges, or stamp it into rounds using a pastry cutter. Transfer the oatcakes to a baking sheet and bake them for about 15 minutes until firm and lightly coloured. Let them cool on the tin for a few minutes, then transfer them to a wire cooling rack. Or serve them straight from the oven, all warm and crumbly.

SCONES AND TEABREADS

EASY WHOLEMEAL SCONES

These scones freeze well after baking.

MAKES 12 F
225g (8oz) plain wholemeal flour
4 teaspoons baking powder
50g (2oz) soft butter
50g (2oz) raw Barbados sugar
8–10 tablespoons milk

Set oven to 230°C (450°F), gas mark 8. Sift flour and baking powder into a bowl; add the bran left in the sieve too. Then rub in the butter, add the sugar and mix to a soft dough with the milk. Roll out 2cm (1in) thick and cut into rounds using a 5cm (2in) round cutter. Place on a floured baking sheet and bake for 12–15 minutes until risen. Cool on a wire rack.

Variations

HONEY SCONES

Leave out the sugar. Use 8 tablespoons milk and 2 tablespoons clear honey, blended together to bind scones.

CHEESE SCONES

Leave out sugar. Sift ½ teaspoon mustard powder with the flour, and add 125g (4oz) grated cheese to the mixture after rubbing in the butter. Some chopped walnuts, say 50g (2oz), are also good in this, or try a cheese, mustard and sesame variation: make as for cheese scones, but roll the mixture out on a board which has been sprinkled with sesame seeds.

BABY SCONES

The scones can be made from the same basic mixture cut out with a tiny round cutter measuring 1cm (½in) across. They are a bit fiddly to make but are very suitable for a buffet or drinks party, split and topped with various sweet and savoury dips. Using a small cutter the quantities above should give about thirty scones and they will take about 10 minutes to cook.

EASY WHOLEMEAL SCONE CIRCLE

A lovely recipe which was given to me by a friend.

MAKES ONE CIRCLE CUTTING INTO 8 F
1 dessertspoon fine oatmeal
125g (4oz) plain wholemeal flour
1 heaped teaspoon baking powder
25g (1oz) brown sugar
pinch salt
25g (1oz) margarine *or* fat
25g (1oz) sultanas
6 tablespoons milk

Set oven to 180°C (350°F), gas mark 4. Mix together oatmeal, flour and baking powder and pinch salt and sugar. Rub in fat until mixture resembles breadcrumbs, mix to a soft pliable consistency with milk. Shape into a round on a floured baking tin and cut across and across into 8 sections. Bake for 15 minutes.

Variation

TREACLE SCONE CIRCLE

Use 1 tablespoon black treacle and only 4 tablespoons milk, blending the two together before adding.

BANANA BREAD

An old favourite.

MAKES ONE 450G (1 LB) LOAF CUTTING INTO 10 SLICES F
225g (8oz) wholemeal flour
2 level teaspoons baking powder
pinch salt
50g (2oz) margarine
50g (2oz) dark Barbados sugar
75g (3oz) golden syrup *or* honey
50g (2oz) walnuts
1 egg
2 bananas

Set oven to 180°C (350°F), gas mark 4. Grease and line a 450g (1 lb) loaf tin with slips of greased greaseproof paper. Sift together flour, baking powder and salt. Melt together margarine, sugar and syrup in a pan over a gentle heat. Chop walnuts; beat eggs, mash bananas. Make a well in the centre of the flour and pour in margarine mixture; mix quickly, then add beaten egg and mashed bananas. Mix very well; pour into greased and lined 450g (1 lb) loaf tin, and bake for 1 hour. Cool on a wire rack.

Variation

DATE AND WALNUT LOAF

Make this in the same way, using 125g (4oz) chopped dates and a little milk instead of bananas.

BRAN, APRICOT AND ALMOND LOAF

I invented this loaf because I wanted an iron-rich, high fibre, quick-to-make tea-bread to help the various internal problems which can be a feature of pregnancy and the early days after the baby's birth! It's a moist fruity loaf. This freezes well after baking.

MAKES ONE 450G (1 LB) LOAF, CUTTING INTO 10 SLICES F
125g (4oz) dried apricots
150ml (5 fl oz) hot water
125g (4oz) plain wholemeal flour
1 teaspoon baking powder
½ teaspoon mixed spice
25g (1oz) bran
125g (4oz) sultanas
75g (3oz) dark or light real Barbados sugar
50g (2oz) almonds, with skins on, chopped
1 egg

Wash apricots in warm water, then shred into small pieces with kitchen scissors or a sharp knife. Put into a bowl and cover with the hot water. Next day, set oven to 180°C (350°F), gas mark 4, and line a 450g (1 lb) loaf tin with strips of non-stick or greaseproof paper and grease well. Then sift the flour, baking powder and spice into another bowl and add the bran, sultanas, sugar, almonds and egg. Now add the apricots, together with the soaking water, and mix everything together well. Spoon into prepared tin. Bake in the centre of the oven for 50–60 minutes, until top springs back when touched, and a skewer inserted in the middle comes out clean. Turn out on to a wire rack to cool. Serve in thick slices, with butter.

QUICK BAKING POWDER LOAF

This is a quickly made 'emergency' loaf, and delicious eaten warm with butter and runny honey. It doesn't keep well, though it makes quite good toast, if you do get some over.

MAKES ONE ROUND LOAF F
225g (8oz) plain wholemeal flour
4 level teaspoons baking powder
150ml (5 fl oz) plus 2 tablespoons milk

Set oven to 220°C (425°F), gas mark 7. Sift the flour and baking powder together into a large bowl. Mix quickly to a soft dough with the milk. Turn on to a floured board and knead lightly for a minute or two till the dough is smooth. Shape into a round with your hands and place on a floured baking sheet. Brush the top with milk to give a nice golden brown crust and bake for 25 to 30 minutes.

Variation

QUICK BAKING POWDER ROLLS

Put small pieces of the above mixture on to a greased baking sheet; bake for 10–15 minutes.

CHAPAATIS

These circles of unleavened bread are delicious with any curry dish; they can also be rolled round salad fillings or stuffed and baked in a similar way to stuffed pancakes.

MAKES 12
250g (9oz) plain wholemeal flour
1½ teaspoons oil, melted butter or ghee
1 teaspoon sea salt
about 150ml (5 fl oz) cold water

Sieve the flour into a bowl, adding also the bran which will be left in the sieve. Mix in the fat, salt and water to make a firm dough. When the dough has formed turn it out on to a very lightly floured board and knead it for about 5 minutes. Then if possible cover it with a damp cloth and leave it to rest for 2–3 hours before kneading it again.

Divide the dough into 12 pieces, form each into a ball with your hands, then roll them out with a rolling pin so that they are 15–20cm (6–8in) across. Fry the chapaatis on both sides in an ungreased frying pan. Pile them up on a plate as they're done and cover them with a piece of foil to prevent them from drying out.

If you like you can brush them over with a little oil, melted butter or *ghee* before serving them.

PURIS

These puffed-up, succulent Indian breads are made from the same basic dough as the chapaatis in the last recipe, but the rounds are made a little smaller and are deep fried.

SERVES 4
250g (9oz) wholemeal flour
1½ teaspoons oil *or* ghee
150ml (5 fl oz) water
oil for deep frying

Make the dough exactly as described for chapaatis, then take pieces of dough about the size of a walnut and roll each into a circle about 7.5cm (3in) diameter. Plunge one of these rounds into really hot, deep oil and fry until golden on the underside, then, using a perforated spoon, turn it over and press it down below the surface of the oil with the spoon. As you do this it will swell up. Lift the puffed-up puri out of the oil and drain on kitchen paper. Fry the remainder in the same way, three or four at a time. Keep the finished puris warm while you make the rest, then serve them immediately.

SUGARLESS AND FATLESS DATE AND WALNUT LOAF

One of my inventions. It is fatless in that it doesn't contain added fat, although there is of course some natural oil in the walnuts.

MAKES ONE 450G (1 LB) LOAF, CUTTING INTO 10 SLICES F
175g (6oz) dates
275ml (10 fl oz) water
175g (6oz) plain wholemeal flour
3 teaspoons baking powder
75g (3oz) walnuts, chopped
1 teaspoon vanilla

Put dates into a saucepan with the water and simmer gently until dates are reduced to a purée. Remove from heat and leave on one side to cool. Set oven to 180°C (350°F), gas mark 4. Line a 450g (1 lb) loaf tin with strips of non-stick paper and grease. Sift flour and baking powder into a bowl, adding the residue of bran from the sieve too. Then add the walnuts, vanilla and cooled date mixture and stir well. Spoon into tin, bake for 50–60 minutes, until centre feels springy and a skewer inserted into the centre comes out clean. Cool on a wire rack. Serve cut into thick slices, and buttered if liked.

SWEETS

ALMOND PASTE SWEETS

The almond paste on page 313 makes good sweets. Colour the almond paste with vegetable colourings if you like and roll it into little fruits or whatever shapes you fancy. If you have young children they will have plenty of ideas but will probably eat most of it. It's good at Christmas as a filling for shiny dates, instead of the stone, or to stick two walnut halves together with or as a thin coating for Brazil nuts which can then be rolled lightly in cocoa or carob powder.

CAROB AND CASHEW SQUARES

These and the following sweets, have been approved by my six year old daughter, Claire, and her friends!

MAKES 21
125g (4oz) cashew nuts
1 tablespoon carob
¼ vanilla pod – optional
1 tablespoon thick honey

Put the cashew nuts, carob and vanilla pod, if used, into a liquidizer or food processor and whizz to a powder. Then add honey and process again to make a stiff paste. Put this into a 20 × 20cm (8 × 8in) shallow tin and press it out so that it is 1 cm (½in) deep (it will only fill about a third of the tin). Put into the fridge to firm up, then make two cuts one way and 7 the other, to make 21 squares.

FRUITY SQUARES

MAKES 64
350g (12oz) mixed dried fruit: dates, peaches,
apricots, raisins
125g (4oz) nuts: cashew, almonds, walnuts, hazels *or*
Brazils
125g (4oz) desiccated coconut (unsweetened)
grated rind of 1 orange *or* lemon
a little orange juice
extra desiccated coconut for coating

Put dried fruit and nuts into a food processor and
process until finely chopped. Then add coconut and
grated rind and process again, adding enough orange
juice to make a firm paste. Sprinkle a little desiccated
coconut in a 20cm (8in) square tin, press mixture on
top, then sprinkle with more coconut and press
down well. Put a weight on top and place in fridge
to firm up. Then slice into 2cm (1in) squares.

NUT, RAISIN AND DATE 'FUDGE'

This isn't quite like real fudge, but it's not a bad
approximation, especially when you consider that it
doesn't contain any added sugar or fat. You need
powdered skimmed milk from health shops, not the
ordinary granules.

MAKES 24 PIECES
125g (4oz) cooking dates from a block
60ml (2 fl oz) water
1 tablespoon carob or cocoa powder
1–2 teaspoons vanilla extract
6 tablespoons skimmed milk powder
4 tablespoons ground almonds
4 tablespoons chopped mixed nuts
50g (2oz) raisins
1–2 teaspoons rum – optional

Cut the dates into pieces and put them into a small
saucepan with the water. Heat gently, stirring often,
until dates have softened to a thick purée. Remove
from heat and mix in the remaining ingredients,
beating well – the mixture will be quite stiff. Spread
into a lightly greased swiss roll tin, making the
mixture about 1 cm (½in) deep (it won't fill the
whole tin). Smooth top and leave on one side for at
least 2 hours to firm up. Cut into squares to serve.

NUTTY GINGER CLUSTERS

These are my favourites, shiny little heaps of
chopped nuts and ginger.

MAKES 8
1 tablespoon clear honey
75g (3oz) chopped nuts
2 pieces of preserved ginger, finely chopped about
40g (1½oz)

Put the honey into a small saucepan and heat gently
for 3–4 minutes, until a little forms a hard ball when
dropped into a saucer of cold water. Stir frequently
and be careful not to let it burn. Remove from the
heat, add the other ingredients. Put little heaps of
the mixture into tiny paper cases or on to waxed
paper and leave to set.

14

BREAD AND YEAST COOKERY, INCLUDING PIZZA

'Breadmaking is easy' we cookery writers say. But what we should add is 'if you do it often'. If, however, you only make bread once in a while, or are attempting to do so for the first time, it's more nerve-wracking. That's mainly because you're not quite sure what the yeast is going to do. But there are only three things which can really go wrong. These are, using stale yeast, which won't rise; getting the mixture too hot, which kills the yeast (though it doesn't mind the cold, and bread will rise slowly in the fridge); and putting too much sugar or salt in the mixture, which also inhibits or kills the yeast.

You can easily avoid these pitfalls, produce wonderful results each time and fill your home with the warm smell of freshly-baked bread. If you're short of time, start with the easiest of all loaf which doesn't even have to be kneaded, the Even Quicker Bread on page 341. Otherwise read on, and I'll take you through the process and try and make it easy for you. Then, once you've got a bit of confidence, try

some of the other lovely things you can make with yeast such as yeasted fruit cake, crumpets and hot cross buns. And don't forget pizza: a homemade one is delicious, and easy to do, either starting from scratch, or using a piece of dough when you're making bread.

HOW TO MAKE PERFECT BREAD

If you're baking for a family, or have a deep freeze, I think it's worth making up a 1.5 kilo (3 lb 5oz) bag of flour. You can use all wholemeal flour, or if your family isn't used to wholemeal flour, you might find it best to use wheatmeal flour, which is flour which has been sieved once by the millers to remove the coarsest part of the grain, and contains 85–90% of the grain, whereas wholemeal or wholewheat (the two names are interchangeable) flour consists of 100%. Or you might find it best to use wheatmeal flour or wholewheat flour with a proportion of strong white flour (preferably unbleached, from the health shop) – half and half is a good mixture to start with.

I advise using dried yeast for your first attempt, because it's more predictable, and I think, easier when you're learning. But it's important that the dried yeast should be fresh, so buy it from a shop which has a quick turnover and, unless you know you're going to do a lot of breadmaking, it's best to buy a small quantity to start with. The 'easy blend' yeast which you can now buy is also excellent and even easier to use. If you're converting a recipe, remember that 25g (1oz) fresh yeast equals 15g (½oz) dried yeast or one 7g (¼oz) sachet of easy blend yeast. If you want to use fresh yeast, or to use it for some of the recipes in this section, you can usually buy it, by the 25g (1oz) weight, from health shops, bakers and some supermarkets. It should be creamy beige in colour, moist, crumbly and sweet-smelling. A dark, mottled colour, sticky or very dry texture, and an 'off' smell mean that the yeast is stale and will not work. Fresh yeast will keep for up to a week in a screw-top jar in the fridge. To use it, just crumble it into the liquid given for the recipe and stir to blend. There's no need to add any sugar to this liquid.

If you've got a warm place like an airing cupboard you can put the bread to rise: close to the pilot light on a gas cooker is another good place. But the bread will rise just as well but more slowly standing on the working surface in the kitchen or even in the fridge – see chart. You don't especially need to put it into a warm place, and it's important not to let it get too hot.

MAKES FIVE 450G (1 LB) LOAVES
275ml (10 fl oz) hand-hot water
½ teaspoon sugar (not needed for easy blend yeast)
2 tablespoons dried yeast *or* 2 sachets easy blend yeast
1.5 kilo (3 lb 5oz) bag of wheatmeal *or* wholemeal flour; *or* a mixture of wholemeal flour and strong white bread flour
2 tablespoons sugar – I use Barbados molasses sugar
4 teaspoons fine sea salt
50g (2oz) butter
575–725ml (1–1¼ pints) hand-hot water (if you're using easy blend yeast you can add this water to the smaller quantity of water to make 850ml–1 litre [1½–1¾ pints])

If you're using easy blend yeast, skip this paragraph. If you're using ordinary dried yeast, put the 275ml (10 fl oz) water into a small jug or bowl and stir in the ½ teaspoon of sugar and the dried yeast. Leave on one side for 5–10 minutes to froth up.

Prepare your loaf tins by greasing them thoroughly with butter or oil, then leave them on one side, in a warm place if there's one handy, but this isn't essential. If you're buying tins, get traditional ones with high slanting sides. But if you're making bread for the first time, or haven't got any, don't worry. You can use any sort of deepish tin – even a round cake tin – just remember to fill it half full of dough.

Now put your flour into a large bowl – the bowl of your electric mixer if this has a dough hook attachment. Add the 2 tablespoons of sugar and the salt and the easy blend yeast if you're using it. Rub in the butter with your fingers. If you're using ordinary dried yeast, by this time you should find that it has frothed up quite dramatically into a lovely volcanic mass and you can add it with the 575–725ml (1–1¼ pints) water, or the 850ml–1 litre (1½–1¾ pints) if you're using easy blend yeast. Only, whichever yeast you're using, don't put in quite all the water; put in the smaller quantity to start with and leave the rest for the moment.

Mix the flour, yeast and water together until the dough forms – add the remaining water now if the dough seems too stiff. It should be firm, but soft enough to handle pleasantly, rather like soft well-worked Plasticine. If you've got a dough hook on your mixer – and I must say it's since I got one that I've managed to make our bread regularly – you can now leave it to knead the dough for 5 minutes. Otherwise, turn the dough out and knead it by hand, pushing and pummelling, folding and refolding it, for 5 minutes or even 10 minutes if you can manage it. As you knead the dough you'll feel it change from a course, lumpy and slightly sticky texture to a beautiful smooth, supple, silky one.

Put the dough back in its bowl, cover it with a damp tea-towel then stand the bowl in a polythene carrier bag and leave it to double in size. I find this takes an hour in a warm place, perhaps slightly longer if the bowl is just standing on the working surface and up to 2 hours if the kitchen is cold (see chart below).

Now punch down the dough with your fist and knead it again a little – just 1–2 minutes this time, to wake the yeast up again. Cut the dough into 5 equal-sized pieces and shape them to fit the tins. I find the best way to do this is to flatten each piece with the palm of my hand, then gently roll it up and pop it into the tin with the fold underneath. Then I press the sides and corners down so that the centre of the loaf is higher, coming up into a nice dome shape. Put the loaves on top of the cooker or in a warm place with the damp cloth again and set the oven to 240°C (475°F), gas mark 9. (If you put the loaves on top of the cooker the heat of the oven as it warms up will help them to rise.)

They'll take about 30 minutes to rise: as soon as the dough is just peeping over the tops of the tins put them into the oven. Don't let them over-rise or they'll collapse in the oven: if there is still some rise left in them the heat from the oven will give them a final boost and they'll have a lovely domed crust.

After 10 minutes turn the heat down to 200°C (400°F), gas mark 6 and bake the loaves for a further 25 minutes. Turn the loaves out of their tins straight away – they should sound hollow when you tap them on the base with your knuckles – and leave them on a wire rack to cool.

You can of course make 2 large loaves and 1 small loaf if you'd prefer; large loaves take about 10 minutes longer to bake.

Once it has risen to double its size, the bread can be baked as it is, or it can be finished by being brushed and sprinkled with various ingredients to give a particularly attractive appearance. For a crusty loaf, brush with salted water (1 part salt to 3 parts water); if you want a shiny golden finish, use top of the milk or beaten egg, or melted butter or margarine for a crisp, crunchy crust. After being brushed with any of these the loaves or rolls can be sprinkled with kibbled wheat, poppy seeds, sesame seeds or other seeds such as caraway or cumin.

GUIDE TO BREAD RISING TIMES

First Rising Times

In a warm place 23°C (74°F) e.g., an airing cupboard, by pilot light on gas cooker	45–60 minutes
At room temperature 18–21°C (65–70°F)	1½–2 hours
In a cool room or larder	8–12 hours
In a refrigerator (brush dough with oil and cover bowl with greased polythene to prevent hard crust forming)	up to 24 hours

Second Rising (Proving) Times

In a warm place 23°C (74°F) e.g., an airing cupboard, by pilot light on gas cooker	30 minutes
At room temperature 18–21°C (65–70°F)	40–50 minutes
In a cool room or larder	2–3 hours

In a refrigerator: brush surface of dough with oil and cover with greased polythene; leave at room temperature for 15 minutes before baking	up to 12 hours

ALMOND PLAIT

A flaky roll with a moist filling of almond paste.

MAKES ONE LARGE PASTRY F
½ quantity of croissant dough (page 338)
225g (8oz) almond paste
2 tablespoons apricot jam, sieved and warmed
2 tablespoons flaked almonds
a little icing sugar

Make flaky dough exactly as described for croissants on page 338; roll out to a rectangle about 35 × 25cm (14 × 10 in). Roll almond paste into a strip 32cm (13in) long and 7.5cm (3in) wide and place down the centre of the dough, so that there is about 7.5cm (3in) of dough either side of it. Make diagonal cuts in these side pieces about 1cm (½in) apart, then fold alternate strips over to make a plaited effect, tucking in the top and bottom ends neatly. Place plait on a baking sheet, cover and leave to rise for about 30 minutes, until puffy. Set oven to 220°C (425°F), gas mark 7. Bake plait for 25–30 minutes. Brush with apricot jam, sprinkle flaked almonds down centre. Cool on wire rack; sprinkle with icing sugar.

BRAN BREAD

This extra high fibre bread tastes good and has a pleasantly light texture.

MAKES TWO 450G (1 LB) LOAVES F
15g (½oz) fresh yeast *or* 2 teaspoons dried yeast and ½ teaspoon sugar
475ml (17 fl oz) warm water
700g (1½ lb) wholemeal flour
50g (2oz) bran
1 tablespoon sugar
2 teaspoons salt
1 tablespoon oil

Dissolve yeast in a cup of the measured water; if using dried yeast add sugar too and leave for 10–15 minutes until frothed up. Mix flour, bran, sugar, salt and oil in a large bowl; add yeast liquid and remaining water and mix to a dough. Knead for 5–10 minutes, cover and leave until doubled in bulk: about 1 hour in a warm place. Knock back, knead lightly, shape and put into greased tins. Cover and leave until dough has doubled in size again; about 30 minutes. Set oven to 230°C (450°F), gas mark 8. Bake bread for 10 minutes, reduce heat to 200°C (400°F), gas mark 6 for a further 25 minutes, then turn on to a wire rack to cool.

EASY BAPS

Quick and easy to make using easy-blend yeast, these are delicious for breakfast or with a savoury filling.

MAKES 8 F
150ml (5 fl oz) milk
150ml (5 fl oz) water
50g (2oz) butter
225g (8oz) wholemeal flour
225g (8oz) strong white flour
1 teaspoon salt
1 teaspoon sugar
7g (1⁄4oz) packet of easy-blend yeast

Heat milk, water and butter gently until butter melts; cool to lukewarm. Mix flours, salt, sugar and yeast in large bowl, add milk mixture and mix to a dough. Knead 5 minutes, put into a bowl, cover and leave in a warm place for about 1 hour, until doubled in bulk. Set oven to 220°C (425°F), gas mark 7. Knock back dough, knead briefly. Divide into 8 pieces, form into smooth rounds, dust with flour and place well apart on a floured baking tray. Cover and leave in a warm place for 15–20 minutes, until well-risen. Bake for 15–20 minutes. Cool on a wire rack.

BREAD ROLLS

Warm home-made rolls are useful for serving with so many dishes and they're really not difficult to make. This recipe is based on half one of the new metric bags of flour containing 1.5 kilos (3 lb 5oz) which is why the amount looks rather strange in the Imperial measurements. If you don't like eggs, you can replace this with a little extra milk.

MAKES 24 F
200ml (7 fl oz) hand-hot water
1 tablespoon dried yeast and 1⁄2 teaspoon sugar or 1 sachet easy-blend yeast
750g (1 lb 101⁄2oz) wholemeal flour
2 teaspoons salt
1 tablespoon sugar
50g (2oz) butter
200ml (7 fl oz) milk
1 egg, beaten
a little extra flour to finish

For easy blend yeast, follow the method given for mixing the dough on page 334.

Otherwise, put the water into a small bowl and stir in the yeast and the 1⁄2 teaspoon of sugar. Leave on one side for 10 minutes to froth up. Meanwhile put the flour, salt and the 1 tablespoon of sugar into a bowl and rub in the butter. Pour the frothed-up yeast into the centre of the flour and add the milk and egg; mix together to make a firm but pliable dough. Turn the dough out and knead it for 10 minutes, then put it back into the bowl, cover with a damp cloth, stand the bowl inside a polythene carrier bag and leave until it's doubled in size. This takes about an hour in a warm place, 1–2 hours just standing on a working surface; depending on how warm the room is.

When the dough has risen set the oven to 220°C (425°F), gas mark 7. Punch down the dough, knead it again lightly then divide it into 24 pieces. Form the pieces into rounds then flatten them with the palm of your hand and place them on greased baking trays, 2.5cm (1in) apart, to allow room for them to spread. Cover them with a damp cloth and leave in a warm place for 20–30 minutes to double in size – I put mine on top of the cooker so that they get the benefit of the heat of the oven as it warms up. Sprinkle the rolls with a little flour then bake them for 15 minutes. Cool on a wire rack.

It's easy to vary these rolls; roll them in flour and place them closer together 1cm (1⁄2in) apart for soft rolls you pull apart, brush with melted butter or beaten egg for a crisp crust. You can also replace the beaten egg in the mixture with a little extra milk if preferred.

Variation

FREEZER ROLLS

It's very convenient to be able to take a batch of partly-cooked rolls from the freezer, finish them off in the oven and serve them fresh and warm. You can do this if you bake them first at a low temperature, then freeze them and finish them off as usual when you need them. Follow the previous recipe, but bake the rolls at 150°C (300°F), gas mark 2, for 20 minutes, just to 'set' the rolls. Cool them completely, then pack in polythene bags and freeze. To use, let the rolls thaw out at room temperature for 45–60 minutes, then bake at 230°C (450°F), gas mark 8 for 10 minutes. They can be cooked while still frozen, if you're desperate, but may take a bit longer, about 15 minutes.

BRIOCHES

These classic French rolls make a delicious breakfast treat.

MAKES 12 [F]
15ml (½oz) fresh yeast *or* 2 teaspoons dried yeast
plus ½ teaspoon sugar
2 tablespoons warm water
225g (8oz) strong plain flour
½ teaspoon salt
1 tablespoon sugar
50g (2oz) soft butter
3 eggs, beaten

Dissolve the fresh yeast in the warm water; if using dried yeast add the sugar too and leave for 10–15 minutes until frothy. Mix flour, salt and sugar; add yeast, butter and eggs to make a sticky dough. Knead dough for 5 minutes, adding a little more flour if necessary. Put dough into a bowl, cover and leave for 1–1½ hours until doubled. Punch down, divide into 12 pieces. Remove a quarter of each piece, roll rest into a ball, place in greased bun tin, make hole in centre with your finger. Roll remaining piece of dough into a small ball, place on top. Cover and leave to rise for 1 hour, until puffed up. Set oven to 230°C (450°F), gas mark 8. Bake brioches for 10 minutes, serve warm.

CHEDDAR AND WALNUT BREAD

Serve this crisp-crusted, richly flavoured bread warm from the oven with home-made soup, pâté or cheese and salad.

MAKES ONE ROUND LOAF [F]
15g (½oz) fresh yeast *or* 2 teaspoons dried yeast and
½ teaspoon sugar
200ml (7 fl oz) hand-hot water
275g (10oz) wholemeal flour
1 teaspoon salt
15g (½oz) butter
75g grated Cheddar cheese
50g (2oz) walnuts, chopped

Dissolve the yeast in the water: for dried yeast, add the sugar too and leave 10–15 minutes until frothy. Mix flour and salt in a bowl; rub in butter. Add yeast liquid and mix to a fairly soft dough. Knead 5–10 minutes, put dough into a bowl, cover and leave until doubled in size: 1 hour in a warm place. Knock back dough and knead in the cheese and nuts. Form into a round loaf, place on greased baking sheet. Cover and leave until well risen: 20–30 minutes. Bake loaf at 230°C (450°F), gas mark 8 for 10 minutes, then turn setting down to 200°C (400°F), gas mark 6 and bake for a further 15–20 minutes. Cool on a wire rack.

CHRISTMAS FRUIT LOAF

The candied fruits make this a pretty, jewelled loaf. It's nice for Christmas because it's festive without being too rich. The best way to get the crushed cardamom is to buy some cardamom pods at a health shop or Indian shop and crush them in a pestle and mortar or with the back of a spoon – the seeds will come out of the pods as you crush them and you keep the seeds and discard the pods. If you can't get it leave it out, but it does give a beautiful flavour and cardamom is a useful flavouring for curries and spicy rice dishes, too.

MAKES 1 LARGE LOAF [F]
100ml (3½ fl oz) lukewarm milk
½ teaspoon caster sugar
2 teaspoons dried yeast
450g (1 lb) 85% wholemeal flour
pinch of salt
50g (2oz) soft brown sugar
125g (4oz) softened butter *or* soft margarine
½ teaspoon crushed cardamom
2 teaspoons vanilla essence
rind of ½ lemon
225g (8oz) mixed candied fruits, chopped – try to get
a nice variety of colours
2 eggs, beaten

First grease a 900g (2 lb) loaf tin with butter. Then put the milk into a small bowl, stir in the caster sugar and yeast and leave on one side to froth up. Meanwhile mix together the flour, salt and sugar and rub in the butter or margarine; add the cardamom, vanilla, lemon, fruit and eggs. Make a well in the centre and pour in the yeast mixture. Mix to a soft dough, adding a little more flour if necessary, then knead for 10 minutes. Put the dough into an oiled bowl, cover with a clean damp cloth then with a polythene carrier bag and leave it in a warm place until doubled in bulk – about 1 hour.

Punch the dough down, knead it again lightly, form into a loaf shape and put into the prepared tin. Cover the loaf with the cloth and polythene bag again and leave in a warm place for about 30 minutes to rise. Set the oven to 180°C (350°F), gas mark 4. When the loaf has come up to the top of the tin, bake it until it's golden and crisp. The loaf should sound hollow when turned out of its tin and tapped on the base. Leave on a wire rack to cool. It's nice served with a rich pudding, like *pashka* (page 303), or sliced and buttered for tea.

CROISSANTS

MAKES 12 [F]
200 g (7oz) butter
25g (1oz) fresh yeast
275ml (10 fl oz) warm water
450g (1 lb) strong plain flour
1 teaspoon sugar
beaten egg to glaze

Mix a bread dough as described on page 334 using 25g (1oz) of the butter and no salt; knead 5 minutes, then roll out to a long rectangle about 1 cm (½in) thick. Dot one third of remaining butter over top two thirds of dough, leaving 1 cm (½in) border. Fold bottom third of dough up over centre, then fold top third down. Turn dough so fold is on right-hand side; press edges with rolling pin to seal. Repeat rolling and folding twice, using rest of butter. Put dough in polythene bag in fridge for 1 hour, then roll into rectangle 54 × 35cm (21 × 14in) and cut in half lengthwise. Cut each strip into six triangles with a 15cm (6in) base. Roll triangles up from base, brush with egg, curve into crescents, place on baking sheet. Prove for 30 minutes. Set oven to 220°C (425°F), gas mark 7. Bake croissants for 15–20 minutes.

CRUMPETS

Crumpets are fun to make and surprisingly quick and easy. If you haven't got crumpet rings you can use egg-poaching rings. I have also successfully used an 18cm (7in) flan ring, cutting the crumpet into quarters for serving!

MAKES ABOUT 12 [F]
15g (½oz) fresh yeast *or* 2 teaspoons dried yeast and
½ teaspoon sugar
300ml (11 fl oz) hand-hot milk and water mixed
225g (8oz) flour
1 teaspoon caster sugar
1 teaspoon salt
butter for greasing

Dissolve yeast in the milk and water; if using dried yeast add sugar too and leave for 10–15 minutes to froth. Combine flour, sugar and salt in a bowl; add yeast liquid, mix to a smooth batter. Cover and leave in a warm place for 45 minutes until frothy. Grease frying pan and crumpet rings with butter. Place rings in frying pan, set over a low heat. Half-fill rings with batter. Cook gently for about 5 minutes until tops are set and covered with little holes. Remove rings, turn crumpets over to cook for 1–2 minutes. Serve immediately or cool then toast.

DANISH PASTRIES

Light, crisp and not-too-sweet, Danish pastries are ideal for serving with coffee on a special occasion. They take time to make, but are not difficut; I found it particularly satisfying to produce a wholemeal version that was light and delicious. They freeze well, but leave the final icing until just before serving.

MAKES 15 [F]
1 quantity of croissant dough (page 338)
50g (2oz) mixed dried fruit
40g (1½oz) caster sugar
1 teaspoon mixed spice
125g (4oz) marzipan
beaten egg to glaze, glacé icing, flaked almonds

Roll dough out 1cm (½in) thick and divide into three equal pieces. Roll one of these into an oblong, 30 × 20cm (12 × 8in), sprinkle with dried fruit, sugar and spice, roll up like a swiss roll. Cut into 6 pieces, make two deep cuts in each, open out slightly. Cut both remaining pieces of dough into 6 and roll each into a square about 10 × 10cm (4 × 4in). Cut marzipan into 12 pieces. Make six of these into 2.5 × 10cm (1 × 4in) strips. Place a strip of marzipan at top edges of 6 squares of dough, roll up, make cuts along length and curl round to make cockscomb. Form rest of marzipan into rounds, place one in centre of each remaining square of dough and fold corners to centre. Brush all with beaten eggs. Set oven to 220°C (425°F), gas mark 7. Leave pastries for 20 minutes, until puffy, then bake for 20 minutes. Cool, then ice and sprinkle with flaked almonds.

FRENCH BREAD

MAKES TWO BAGUETTES [F]
25g (1oz) fresh yeast *or* 15g (½oz) dried yeast and ½
teaspoon sugar
275ml (10 fl oz) hand-hot water
700g (1½ lb) strong, plain, unbleached, white flour
2 teaspoons salt
2 teaspoons sugar
25g (1oz) soft butter
yellow cornmeal *or* extra flour for coating

Dissolve the yeast in the water; if using dried yeast,
add sugar too and leave for 10–15 minutes until
frothy. Combine flour, salt and sugar in a large
bowl; rub in butter. Add yeast liquid, mix to a
dough, adding a little more liquid if necessary.
Knead for 10 minutes, then put dough into a clean
bowl, cover and leave until doubled in size: 1 hour
in a warm place. Knock back, knead briefly, put
dough back into bowl and rise again: 40–45 minutes.
Knock back, divide dough in two, sprinkle working
surface with cornmeal, roll dough into two long thin
baguettes. Place on greased baking sheet, cover and
prove for 30 minutes. Brush with cold water, bake
at 200°C (400°F), gas mark 6, for 1 hour, brushing
crust with cold water every 10–15 minutes.

GRANARY COB

This crusty round loaf is delicious with butter and
honey.

MAKES ONE 900G (2 LB) LOAF [F]
25g (1oz) fresh yeast *or* 15g (½oz) dried yeast
and ½ teaspoon sugar
425ml (15 fl oz) hand-hot water
700g (1½ lb) Granary flour
1 tablespoon sugar
1½ teaspoons salt
25g (1oz) butter
kibbled wheat for topping

Dissolve yeast in a cup of the measured water; if
using dried yeast add ½ teaspoon sugar and leave
for 10–15 minutes until frothed up. Put flour, sugar
and salt into a large bowl; rub in butter, then pour
in yeast liquid and remaining water and mix to a
dough. Knead for 5–10 minutes, put back in bowl,
cover with polythene or cling film and leave until
doubled in bulk: 1 hour in a warm place. Knock
back, knead lightly, shape into a round. Sprinkle
with kibbled wheat. Place on greased baking sheet,
then cut a deep cross in the top. Cover and leave in
a warm place for 30 minutes until well risen. Set
oven to 200°C (425°F), gas mark 7. Bake for 40–45
minutes. Cool on rack.

HERB BREAD

Served warm from the oven, fragrant herb bread
is delicious with soup, especially the artichoke or
cauliflower soup. This bread takes just 2 hours to
make from start to finish.

MAKES ONE 450G (1 LB) LOAF
6 tablespoons milk
6 tablespoons hot water
15g (½oz) fresh yeast *or* 2 teaspoons dried yeast and
½ teaspoon sugar
275g (10oz) wholemeal flour
4 teaspoons sugar
1 teaspoon salt
25g (1oz) soft butter *or* margarine
1 small onion, peeled and grated
½ teaspoon each oregano and rosemary

Mix milk and water, blend in yeast. If using dried
yeast add sugar too and leave for 10–15 minutes to
froth. Combine flour, sugar and salt in large bowl,
rub in butter or margarine, add onion and herbs.
Pour in yeast and mix to a dough; knead for 5–10
minutes. Put dough back in mixing bowl, cover and
leave until doubled: 45 minutes in a warm place. Set
oven to 230°C (450°F), gas mark 8. Knock back
dough, shape and place in greased 450g (1 lb) loaf
tin. Cover, leave 20–30 minutes to rise. Bake for 10
minutes, then reduce setting to 200°C (400°F), gas
mark 6, for 25 minutes. Serve warm.

HOT CROSS BUNS

Fragrantly spiced buns, fun to make, and delicious
served warm.

MAKES 12 [F]
1 quantity bread roll dough (page 336) kneaded and
risen once
½ teaspoon each mixed spice, cinnamon, grated
nutmeg
75g (3oz) currants
40g (1½oz) chopped mixed peel
25g (1oz) sugar
75g (3oz) shortcrust pastry
2 tablespoons milk
25g (1oz) sugar

Knock back dough, add the spices, currants, peel
and sugar and knead dough until they're mixed in.
Divide dough into 12 pieces, form into rounds, place
2.5cm (1in) apart on greased baking sheet. Cover
and put in warm place for 30 minutes until well
puffed up. Set oven to 220°C (425°F), gas mark 7.

To make crosses, roll pastry thinly, cut into strips and arrange in crosses on top of buns (or just cut crosses). Bake for 20 minutes. Heat milk and sugar until sugar is dissolved; brush over buns. Cool on rack.

MIXED GRAIN BREAD

This bread has a delicious flavour and chewy texture and is a great favourite with my youngest daughter, Claire.

MAKES ONE 450G (1 LB) LOAF [F]
15g (½oz) fresh yeast *or* 2 teaspoons dried yeast and
½ teaspoon sugar
200ml (7 fl oz) hand-hot water
175g (6oz) wholemeal flour
75g (3oz) rye flour
25g (1oz) kibbled wheat
75g (3oz) medium oatmeal
1 teaspoon salt
1 tablespoon oil

Dissolve the yeast in the water; if using dried yeast stir in the sugar too and leave in a warm place for 10–15 minutes until frothy. Combine the flours, wheat, oatmeal, salt and oil in a large bowl; add the yeast liquid and mix to a dough. Knead 10 minutes, place in bowl, cover and leave until doubled in bulk: 1 hour in a warm place. Knock back, knead briefly, shape and put into a greased 450g (1 lb) loaf tin. Cover and leave in a warm place until doubled in size. Bake loaf at 220°C (425°F), gas mark 7, for 10 minutes then reduce to 200°C (400°F), gas mark 6, for a further 20 minutes. Cool on a wire rack.

NUT, RAISIN AND HONEY BREAD

A slightly sweet bread that's delicious sliced and buttered for tea.

MAKES ONE 450G (1 LB) LOAF [F]
15g (½oz) fresh yeast *or* 2 teaspoons dried yeast and
½ teaspoon sugar
150ml (5 fl oz) warm water
225g (8oz) wholemeal flour
1 teaspoon salt
15g (½oz) butter
50g (2oz) each flaked almonds, raisins and honey

Dissolve the yeast in the water; for dried yeast add sugar too and leave 10–15 minutes until frothy. Mix flour and salt in a bowl, rub in butter. Mix to a

dough with the yeast liquid, knead 5–10 minutes. Put dough in bowl, cover, leave until doubled in size: 1 hour in a warm place. Knock back, then knead in the almonds, raisins and honey. Shape and place in greased 450g (1 lb) loaf tin. Cover and leave until centre of bread is 2.5cm (1in) above top of tin. Bake at 230°C (450°F), gas mark 8, for 10 minutes, then turn down to 200°C (400°F), gas mark 6, for a further 20–25 minutes. Turn out on to a wire rack to cool.

PEAR BREAD

Slices of this pear bread, the recipe for which comes from Switzerland, are lovely served warm with coffee, or if you serve it hot with single cream it makes a very good pudding. I think it goes rather well after a fondue because it's sweet without being rich. You can leave out the kirsch and wine but they do give a beautiful flavour for a special occasion. You will probably be able to get dried pears at a health shop; they're also nice in fruit compôtes.

MAKES 1 LARGE LOAF [F]
5 tablespoons lukewarm water
¼ teaspoon caster sugar
1 teaspoon dried yeast
150g (5oz) plain wholemeal flour
150g (5oz) plain white flour
pinch of salt
50g (2oz) butter *or* soft margarine
50g (2oz) soft brown sugar
1 egg, beaten
275ml (½ pint) water
125g (4oz) dried stoned prunes
225g (8oz) dried pears
50g (2oz) seedless raisins
rind and juice of ½ lemon
50g (2oz) soft brown sugar
a little ground cinnamon
grated nutmeg
1 tablespoon each of dry red wine and kirsch –
optional
a little beaten egg

Grease a large baking sheet with butter; leave on one side. First make the dough. Put the milk into a small bowl and stir in the caster sugar and yeast. Leave in a warm place for the yeast to froth up. Put the flours and salt into a large bowl; rub in the butter or margarine and add the sugar. Make a well in the centre and pour in the yeast and milk, together with the beaten egg. Mix everything together to make a smooth, soft dough, adding a little more flour if necessary. Turn the dough on to a floured board and knead it for 10 minutes, then put the dough into a clean, oiled bowl, cover it with a clean damp cloth then put the bowl inside a large polythene carrier bag and leave it in a warm place for about an hour or until it has doubled in bulk.

While this is happening make the filling. Put the water, prunes, pears and raisins into a small pan and heat gently until soft, thick and dry. Sieve, finely chop or liquidize the mixture, then add the lemon and sugar and some cinnamon and nutmeg to taste – about ¼ teaspoonful of each – and the wine and kirsch if you are using them. Don't make the mixture too liquid – it should hold it's shape.

To assemble the pear bread take the risen dough and knead it for a minute or two, then put it on to a lightly floured board and roll out into a large square, about 38 × 38cm (15 × 15in) and not more than 6mm (¼in) thick. Spread the fruity filling over the square to within about 2.5cm (1in) of the edges. Fold the edges over to enclose the filling, then roll it firmly like a swiss roll and put it on to the prepared baking sheet. Prick the pear bread all over, cover it with a clean cloth and put it into a warm place for 20 minutes to rise. About 15 minutes before the pear bread is ready, set the oven to 180°C (350°F), gas mark 4. Then brush the bread over with beaten egg and bake it in the centre of the oven, for about 35 minutes, or until it's golden brown and crisp. Serve warm.

POPPY SEED PLAIT

MAKES 1 LARGE PLAIT F
25g (1oz) fresh yeast *or* **15g (½oz) dried yeast plus**
½ teaspoon sugar
425ml (15 fl oz) warm milk
700g (1½ lb) strong plain flour
1½ teaspoons salt
1½ teaspoons sugar
50g (2oz) butter
beaten egg, to glaze
poppy seeds

Blend yeast into the milk; for dried yeast add sugar too and leave for 10–15 minutes until frothy. Put flour, salt and sugar into a large bowl, rub in butter. Add yeast liquid, mix to a dough. Knead for 10 minutes, put into a bowl, cover and leave until doubled in bulk: 1 hour in a warm place. Knock back, knead briefly, then make a plait: divide the dough into three equal pieces, roll each into a sausage about 30cm (12in) long, fat in the middle and tapering at the ends. Start plaiting from the centre, finish the ends off to a neat point. Put on greased baking sheet, cover and prove for 30

minutes, until puffy. Set oven to 230°C (450°F), gas mark 8. Brush plait with beaten egg, sprinkle with poppy seeds and bake for about 35 minutes. Cool on wire rack.

QUICK BREAD

You can reduce breadmaking time dramatically by adding ascorbic acid or vitamin C to the dough: this speeds up fermentation so that the bread can be ready in 1¾ hours.

MAKES ONE 900G (2 LB) LOAF OR TWO
450G (1 LB) F
25g (1oz) fresh yeast
425ml (15 fl oz) warm water
25mg ascorbic acid tablet, crushed, from chemists
700g (1½ lb) strong flour
1 tablespoon salt
1 teaspoon sugar
15g (½oz) butter or margarine

Dissolve yeast in the water, add ascorbic acid. Mix flour, salt and sugar, rub in the butter or margarine. Make a well in the middle, pour in yeast liquid, mix to form a dough. Knead for 5–10 minutes, then put dough in a bowl, cover and leave 5 minutes – dough will increase by one third. Knock back, knead briefly, shape and place in tins. Cover bread and put in a warm place until doubled in size: 40–45 minutes. Bake at 230°C (450°F), gas mark 8, for 30–35 minutes for small loaves, 40–45 minutes for large ones. Cool on a wire rack.

EVEN QUICKER BREAD

If you've never made bread before, this is the one to start with. It doesn't need kneading and it really is as quick as making a simple cake. The texture is a little different from ordinary bread, being moister, which means that the bread keeps well and the flavour is very good. It is sometimes called the 'Grant Loaf', after its inventor, Doris Grant, one of the pioneers of healthy eating. This quantity makes two 450g (1 lb) loaves. You can bake it all in one 900g (2 lb) loaf tin, but I think it comes out better in two smaller tins. You do need to use all 100% wholemeal flour, by the way, for this particular recipe to work.

MAKES TWO 450G (1 LB) LOAVES [F]
425ml (15 fl oz) hand-hot water
1 tablespoon dried yeast and ½ teaspoon sugar *or* 1
sachet of easy blend
500g (1 lb 2oz) wholemeal flour
1½ teaspoons sugar
1½ teaspoons salt
kibbled wheat for topping

If you're using dried yeast put the water into a jug or bowl and stir in the ½ teaspoon sugar and yeast. Leave on one side for 10 minutes – it will froth up like a glass of beer. Thoroughly grease two 450g (1 lb) loaf tins or one 900g (2 lb) tin – I think butter is the best fat to use for this as it does seem to prevent the loaves from sticking to the tins.

Put the flour, 1½ teaspoons sugar and salt and the easy blend yeast, if you're using that kind, into a large bowl, or the bowl of your electric mixer. Pour in the frothy yeast mixture or just water, for easy blend yeast, and mix well to a smooth but sticky dough – it won't be firm enough to knead. Spoon the dough into the tins or tin – it should come halfway up the sides. Sprinkle with some kibbled wheat, pressing it down lightly with the back of a spoon. Cover the bread lightly with a piece of polythene and leave it to rise. It should come to within 1cm (½in) of the top of the tin and I find this takes 30 minutes at room temperature. (The bread will rise a bit more when it gets into the oven).

Set the oven to 200°C (400°F), gas mark 6 after the bread has been rising for 15 minutes. Bake the bread for 30 minutes for small loaves, 40 minutes for large. Turn out the bread and cool on a wire rack.

If you like this bread you might like to make a larger batch. Use a whole 1.5kg (3 lb 5oz) bag of flour, and treble all the ingredients except the yeast: 1.3 litres (2¼ pints) water, 2 level tablespoons sugar, a slightly rounded tablespoon of salt and 2 tablespoons (or one sachet) of dried yeast or 2 sachets easy blend yeast. These quantities make 6 small or 3 large loaves.

RYE BREAD WITH TREACLE AND CUMIN

MAKES TWO ROUND LOAVES [F]
25g (1oz) fresh yeast *or* 15g (½oz) dried yeast plus
½ teaspoon sugar
375ml (13 fl oz) warm water
350g (12oz) rye flour
350g (12oz) wholemeal flour
1 tablespoon salt
15g (½oz) butter
125g (4oz) black treacle
2 teaspoons cumin seeds

Dissolve yeast in the water; if using dried yeast add sugar too and leave 10–15 minutes to froth. Mix flours and salt, rub in butter, then add treacle, cumin and yeast liquid. Mix to a dough, knead 5–10 minutes. Place in a bowl, cover and leave until doubled in size: 1 hour in a warm place. Knock back, re-knead briefly. Form into two round loaves, place on greased baking sheets, cover and leave for 30 minutes, until well-risen. Set oven to 230°C (450°F), gas mark 8. Bake loaves for 10 minutes, then reduce setting to 200°C (400°F), gas mark 6 and bake for 25 minutes. Cool.

SWEDISH TEA RING

A pretty semi-sweet yeast cake made in the form of a ring and decorated with icing, cherries and almonds.

SERVES 8–10 [F]
1 quantity of dough as given for poppy seed plait
(page 341) kneaded and risen once
50g (2oz) melted butter
50g (2oz) soft brown sugar
1 teaspoon cinnamon
white glacé icing, glacé cherries and flaked almonds

Knock back dough, then roll dough to a rectangle 22 × 30cm (9 × 12in). Brush with melted butter, sprinkle with the sugar and cinnamon. Roll up like a swiss roll then form into a ring. Place on a greased baking sheet and with scissors make slashes at an angle 2.5cm (1in) apart, and pull out the cut sections. Cover and leave in a warm place until puffy: about 30 minutes. Set oven to 190°C (375°F), gas mark 5. Bake ring for 30–35 minutes. Decorate with glacé cherries and nuts.

SAVARIN

A wonderfully impressive pudding that's easy to make.

SERVES 8–10 F
1 level tablespoon dried yeast
6 tablespoons lukewarm milk
150g (5oz) sugar
225g (8oz) flour
1 teaspoon salt
4 eggs
125g (4oz) soft butter
4 tablespoons each water and rum
4 tablespoons apricot jam, sieved and warmed

Put dried yeast, milk, 25g (1oz) sugar and 50g (2oz) of the flour into a bowl and mix. Cover, leave in warm place until sponge-like: 30–40 minutes. Then add the rest of the flour, salt, eggs and butter. Beat vigorously for 4–5 minutes. Pour into greased 20–22cm (8–9in) ring mould; it should half-fill it. Cover, leave 30–40 minutes until risen almost to top. Bake at 200°C (400°F), gas mark 6 for 20–25 minutes. Turn out on to wire rack, cool, then prick with skewer. Heat remaining sugar in water until dissolved; add rum, pour over cake, brush with apricot jam. Fill centre with fresh or poached fruit, decorate with whipped cream.

WHOLEMEAL STICK

MAKES ONE LOAF F
15g (½oz) fresh yeast or 2 teaspoons dried yeast and
½ teaspoon sugar
275ml (10 fl oz) warm water
450g (1 lb) wholemeal flour
1 teaspoon salt
15g (½oz) butter or margarine
kibbled wheat

Blend yeast with water; if using dried yeast add ½ teaspoon sugar and leave 10–15 minutes to froth. Combine flour and salt in large bowl, rub in butter or margarine. Add yeast liquid, mix to a dough. Knead for 5–10 minutes, until smooth, then put dough into a bowl, cover and leave until doubled in bulk: 1 hour in a warm place. Knock back dough. Knead briefly, then roll dough into a long stick, sprinkle with kibbled wheat, place on a greased baking tray. Slash top of stick several times with a sharp knife, then cover with polythene and leave in a warm place for 30–45 minutes, until puffy. Set oven to 220°C (425°F), gas mark 7. Bake stick for 25–30 minutes, until it sounds hollow when tapped. Cool on a wire rack.

YEASTED FRUIT CAKE

This light, semi-sweet cake is easy to make and good with coffee.

MAKES ONE 20CM (8IN) CAKE F
1 level tablespoon dried yeast
6 tablespoons lukewarm milk
25g (1oz) sugar
225g (8oz) flour
1 teaspoon salt
2 eggs
125g (4oz) soft margarine
grated rind of 1 orange
225g (8oz) mixed dried fruit
3 tablespoons demerara sugar

Put dried yeast, milk, sugar and 50g (2oz) of the flour into a bowl and mix. Cover, leave in a warm place until sponge-like: 30–40 minutes. Then add rest of ingredients, beat vigorously for 4–5 minutes. Pour into greased 20cm (8in) round tin. Cover, leave 30–40 minutes until doubled in size. Sprinkle with demerara sugar. Bake at 200°C (400°F), gas mark 6 for 30–35 minutes. Cool on wire rack.

PIZZA

Pizza makes a very good vegetarian meal. It's filling and tasty and looks and smells so appetizing with its topping of red tomatoes, golden cheese and black olives, and its mouth-watering aroma of home-made bread. Although it sounds complicated pizza isn't really too difficult or time-consuming to make and only needs a crunchy green salad to accompany it. Pizza freezes very well. Place the uncooked pizza in the freezer and open-freeze until firm, then wrap in foil or polythene. To use the pizza, remove the coverings, leave for 15–30 minutes to defrost while the oven heats up and then bake as usual.

SERVES 4–8 F
For the dough:
½ teaspoon sugar
2 teaspoons dried yeast
125ml (4 fl oz) warm water
275g (10oz) plain wholemeal or wheatmeal flour
pinch of salt
40g (1½oz) soft butter or margarine
1 egg
(List of ingredients continued overleaf)

For the topping:
2 large onions
2 tablespoons oil
792g (1 lb 2oz) can tomatoes
125g (4oz) mozzarella *or* Lancashire cheese
sea salt
freshly ground black pepper
8–12 black olives, stoned and halved
a little olive oil

To make the dough first put the sugar, yeast and warm water into a small bowl and mix them briefly with a fork. Leave on one side for about 10 minutes for the yeast to froth up. While this is happening put the flour and salt into a bowl and rub in the butter or margarine. Add the yeast to the flour, also the egg, mixing them with your hands to make a dough. It should be soft enough to knead without effort but firm and pliable. Add a tiny bit more flour or water if necessary to adjust the consistency, then turn the dough on to a clean board or working surface and knead for about 5 minutes. Put the kneaded dough into a bowl, cover with a clean damp cloth then put the bowl under a polythene carrier bag if you have one and leave in a warm place to double in size – this takes 45–60 minutes.

While you're waiting for the dough make the topping. Peel and slice the onions and fry them gently in the oil for about 10 minutes until they're soft but not browned. Drain and chop the tomatoes, reserving the juice; cut the cheese into thin slices.

When the dough has doubled in size punch it down with your hand and turn it out on to a lightly floured board. Knead the dough briefly, then divide it into two or four pieces and roll each out to fit your plate or tin. Brush the plates or tins with oil and lay the dough on them, pressing it down and tucking in the edges to fit. Cover the top of the dough with the chopped tomatoes, adding a little of the juice as necessary to moisten, then arrange the fried onions and sliced cheese on top and decorate with the olives. Sprinkle a little oil over the top of the pizza and brush some over the edges of the dough. Season with salt and pepper.

Set oven to 200°C (400°F), gas mark 6. Put the pizzas (uncovered) on one side to 'prove' for 15 minutes while the oven is heating up. I stand mine on top of the cooker so that they get the benefit of the heat from the oven as it warms up, but this isn't essential. Bake the pizzas for 15–20 minutes until the base is puffed up and the cheesy topping all golden brown and delicious-looking.

Variations

MUSHROOM PIZZA

Make this as above, but omit the olives. Instead arrange on top of the pizza 125g (4oz) washed and finely sliced button mushrooms, brushed lightly with olive oil.

HERBY PIZZA

Sprinkle the top of the tomato pizza with plenty of dried oregano or marjoram; drip a little olive oil over the top to moisten the herbs.

GREEN PEPPER PIZZA

Wash and de-seed a large green pepper or red pepper. Cut the pepper into strips and fry these with the onions, adding them to the saucepan after 5 minutes. Arrange the slices on top of the pizza with the onions – you can make a very pretty pizza with a lattice of pepper strips on top.

ARTICHOKE PIZZA

Finely slice 3 or 4 canned artichoke hearts; arrange the slices on top of the tomato mixture. Omit the olives but keep the fried onions.

INDIVIDUAL PIZZAS

I find it very handy to have some small pizzas in the deep freeze, ready to be heated up quickly from frozen when people come in at odd times for meals. This recipe will make eight such pizzas: divide the mixture into eight pieces, roll each into a circle about 10cm (4in) across. Complete each with the topping, as described above, then open-freeze the pizzas. When they're frozen they can be packed in a polythene bag and used one by one as required. They can be cooked in a frying pan and finished off under the grill, and take about 15 minutes from frozen. When I'm feeling keen I make a double batch (twice the quantities given above) and stock up the freezer – but they don't last long!

NOTE ON MEASUREMENTS

Throughout this book I've given both metric and Imperial measurements. As long as you keep to either one set of measurements or the other in a recipe you should find that all is well. I have used the standard equivalents, listed below, but as you will see, for some of the Imperial measurements there are two possible metric equivalents and sometimes I have used one and sometimes the other, depending on which is the more accurate for a particular recipe. This mainly applies to sauces and pastries, where proportions are important.

With liquids I have generally used pints and fractions of a pint as the Imperial equivalent to millilitres, but again, in one or two recipes, where accuracy is particularly important, or where there is no near fractional equivalent, I've used fluid ounces as the equivalent. Measuring liquids is easy with a good measuring jug marked in millilitres, pints and fluid ounces.

The tablespoons and teaspoons used in the recipes are standard size, 15ml and 5ml respectively, and level unless otherwise stated.

The eggs used are always standard, size 3.

Measurement Equivalents

Grams (g)	Ounces (oz)	Millilitres (ml)	Fluid ounces (fl oz)
25	1	25	1
40	1½	50	2
50	2	75	3
60	2½	125	4
75	3	150	5 (¼ pint)
100	4 } (¼ pound)	175	6
125	4	200	7
150	5	225	8
175	6	250	10 } (½ pint)
200	7	275	10
225	8 (½ pound)	300	11
250	9	350	12
275	10	375	13
300	11	400	15 } (¾ pint)
350	12 (¾ pound)	425	16
375	13	450	17
400	14	475	18
425	15	500	20 } (1 pint)
450	16 (1 pound)	550	20
475	17	575	(1½ pints)
500	18	850	35
700	24 (1½ pounds)	1000 (1 litre)	(2 pints)
1000 (1 kilo)	2–2¼ pounds	1.2 litres	

Oven Temperatures

Temperature	Centigrade (°C)	Fahrenheit (°F)	Gas Mark
	70	150	
	80	175	
	100	200	
Very Cool	110	225	¼
	120	250	½
	140	275	1
Cool	150	300	2
Warm	160	325	3
Moderate	180	350	4
Fairly Hot	190	375	5
	200	400	6
Hot	220	425	7
	230	450	8
Very Hot	240	475	9
	260	500	9

EQUIVALENTS FOR NORTH AMERICAN READERS

Ingredients

Aubergine	Egg plant
Beetroot	Beet
Biscuits	Cookies
Black treacle	Molasses
Caster sugar	Fine sugar
Cornflour	Cornstarch
Courgette	Zucchine
Double cream	Heavy cream
Grill	Broiler
Hazel nuts	Filberts
Icing sugar	Confectioner's sugar
Marmite	Savita
Marrow	Squash/very large zucchini
Single cream	Light cream
Spanish onion	Bermuda onion
Spring onion	Scallion

Measurements

1 pint (20 fl oz/575 ml)	2¼ cups
25g (1oz) chopped nuts	2 tablespoons
25g (1oz) fat/butter/margarine	2 tablespoons
25g (1oz) flour	2 tablespoons
25g (1oz) grated cheese	4 tablespoons
25g (1oz) caster sugar	2 tablespoons
450g (1lb) fresh breadcrumbs	8 cups
450g (1lb) large beans	3 cups
450g (1lb) small beans	2 cups
450g (1lb) bulgur wheat	2 cups
450g (1lb) cottage/cream/curd cheese	2 cups
450g (1lb) grated whole nuts	4 cups
450g (1lb) macaroni	3 cups
450g (1lb) mashed potato	2 cups
450g (1lb) cooked/uncooked rice	2 cups
450g (1lb) semolina	2 cups
450g (1lb) wholemeal flour	4 cups

Centimetres to Inches

Centimetres	Inches	Centimetres	Inches
6 mm	¼ in	15 cm	6 in
1 cm	½ in	18 cm	7 in
2.5 cm	1 in	20 cm	8 in
5 cm	2 in	23 cm	9 in
7.5 cm	3 in	25 cm	10 in
10 cm	4 in	28 cm	11 in
12.5 cm	5 in	30 cm	12 in

INDEX